Brief Contents

i

Touchstones

A Guided Approach to Writing Paragraphs and Essays

Chris Juzwiak

Glendale Community College

Bedford/St. Martin's

Boston ◆ New York

For Bedford/St. Martin's

Executive Editor for Developmental Studies: Alexis Walker
Developmental Editors: Joelle Hann and Randee Falk
Senior Production Editor: Ryan Sullivan
Assistant Production Manager: Joe Ford
Senior Production Supervisor: Nancy Myers
Senior Marketing Manager: Christina Shea
Editorial Assistants: Emily Wunderlich, Nicholas McCarthy, and Amy Saxon
Copy Editors: Alice Vigliani and Steven Patterson
Indexer: Melanie Belkin
Photo Researcher: Julie Tesser
Permissions Manager: Kalina K. Ingham
Art Director: Lucy Krikorian
Text Design: Claire Seng-Niemoeller and Cenveo® Publisher Services
Cover Art and Design: Billy Boardman
Composition: Cenveo® Publisher Services
Printing and Binding: RR Donnelley and Sons

President, Bedford/St. Martin's: Denise B. Wydra
Presidents, Macmillan Higher Education: Joan E. Feinberg and Tom Scotty
Editor in Chief: Karen S. Henry
Director of Development: Erica T. Appel
Director of Marketing: Karen R. Soeltz
Production Director: Susan W. Brown
Associate Production Director: Elise S. Kaiser
Managing Editor: Shuli Traub

Manufactured in the United States of America.

8   7   6   5   4   3

f   e   d   c   b   a

For information, write: Bedford/St. Martin's, 75 Arlington Street, Boston, MA 02116
(617-399-4000)

ISBN 978-0-312-61222-1 (Student edition)
ISBN 978-1-4576-2292-2 (Instructor's annotated edition)
ISBN 978-1-4576-3089-7 (Loose-leaf edition)

Acknowledgments

Preface

If your teaching experiences are like mine, many of the students entering your classroom have encountered difficulty in past classes. They may have had negative experiences learning writing and grammar, finding these pursuits boring or confusing. Often, they have been given minimal examples and activities, or they have been asked to make big leaps in skill level without proper support. They frequently become frustrated, and many of them give up.

Touchstones addresses these challenges head-on. It was designed with the unflagging conviction that learners who feel both safe and stimulated are likely to succeed. The word *touchstone*, originating in small tablets that ancient Greeks used to test the purity of precious metals, refers to a standard of excellence and also to basic, essential properties. The title of the book uses the word in both these senses: we encourage students to achieve excellence by first mastering the essential skills they need to do so.

The "touchstones" in this book are a series of innovations and refinements to traditional composition pedagogy that will enable your students to acquire all the skills that are essential for good academic writing and to move from writing paragraphs to writing academic essays. Thus, in this book you will find unique chapters on organization, outlining, and developing details—part of a new systematic approach to writing paragraphs and essays. In addition, an original "build it / fix it" approach to grammar enables students to both analyze and synthesize the sentences that comprise the paragraphs and essays they write.

At the core of the instruction, you will find carefully honed *incremental learning sequences*, which ensure that all learners—whether struggling or advanced—will persist at, master, and retain the material. Indeed, at every step of the writing process, your students should feel a sense of progression and gradual mastery—and of intellectual excitement. Their enthusiasm and progress should never be thwarted by inconsistencies and gaps in instruction, abstruse terminology, or uninspired activities.

If you are new to basic writing instruction, I hope this book will provide a reliable touchstone for measuring and confirming your confidence and interest in the discipline. Ideally, it will help you to grasp and experience the genuine intellectual appeal that basic writing instruction can have for both you and your students. If you are a veteran writing instructor, you may be looking for fresh approaches to the discipline. As you use the book in the classroom, I hope that its innovative pedagogical approach will confirm your commitment to—and enthusiasm for—teaching writing.

BACKGROUND ON THE PEDAGOGY

Like *Stepping Stones*, the sentence-to-paragraph-level book in this series, *Touchstones* has benefitted from more than a decade of grant-sponsored pedagogical research, from sustained conversation and collaboration with colleagues across the nation, and from five years of designing and implementing the pedagogy that informs it.

Starting in 2004, I directed a three-year Carnegie Foundation SPECC (Strengthening Pre-Collegiate Education in Community Colleges) grant in which my colleagues and I were able to test materials that I developed and to study students' writing and learning processes. We spent hundreds of hours observing students as they wrote and completed exercises, and even more time watching videos of students working at computers, noting how they started and stopped compositions; cut, added, and moved text; and generally worked through their individual composing processes. We also interviewed students about their writing processes and responses to various learning materials. The students in the study responded enthusiastically, and their skills improved markedly. Through this research, my colleagues and I became convinced that developmental learners flourish when their critical thinking and imagination are challenged with fresh, precisely honed sequences of instruction and activities—the key insight that eventually gave rise to both *Stepping Stones* and *Touchstones*.

Subsequent research from 2008 to 2012 was funded by grants from the California Basic Skills Initiative (CBSI) and the Hewlett Foundation. At my campus, twelve developmental writing instructors and a host of student co-inquirers participated in IMPACT (Incremental, Motivational Pedagogy and Assessment Cycles Training), a program developed with funds from CBSI. We confirmed that developmental students thrive on clear, carefully structured *learning sequences* that move seamlessly from basic to advanced levels, providing ample activities. (We like to call it "drill and *thrill*" to challenge the misconception that sustained practice is inevitably boring.) Our instructional innovations have realized a solid 15 percent increase in student success in our college's basic writing programs. *Touchstones* incorporates many of the best features of this progressive pedagogy, such as training in "organizational cognition" (critical thinking about outlines) and the "build it / fix it" approach to sentence construction and grammar.

Throughout this decade of grant-funded research—and during a year-long sabbatical—I was able to attend conferences and visit campuses in ten states, discussing basic skills pedagogy with scores of dedicated and talented faculty. Countless refinements in the pedagogy that informs this book resulted from these dialogues. In fact, of all the influences that shaped *Touchstones*, the contributions of fellow faculty were the richest and most crucial.

FEATURES

In *Touchstones*, coverage, organization, and features are designed to work together to scaffold students' learning and to help students move from writing effective academic paragraphs to writing effective academic essays.

Unusually Thorough Writing Coverage Helps Students Generate and Organize Ideas with Confidence

Recognizing that two of the most serious challenges that developmental writers face are, first, coming up with solid ideas and, second, organizing those ideas, I wanted *Touchstones* to give more help with these tasks than other texts do.

Chapters 2 and 3 help students become more invested in the *dynamics* of clustering, listing, questioning, and freewriting. Chapter 2 helps students determine whether certain idea-generating techniques might be especially suited to their learning styles. Chapter 3 helps students first choose a topic that matters to them and then, through a sequential, color-coded demonstration of the "layering" process that occurs during brainstorming, internalize key idea-generating techniques.

THE BRAINSTORMING PROCESS

Start your brainstorming by writing down your **narrowed topic** at the top of the page (for listing, freewriting, and flowcharting) or in a bubble in the center of the page (for clustering). Several obvious or **big ideas** related to your topic will usually pop into your head right away. Then, as you focus on each of these big ideas individually, some **related examples** should come to mind to support those ideas. Finally, if you focus on each of these examples one at a time, you may recall some **specific details** to illustrate and support the examples.

To get a general idea of the brainstorming process, take a look at the graphic below. The colors correspond to the layers of information that get revealed in the process of brainstorming on your topic.

NARROWED TOPIC	States your position on the writing assignment
BIG IDEAS	Present ideas related to the topic
RELATED EXAMPLES	Provide support for each of your big ideas
SPECIFIC DETAILS	Clarify the examples and bring them to life

Two dedicated chapters—Chapters 4 and 5—give students unusually thorough guidance in organizing and outlining their ideas. Chapter 4 starts with the basics of ordering, grouping, and eliminating words, phrases, and sentences, in preparation for in-depth instruction in outlining in Chapter 5.

Step 1: Write the main idea.

Steps 2–4: Write the three support points, beginning each with a transitional expression.

Main Idea: College students experience several financial problems.

Support Point 1: First, the cost of education keeps going up.

    Related Examples: rising tuition
                  books and supplies cost more
                  increase in parking and lab fees

    Step 5: Write the examples for support point 1.

Support Point 2: Next, students have fewer sources of income.

    Related Examples: low-paying jobs
                  loans being cut
                  no help from family

Support Point 3: Last, students suffer because of money trouble.

    Related Examples: eating cheap, unhealthy food
                  no money for emergencies
                  pressure of debt

Step 6: Write the examples for support points 2 and 3.

An Incremental Writing Sequence Helps Students Develop the Tools They Need for Academic Writing

By connecting writing concepts across chapters, the book ensures that there are no gaps to confuse or discourage students. Instead, students will emerge with the tools—and confidence—they need to complete writing assignments for college courses.

- Chapter 1 provides students with the "big picture" of writing in college, covering the **differences between academic and popular or informal writing**.
- Chapters 2 through 5 offer incremental instruction in **idea generation, organization, and outlining**.
- Chapters 6 and 7 enable students to draft and revise **well-developed paragraphs**.
- Chapter 8 shows students concretely how their paragraph writing can be the basis for **essay writing**, and Chapter 9 expands paragraph revision strategies to cover the various **elements of essays** from thesis statement through conclusion.
- Chapter 10 encourages students to refine their writing by adding **specific details**.
- Chapters 11 and 12 introduce students to the use of the **rhetorical modes** to strengthen both paragraph and essay writing.
- Chapters 13 and 14 show students how to work with **paraphrase and summary** and introduce them to **research writing**.

Carefully Sequenced Grammar Chapters Use an Innovative Color-Coding System to Help Students Master Sentence Patterns

Ample practice that grows incrementally more challenging builds competency in all learners, including ESL and Generation 1.5 students.

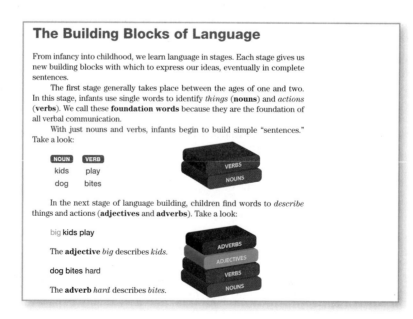

The Building Blocks of Language

From infancy into childhood, we learn language in stages. Each stage gives us new building blocks with which to express our ideas, eventually in complete sentences.

The first stage generally takes place between the ages of one and two. In this stage, infants use single words to identify *things* (**nouns**) and *actions* (**verbs**). We call these **foundation words** because they are the foundation of all verbal communication.

With just nouns and verbs, infants begin to build simple "sentences." Take a look:

NOUN	VERB
kids	play
dog	bites

In the next stage of language building, children find words to *describe* things and actions (**adjectives** and **adverbs**). Take a look:

big kids play

The **adjective** *big* describes *kids.*

dog bites hard

The **adverb** *hard* describes *bites.*

Students learn about the building blocks of sentences—the parts of speech—in the first grammar chapter.

Students continue to use the building blocks in progressively longer and more complex sentences, with each sentence type presented in its own chapter. At the start of each chapter, students get a visual overview of the sentence patterns they will be asked to create.

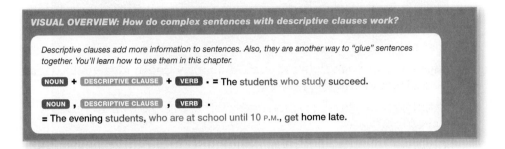

The same color coding is used within examples throughout the grammar chapters, so students see how the same types of words work together in different patterns of effective sentences (noun + verb; noun + verb + comma + conjunction + noun + verb; etc.).

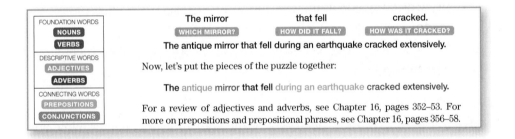

With the "Build It / Fix It" Model, Grammar Problems Are Covered in Context—Not as Isolated Errors

Touchstones **addresses problems such as fragments, run-ons, and comma splices in the context of the sentence patterns in which they are most common** (for example, dangling modifiers are covered in the chapter on sentences with modifiers). This approach focuses students on their abilities as problem-solvers, rather than on their sense of themselves as writers with problems. It also builds students' awareness of situations in which errors are most likely to occur, making them better editors of their own writing.

Grammar chapters are divided into a "Build It" section on the sentence pattern and a "Fix It" section on watching for and fixing mistakes in the sentence pattern. This model is used not only in the chapters on sentence types but also in three special chapters that focus on particular problem areas: parallelism, verb use, and pronoun use.

A Precise and Colorful Design Appeals to Visual Learners

Touchstones **uses color and visuals to make information clearer and more appealing** to visual learners and, indeed, to all students. In addition to

coding the building blocks of sentences, color is used to identify main ideas, support points, and other key elements of writing to make clear for students the structure of effective writing. Color photographs and illustrations engage students and clarify important concepts.

Hundreds of Engaging Exercises Provide Abundant Options for Skill Practice and for Self-Assessment and Review

Like instruction, exercises are carefully sequenced.

"What Do You Know?" pre-tests at the start of every chapter allow students to identify areas that need work.

CHAPTER 18

The Complex Sentence

Before you read this chapter, it's a good idea to test your understanding of complex sentences. You may know more than you think.

WHAT DO YOU KNOW?

Circle "Yes" if each word group below is a complete, correct sentence. Circle "No" if it is incomplete. Then, explain your choice.

1. **When fog blanketed the airport; all flights were postponed.**

    Yes   No

    Explanation: _____

"Challenge Meters" (see top of next page) chart the progression in the level of difficulty of exercises within chapters and within sections of chapters. Students can use them to see the difficulty level of exercises, from "warmup" early in sections and chapters, to "mastery" at the end.

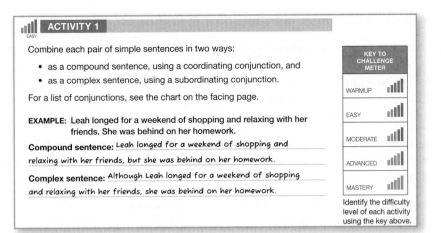

"Bringing It All Together" reviews at the end of every chapter help students review their learning and promote retention. More quizzes on the companion Web site provide additional practice, with a gradebook that lets instructors track student progress.

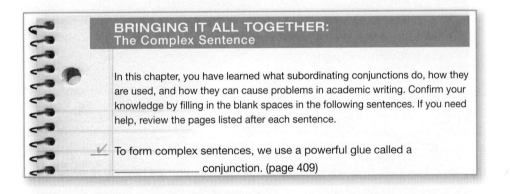

End-of-Book Materials Offer ESL Advice and At-a-Glance Help for Key Grammar Issues

An appendix for ESL writers condenses advice most useful for non-native speakers and Generation 1.5 students.

"Quick Guides" to comma usage, fragments, run-ons and comma splices, sentence types, and verb usage offer brief visual overviews of critical information.

A Thematic Reader Offers 16 Readings Selected for Their Appeal to Student Writers

Contemporary authors such as Sherman Alexie, Michaela Angela Davis, and Edwidge Danticat are represented in a collection organized around **topics students want to think, talk, and write about**, including family heritage, wealth and poverty, responses to violence, and music.

Thoughtful apparatus accompanying the readings offers prompts for peer discussion, paragraph and essay writing, and discussion of the rhetorical modes.

Touchstones *Comes with Support for Instructors*

Touchstones **gives instructors flexibility,** letting them teach the class their students need. Instructors can vary the proportions of paragraph and essay writing and the extent to which they include various higher-level writing skills, can cover more or fewer grammar topics, and can incorporate reading to the extent they choose.

The complimentary Instructor's Annotated Edition offers "Time-to-Teach" tips for all writing and grammar chapters, each of which comprises a built-in lesson plan with options.

Video chats with Chris Juzwiak on the companion Web site offer ideas for teaching in the developmental classroom, including how to access students' "intellectual humanity" and sequence exercises for maximum skill retention.

Chris Juzwiak
Glendale Community College

Answers to all exercises are available to instructors on the free companion Web site (in a complete set as well as an odd-numbered set), in formats that allow for easy printing or posting for students' use, as instructors see fit.

YOU GET MORE CHOICES WITH *TOUCHSTONES*

Touchstones doesn't stop with a book. Online and in print, you'll find free and affordable premium resources to help students get even more out of the book and your course. You'll also find convenient instructor resources, such as a downloadable instructor's manual, additional exercises, and PowerPoint slides.

This section provides information for ordering and ISBNs for packaging these resources with your students' books. You can also contact your Bedford/ St. Martin's sales representative, e-mail sales support (**sales_support@bfwpub .com**), or visit **bedfordstmartins.com/touchstones/catalog**. For questions related to content in our textbooks for basic reading and writing courses, please e-mail **developmental@bedfordstmartins.com**.

[icon] = Print [icon] = Online [icon] = CD-ROM

Free Instructor Resources

You have a lot to do in your course. Bedford/St. Martin's wants to make it easy for you to find the support you need.

[icon] **The Instructor's Annotated Edition** of *Touchstones* contains answers to all practice exercises, in addition to numerous teaching ideas, reminders, and cross-references that are useful to teachers at all levels of experience. ISBN: 978-1-4576-2292-2.

[icon] [icon] *Resources for Teaching Touchstones* offers advice for teaching developmental writing from five expert instructors, including lead author Chris Juzwiak. Contributors cover such practical topics as different teaching approaches, working with ESL and Generation 1.5 students, and supporting students with disabilities. Available as a print booklet or as a downloadable PDF from the book's companion Web site. ISBN: 978-1-4576-2622-7.

[icon] [icon] *Diagnostic Tests and Exercises for Touchstones* provides diagnostic pre- and post-tests and additional exercises to build students' writing and grammar skills. Answers are provided at the back. Available as a print booklet or as a downloadable PDF from the book's companion Web site. ISBN: 978-1-4576-2619-7.

[icon] **Presentation Slides (in PowerPoint) for** *Touchstones* cover 16 significant topics—such as commonly confused words and dangling modifiers—and are designed to help spark class discussion. Formatted as multiple-choice questions, followed by answers, this resource is available for free on the instructor's side of the companion Web site at **bedfordstmartins.com/touchstones**.

[icon] **Bedford Coursepacks** allow you to plug Bedford/St. Martin's content into your own course management systems. For details, visit **bedfordstmartins .com/coursepacks**.

[icon] *Testing Tool Kit: Writing and Grammar Test Bank* CD-ROM allows instructors to create secure, customized tests and quizzes from a pool of nearly 2,000 questions covering 47 topics. It also includes 10 prebuilt diagnostic tests. ISBN: 978-0-312-43032-0.

[icon] *Teaching Developmental Writing: Background Readings,* **Fourth Edition,** is edited by Susan Naomi Bernstein, former cochair of the Conference on Basic Writing. This professional resource offers essays on topics of interest to basic writing instructors, along with editorial apparatus pointing out practical applications for the classroom. ISBN: 978-0-312-60251-2.

[icon] *Teaching Developmental Reading: Historical, Theoretical, and Practical Background Readings,* **Second Edition,** by Norman Stahl, Hunter Boylan, and Sonya Armstrong, offers a collection of professional essays by writers such as Katie Hern, Michele Simpson, and Dolores Perin, on topics that will engage teachers of basic reading. ISBN: 978-1-4576-5895-2.

[icon] *Teaching Study Strategies in Developmental Education: Readings on Theory, Research, and Best Practice,* edited by Russ Hodges, Michele Simpson, and Norman Stahl, presents 29 selections that discuss the theory and practice of teaching college students to be efficient and effective

learners. Topics include the needs of students in developmental education and learning assistance programs, current psychological and sociological principles that promote—or hinder—learning, and the role of effective learning strategies and assessment on instruction and student learning. ISBN: 978-0-312-66274-5.

The Bedford Bibliography for Teachers of Basic Writing, **Third Edition** (also available online at **bedfordstmartins.com/basicbib**), has been compiled by members of the Conference on Basic Writing under the general editorship of Gregory R. Glau and Chitralekha Duttagupta. This annotated list of books, articles, and periodicals was created specifically to help teachers of basic writing find valuable resources. ISBN: 978-0-312-58154-1.

TeachingCentral at **bedfordstmartins.com/teachingcentral** offers the entire list of Bedford/St. Martin's print and online professional resources, all in one place. You will find landmark reference works, sourcebooks on pedagogical issues, award-winning collections, and practical advice for the classroom—all free for instructors.

Student Resources

FREE AND OPEN

The free companion Web site for *Touchstones* at **bedfordstmartins .com/touchstones** offers an abundance of resources for instructors and students, including downloadable diagnostic and mastery tests, access to hundreds of book-specific exercises on *Exercise Central*, PowerPoint slides for in-class review, and access to useful forms for brainstorming, outlining, and peer review. Also available are more models of student writing, tutorials on avoiding plagiarism and doing research, and more.

Exercise Central 3.0 at **bedfordstmartins.com/exercisecentral** is the largest database of editing exercises on the Internet. This comprehensive resource contains more than 9,000 exercises that offer immediate feedback; the program also recommends personalized study plans and provides tutorials for common problems. Best of all, students' work reports to a gradebook, allowing instructors to track students' progress quickly and easily.

FREE WITH PRINT TEXT

The Bedford/St. Martin's ESL Workbook, **Second Edition,** includes a broad range of exercises covering grammatical issues for multilingual students of varying language skills and backgrounds. Answers are at the back. **Free** when packaged with the print text. Package ISBN: 978-1-4576-5736-8.

Exercise Central to Go: Writing and Grammar Practices for Basic Writers **CD-ROM** provides hundreds of practice items to help students build their writing and editing skills. No Internet connection is necessary. **Free** when packaged with the print text. Package ISBN: 978-1-4576-5737-5.

Make-a-Paragraph Kit is a fun, interactive CD-ROM that teaches students about paragraph development. It also contains exercises to help students build their own paragraphs, audiovisual tutorials on four of the most common errors for basic writers, and the content from *Exercise Central to Go: Writing and Grammar Practices for Basic Writers.* **Free** when packaged with the print text. Package ISBN: 978-1-4576-5738-2.

📖 *The Bedford/St. Martin's Planner* includes everything that students need to plan and use their time effectively, with advice on preparing schedules and to-do lists plus blank schedules and calendars (monthly and weekly). The planner fits easily into a backpack or purse, so students can take it anywhere. **Free** when packaged with the print text. Package ISBN: 978-1-4576-5734-4.

📖 *Journal Writing: A Beginning* is designed to give students an opportunity to use writing as a way to explore their thoughts and feelings. This writing journal includes a generous supply of inspirational quotations placed throughout the pages, tips for journaling, and suggested journal topics. **Free** when packaged with the print text. Package ISBN: 978-1-4576-5733-7.

📖 *From Practice to Mastery* (study guide for the Florida Basic Skills Exit Tests) gives students all the resources they need to practice for—and pass—the Florida tests in reading and writing. It includes pre- and post-tests, abundant practices, many examples, and clear instruction in all the skills covered on the exams. **Free** when packaged with the print text. Package ISBN: 978-1-4576-5739-9.

PREMIUM

🖥 *WritingClass* provides students with a dynamic and interactive online course space preloaded with exercises, diagnostics, video tutorials, writing and commenting tools, and more. *WritingClass* helps students stay focused and allows instructors to see how they are progressing. It is available at a significant discount when packaged with the print text. To learn more about *WritingClass*, visit **yourwritingclass.com**. Package ISBN: 978-1-4576-5731-3.

🖥 *SkillsClass* offers all that *WritingClass* offers, plus guidance and practice in reading and study skills. This interactive online course space comes preloaded with exercises, diagnostics, video tutorials, writing and commenting tools, and more. It is available at a significant discount when packaged with the print text. To learn more about *SkillsClass*, visit **yourskillsclass .com**. Package ISBN: 978-1-4576-5730-6.

📖 *The Bedford/St. Martin's Textbook Reader,* **Second Edition,** by Ellen Kuhl Repetto gives students practice in reading college textbooks across the curriculum. This brief collection of chapters from market-leading introductory college textbooks can be packaged inexpensively with *Touchstones*. Beginning with a chapter on college success, the *Textbook Reader* also includes chapters from current texts on composition, mass communication, history, psychology, and environmental science. Comprehension questions and tips for reading success guide students in reading college-level materials efficiently and effectively. Package ISBN: 978-1-4576-5735-1.

🖥 *Re:Writing Plus,* **now with VideoCentral,** gathers all of our premium digital content for the writing class into one online collection. This impressive resource includes innovative and interactive help with writing a paragraph; tutorials and practices that show how writing works in students' real-world experience; VideoCentral, with more than 140 brief videos for the writing classroom; the first-ever peer review game, *Peer Factor*; *i-cite: visualizing sources*; plus hundreds of models of writing and hundreds of readings. *Re:Writing Plus* can be purchased separately or packaged with *Touchstones* at a significant discount. Package ISBN: 978-1-4576-5729-0.

Alternatives to Print: e-Books and Loose-Leaf Editions

Bedford/St. Martin's e-books let students do more and pay less. For about half the price of a print book, the e-book for *Touchstones* offers the complete text of the print book combined with convenient digital tools such as highlighting, note-taking, and research. Both online and downloadable options are available in popular e-book formats for computers, tablets, and e-readers. For details, visit **bedfordstmartins.com/ebooks**.

Touchstones is also available in a loose-leaf (unbound and three-hole-punched) version that costs 45 percent less than the bound print text. ISBN: 978-1-4576-3089-7.

ORDERING INFORMATION

To order any ancillary or ancillary package for *Touchstones*, contact your local Bedford/St. Martin's sales representative, e-mail **sales_support@bfwpub .com**, or visit our Web site at **bedfordstmartins.com**.

ACKNOWLEDGMENTS

Touchstones would not have been possible without the diligence, insights, and plain hard work of a large number of instructors, students, and other contributors.

Reviewers

Throughout the development of this book, a dedicated group of instructors reviewed every page of the manuscript, offering helpful comments and fresh ideas to make the book more useful to students and other teachers. A few of these instructors are expert in teaching ESL and Generation 1.5 students, and their comments helped us address the needs of those students throughout the text. I am indebted to the following insightful instructors: Angelina Arellanes-Nunez, El Paso Community College; Daniel T. Bahner, Crafton Hills College; Steven J. Belluscio, Borough of Manhattan Community College; Ruby Lane Blackwell, Northwest-Shoals Community College; Candace Boeck, San Diego State University; Tamara Kuzmenkov Bohner, Tacoma Community College; Kathleen Chescattie, Harrisburg Area Community College; Christina M. Devlin, Montgomery College; Deborah DeVries, Oxnard College; Jessica Felizardo, Bay State College; Jennifer Ferguson, Cazenovia College; Kristin Georgine, Colorado Mountain College; Julie Gibson, Greenville Technical College; Lynn Gold, Bergen Community College; Kendra L. Haggard, Northeastern State University; Donna Hill, Ouachita Technical College; Alexander N. Howe, University of the District of Columbia; Paige Huskey, Clark State Community College; Wayne H. Johnson, Odessa College; Timothy J. Jones, University of Oklahoma; Kathy Lamos, Westwood College; Erlinda Legapsi, City College of San Francisco; Alexandra Leyton, City College of San Francisco; Carl Mason, University of Massachusetts–Lowell; Jennifer McCann, Bay College; Katheryn Ann McCoskey, Kansas State University; Carolyn Mello, Lamar

State College–Orange; Nailah S. Muttalib, Columbia College Chicago; Caryn Newburger, Austin Community College; Brit Osgood-Treston, Riverside City College; Sandra Padilla, El Paso Community College; Brenda Reeves, Northeast Alabama Community College; Sarah Schwendimann, Glendale Community College; James Soular, Flathead Valley Community College; Joan Parr Tucker, Northeast Alabama Community College; Erica Tupone, Brooklyn College; Christine Tutlewski, University of Wisconsin–Parkside; Kathryn Tyndall, Wake Technical Community College; Marisol Varela, Miami Dade College; and Stephanie Zerkel-Humbert, Maple Woods Community College.

Students

Several student writers contributed paragraphs and essays to this book and its supplements. I am grateful for their dedication and for their willingness to share their work. These students include Gina Aslanyan, Doorga Ghosh, May Hampton, Anallely Orozco-Posadas, Shelby Potts, Jacqueline Ramirez, Bridgette Reed, Janice Robinson, and Hongjie Zhang.

Other Contributors

I am also grateful to a number of other people whose hard work made this book possible. Bruce Thaler carefully and energetically crafted exercises for both the book and its supplements, while Denise Ezell, assistant professor at Glendale Community College, crafted hundreds of invaluable new exercises for the book's companion Web site. Julie Tesser researched images and also cleared art permissions, while Linda Winters cleared text permissions. Brian DeTagyos created colorful illustrations to aid students' understanding of writing and grammar points.

For their insightful contributions to *Resources for Teaching Touchstones*, I would like to thank Matthew Fox of Monroe Community College, Sally Gearhart of Santa Rosa Junior College, Erin M. O'Brien of the University of Massachusetts–Boston, and Susan Brown Rodriguez of Hillsborough Community College.

At Glendale Community College, several colleagues inspired me to think outside the pedagogical box. For their guidance, I am grateful to Hasmik Barsamian, Denise Ezell, Linda Griffith, Elena Grigori, Lara Kartalian, Darren Leaver, Mark Maier, Sarah McLemore, Alice Mecom, Brett Miketta, Nancy Nevins, Ellen Oppenberg, Chris Pasles, Hollie Stewart, and Monette Teirnan.

Bedford/St. Martin's and Beyond

At Bedford/St. Martin's, a large number of people were part of bringing *Touchstones* into being. Executive Editor Alexis Walker shared market knowledge and other insights and helped to shape a strong message for the book. Throughout the book's development, Macmillan Higher Education President Joan E. Feinberg, Bedford/St. Martin's President Denise B. Wydra, and Editor in Chief Karen S. Henry have generously contributed many wise ideas and thoughtful suggestions for *Touchstones* based on years of experience listening to, and responding to the needs of, writing instructors. Throughout the development process, editorial assistants Amy Saxon, Emily Wunderlich, and Nicholas McCarthy assisted with countless tasks large and small, from helping to find engaging readings to running numerous review programs and managing a multitude of administrative details. Director of Development Erica T. Appel oversaw the book's entire development, offering invaluable guidance on the daily tasks involved in getting a big job done.

Making *Touchstones* colorful and engaging while ensuring its ease of use was a design challenge ably met by Art Directors Anna Palchik and Lucy Krikorian, designer Claire Seng-Niemoeller, and the design team at Cenveo Publisher Services. Their creativity, energy, and problem-solving skills resulted in a design as attractive as it is practical. Additionally, Elise Kaiser, Shuli Traub, Nancy Myers, and Joe Ford oversaw many details regarding the production of the book. Senior Production Editor Ryan Sullivan skillfully guided the book through the production process, offering many practical suggestions and helping to solve a range of problems with patience, intelligence, and good humor. Ryan brought on Alice Vigliani and Steven Patterson as copyeditors and Judy Kiviat, Will Rigby, and Julie Nemer as proofreaders, all of whom deserve praise for their thoroughness and careful eye for details. Also contributing to the look of the book was Billy Boardman, who designed the appealing cover for this edition. Several talented people helped to shape and produce the Web site and electronic ancillaries, namely, Marissa Zanetti, Rebecca Merrill, and Lindsey Jones, guided by the expertise of Harriet Wald, and the entire New Media team. In marketing, sincere thanks go to Karen R. Soeltz, Jane Helms, and Senior Marketing Manager Christina Shea for their creative ideas in getting out the word on *Touchstones* and coordinating a number of sales efforts to help the book reach its audience.

My enduring gratitude goes to Joelle Hann, who brought formidable rigor and vision to the book. I learned so much from her example of uncompromising excellence, equanimity, and intellectual stamina. Randee Falk contributed her energy and expertise to the crucial later stages of the book's development and production.

I also want to thank my family members and friends, whose unflagging enthusiasm and patience were as crucial to this work as any other component: Doug Mann, Lael Mann, Estella Martinez, Ruth Owens, Sandra and Ernie Gomez, Catherine Leh, James Geyer, Shelley Aronoff, Michael Ritterbrown, Christine Menardus, George Gharibian, Ildy Lee, and Marilyn Selznick. Your support made all the hard work worthwhile.

Chris Juzwiak

Contents

7   Revising   149

8   Moving from Paragraphs to Essays   173

9   Composing and Revising Your Essay   195

PART TWO   Expanding Your Academic Writing   227

10   Using Language Effectively   229

11   Basic Writing Patterns   255

PART THREE Grammar for Academic Writing   335

PART FOUR   **Reading for Academic Writing**   557

25   Introduction to Academic Reading   559

26   On Family Heritage   569

27   On Looking Out for One Another   580

28   On Rich and Poor   585

Readings by Patterns of Development

This table of contents organizes the readings in Part Four of *Touchstones* ("Reading for Academic Writing") according to the patterns of development they use. (Within each category, readings are listed in order of appearance. Each reading may appear in more than one category.) For more information on the patterns of development, see Chapters 11 and 12.

Comparison and Contrast

Argumentation

PART ONE

Writing for College: Academic Paragraphs and Essays

CHAPTER 1

Seeing the Big Picture: Paragraphs, Essays, Purpose, and Audience

Test your understanding of paragraphs, essays, purpose, and audience by completing this quiz. You may know more than you think.

For each question, select all the answers that apply.

WHAT DO YOU KNOW?

1. **An "academic paragraph" is an important writing format. Where is an academic paragraph found?**

    ___ in notes to friends
    ___ in scholarly journals
    ___ in magazines and newspapers
    ___ in essays written for class

2. **An "academic essay" is also an important writing format. What elements does it contain?**

    ___ conclusion
    ___ introduction
    ___ abbreviations
    ___ body paragraphs
    ___ slang words

3. **If your instructor asks you to write an essay that argues for better school lunches, what would the purpose of your essay be?**

    ___ to entertain
    ___ to persuade
    ___ to explain
    ___ to discuss

4. **If you text a friend, asking her to join you for dinner, what type of audience are you addressing?**

    ___ professional
    ___ academic
    ___ personal
    ___ journalistic

5. **What should you be sure to do in every writing situation?**

    ___ Use formal English.
    ___ Use language that is appropriate for your audience.
    ___ Assume that all audiences have the same expectations.
    ___ Provide information that is appropriate for your audience.

Understanding Academic Paragraphs

Writing is essential in college. Strong academic writing allows you to demonstrate what you know clearly and effectively, convincing other people—such as your instructors and your peers—that you know what you're talking about. It is also an important life skill that helps you communicate with your colleagues, family, and community. The goal of this book is to help you learn to write confidently in all areas of your life.

Let's begin with an obvious question: What is college writing? Usually college writing is a well-developed paragraph or an essay that responds to an assignment from an instructor. To become a confident writer, it's helpful to know all the parts that make up a paragraph or an essay. For example, it's helpful to know that all essays—including college essays—are *a series of paragraphs*. For this reason, it's essential that you learn the basics of paragraph writing before attempting to write a complete essay.

The academic paragraph is a very important form. It is much more than a string of thoughts hastily put on paper. Rather, an academic paragraph is a carefully formulated "unit of thinking" with a main idea, support points, related examples, and details.

Take a look at the following paragraph:

> Investing in a college education has rewarded me in many ways; however, in order to attend college, I have had to give up many things. First, I had to give up spending time with family. For instance, I used to enjoy cooking dinner and watching television with my three kids in the evening. We would sit down in front of *The Simpsons* or *The Office* to eat and laugh together. Now, I pick up fast food or cook a quick meal and then go into another room to study after we've eaten. In addition, on weekends we often had picnic lunches at a nearby park. These days, though, I usually stay home and read or prepare for exams. Another thing I have given up is my hobbies. For instance, before starting school, I used to spend hours each week knitting. I would make baby clothes, or scarves and sweaters as presents for my friends. Once I enrolled in school, however, I needed all my spare time for classes and homework. Finally, returning to college meant giving up something else I value: sleep. I used to go to sleep at 10:00 P.M. and wake up around 6:30 A.M. to get my kids to school before going to work. Now, I often stay up until midnight and set my alarm for 5:30 or 6:00 A.M. to get my assignments done on time. I wake up early even on weekends. Therefore, even though I'm happy that I'm in college, I have had to sacrifice a number of things I value to get my degree.

Power Tip
Some students have observed that an academic paragraph is like a "mini-essay," and they are right! Like an essay, a paragraph contains a main idea, support points, transitions, and a conclusion. If it is helpful, keep this comparison in mind as you develop and compose your paragraphs.

ACTIVITY 1

Evaluate the sample paragraph by completing the following prompts.

1. Highlight or underline the sentence that contains the *main idea*. Then, state the main idea in your own words on the lines below.

4

Main idea: _____

_____

2. Highlight or underline the *three main support points* that develop the writer's main idea. Then, write them on the lines below.

   Support point: _____

   Support point: _____

   Support point: _____

3. Highlight or underline each *transitional expression* in the paragraph (the word or phrase that introduces a new support point). Then, write the expressions on the lines below.

   _____

   _____

4. Highlight or underline the *related examples* that illustrate the writer's support points.

5. Each example in the paragraph includes some *precise and colorful details*. Identify and then write some of the best examples below:

   _____

   _____

6. Identify the writer's *concluding thought* in the paragraph. Then, in your own words, write it on the lines below.

   _____

   _____

   _____

ACADEMIC AND POPULAR PARAGRAPHS

In your reading experiences, you may have noticed that paragraphs come in a variety of shapes and sizes.

Some paragraphs are quite long, with many sentences. In general, they have a main idea and plenty of supporting examples and details. For convenience, we will call these **academic** paragraphs. They are commonly found in textbooks, college essays, and scholarly journals. Academic paragraphs encourage readers to *slow down* and reflect on the ideas being discussed.

Other paragraphs are quite short, with only a few sentences. These paragraphs may or may not contain a main idea, and they may or may not have supporting examples and details. We will call these **popular** paragraphs.

scholarly journal: a publication — similar to a magazine, but often without advertising — in which scholars, professors, and specialists publish their research and their ideas

They are commonly found in newspapers, magazines, Web sites, and personal communication, such as e-mails. Popular paragraphs allow readers to *move quickly*, grabbing key pieces of information as they go.

The following writing samples illustrate the difference between popular and academic paragraphs. Although the articles are about the same length, the one on the left contains only two (academic) paragraphs, while the one on the right contains eleven (popular) paragraphs. Take a look and then complete the activities that follow.

Academic

The Axial Age marks the beginning of humanity as we now know it. During this period, men and women became conscious of their existence, their own nature, and their limitations in an unprecedented way. Their experience of utter impotence in a cruel world impelled them to seek the highest goals and an absolute reality in the depths of their being. The great sages of the time taught human beings how to cope with the misery of life, transcend their weakness, and live in peace in the midst of this flawed world. The new religious systems that emerged during this period—Taoism and Confucianism in China, Buddhism and Hinduism in India, monotheism in Iran and the Middle East, and Greek rationalism in Europe—all shared fundamental characteristics beneath their obvious differences. It was only by participating in this massive transformation that the various peoples of the world were able to progress and join the forward march of history. Yet despite its great importance, the Axial Age remains mysterious. We do not know what caused it, nor why it took root only in three core areas: in China; in India and Iran; and in the eastern Mediterranean. Why was it that only the Chinese, Iranians, Indians, Jews and Greeks experienced these new horizons and embarked on this quest for enlightenment and salvation? The Babylonians and Egyptians also created great civilizations, but they did not evolve an Axial ideology at this point, and only participated in the new ethos later: in Islam or Christianity, which were restatements of the original Axial impulse. But in the Axial countries, a few men sensed fresh possibilities and broke away from the old traditions. They sought change in the deepest reaches of

Popular

During the recession, consumer dependence on credit cards decreased while more and more patrons chose to use debit cards or cash.

Be that as it may, on Black Friday the amount of purchases made with credit cards rose 7.4% from last year, whereas payments made with debit cards increased by only 3.4%, First Data reports.

However, college students are still hesitant to whip out the plastic.

In February 2010, the Credit Card Accountability, Responsibility, and Disclosure Act (CARD Act) took effect, making it much more difficult for those under 21 to obtain a credit card, and thus begin building credit. With the implementation of the CARD Act, the number of credit card accounts opened through colleges and alumni associations fell 17%, according to a Federal Reserve survey.

Emory University sophomore Arielle Fradkin has two credit cards, which are linked to her parents' accounts. While she has her own debit cards, Fradkin says she does not have her own credit cards because she is still financially dependent on her parents.

"I use my credit cards for bigger things like groceries, school supplies, anything that I think my parents should pay for," Fradkin said. "I use my debit cards for smaller things like frozen yogurt or coffee, and also to pay for things I order online."

However, Fradkin does not fall into the trap of charging too much to the credit cards. To her, there's not much of a difference between credit and debit cards.

"I don't think I pay less attention to what I'm spending when I use a credit card," Fradkin

their beings, looked for greater inwardness in their spiritual lives, and tried to become one with a reality that transcended normal mundane conditions and categories. After this pivotal era, it was felt that only by reaching beyond their limits could human beings become most fully themselves.

Recorded history only begins in about 3000 B.C.E.; until that time we have little documentary evidence of the way human beings lived and organized their societies. But people always tried to imagine what the 20,000 years of prehistory had been like, and to root their own experience in it. All over the world, in every culture, these ancient days were depicted in mythology, which had no historical foundation but which spoke of lost paradises and primal catastrophes. In the Golden Age, it was said, gods had walked the earth with human beings. The story of the Garden of Eden, recounted in the Book of Genesis, the lost paradise of the West, was typical: once upon a time, there had been no rift between humanity and the divine: God strolled in the garden in the cool of the evening. Nor were human beings divided from one another. Adam and Eve lived in harmony, unaware of their sexual difference or of the distinction between good and evil. It is a unity that is impossible for us to imagine in our more fragmented existence, but in almost every culture, the myth of this primal concord showed that human beings continued to yearn for a peace and wholeness that they felt to be the proper state of humanity. They experienced the dawning of self-consciousness as a painful fall from grace. The Hebrew Bible calls this state of wholeness and completeness *shalom*; Gotama spoke of Nibbana and left his home in order to find it. Human beings, he believed, had lived in this peace and fulfillment before, but they had forgotten the path that led to it.

Karen Armstrong, *Buddha*

said. "My parents always instilled in me the idea that 'money is money is money.' It's not less if I use a credit card, or it doesn't seem like less to me. I think about all my purchases the same way whether I use a debit card, credit card, or cash. But I do try to pay with my debit cards when possible."

Emory University sophomore Devin McKissic has three credit cards, each of which is her own. McKissic and her parents decided she should have her own credit cards when she entered college so she could start building credit.

McKissic reserves her credit cards for when she doesn't have enough money in her checking account to make a purchase. The thought of looming charges makes her uneasy, so she pays for the charges within a week or two.

With the unstable economy and never-ending stories about credit card debt, McKissic, like other college students, always thinks twice before charging something.

Erica Petri,
"College Students Are Still Hesitant
to Whip Out the Plastic"

ACTIVITY 2

In each writing sample on pages 6–7, count the *number of sentences* in each paragraph. Write this number in the space provided. Then, read one or more paragraphs to get an idea of what kind of information the author includes.

CONTINUED >

Finally, in the space provided, write your own definition or description of an academic or popular paragraph.

1. *Buddha*, by Karen Armstrong

   Paragraph 1: _____

   Paragraph 2: _____

   An academic paragraph is _____

   _____

   _____

2. "College Students Are Still Hesitant to Whip Out the Plastic," by Erica Petri

   Paragraph 1: _____

   Paragraph 2: _____

   Paragraph 3: _____

   Paragraph 4: _____

   Paragraph 5: _____

   A popular paragraph is _____

   _____

   _____

ACTIVITY 3

For each of the following writing samples, identify whether the author is using popular or academic paragraphs. Then, in the space provided, explain why the paragraphs are popular or academic.

EXAMPLE:

Overdue books meant much-needed food Tuesday as Ozarks Food Harvest collected donations given to Springfield Public Libraries as part of the library's Food for Fines program.

Kathleen O'Dell, library spokesperson, said that 4.8 tons of food were collected, or enough for approximately 7,406 meals. The collection of cans and other food items at Library Station on North Kansas Expressway was about 8 feet by 15 feet, and it was 4 feet high.

This is the third year the library has done Food for Fines. This year the drive ran from Jan. 22 to 28. For each nonperishable food item brought in by a patron, overdue fines were reduced by 50 cents.

Type of paragraphs: *popular*

Explanation: The paragraphs have only one to three sentences. The writer wants the readers to move quickly, grabbing key pieces of information as they go.

1.   A bicyclist suffered minor injuries when she was hit by a U.S. Postal Service truck Tuesday in San Francisco's Richmond District, police said.

     The 39-year-old cyclist was traveling east on Clement Street at 4:48 P.M. when she was hit by the mail truck, which was heading north on 18th Avenue, police said.

     The cyclist, who was not wearing a helmet, suffered minor head trauma and was released from San Francisco General Hospital an hour after the crash, said Officer Albie Esparza, a police spokesman.

Type of paragraphs: _____

Explanation: _____

_____

_____

2.   Emotion doesn't only affect how memories are stored; it also affects how they are recalled. Recall from Chapter 3 the concept of *transfer-appropriate processing,* in which chances of recall are increased if the cues available at retrieval are similar to the cues available at testing. It is likewise easier to retrieve memories that match our current mood or emotional state; this effect is termed **mood-congruency of memory**. For example, in one study, students first listened to music and reported whether it made them feel happy or sad. They then saw a list of words (SHIP, STREET, etc.) and were asked to recall an autobiographical memory associated with each word. Students who had reported being in a happy mood tended to generate mostly positive memories, and relatively few neutral or negative

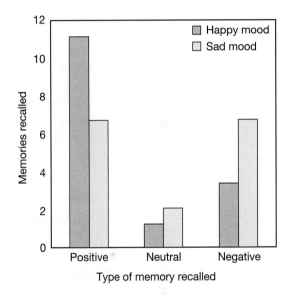

memories, as shown in Figure 10.5 (Eich, Macaulay & Ryan, 1994). Students in a sad mood recalled fewer positive and more negative memories. Few students in either mood generated neutral memories — consistent with the general principle that our strongest memories tend to be associated with strong emotions, whether those emotions are positive or negative.

Type of paragraph: _____

Explanation: _____

_____

_____

3.   Please join me in welcoming Tom Parenti, who has officially joined the custom publishing group as Editorial Assistant. Since last February, Tom has been working as our temporary intern, adapting well to a variety of tasks in a demanding, fast-paced environment.

CONTINUED >

We have quickly grown to value Tom's intelligence, wit, and calm demeanor, and especially his willingness to take on whatever the moment requires — from assisting with manuscript preparation and checking page proofs, to clearing permissions and following up on outstanding invoices, to formatting custom content. During the past few months, Tom has also stepped in as coordinator of our Select texts department.

We look forward to working with Tom on a more permanent basis, and we hope you share our enthusiasm in having him as part of our team.

Type of paragraphs: _____

Explanation: _____

_____

_____

4.   Many people think of knights as being the heroes of medieval Europe. However, they sometimes behaved more as villains, like the Mafia. They were cruel to members of the lower classes and forced the peasants to pay them "protection money." If the peasants didn't or couldn't pay, the knights would punish them. They would beat up the peasants, threaten them, and sometimes even kidnap the peasants and force them to obey the knights' orders. Sometimes, if one or two peasants made knights mad, the knights would lay waste their whole town, and no one had any power to fight back.

Type of paragraph: _____

Explanation: _____

_____

_____

Understanding Academic Essays

An academic essay is *a series of paragraphs*: an introduction, one or more "body" paragraphs that support and develop the essay's main idea, and a conclusion. In some cases, the introduction or the conclusion may be brief; however, each of the body paragraphs must be a fully developed and carefully organized academic paragraph—a complete "unit of thinking." Take a look at the following example of an academic essay.

Cheating in College

Today, cheating pops up everywhere we look. Athletes use performance-enhancing drugs, and big banks and corporations cheat people on their mortgages and investments. Like the rest of the world, students also cheat, and they do so for many reasons. They feel pressure to do well, and the competition is tough. By comparison, cheating seems easy. However, although cheating may seem to save time and produce higher grades, it is never worth the cost. In the end, cheating creates bigger problems such as a loss of respect, time, and money, and it encourages bad habits that follow students into their work life.

The first reason that cheating is not worth it is loss of respect. For one thing, if a student is caught cheating, he will lose the respect of his instructors. They will wonder about other assignments that the student has already turned in. It will become difficult for a teacher to trust that student. For example, instructors may not allow him extra time for an assignment or write him letters of recommendation for jobs or scholarships. As well, a student who gets a zero on a test or paper will disappoint his parents, who most likely hope that he is honest and hardworking. They will be ashamed if their son gets dropped from a class, or even expelled from his college. If they are paying his tuition, or if he is living at home, the consequences of cheating will also be especially intense. In addition, even if the student does not get caught, he may lose self-respect because he knows that he did not truly earn his grades. His conscience will bother him, and he might question his own abilities. Losing respect in the face of instructors, parents, and oneself makes cheating not worth the risk.

Another reason that cheating is not worth it is the loss of money and time. The rewards of cheating might be tempting: higher grades and the admiration of peers, parents, and faculty. However, if a student is caught, she might be expelled from a class—or even from the school. Imagine taking out student loans, or working multiple jobs, just to get expelled! It's like deliberately throwing away all that hard-earned money. Without a degree, a student's education doesn't add up to much. In addition, even if a student isn't expelled, being caught cheating might mean that she loses her scholarship. Without this financial support, she may not be able to continue working toward her degree. This is a waste of all the time the student already spent on that class and all the classes she has already completed. Furthermore, once she loses her classes or her financial support, she also loses the opportunity to continue her education. She may not get a chance to finish any degree. This is a huge risk and certainly not one worth taking.

A third reason that cheating in college is a bad idea is that it creates negative habits that will follow students throughout their school and work lives. When people cheat, they don't learn anything from the assignment or the class. Even if they can complete Introduction to Algebra by cheating, what happens in Algebra I when they don't know the fundamentals? They will be lost. In addition, when students with good GPAs do not live up to their reputations in the workplace, their jobs will be threatened. Employers expect much of high-ranking students, but cheaters can't deliver. They may not really know how to work hard to get things done at their jobs, either. Not to mention that if they pursue another degree, they won't know how to learn in more difficult classes. Cheating students have not learned to work hard to get things done, and this bad habit will eventually hurt them.

Even though students have reasons to cheat, it's not worth it in the end. Students lose respect, waste money and time, and learn nothing but how to cheat. Those who work hard for their grades are also cheated, and grades and diplomas become meaningless. Cheating may offer students something in the short term, but in the long run, no one wins.

Power Tip
You will learn about the parts and organization of a short essay in Chapter 8.

ACTIVITY 4

To see how much you already know about essays, evaluate the sample essay above, and then complete the following prompts.

1. Highlight or underline the sentence that contains the main idea for the essay (the thesis statement). Then, state the main idea in your own words on the lines below, and indicate what paragraph it appears in.

   Thesis statement: _____

   _____

   _____

   Appears in paragraph: _____

2. Highlight or underline the main support points that develop the writer's thesis sentence. Then, write them on the lines below and indicate what paragraph they appear in.

   Support point: _____

   _____

   Appears in paragraph: _____
   Support point: _____

   _____

   Appears in paragraph: _____
   Support point: _____

   _____

   Appears in paragraph: _____

3. Each support point is elaborated with some examples. Identify at least one or two for each support point and then write four or five of them below.

   _____

   _____

   _____

   _____

   _____

   _____

4. Identify the writer's concluding thought in the essay. Then, in your own words, write it on the lines below.

_____

_____

_____

ACTIVITY 5: Teamwork

You might already have some ideas about how paragraphs and essays are related. Get together with a classmate and answer the following questions.

- How are paragraphs and essays similar?
- How are paragraphs and essays different?

Understanding Your Purpose in Academic Writing

Every time you write, you write for a reason, or **purpose**. It is hard to imagine writing anything without a reason for doing so. To illustrate this simple point about writing with a purpose, complete the following activity.

ACTIVITY 6: Teamwork

Identify the author's likely reason, or purpose, for writing each of the following items. Then, write the reason in the space provided.

EXAMPLE: an essay for your art history class on Renaissance religious figures

Purpose(s): _to demonstrate your knowledge of the topic_

1. a letter from a credit card company to a customer who is behind in his payments

Purpose(s): _____

_____

2. a friend's description of his vacation on his Facebook page

Purpose(s): _____

_____

3. a letter from a U.S. soldier in Afghanistan to her children

Purpose(s): _____

_____

CONTINUED >

4. an e-mail to your professor telling her that you were at home sick yesterday

Purpose(s): _____

_____

5. a memo to your employer listing your achievements for the year

Purpose(s): _____

_____

WRITING TO INFORM, EXPLAIN, OR PERSUADE

As a college writer, you should have a clear sense of purpose for your academic writing assignments. Knowing your purpose will help you make intelligent choices about the information you include and how to present it most effectively.

In the broadest sense, the purpose of all writing is to communicate information and ideas. However, there are three key purposes for much of the writing that you will do in college. They are: **to inform**, **to explain**, and **to persuade**.

To Inform

Many of your college writing assignments may ask you to *present basic information* about a specific topic or issue. The information that you select will show your instructor how well you understand the topic. Here are some examples of topics that ask you to provide basic information on an issue:

- *Describe* a photograph of women marching on Washington.
- *Summarize* an article about health care to show its main points.
- *Identify* the events leading up to the Vietnam War.
- *Narrate* a story about your family's history.
- *Respond to* an assigned chapter on stem cells.

To Explain

Many of your instructors will ask you to do more than present basic information; they will ask you to *explain the meaning or importance of that information.* In this type of writing, you are required to explain, discuss, or interpret the meaning or importance of the information you provide. Here are some examples of topics that ask you to explain an issue to the reader:

- *Explain* the meaning of a photograph of women marching on Washington.
- *Interpret* the author's motive for writing an article on health care.
- *Analyze* the importance of each event leading up to the Vietnam War.

- *Discuss* how an event in your family's history changed your life.
- *Evaluate* what information in the assigned chapter on stem cells is most important.

To Persuade

As you advance in your college studies, you will be asked to do more than inform your readers or explain the meaning of things; you will be asked to *challenge—and perhaps change—your reader's opinion on a topic or issue.* In order to do this successfully, you will have to show clear thinking and provide good evidence for your position. You may also need to evaluate the arguments and opinions of experts on an issue. Here are some examples of topics that ask you to argue your point of view:

- *Argue* whether a photograph of women marching on Washington helped or hurt the feminist movement.
- *Agree or disagree* with the author's key points in an article on health care.
- *Persuade* your reader that the Vietnam War could or could not have been prevented.
- *Take a stand* on whether divorce is beneficial or harmful to the children in a family.
- *Defend your position* on the importance of stem cells for research.

Here is a chart that will help you recognize and understand the purposes for college writing:

PURPOSE	REQUIREMENT(S)	KEY WORDS
To inform	1. Provide (basic) information	Describe . . . Summarize . . . Identify . . . Narrate . . . Respond to . . .
To explain	1. Provide information 2. Explain the importance or meaning of the information	Explain . . . Interpret . . . Analyze . . . Discuss . . . Evaluate . . .
To persuade	1. Provide information 2. Explain the importance or meaning of the information 3. Argue different positions or viewpoints on the information	Argue . . . Agree/Disagree . . . Persuade . . . Take a stand . . . Defend your position . . .

CREATING A PURPOSE STATEMENT

Whenever you are given a writing assignment for college, it's helpful to take a few minutes to understand what the assignment requires. Without a clear sense of purpose, your response might become confusing, or it might stray from the topic.

Start by identifying key words in the topic (such as *describe, explain, argue,* and so on). Then, decide what kind of information you will need to include or what questions you will need to answer. Finally, write a brief statement of purpose for the assignment.

A purpose statement includes:

- **key words** (from the assignment)
- **purpose** for the writing (to inform, explain, persuade)
- **a statement** of the requirements needed to complete the assignment

ACTIVITY 7

Power Tip
Some writing assignments may have multiple purposes. However, you should identify which of these purposes is your primary purpose. Keep this in mind as you develop your ideas.

Analyze each of the following writing assignments to understand its purpose. First, underline key words in the assignment that help you identify the purpose. Then, in the space provided, write down the purpose and a statement that spells out the requirements for the assignment. If it is helpful, refer to the chart on page 15.

EXAMPLE: Select a photo by the American documentary photographer Dorothea Lange. <u>Analyze</u> the details in the image and <u>interpret</u> what they imply about life in America.

Key word(s): *analyze, interpret*

Purpose: *to explain*

Statement: *Provide information about a photograph by Dorothea Lange and explain the meaning or importance of it.*

1. Describe a place that makes you feel especially happy or calm. Be sure to include plenty of details to re-create the place in your reader's mind.

    Key word(s): _____

    Purpose: _____

    Statement: _____

    _____

2. Evaluate the advantages and disadvantages for the U.S. economy of outsourcing jobs to foreign countries.

    Key word(s): _____

    Purpose: _____

Statement: _____

_____

_____

3. Advertisements often use humor to hold the audience's attention and to make a product memorable. Choose a humorous ad from television, the Web, or another source and evaluate its use of humor. What visual, auditory, or textual elements make the ad funny—and why?

Key word(s): _____

Purpose: _____

Statement: _____

_____

_____

4. Think of a decision or action in your past that you regret — for instance, dropping out of school, stopping an exercise plan, or cheating. Now, think of someone who is about to make the same decision. Persuade him or her not to, using detailed evidence from your personal experience.

Key word(s): _____

Purpose: _____

Statement: _____

_____

_____

5. The "three strikes" laws require tough sentences for citizens convicted of three felonies. Supporters of these laws argue that they deter criminals. Opponents argue that they bypass fairer forms of justice. Argue for or against the "three strikes" laws, drawing on evidence from this course's textbook and lectures, and from your own research.

Key word(s): _____

Purpose: _____

Statement: _____

_____

_____

ACTIVITY 8: Teamwork

Use one of the following expressions to complete each writing topic. (Use each expression only once.) If it is helpful, use the chart on page 15 to review the key words, the purposes for college writing, and the requirements that go with each purpose.

CONTINUED >

EXAMPLE: Narrate/Interpret/Argue

_____Interpret_____ the effect or impact that the adult's actions had on you.

_____Argue_____ for a reward or a punishment that the adult deserves for his/her actions.

_____Narrate_____ something that an adult did to you as a child that hurt or helped you.

1. Summarize/Evaluate/Take a stand on

   _____ whether these parking rules, violations, and penalties should be changed.

   _____ the parking rules, violations, and penalties on your college campus.

   _____ the purpose and usefulness of these parking rules, violations, and penalties.

2. Describe/Discuss/Agree or Disagree

   _____ when, where, and how many people smoke on your college campus.

   _____ that smoking should be banned on your college campus.

   _____ your feelings about people smoking on your college campus.

3. Identify/Explain/Persuade

   _____ the reasons for your English instructor's policy on cell phones in the classroom.

   _____ your English instructor to keep or change this policy.

   _____ your English instructor's policy on cell phones in the classroom.

ACTIVITY 9

Pick one of the following topics and, on a separate piece of paper, respond briefly to each purpose. Moving from purpose to purpose in this way will help you understand the different requirements of each one.

Topic 1: Your reasons for being in college

Purpose 1: Summarize your reasons for being in college.

Purpose 2: Explain whether you think these reasons are important.

Purpose 3: Argue that being in college right now is or is not the best thing you could be doing with your life.

Topic 2: The cost of college textbooks

Purpose 1: <u>Identify</u> how much you spent on your textbooks this semester.

Purpose 2: <u>Evaluate</u> the quality of the textbooks you bought.

Purpose 3: <u>Take a stand on</u> whether textbooks are or are not a good value.

Topic 3: The college classes you are taking this semester

Purpose 1: <u>Describe</u> the classes that you are taking this semester.

Purpose 2: <u>Discuss</u> how you feel about the classes you are taking.

Purpose 3: <u>Argue</u> whether college students should or should not have to take required classes.

ACTIVITY 10: Teamwork

With a small group of your classmates, respond to each of the following assignments. Be prepared to share your ideas with the entire class.

Purpose 1: <u>Describe</u> what you did in the last activity.

Purpose 2: <u>Explain</u> what the last activity helped you to understand.

Purpose 3: <u>Argue</u> whether the last activity is or is not a useful learning experience.

Understanding Your Audience

Whenever you write, you always write for *someone*. If you are writing in a diary or journal, you will probably be writing for *yourself*. However, with most writing projects, you will be writing *for someone else*—your **audience**, or readers.

As a college writer, you should be aware of three general types of audiences: personal, professional, and academic.

In your personal writing, you communicate with family, friends, and casual acquaintances. These people can be considered your **personal audience**. Today, much of our personal writing is done electronically through e-mail, text messaging, and social networking sites, such as Facebook and Twitter.

Professional writing is used for business, journalism, and most forms of public communication. When you write for a **professional audience** (employers, employees, customers, clients, newspaper readers, and so on), your goal is to communicate public—not personal or private—information.

Finally, when you write assignments for college or university classes, you will be writing for an **academic audience**. In this situation, your main academic audience will be your instructors. However, the larger academic audience includes students, faculty, scholars, and researchers; forms of academic writing include college essays, textbooks, and scholarly journals and books.

Power Tip
There are other audience types besides personal, professional, and academic. For example, if you take a creative writing class in college, you will be addressing a *literary audience*. In this case, you will have much greater freedom in selecting the language and information you include in your writing.

ACTIVITY 11

For each of the following pieces of writing, identify who the specific audience is (personal, professional, or academic) and write it in the space provided.

EXAMPLE: a letter to your city's department of water and power asking for a limited-income discount on your usage

Type of audience: _professional_

1. a résumé and cover letter for a job application

   Type of audience: _____

2. a text message asking for directions to a restaurant

   Type of audience: _____

3. a take-home examination for an American history class

   Type of audience: _____

4. an article on new Alzheimer's treatments in the *Journal of the American Medical Association*

   Type of audience: _____

5. an acceptance letter from a college or university

   Type of audience: _____

Power Tip

More and more students are allowing text messaging abbreviations and slang to slip into their college writing. To discourage this habit, some instructors will take points off your grade. Be sure to edit your essays carefully in order to eliminate any inappropriate abbreviations or slang.

Power Tip

For a more in-depth explanation of Standard and Non-standard English, see Chapter 23, Using Verbs Correctly, pages 508–9.

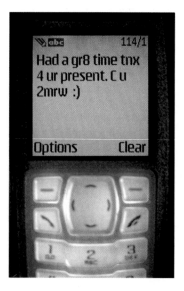

REACHING YOUR AUDIENCE

Knowing the audience for your writing can help you make important decisions about how to communicate effectively. Specifically, you should: (1) use **language** that is appropriate for your audience, and (2) provide **information** that is appropriate for your audience.

Use Language That Is Appropriate for Your Audience

If you are writing an e-mail or text message to a friend, you can use abbreviations (like CU for "*see you*" or UR for "*you are*") that make your writing fast and fun. You will probably use some slang, and you may break grammar rules.

However, if you are writing a letter to your manager at work, you will want to avoid abbreviations, slang, and any profanity that could offend or confuse your manager. Although you will want your writing to be clear and easy to understand, your grammar will probably be "relaxed"—correct enough for clear communication, but not perfect.

Finally, if you are writing an essay on cloning for your ethics class, your instructor will expect you to use more formal language and grammar, often referred to as "Standard English" (the form of written English expected in most school and work settings). In addition, you may need to use some technical language related to the topic of cloning. Because your audience (the instructor) will be knowledgeable about the topic, such language will be acceptable, even expected. You will also need to follow grammar rules carefully and to write complete, correct sentences.

The following chart summarizes the expectations of a few common audiences for whom you will write.

Different Audience Expectations for Writing

AUDIENCE TYPE	EXAMPLES	GRAMMAR	VOCABULARY
Personal	family, friends, Facebook users, etc.	Correct grammar is optional.	Informal English: slang and abbreviations are acceptable.
Professional	boss, credit card company, newspaper readers, etc.	Correct grammar is appreciated or expected.	Standard English
Academic	instructors, professors, other students, scholars, etc.	Correct grammar is required.	Standard English, sometimes with technical or specialized vocabulary

ACTIVITY 12

Identify what type of language (grammar and vocabulary) would be appropriate for each of the following pieces of writing, given its audience. Then, describe the language, referring to the previous chart.

EXAMPLE: a letter from an employer to an employee explaining why his job is being terminated

Appropriate language: _Standard English and correct grammar_

1. an invitation to your friends on Facebook for a New Year's Eve party

   Appropriate language: _____

2. an in-class exam for your art history class

   Appropriate language: _____

3. a letter to your city council representative asking for stronger police enforcement of neighborhood security

   Appropriate language: _____

4. an essay on women's rights in late-nineteenth-century America

   Appropriate language: _____

5. a short letter to your son's high school teacher asking for a meeting to discuss your son's learning difficulties

   Appropriate language: _____

Power Tip

The type of grammar and vocabulary you use will also determine the *tone* of your writing. Personal writing is usually conversational, professional writing is usually businesslike, and academic writing is usually formal.

Power Tip

Keep in mind that the formal tone of academic writing should come from carefully constructed sentences and carefully chosen vocabulary — not from overly complicated sentences or unnecessary "big" words.

Include Information That Is Appropriate for Your Audience

If your audience has little knowledge about your topic, you will need to include the most **basic information** possible. For example, if you are giving car maintenance advice to someone who knows little about cars, you will need to provide very basic advice, such as the need to change the oil regularly.

If your audience has a lot of knowledge or experience, you may skip very basic information and move directly to more **advanced information**. A car expert would already know about the need for regular oil changes but might want to hear about the latest technology for increasing engine efficiency.

If your audience is somewhere in between, you will need to provide an **intermediate level of information**—not too simple, and not too advanced. If the information you provide is too simple for your audience, you may lose their interest. If the information is too advanced for your audience, they may not understand your writing.

To decide what kind of information is appropriate for your audience, always answer this question: How much experience or knowledge does my audience have on the topic?

Whether the information you provide is basic, intermediate, or advanced, be sure that it is as precise and accurate as possible.

ACTIVITY 13

Write down the type of information (basic, intermediate, or advanced) that would be appropriate for the following audiences.

EXAMPLE: a lesson on making a soufflé for students in their first semester of culinary school

Appropriate information: _____basic_____

1. a description of the features of a new mountain bike for the owner of a bicycle shop

   Appropriate information: _____

2. instructions on how to use Excel spreadsheets for accounting students in their second year of accounting school

   Appropriate information: _____

3. a research essay on volcanoes for your geography class

   Appropriate information: _____

4. a letter to your younger brother who just started college, giving suggestions on how to successfully balance his schedule

   Appropriate information: _____

5. a class on dog obedience to a group of first-time dog owners

   Appropriate information: _____

CREATING AN AUDIENCE PROFILE

Whenever you are given a writing assignment for college, it's helpful to take a few minutes to create an "audience profile." Without a clear sense of who you are writing for, your response might become confusing or stray from the topic. In this brief profile, you will identify the type of audience for whom you are writing and what language and information are appropriate for that audience. An audience profile includes:

- type of **audience**
- type of **grammar** you will use for the audience
- type of **vocabulary** you will use for the audience
- type of **information** you will provide for the audience

ACTIVITY 14: Teamwork

With a small group of your classmates, make an audience profile for each of the following writing assignments. You may use the chart on page 21.

EXAMPLE: Write a letter to your aunt asking for a small loan to buy a car.

Type of audience: personal

Grammar you will use: Correct grammar is optional.

Vocabulary you will use: Informal English is okay.

Type of information you will provide: basic

1. Write a letter to the editor of your college newspaper complaining about the rise in tuition costs. You goal is to have the letter published in the newspaper so that your college's administration will read your complaint and take it seriously.

   Type of audience: _____

   Grammar you will use: _____

   Vocabulary you will use: _____

   Type of information you will provide: _____

2. For an art history class, write a presentation on the different types of gargoyles (stone creatures) used on churches and on the purposes of these creatures. Your goal is to convince your instructor that you understand an aspect of architecture: in this case, gargoyles.

   Type of audience: _____

   Grammar you will use: _____

   Vocabulary you will use: _____

   Type of information you will provide: _____

CONTINUED >

3. Write a Facebook posting to a friend about a funny movie you saw. Your goal is to persuade your friend to see the movie.

   Type of audience: _____

   Grammar you will use: _____

   Vocabulary you will use: _____

   Type of information you will provide: _____

4. Write a ten-minute speech to give to your local city council to describe the dangers of an intersection near your house. Your goal is to convince the council members that a traffic light should be installed at the intersection.

   Type of audience: _____

   Grammar you will use: _____

   Vocabulary you will use: _____

   Type of information you will provide: _____

5. For a business-writing class, write a letter to your credit card company to complain about an unfairly high interest rate. Your goal is to get the company to lower the rate.

   Type of audience: _____

   Grammar you will use: _____

   Vocabulary you will use: _____

   Type of information you will provide: _____

ACTIVITY 15: Teamwork

The following topic has been written three different ways, with three different audiences in mind: one personal, one professional, and one academic. With your classmates, read each passage out loud. Then, discuss and identify the language and information that make the passage appropriate for a certain type of audience. Finally, in the spaces provided, write down the type of audience and the type of language and information used in the passage.

Topic: The year-round school year versus ten-month school year

1. Although more and more U.S. schools are moving from a ten-month school year to a year-round schedule, this practice remains controversial. In a typical year-round schedule, students attend school at intervals throughout the year, getting breaks in between. A typical interval is 45 days of school followed by 15 days of break. Proponents of year-round education say that it makes students less likely to forget important information needed to advance in school. Also, brief breaks between school sessions can allow students who are struggling with a subject to get extra help with it right when they need it, rather than waiting for summer school. Finally, students avoid the boredom that can come with long summer breaks. Those who oppose year-round education say that there is no proof that it improves student

performance. Additionally, opponents argue that students are just as likely to forget information over short breaks as over long summer breaks. Finally, year-round students might be "out of sync" with camps and other summer programs, as well as employers looking for summer help. Researchers are trying to gather more evidence about the effectiveness of year-round school. In the meantime, school districts continue to debate the practice, with input from parents, teachers, and students.

Type of audience: _____

Type of grammar: _____

Type of vocabulary: _____

Type of information: _____

2.   Briarwood Public Schools will hold an open meeting to hear citizen comments about a proposal for year-round school for BPS students. The meeting will take place at 8 P.M. on Monday, March 23, in the Penman School auditorium. Specifically, the proposal is for a twelve-month school year with cycles of 45 days on and 15 days off. A briefing sheet on the proposal is available on the BPS Web site. The briefing describes positive aspects of year-round schooling, including the possibility that it keeps "educational momentum" going, allows students to get help when they need it, and avoids summertime boredom. Potentially negative aspects include possible difficulties in scheduling extracurricular activities and in obtaining summer employment. We encourage you to read the briefing in advance of the meeting and to come with your own questions, comments, and concerns.

Type of audience: _____

Type of grammar: _____

Type of vocabulary: _____

Type of information: _____

3.   Donna, did you see that bulletin on the BPS proposal and meeting? I want to go to the mtg, and I'm hoping maybe you'll want to join me. As you know, Carlo is at a BPS school, but Gina is at the Thayer School, which isn't considering the year-round thing, so I have no idea what it'll mean for work scheds, school scheds, etc. if this proposal goes through. I see the good points of it, but the scheduling stuff could be a total nightmare. What do you think about this whole thing? Let me know if you wanna join me for the meeting. I need to get off the computer now (kids need homework help), but I'll look for a message from you when I'm back on tomorrow.

Type of audience: _____

Type of grammar: _____

Type of vocabulary: _____

Type of information: _____

BRINGING IT ALL TOGETHER:
Seeing the Big Picture

In this chapter, you have learned about academic paragraphs and essays, as well as the purpose and audience for your college writing. Confirm your understanding by filling in the blank spaces in the sentences below. If you need help, review material in the chapter using the page numbers given. Finally, check off each item that you have mastered.

✔ An academic paragraph is an important writing format. It is a complete unit of _____, with a _____, _____, _____, and _____. (page 4)

✔ An academic essay has an introduction and a conclusion and one or more _____ paragraphs. (page 10)

✔ Three important purposes for academic writing are: _____, _____, and _____. (page 14)

✔ An assignment that asks for basic information about an issue might include the following key words: _____, _____, _____, _____, or _____. (pages 14–15)

✔ An assignment that asks for an explanation of the meaning or importance of information might include the following key words: _____, _____, _____, _____, or _____. (pages 14–15)

✔ An assignment that asks for an argument or a point of view might include the following key words: _____, _____, _____, _____, or _____. (page 15)

✔ Three types of audiences are: _____, _____, and _____. (page 19)

✔ Three types of information are: _____, _____, and _____. (page 22)

✔ An audience profile for a college writing assignment will consider the appropriate type of _____, _____, _____, and _____ for the assignment. (page 23)

Journal Writing

Besides the formal writing that you do for your college classes, some *informal* writing in a personal journal can be both enjoyable and beneficial. Spending as little as ten minutes a day writing down your thoughts can help you become more aware of yourself, your relationships, and your surroundings. At the same time, it can help you integrate the writing skills you are learning in your college classes and can help you improve your time and stress management. Occasionally, it can even feel like taking a break from the hectic pace of college life.

To begin your journal, take out a fresh sheet of paper, open a blank computer screen, or begin a new notebook dedicated to journal writing. Give yourself 10 or 15 minutes and write without stopping. Simply write down what happened and explain how you feel about the events. (Remember, journal writing is informal writing. You should not worry about grammar or organization; just let your ideas flow.)

Since college can be an especially challenging experience, writing about it on a regular basis can help you become a more relaxed, confident, and successful student.

JOURNAL WRITING: 10–15 minutes

Write about an unforgettable experience you've had. For example, discuss something unique or engaging that happened to you at work, at school, at home, or on the street. Perhaps one of your classes has been particularly helpful or interesting so far; if so, write about its effect on you.

CHAPTER 2

Getting Your Ideas Down

Test your understanding of how to get ideas down by completing this quiz. You may know more than you think.

For each question, select all the answers that apply.

WHAT DO YOU KNOW?

1. **Which of the following methods are commonly used for generating ideas?**
   ___ clustering
   ___ freewriting
   ___ revising
   ___ listing

2. **A person's way of thinking and processing information is sometimes called his or her:**
   ___ learning style.
   ___ brainstorming.
   ___ intelligence quotient (I.Q.).
   ___ writing process.

3. **If you are a visual learner, you usually:**
   ___ write precise class notes.
   ___ enjoy drawing and images.
   ___ sketch or doodle while taking class notes.
   ___ like to make or read charts of information.

4. **If you are a verbal learner, you usually:**
   ___ are very interested in word games.
   ___ enjoy reading and writing.
   ___ are curious about colors and color combinations.
   ___ remember faces more than names.

5. **If you prefer solving problems in an orderly, step-by-step fashion, which of the following may describe you?**
   ___ right-brain dominant
   ___ left-brain dominant
   ___ a balanced brain
   ___ a no-brainer

Evaluating Your Learning Style

The first step in the writing process is often called *brainstorming*—getting your initial ideas down on paper. As you will see—here and in more depth in Chapter 3—there are several popular methods for brainstorming: **clustering**, **listing**, **freewriting**, and **flowcharting**. Each method is available to all writers. However, some may correspond more closely to your particular learning style—the way you think and process information most effectively. If you select methods that correspond well to your learning style, your brainstorming may go more smoothly.

In this chapter, you'll have an opportunity to evaluate your learning style and hemispheric (brain) dominance. This information will help you select one or more recording methods that may help you brainstorm effectively.

ARE YOU VERBAL OR VISUAL?

When we learn, we use a combination of our visual and verbal abilities. However, some students learn better through words and language, while others learn better through images and objects. If you prefer words, you may be a strong **verbal learner**; if you prefer images, you may be a strong **visual learner**. If you work equally well with words and images, you may have a **balanced learning style**.

ACTIVITY 1: Teamwork

Look at the two images below and decide which one grabs your attention more. Then, pair with a classmate and discuss why you find one image more interesting to look at than the other. Use the questions that follow to guide your discussion.

agency apart **baradell**
belo billion blog brand business calls
clients com
communications
company competitors
corporate creative customers
employees executive experience expertise firm
grove idea idea grove
industry investors marketing
media message news offering pr
president product programs
public relations
revenues sales served services strategic
strategy technology vice web wireless work

CONTINUED >

1. The image on the left / right (circle one) grabs my attention the most because _____

   _____ .

2. As I look closer at this image, I am intrigued by _____

   _____ .

3. This image holds my attention for quite a while because _____

   _____ .

4. The other image is less interesting to me because _____

   _____ .

5. After talking to my classmate about the other image, I understand that it is appealing to him/her because _____

   _____ .

Power Tip
If you want to learn more about learning styles, do a quick Internet search by typing in any of the following phrases: *learning styles, multiple intelligences, right brain, left brain, verbal learner, visual learner.*

ACTIVITY 2

Complete the following survey to understand whether you may be more verbal or visual in your learning style.

1. Would you prefer to take a creative writing class or a class in drawing and painting?

Definitely creative writing	Maybe creative writing	No preference	Maybe drawing/ painting	Definitely drawing/painting
❑	❑	❑	❑	❑
1	2	3	4	5

2. When you are following an instruction booklet, do you start reading the instructions first to figure out what to do or do you look at the pictures first?

Definitely read instructions first	Maybe read instructions first	No preference	Maybe look at pictures first	Definitely look at pictures first
❑	❑	❑	❑	❑
1	2	3	4	5

3. Are you better at remembering people's names or faces?

Definitely remember people's names	Maybe remember people's names	No preference	Maybe remember people's faces	Definitely remember people's faces
❑	❑	❑	❑	❑
1	2	3	4	5

Power Tip
Try opening a newspaper and see if your attention is drawn more to the headlines or to the illustrations and photos. This is a quick way to begin thinking about your learning style preferences.

4. Do you "doodle" (draw pictures or designs) a lot when you are taking notes for a class?

Definitely do not doodle	Maybe do not doodle	No preference	Maybe doodle	Definitely doodle
❑	❑	❑	❑	❑
1	2	3	4	5

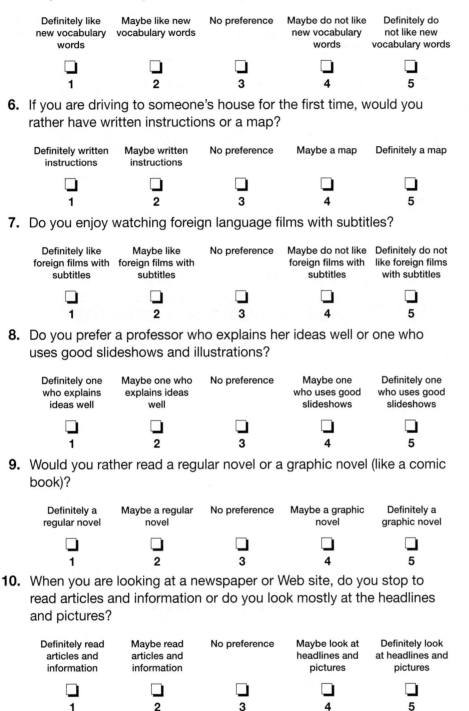

5. Do you like learning new vocabulary words?

Definitely like new vocabulary words	Maybe like new vocabulary words	No preference	Maybe do not like new vocabulary words	Definitely do not like new vocabulary words
❏	❏	❏	❏	❏
1	2	3	4	5

6. If you are driving to someone's house for the first time, would you rather have written instructions or a map?

Definitely written instructions	Maybe written instructions	No preference	Maybe a map	Definitely a map
❏	❏	❏	❏	❏
1	2	3	4	5

7. Do you enjoy watching foreign language films with subtitles?

Definitely like foreign films with subtitles	Maybe like foreign films with subtitles	No preference	Maybe do not like foreign films with subtitles	Definitely do not like foreign films with subtitles
❏	❏	❏	❏	❏
1	2	3	4	5

8. Do you prefer a professor who explains her ideas well or one who uses good slideshows and illustrations?

Definitely one who explains ideas well	Maybe one who explains ideas well	No preference	Maybe one who uses good slideshows	Definitely one who uses good slideshows
❏	❏	❏	❏	❏
1	2	3	4	5

9. Would you rather read a regular novel or a graphic novel (like a comic book)?

Definitely a regular novel	Maybe a regular novel	No preference	Maybe a graphic novel	Definitely a graphic novel
❏	❏	❏	❏	❏
1	2	3	4	5

10. When you are looking at a newspaper or Web site, do you stop to read articles and information or do you look mostly at the headlines and pictures?

Definitely read articles and information	Maybe read articles and information	No preference	Maybe look at headlines and pictures	Definitely look at headlines and pictures
❏	❏	❏	❏	❏
1	2	3	4	5

ACTIVITY 3

Figure out your total score from Activity 2 by adding the numbers below each of your answers. Enter your total on the line below. Then, use the graph below to think about your learning preference.

CONTINUED >

Total Score: _____   **I am a** _____ **learner.**

Strong verbal learner	Moderate verbal learner	Balanced learning style	Moderate visual learner	Strong visual learner

10   15   20   25   30   35   40   45   50

ACTIVITY 4: Teamwork

Power Tip

If you are working on these activities as homework, ask a friend or family member to take the ten-question survey in Activity 2 and total the points. Then, do the teamwork Activity 4 with that person. It's more fun and informative to share your results and opinions with others who've taken the survey.

Pair with a classmate and discuss whether you agree or disagree with the results of the survey you just completed in Activities 2 and 3. Then, look at the chart below and discuss whether you have a verbal, visual, or balanced learning style.

General Characteristics of Verbal and Visual Learners

VERBAL LEARNER	VISUAL LEARNER
• Enjoys reading and writing	• Enjoys drawing and pictures
• Is curious about new vocabulary words	• Is curious about colors and color combinations
• Takes accurate notes during class	• Sketches or doodles while taking class notes
• Is comfortable with foreign languages	• Is comfortable with abstract and modern art
• Is intrigued by word puzzles or games	• Is intrigued by picture or object puzzles
• Asks for directions, tends to get lost	• Uses a map and instinct, rarely gets lost
• Remembers names of people and places	• Remembers faces and scenes very well
• Prefers written communication (blogs, e-mail, letters)	• Prefers pictorial communication (photos, icons, abbreviations, etc.)
• Likes talking, debating, and storytelling	• Likes observing, watching, daydreaming

ARE YOU RIGHT BRAINED OR LEFT BRAINED?

When we learn, we use a combination of our left- and right-brain functions. If you prefer solving problems in an orderly, step-by-step fashion, you may rely more on your **left brain**. If you prefer using your imagination and intuition to find solutions, you may rely more on your **right brain**. If you use your reasoning and imaginative abilities equally well, you may be using your brain functions equally well. In this case, you have a **balanced learning style**.

ACTIVITY 5: Teamwork

Look at the image below and see if you can recognize some of your study habits in either the left- or the right-brain image. Then, pair with a classmate and explain why you see yourself more in one image than the other — or between the two.

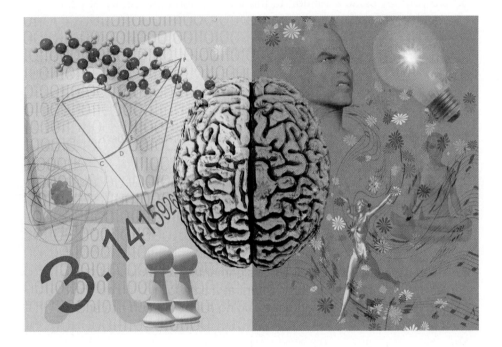

ACTIVITY 6

Complete the following survey to understand whether you may be more left-brain or right-brain dominant. Then, in the next activity, you can add up your score to determine your type.

1. Are your class notes neatly organized with different sections for each class?

Definitely neatly organized	Somewhat neatly organized	Not sure	Somewhat disorganized	Definitely disorganized
❏	❏	❏	❏	❏
1	2	3	4	5

2. Do you prefer a test with multiple-choice or short-answer questions?

Definitely multiple-choice questions	Maybe multiple-choice questions	No preference	Maybe short answers	Definitely short answers
❏	❏	❏	❏	❏
1	2	3	4	5

CONTINUED >

3. When you get a "crazy idea," are you more likely to talk yourself out of it or "go for it"?

Definitely talk myself out of it	Maybe talk myself out of it	Not sure	Maybe go for it	Definitely go for it
❏	❏	❏	❏	❏
1	2	3	4	5

4. Do you pay close attention to the time, looking frequently at your watch or clocks?

Definitely pay close attention to time	Maybe pay close attention to time	No preference	Maybe do not pay close attention to time	Definitely do not pay close attention to time
❏	❏	❏	❏	❏
1	2	3	4	5

5. If someone is telling you a story, do you become impatient if he rambles and doesn't get to the point?

Definitely impatient with rambling	Maybe impatient with rambling	No preference	Maybe not impatient with rambling	Definitely not impatient with rambling
❏	❏	❏	❏	❏
1	2	3	4	5

6. If you have a lot of homework assignments to complete, do you patiently complete one assignment at a time, or do you go back and forth between assignments, doing a little of each one at a time?

Definitely complete one at a time	Maybe complete one at a time	No preference	Maybe go back and forth	Definitely go back and forth
❏	❏	❏	❏	❏
1	2	3	4	5

7. If you found an expensive item of clothing that you loved, would you go away and think about whether or not you should buy it or would you buy it on impulse?

Definitely go away and think about it	Maybe go away and think about it	No preference	Maybe buy it on impulse	Definitely buy it on impulse
❏	❏	❏	❏	❏
1	2	3	4	5

8. If you got a new cell phone, MP3 player, or other device, would you read the instruction booklet first or just start playing around with the device?

Definitely read instructions first	Maybe read instructions first	No preference	Maybe start playing around with the device	Definitely start playing around with the device
❏	❏	❏	❏	❏
1	2	3	4	5

9. When you first visit a Web site, do you study the items on the homepage first, or do you start clicking on interesting links right away?

Definitely study the items on homepage	Maybe study the items on homepage	No preference	Maybe start clicking on interesting links	Definitely start clicking on interesting links
❑	❑	❑	❑	❑
1	2	3	4	5

10. Do you prefer studying in a quiet, secluded place (a library, your bedroom) or in a busy, active place (the school cafeteria, Starbucks, etc.)?

Definitely in a quiet, secluded place	Maybe in a quiet, secluded place	No preference	Maybe in a busy, active place	Definitely in a busy, active place
❑	❑	❑	❑	❑
1	2	3	4	5

ACTIVITY 7

Figure out your total score from Activity 6 by adding the numbers below each of your answers. Enter your total on the line below. Then, use the graph below to think about which part of your brain you use the most.

Total Score: _____ I have a _____ brain function.

Strong left brain	Moderate left brain	Balanced brain function	Moderate right brain	Strong right brain

10   15   20   25   30   35   40   45   50
■ ■

ACTIVITY 8: Teamwork

Pair with a classmate and discuss whether you agree or disagree with the results of the survey you just completed. Then, look at the chart below and discuss whether you have a left-, right-, or balanced brain function.

General Characteristics of Left- and Right-Brain Dominance

LEFT-BRAIN DOMINANCE	RIGHT-BRAIN DOMINANCE
• Prefers step-by-step tasks	• Lacks patience with step-by-step tasks
• Pays close attention to details	• Doesn't worry much about details
• Follows the rules	• Ignores the rules
• Likes using reasoning and logic	• Likes using imagination and intuition (feeling)
• Wants to know the answers	• Wants to ponder and ask interesting questions
• Plans ahead, plays it safe	• Goes with the flow, takes risks
• Thinks about past mistakes	• Lives in the moment

Power Tip
If you are working at home, ask a friend or family member to take the ten-question survey in Activity 6 and total the points. Then, do the teamwork Activity 8 with that person. It's more fun and informative to share your results and opinions with others who've also taken the survey.

Recognizing Brainstorming Methods

As you begin to gather ideas for a writing assignment, you will want to record your ideas—that is, *get them down on paper*—as quickly and effectively as possible. Students who try to keep ideas in their head usually lose valuable time and information in completing assignments.

You are probably already familiar with one or more of these brainstorming methods—and they will be covered in more depth in the next chapter (see pages 48–56). Knowing which method or methods work best for you can greatly enhance the success of your work. This section will give you ideas and practice that can help you determine which method—or methods—you prefer.

Below are four basic approaches to writing down your ideas: *clustering, listing, freewriting,* and *flowcharting.*

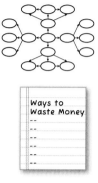

- A **cluster** begins in the center of the page with a main idea and moves outward into smaller and smaller parts.
- **Listing** is similar to taking notes in class. You write down just the essential words to capture each idea, and then you move to a new line for the next idea. You may have one long list or a series of smaller lists with or without headings.
- **Freewriting** is like writing in a personal journal or diary. You write down your thoughts as though you are having a conversation with yourself or writing a letter to a friend. Just let your thoughts flow—writing anything that comes to mind—without worrying about spelling, grammar, or typing errors.
- A **flowchart** starts at the top of the page with a main idea and breaks into smaller and smaller parts as it moves down the page.

FINDING YOUR PREFERRED BRAINSTORMING METHOD

Now, use the results from the two surveys you took on pages 30 and 33, plus the grid below, to determine which brainstorming method may be best for you.

Verbal Learner Left Brain <div align="right">LISTING</div>	Verbal Learner Right Brain FREEWRITING
<div align="right">FLOWCHARTING</div> Visual Learner Left Brain	CLUSTERING <div align="right">Visual Learner Right Brain</div>

If you are a strong *verbal learner*, you may prefer using one of the more text-based methods (listing or freewriting). If you are a strong *visual learner*, you may prefer using one of the more graphics-based methods (clustering or flowcharting).

If your *left brain* is dominant, you may prefer recording your ideas in an organized, step-by-step sequence. In this case, try using listing or flowcharting, as both of these methods can guide your thinking in a more ordered fashion. If your *right brain* is dominant, you may prefer allowing your ideas to flow naturally, without too much organizational restraint. In this case, try freewriting or clustering, as both of these methods encourage your mind to "unfold" and explore all the possibilities.

Power Tip

If you want to do clustering or flowcharting efficiently on a computer, you may need special software (such as Inspiration, Mindjet, or Cornerstone). Check with your college's learning center to see if it has such software installed for student use.

TEST-DRIVING THE METHODS

Now, it's time to "test-drive" the four brainstorming methods reviewed in this chapter and get a feel for each one. (For more detailed instruction in how to use these methods, see Chapter 3, pages 48–56.)

Practice Clustering

ACTIVITY 9

Imagine that your instructor would like your personal recommendation for a great source of entertainment. Pick one from the list below and convince your instructor that he or she <u>must</u> try it out. You may choose:

- an album or a song
- a movie or TV show
- a book
- a video game
- a Web site

On a blank sheet of paper, draw the following cluster to get started. In the center circle, write the name of your personal recommendation for a great source of entertainment.

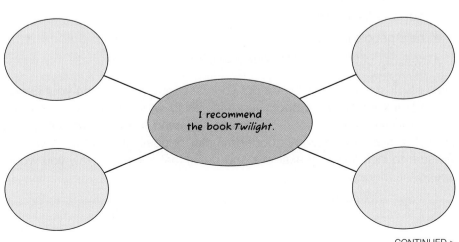

I recommend
the book *Twilight*.

CONTINUED >

To download a premade clustering diagram, go to **bedfordstmartins.com /touchstones** and click on Useful Forms.

Take about ten minutes to write down as many ideas as you possibly can. Keep expanding the cluster by adding new circles. You should try to include every example and detail that will convince your instructor to try out your recommendation.

Practice Listing

ACTIVITY 10

Among the following topics, pick the <u>one</u> that you have the most to say about:

Ways to Waste Money
- --
- --
- --
- --
- --
- --

- spending hours on the Internet
- qualities your soul mate must have
- ways to waste money
- bad fashion statements
- a celebrity whom you admire or detest

On a separate sheet of paper, write down the title for your own list. Take about ten minutes to write down as many ideas as you can. Keep expanding the list by adding new ideas. Express each idea with just a few key words and move quickly from one idea to the next. Be sure to include every example and detail that will show your knowledge of the topic.

Practice Freewriting

ACTIVITY 11

Surprise! You have just won a $5,000 prize to do one of the following things:

I would like to use my $5,000 to go on a shopping spree.

- go on a dream trip
- go on a shopping spree
- get your life in order
- help people in need
- _____ (Fill in your own idea.)

On a blank sheet of paper, write out your first sentence, putting your choice in the blank space. Take about ten minutes to write down as many ideas as you can. As you explore your fantasy, pretend that you are writing in a journal or diary. Don't worry about grammar or spelling — just keep writing. Be sure to include every example and detail that will show how you would spend the money.

Practice Flowcharting

ACTIVITY 12

Do the habits of some people get on your nerves? From the following groups, pick a person or group of persons whose habits annoy you:

- co-workers or boss
- classmates or teacher
- teammates or coach
- siblings or parent
- anyone else who annoys you

On a blank sheet of paper, draw a flowchart diagram similar to the one below to get started. In the box at the top of the diagram, write down the person or people whose habits annoy you.

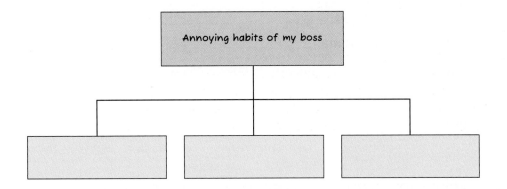

Take about ten minutes to write down as many ideas as you can. Keep extending the flowchart by adding additional boxes. Be sure to include every example and detail that will explain how the person or people get on your nerves.

ACTIVITY 13: Teamwork

Team up with a small group of your classmates and discuss your experience with each brainstorming method. Working together, try to identify what you like (pros) or don't like (cons) about each method. Write your ideas in the blank spaces below.

1. **Clustering**

    Pros: _____

    Cons: _____

CONTINUED >

2. **Listing**

   Pros: _____

   Cons: _____

3. **Freewriting**

   Pros: _____

   Cons: _____

4. **Flowcharting**

   Pros: _____

   Cons: _____

ACTIVITY 14

Now, take a moment to write out your preferred brainstorming method. Take a moment to also explain why it works for you.

Preferred method: _____

Why it works for me: _____

_____

_____

BRINGING IT ALL TOGETHER:
Getting Your Ideas Down

In this chapter, you have learned about learning styles and which brainstorming methods might work best for you. Confirm your understanding by filling in the blank spaces in the sentences below. If you need help, review the pages listed.

✔ If you learn better through words and language, you may have a _____ learning style. (page 29)

✔ If you learn better through images, you may have a _____ learning style. (page 29)

✔ If you prefer solving problems in an orderly, step-by-step fashion, you may rely more on your _____ brain. (page 32)

✔ If you prefer using your imagination and intuition to find solutions, you may rely more on your _____ brain. (page 32)

✔ If you use your reasoning and imaginative abilities equally well, you may have a _____ learning style. (page 32)

✔ Among the four popular brainstorming methods, _____ begins in the center of the page with a main idea and moves outward into smaller and smaller parts. _____ your ideas is similar to taking notes in class. _____ is like writing in a personal journal or diary. A _____ starts at the top of the page with a main idea and breaks into smaller and smaller parts as it moves down the page. (page 36)

✔ Two text-based methods of getting your ideas down are called _____ and _____. These brainstorming methods are often preferred by _____ learners. (page 37)

✔ Two graphics-based methods of getting your ideas down are called _____ and _____. These brainstorming methods are often preferred by _____ learners. (page 37)

JOURNAL WRITING: 10–15 minutes

If you have completed the activities in this chapter, you now have a lot of information about learning styles, brain dominance, and brainstorming methods. Write, without stopping, about what you have learned and how your attitudes may have changed about any of these methods. What do you think of your own learning processes now?

CHAPTER 3

Developing a Topic

Test your understanding of how to develop a topic by completing this quiz. You may know more than you think.

For each question, select all the answers that apply.

WHAT DO YOU KNOW?

1. **Which one of the following types of writing topics will give you the most choice in what to write about?**
   ___ a limited topic
   ___ a broad topic ✓
   ___ a narrow topic

2. **Which of the following topics would be considered the narrowest?**
   ___ *Discuss education.*
   ___ *Discuss required classes for college freshmen.*
   ___ *Discuss a professor you like.* ✓

3. **When brainstorming for ideas on a topic, what step should you do first?**
   ___ Make an outline of big ideas and related examples.
   ___ Freewrite, make lists, cluster, or make flowcharts to explore your thoughts.
   ___ Research your topic.

4. **Which of the following might make a writing topic work for you?**
   ___ The topic is very broad.
   ___ The topic appeals to you.
   ___ You know very little about the topic.
   ___ You would like to talk about the topic with others.

5. **What are some good questions to ask if you get stuck in your brainstorming and need a "jump start"?**
   ___ Who?
   ___ Where?
   ___ When?
   ___ What?
   ___ Why?

Understanding Broad, Limited, and Narrow Topics

In Chapter 1, you learned about different types of paragraphs, purposes, and audiences. As you now know, in college you will typically write academic paragraphs and essays in response to specific assignments.

Some assignment topics are very **broad** or general, giving students a lot of choice in what to write about. Other topics are more carefully defined, giving students a **limited** choice in what to write about. In other cases, a topic may be very **narrow**, giving students very little choice in what to write about.

As a college student, you should be able to recognize the type of topic you have been assigned. To work effectively, you should know how much choice you have and how much further narrowing, if any, you will have to do with a topic.

Now, let's look at some sample college writing assignments. The instructor might make the writing assignment broad, limited, or narrow:

BROAD TOPIC   Discuss the financial reality of attending college.

This topic is broad because there are so many different parts of the "financial reality" of going to college. You could focus on tuition costs, housing costs, textbooks and supplies, loans and scholarships, financial contributions from family or loved ones, work-study programs, working part-time or full-time while going to school, living on a fixed income, long-term debt, and so on. Clearly, this topic will require you to make some careful choices in what you wish to write about.

LIMITED TOPIC   Discuss financial aid for college students.

Like the broad topic, this topic is also about student finances. However, the focus has been determined more carefully: you must write about financial aid at college. Here, you still have quite a bit of choice: you can write about state or federal financial aid, private loans, merit-based or financial need–based loans, private or public scholarships, and so on.

NARROW TOPIC   Discuss how much you spent on your college textbooks this semester and whether this was a good value.

This topic has already been narrowed by your instructor. You must specify how much you spent on your textbooks this semester and explain whether you believe this expenditure was a good value for you. You don't have much choice in what to write about—just present the facts and give your opinion.

Some students prefer broad topics that give them plenty of choice. However, this freedom of choice comes at a cost. You must work harder to narrow a broad topic to a manageable scope for your assignment.

ACTIVITY 1: Teamwork

Examine each of the following groups of topics. Then, decide which topic offers the most choice in what to write about, which one offers a limited choice, and which one offers little choice. In the space provided, label each topic *broad*, *limited*, or *narrow*.

CONTINUED >

EXAMPLE: Discuss reality television.   broad

Discuss the TV show *The Bachelor.*   limited

Discuss last night's episode of *Real
Housewives of Beverly Hills.*   narrow

1. Discuss the advantages and/or disadvantages
   of having a cat rather than a dog.   _____

   Discuss a low-maintenance pet.   _____

   Discuss pets.   _____

2. Discuss the behavior of a celebrity athlete.   _____

   Discuss how celebrity athletes have changed
   professional sports.   _____

   Discuss celebrity athletes.   _____

3. Discuss a professor who assigns too much work.   _____

   Discuss college professors.   _____

   Discuss how college professors don't understand
   the needs of their students.   _____

4. Discuss dating.   _____

   Discuss appropriate first-date behavior.   _____

   Discuss the risks and benefits of Internet dating.   _____

5. Discuss how the Internet can be harmful
   for children.   _____

   Discuss children and the Internet.   _____

   Discuss a good Internet site for children.   _____

6. Discuss Hillary Clinton.   _____

   Discuss Hillary Clinton's role as a politician
   in the United States.   _____

   Discuss a campaign that Hillary Clinton
   undertook and how effective it was.   _____

7. Discuss the history of the International Soccer Cup.   _____

   Discuss your favorite soccer player.   _____

   Discuss soccer.   _____

8. Discuss the artistic movement known
   as impressionism.   _____

   Discuss the innovations of the impressionist
   painters.   _____

   Discuss Van Gogh's impressionist painting
   Starry Night.   _____

Narrowing a Topic

If you are assigned a broad topic, you will probably need to narrow it to a more manageable scope to write an academic essay, and even more for an academic paragraph. The scope of your topic should fit the required length of the composition, which is usually set by your instructor. Here are some common lengths (typed and double-spaced) for college writing assignments:

- an academic paragraph (one page or less)
- a short essay (one to three pages)
- a standard essay (three to five pages)
- a research essay (more than five pages)

As you narrow a topic, make sure that the information you need to include will fit comfortably within the required page length. Also, make sure that your topic is not *too narrow*. Otherwise, you might not have enough ideas to fulfill the length requirement.

Now, suppose that you have been assigned the following topic:

BROAD TOPIC   Write about the neighborhood you live in.

Clearly, this topic is too broad for a paragraph or an essay. There are so many aspects of your neighborhood that you could discuss—its history, its location, its buildings and architecture, its residents, its community groups and functions, and so on. If you covered all of these points, you might end up with a 10- or 12-page paper. It would be impossible to include them all in a successful paragraph or short essay.

Now, here is how the topic could be narrowed for a short essay of one to three pages:

LIMITED TOPIC   I'll write about <u>the interesting people</u> who live in my neighborhood.

In a short essay of one to three pages, you could carefully discuss several interesting people who live in your neighborhood. You would have plenty of room to provide specific examples and details to illustrate each of these people. However, for a paragraph-length writing assignment (one page or less) you would need to narrow the topic even more:

NARROW TOPIC   I will write about <u>the neighborhood watch group</u> on my street.

In one page or less, you could carefully describe the activities of your neighborhood watch group, its members, and even a bit about its history.

ACTIVITY 2: Teamwork

With a small group of your classmates, discuss possibilities for narrowing each of the following broad topics. When you have discovered a narrowed topic that you like, write it in the space provided. You may use the same topics as other members of your group, or you may find topics that are of specific interest to you.

CONTINUED >

EXAMPLE: **Broad:** Write about dreams.

    Limited: I like to analyze my dreams to learn about my life.

    Narrow: I've had the same scary dream since I was eight years old.

1. **Broad:** Write about food.

    Limited: _____

    _____

    Narrow: _____

    _____

2. **Broad:** Write about money.

    Limited: _____

    _____

    Narrow: _____

    _____

3. **Broad:** Write about friendship.

    Limited: _____

    _____

    Narrow: _____

    _____

4. **Broad:** Write about college life.

    Limited: _____

    _____

    Narrow: _____

    _____

5. **Broad:** Write about expectations.

    Limited: _____

    _____

    Narrow: _____

    _____

Selecting a Topic That Works for You

When you have a choice of topics, be sure to consider which topic will work best for you. In other words, decide which topic will *motivate* you to write and give you the *best results*. Here is a list of criteria that you can use to evaluate topics:

- Does the topic appeal to you immediately? Does it seem interesting, exciting, or fun? (A topic that grabs your interest will motivate you.)
- What can you learn from this topic about yourself or the world you live in? Would you like to explore this topic and learn more? (Intellectual curiosity—your desire to learn more—will also motivate you.)
- Do you know a lot about this topic? Do you have a lot to say about it? (Having a lot to say about a topic will motivate you.)
- Is this a topic that you would like to discuss with other people? Would you like to show your finished composition to others? (The desire to share your ideas with other people will motivate you.)

ACTIVITY 3

For this activity, write each of your narrowed topics from Activity 2 on the line that says "Narrowed Topic." Score each topic according to the four criteria listed, using the following key: **3** = definitely   **2** = somewhat   **1** = not really. Finally, add the four scores together to find out the total score.

1. Narrowed Topic _____

The topic seems exciting or fun.	3 2 1
I would like to learn something from this topic.	3 2 1
I know a lot about this topic.	3 2 1
I would like to share my ideas about this topic with others.	3 2 1

Total score: _____

2. Narrowed Topic _____

The topic seems exciting or fun.	3 2 1
I would like to learn something from this topic.	3 2 1
I know a lot about this topic.	3 2 1
I would like to share my ideas about this topic with others.	3 2 1

Total score: _____

3. Narrowed Topic _____

The topic seems exciting or fun.	3 2 1
I would like to learn something from this topic.	3 2 1
I know a lot about this topic.	3 2 1
I would like to share my ideas about this topic with others.	3 2 1

Total score: _____

4. Narrowed Topic _____

The topic seems exciting or fun.	3 2 1
I would like to learn something from this topic.	3 2 1

CONTINUED >

I know a lot about this topic.   3 2 1

I would like to share my ideas about this topic with others.   3 2 1

Total score: _____

5. Narrowed Topic _____

The topic seems exciting or fun.   3 2 1

I would like to learn something from this topic.   3 2 1

I know a lot about this topic.   3 2 1

I would like to share my ideas about this topic with others.   3 2 1

Total score: _____

ACTIVITY 4: Teamwork

With a few of your classmates, identify which of your topics in Activity 3 scored the highest. Then, explain why you believe these topics would (or would not) motivate you to write and help you get the best results in your composition.

Power Tip
If you would like more information on the kind of brainstorming method that is right for you, see Chapter 2. There, you can take surveys that will help you identify what your preferred learning style is and how to use it most effectively.

Gathering Ideas for Your Narrowed Topic

Once you have decided on a narrowed topic for your writing, it's time to brainstorm more extensively. Whether you prefer clustering, listing, freewriting, or flowcharting, it may be helpful to think of brainstorming as a process in which your ideas reveal more and more layers of information. This additional information will make the writing process much easier. You will know what you want to say from the beginning.

THE BRAINSTORMING PROCESS

Start your brainstorming by writing down your **narrowed topic** at the top of the page (for listing, freewriting, and flowcharting) or in a bubble in the center of the page (for clustering). Several obvious or **big ideas** related to your topic will usually pop into your head right away. Then, as you focus on each of these big ideas individually, some **related examples** should come to mind to support those ideas. Finally, if you focus on each of these examples one at a time, you may recall some **specific details** to illustrate and support the examples.

To get a general idea of the brainstorming process, take a look at the graphic below. The colors correspond to the layers of information that get revealed in the process of brainstorming on your topic.

NARROWED TOPIC	States your position on the writing assignment
BIG IDEAS	Present ideas related to the topic
RELATED EXAMPLES	Provide support for each of your big ideas
SPECIFIC DETAILS	Clarify the examples and bring them to life

Getting Messy

Of course, in a perfect situation, these layers would flow in a clear and logical order from your brain to the page. However, brainstorming is not always an orderly process, as these samples of student clustering and listing show.

Sample Clustering Diagram

While brainstorming, ideas are likely to pop up randomly, and some of these ideas may not ultimately fit with your topic. Here are some things to remember during the brainstorming process:

- *Do not worry about organizing your thoughts.* This "messy" part of brainstorming is natural and can often be valuable.

- Ideas are likely to pop into your head rapidly and randomly. Just *let your thoughts flow*, write them down, and keep moving. Do not worry too much about how appropriate they are.

- *Do not worry if you repeat some ideas.* Repetition during brainstorming can help you identify ideas that are especially important for your topic. Later—when you organize and outline your ideas—you can eliminate any ideas that do not fit and any repetitious ideas.

- Try to fill up your page with thoughts, and *do not stop working too soon*. It is often during the last minutes of your brainstorming that you discover your most powerful ideas.

Sample Listing Diagram

Rock climbing photo 6

Drive
test of manhood   weather change
Strenuous vacation   dark, winds, drizzling
China, Australia, Brazil
group of close friends   could not believe
falling down   midlife crisis
250-to-300-foot walk   ~~they would look down~~
money at stake   lucky hat
extreme sports   he was respected and
Fathers all ~~age~~ ages   he was the one that was
at-home dads   scared to do things

Emotions   Senses
scared   * Smell = mist fresh air
fired up   ** ~~sig~~ sights = th friend the other end
nauseous   * Sound = deer, wind, animals,
~~evil~~   music, MP3
focus   * Taste = the last meal, vomit
sweating   touch = rope, ruff shirt wet, sweat
live or dead   6th sense = visualize himself
upset, how did I get into this?   somewhere else

lesson
no limits
challenge
better confidence
inspirational

Don't be discouraged if your thoughts don't come out perfectly arranged on the first try. The most important thing you can do is to get all of your ideas down on paper. That way, you avoid getting "stuck," and you have a lot of material to work with.

Now, let's see how this layering process occurs within the four brainstorming methods.

CLUSTERING

Clustering involves using a series of bubbles and connecting lines to record your thoughts. Clustering is especially helpful for students who have trouble organizing their ideas, since the bubbles and lines help group related items together.

The following example of clustering uses the color coding illustrated on page 48. Notice that the narrowed topic, *Why cheating isn't worth it,* is placed in a bubble in the center of the page, and the big ideas are connected to it.

Power Tip
Clustering is especially useful for students who are strong *visual learners*.

Next, focus on one big idea at a time and provide related examples.

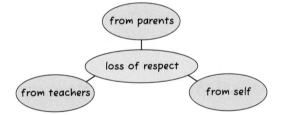

Finally, focus on one example at a time, adding specific details to illustrate each example. When you reach this final layer of ideas, remember to look back at your topic to stay focused.

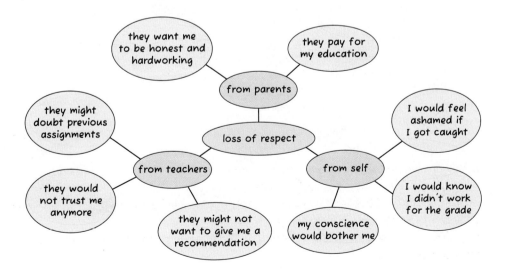

ACTIVITY 5

Answer the following questions about the cluster immediately preceding this activity.

1. What are the three related examples of "loss of respect"? _____

    _____

    _____

2. What are details of "loss of respect from teachers"? _____

    _____

    _____

3. What specific details are related to "loss of respect from self"?

    _____

    _____

4. How many specific details about loss of respect from parents are mentioned? _____

ACTIVITY 6

Complete the cluster below. Follow these steps:

1. Write the name of one of your favorite things (favorite restaurant, college class, book, video game, sport, etc.) in the center bubble.
2. Fill in the *green* bubbles with big ideas about why this is your favorite thing.
3. Fill in the *purple* bubbles with examples to support your big ideas.

NOTE: You may leave some bubbles empty or add extra bubbles if necessary.

LISTING

Some students do not like using bubbles and lines to record and connect their ideas. Instead, they prefer to list ideas on paper or a computer screen. If you use this method, it is helpful to think of your list as a *series of short lists*, with each list headed by a big idea. This will help you group related ideas together.

Here is an example of listing using color coding. Notice that the narrowed topic is at the top of the page, and the big ideas are listed below, with space between each one for adding examples and details. The first big idea has been expanded into related examples and specific details.

Power Tip
Listing is often popular with *verbal* or mathematically oriented *learners*.

<u>Why cheating isn't worth it</u>

<u>loss of respect</u>

<u>from parents</u> — they want me to be honest and hardworking, they pay for my education

<u>from teachers</u> — they wouldn't trust me anymore, they might wonder if I cheated on all my other assignments in the class, they might not want to write me a positive recommendation if I needed it

<u>from self</u> — I would feel ashamed if I got caught, I would know that I didn't work to get a good grade, my conscience would always bother me

<u>loss of time, money, learning opportunities</u>

<u>creates negative habits</u>

From this point, the student would continue to build her list by working on the other big ideas. For each big idea, she would give herself at least five minutes to note down related examples and specific details.

ACTIVITY 7

Use listing to brainstorm on *how other people see you and feel about you.* Follow these steps:

1. Write your topic at the top of a fresh sheet of paper.

2. As big ideas come to mind, write them down as "headings" for individual lists, leaving enough space between each one for examples and details.

CONTINUED >

3. Select ONE of those big ideas and start adding related examples.

4. For each example, add any specific details that come to mind.

5. Repeat steps 2–4, continuing the exercise until you have fully explored your big ideas for the topic.

FREEWRITING

Power Tip
You might start with freewriting to warm up your brain, then switch to clustering or listing when the ideas start to come faster.

Another method of generating ideas is called freewriting. With freewriting, you simply write down your thoughts as you would in a diary or personal journal without worrying about grammar, spelling, or punctuation. Write down whatever comes to mind, even if it seems silly or disconnected at first. This process gives your mind time to warm up and may help you uncover more ideas than you thought you had on a topic.

Here is an example of freewriting on the narrowed topic, *Why cheating isn't worth it*:

I can honestly say I've never cheated, but I have been tempted many times—and the temptation keeps getting stronger. There is a lot of pressure from many different places. But it would be terrible to get caught. I would feel really embarrassed if I got caught—I like my teachers, and I think they would be really upset with me. Professor McDougall and I get along, even though she's really tough, and she would totally not respect me anymore if I got caught cheating in her class. And anyway, I might get expelled from her class, which means that I spent a lot of time working in the class that was wasted by just one assignment.

Power Tip
Freewriting is especially useful for students who are strong *verbal learners*.

The next step in freewriting is to read what you have written and circle or highlight two or three big ideas that you would like to explore further. Remember to select ideas that are closely connected to your topic (in this case, *Why cheating isn't worth it*). Here is what this student circled in his original freewriting:

I can honestly say I've never cheated, but I have been tempted many times—and the temptation keeps getting stronger. There (is a lot of pressure from many different places.) But it would be terrible to get caught. I would feel really embarrassed if I got caught—I like (my teachers,) and I think they would be really upset with me. Professor McDougall and I get along, even though she's really tough, and she (would totally not respect me anymore) if I got caught cheating in her class. And anyway, I (might get expelled from her class,) which means that I spent a lot of time working in the class that (was wasted by just one assignment.)

Power Tip
Freewriting generally requires more time than the other methods, so it may not be ideal for timed writing assignments in class. Make sure you practice one of the other methods as a backup for timed writing assignments.

This student's next step is to select one of these ideas and freewrite about it for five minutes. Once again, the idea is to *just keep writing* until the time is up. Here is what the student wrote:

I would gain a good grade or two from cheating, but I really think I would lose a lot more. It would be such a (waste of time to get caught) and then expelled,

because I (don't really cheat all the time,) but that probably wouldn't matter.
I heard from a friend of mine that even if they catch you cheating once,
(they can expel you from that class — or even the school.) There is no way I
could afford to go through the process of applying to schools again, especially
(if I lost my scholarships.) I heard that happens sometimes, too.

Next, read what you have written and circle one or two of the most powerful
ideas. Then, select one idea from *either* your first or second freewriting and
freewrite about that idea for five minutes.

Continue this process of freewriting, reading, circling, and freewriting
again until you have explored all your ideas about the topic or until you run
out of time.

Power Tip
Remember that freewriting does not count as a draft of your composition. After you complete your freewriting activity, you will still need to write an outline for your composition and *then* write your first draft.

ACTIVITY 8

Using freewriting, discuss *what you plan to do when you graduate and why*.
Follow these steps:

1. Freewrite for ten minutes on the topic.

2. Read what you wrote and circle two or three big ideas that you would
    like to develop.

3. Select ONE of those ideas and freewrite on it for five minutes.

4. Read what you wrote and circle one or two big ideas that you would
    like to develop.

5. Select ONE idea from either your first or second freewriting. Then,
    freewrite on this idea for five minutes.

6. If you wish, continue this exercise until you have fully explored your
    ideas on the topic.

ACTIVITY 9

Select one of your narrowed topics from Activity 2. (Do not select a topic that
you have already used in a previous exercise.) On a blank sheet of paper,
generate more ideas for your narrowed topic using the freewriting method
illustrated on the previous pages.

FLOWCHARTING

When you create a flowchart, you use boxes and lines to write down your
ideas and keep related ideas connected. With flowcharting, the narrowed
topic is at the top of the page, and the big ideas are added horizontally across

Power Tip
Flowcharting is especially useful for students who are strong *visual learners*.

the first row. To have enough room for all your big ideas, you may want to turn your sheet of paper sideways so that it is wider than it is long.

Here is an example of flowcharting using color coding.

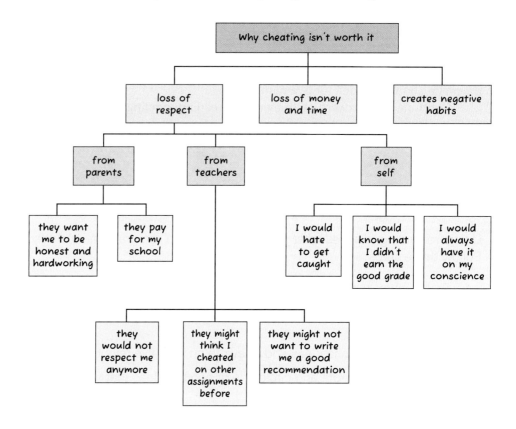

ACTIVITY 10

Use flowcharting to explore *the possible causes behind students dropping out of college*. Follow these steps:

1. Write your topic at the top of a fresh sheet of paper.

2. Make branches from the topic to three to four big ideas that you would like to develop.

3. Select ONE of those ideas and make a branch down to two or three examples.

4. From those examples, create branches down to specific details that support the examples.

5. Repeat steps 2–4, continuing the exercise until you have fully explored your ideas for the topic.

ACTIVITY 11: Teamwork

Team up with classmates who preferred the same brainstorming method that you did. Compare what you wrote as big ideas and examples for the corresponding activity (either Activity 6, 7, 8, or 10). See if your classmates found good examples that you might be able to use in your brainstorming as well. Then, discuss whether you could add some specific details (yellow points) to some of the examples (purple points).

Jump-Starting Your Thinking with the Five *W*s

Sometimes, during the brainstorming process, your brain may stall — like a car motor that won't start. In these instances, you can use a helpful strategy to jump-start your thinking: Just insert one or more of the five *W* questions (*Who? Where? When? What? Why?*) into your clustering, listing, freewriting, or flowcharting. These questions are typically used by reporters and investigators to uncover better details on a story or a case. The questions can help you get below the surface of your topic and look at it from different points of view.

- **Who** are the important people involved in my topic?
- **Where** did events connected to my topic take place?
- **When** did the experiences in my topic happen?
- **What** important things happened in relation to my topic?
- **Why** did these things happen? **Why** did people act the way they did?

> **Power Tip**
> You may use the five *W*s in any order you like, but try to *start with one that is easy for you*. Many students find it easy to begin with *who, where,* or *when*.

Remember, you can add a *W* question at any point in your brainstorming process. In the following cluster, the question *Who?* has been added in place of a big idea in order to help the student gather more information on her topic:

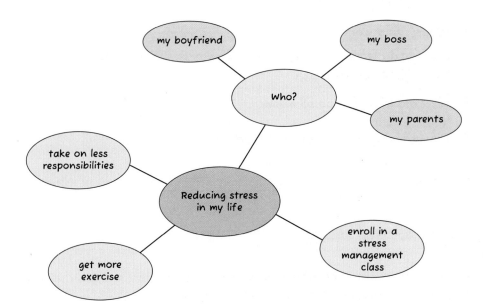

Power Tip
Not all the questions work for every topic. Generally, you should be able to use three or four of the *W*s for a given topic. If one *W* does not make sense for your topic, move on to the next *W*.

You can also *begin* your brainstorming by using all five *W*s as your big ideas. Take a look at the following example that uses the five *W*s with the flowcharting technique:

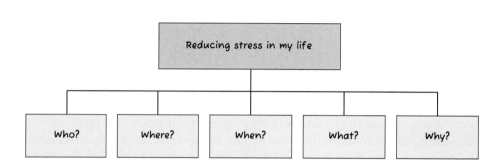

You may use the five *W* questions in the same ways for all methods of brainstorming, or whenever you get stuck in generating ideas for your topic. Remember, the five *W*s should jump-start your brainstorming, but they should not restrict the free movement of your thinking. Once your brain warms up, you may decide to start clustering or listing instead.

ACTIVITY 12: Teamwork

With your classmates, complete each of the following questions for the topics provided. There may be more than one way to complete some of the questions.

EXAMPLE: Discuss a job that you had that you either liked or disliked very much.

Who *did I work with?*

Where *did I work?*

When *did I work?*

What *did I do at my job?*

Why *did I like my job so much?*

Power Tip
Sometimes, two Ws will produce similar answers or ideas. This is fine. Repetition can be useful because it can help you identify ideas that might be especially important for your topic.

1. Discuss a big mistake that you made.

Who _____

Where _____

When _____

What _____

Why _____

2. Discuss your reasons for being in college.

Who _____

Where _____

When _____

What _____

Why _____

3. Discuss the best relationship you ever had.

Who _____

Where _____

When _____

What _____

Why _____

ACTIVITY 13

Now, it's your turn to put all the brainstorming strategies together to work on a narrowed topic. You'll need a separate piece of paper. Then, do the following:

- Select one of the broad topics listed below and narrow it; OR select one of the narrowed topics on the next page.
- Decide which brainstorming method (clustering, listing, freewriting, or flowcharting) you will use to get your ideas down. (If you still need help deciding which one is best for you, see Chapter 2.)
- On a blank sheet of paper, write down your narrowed topic at the top of the page (or in the center of the page for clustering).
- Start writing down any big ideas that come to mind about your topic.
- Start adding layers (of related examples and specific details) to expand your brainstorming. Keep working until you have a full or nearly full page of ideas.
- If you get stuck, use one or more of the five _W_ questions.
- Save your work to use with the activities in the next chapter.

Broad topics

my self-image	powerful emotions
romantic relationships	entertainment
personal sacrifice	stress
social networking	authority figures
family challenges	life-changing events

CONTINUED >

Narrowed topics

1. I never thought I would tell anybody about _____.

2. If I have learned one important rule in life, it is _____.

3. If I am an expert in one thing, it would be _____. *(examples: giving advice on love, getting into debt, making people laugh, etc.)*

4. Above all else, _____ keeps me going when I feel like giving up.

5. _____ is something many people take for granted, but I know what it means to live without it.

6. If I could live my life over as someone else, that person would be _____.

7. _____ is a song, album, or performer that brings back powerful memories for me.

8. If I could convince my audience to do one thing, it would be to _____.

9. If I could change one thing about my world, it would be _____.

10. I would like to invent a machine that could _____.

BRINGING IT ALL TOGETHER:
Developing a Topic

In this chapter, you have learned how to explore your ideas for a writing topic — how to narrow topics, and how to generate ideas that will support and develop your academic writing. Confirm your knowledge by filling in the blank spaces in the following sentences. If you need help, review the pages listed. Finally, check off each item to confirm your understanding of the material.

✔ Topics that give students a lot of choice in what to write about are called _____ topics. Topics that give students very little choice in what to write about are called _____ topics. Topics that give students a moderate amount of choice — not a lot or a little — are called _____ topics. (page 43)

✔ When you are given a topic, you should be aware of how much choice you have in your topic and how much _____, if any, you will have to do. (page 45)

✔ When narrowing a topic for a writing assignment, you should consider the required length of the assignment. Four common length requirements for college writing are: 1) _____, 2) _____, 3) _____, and 4) _____. (page 45)

✔ When selecting a writing topic, you should select one that will motivate you to write and help you get the best results. To determine which topic will work well for you, you can ask four questions. These questions are: 1) _____, 2) _____ _____, 3) _____, and 4) _____ _____ (pages 46–47)

✔ When gathering more ideas for a narrowed topic, you can use any of four methods for getting your ideas down on paper. These methods are: 1) _____, 2) _____, 3) _____, and 4) _____. (page 48)

✔ Brainstorming often reveals more layers to your topic. These layers are: 1) _____, 2) _____, 3) _____, and 4) _____. (page 48)

✔ During brainstorming, your most powerful ideas may come forth _____. For this reason, you should be patient with the process and not give up too soon. (page 50)

✔ After you freewrite, you should go back and circle two or three _____ that you will want to explore further. (page 54)

✔ If you get stuck in your brainstorming, you can use the _____ to help jump-start the process. These questions are 1) _____, 2) _____, 3) _____, 4) _____, and 5) _____. (page 57)

JOURNAL WRITING: 10–15 minutes

Many students establish lasting relationships in college: best friends, life partners, educational and professional mentors, and so on. Write about one or two significant individuals you've met so far in college. (They could be students, tutors, counselors, coaches, instructors, etc.) Describe these individuals and discuss your relationship with them. How do you think these relationships will affect you over time?

CHAPTER 4

Organizing Your Ideas

Test your understanding of how to organize your ideas by completing this quiz. You may know more than you think.

For each question, select all the answers that apply.

1. **Which of the following sentences expresses a general or *big idea*? (Hint: The other three are *related examples*.)**

    ___ High-quality hair products prevent damage, such as split ends.

    ___ A healthy diet ensures that hair gets essential nutrients.

    ___ Beautiful hair needs regular maintenance.

    ___ Gentle brushing keeps hair strong and elastic.

2. **Which of the following sentences are *related examples*? (Hint: The other item is a general or *big idea*.)**

    ___ Take the stairs instead of an elevator.

    ___ Get off the bus one stop early and walk.

    ___ Get your daily exercise without going to the gym.

    ___ Put on some music and dance in your room.

3. **When you are arranging a list of items, which ones will generally come first?**

    ___ big ideas

    ___ related examples

    ___ colorful details

4. **Which of the following strategies requires you to recognize an example that doesn't fit in a group of examples?**

    ___ grouping

    ___ ordering

    ___ eliminating

5. **Which of the following examples does not fit with the other three examples?**

    ___ going to the movies

    ___ going to a museum

    ___ going to the train station

    ___ going out for dinner

Organizing Basics

In Chapter 3, you practiced exploring and writing down your ideas for a topic. In this chapter, you will learn some basic strategies for organizing your ideas in preparation for writing outlines.

As you move from *brainstorming* (a fast and random flow of your ideas) to *outlining* (a carefully organized presentation of your ideas), you will be required to use several strategies:

- **ordering:** arranging ideas in a logical way
- **grouping:** putting related ideas together
- **eliminating:** removing ideas that are not related to your topic

Often, these activities are like solving a puzzle, and they can be a lot of fun. The more you practice them, the more your organizational awareness and skills are likely to improve.

ORDERING

The first skill to practice is **ordering**. To order your ideas effectively, you will need to be able to recognize the difference between general or **big ideas** and **related examples**. Big ideas usually come first, and they are followed by related examples. Take a look:

pens
ballpoint
erasable
felt-tip
fountain

The word *pens* expresses a big idea because there are many types of pens. The words *ballpoint, erasable, felt-tip,* and *fountain* are examples of pens.

Ordering Words and Phrases

As shown above, a *single word* can express either a *big idea* or a *related example*. Take a look at the following lists and decide which one is ordered correctly.

pizza	**fast-food**
burger	burger
fast-food	pizza
taco	taco

The second list is correct: the word *fast-food* expresses a big idea because there are many types of fast-food. *Burger, pizza,* and *taco* are examples of fast-food.

A phrase can also express a big idea or a related example. Take a look at the following brief phrases and decide which list is ordered correctly.

filling out the form
writing the project description
entering a contest
sending in the application

entering a contest
filling out the form
writing the project description
sending in the application

Again, the second list is correct: the phrase *entering a contest* expresses a big idea because there are many steps involved in this process. *Filling out the form, writing the project description,* and *sending in the application* are examples of how to enter a contest.

Power Tip
While working through the activities in this chapter, use a dictionary to look up the meaning of any words you do not recognize. Doing this will help you complete the activities successfully and build your vocabulary at the same time.

ACTIVITY 1

Study the clusters below, and then draw lines from the *big idea* to the *related examples*. Next, move the items to a list, putting the big idea first.

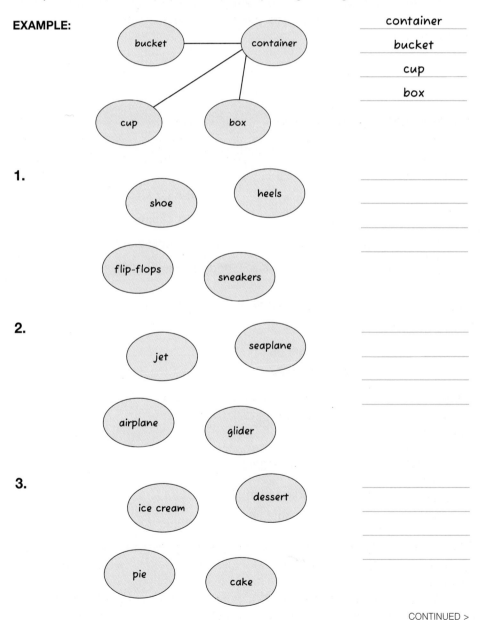

EXAMPLE:

container
bucket
cup
box

1.

2.

3.

CONTINUED >

4.

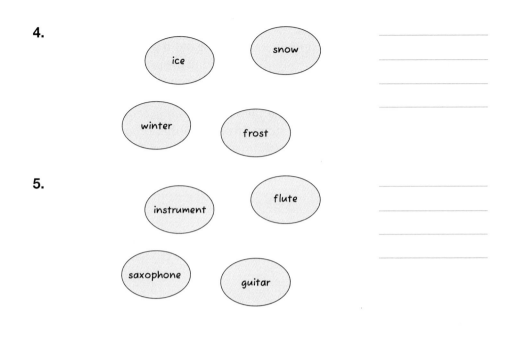

ice

snow

winter

frost

_____

_____

_____

5.

instrument

flute

saxophone

guitar

_____

_____

_____

_____

ACTIVITY 2

Rewrite each of the following lists, putting the general or *big idea* first. If a list is correct as is, write "OK" on the first line.

EXAMPLE: replacing cabinets

installing appliances

renovating a kitchen

adding energy-efficient lights

renovating a kitchen

replacing cabinets

installing appliances

adding energy-efficient lights

1. reality TV involving housewives

crime investigation shows

highly rated television series

daytime talk shows like *Ellen*

2. mouth-to-mouth resuscitation

clearing the breathing passage

administering first aid

checking the pulse

3. ironing shirts before folding them

packing a suitcase efficiently

stuffing socks inside shoes

buying travel-size toiletries

4. listen to language tapes

use flash cards

learn a foreign language

converse with native speakers

5. ensure that your dog is a good pet

visit dog parks to socialize the dog

give rewards to reinforce good behavior

hire a professional dog trainer

ACTIVITY 3

Study the clusters below and then draw lines from the general or *big idea* to the related examples. Next, move the items from the cluster to a list, putting the big idea on the first line.

EXAMPLE:

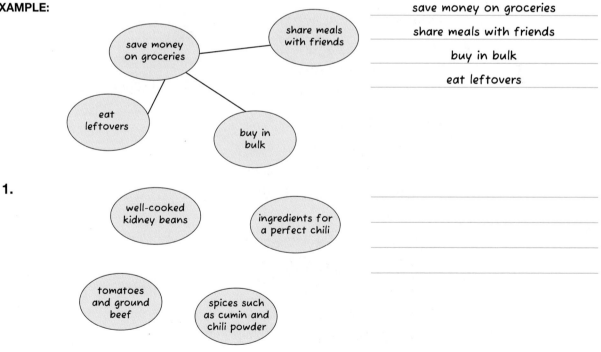

save money on groceries

share meals with friends

buy in bulk

eat leftovers

1.

CONTINUED >

2.

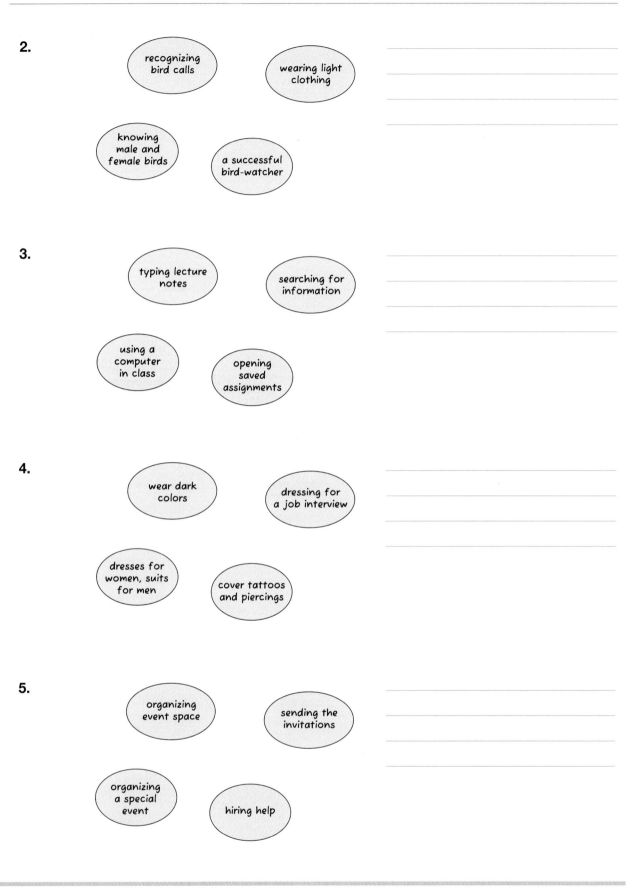

(recognizing bird calls)   (wearing light clothing)

(knowing male and female birds)   (a successful bird-watcher)

_____

3.

(typing lecture notes)   (searching for information)

(using a computer in class)   (opening saved assignments)

_____

4.

(wear dark colors)   (dressing for a job interview)

(dresses for women, suits for men)   (cover tattoos and piercings)

_____

5.

(organizing event space)   (sending the invitations)

(organizing a special event)   (hiring help)

_____

Ordering Sentences

You will sometimes need to order complete sentences during your brainstorming or writing process. It may be trickier to identify the general or *big idea* in complete sentences because you are working with more words—and more words mean more ideas to consider. Like words and phrases, however, a complete sentence can also express a big idea or related examples.

With complete sentences, there will be *two or more key words* that define the idea. Get in the habit of marking these key ideas. This will help you decide what types of examples you can use.

First, take a look at the following group of items and see if you can identify the general or big idea:

A good interviewer is a good judge of character.
A good interviewer can ask meaningful questions.
A good interviewer should have several important skills.
A good interviewer can put the interviewee at ease.

Did you find it? The general or big idea here is the third item on the list, "A good interviewer should have several important skills." This sentence identifies a general topic, *a good interviewer*, and the author's original point about the topic, *should have several important skills*. The other sentences each provide an example of a skill that an interviewer should have. Take a look:

A good interviewer should have <u>several important skills</u>.
A good interviewer is a <u>good judge of character</u>.
A good interviewer can <u>ask meaningful questions</u>.
A good interviewer can <u>put the interviewee at ease</u>.

As this example shows, it can be very helpful to find key words or phrases *within a complete sentence* to help you distinguish between big ideas and related examples.

ACTIVITY 4: Teamwork

Working with one or two classmates, identify and underline the *key words* that define the general or *big idea* in each sentence. Each sentence will have at least two key words.

EXAMPLE: The mangrove <u>swamps</u> of southwestern Florida provide a <u>home</u> for many types of <u>birds</u>.

1. Several factors determine whether an elderly relative should move into an assisted living facility.

2. Learning to play a musical instrument can be made easier by following these three guidelines.

3. Trees can add to the financial and aesthetic value of a home.

CONTINUED >

4. A number of factors make a man or woman a good choice for a long-term relationship.

5. Horseback-riding therapy ("equine therapy") can benefit certain kinds of patients.

ACTIVITY 5

In each of the following groups, identify the general or *big idea*. You may underline or highlight key words or phrases within each sentence to help you differentiate between big ideas and related examples. Then, put the big idea on the first line and write the related examples under it in any order.

EXAMPLE: Mountain climbers should have well-conditioned muscles and little body fat.

Mountain climbers should be in top physical condition.

Mountain climbers should have good balance and quick reflexes.

Mountain climbers should have strong lungs.

Mountain climbers should be in top physical condition.

Mountain climbers should have well-conditioned muscles and little body fat.

Mountain climbers should have good balance and quick reflexes.

Mountain climbers should have strong lungs.

1. Many people add hazelnut or vanilla syrup to their coffee.

   Shots of espresso are frequently added to ordinary coffee.

   Lattes and cappuccinos are big sellers at Starbucks.

   Specialty coffee drinks have become popular.

2. Swimming strengthens bones and joints.

   Swimming works out both the upper and lower body.

   Swimming enhances one's physical fitness.

   Swimming conditions both the heart and muscles.

3. The Kindle's lighted screen encourages people to read in the dark.

_____

The Kindle allows one to download many books for free.

_____

The Kindle has made reading a more popular pastime.

_____

The Kindle allows people to carry many books with them on one lightweight screen.

_____

4. Just five hours of vigorous exercise per week can help to prevent cancer.

_____

Research has shown that people can take actions to prevent cancer.

_____

Drinking green tea on a regular basis can help to prevent cancer.

_____

Eating lots of leafy green vegetables can help to prevent cancer.

_____

5. Medical marijuana has become more accepted recently.

_____

Medical marijuana is now legal in at least 17 states.

_____

Medical marijuana can be purchased legally in special shops and clinics.

_____

Doctors can prescribe medical marijuana for the treatment of cancer and AIDS.

_____

GROUPING

The second skill that is useful for organizing your ideas is **grouping**. To group items successfully, you will need to be able to recognize items that are *related to one another*. Often, when we brainstorm, our ideas come to us in random order. When we organize these ideas, we need to sort through them and put them in distinct groups.

Grouping Words and Phrases

The following example shows how one group of items can be sorted into two groups.

Items to be grouped: eagles / robins / sparrows / hummingbirds / falcons / pelicans

Group 1: small birds	**Group 2:** large birds
robins	eagles
sparrows	falcons
hummingbirds	pelicans

Notice that as you group items, you begin to develop a sense of the *big idea* that connects the items to one another. For example, the big idea that connects the items in group 1 is *small birds*. The big idea that connects the items in group 2 is *large birds*.

Now take a look at another example, one that sorts phrases into two groups:

Items to be grouped: rereading the assignment / doing homework / listening to the professor / taking good notes / using flash cards / sitting in the front

Group 1: good study habits in class	**Group 2: good study habits outside of class**
listening to the professor	rereading the assignment
taking good notes	doing homework
sitting in the front	using flash cards

As you group the items, the big idea begins to become apparent. In this example, the big idea that connects the items in group 1 is *good study habits in class*. The big idea that connects the items in group 2 is *good study habits outside of class*.

ACTIVITY 6

Rearrange each of the following sets of items into two groups. Follow these steps:

- At first, leave the general or *big idea* blank.
- Separate the items into two groups, keeping related items together. Write the items in the spaces provided.
- Think of a big idea that connects the items in each group. Write it in the space provided.

1. tugboats / powerboats / rowboats / kayaks / canoes / ocean liners

    Group 1:   **Group 2:**

    Big idea: _____   **Big idea:** _____

    _____   _____

    Examples: _____   **Examples:** _____

    _____   _____

    _____   _____

2. plastic / wood / ceramic / rubber / polyurethane / stone / Astroturf

    Group 1:   **Group 2:**

    Big idea: _____   **Big idea:** _____

    _____   _____

    Examples: _____   **Examples:** _____

    _____   _____

    _____   _____

3. salmon / tuna / blue whale / jellyfish / octopus / dolphin

    Group 1:   **Group 2:**

    Big idea: _____   **Big idea:** _____

    _____   _____

    Examples: _____   **Examples:** _____

    _____   _____

CONTINUED >

4. flossing regularly / filling a cavity / getting a root canal / having professional cleanings / wearing braces / using an electric toothbrush

Group 1:	Group 2:
Big idea: _____	**Big idea:** _____
_____	_____
Examples: _____	**Examples:** _____
_____	_____
_____	_____
_____	_____
_____	_____

5. take regular breaks / have a good lighting source / join a college club / get a study partner / try out for a sports team / have lunch with friends in the cafeteria

Group 1:	Group 2:
Big idea: _____	**Big idea:** _____
_____	_____
Examples: _____	**Examples:** _____
_____	_____
_____	_____
_____	_____
_____	_____

6. posting on Facebook / composing in a text program / keeping track of expenses in a spreadsheet / protecting with an antivirus system / bidding on eBay / downloading from iTunes

Group 1:	Group 2:
Big idea: _____	**Big idea:** _____
Examples: _____	**Examples:** _____
_____	_____
_____	_____
_____	_____
_____	_____

As you learned in Chapters 2 and 3, clustering is a method that helps you group related ideas. The bubbles and lines are a visual reminder to keep related ideas in separate groups or clusters. Here is an example:

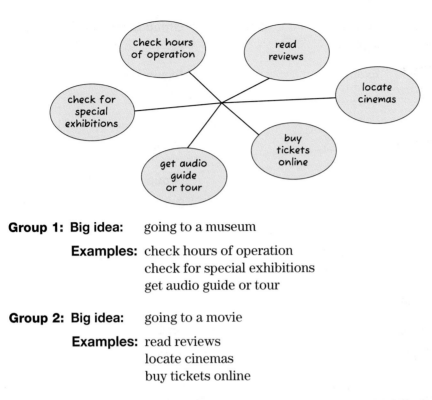

Group 1: Big idea: going to a museum

         Examples: check hours of operation
                       check for special exhibitions
                       get audio guide or tour

Group 2: Big idea: going to a movie

         Examples: read reviews
                       locate cinemas
                       buy tickets online

Lists can also be used to group phrases, as shown in the examples below the cluster. Notice that a big idea connects the items in each group.

    Keep in mind that clusters are rarely this simple and neat. As you move from a cluster to a list (and to an outline), be on the lookout for items that are incorrectly grouped together.

ACTIVITY 7

Move the items from each of the following clusters into separate groups, being careful of items that are clustered incorrectly. Follow these steps:

- At first, leave the "Big idea" line after "Group 1" and "Group 2" blank.
- Fill in the other lines with the items that should go in each group, making sure to keep related items together.
- Think of a *big idea* that connects the items in each group. Write the big ideas in the spaces provided.

1.

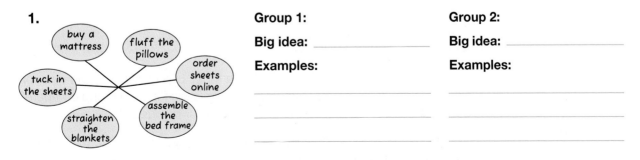

Group 1:

Big idea: _____

Examples:

_____

_____

_____

Group 2:

Big idea: _____

Examples:

_____

_____

_____

CONTINUED >

2.

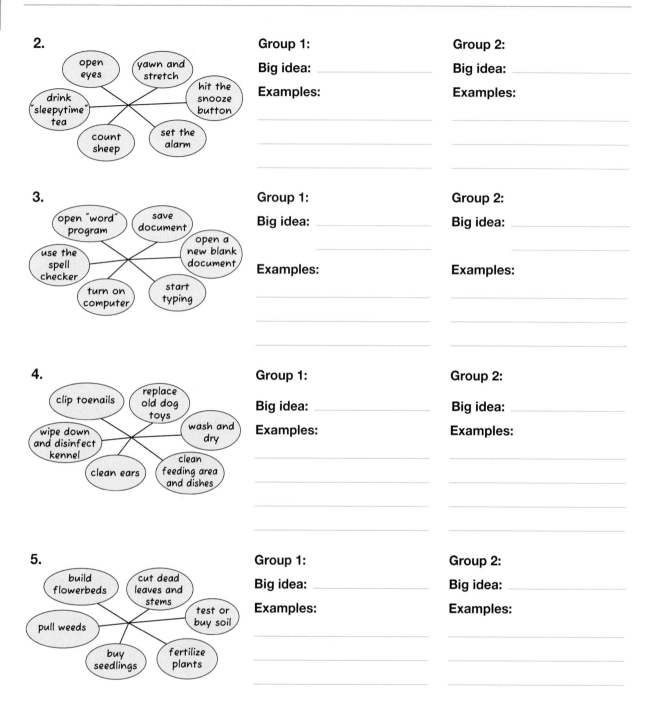

Group 1:

Big idea: _____

Examples:

_____

_____

_____

_____

Group 2:

Big idea: _____

Examples:

_____

_____

_____

_____

3.

Group 1:

Big idea: _____

Examples:

_____

_____

_____

_____

Group 2:

Big idea: _____

Examples:

_____

_____

_____

_____

4.

Group 1:

Big idea: _____

Examples:

_____

_____

_____

_____

Group 2:

Big idea: _____

Examples:

_____

_____

_____

_____

5.

Group 1:

Big idea: _____

Examples:

_____

_____

_____

_____

Group 2:

Big idea: _____

Examples:

_____

_____

_____

_____

ACTIVITY 8: Teamwork

Exchange your answers to Activity 7 with those of a classmate. Did you sort any of the items differently? How do your *big ideas* for each group compare? Can you find any ways to refine or improve your big ideas?

Grouping Sentences

Like words and phrases, complete sentences can also be grouped together by topic. To come up with a general or *big idea* to connect sentence groups, it's good to circle the key words in the sentences and ask yourself how those words are related. You may want to highlight or underline key words or phrases to help you identify related items. Take a look:

Items to be grouped:

- Order items from the <u>dollar menu</u>.
- When possible, buy <u>products in bulk</u>.
- <u>Drink water</u> instead of ordering expensive soft drinks.
- Split <u>combo or family meals</u> with friends.
- Clip <u>newspaper coupons</u> for savings on many items.
- Make sure you have a <u>supermarket club card</u> for in-store specials.

Group 1: There are several ways to save money when eating at a fast-food restaurant.

- Order items from the dollar menu.
- Drink water instead of ordering expensive soft drinks.
- Split combo or family meals with friends.

Group 2: There are several ways to save money when grocery shopping.

- When possible, buy products in bulk.
- Clip newspaper coupons for savings on many items.
- Make sure you have a supermarket club card for in-store specials.

Highlighting the phrases *dollar menu*, *drink water*, and *combo or family meals* makes it easier to recognize that all of these sentences relate to saving money while eating at fast-food restaurants. The phrases *products in bulk*, *newspaper coupons*, and *supermarket club card* suggest that these sentences all relate to saving money when grocery shopping.

ACTIVITY 9

Rearrange each of the following sets of items into two groups. Follow these steps:

- At first, leave the "Big idea" lines blank.
- Separate the items into two groups, keeping related items together. (You may highlight or underline key words or phrases to identify related items.) Write the items in the spaces provided.
- Think of a *big idea* that connects the items in each group. Write the big ideas in the spaces provided.

CONTINUED >

EXAMPLE: Many colleges have career centers to help you explore career choices.

Making a lot of money should not be your primary criterion in a career.

If you like working with other people, you might choose a service-oriented career such as nursing or hotel management.

You can take a "career inventory test" to help you identify your interests.

Many companies offer apprenticeships so that you can see if you like what they do.

If you have a special talent, pick a career that lets you use it.

Group 1:

Big idea: Ways to explore the right career for you

Examples:

Many colleges have career centers to help you explore career choices.

You can take a "career inventory test" to help you identify your interests.

Many companies offer apprenticeships so that you can see if you like what they do.

Group 2:

Big idea: How to make a good career choice

Examples:

Making a lot of money should not be your primary criterion in a career.

If you like working with other people, you might choose a service-oriented career such as nursing or hotel management.

If you have a special talent, pick a career that lets you use it.

1. In any semester, try to balance difficult classes with some easier ones.

When picking a class, consider the reputation of the professor who will be teaching it.

Avoid scheduling a late-night class followed by an early-morning class the next day.

Make sure to have time between classes so that you can review, relax, and prepare for the next class.

Be sure to take a math placement exam so that you get into the right math class for you.

When selecting classes, consider the graduation requirements for your major.

Group 1:

Big idea: _____

Examples:

_____
_____
_____
_____
_____

Group 2:

Big idea: _____

Examples:

_____
_____
_____
_____
_____

2. Making homemade gifts for the holidays can save money and create more original presents.

   Ordering online avoids parking hassles and crowded stores.

   Shopping on sites like eBay can save buyers hundreds of dollars over shopping at department stores.

   Flying or driving during non-peak times can ease the strain of holiday travel.

   Knowing that holidays can be stressful can help people to keep calm when others act badly.

   Shopping at thrift stores and consignment stores can help shoppers find unusual and inexpensive gifts.

   Group 1:   **Group 2:**

   Big idea: _____   **Big idea:** _____

   _____   _____

   Examples: **Examples:**

   _____   _____

   _____   _____

   _____   _____

   _____   _____

   _____   _____

   _____   _____

   _____   _____

3. Even if you don't like the meal you are served, you may need to compliment it.

   Getting along with your boyfriend's or girlfriend's family may mean dressing more conservatively than you like.

   Discussing religion can sometimes create unpleasant tension.

   You may need to laugh at jokes you don't find funny or watch a sports game you aren't interested in.

   If you know about a private family matter, don't mention it unless the family brings it up first.

   Political differences should be kept to a minimum until you really know the family better.

   Group 1:   **Group 2:**

   Big idea: _____   **Big idea:** _____

   _____   _____

   _____   _____

   Examples: **Examples:**

   _____   _____

   _____   _____

   _____   _____

   _____   _____

CONTINUED >

_____   _____
_____   _____
_____   _____

4. Make perfect attendance a priority for all your college classes.

Many students find that their study habits improve as they advance in college.

Anyone can learn good study skills with enough effort.

There are published guides that teach students good study habits.

Do not neglect your assignments until the last minute.

Take advantage of the free study resources on your campus such as tutoring, labs, and library workshops.

Group 1:   **Group 2:**

Big idea: _____   **Big idea:** _____

Examples: **Examples:**

_____   _____
_____   _____
_____   _____
_____   _____
_____   _____

ACTIVITY 10: Teamwork

Exchange your answers to Activity 9 with those of a classmate. Did you sort any of the items differently? How do your *big ideas* for each group compare? Can you find any ways to refine or improve your big ideas?

ELIMINATING

One of the most important skills you will need for organizing your ideas is **eliminating**. When you brainstorm, you write down all the ideas that come to mind, without judging their individual value. However, as you move from brainstorming to outlining, you will need to select your best ideas (those that are most appropriate for the topic) and eliminate those that are weak (ideas that do not fit the topic especially well). Generally, you will want to look for groups of related items that clearly support the topic and you will want to eliminate isolated items that do not fit. With practice, your ability to recognize and eliminate these items will improve.

Eliminating Words and Phrases

In the list below, most of the points are related. However, one phrase is not. Can you find it?

Big idea: extracurricular opportunities for college students

- student government
- faculty committees
- team sports
- the college newspaper

College students can be involved in student government, team sports, and the college newspaper. However, it is unlikely that students will participate in *faculty committees*. Therefore, this item should be eliminated.

ACTIVITY 11

For each group of items, do the following:

- Cross out the one item that does not fit.
- For the remaining items, think of a general or *big idea* that connects them and write it on the first line.
- Add the remaining items to this new list, using any order of your choice.

EXAMPLE: Big idea: _warning sounds_

siren	_siren_
alarm	_alarm_
horn	_horn_
~~radio~~	

1. Big idea: _____

loans _____

credit cards _____

mortgage _____

savings

2. Big idea: _____

paperback _____

e-book _____

laptop _____

textbook

3. Big idea: _____

credit cards _____

passport _____

driver's license _____

student ID

4. Big idea: _____

overdue books _____

parking ticket _____

cell phone overage _____

snacks in a bar

CONTINUED >

5. Big idea: _____

   garage sale   _____

   thrift shop   _____

   eBay auctions   _____

   hardware store _____

6. Big idea: _____

   hot fudge
   sundae   _____

   steamed
   broccoli   _____

   deep-fried
   cheese

   french fries

ACTIVITY 12

Examine each of the following clusters and then do the following:

- Cross out one item that does not fit.
- For the remaining items, think of a general or *big idea* that connects the examples and write it in the middle bubble and on the first line.
- Add the remaining items (the examples) to the list in the order you choose.

EXAMPLE:

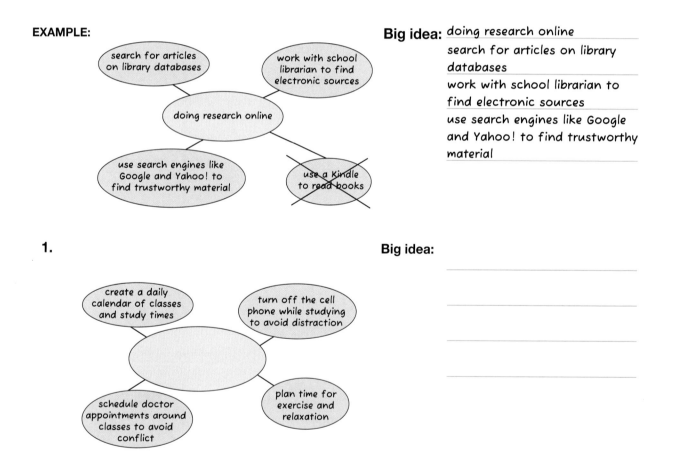

Big idea: doing research online

search for articles on library databases

work with school librarian to find electronic sources

use search engines like Google and Yahoo! to find trustworthy material

1.

Big idea: _____

2.

change the oil and filters on a regular basis

have the ignition and transmission checked every 30,000 miles

rotate the tires and check the brakes

wash the car when it's very dirty

Big idea: _____

_____

_____

_____

3.

wear boots if there is deep snow

block possible drafts in doors and windows

wear warm clothes in the house

use portable room-heaters instead of heating the whole house

Big idea: _____

_____

_____

_____

4.

have cough drops handy if attending a movie with a cold

do not stuff yourself on popcorn and candy

sit in an aisle seat if you're likely to use the restroom frequently

do not talk during the film

Big idea: _____

_____

_____

_____

5.

serve the cake when still slightly warm

pre-heat the oven

make sure the ingredients are fresh

follow a recipe

Big idea: _____

_____

_____

_____

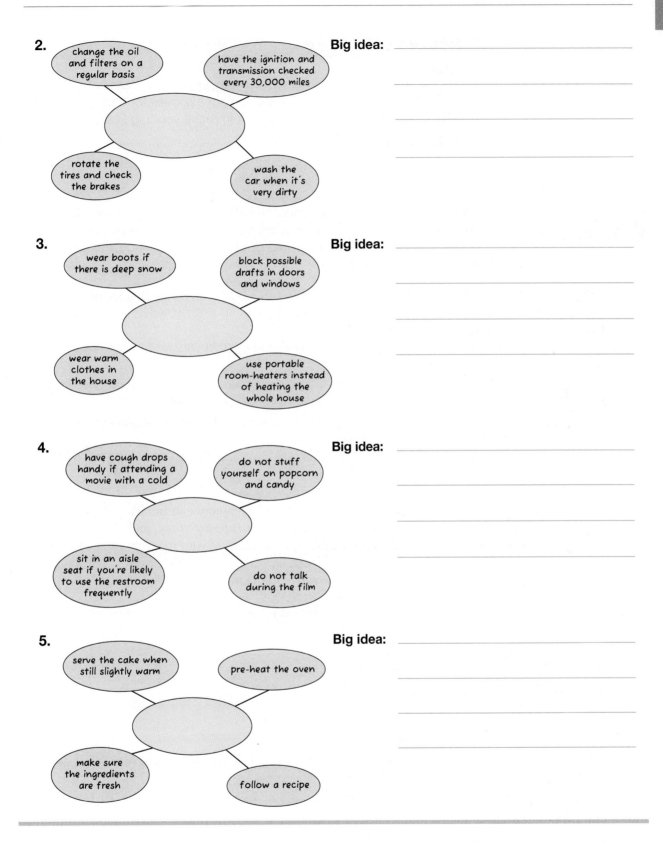

ACTIVITY 13: Teamwork

Exchange your answers to Activity 12 with those of a classmate. Did you sort any of the items differently? How do your *big ideas* for each group compare? Can you find any ways to refine or improve your big ideas?

Eliminating Sentences

Like words and phrases, sentences that do not fit also need to be eliminated. To come up with a big idea to connect the remaining sentences, you may need to highlight or underline key words or phrases to help you figure out which items do not fit. Take a look:

Big idea: Credit card companies can punish you for getting behind in your payments.

- If you get behind in your payments, credit card companies can put a hold on your account.
- If you get behind in your payments, credit card companies can lower your monthly payments.
- If you get behind in your payments, credit card companies can raise your interest rates.
- If you get behind in your payments, credit card companies can damage your credit rating.

Three examples of how a credit card company can punish you are *putting a hold on your account, raising your interest rates*, and *damaging your credit rating*. However, if the company lowers your monthly payments, this is not a penalty but an offer of assistance. Therefore, the second item should be eliminated since it does not relate to the topic.

- ~~If you get behind in your payments, credit card companies can lower your monthly payments.~~

ACTIVITY 14

For each group of items, do the following:

- Cross out the one item that does not fit. (If helpful, highlight or underline key words or phrases within the complete sentences.)
- For the remaining items, think of a *big idea* that connects them and write it on the first line in a complete sentence.
- Add the remaining items to the list, using any order of your choice.

EXAMPLE: Make sure that you can afford veterinarian bills and pet food.

Make sure that other family members or roommates feel comfortable with a pet.

~~Make sure that you visit a local animal shelter.~~

Make sure that you have adequate time to spend with your pet.

Big idea: Before adopting a pet, make sure you can manage the responsibility.
Make sure that you can afford veterinarian bills and pet food.
Make sure that other family members or roommates feel comfortable with a pet.
Make sure that you have adequate time to spend with your pet.

1. You may be required to separate plastic items, paper items, and glass items.

You may need to take your recyclable items to a recycling center.

You may receive some money in exchange for your recyclable items.

You may have to rinse some items before recycling them.

Big idea: _____

_____

_____

_____

_____

2. If a co-worker talks too much, politely excuse yourself from the conversation and go back to work.

If a co-worker tends to gossip, avoid taking sides on issues he or she brings up.

If a co-worker offers to help you with a project, show your gratitude and accept his/her help if it is appropriate.

If a co-worker is always unpleasant, be polite during interactions but keep contact to a minimum.

Big idea: _____

_____

_____

_____

_____

_____

_____

CONTINUED >

3. Date or live together for several years to see how well you get along day-to-day.

Marriage is a long-term commitment and should be taken seriously.

Finish your education and start your careers before having children.

Instead of spending a fortune on a wedding, use that money for a down payment on a house or apartment.

Big idea: _____

4. Calling and Skyping regularly can make the distance seem like less of an obstacle.

Long-distance romances used to be more difficult before modern technology.

Planning regular visits to each partner's town will give the couple something to look forward to.

Writing love letters to each other keeps the romance alive.

Big idea: _____

5. Browse fashion magazines in bookstores.

Shop at seasonal sales, sample sales, and thrift stores for the rare and inexpensive finds.

Make one piece of clothing work several ways so that it lasts longer.

Avoid buying expensive shoes or accessories that will only last one season.

Big idea: _____

COMBINING STRATEGIES

In most writing situations, you will need to use all the organizing strategies (ordering, grouping, eliminating) at the same time. In other words, you will need to:

1. **group** the items into related groups

2. **order** the items in each group by putting the big idea first and the examples in any order of your choice

3. **eliminate** any items that do not fit well in either group

ACTIVITY 15

In this activity, you will need to form three ordered lists from three scrambled lists. Each list should begin with a *big idea*. You will be given one of the big ideas. For each set of lists, do the following:

- Determine the missing big idea.
- Write each big idea in the space provided.
- Add the examples under the appropriate big ideas.
- Eliminate any items that do not fit and write them in the space provided.

EXAMPLE: bears / elk / moose / deer / wolves / foxes / ranger

Group 1:

Big idea: wildlife with hooves

Examples: elk

moose

deer

Group 2:

Big idea: wildlife with paws

Examples: bears

wolves

foxes

Eliminate one item: ranger

1. poem / memo / story / novel / ticket / newsletter / memo / report

    Group 1:

    Big idea: literary writing

    Examples:

    Group 2:

    Big idea:

    Examples:

    Eliminate one item:

CONTINUED >

2. tea / fruit juice / coffee / hot chocolate / fresh bread / water / vegetable juice

   Group 1:

   Big idea: hot drinks

   Examples: _____

   _____

   _____

   Group 2:

   Big idea: _____

   Examples: _____

   _____

   Eliminate one item: _____

3. speeches / candidates / government / voting / cars / policy / city services / legislation

   Group 1:

   Big idea: election

   Examples: _____

   _____

   _____

   Group 2:

   Big idea: _____

   Examples: _____

   _____

   Eliminate one item: _____

4. check IV / visit a relative / perform surgery / take vital signs / give medications / give instructions to nurses

   Group 1:

   Big idea: nurses' duties

   Examples: _____

   _____

   _____

   Group 2:

   Big idea: _____

   Examples: _____

   _____

   Eliminate one item: _____

5. turn on siren / show driver's license / pull off road carefully / don't exceed speed limit / approach car and driver with caution / turn off engine and stay in car / follow car to safe stop

   Group 1:

   Big idea: police stopping driver

   Examples: _____

   _____

   _____

   _____

   Group 2:

   Big idea: _____

   Examples: _____

   _____

   Eliminate one item: _____

ACTIVITY 16: Teamwork

Each of the following items consists of two joined clusters. In each cluster, the big idea appears in a central (green) bubble. Work with one or two classmates to do the following:

- For each group, write the *big idea* on the first line.
- Add the related examples under each big idea, eliminating any items that do not fit.
- Watch out for items that are clustered incorrectly.

EXAMPLE:

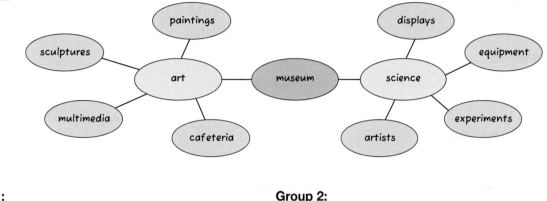

Group 1:

Big idea: art museum

Examples: paintings

sculptures

multimedia

Group 2:

Big idea: science museum

Examples: experiments

equipment

displays

Eliminate two items: cafeteria, artists

1.

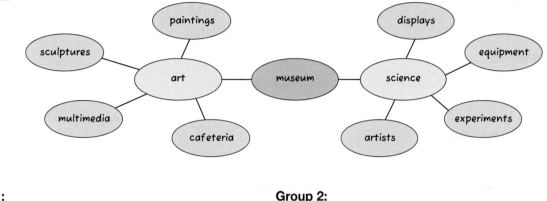

Group 1:

Big idea: _____

Examples: _____

_____

_____

Group 2:

Big idea: _____

Examples: _____

_____

_____

Eliminate two items: _____

CONTINUED >

2.

Group 1:

Big idea: _____

Examples: _____

_____

_____

Group 2:

Big idea: _____

Examples: _____

_____

_____

Eliminate two items: _____

ACTIVITY 17

Although *big ideas* should appear in green bubbles, we sometimes put them in the wrong place by accident. The following clusters are trickier because more items are incorrectly clustered, including some of the *big ideas*. For this activity, you will need to unscramble the clusters and move the items into well-organized lists. For each item, do the following:

- Write the big idea for each group in the space provided.
- Add the related examples under each big idea.
- Eliminate the items that do not fit. Write them in the space provided.

1.

Group 1:

Big idea: _____

Examples: _____

_____

_____

Group 2:

Big idea: _____

Examples: _____

_____

_____

Eliminate two items: _____

2.

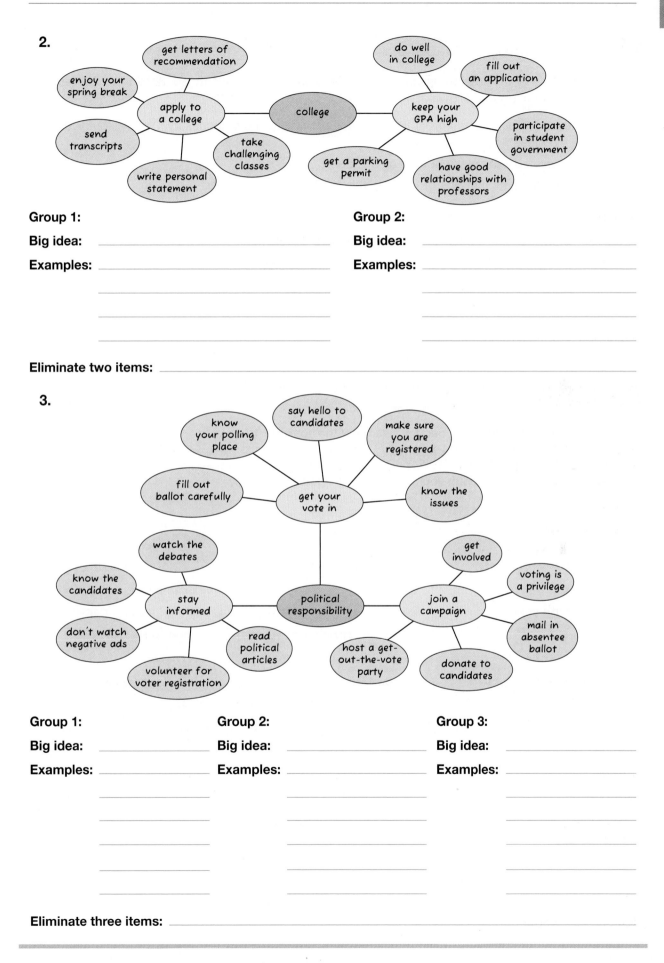

Group 1:

Big idea: _____

Examples: _____

_____

_____

_____

Group 2:

Big idea: _____

Examples: _____

_____

_____

_____

Eliminate two items: _____

3.

Group 1:

Big idea: _____

Examples: _____

_____

_____

_____

_____

Group 2:

Big idea: _____

Examples: _____

_____

_____

_____

_____

Group 3:

Big idea: _____

Examples: _____

_____

_____

_____

_____

Eliminate three items: _____

ACTIVITY 18: Mastery Test or Teamwork

For this activity, you will need to unscramble the list of items and move those items to well-organized lists. For each item, do the following:

- Write the *big idea* for each group in the space provided, where necessary. (You will be given two of the big ideas.)
- Add the related examples under each big idea.
- Eliminate the items that do not fit. Write them in the space provided.

EXAMPLE: **Topic: Being a responsible roommate**

Show genuine empathy for your roommates' problems.

If you want to have a party, ask your roommates first.

Always lock the apartment door when you leave.

Pay your share of the utility bills on time.

Don't ask your roommates if you can borrow money.

Throw out your spoiled food items from the refrigerator.

Don't fight with your roommates over unimportant problems.

Deep-clean the bathroom every week.

If sick, don't spread your germs around the apartment.

Don't eat your roommates' groceries.

Don't stay angry with your roommates — apologize quickly.

Group 1:

Big idea: Be an emotionally mature roommate.

Examples:

Don't fight with your roommates over unimportant problems.

Don't stay angry with your roommates — apologize quickly.

Show genuine empathy for your roommates' problems.

Group 2:

Big idea: Be a financially responsible roommate.

Examples:

Don't ask your roommates if you can borrow money.

Pay your share of the utility bills on time.

Don't eat your roommates' groceries.

Group 3:

Big idea: Be a clean roommate.

Examples:

Throw out your spoiled food items from the refrigerator.

Deep-clean the bathroom every week.

If sick, don't spread your germs around the apartment.

Eliminate two items:

Always lock the apartment door when you leave.

If you want to have a party, ask your roommates first.

1. **Topic: Being a good parent**

   Parents should know where their children are at all times.

   Parents should warn their children about dangerous strangers.

   Parents should explain their rules clearly to their children.

   Parents should praise their children's academic efforts.

   Parents should listen carefully when their children have problems.

   Parents should take precautions against Internet intruders.

   Parents should read books on raising children.

   Parents should help their children with homework each night.

   Parents should meet with teachers on a regular basis.

   Parents should set a good example for their children.

   Parents should initiate daily conversation with their children.

Group 1:	Group 2:	Group 3:
Big idea: _____	Big idea: Good parents communicate effectively with their children.	Big idea: Good parents get involved in their children's education.
_____		
_____		
Examples:	Examples:	Examples:
_____	_____	_____
_____	_____	_____
_____	_____	_____
_____	_____	_____
_____	_____	_____
_____	_____	_____
_____	_____	_____
_____	_____	_____

Eliminate two items:

_____

_____

2. **Topic: Living a balanced life**

   Pick a job that is enjoyable and rewarding.

   Pick a spouse with a sense of humor.

   Trips to exotic places can open your mind.

   Regular exercise decreases stress.

   Don't work a lot of stressful overtime.

CONTINUED >

Surround yourself with positive people.

Avoid a workplace where employees aren't respected.

Having a pet is one of life's greatest joys.

Vitamin supplements can prevent illness.

Meditation can improve mental health.

Develop meaningful friendships.

Group 1:	Group 2:	Group 3:
Big idea: _A balanced life includes good relationships._	**Big idea:** _A balanced life includes good health._	**Big idea:** _____
Examples:	**Examples:**	**Examples:**

Eliminate two items:

_____

_____

ACTIVITY 19: Mastery Test

Go back to one of the clusters you generated in Chapter 3 and do the following:

- Make sure that the ideas are *grouped* in a way that makes sense. (You can write your changes on the cluster or list, or you can transfer your work to a fresh sheet of paper.)
- Make sure that there is a *big idea* that connects the items in each group.
- Make sure that the ideas are *ordered* in a way that makes sense, especially if you are working with a list.
- *Eliminate* any items that do not fit your topic.

BRINGING IT ALL TOGETHER:
Organizing Your Ideas

In this chapter, you have learned about basic strategies for organizing your ideas. Confirm your knowledge by filling in the blank spaces in the following sentences. If you need help, review the pages listed after each sentence. Finally, check off each item to confirm your understanding of the material.

✔ Three strategies for organizing ideas are _____, _____, and _____. (page 64)

✔ To order your ideas effectively, you will need to be able to recognize the difference between _____ or _____ and _____. (page 64)

✔ With complete sentences, there will be _____ that define the idea. Get in the habit of marking these _____. (page 69)

✔ To group items successfully, you will need to be able to recognize items that are _____. (page 72)

✔ When organizing your ideas, you will want to look for groups of related items that clearly support the topic and you will want to _____ isolated items that do not fit. (page 80)

✔ In most writing situations, you will need to use _____ organizing strategies (ordering, grouping, eliminating) at the same time. (page 87)

JOURNAL WRITING: 10–15 minutes

An important part of college success is learning to manage your emotions. In particular, you may experience anxiety and even fear about your intelligence and ability to succeed in college. For this journal entry, discuss any anxiety you've experienced so far in college. Explain how these emotions have affected you and your academic performance, how you have managed the emotions, and whether you think these experiences will prepare you for future challenges in college.

CHAPTER 5

Outlining Your Paragraph

Test your understanding of how to outline paragraphs by completing this quiz first. You may know more than you think.

For each question, select all the answers that apply.

WHAT DO YOU KNOW?

1. **All outlines have the same basic key features even if they look different. What are these features?**

   ___ a main idea

   ___ a topic sentence

   ___ support points

   ___ related examples

2. **What are some strategies for filling in outlines?**

   ___ transferring ideas from your brainstorming to your outline

   ___ adding or changing any ideas that you missed during brainstorming

   ___ ignoring your brainstorming and starting afresh

   ___ eliminating weaker ideas that do not fit with the topic

3. **When finalizing your *main idea* for an outline, what strategy is helpful?**

   ___ using colorful details

   ___ expressing your idea as a complete sentence

   ___ adding a transitional expression

4. **When writing the *support points* in your outline, what strategies are helpful?**

   ___ writing each support point as one word

   ___ writing each support point as a complete sentence

   ___ beginning each support point with a transitional expression

   ___ not beginning each support point with a transitional expression

5. **What can including *transitional expressions* in your outline help you with?**

   ___ finalizing your main idea

   ___ moving smoothly from one support point to another

   ___ remembering to use transitional expressions in your final paragraph

   ___ making your outline look bigger than it really is

Outlining Basics

In the previous chapter, you learned how to organize your ideas. In this chapter, you will learn about outlining, an important process for planning paragraphs and other writing assignments. All outlines have the same basic functions, which you are already familiar with:

- They **order** ideas, starting with the big ideas (which become support points) and moving to related examples.
- They **group** items that are related to one another.
- They **eliminate** items that do not fit together.

As you move ahead in your college education, you will probably be required to use a variety of outline types. Even though these outlines may *look* quite different from one another, they all have the same basic parts:

- a main idea
- support points
- related examples

In this book, you will use a simple outline form that has all of these parts. You will use a similar form for writing both paragraphs and short essays. Once you understand the basic features of this form, you will be able to work confidently with other types of outlines required in your other classes. (As you will see in the pages that follow, specific details are not usually included in an outline because they can easily clutter it. Instead, specific details are added to a composition during the draft stage.)

Take a look at the following outline in which the key features are highlighted:

Power Tip
You may think that making outlines is a waste of time, but organizing your ideas before you write can actually save time, especially if you are writing under a deadline.

ASSIGNED TOPIC	*Discuss a special friend you've had.*
MAIN IDEA	My 92-year-old neighbor became an unlikely friend.
SUPPORT POINT 1	To begin with, helping her out makes me feel useful.
RELATED EXAMPLES	– She needs help with her dog. – She needs help shopping. – She needs help with her groceries.
SUPPORT POINT 2	Next, she offers me a sanctuary in her apartment.
RELATED EXAMPLES	– I can do homework there in peace. – ~~I don't have my own apartment.~~ – We watch old movies together. – I sleep over when I need space from family.
SUPPORT POINT 3	Last, she shares her experience and wisdom with me.
RELATED EXAMPLES	– about romantic relationships. – about education and career. – ~~about everything~~

The **main idea** responds to your assigned topic. It connects all the support points and examples that follow.

The **support points** are based on the *big ideas* from your brainstorming, and they back up your main idea.

The **related examples** are grouped under each support point.

Any **items that do not fit** are eliminated.

ACTIVITY 1

Refer to Activity 18 in Chapter 4, page 92, to complete this activity.

- First, look at topic 2 (*Living a balanced life*).
- Then, move the items that you wrote for topic 2 onto the outline form that appears below. You can use the outline on page 97 as a model. To get you started, the main idea has been filled in for you.
- Additionally, turn each big idea from topic 2 into a support point. (The first support point has been done for you.)
- Be sure to write each support point as a complete sentence.
- Then, write three related examples below each support point. These examples can be left as short phrases.

MAIN IDEA   Several factors contribute to living a balanced life.

SUPPORT POINT 1   A balanced life includes good relationships.

SUPPORT POINT 3

SUPPORT POINT 2

UNDERSTANDING KEY FEATURES OF OUTLINES

The following sections give more details on the four key features of outlines: the main idea, the support points, the related examples, and transitional expressions.

Feature 1: The Main Idea

In college, each paragraph that you write must contain a *main idea* that responds directly to an assigned topic. Consider the following assignment:

> *Discuss the college class in which you have learned the most valuable skills or knowledge.*

In writing a main idea for this topic, you should do all of the following:

- Identify a college class of your choice.
- Use some *key words* from the assigned topic (*college class, most valuable, skills, knowledge,* etc.).
- Express your idea as *a complete sentence.*

Here are three students' main ideas that respond to this assigned topic:

- The most valuable knowledge I've gained in college so far was in my art history class.
- My business writing class gave me the most valuable skills I've acquired in college.
- Of all my college classes, Women's Studies 101 has given me the most valuable knowledge.

Notice that each main idea identifies a specific class. Also, each one uses key words from the assigned topic (*most valuable, knowledge, skills*). Finally, each main idea is expressed as a complete sentence.

ACTIVITY 2

For each of the following assigned topics, provide a main idea, and then do the following:

- In the main idea, underline any words repeated from the assigned topic.
- In the main idea, circle the key phrase that responds to the assigned topic.
- To ensure that the main idea is expressed as a complete sentence, put a check mark over the capital letter at the beginning of the sentence and over the period at the end of the sentence.

EXAMPLE:

Assigned topic: Identify a talent you wish you had.

Main idea: One talent I wish I had is (gardening).

1. **Assigned topic:** Discuss how you manage your time.

   Main idea: _____

2. **Assigned topic:** Discuss a role you play in your family.

   Main idea: _____

CONTINUED >

Power Tip

Whenever you have trouble coming up with a main idea, look back at ideas that you've brainstormed in response to an assigned topic. You might circle words in your brainstorming that directly respond to the topic. Then, use these words in your main idea. In Chapter 6, you will learn how to turn main ideas into a *topic sentence*, an important feature of effective paragraphs.

3. **Assigned topic:** Describe something that motivates you.

   Main idea: _____

   _____

4. **Assigned topic:** Explain why you decided to enroll in college.

   Main idea: _____

   _____

5. **Assigned topic:** Discuss your attitude about teachers who routinely arrive late.

   Main idea: _____

   _____

Feature 2: The Support Points

Power Tip
Sometimes, you may only have two support points. At other times, you may have more than three support points. Ask your instructor for suggestions if you're not sure that you have adequate support, or if you think you have too much.

In an outline, you'll need to include *support points* that back up your main idea. Often, these are taken from the *big ideas* in your clusters and lists. Make sure to state the support points as complete sentences.

Compare the following (partial) cluster with the (partial) outline that follows. Notice that the first support point is based on the big idea "too much pressure."

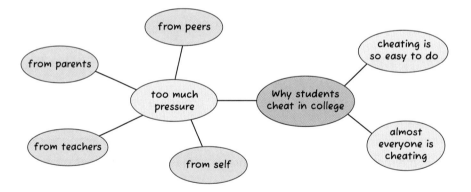

Here is the start of an outline that turns a big idea into a support point:

MAIN IDEA   College students cheat for three key reasons.

SUPPORT POINT 1   To begin with, they cheat because of excessive pressure.
   – pressure from parents
   – pressure from instructors
   – pressure from peers
   – pressure from oneself

Often, adding the word *because* to the end of your main idea will help you develop support points that make sense. For example, suppose your main idea is

College students cheat (*because* . . .)

Now, you will have to complete this thought with a support point that makes sense. Here are several examples of how you might complete this idea:

They are under so much pressure.
Cheating has become so easy to do.
Everyone appears to be doing it.

Notice that each support point is expressed as *a complete sentence* and connects clearly with the main idea. You should always verify that each support point makes sense by reading it in conjunction with the main idea. For example:

College students cheat *because* they are under so much pressure.

This idea makes clear sense. However, suppose you tried to express your support point as a single word (like *pressure*) or as a short phrase (like *under pressure*). When you connect a single word or short phrase to your main idea, it will not make sense:

College students cheat *because* pressure.
College students cheat *because* under pressure.

ACTIVITY 3

Using the items from this cluster, fill in the outline form that follows. Remember to write the main idea and the support points as *complete sentences*.

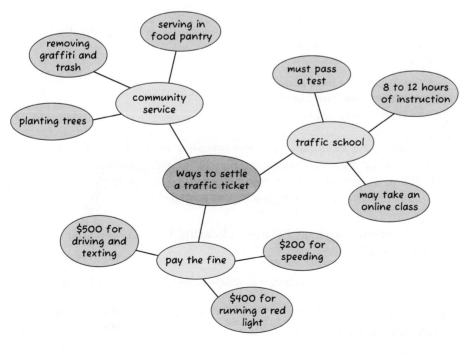

CONTINUED >

MAIN IDEA _____

SUPPORT POINT 1 _____   SUPPORT POINT 3 _____

_____   _____

RELATED EXAMPLES _____   RELATED EXAMPLES _____

_____   _____

_____   _____

_____   _____

SUPPORT POINT 2 _____

_____

RELATED EXAMPLES _____

_____

_____

_____

Feature 3: The Related Examples

For each support point in your outline, you will need to provide *related examples* to illustrate your point. For example, if you say,

> **College students cheat because they are under so much pressure.**

your readers will expect you to name some *related examples* of the types of pressure college students are under. For example:

> **pressure from parents**
> **pressure from instructors**
> **pressure from peers**

In an outline, your examples may be expressed as *short phrases* or even as *single words*. Be sure that your examples fit with the point you are trying to prove. If you are not sure what kind of examples fit, circle the key words in the support point to help you focus. For example:

> **Many students cheat because (cheating) has become so (easy to do) successfully.**

For this support point, you should provide examples of how cheating is easy to do. For example:

> **texting answers**
> **buying essays online**

For more practice with outlining, visit **bedfordstmartins .com/touchstones**.

ACTIVITY 4

Circle the key word or words in the following support points. Then, provide two or three related examples for each point.

MAIN IDEA   I like spending time with friends (because...)

SUPPORT POINT 1   I can be myself around them.

RELATED EXAMPLES

_____

_____

_____

_____

SUPPORT POINT 3   They help me in different ways.

RELATED EXAMPLES

_____

_____

_____

_____

SUPPORT POINT 2   We have a lot of fun together.

RELATED EXAMPLES

_____

_____

_____

_____

_____

USING TRANSITIONAL EXPRESSIONS IN OUTLINES

Moving from one support point to another requires a **transitional word or expression** such as *To begin with*, *In the second place*, and *Finally*. Transitional words or expressions are an essential feature of academic writing. They help your reader follow the development of your ideas from point to point.

Although you can add transitional expressions while drafting your paragraph, it is a much better practice to add them *directly on your outline* beside each support point. This simple step will ensure that you include the transitional expressions when drafting your paragraph.

MAIN IDEA   _____

To begin with, _____

SUPPORT POINT 1   _____

RELATED EXAMPLES   _____

_____

Transitional Expressions

↓

Group 1

First,
To begin with,
For starters,
In the first place,

Group 2 ────────────────────→ Second,

Second,
Next,   **SUPPORT POINT 2** _____
In the second place,
Equally important,   **RELATED EXAMPLES** _____

_____

_____

Group 3 ───────────
                       ────────→ Last,
Finally,
Last,   **SUPPORT POINT 3** _____
Third,
Most important,   **RELATED EXAMPLES** _____

_____

_____

_____

FILLING IN OUTLINES

If you have brainstormed thoroughly for your topic, filling in an outline can be managed quite easily. It is a step-by-step process that requires you to transfer ideas from your brainstorming to your outline form. Sometimes, you may need to change some of your ideas or add new ideas that did not come to mind during your brainstorming. Finally, you may need to eliminate some weaker ideas and any ideas that do not fit with the topic.

As an example of this process, let's review one student's brainstorming and then follow his step-by-step completion of the outline form. Notice that the student has used *listing* and the *five* Ws to explore and write down his ideas.

ASSIGNED TOPIC   *Discuss some common problems that college students experience.*

NARROWED TOPIC   *financial problems of college students*

WHO?

—me!...too many loans, no money for books after tuition, no money for dates

—my brother Stan...working two jobs after school, maxed out credit card, lives on noodles and peanut butter

—my girlfriend, Luce...can afford only two classes per semester, gave up cable, can't fix 20-year-old car

WHERE?

—at school...grades suffer because of the need to work, students have to reduce course loads because of $, some can't even afford snacks at the school cafeteria

—at home...chores don't get done because of the need to work, no $ for home repairs, no $ for home decor and other extras

—at work...need more hours but can't always get them, pay cuts, layoffs

WHEN? (financial stresses are worst)

—at the beginning of the semester...fees due, books and supplies need to be purchased

—when we are expected to spend $ on others...on holidays, at the start of children's school year, for birthdays

WHAT?

—minimal money for day-to-day expenses...food, gasoline, child care

—excessive debt...in student loans, on credit cards, doctor bills

—nonexistent savings...no savings account, no money under the mattress, no money that anyone owes me

WHY? (financial problems arise)

—not enough income...low-paying jobs, not enough hours, no spouse or friend to bring in $

—high education costs...increasing tuition, costs of books and supplies, parking fees

—not enough student aid...loans being cut, scholarships more competitive, qualifications for aid becoming stricter

Step 1: Write Your Main Idea

Looking at your brainstorming, find your narrowed topic. (It will be in the center of your cluster or at the top of the page for a list, flowchart, or freewrite.) Next, write this idea at the top of the outline form as a complete sentence:

Main Idea: College students experience several financial problems.

Step 2: Write Your First Support Point

Your first support point should be one of the *big ideas* that you have about the topic. Start by asking yourself this question: "If I could only talk about one major idea to support my topic, which idea would be the most powerful or important?" Look carefully over your cluster, list, flowchart, or freewrite until you find this idea.

Power Tip
Some useful transitional expressions to start with are:
- First,
- In the first place,
- For starters,
- For openers,
- To begin with,

Next, write the idea on your outline as a *complete sentence*, starting with a *transitional expression*. Take a look:

Main Idea: College students experience several financial problems.

Support Point 1: First, the cost of education keeps going up.

Step 3: Write Your Second Support Point

Your second support point should be another *big idea* you have about your topic. Try asking yourself this question: "If I could talk about only one more idea to support my topic, which idea would be the most powerful or important?" Now, look carefully over your cluster, list, flowchart, or freewrite until you find this next big idea.

Write the idea on your outline as *a complete sentence*, starting with a *transitional expression*. Take a look:

Power Tip
Some useful transitional expressions in the middle of a paragraph or essay are:
- Second,
- Next,
- In the second place,
- Equally important,
- More important,

Main Idea: College students experience several financial problems.

Support Point 1: First, the cost of education keeps going up.

_____

_____

_____

Support Point 2: Next, students have fewer sources of income.

Step 4: Write Your Third Support Point

Now, ask yourself this question: "If I could talk about only one more idea to support my topic, which idea would be the most powerful or important?" Look carefully over your cluster, list, flowchart, or freewrite until you find this big idea.

Write the idea on your outline as a *complete sentence*, starting with a *transitional expression*. Take a look:

Main Idea: College students experience several financial problems.

Support Point 1: First, the cost of education keeps going up.

_____

_____

_____

Support Point 2: Next, students have fewer sources of income.

_____

_____

_____

Support Point 3: Last, students suffer because of money trouble.

_____

_____

_____

Power Tip

Some useful transitional expressions in the final stages of a paragraph or essay are:
- Third,
- Last,
- Finally,
- Ultimately,
- In the third place,
- More important,
- Most important,

Once you have written in your three support points, you may now decide to change their order. If you've followed the instructions so far for filling in your outline, your first support point will be your most important or powerful one. However, some students like to *end* with their most powerful support point, building up to it. Both approaches can work effectively.

Step 5: Write the Related Examples for the Support Points

You should provide at least one related example for each support point on your outline. However, if possible, provide two or even three examples for each support point. The examples do not have to be complete sentences, and no transitional expressions are required. Watch out for items that do not fit.

You can look again at the brainstorming on pages 104–5 to see where the student got his examples for the first support point.

Main Idea: College students experience several financial problems.

Support Point 1: First, the cost of education keeps going up.

Related Examples: rising tuition
books and supplies cost more
increase in parking and lab fees

The **sixth step** is to write the related examples for the remaining support points, following the instructions above.

The Steps at a Glance

Now, you can take a look at the completed outline and the steps that lead to its completion:

Step 1:
Write the
main idea.

Steps 2–4:
Write the
three support
points, begin-
ning each with
a transitional
expression.

<u>Main Idea</u>: College students experience several financial problems.

<u>Support Point 1</u>: First, the cost of education keeps going up.

    <u>Related Examples</u>: rising tuition
                        books and supplies cost more
                        increase in parking and lab fees

Step 5: Write
the examples
for support
point 1.

<u>Support Point 2</u>: Next, students have fewer sources of income.

    <u>Related Examples</u>: low-paying jobs
                        loans being cut
                        no help from family

Step 6: Write
the examples
for support
points 2 and 3.

<u>Support Point 3</u>: Last, students suffer because of money trouble.

    <u>Related Examples</u>: eating cheap, unhealthy food
                        no money for emergencies
                        pressure of debt

ACTIVITY 5

Go back to at least one of the clusters you generated in Chapter 3 and do the following:

- Print a blank outline from this book's Web site at **bedfordstmartins .com/touchstones** (see Useful Forms), or create your own.
- Move the items from the list or cluster to the outline form by following the six steps. Start by filling in the *main idea* and the *support points*, putting the support points in an order that makes sense to you.
- Remember that both the main idea and the support points should be stated as complete sentences.
- Go back and fill in the related examples for each support point, eliminating items that do not fit.

ACTIVITY 6

Unscramble the list of items on the left and fill in the outline form on the right. Do the following:

- First, look through the list for a ***main idea*** that responds directly to the assigned topic. Write the main idea on the outline form.
- Next, look through the list for three ***big ideas*** that support the main idea. Write these ideas on the outline form as the three support points. Be sure to add a transitional expression to each one.

- Then, look through the list and find three examples that fit the first support point. Write them on the outline.
- Find the examples that fit with support points 2 and 3, and write them on the outline.
- Finally, write the two items to be eliminated in the spaces provided.

Assigned topic 1: Discuss changes you would make at your college.

I'd keep the library open on Sunday.   **MAIN IDEA**   _____

I'd keep the campus cleaner.   **SUPPORT POINT 1**   _____

I'd plant more trees along the sidewalks.

I'd add two new lots for cars.   **EXAMPLES**   _____

I'd have litter picked up regularly.   _____

I'd reduce the cost of passes.   _____

I'd add grassy areas with benches.   **SUPPORT POINT 2**   _____

I'd add more spaces for motorcycles.   **EXAMPLES**   _____

I'd put fresh paint in classrooms.   _____

I'd start a rose garden by the library.   _____

I'd remove graffiti from bathrooms.   **SUPPORT POINT 3**   _____

I'd change campus parking.   _____

I'd change three things at my college.   **EXAMPLES**   _____

I'd offer more classes in the summer.   _____

I'd add more green spaces.   _____

Eliminate two items:

_____

_____

Assigned topic 2: Discuss something you would avoid at all costs.

Drug addiction can lead to bigger problems.   **MAIN IDEA**   _____

SUPPORT POINT 1   _____

All your money is spent on drugs.   _____

Drug addiction is a huge problem in America.   **EXAMPLES**   _____

My uncle's addiction cost him his life.   _____

You deal drugs to support your habit.   _____

Amos dropped out of school because of drugs.   _____

Drug addiction takes over your life.   _____

I would avoid getting hooked on drugs.   **SUPPORT POINT 2**   _____

You don't care about school anymore.   _____

I've seen what drug addiction can do to people.   **EXAMPLES**   _____

CONTINUED >

Some drug addictions are worse than others.

A pregnant woman on drugs hurts her baby.

SUPPORT POINT 3

You go to jail on drug charges.

You steal to get money for drugs.

EXAMPLES

You'd rather get high than go to work.

Eliminate two items:

_____

_____

Assigned topic 3: Discuss how you stay motivated.

I eat a healthy diet.

MAIN IDEA

I am always looking for new motivational strategies.

SUPPORT POINT 1

My best friends challenge and support me.

I keep myself motivated by using several strategies.

EXAMPLES

I meditate twice a day for 20 minutes.

I make a list of things I want to accomplish.

SUPPORT POINT 2

I prepare each night for the next day's challenges.

I associate with other highly motivated people.

EXAMPLES

I pray for strength while falling asleep.

I participate in motivated study groups.

SUPPORT POINT 3

I stay physically and mentally fit.

I work out with a high-energy trainer.

EXAMPLES

I wasn't always as motivated as I am now.

I get to bed early to wake up fresh.

I work out five times a week at the gym.

Eliminate two items:

_____

THE ELASTIC OUTLINE

It is important to remember that an outline form provides a *starting point* for the organization of your ideas, not a one-size-fits-all formula that you must match exactly. You should be able to *stretch* it, *shrink* it, and *reshape* it according to the writing project, the topic, and your ideas. Think of your outline as being like a shape-changing mirror at a fun house. Take a look:

In the photo above, notice that the mirror has stretched and reshaped the girls' reflections. Similarly, you can stretch, shrink, and reshape an outline, depending on the particular needs of your topic and assignment. There are basically two ways to stretch, shrink, or reshape an outline:

1. by adding or subtracting support points
2. by adding or subtracting related examples

In other words, your outline may have just two support points or as many as your instructor allows. For each support point, you should have at least one related example, but having two or three will help you develop your composition more fully and effectively.

Solving Problems in Outlines

After completing your outline—and before drafting your composition—it is a good idea to double-check the outline to make sure that it is free of three common problems:

- an item that does not fit
- an item that repeats another item
- an item that is unclear

An Item That Does Not Fit

One problem that can occur with your outline is including *an item that does not fit.* An item does not fit when it is not clearly connected to a main idea or support point.

Take a look at the following outline, in which just the first support point has been developed with examples. Can you see a problem with one of the examples?

MAIN IDEA	I have learned to manage my anger effectively.
SUPPORT POINT 1	My weekly anger management class helps me control my anger.
	– Sharing stories with other angry people helps me.
	– We role-play situations that might cause anger.
	– The class meets on Friday afternoon for two hours.
SUPPORT POINT 2	I proactively avoid or modify situations that are likely to make me angry.
SUPPORT POINT 3	I exercise vigorously to reduce my anger.

You might have noticed that the third example (*The class meets on Friday afternoon for two hours*) doesn't fit with the main idea (*I have learned to manage my anger effectively*) or with the support point it's under (*My weekly anger management class helps me control my anger*) because the day and time that the class meets doesn't illustrate how the writer is learning to manage his anger. A better example would be, *We spend time writing in our anger management diary.*

When you have finished an outline, first read each support point together with the main idea to make sure the point fits the main idea. Then, check the related examples under each support point to make sure they belong. If they do not, change them so that they fit better.

ACTIVITY 7

In the following outlines, cross out any item that does not fit.

1.	**MAIN IDEA**	Playing on my college's football team was not a good experience.
	SUPPORT POINT 1	To begin with, football took too much time.
		We practiced 10 to 15 hours per week.
		First-string players always have to be there.
		We spent whole weekends away for games.
	SUPPORT POINT 2	Second, it was hard on my body.
		I injured my ankle during a tackle.
		I work out at the gym to stay tough.
		The competition gave me an upset stomach.
	SUPPORT POINT 3	College is more demanding than high school.
		I missed classes because of "away" games.

Practice interfered with my homework.

Some professors treated me like a "dumb jock."

2. **MAIN IDEA**   Organizing one's home can be beneficial.

SUPPORT POINT 1   First, organize one's closet for easy selection.

Organize clothes by color.

Separate shoes for work and play.

Put accessories in labeled boxes.

Buy clothes at thrift stores.

SUPPORT POINT 2   Next, organize one's desk for efficiency.

Create a place for bills that need to be paid.

Keep scissors away from children.

Make a file for each of your college classes.

SUPPORT POINT 3   Third, organize the living room for comfort.

Separate canned goods from fresh items.

Have separate bins for recyclables.

Keep all pots and pans close together.

ACTIVITY 8: Teamwork

Working with a classmate, compare the items that you crossed out in the last activity. Discuss your choices and explain why the crossed-out items do not fit.

An Item That Repeats Another Item

Another problem that occurs with outlines is *an item that repeats another item.* Sometimes, we express the same idea more than once, but we do not recognize this because we have changed the words. Take a look at this example:

MAIN IDEA   I like buying used parts for my '66 Mustang.

SUPPORT POINT 1   There is a big selection of used parts.

SUPPORT POINT 2   There are plenty of used parts to choose from.

SUPPORT POINT 3   Many sellers list hundreds of used parts.

Even though each support point uses different words, each one repeats the same idea: that a large number of used parts are available. Repetitions are not always this easy to spot, so you have to be very careful about the ideas and words that you use. Now, here is an example of three *distinct* support points:

MAIN IDEA   I like buying used parts for my '66 Mustang.

SUPPORT POINT 1   There is a big selection of used parts.

| SUPPORT POINT 2 | I can buy the used parts very cheaply. |
| SUPPORT POINT 3 | I discover parts that I did not know about. |

ACTIVITY 9

In the following outlines, cross out any item that repeats another item.

1. **MAIN IDEA**   Finding an academic mentor can help you succeed in college.

   SUPPORT POINT 1   For starters, a mentor can share her experiences with you.

   how she recovered from setbacks

   how she selected a major

   how she got financial aid

   how she got through hard times

   SUPPORT POINT 2   Next, a mentor can make recommendations to you.

   She can recommend professors.

   She can recommend classes.

   She can recommend the best instructors.

   She can recommend study strategies.

   SUPPORT POINT 3   Last, a mentor has a lot of experience.

   She can reassure you when you feel fear or anxiety.

   She can listen to your dreams and encourage them.

   She can hold your hand when you are scared of failing.

2. **MAIN IDEA**   Drinking water regularly contributes to better health, improved appearance, and a happy mood.

   SUPPORT POINT 1   First, drinking lots of water is physically healthy.

   reduced risk of colon and bladder cancer

   fewer cramps and sprains with hydrated joints

   better physical condition

   SUPPORT POINT 2   Furthermore, staying hydrated improves one's looks.

   glowing skin

   look better

   helps with weight control

   youthful complexion

   SUPPORT POINT 3   Finally, drinking water improves one's mental outlook.

   increased concentration and alertness

   more ability to focus at work

   minimizes stress

ACTIVITY 10: Teamwork

Working with a classmate, compare the items that you crossed out in the last activity. Discuss your choices and explain why the crossed-out items repeat other items.

An Item That Is Unclear

The last major problem that can occur in outlines is the use of *an item that is unclear.* Often, items are unclear because they express an idea that is not specific enough. Be especially careful about single-word items in your outline; it is common for single-word items to be unclear.

An unclear item in your outline can lead to a serious breakdown of organization in your paragraph. Always try to correct any unclear items *before* you attempt to write your paragraph. In the examples below, compare the unclear words (in bold) with the specific examples in the revision. Can you see the difference?

UNCLEAR	During my first year at the police academy, I learned **a lot of important stuff**.
SPECIFIC	During my first year at the police academy, I learned strategies for avoiding conflict.
UNCLEAR	My employer uses **some good policies**.
SPECIFIC	My employer uses employee-centered policies.

For unclear (imprecise) words to look out for, see Chapter 10, pages 230–31.

ACTIVITY 11: Teamwork

Working with a classmate, cross out any unclear items in the following outlines.

1. MAIN IDEA   A big pot of vegetable soup is my favorite food.

SUPPORT POINT 1   In the first place, it's economical.

I use marked-down vegetables.

Much of soup is water, which is free.

It's always a good deal.

SUPPORT POINT 2   Furthermore, it's convenient.

a complete meal in one dish

never a problem

easy to make and reheat

SUPPORT POINT 3   Last, it's a pleasure to eat.

It's my favorite.

It's nutritious and delicious.

It's comfort food that warms the soul.

CONTINUED >

2.   **MAIN IDEA**   The *Star Wars* films became an American pop classic.

SUPPORT POINT 1   To begin with, the special effects were innovative.

No one had seen anything so awesome.

computer-designed scenery

holographic images with human actors

light sabers

SUPPORT POINT 2   Furthermore, a lot of stuff comes from *Star Wars*.

"Evil Empire"

"May the Force be with you."

missile defense project called "Star Wars"

SUPPORT POINT 3   Last, *Star Wars* combined several storytelling traditions.

science fiction

westerns

myth

only the best

ACTIVITY 12: Teamwork

Working with a classmate, compare the items that you crossed out in the last activity. Discuss your choices and explain why the crossed-out items are unclear.

Combined Problems

Often, an outline will have more than one problem. The following activity will give you practice in identifying multiple problems in an outline.

ACTIVITY 13: Mastery Test or Teamwork

In each outline below, cross out and label any item that 1) does not fit, 2) repeats another item, or 3) is unclear.

1.   **MAIN IDEA**   To make your travel experience more pleasant, follow some simple guide-lines at the airport.

SUPPORT POINT 1   To begin with, arrive at the airport prepared and early.

Get to the airport even earlier than the airline recommends.

Have your ticket already printed.

Bring carry-on items only, if possible.

Only 70 percent of planes leave on time.

SUPPORT POINT 2 Second, make getting through security as easy as possible.

Wear shoes, belt, and jewelry that are easy to remove.

Security guards are often overworked and tired.

Put liquid items in a clear plastic bag.

Put laptop and other electronic items in a separate tray.

SUPPORT POINT 3 Third, use your time at the gate wisely.

Organize all your belongings in preparation for boarding.

Listen carefully to boarding instructions and follow them.

There are a lot of things you can do while waiting.

Don't rush off to buy snacks at the last minute.

2. **MAIN IDEA** Many oils distilled from trees have valuable medicinal benefits.

SUPPORT POINT 1 To begin with, pine tree oil is used for respiratory illnesses.

colds and flu

sinus infections

asthma

detergents and room sprays

SUPPORT POINT 2 Furthermore, tea tree oil is applied to the skin for healing.

athlete's foot

acne and cold sores

skin problems

cuts and bruises

SUPPORT POINT 3 Last, eucalyptus oil is good too.

fragrant flower arrangements

skin infections

sinus infections

muscle pain

3. **MAIN IDEA** Edgar Allan Poe's life was unusual and fascinating.

SUPPORT POINT 1 To begin with, Poe's family life was unusual.

Poe's parents were both actors.

Poe was raised by his godfather.

Things were rough for Poe.

Poe married his 13-year-old cousin when he was 27.

CONTINUED >

SUPPORT POINT 2 Furthermore, Poe wrote weird stuff.

Poe's narrators often used opium.

Poe visited "dark" places, like opium dens.

Poe wrote about psychological disorders.

SUPPORT POINT 3 Poe's last days are surrounded by mystery.

Poe was found delirious in the streets of Baltimore.

His corpse was dressed in a stranger's suit.

Rumors about his murder or suicide spread quickly.

Poe's clothing at time of death was bizarre.

ACTIVITY 14: Teamwork

Working with a classmate, compare the items that you crossed out in the last activity. Discuss your choices and explain why each crossed-out item does not fit, repeats another item, or is unclear.

BRINGING IT ALL TOGETHER:
Outlining Your Paragraph

In this chapter, you have learned how to organize your ideas and complete an outline. Confirm your knowledge by filling in the blank spaces in the following sentences. If you need help, review the pages listed after each sentence. Finally, check off each item to confirm your understanding of the material.

✔ All outlines have the same basic parts. They are _____, _____, and _____. (page 97)

✔ Moving from one support point to another requires _____ _____, to help your reader follow the development of your ideas. (page 103)

✔ The first step in completing an outline is _____. (page 105)

✔ In steps 2, 3, and 4 of completing an outline, you write _____. (pages 105–6)

✔ In steps 5 and 6 of completing an outline, you write _____ _____. (page 107)

✔ You can stretch, shrink, or reshape outlines by _____

_____ or by _____. (page 111)

✔ Three common problems in outlines are 1) _____,

2) _____, and 3) _____.

(page 111)

JOURNAL WRITING: 10–15 minutes

For this journal entry, discuss how your friends and family support or do not support your role as a college student. First, discuss their attitudes about your attending college. Then, give examples of what they do — or do not do — to help you succeed in college. Finally, suggest other things you would like your family and friends to do to support your effort to get a college education.

CHAPTER 6

Composing Your Paragraph

Test your understanding of composing paragraphs by completing this quiz first. You may know more than you think.

For each question, select all the answers that apply.

WHAT DO YOU KNOW?

1. **In an academic paragraph, the topic sentence should do two things. What are these two things?**
    ___ state the name of the class and the assignment
    ___ ask a general question
    ___ respond clearly to the assigned topic
    ___ express an original point about the assigned topic

2. **When moving from your outline to your draft of the paragraph, what should you avoid?**
    ___ adding unrelated information
    ___ changing key words
    ___ adding the support points
    ___ adding the related examples

3. **What will happen if you write your topic sentence as a question?**
    ___ You will make a grammatical mistake.
    ___ Your original point on the assigned topic may not be clear.
    ___ Your topic sentence may sound incomplete.
    ___ Nothing will happen.

4. **When developing the related examples in your draft, what should you do?**
    ___ Discuss the examples one at a time.
    ___ Use at least one separate sentence for each example.
    ___ Add specific details to each example.
    ___ Use minor transitional expressions to move from example to example.

5. **Which of the following should you avoid when writing a concluding sentence?**
    ___ using expressions like *In conclusion* and *To sum up*
    ___ sounding mechanical and simplistic
    ___ showing sincerity and conviction
    ___ going off topic

Moving from Outline to Paragraph: An Opening Example

In Chapter 5, you learned how to develop a complete and problem-free outline. In this chapter, you will learn how to use your outline to draft an academic paragraph. Remember, if you have a complete and problem-free outline, you are already half the way to writing a successful paragraph.

As an example, let's see how one student drafted a paragraph by following his outline step by step.

As if learning about economics and world history is not hard enough, college students face increasing financial challenges that interfere with their academic and personal well-being. First, the cost of education keeps going up. For example, tuition at my community college was increased 20 percent in the fall semester. Many students cannot afford such a sudden cost hike. Also, our student bookstore marks up the textbooks 25 percent, compared to 18 percent just one year ago. Pens and notebooks for one term cost me close to $50. In addition, parking fees are now $60 a semester, so I am taking the bus. And my biology lab fee was so expensive that I had to drop the class. Next, most college students have fewer sources of income. With the U.S. financial crisis, part-time jobs are harder to find, and students are willing to work for the lowest pay just to have some income, no matter how small. For instance, I make minimum wage at a burrito stand, which nets me about $105 a week. Furthermore, my family is struggling too, because my dad lost his job; as a result, they can't offer me any financial support with school. When I applied for financial aid at my college, they said I'd have to be on a waiting list because several state-funded scholarships had been discontinued by the state. Last, college students suffer because of their money problems. As an example, many students live off rice, pasta, and bread—all simple carbohydrates that aren't very healthy. I, for one, would like to be able to afford lean proteins and fresh vegetables. Plus, we never have any money put aside for emergencies. Since I can't afford health insurance, I always worry that I will get into an accident and not be able to afford a doctor. Add to all of this the constant worry about debt that I have no realistic way of paying off in less than 20 years. Often, I wonder what my educational experience would be like if college were absolutely free and the financial burdens no longer interfered with the opportunity to learn.

MAIN IDEA
College students face several financial challenges.

SUPPORT POINT 1
First, the cost of education keeps going up.
– rising tuition
– books and supplies cost more
– increase in parking and lab fees

SUPPORT POINT 2
Next, students have fewer sources of income.
– low-paying jobs
– loans being cut
– no help from family

SUPPORT POINT 3
Last, students suffer because of money trouble.
– eating cheap, unhealthy food
– no money for emergencies
– pressure of debt

Writing an Effective Topic Sentence

The topic sentence expresses the main idea of a paragraph, and it is often the *first sentence* of a paragraph. To write a topic sentence, simply transfer the main idea from your outline, making sure that it is a complete sentence with a subject and a verb. You may modify the language in the sentence to make it more original and interesting, but do not accidentally change the meaning.

Once you have written the topic sentence, you should verify that it does two things: 1) it identifies the topic, and 2) it expresses your particular idea, point of view, or feeling about the topic.

In each of the following topic sentences, the topic has a single underline and the student's particular idea, point of view, or feeling has a double underline.

ASSIGNED TOPIC   *Discuss college.*

MAIN IDEA   Successful college students need strategies.

TOPIC SENTENCE   Successful college students use several strategies to achieve their success.

ASSIGNED TOPIC   *Discuss a place you are very familiar with.*

MAIN IDEA   The neighborhood where I grew up gave me street smarts.

TOPIC SENTENCE   The neighborhood where I grew up taught me how to be street smart.

ASSIGNED TOPIC   *Discuss electronic communication.*

MAIN IDEA   I use text messaging to communicate with my family and friends.

TOPIC SENTENCE   Text messaging helps me communicate more effectively with family and friends.

ACTIVITY 1

In each of the following topic sentences, underline the topic once and double-underline the student's particular idea, point of view, or feeling about the topic.

EXAMPLE:

ASSIGNED TOPIC   *Discuss your friends.*

MAIN IDEA   My friends have some good qualities in common.

TOPIC SENTENCE   My closest friends all have several good qualities, including patience and respect.

1. **ASSIGNED TOPIC**   *Discuss a family member.*

   MAIN IDEA   My grandmother tells good stories.

   TOPIC SENTENCE   My grandmother is the best storyteller in our family.

2. **ASSIGNED TOPIC**   *Discuss something you know how to do well.*

   MAIN IDEA   An elegant dinner for two is easily made.

   TOPIC SENTENCE   An elegant dinner for two can be prepared in less than a half hour.

3. ASSIGNED TOPIC   *Discuss people you admire.*

MAIN IDEA   I admire courageous people.

TOPIC SENTENCE   I admire people who have the courage to stand up for their beliefs.

4. ASSIGNED TOPIC   *Discuss a quality you would like your partner to have.*

MAIN IDEA   Humor is a quality I would like my partner to have.

TOPIC SENTENCE   My life partner needs to be a good person all-around, but a sense of humor is the one quality he must have.

5. ASSIGNED TOPIC   *Discuss a positive change you have made in your life.*

MAIN IDEA   I got rid of my TV.

TOPIC SENTENCE   Giving away my television improved my life in ways I never imagined.

6. ASSIGNED TOPIC   *Discuss something that you have learned to do.*

MAIN IDEA   I learned to dance the tango.

TOPIC SENTENCE   When learning to dance the tango, a positive and relaxed attitude is essential.

7. ASSIGNED TOPIC   *Discuss a law that you agree or disagree with.*

MAIN IDEA   I agree with texting-while-driving laws.

TOPIC SENTENCE   Laws against texting while driving should be enforced nationwide.

8. ASSIGNED TOPIC   *Discuss a social service that you are familiar with.*

MAIN IDEA   Welfare helps single moms.

TOPIC SENTENCE   Welfare is a social service that benefits single mothers.

ACTIVITY 2

Using one of your completed outlines from Chapter 5, write your topic sentence. (Note: Throughout the first half of this chapter, you will continue to draft this paragraph.) Watch for the pencil icon beside the activity number; it will indicate a composition exercise.

Avoiding Problems in the Topic Sentence

The most important function of a topic sentence is to state your main idea *clearly*. In order to do this, you should avoid four common errors when you compose your topic sentence:

- accidentally changing the meaning of your main idea
- asking a question
- making an announcement
- writing the topic sentence as a fragment

ACCIDENTALLY CHANGING THE MEANING OF YOUR MAIN IDEA

When you move from outline to draft, be careful not to change the meaning of your main idea. Students sometimes do this by accidentally leaving out key words, changing key words, or adding new information. In each of the following topic sentences, the student's main idea is not clear because key words have been left out or changed, or new information has been added. Take a look:

ASSIGNED TOPIC	*Discuss a type of conflict.*
MAIN IDEA	Family conflict is on the rise.
TOPIC SENTENCE	Families always have difficulties.
PROBLEM	*Difficulties* and *conflict* do not have the same meaning. A family can have difficulties without having conflict. Also, *always* is different in meaning from *on the rise*.
TOPIC SENTENCE	Conflict comes in many forms and touches many people.
PROBLEM	The key word *family* has been left out, so the meaning is much more general.
TOPIC SENTENCE	Jealousy often leads to conflict.
PROBLEM	*Jealousy* is not necessarily a *family* conflict.
TOPIC SENTENCE	Family conflict and divorce are on the rise.
PROBLEM	The added information *divorce* changes the main idea for the paragraph.

ACTIVITY 3

In each of the following topic sentences, explain what key words have been changed or left out, or what new information has been added.

EXAMPLE:

ASSIGNED TOPIC   *Discuss a type of vacation.*

MAIN IDEA   I can relax and forget my troubles when I take inexpensive vacations.

TOPIC SENTENCE   Beach vacations are my favorite way to relax and forget my troubles.

PROBLEM   The key word "inexpensive" has been left out. The writer has changed the focus to beach vacations.

---

1. ASSIGNED TOPIC   *Discuss a tradition.*

   MAIN IDEA   Wedding traditions differ a lot across cultures.

   TOPIC SENTENCE   Traditions vary widely across cultures.

   PROBLEM

---

2. ASSIGNED TOPIC   *Discuss something fascinating.*

   MAIN IDEA   UFOs are fascinating.

   TOPIC SENTENCE   UFOs and vampires have fascinated people for decades.

   PROBLEM

---

3. ASSIGNED TOPIC   *Discuss pets.*

   MAIN IDEA   Guinea pigs are good pets for small homes.

   TOPIC SENTENCE   Guinea pigs make good pets for small children.

   PROBLEM

---

4. ASSIGNED TOPIC   *Discuss divorce.*

   MAIN IDEA   There are many reasons for divorce.

   TOPIC SENTENCE   Divorce affects children throughout their lives.

   PROBLEM

---

5. ASSIGNED TOPIC   *Discuss a form of transportation.*

   MAIN IDEA   High-speed train service can reduce highway traffic.

   TOPIC SENTENCE   High-speed train service would take many cars off our crowded highways, and it would be really cool.

   PROBLEM

ASKING A QUESTION IN YOUR TOPIC SENTENCE

If you write your topic sentence as a question, your particular idea, point of view, or feeling about the topic may not be clear. Notice how this is the case in the following sample topic sentences:

ASSIGNED TOPIC	*Discuss a place you know very well.*
MAIN IDEA	Everyone knew each other in the Harlem neighborhood where I grew up.
TOPIC SENTENCE	What was the neighborhood that I grew up in like?
PROBLEM	This question does not express a particular idea, point of view, or feeling about the topic.
REVISED TOPIC SENTENCE	The Harlem neighborhood where I grew up is like one big family.

ASSIGNED TOPIC	*Discuss a strategy for personal success.*
MAIN IDEA	Time management can lead to personal success.
TOPIC SENTENCE	How can I succeed if I manage my time better?
PROBLEM	This question does not express a particular idea, point of view, or feeling about the topic.
REVISED TOPIC SENTENCE	Good time management leads to several types of personal success.

ACTIVITY 4

Rewrite each question as a topic sentence that clearly states a particular idea, point of view, or feeling about the topic. If you wish, you may use key words from the questions to help you get started.

EXAMPLE: What is a good friend?

A good friend knows when to be there for you and when to give you space.

1. What is a good job?

   A good job _____

2. How important is friendship in my life?

   Friendship _____

3. Are good manners a useful tool for success?

   Good manners _____

4. Should pets be allowed on college campuses?

   Pets _____

5. If we can't help the environment in big ways, can we help it in small ways?

We _____

MAKING AN ANNOUNCEMENT IN YOUR TOPIC SENTENCE

If you write a topic sentence like an announcement, you are likely to leave out your particular idea, point of view, or feeling about the topic. Notice how this is the case in the following topic sentences:

MAIN IDEA	Academic success in college requires some personal sacrifices.
TOPIC SENTENCE	In this essay, I will discuss personal sacrifices that college students have to make.
TOPIC SENTENCE	The topic of my paragraph is the personal sacrifices of college students.
TOPIC SENTENCE	I am going to write about the personal sacrifices of college students.
PROBLEM	In each version of the topic sentence, the student forgets to express a particular idea, point of view, or feeling about the topic.
REVISED TOPIC SENTENCE	College students must make a number of personal sacrifices in order to succeed academically.

ACTIVITY 5

Rewrite each announcement as a topic sentence that clearly states a particular idea, point of view, or feeling about the topic.

EXAMPLE: In this paragraph, I will discuss the benefits of regular exercise.

Regular exercise reduces stress and increases energy levels.

1. I would like to talk about steroids in professional sports.

_____

_____

2. My topic today is gossip.

_____

_____

3. I have been asked to write about a type of pollution.

_____

_____

CONTINUED >

4. In this essay, I am going to discuss my reasons for going to college.

_____

_____

5. The main idea for my paragraph is secondhand smoke.

_____

_____

WRITING THE TOPIC SENTENCE AS A FRAGMENT

In order to be grammatically correct, a topic sentence needs to have both a subject and a verb, and it must express a complete thought. If any of these elements is missing, your topic sentence will be a _**fragment**_. (For more information on fragments, see Chapter 16, pages 361–64.) If you write a fragment for your topic sentence, you may leave out your particular idea, point of view, or feeling about the topic. Take a look:

MAIN IDEA	Car accidents have several main causes.
TOPIC SENTENCE	The causes of car accidents.
TOPIC SENTENCE	Automobile accidents and their causes.
TOPIC SENTENCE	The different causes of car collisions.

PROBLEM   In each version of the topic sentence, the student forgets to include a verb, thus creating a fragment. Also, the student forgets to express a particular idea, point of view, or feeling about the topic.

REVISED TOPIC SENTENCE

SUBJECT   **VERB**

All drivers should know the primary causes of car accidents.

Power Tip
Notice that when the topic sentence is written as a fragment, it sounds more like a title than an opening sentence with a complete thought.

ACTIVITY 6

Rewrite each fragment as a topic sentence that clearly states a particular idea, point of view, or feeling about the topic.

EXAMPLE: Home cooking and its benefits.

Cooking at home saves money and calories.

1. Big dogs in small apartments.

_____

_____

2. Smoking and its consequences.

_____

_____

3. The reasons that friends grow apart.

_____

_____

4. The benefits of reading to children.

_____

_____

5. Reasons to get a college degree.

_____

_____

ACTIVITY 7

For each of the following topic sentences, identify the error and explain why it creates a problem. Possible errors include changing the meaning of the main idea, asking a question, making an announcement, or writing a fragment.

EXAMPLE: Main idea: Racial profiling can result in a great deal of harm to individuals.

Topic sentence: Do you know what racial profiling is?

Error: The topic sentence has been written as a question. The student's original point about the topic is not clear.

1. Main idea: Certain careers are especially good for working parents.

Topic sentence: My topic is good careers for working parents.

Error: _____

_____

2. Main idea: There are several reasons for lengthening the school year.

Topic sentence: Should children stay in school year-round?

Error: _____

_____

3. Main idea: Our school needs an improved student health clinic.

Topic sentence: In this essay, I will discuss the need for an improved student health clinic.

Error: _____

_____

CONTINUED >

4. **Main idea:** Raising the driving age is a good idea for several reasons.

   Topic sentence: Reasons for raising the driving age.

   Error: _____

   _____

5. **Main idea:** There are many reasons why online dating is challenging.

   Topic sentence: Dating after a divorce is challenging for many reasons.

   Error: _____

   _____

6. **Main idea:** It is important for us to vote.

   Topic sentence: Why should we bother to vote?

   Error: _____

   _____

7. **Main idea:** The benefits of urban gardening include saving money and getting exercise.

   Topic sentence: Gardening is a good way to save money and get some exercise.

   Error: _____

   _____

8. **Main idea:** Road rage has several causes.

   Topic sentence: The causes of road rage.

   Error: _____

   _____

ACTIVITY 8

Check the topic sentence that you wrote for your draft and make sure that it is free of any problems.

Grabbing Your Reader's Attention with the Topic Sentence

The second most important function of a topic sentence is to grab your reader's attention. In other words, you want to get your reader (probably your instructor) interested in your paragraph immediately from the first sentence. To make your topic sentences more interesting, you can try these strategies:

- Create a contrast.
- Identify the support points.
- Use a creative idea or image.

CREATING A CONTRAST IN YOUR TOPIC SENTENCE

To form this type of topic sentence, you will need to write a complex sentence beginning with *although, even though,* or *while.* A sentence with a contrast requires your audience to read more actively; a simple sentence without a contrast allows your audience to read more passively. Therefore, using a contrast in your topic sentence will grab and focus your audience's attention from the moment they start reading. Take a look at the following examples and explanations:

Power Tip
To understand more about complex sentences, see Chapter 18.

ASSIGNED TOPIC	*Discuss a sport.*
MAIN IDEA	Professional soccer is becoming increasingly popular.
BASIC TOPIC SENTENCE	Professional soccer is becoming more popular.
TOPIC SENTENCE WITH A CONTRAST	While football, baseball, and basketball still dominate sports in America, professional soccer is becoming more popular.
BENEFIT	In the topic sentence with a contrast, the word *while* tells the reader to prepare for a contrast. The reader is likely to pay close attention so that the second part of the sentence will make sense. The version without a contrast is so simple that the reader is less likely to be interested or to have to pay close attention.

Here is another example:

ASSIGNED TOPIC	*Discuss a human hardship.*
MAIN IDEA	Prison inmates face many hardships.
BASIC TOPIC SENTENCE	I can imagine the hardships that inmates face.
TOPIC SENTENCE WITH A CONTRAST	Even though I have never set foot inside a prison, I can imagine the hardships that inmates face.

ACTIVITY 9: Teamwork

Rewrite each of the following topic sentences using a contrast.

EXAMPLE: The best advice my parents gave me is to always tell the truth.

Although my parents taught me all the values I need to live a good life, the most important advice they gave me is to always tell the truth.

1. Facebook makes it easier to stay in touch with family and friends.

CONTINUED >

2. The "American Dream" is a reality for some Americans.

_____

_____

3. Most instructors expect students to do two hours of homework for each hour of class time.

_____

_____

_____

IDENTIFYING THE SUPPORT POINTS IN YOUR TOPIC SENTENCE

This type of topic sentence includes the main idea and briefly identifies the support points that you will develop in your paragraph. When you give your readers a peek at what's to follow, you spark their anticipation. This is like the trailer for a movie that shows viewers the highlights and makes them want to see the film. Take a look at the following example:

ASSIGNED TOPIC	_Discuss something that is harmful for students._
MAIN IDEA	Energy drinks are harmful for students.
SUPPORT POINT 1	contain too much caffeine
SUPPORT POINT 2	have bad after-effects
SUPPORT POINT 3	are addicting
TOPIC SENTENCE	The so-called "energy drinks" that are popular among students are harmful because they contain too much caffeine, have bad after-effects, and are addicting.
BENEFIT	Identifying the support points lets the reader know what to expect and arouses his or her curiosity.

Power Tip
Writing this type of topic sentence requires that you use correct parallel structure. For information on parallel structure, see Chapter 22.

ACTIVITY 10

For each of the following items, write a topic sentence that includes the main idea and major supports.

EXAMPLE: **Main idea:** My favorite sport is surfing.

Support point 1: It is fun.

Support point 2: It gets me outdoors.

Support point 3: It keeps me fit year-round.

Topic sentence: Surfing is my favorite sport because it is fun, it gets me outdoors, and it keeps me fit year-round.

1. **Main idea:** There are various reasons to plant trees.

   Support point 1: They beautify surroundings.

   Support point 2: They help to offset carbon emissions.

   Support point 3: They provide homes for birds and other wildlife.

   Topic sentence: _____

   _____

2. **Main idea:** Billboards should not be allowed because of the problems they create.

   Support point 1: They block natural scenery.

   Support point 2: They interfere with plant and animal habitats.

   Support point 3: They distract drivers.

   Topic sentence: _____

   _____

3. **Main idea:** Adopting pets from shelters makes sense.

   Support point 1: It is free or inexpensive.

   Support point 2: It can save an animal's life.

   Support point 3: It gives neglected animals a second chance.

   Topic sentence: _____

   _____

USING A CREATIVE IDEA OR IMAGE IN YOUR TOPIC SENTENCE

This type of topic sentence requires you to use some imagination. Instead of stating your main idea in an obvious way, you can spark your reader's curiosity with a clever idea, image, or comparison. If you "hook" your reader in this way, you will have a much more attentive audience. Take a look at two examples:

ASSIGNED TOPIC	*Discuss an electronic device.*
MAIN IDEA	I need my iPad.
BASIC TOPIC SENTENCE	I could not live without my iPad.
CREATIVE TOPIC SENTENCE	Like a CEO's office suite, my iPad is where all my business gets done, and I couldn't function without it.

BENEFIT	The creative topic sentence sparks the reader's imagination and makes him or her much more curious about what's to come.

ASSIGNED TOPIC   *Discuss a world event.*

MAIN IDEA   The World Cup championship game was exciting.

BASIC TOPIC SENTENCE   The World Cup championship game between Spain and the Netherlands was a good game.

CREATIVE TOPIC SENTENCE   The World Cup championship game between Spain and the Netherlands rocked the stadium and the world.

BENEFIT   The creative topic sentence sparks the reader's imagination and makes him or her much more curious about what's to come.

ACTIVITY 11: Teamwork

Rewrite each of the following topic sentences to include an unusual idea, image, or comparison.

EXAMPLE: Main idea: my first date in college

Obvious topic sentence: I was attracted to my first date in college.

Creative topic sentence: My first date in college was as handsome and mysterious as Johnny Depp.

1. **Main idea:** my best teacher

   Obvious topic sentence: My algebra teacher is good.

   Creative topic sentence: _____

2. **Main idea:** a form of entertainment

   Obvious topic sentence: *Dancing with the Stars* entertains me a lot.

   Creative topic sentence: _____

3. **Main idea:** a place you would love to visit

   Obvious topic sentence: I would like to visit the Grand Canyon.

   Creative topic sentence: _____

✎ ACTIVITY 12

Look again at the topic sentence that you wrote for your draft. Now, rewrite that topic sentence three different ways, using the three strategies described on pages 130–34. Finally, decide which topic sentence is the most effective and keep it for your paragraph.

Writing the First Support Point

After you have written an error-free topic sentence, it is time to develop your first support point. Follow these steps:

- From your outline, copy the transitional expression that introduces your first support point. If your outline doesn't include a transitional expression, add one. Put a comma after this expression.
- Follow the transitional expression with the first support point from your outline, making sure that it is a complete sentence with a subject and a verb.

Power Tip
For more on transitional expressions, see Chapter 5, pages 103–7, and page 136 of this chapter.

Now, take a look at this example from the paragraph that started this chapter (page 121). The first support point is underscored in green, and the transitional expression is underscored in grey:

MAIN IDEA College students face several financial challenges. **TRANSITIONAL EXPRESSION** First, **SUPPORT POINT 1** the cost of education keeps going up.	As if learning about economics and world history is not hard enough, college students face increasing financial challenges that interfere with their academic and personal well-being. First, the cost of education keeps going up.

As with the topic sentence, you may change the word order or add words, but be careful not to change the meaning of the support point. Be aware of four common problems that can occur with the support points when you move from outline to draft:

- forgetting transitional expressions
- accidentally changing the meaning of the support points
- writing the support points as fragments
- combining a support point with an example

These problems usually occur when you are working quickly and not following your outline carefully. Remember, the outline is your navigation system: You should refer to it closely throughout the writing process. If you ignore it, you may get lost while writing the paragraph, or your reader might get lost while reading it.

ACTIVITY 13

Return to the draft of your paragraph that you began in Activity 2. Immediately following your topic sentence, write a transitional expression and your first support point.

REMEMBER TRANSITIONAL EXPRESSIONS

As you learned in Chapter 5, transitional expressions are essential for good academic writing; they help the reader follow your ideas, especially in a long paragraph. If you forget transitional expressions, your reader may have difficulty following your thoughts. If you are worried about this, use a highlighter to mark transitional expressions on your outline.

Here is a chart of major transitional expressions that help introduce support points:

SUPPORT POINT 1	SUPPORT POINT 2	SUPPORT POINT 3
First,	Second,	Third,
In the first place,	In the second place,	Last,
For starters,	More important,	Most important,
To begin with,	To follow,	Finally,
One reason is . . .	Another reason is . . .	A final reason is . . .

For more on transitional expressions, see Chapter 5, pages 103–7, and pages 141–42 of this chapter.

DO NOT ACCIDENTALLY CHANGE THE MEANING OF THE SUPPORT POINT

In order to stay on topic when writing support points—and avoid accidentally changing their meaning—follow the same guidelines that you learned for the topic sentence:

- Do not leave out key words from the support point.
- Do not change key words from the support point. (However, you may use words with similar meanings in some cases.)
- Do not add inappropriate new information to the support point.

Consider the following example:

Power Tip
See page 124 of this chapter for more information on how you might accidentally change the meaning of an idea when moving from outline to draft.

MAIN IDEA College students face several financial challenges. **TRANSITIONAL EXPRESSION** First, **SUPPORT POINT 1** the cost of education keeps going up.	<u>As if learning about economics and world history is not hard enough, college students face increasing financial challenges that interfere with their academic and personal well-being.</u> <u>First, things are getting more expensive.</u>

Explanation of the problem: *Things* does not have the same meaning as *the cost of education*. This will confuse your reader about what's to follow.

DO NOT WRITE THE SUPPORT POINT AS A FRAGMENT

When you begin a sentence with a transitional expression, you may sometimes forget to include both a subject and a verb in the sentence.

Consider the following example:

Power Tip
The *subject* is the main actor in a sentence; it is *who* or *what* the sentence is about. A *verb* expresses an action or a state of being. For more on subjects and verbs, see Chapter 15, The Building Blocks of Language, and Chapter 16, The Simple Sentence.

MAIN IDEA College students face several financial challenges. **TRANSITIONAL EXPRESSION** First, **SUPPORT POINT 1** the cost of education keeps going up.	<u>As if learning about economics and world history is not hard enough, college students face increasing financial challenges that interfere with their academic and personal well-being.</u> <u>First, the cost of education.</u>

When you begin a sentence with a transitional expression, remember that what follows the comma must be a complete sentence with a subject and a verb. Do not let the presence of the transitional expression cause you to write a fragment.

INCORRECT   First, the cost of education.

CORRECT   First, the **SUBJECT** cost of education **VERB** keeps rising.

AVOID COMBINING THE SUPPORT POINT WITH THE FIRST EXAMPLE

When you move from the outline to the paragraph, you might accidentally combine two items that should be expressed in separate sentences. This can cause confusion for your reader. When you write a support point, be sure not to mention the first example in the same sentence. Take a look at the following example of this error:

MAIN IDEA
 	
College students face several financial challenges.
 	
TRANSITIONAL EXPRESSION
 	
First,
 	
SUPPORT POINT 1
 	
the cost of education keeps going up.
 	
   – rising tuition
   – books and supplies cost more
   – increase in parking and lab
     fees
	<u>As if learning about economics and world history is not hard enough, college students face increasing financial challenges that interfere with their academic and personal well-being.</u> <u>First, the cost of tuition is on the rise.</u>

Here, the writer has combined the first support point (*the cost of education keeps going up*) with the first related example (*rising tuition*). This error will cause significant confusion for readers because they will assume that the support point here is about tuition costs instead of the educational costs in general.

ACTIVITY 14: Teamwork

Look at the following partial outline (a main idea, the first support point, and three examples). Then, read the support points that follow it, identifying the problem with each. Possible problems include forgetting the transitional expression, changing the meaning of the support point, writing a fragment, and combining the support point and an example.

EXAMPLE: **Main idea:** Atlanta's summer-jobs program should be funded for another year.

    Support point: First, the program improves the lives of at-risk youth.

          — It gives them valuable job experience.

          — It improves their financial situation.

          — It gives them a sense of pride and accomplishment.

    Support point: The program improves the lives of at-risk youth.

    Problem: The transitional expression has been left out.

1. **Support point:** First, the program improves the lives of at-risk youth by giving them valuable job experience.

   Problem: _____

   _____

2. **Support point:** First, the program improves the lives of everyone in our city.

   Problem: _____

   _____

3. **Support point:** First, improves the lives of at-risk youth.

   Problem: _____

   _____

4. **Support point:** First, the program improves the lives of at-risk youth by giving them a sense of accomplishment.

   Problem: _____

   _____

5. **Support point:** First, the program gives jobs to at-risk youth.

   Problem: _____

   _____

ACTIVITY 15

Return to the draft of your paragraph. Check your first support point to make sure that it is free of any errors.

Writing the Related Examples

After writing the first support point, it is time to develop your related examples. Follow these guidelines:

- Discuss the examples *one at a time.*
- Write at least one complete sentence for each example.
- Add some specific details to each example.
- Use *minor* transitional expressions to move from example to example.

DISCUSS THE EXAMPLES ONE AT A TIME

As you learned in Chapter 1, academic paragraphs typically contain more than five sentences, and sometimes they have as many as ten or fifteen sentences. To achieve this level of development in your paragraph, you will need to discuss the examples one at a time, writing at least one complete sentence for each example. If you rush and combine all your examples into only one or two

Power Tip
Be aware that some graders of standardized tests and exit tests will assign a lower score to even a well-written paragraph if it is very brief.

sentences, you will not meet the minimum length requirement for the paragraph. More important, your paragraph may appear to be poorly developed and superficial.

Below, the three examples have been squeezed into one sentence:

MAIN IDEA
 	
College students face several financial challenges.
 	
TRANSITIONAL EXPRESSION
 	
First,
 	
SUPPORT POINT 1
 	
the cost of education keeps going up.
 	
   – rising tuition
   – books and supplies cost more
   – increase in parking and lab fees
	As if learning about economics and world history is not hard enough, college students face increasing financial challenges that interfere with their academic and personal well-being. First, the cost of education keeps going up. For example, tuition, books, supplies, parking fees, and lab fees are getting more expensive.

Here, the writer has merged all the examples into one sentence. As a result, the paragraph feels rushed and superficial. Students who find themselves in this situation often feel stuck and do not know how to move ahead. To avoid this problem, discuss the examples one at a time, giving each its own sentence.

Now, let's see a revision of the previous paragraph, with each example discussed in a separate, complete sentence:

MAIN IDEA
 	
College students face several financial challenges.
 	
TRANSITIONAL EXPRESSION
 	
First,
 	
SUPPORT POINT 1
 	
the cost of education keeps going up.
 	
   – rising tuition
   – books and supplies cost more
   – increase in parking and lab fees
	As if learning about economics and world history is not hard enough, college students face increasing financial challenges that interfere with their academic and personal well-being. First, the cost of education keeps going up. For example, tuition has increased 20 percent at my college. Textbook prices are now marked up 25 percent. Also, parking fees and lab fees are rising each semester.

Here, one complete sentence illustrates each example. Not only does this method allow the student to illustrate each example more effectively, but it also ensures that the paragraph will be fully developed.

ADD SOME SPECIFIC DETAILS TO EACH EXAMPLE

In your outline, you generally write related examples as short phrases. However, as you present examples in your paragraph, try to develop them with specific details that bring the examples to life and give them *personality*.

Below, the writer has added specific details to each of the examples:

MAIN IDEA
 	
 College students face several financial challenges.
 	
 TRANSITIONAL EXPRESSION
 	
 First,
 	
 SUPPORT POINT 1
 	
 the cost of education keeps going up.
 	
  – rising tuition
  – books and supplies cost more
  – increase in parking and lab fees
	<u>As if learning about economics and world history is not hard enough, college students face increasing financial challenges that interfere with their academic and personal well-being.</u> <u>First, the cost of education keeps going up.</u> For example, tuition at my community college was increased 20 percent in the fall semester. Many students cannot afford such a sudden cost hike. Also, our student bookstore currently marks up the textbooks 25 percent, compared to 18 percent just one year ago. Pens and notebooks for one term cost me close to $50. In addition, parking fees are now $60 a semester, so I am taking the bus. And my biology lab fee was so expensive that I had to drop the class.

Power Tip

You do not necessarily have to develop specific details for every example, especially if you are writing a timed composition. However, it's always a good idea to look back at all of your examples and ask which ones could be made more vivid through added details.

Here, we get a vivid and convincing picture of the financial hardships experienced by the student. The specific details bring the examples to life and give the writing personality. In Chapter 10, you will learn some fun and effective strategies for developing details in your writing.

USE MINOR TRANSITIONAL EXPRESSIONS TO MOVE FROM EXAMPLE TO EXAMPLE

In addition to the major transitional expressions that you use to introduce your support points, you will need a variety of minor transitional expressions to help you move smoothly from example to example. In the writing sample above, notice that the writer has included three minor transitional expressions: *for example, also, in addition.*

Remember, writing a paragraph is a process of constant movement or transition from one idea to another. Without transitional expressions, some of your ideas may seem "stuck together" rather than smoothly developed.

Here is a chart of useful minor transitional expressions:

MINOR TRANSITIONAL EXPRESSIONS	
For example,	For instance,
As an example,	Then,
Another example . . .	In fact,
In particular,	Once,
Specifically,	One time,
To illustrate,	Another time,
Another illustration . . .	Sometimes,
In addition,	Also,
Next,	Plus,
Furthermore,	Moreover,

In the chart below, notice how three minor transitional expressions (underscored in grey) help the writer to introduce the first example and to move smoothly from one example to another:

MAIN IDEA
 	
College students face several financial challenges.
 	
TRANSITIONAL EXPRESSION
 	
First,
 	
SUPPORT POINT 1
 	
the cost of education keeps going up.
 	
  – rising tuition
  – books and supplies cost more
  – increase in parking and lab fees
	As if learning about economics and world history is not hard enough, college students face increasing financial challenges that interfere with their academic and personal well-being. First, the cost of education keeps going up. For example, tuition at my community college was increased 20 percent in the fall semester. Many students cannot afford such a sudden cost hike. Also, our student bookstore currently marks up the textbooks 25 percent, compared to 18 percent just one year ago. Pens and notebooks for one term cost me close to $50. In addition, parking fees are now $60 a semester, so I am taking the bus. And my biology lab fee was so expensive that I had to drop the class.

ACTIVITY 16: Teamwork

First, review the partial outline below. Then, read each version of the paragraph and identify any problem with the way the examples have been written. Possible problems include not discussing the examples one at a time or in a full sentence each, forgetting to add specific details, and forgetting minor transitional expressions.

EXAMPLE: **Main idea:** Atlanta's summer-jobs program should be funded for another year.

Support point: First, the program improves the lives of at-risk youth.

— It gives them valuable job experience.

— It improves their financial situation.

— It gives them a sense of pride and accomplishment.

Paragraph: Atlanta's summer-jobs program should be funded for another year. First, the program improves the lives of at-risk youth. For instance, it gives them valuable work experience, improves their financial situation, and gives them a sense of pride and accomplishment.

Problem: The examples have been written as one sentence.

1.   Atlanta's summer-jobs program should be funded for another year. First, the program improves the lives of at-risk youth. For example, it gives them valuable job experience. In addition, it improves their financial situation. Also, it gives them a sense of pride and accomplishment.

Problem: _____

2.   Atlanta's summer-jobs program should be funded for another year. First, the program improves the lives of at-risk youth. For example, it gives them valuable job experience. In addition, the program improves their financial situation, and it gives them a sense of pride and accomplishment.

Problem: _____

3.   Atlanta's summer-jobs program should be funded for another year. First, the program improves the lives of at-risk youth. It gives them valuable job experience in all types of fields, from community service to parks management. It improves participants' financial situation, helping them to earn as much as $3,000 over the course of the summer. It gives participants a sense of pride and accomplishment: They know that they have done good works in their community and that they are valued members of society.

Problem: _____

✏️ **ACTIVITY 17**

Return to the draft of your paragraph and add related examples to your first support point. Remember the guidelines for writing examples:

- Discuss the examples *one at a time*.
- Write at least one complete sentence for each example.
- Add some specific details to each example. (See Chapter 10 for suggestions.)
- Use minor transitional expressions to introduce the first example and to move from one example to another.

Completing the Paragraph

Power Tip
Once you have written your first support point with its related examples, you will probably be warmed up and writing a bit faster. While you have this momentum, make good use of it by moving immediately to your second support point. If you take a break now and come back to your paragraph later, you may lose valuable energy and focus.

Now, you have only three things to do to complete your paragraph:

- Write the second support point with the related examples.
- Write the third support point with the related examples.
- Write the concluding sentence. (More on this below.)

WRITE THE SECOND AND THIRD SUPPORT POINTS WITH THE RELATED EXAMPLES

When writing your examples, remember to do the following:

- Discuss the examples one at a time.
- Write at least one complete sentence for each example.
- Add some specific details to each example.
- Use minor transitional expressions to introduce your examples, and to move from one example to another.

✏️ **ACTIVITY 18**

Return to the draft of your paragraph. Remember to have your outline nearby and follow it carefully. Write out your second and third support points and the related examples.

WRITE THE CONCLUDING SENTENCE

The last sentence of a paragraph should restate or summarize your main idea in a fresh, thoughtful manner. An unimaginative or missing concluding sentence can indicate your lack of commitment and may leave the reader unsatisfied or confused. Instead, restate your main idea in a way that expresses your sincerity and enthusiasm about the ideas discussed in the paragraph. Follow these guidelines for writing the concluding sentence:

- Do not repeat the topic sentence in an overly simple or mechanical way.
- Do not introduce new information or go off topic.
- Find creative, persuasive ways to restate the main idea.
- Never omit the concluding sentence, even if your paragraph has met any length requirement provided by your instructor.

Now, let's look at several versions of a concluding sentence—two versions that do not work and one that does. First, review the topic sentence that opens the paragraph:

TOPIC SENTENCE	Riding my bike to school has several important advantages.
CONCLUDING SENTENCE	Clearly, there are several advantages to riding my bike to school.
PROBLEM	This concluding sentence repeats the main idea in a simple, mechanical way.
CONCLUDING SENTENCE	Biking to school is cool, but I may try taking the bus to see what advantages it has to offer.
PROBLEM	This concluding sentence introduces new information and goes off topic.
CONCLUDING SENTENCE	The humble act of riding my bike to school has made me a better person, a better citizen, and a better student.
PROBLEM	This is an effective concluding sentence that shows sincerity and enthusiasm about the topic.

Power Tip
Some writers begin concluding sentences with expressions like *For these reasons*, *In conclusion*, or *To sum up*. Although these are acceptable transitions, make sure that what follows them is not a mechanical restatement of your main idea. Try to think of creative ways to end your paragraphs.

ACTIVITY 19

Following are different concluding sentences written for a single topic sentence. Identify whether each concluding sentence is effective or ineffective. If it is ineffective, identify the problem.

EXAMPLE: Topic sentence: Though caring for my elderly mother at home was difficult, I consider the experience to be one of the most rewarding times of my life.

Concluding sentence: Caring for my elderly mother has been rewarding.
This concluding sentence is too simple and mechanical to be effective.

CONTINUED >

Concluding sentence: The experience of caring for my elderly mother enhanced my life, and I will always be grateful for it.
This is an effective concluding sentence. It shows sincerity.

Concluding sentence: Care of the elderly should be left to families, not to impersonal public institutions.
This is an ineffective concluding sentence because it is off topic.

1. **Topic sentence:** Although the Internet is great for research, the college library has several important resources.

   Concluding sentence: However, many college libraries have cut back on their resources because of budget restraints.

   _____

   Concluding sentence: Although I used to avoid going to the college library, I am now a knowledgeable patron and advocate for its resources.

   _____

   Concluding sentence: The college library has some useful resources.

   _____

2. **Topic sentence:** I believe the disadvantages of being a single child outweigh the benefits.

   Concluding sentence: Being a single child is not really that great.

   _____

   Concluding sentence: I grew up a single child, but I hope to have more than one child when I get married.

   _____

   Concluding sentence: As a single child, I was pampered and privileged but alone and lonely most of the time.

   _____

3. **Topic sentence:** Even a poor college student can begin to manage his or her financial future.

   Concluding sentence: Although I never have much money as a college student, I have a clear vision of my financial future and am taking small steps to get there successfully.

   _____

Concluding sentence: Even wealthy CEOs need to have solid finan-cial planning.

_____

_____

Concluding sentence: If you're a college student, you can begin to manage your financial future.

_____

_____

ACTIVITY 20

Return to the draft of your paragraph and write the concluding sentence. You may have to experiment with various ideas and revise a few times to find a sentence that concludes your paragraph with sincerity and enthusi-asm. Avoid a simple, mechanical ending, and be sure to stay on topic.

BRINGING IT ALL TOGETHER:
Composing Your Paragraph

In this chapter, you have learned how to draft an academic paragraph. Confirm your knowledge by filling in the blank spaces in the following sentences. If you need help, review the pages listed after each sentence. Finally, check off each item to confirm your understanding of the material.

✔ To be complete, a topic sentence must do two things. It must
1) _____ and 2) _____
_____. (page 122)

✔ There are four common errors that can occur when writing a topic sen-tence. These errors are: 1) _____
_____, 2) _____, 3) _____,
and 4) _____. (page 124)

✔ There are three strategies for grabbing your reader's attention with the
topic sentence. These strategies are: 1) _____,
2) _____, and 3) _____.
(page 130)

CONTINUED >

✔ Name four common problems that can occur when writing the support points in a paragraph: 1) _____, 2) _____, 3) _____, and 4) _____. (page 135)

✔ When writing the examples and details in a paragraph, it is important to: 1) _____, 2) _____, 3) _____, and 4) _____. (page 139)

✔ When writing a concluding sentence, avoid 1) _____, 2) _____, and 3) _____. (page 145)

✔ A concluding sentence in a paragraph should restate your main idea in a way that expresses your _____ and _____ about the ideas discussed in the paragraph. (page 145)

JOURNAL WRITING: 10–15 minutes

For this journal entry, you will need to visit one of your college instructors during his or her office hours. During this visit, introduce yourself to your instructor, explain some of your educational goals, and discuss your progress and any difficulties you are having in the class so far. After your visit, write about the experience in your journal. Explain what happened during the visit, how you feel about it, and whether you are likely to visit the instructor again. In general, what are your feelings now about meeting with an instructor during office hours?

CHAPTER 7

Revising

Test your understanding of how to revise a paragraph by completing this quiz first. You may know more than you think.

For each question, select all the answers that apply.

WHAT DO YOU KNOW?

1. **A successful academic paragraph should contain which of the following?**

   ___ a topic sentence
   ___ transitional expressions
   ___ support points
   ___ unity

2. **Which of the following are common problems in an academic paragraph?**

   ___ a flawed topic sentence
   ___ an unstated or unclear support point
   ___ a missing transitional expression
   ___ details that do not fit

3. **Which of the following strategies are helpful when participating in peer review?**

   ___ Don't offer any opinions if your partner is shy.
   ___ Let your partner do most or all of the talking.
   ___ Offer suggestions and ask questions.
   ___ Do most or all of the talking yourself.

4. **When using spell checkers or grammar checkers, what problems might you encounter?**

   ___ The checkers can sometimes cause plagiarism.
   ___ The checkers sometimes flag sentences that have no errors.
   ___ The checkers can suggest wrong words to replace your misspelled word.
   ___ The checkers won't catch errors in meaning.

5. **When proofreading your writing, which of the following are useful strategies?**

   ___ Proofread on the computer monitor *and* on the printed page.
   ___ Use a combination of pen, pencil, and highlighter to mark your errors.
   ___ Proofread late at night when you are tired.
   ___ Double-space your composition so that it is easier to read.

Understanding the Revision Process: An Overview

The chapters preceding this one showed you how to organize and compose an academic paragraph.

When you have gained some mastery over these parts of the writing process, you will be able to produce **unified** paragraphs that stay on track and include only information that supports the main idea. However, the act of writing is not always orderly and predictable, and even experienced writers can get off track. Sometimes, you may become so closely involved with your ideas that you skip a key piece of your outline or get lost in your examples and details. Also, you might make grammar mistakes and other errors. For these reasons, dedicated writers recognize that the final step of the writing process — **revision** — is just as important as the earlier steps.

Revision ("re" + "vision") means looking over your writing with a fresh eye to identify and fix any problems with unity. You will also want to check carefully for problems with grammar, mechanics (spelling, punctuation, formatting), and word choice.

The best way to make sure that you've fixed these problems is to perform your revision as carefully as you have performed the other steps in the writing process. Many students rush their revision or skip it altogether, which can seriously harm their finished product.

Revising for Unity

Again, **unity** means that a paragraph stays on track and includes only information that supports the main idea. Because unity is so important to effective writing, it's a good idea to check for it before you look for errors in individual words and sentences.

FOUR MAJOR PROBLEMS WITH UNITY

As you learned in Chapters 5 and 6, there are several ways that you can get off track when outlining and writing a paragraph. The resulting problems with unity include:

- a flawed topic sentence — from changing your main idea when you write the topic sentence
- an unstated or unclear support point — from changing a support point, combining it with an example, or forgetting it altogether
- a missing transitional expression
- details that do not fit

To see each of these problems in action, let's look at an academic paragraph. Here is the outline for the paragraph, complete and error-free:

ASSIGNED TOPIC   *Discuss ways to stay informed about current events.*

MAIN IDEA   The best way to stay informed about current events is to use a variety of media.

TRANSITIONAL EXPRESSION   For starters,

SUPPORT POINT 1   use the Internet to stay informed.
- Yahoo.com
- Slate.com
- MoveOn.org

TRANSITIONAL EXPRESSION   In the second place,

SUPPORT POINT 2   use print media to stay informed.
- newspapers
- magazines

TRANSITIONAL EXPRESSION   Third,

SUPPORT POINT 3   use radio and television to stay informed.
- National Public Radio
- CNN
- PBS

Below is an academic paragraph based on this outline. After drafting the paragraph, the student who wrote it compared it very carefully to the outline. She identified four problems with her unity. The problems are numbered and underlined below, and they are discussed in more detail in the following sections.

    <u>Today, almost everyone uses the Internet instead of reading newspapers or watching television.</u> For starters, the Internet is probably the fastest, most convenient way to stay informed. For instance, each time I turn on my computer, my browser's homepage is set to Yahoo.com. Yahoo is a great source for up-to-the-minute news, and it's very efficient, too. You can scan the headlines, read synopses of stories, and then click on interesting topics for fuller coverage. If you're looking for more intellectual and cutting-edge journalism, you can go to Slate.com. This Web site features insightful articles on politics, technology, and business by some of America's top reporters. In addition, if your political interests are liberal, MoveOn.org offers the most in-depth and provocative political commentary on the Web. <u>In the second place, I try to stop by my college library and read a newspaper each day between classes.</u> I especially like the *Wall Street Journal* and the *New York Times*. Newspapers are different from Internet sites because I see a lot of information on the page and end up reading whole articles that I wouldn't necessarily navigate to on a Web site. I also like to read newsmagazines like *Time* and *Newsweek*. Because these magazines publish only once a week, they give a more comprehensive overview of events. <u>Radio and television work hard to make their coverage of current</u>

❶

❷

❸

④ events competitive with the Internet. I love the political debates on National Public Radio. Shows like *Left, Right, and Center* and *To the Point* feature brilliant and opinionated guests. Similarly, Public Broadcasting has some of the most unbiased news coverage on the air. The *News Hour* and *Bill Moyers* are my favorite shows for understanding national and world politics. However, if I just want a quick update on current events, I can tune in 24/7 to CNN. <u>Sometimes, I feel like I watch too much television, but it's a habit I haven't been able to break.</u> With all these excellent sources of news and information, how can any interested person not stay well informed?

Problem 1: A Flawed Topic Sentence

When the student began composing her paragraph, she was excited and confident about her ideas. As a result, she wrote a bold topic sentence:

Today, almost everyone uses the Internet instead of reading newspapers or watching television.

While this is a powerful claim, it misrepresents the main idea for her paragraph. According to this topic sentence, the entire paragraph should focus on *how the Internet has replaced newspapers and television.* However, the paragraph actually discusses the Internet, newspapers, and television as good ways to stay informed about current events. With this topic sentence, the reader will be confused by the support points and examples that follow.

Remember, the topic sentence is an especially important feature of your paragraph. If you misstate your main idea in the topic sentence, the rest of the paragraph may not make sense to your reader. <u>Always double-check your topic sentence during the revision process.</u>

Fix this problem by rewriting the topic sentence so that it clearly expresses your main idea for the paragraph. (For a detailed review of problems with topic sentences and how to fix them, see Chapter 6, pages 124–28.)

Problem 2: An Unstated or Unclear Support Point

In rereading her paragraph and comparing it to her outline, the student noticed that something was missing: She forgot to state her second support point, skipping directly to her first example:

In the second place, I try to stop by my college library and read a newspaper each day between classes.

This error will be quite confusing for readers, who will expect that all the examples following this sentence will relate to reading a newspaper. However, when the writer discusses reading magazines like *Time* and *Newsweek*, the unity will be disrupted.

Remember, each support point is a major feature of your paragraph. If you forget or misstate a support point, it can damage the unity of your writing. <u>Always double-check your support points during the revision process.</u>

Fix this problem by rewriting the support point so that it clearly expresses your idea and accurately sets up the examples that follow it. Often, you will need to separate the support point from the first example and rewrite each as a separate sentence. (For more information on common problems with support points, see Chapter 6, pages 135–38.)

Problem 3: A Missing Transitional Expression

The author of the paragraph noticed that at one point in her writing, the ideas seemed jumbled; they did not flow as smoothly as she wanted. Then, she realized that she had forgotten her third transitional expression (introducing the third support point):

Radio and television work hard to make their coverage of current events competitive with the Internet.

For the reader, the missing transitional expression is a large gap in the unity: The abrupt shift from the description of magazines like *Time* and *Newsweek* to the third support point (that radio and television are good ways to stay informed) will be confusing.

Remember, the reader cannot anticipate when you will shift to a new support point or to a new example. You must include transitional expressions to make this shift smooth and logical for your reader. <u>Always double-check your transitional expressions during the revision process.</u>

Fix this problem by adding the missing transitional expression. (For more information on adding transitional expressions, see Chapter 6, pages 136 and 142.)

Problem 4: Details That Do Not Fit

As the writer was describing tuning in to CNN, she included an unrelated detail about her habit of watching too much television:

Sometimes, I feel like I watch too much television, but it's a habit I haven't been able to break.

This is such a powerful idea in the writer's mind that it takes momentary control of her development. However, this detail does not fit with her support point—that radio and television are good ways to stay informed about current events.

Remember, details that do not fit can be especially confusing for your reader. When composing your paragraph, keep a close eye on your outline and don't let unrelated details get you off track. <u>During the revision process, always double-check for details that do not fit.</u>

Fix this problem by eliminating unrelated details. If taking out these details leaves your paragraph underdeveloped, add new details that fit your support point. (To review the process of eliminating unrelated ideas, see Chapter 4, pages 80–84.)

Power Tip

If you try to revise your paragraph immediately after writing it, you may be too close to the material to see any problems. Try taking a break before revising it. Do something to relax your mind: Get some exercise, do some chores, take a nap. If possible, wait one day before you look over your work. Having fresh eyes will help you spot errors in your writing.

The Revised Paragraph

In her revision, the writer corrected each of the problems with unity. Take a look:

Topic sentence rewritten ⟶

The best way to stay informed about current events is to use a variety of media, such as the Internet, print media, and radio and television. For starters, the Internet is probably the fastest, most convenient way to stay informed. For instance, each time I turn on my computer, my browser's homepage is set to Yahoo.com. Yahoo is a great source for up-to-the-minute news, and it's very efficient, too. You can scan the headlines, read synopses of stories, and then click on interesting topics for fuller coverage. If you're looking for more intellectual and cutting-edge journalism, you can go to Slate.com. This Web site features insightful articles on politics, technology, and business by some of America's top reporters. In addition, if your political interests are liberal, MoveOn.org offers the most in-depth and provocative political commentary on the Web.

Missing support point added ⟶

In the second place, don't forget to scan the print media whenever you have the chance. For example, between classes, I try to stop by my college library and read a newspaper. I especially like the *Wall Street Journal* and the *New York Times*. Newspapers are different from Internet sites because I see a lot of information on the page and end up reading whole articles that I wouldn't necessarily navigate to on a Web site. I also like to read newsmagazines like *Time* and *Newsweek*. Because these magazines publish only once a week, they give a more comprehensive overview of events. Although print media seems to be losing popularity, it's still a unique source for news.

Missing transitional expression added ⟶

Finally, radio and television work hard to make their coverage of current events competitive with the Internet. I love the political debates on National Public Radio. Shows like *Left, Right, and Center* and *To the Point* feature brilliant and opinionated guests. Similarly, Public Broadcasting has some of the most unbiased news coverage on the air. The *News Hour* and *Bill Moyers* are my favorite shows for understanding national and world politics.

Detail rewritten to fit support point ⟶

However, if I just want a quick update on current events, I can tune in 24/7 to CNN. Not only is CNN the original all-news network, but it continues to provide the most reliable reporting. With all these excellent sources of news and information, how can any interested person not stay well informed?

Caution: Unrevised paragraph

Caution!   A paragraph without unity can be a hazardous reading experience: The large gaps, abrupt shifts, and unexpected digressions can cause your reader to stumble and fall. To protect your reader from such hazards, always take the revision stage of the writing process seriously.

ACTIVITY 1

Following is an outline and paragraph pairing. The paragraph has five problems with unity. Do the following:

- Review the outline.
- Read the paragraph, comparing it carefully with the outline.

- Underline or highlight any problems with unity.
- In the spaces between the lines (or in the margins), write a revision to correct each problem.

| MAIN IDEA | Meeting with my psychology professor to discuss my work was extremely helpful. |

TRANSITIONAL EXPRESSION To begin with,

SUPPORT POINT 1 I realized she is a normal human being.
- She has children my age.
- She struggled in college, too.
- She is very sweet and supportive.

TRANSITIONAL EXPRESSION Second,

SUPPORT POINT 2 she gave me valuable study tips.
- reading strategies
- class participation strategies
- study group

TRANSITIONAL EXPRESSION Last,

SUPPORT POINT 3 she offered to go over my exam.
- my thesis statement
- my evidence
- my commentary

In the sixth week of the semester, I finally went to meet with my psychology professor during her office hours. To begin with, meeting Professor Ramirez face-to-face helped me understand that she is a normal human being. For example, she has two college-age children, so she has a lot of sympathy for the struggles of students like me. She told me about her daughter, who has math anxiety, and that personal story helped me relax. Then, Professor Ramirez talked about her own fear as a college freshman, when she wasn't sure she was "college material." She was so sweet to share her personal experiences, and her support came through loud and clear. She even gave me valuable study tips, like using a highlighter and taking notes while I read the textbook. Furthermore, she suggested that I always sit in the front of the classroom, so that she can see when I need help. She encouraged me to ask at least one question during each lecture—even a simple

CONTINUED >

Power Tip
Many students put aside their outline after composing the paragraph. This is like putting away the map before reaching your final destination. Instead, keep your outline beside your paragraph to check for unity during revision. Cross-check each part of the paragraph with the corresponding items in the outline. Watch for missing, misplaced, or accidentally changed features.

For more practice with unity and other topics covered in this chapter, visit **bedfordstmartins .com/touchstones.**

question. Also, she advised me to join a study group outside of class. I was in a study group once for my sociology class, but I thought two of the students in my group were arrogant and not interested in my learning. So I quit the group and haven't belonged to another study group since then. Last, Professor Ramirez got down to business. In particular, she reviewed my thesis statement and showed me how to revise it. In the revision, she showed me how to add stronger vocabulary. Then, she discussed the evidence I had provided to support my points. While some of my evidence was good, I had not selected the most powerful quotations that were available to me. She opened the textbook and showed me the stronger evidence. In addition, she explained how I could write commentary that connected more clearly to my thesis statement. When I left Professor Ramirez's office, I felt optimistic and empowered, ready to succeed in college like she had done.

Using Peer Review as a Revision Strategy

One of the best strategies for revising your paragraph is to exchange papers with a peer (a classmate or fellow student who is at the same level of English as you) to comment on each other's work. This process is known as **peer review**.

Sometimes, your instructor may pair you with another student during class for peer review. If you are not given this opportunity, you can arrange to meet with another student outside of class and conduct your own peer review.

Start by inviting a fellow student who is mature and dedicated to the work. Meet in a quiet place, like the library or an empty classroom. Plan to spend at least half an hour for the peer review. You should bring your paragraph, your outline, and the peer review form on pages 157–58. Then, follow this process:

1. Exchange paragraphs, outlines, and peer review forms with your peer.
2. Carefully examine each other's paragraphs and outlines, completing the review form as you go.
3. Exchange and discuss the review forms and the paragraphs.

ATTITUDE AND INTELLECTUAL HONESTY IN PEER REVIEW

Remember that many people are sensitive to criticism. You, too, might be more sensitive than you think. Be polite and constructive in your comments about any paper. For example, it's better to say "I think there may be a problem here" than "You messed up." Also, specific remarks are always more helpful than general ones; for example:

GENERAL   I'm confused.

SPECIFIC   I don't understand what you mean by "important reason." Can you provide more of a description?

Remember that your job is to provide constructive feedback; it is the writer's job to make decisions and corrections.

Do not try to force your opinion or act like a know-it-all. On the other hand, don't be shy or lazy about identifying potential problems. If you are overly concerned about hurting the other person's feelings, or if you aren't serious about the work, your peer review may be ineffective.

When it's your turn to get comments on your work, pay attention to what the reviewer says and try not to be defensive. If you don't understand something, ask questions. Remember, the review process is a great opportunity to improve your work, so take full advantage of it.

PEER REVIEW FORM

1. Identify the topic sentence. How well does it express the main idea of this paragraph? If the topic sentence does not clearly express the main idea, what specific problems do you see?

2. Where might transitional expressions be added to the paragraph? Should any existing transitions be revised? If so, how?

3. List the support points. Is each one clearly stated in its own sentence? If not, describe the problem(s)?

4. How well do the support points back up the main idea (topic sentence)? Does any support seem to be missing? If so, what type of additional support might be helpful?

5. Does the paragraph have any details that do not fit? If it does, identify them.

6. Did you find anything confusing? If so, what specifically?

Power Tip
For lists of transitional expressions, see Chapter 6, pages 136 and 142.

Power Tip
If a peer believes that your main idea is inadequately supported, you might try some of the strategies discussed in Chapter 10 to generate more precise and colorful details for your topic.

CONTINUED >

This peer review form is also available at **bedfordstmartins.com /touchstones** under Useful Forms.

Power Tip
Feel free to add your own questions to the peer review form, especially if you have concerns that are specific to a certain piece of writing (for example, "Did you laugh or groan at my description of my uncle's clothes?").

7. What do you like best about this paragraph?

8. Do you have other recommendations for improving this paragraph? If so, what are they?

ACTIVITY 2: Teamwork

Choose a paragraph or short essay that you wrote recently, perhaps in response to one of the activities in this book. Then, follow these steps:

- Pair up with another student who has also chosen a paragraph.
- Trade papers and evaluate each other's writing, using the peer review form above.
- Next, return the review forms and paragraphs, and ask each other any questions about the evaluations. (For example, if something isn't clear, you might say, "I'm not sure what you mean by _____. Could you please explain or give me an example?")
- Revise your paragraphs, based on the feedback.

Proofreading for Grammar, Mechanics, and Word Errors

You may recognize this scenario: An hour before class, you begin to write a paper in response to an assignment. Surprisingly, you find the topic interesting and hammer out some original ideas. With seconds left on the clock, you print your work and dash off to class. A week later, when it's time to get your paper back from your instructor, you are hopeful that the grade will reflect your original thinking. Imagine your shock when you see the paper covered in red ink, with a C+ at the top. The instructor's comment says it all: "Great ideas, but too many errors."

What went wrong? The answer is simple: You did not proofread. That is, you did not read your writing slowly and carefully (word by word), as if with an imaginary magnifying glass, to identify mistakes. If you had reserved 10 or 15 minutes to review your composition for errors, your grade might have been significantly better.

This experience is all too common in college. Because we are busy or because we see proofreading as optional, we may skip this important final step of the revision process. However, not taking the time for this step is often the number one cause of grammar, mechanical, and wording errors in student writing. Proofreading is not difficult; with even a modest effort, most writers can identify and fix many errors in their writing. More difficult is the task of training ourselves to proofread every time we write.

PROOFREADING FOR GRAMMAR AND MECHANICS

Grammar problems are discussed in detail in Part Three of this book, so we will not address them in depth here. However, the chart below previews important errors to be aware of.

When proofreading for grammar, look at the words between periods to make sure that they are, in fact, complete, correct sentences. Also, make sure that verbs are in the correct tense and properly formed.

Mechanics issues include spelling, punctuation, and formatting (such as using double-spacing when required). Spelling is discussed on pages 160–62 in the charts showing commonly confused words. For a review of punctuation, see Appendix C.

Power Tip

For frequently misspelled words and frequent grammar errors, try keeping a *spelling log* and a *grammar log*. Recording your errors will help you recognize them and eliminate them from your writing. Samples may be found at **bedfordstmartins .com/touchstones** under Useful Forms.

PROBLEM (and where it is covered in this book)	DEFINITION	EXAMPLE
Fragments (Chapter 16, page 361; Chapter 18, page 423; Chapter 19, page 443; Quick Guide, page R-3)	word groups that are missing a subject or a verb or that do not express a complete thought	The fastest runner. [*The fastest runner* could be the subject of a sentence, but there is no verb expressing an action.] **Corrected:** The fastest runner won.
Run-ons (Chapter 17, page 391; Quick Guide, page R-4)	sentences joined together with no punctuation or linking words	The movie ended we left. **Corrected:** The movie ended. We left. OR The movie ended, so we left. The movie ended; we left.
Comma splices (Chapter 17, page 391; Quick Guide, page R-4)	sentences joined together with just a comma	The movie ended, we left. **Corrected:** The movie ended. We left. OR The movie ended, so we left. The movie ended; we left.
Mistakes in verb usage (Chapter 23; Quick Guide, page R-6)	These include a wide variety of errors, such as using the wrong tense (time) of a verb, the wrong form of a verb, or a verb that does not agree with (match) a subject in number.	Yesterday, I go to the movies. [The sentence is in the past time, but *go* is a present tense verb.] **Corrected:** Yesterday, I went to the movies.

PROOFREADING FOR WORD CHOICE

When proofreading for word choice, look at every word in your writing to make sure that it exactly expresses the meaning that you intended. (When you are unsure of a word's meaning, check the definition in a dictionary.) As discussed in previous chapters, you should also make sure that your words are

- appropriate for your audience (see Chapter 1, pages 20–21) and as precise as possible (Chapter 10, page 231).
- as original as possible; in other words, avoid overused expressions, or clichés. (See Chapter 10, page 236.)

Also, look out for words that are often confused because they sound alike. The following chart lists the words that are the most commonly confused. Pay special attention to these words in your writing, and check their definitions and uses against the charts.

The Most Commonly Confused Words

WORDS/COMMON DEFINITIONS	EXAMPLES
its: a possessive (showing ownership) form of *it* **it's:** a combination (contraction) of *it is* or *it has*	The company lost <u>its</u> lawsuit against the town. <u>It's</u> clear that couples therapy has improved my marriage.
loose: not tight; not fully attached **lose:** to misplace; to be defeated	The <u>loose</u> shingle flapped in the wind. I <u>lose</u> a cell phone every year.
than: a word used in comparisons **then:** at another time (not now); next	Doug is funnier <u>than</u> Kyle. They were not as wealthy <u>then</u>. Peel the apples. <u>Then</u>, cut them into thin slices.
their: belonging to them **there:** at a certain location; not here **they're:** a combination (contraction) of *they are*	<u>Their</u> car broke down twice this month. Please sit <u>there</u>. <u>They're</u> still in shock about winning the lottery.
your: belonging to you **you're:** a combination (contraction) of *you are*	<u>Your</u> phone is ringing. <u>You're</u> my best friend.

Get regular practice with the most commonly confused words so that you can use them correctly every time. Take one or two quizzes every day, if possible. Quizzes are available at **bedfordstmartins.com/touchstones**. Also, take the time to get familiar with other words that are commonly confused by studying the additional chart that follows.

More Commonly Confused Words

WORDS/COMMON DEFINITIONS	EXAMPLES
accept: to take; to agree to **except:** excluding	I <u>accept</u> responsibility for the accident. Mara likes all vegetables <u>except</u> broccoli.
advice: a recommendation; words intended to be helpful **advise:** to give advice	We took your financial <u>advice</u>. You <u>advise</u> us to save more money.
affect: to have an impact on **effect:** an outcome or result	The storm did not <u>affect</u> our travel plans. The drugs had little <u>effect</u> on the patient.

WORDS/COMMON DEFINITIONS	EXAMPLES
brake: to stop or slow; a device used for this purpose	I <u>brake</u> my car before sharp turns.
break: to smash or cause something to stop working; a period of rest or an interruption in an activity	Be careful not to <u>break</u> the crystal vase. The factory workers took a <u>break</u>.
breath: air inhaled (taken in) and exhaled (pushed out)	I am always out of <u>breath</u> after the 5K race.
breathe: to inhale and exhale	It was hard to <u>breathe</u> in the hot, crowded room.
buy: to purchase **by:** next to	We <u>buy</u> a gallon of milk every week. Martino always sits <u>by</u> the door.
hear: to detect with the ears **here:** present; at this location	I <u>hear</u> our neighbor's car stereo every morning. Is Jeremy <u>here</u>, or did he already leave for work?
knew: past tense of *know* (see below) **new:** recently introduced or created	Even as a child, I <u>knew</u> my parents were not perfect. The <u>new</u> convertible gleamed in the sunlight.
know: to understand or comprehend; to be acquainted with **no:** a negative expression (the opposite of *yes*)	I <u>know</u> how to swim. You <u>know</u> Jim. <u>No</u>, I can't go to the game with you.
lie: to recline **lay:** to put something down	Don't <u>lie</u> in the sun too long. <u>Lay</u> the clothes on the bed, not on the floor.
mind: the part of a person that thinks and perceives **mine:** belonging to *me*	I couldn't get my <u>mind</u> around those math formulas. Those gloves on the chair are <u>mine</u>.
passed: went by (past tense of *pass*) **past:** the time before now	We <u>passed</u> the house twice before we realized it was Josie's. In the <u>past</u>, I drove to work every day.
peace: lack of conflict or war; a state of calm **piece:** a part of something	We must work for <u>peace</u> in a violent world. Have a <u>piece</u> of this delicious pie.
principal: the leader of a school or other organization; main or major **principle:** a law or standard	The <u>principal</u> addressed the school assembly. Our <u>principal</u> complaint is that we waited two hours for service. Professor Bates lectured on economic <u>principles</u>.
quiet: soundless or low in sound **quite:** very; fully **quit:** to stop	The room was <u>quiet</u> because the children were sleeping. We are <u>quite</u> happy with the decision. We are not <u>quite</u> there yet. Joe <u>quit</u> smoking a year ago.
right: correct; opposite of *left* **write:** to put words down in a form that can be read (on paper or on a computer screen)	Margo is <u>right</u> that our seats are on the <u>right</u> side of the concert hall. The soldier's daughter promised to <u>write</u> him an e-mail every day.

CONTINUED >

WORDS/COMMON DEFINITIONS	EXAMPLES
set: to put something somewhere **sit:** to be seated	I <u>set</u> the glasses on the counter. Please <u>sit</u> down.
threw: past tense of *throw* **through:** finished; going in one side and out the other	Shontelle <u>threw</u> the ball to Dave. We are <u>through</u> with exams. The Cartullos drove <u>through</u> the snowstorm.
to: in the direction of; toward **too:** also **two:** the number between one and three	Christina ran <u>to</u> the lake and back. My daughter wants to go to the movies <u>too</u>. <u>Two</u> swans glided on the pond.
use: to put into service or employ **used:** past tense of *use*; accustomed	I <u>use</u> a rubber glove to open jars that are stuck. Bill <u>used</u> butter in his cooking before his cholesterol got too high. Kent is <u>used</u> to getting up early.
weather: climate (pertaining to the absence or presence of sun, wind, rain, and so on) **whether:** a word used to present alternatives	The <u>weather</u> was beautiful during our vacation. I can't decide <u>whether</u> or not to go to the party.
whose: the possessive form of *who* **who's:** a combination (contraction) of *who is* or *who has*	I don't know <u>whose</u> car is parked in front of our house. <u>Who's</u> the actor <u>who's</u> just divorced his fifth wife?

ACTIVITY 3

For each sentence, decide which words in parentheses are correct. Then, circle your choices.

EXAMPLE: (Their / (They're)) not willing to go (their / (there)) on vacation.

1. You will (loose / lose) your mind if you keep all of your papers (loose / lose) in your backpack.

2. The student corrected her (passed / past) failures when she (passed / past) all her classes.

3. If (your / you're) out late with your friends, you won't be able to complete (your / you're) homework.

4. Divorce can (affect / effect) children in many ways, but the most common (affect / effect) may be a lack of confidence in intimate relationships.

5. Tasha could not (accept / except) that the professor gave everyone a passing grade (accept / except) her.

6. (It's / Its) a shame that the biology book does not have (it's / its) own companion Web site.

7. After the garage band (quiet / quite / quit) practicing, the neighborhood became (quiet / quite / quit) peaceful.

Use the online quizzes at **bedfordstmartins.com /touchstones** to practice your awareness of the most commonly confused words.

8. (Whose / Who's) the student in our history class (whose / who's) cell phone is constantly beeping?

9. The counselor will certainly (advice / advise) Ivan to take her (advice / advise) seriously.

10. You can (lie / lay) down on the couch, but please (lie / lay) your dirty shoes on the doormat first.

PROOFREADING FOR MISSING WORDS

It is very common for writers to leave out words, especially when they are working quickly. Therefore, it is extremely important to look for missing words when proofreading your draft.

Take a look at the following excerpt from a student paragraph and see if you can detect four missing words.

> Benjamin keeps his connections strong by a good friend in every way. For starters, he is the best listener I've ever known. Whenever I've had a problem, he has stopped what he was doing to lend an ear. At these times, he never criticizes or offers unwelcome advice. He understands that, sometimes, friends just to be heard. Next, Ben would do anything for a friend in need. One time, I was so sick I couldn't even out of bed to heat a can of soup. When Ben stopped by and saw how ill I was, he ran out to buy my favorite soup the local deli. He also got six bottles of Gatorade so I wouldn't become dehydrated.

Keep in mind that missing words are often difficult to spot, so you may have to use some special proofreading strategies. Always proofread your writing on a printed page, not just on the computer monitor. Also, you can proofread backwards, one sentence at a time. (You'll read more about these strategies below.) Now, reread the previous excerpt with the missing words added:

> Benjamin keeps his connections strong by **being** a good friend in every way. For starters, he is the best listener I've ever known. Whenever I've had a problem, he has stopped what he was doing to lend an ear. At these times, he never criticizes or offers unwelcome advice. He understands that, sometimes, friends just **want** to be heard. Next, Ben would do anything for a friend in need. One time, I was so sick I couldn't even **get** out of bed to heat a can of soup. When Ben stopped by and saw how ill I was, he ran out to buy my favorite soup **from** the local deli. He also got six bottles of Gatorade so I wouldn't become dehydrated.

Power Tip
So that you do not overlook errors, consider proofreading for only one issue at a time. For example, you might proofread for grammar first, then for mechanics, then for word choice, and then for missing words.

SOME HELPFUL PROOFREADING STRATEGIES

The following four strategies have helped thousands of students to produce better writing.

Identify Your Style of Proofreading

To a certain degree, the way you proofread is a matter of personal style and choice. Some writers proofread *when they write*: Sentence by sentence, they check their grammar, spelling, punctuation, and so on. As a result, their final, overall proofreading requires less time. Other writers prefer to get their ideas down quickly, *without stopping* to proofread each sentence. For these writers, the final, overall proofreading will be a more demanding job, and they must reserve extra time for it.

Identifying your style of proofreading can help you focus your energy and manage your time during the writing process. Whatever your preference, remember that a final, overall proofreading is essential for a polished composition.

Spelling and Grammar: English (U.S.)   ? ☒

Not in Dictionary:

Karin knew I'd be too ashamed to say it was missing, or it was equally possible that she'd been too embarrassed to reveel it as something she'd found worth taking.

Suggestions:

revel
reveal
ravel
revels
reveled
revile

☐ Check grammar

Options... | Undo | Cancel

Ignore Once | Ignore All | Add to Dictionary
Change | Change All | AutoCorrect

Power Tip

It is helpful to keep a grammar guide beside you when proofreading. You can use the Quick Guides at the back of this book, or you can use a separate grammar handbook. If you use a handbook, you should flag pages that cover important errors, such as fragments, run-ons, and verb errors.

Use Spelling and Grammar Checkers—but Cautiously

Many students who compose on a computer rely on spelling and grammar checkers to eliminate errors. However, it is important to use them with caution. For example, spell checkers may not always make the right choice, as in the example on the left, in which the correct replacement should be *reveal*, not *revel*.

Do not automatically select the first word on the replacement list. Instead, examine each word until you have found the best match. If you are still unsure about the right choice, ask your instructor or a peer for advice, or check a dictionary. Also, spell checkers will not identify words that are spelled correctly but misused, as often happens with the commonly confused words listed on pages 160–62.

Grammar checkers highlight possible grammar errors in your writing — for instance, with a green line. Often, this highlighting indicates major grammar errors, such as fragments, run-ons, comma splices, or subject-verb agreement problems. The checker also may prompt you with suggestions for fixing these errors. Once again, you should develop the habit of examining each proposed correction. Not only will this help you make the right choice, but it will also build your grammar skills for those times when you do not have access to a grammar checker.

Finally, keep in mind that grammar checkers are not 100 percent accurate; they sometimes underline a sentence that is perfectly correct. Do not automatically assume that the grammar checker is right and your sentence is flawed. As your grammar awareness grows, you should begin to rely on your own judgment as much as you rely on the electronic correction tools.

Proofread in Two Views

Whenever possible, proofread your writing in two views: on the computer monitor and on the printed page. Each of these visual media will help you notice different details in your writing. If you proofread only on the screen, your eyes may miss quite a few errors.

After writing your composition and reading it on-screen, always print a draft and proofread on the page. It's a good idea to double-space your writing before you print it so that it's easier to read. Then, use a combination of pen, pencil, and/or highlighter to mark your errors. For example, you might highlight words whose spelling you need to look up in the dictionary, put a colored star by items you want to ask your instructor about, and use pencil to add missing words or make other edits. Next, go back to the computer and make any necessary corrections, consulting your instructor or other resources as needed.

Proofread Backwards

Most people would not think of riding a bicycle backwards down the street. However, it would certainly raise your awareness about your own body, the parts of your bicycle, and your surroundings. To advance safely and successfully, you would need to go slowly and pay careful attention to every part of the experience.

Similarly, most students would not think of proofreading their writing backwards, one sentence at a time. However, writers who use this strategy find that it raises their awareness about their grammar, word choice and word order, spelling, and punctuation.

When we proofread a composition in the customary way—from top to bottom—we get caught up in the flow of our ideas. This momentum—just like the momentum of riding a bicycle forward—makes it difficult for us to slow down and pay careful attention to the fine points of our writing. When we proofread backwards, we interrupt the flow of our ideas, allowing us to focus more effectively on our sentence construction. Try proofreading sentence by sentence, beginning with the last sentence.

ACTIVITY 4: Mastery Test or Teamwork

Proofread the following paragraph for eight misspelled words (all from the chart on page 160) and seven missing words. If you are not able to find all 15 errors, try proofreading the paragraph *backwards*, one sentence at a time.

When you give a speech, people are not only listening to what you say; they are also your face and body as you speak. Body language is an important part of successful public speaking. First, good public speakers should pay attention to they stand. For example, standing tall and erect shows that your confident, and the audience will find your message more believable. Also, leaning forward slightly during important parts of the speech can show your connected with your audience. However, standing stooped might suggest a lack of confidence, and slouching may suggest you don't care; either of these postures may cause you to loose the attention of your audience.

CONTINUED >

In addition, moving around too much may be distracting to those watching the speech. Next, a second way to use body language effectively is to attention to how you gesture. Its important to use your hands to emphasize key and express emotions. Think about mimes and dramatic actors. They lift there arms, use their hands, and even stomp their feet to anger, passion, and joy. People relate easily to these gestures, so using them will help your audience feel your emotions. Also, don't forget to use your fingers for additional emphasis. For instance, holding up your right index finger as you say "My first reason" reinforces that this is the beginning of a series, and the audience will anticipate your upcoming points. Finally, facial expressions can show your passion for your topic and create a with your audience. The most important part of your facial expression during a speech is eye contact. Its not only polite to look at your audience, but it also holds there attention. Furthermore, raising your eyebrow can show that certain facts or ideas are surprising. In fact, an arched eyebrow can be more dramatic then raising your voice or shouting. Your mouth can obviously reveal pleasure through a smile, disgust through a grimace, sadness in a down-turned lip, and horror or shock in a dropped jaw. Your face can echo your ideas and reinforce them. Paying attention to body language will make your speech more and will help you relate more effectively to your audience.

ACTIVITY 5

Use a paragraph or short essay that you wrote for Chapter 4 or 6. Proofread your writing backwards, slowly and carefully, one sentence at a time. Fix any errors that you find.

BRINGING IT ALL TOGETHER:
Revising

In this chapter, you have learned about revising and proofreading strategies that will help you improve your writing. Confirm your knowledge by filling in the blank spaces in the following sentences. If you need help, review the pages listed after each sentence. Finally, check off each item to confirm your understanding of the material.

✔ A paragraph that stays on track and includes only information that supports the main idea is called a _____ paragraph. (page 150)

✔ _____ means looking over your writing with a fresh eye to identify and fix any problems. (page 150)

✔ The unity of your paragraph can be disrupted when there is a _____ topic sentence, an _____ support point, a _____ transitional expression, or details that _____. (page 150)

✔ When doing peer review with a classmate, it is your job to provide _____. It is the writer's job to make _____. (page 157)

✔ When proofreading your draft, proofread for _____ and _____ and for _____ errors. (page 158)

✔ Four strategies can improve your proofreading. First, identify your _____. Second, use _____ cautiously. Third, proofread in two _____, and finally, proofread _____, one sentence at a time. (pages 163–65)

JOURNAL WRITING: 10–15 minutes

For this journal entry, write about what you would like to improve in your composition process, and what you have learned about the revision process after trying some of the strategies in this chapter.

Case Study: Writing a Successful Academic Paragraph

To get a clear sense of how the writing process works, take a look at the following case study that outlines Silvia R.'s process of brainstorming, drafting, composing, and revising her academic paragraph.

To begin, Silvia was assigned the following broad topic:

Discuss something that you would avoid at all costs.

NARROWING

Power Tip
To review brainstorming techniques and how to narrow your ideas for a topic, see Chapter 3, pages 48–57.

Silvia knew that her favorite method for getting her ideas down was *listing*. In order to narrow her broad topic, she produced the following list:

Something I would avoid at all costs:

- becoming a couch potato
- being poor
- having a job I don't like
- getting married at a young age
- letting a man dictate my life

After carefully reviewing her options, Silvia selected the following narrowed topic for her paragraph:

Something I would avoid at all costs is getting married at a young age.

BRAINSTORMING

To explore her narrowed topic, Silvia once again used *listing*. Notice that her list is actually *a group* of short lists:

<u>I will avoid getting married at a young age</u>

My education might suffer:
- less or no time for school
- less or no money for school
- my husband's education might come first

Marriage could compromise my self-development:
- I'd become a "wife" instead of a person
- I'd become a "mother" instead of a person
- I'd become a "daughter-in-law" instead of a person

I might lose my independence:
- I'd have to make decisions with my husband
- I couldn't just take off and go where I want
- I'd have to check with my husband before spending my money

I would give up my youth:
- dating
- time alone to dream
- slumber parties
- shopping days with girlfriends

My mother got married at 16:
- she had her first baby at 17
- she had two more babies after that
- my father was mean to her
- I have learned from her mistakes

OUTLINING

After exploring her narrowed topic, Silvia followed the steps to complete her outline form:

- First, she filled in the main idea.
- Then, she picked her support points one at a time and wrote them down as complete sentences.
- She remembered to add a transitional expression to each support point.
- Finally, she added related examples for each support point.

Before drafting her paragraph, Silvia reviewed her outline carefully for problems. She checked for:

- items that did not fit
- items that repeated other items
- items that were vague

Power Tip
To review how to outline your ideas, see Chapter 5, pages 104–8.

MAIN IDEA	I will never get married at a young age.
SUPPORT POINT 1	To begin with, I have learned from my mom's mistakes.

RELATED EXAMPLES
- had three babies right away
- ~~I am a lot like my mother~~
- my father was not supportive

item does not fit ——————————

SUPPORT POINT 2	Next, I don't want to give up my youth.

RELATED EXAMPLES
- dating
- spending time with girlfriends
- ~~going out with guys~~

item repeats another item ——————————

SUPPORT POINT 3	Finally, my education comes first right now.

RELATED EXAMPLES
- in a marriage, no money for college
- in a marriage, no time for college
- ~~other things might get in the way~~

item is vague ——————————

Then, Silvia corrected the errors that she found in her outline:

MAIN IDEA	I will never get married at a young age.
SUPPORT POINT 1	To begin with, I have learned from my mom's mistakes.

RELATED EXAMPLES
- had three babies right away
- lost her independence
- my father was not supportive

SUPPORT POINT 2	Next, I don't want to give up my youth.

RELATED EXAMPLES
- dating
- spending time with girlfriends
- having time alone

SUPPORT POINT 3	Finally, my education comes first right now.

RELATED EXAMPLES
- in a marriage, no money for college
- in a marriage, no time for college
- my husband's education might come first

Power Tip
To review the steps of composing a paragraph, see Chapter 6.

COMPOSING

Finally, Silvia followed her outline step by step to write the following draft of her paragraph. You can see her proofreading and editing comments, which she added after composing the paragraph.

Did I change the meaning of my main idea? ——————————

Getting married at a young age can be a mistake. For starters, I have learned so much about the perils of marrying young from my mother, who wed my father when she was just 16 years old. Within a few months, she was pregnant with her first child. It was a difficult pregnancy she had to stay in

Is this a run-on?

the house and was alone most of the time. After my brother was born, Mom was pregnant again within one month. At that point, she became very depressed about her isolation and loss of independence. No close friendships. She couldn't even buy a pair of shoes without my father's permission. My father refused to take her depression seriously. He said she would feel better if she took more pride in cleaning the house. For years, my mother has shared these stories with me so that I would not make the same mistakes she made. I do not want to give up my youth by marrying too early. For example, if I got married, I would not be able to date anymore, and I enjoy dating. I once dated this guy named Enrique, and he took me to Disneyland on our first date. It was my worst experience ever at Disneyland. In addition, my girlfriends are my tribe. We spend whole days and weekends together shopping, gossiping, and just being girls. If I got married, I don't think my husband would understand or accept our tribal customs. Moreover, being young means spending time alone, dreaming, and imagining my future. I doubt my husband would tolerate this need. Finally, I am a college student. My parents have already said that if I get married, they will stop paying my college expenses, and I can't necessarily count on my husband to have money for that. Plus, as a wife, I will have duties that may distract me from my studies. And in many hispanic marriages, the husband's education comes first. Perhaps my husband would be more progressive, but if money is tight, we might put my education on hold for his. I can't risk this possibility. In conclusion, I do not plan to get married at a young age.

Is this a fragment?

Add a transitional expression.

Did I lose focus in developing my details here?

Did I accidentally change my support point?

Should this word be capitalized?

Does my concluding idea show sincerity and conviction?

REVISING

Finally, Silvia revised her paragraph, correcting her errors and making the necessary changes. She submitted the following finished paragraph. (Note: Her corrections are underlined.)

Although I hope to marry the man of my dreams one day, I will definitely avoid getting married at a young age. For starters, I have learned so much about the perils of marrying young from my mother, who wed my father when she was just 16 years old. Within a few months, she was pregnant with her first child. Since it was a difficult pregnancy, she had to stay in the house and was alone most of the time. After my brother was born, Mom was pregnant again within one month. At that point, she became very depressed about her isolation and loss of independence. She no longer had close friendships, and she couldn't even buy a pair of shoes without my father's permission. My father refused to take her depression seriously. He said that she would feel better if she took more pride in cleaning the house. For years, my mother has shared these stories with me so that I would not make the same mistakes she made. Next, I do not want to give up my youth by marrying too early. For example, if I got married, I would not be able to date anymore, and I enjoy dating. For me, nothing is more fun than dressing up and going out, getting to know a new guy and exploring the friendship. In addition, my girlfriends are my tribe. We spend whole days and weekends together shopping, gossiping, and just being girls. If I got married, I don't think my husband would understand or accept our tribal customs. Moreover, being young means spending time alone, dreaming, and imagining my future. I doubt my husband would tolerate this need. Finally, getting married might compromise my education, which is a priority for me right now. My parents have already said that if I get married, they will stop paying my college expenses, and I can't necessarily count on my husband to have money for that. Plus, as a wife, I will have duties that may distract me from my studies. And in many Hispanic marriages, the husband's education comes first. Perhaps my husband would be more progressive, but if money is tight, we might put my education on hold for his. I can't risk this possibility. In truth, I don't know exactly what age is right for me to get married (22? 25? 28?), but I do know that I will wait until I have fulfilled my youth, finished my education, and gotten my mother's approval.

CHAPTER 8

Moving from Paragraphs to Essays

Test your understanding of how to move from writing paragraphs to writing essays by completing this quiz first. You may know more than you think.

For each question, select all the answers that apply.

WHAT DO YOU KNOW?

1. **What features do an academic paragraph and an academic essay have in common?**
   ___ They are well developed.
   ___ They both have a thesis statement.
   ___ They are carefully organized.
   ___ They are grammatically correct.

2. **How is an essay different from an academic paragraph?**
   ___ It has an introduction with a thesis statement.
   ___ It has two or more body paragraphs.
   ___ It has a concluding paragraph.
   ___ It has support points and examples.

3. **In which two ways are a topic sentence (paragraph) and a thesis statement (essay) similar?**
   ___ They provide related examples.
   ___ They state the general topic.
   ___ They express an original point about the topic.
   ___ They avoid using key words from the topic.

4. **An academic essay includes which of the following?**
   ___ an introduction and a conclusion
   ___ only one body paragraph
   ___ two or more body paragraphs
   ___ either an introduction or a conclusion

5. **What are some major errors found in essay outlines?**
   ___ an item that does not fit
   ___ an item that supports another item
   ___ an item that repeats another item
   ___ an item that is unclear

Understanding the Relationship between Paragraphs and Essays

So far, you have learned the basic features of an academic paragraph:

- It is well developed, usually with more than five sentences.
- It is carefully organized, with a main idea and a series of support points.
- It is grammatically correct.

Notice now that the academic essay (a freshman-level college essay) has similar features:

- It is well developed, usually with three or more pages.
- It is carefully organized, with a main idea and a series of support points.
- It is grammatically correct.

In addition, most instructors will require a standard college essay to include the following:

- **an introduction:** an opening paragraph that includes a thesis statement (a statement containing the essay's main idea)
- **two or more "body" paragraphs:** fully developed academic paragraphs that develop the essay's support points
- **a conclusion:** a paragraph that may restate the main idea or make a related observation

Because you have already mastered the basics of the academic paragraph, you have a strong sense of what goes into good writing. This understanding will help you to master the academic essay as well.

To help you visualize the differences—and similarities—between paragraphs and essays, look carefully at the two images on the facing page. The one on the left is a model for a 300-square-foot studio apartment; the one on the right is a model for a 3,000-square-foot house.

A paragraph, like a studio (one-room) apartment, is a self-contained unit. Even though it is small, it has all of the essential elements of well-developed writing—a main idea (in the form of a topic sentence), support points, examples, unity, and grammatical correctness (just the way a small apartment has a sleeping area, living area, bathroom, front door, and so on).

An essay, like a house, shares the same essential elements with a paragraph although it is more spacious and more fully developed. It has a main idea (in the form of a thesis statement), support points, examples, unity, and grammatical correctness. But instead of just one small area, an essay covers more ground. It likely has four or more paragraphs (rooms), as well as a main idea that is broad enough to require more extensive development (just as a house has at least one living area, a bathroom, front door, garage, and so on, to allow more people to live comfortably in it).

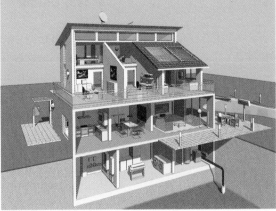

In essence, the main differences between a paragraph and an essay are the scope of the topics covered and the amount of information provided.

Now, read the descriptive paragraph and essay below. The paragraph describing the apartment is followed by the essay describing the house.

Power Tip
For more information on the *patterns of development* — of which *description* is one — see Chapters 11 and 12.

The Paragraph

My tiny studio apartment is ideal for a single college student. First, the living and sleeping area has everything I need to keep myself productive, entertained, and well rested. In a corner of this area is my desk, which gives me plenty of room to write, read, and work on my computer. The desk is in front of a large window that offers plenty of light. In the middle of my room is a comfortable sofa and, in front of it, a coffee table and a flat-screen television. This part of the room is what I call the "entertainment center," and here I watch my favorite sports and hang out with friends. The couch has a comfortable foldout bed, and I always get a good night's rest on it. Second, I love my miniature kitchen, which has everything I need to prepare my meals. A counter area next to the stove gives me a place to chop vegetables and other items in preparation for cooking. Also, a rolling butcher-block table gives me even more work space. Though small, my appliances all work very well. I especially like my two-burner gas stove, which allows me to adjust the intensity of the cooking flames. In addition, there is a mini-refrigerator that has enough space for a week's worth of groceries. Finally, my bathroom is comfortable and well equipped. Surprisingly, it has a deep, old-fashioned bathtub that's great for soaking myself after a long day. There is also a showerhead that lets me wash up quickly before class or work. In addition, the bathroom has a storage unit with enough room for my toiletries and towels. I feel very lucky to have such a comfortable little apartment, and I'd be happy to stay here until I graduate from college.

The Essay

While I was growing up, I took my family's beautiful Victorian house largely for granted; it was just the place where I lived. As I've gotten older, however, I've grown to realize how special that first home was. Every part of it was grand, spacious, and unusual.

I remember the looks on my friends' faces when they first saw the main parlor downstairs—the largest and most impressive room of the house. Back then, I was so used to this room that I didn't understand why other kids' eyes would get so wide. Now that I've lived in a series of bland apartments, I get it. Standing in the entryway to this room, visitors would take in the expanse of polished wood floors, the pink-and-orange marble fireplace, and the delicately carved woodwork around the built-in bookcases. In addition, bay windows jutted out from the room, shining warm light onto the floors and making the room even larger. My parents were careful to decorate the parlor with Victorian antiques, so there were lots of interesting odds and ends to look at. These included beaded lamps, a player piano, and a bronze statue of the hunter-goddess Diana, who carried a realistic-looking bow and arrow. As children, we weren't allowed to play in this room, but it was enough to watch people's reactions to it.

Down the hall from the parlor was a huge kitchen that kept six children fed and two parents sane, for it was everything a kitchen should be. The center of the room—and probably of the whole house—was a long cherry table where we ate most of our meals. The table had room for every member of our family and all the food we wanted to eat, which was a lot. It also was a favorite place to play games, draw, or have conversations over cups of coffee or cocoa. Moreover, the table and the floor under it made up the house's one "free crumb zone," as my mother called it. Here we could drop crumbs and spill to our hearts' content, as long as the messes were cleaned up by bedtime. The working part of the kitchen had plenty of counter space for chopping and other food preparation and a deep sink for soaking dishes and scrubbing vegetables. Also, we had a large six-burner stove and a super-size refrigerator so that Mom and Dad could put together all the large meals that a large family required. For a long time we didn't have a dishwasher because of the big sink, but my parents finally got one when I was a teenager, and it made a great room perfect.

Upstairs were five huge bedrooms, but I'm going to talk about mine because it was the most unusual. The bedroom was almost as big as the parlor, so there was more than enough room for me and my sister Rachel. Like the parlor, it also had bay windows. Now, here is the unusual part: the bedroom had a hidden chamber like the kind sometimes shown in old movies about haunted houses. Opening the chamber required turning a lever hidden behind a little door. Then, a larger panel in the far wall would open, revealing a tiny room with bookshelves, as well as a miniature piano and desk that we discovered when we moved in. Rachel and I loved to discuss possible reasons for the little room, but nothing satisfied us. Finally, we decided that a little-girl ghost lived in there. Sometimes, Rachel and I would swear we heard her playing the piano at night, and we'd squeal and grab on to each other under the covers. Then, my mother would come into our room and say the noise was probably just a mouse running across the keys. Aside from the hidden chamber, another unusual feature of the bedroom was its stained-glass windows. These pictured red and orange flowers blooming on twisting green vines.

I am writing this essay in a plain-looking room with white sheet-rock walls that are so thin I can hear my neighbor gargling in his bathroom. Never have I been more aware of how lucky I was to have lived in such a beautiful old house. I can't go back to the house because my parents had to sell it. Nevertheless, its rooms remain as much a part of me as the chambers of my heart.

Understanding Key Features of Essays

In truth, the academic paragraph and the academic essay are more alike than different. Specifically, the organization of the paragraph mirrors the organization of the essay. Each part of the paragraph (topic sentence, support points, and related examples) corresponds to a similar part of the essay. However, we give different names to the parts of an essay even though these parts serve the same function that they do in the paragraph. Take a look at this chart that identifies the different names for these parts.

Power Tip

It is easy to get confused about these terms (*topic sentence, thesis statement,* etc.) because they are so similar and yet different. More important than memorizing these terms right now is getting a clear sense of how similar the organization of a paragraph and the organization of an essay are. The activities in this chapter will help make this clear for you.

FEATURE	. . . IN A PARAGRAPH	. . . IN AN ESSAY
Main idea ⟶	Topic sentence ⟶	Thesis statement
Support point 1 ⟶	Support point 1 ⟶	Topic sentence 1
Support point 2 ⟶	Support point 2 ⟶	Topic sentence 2
Support point 3 ⟶	Support point 3 ⟶	Topic sentence 3
Conclusion ⟶	Concluding sentence ⟶	Concluding paragraph

ACTIVITY 1

Fill in the two outlines on the next page based on the sample paragraph on page 175 and the sample essay on pages 176–77. Do the following:

- Fill in the paragraph outline first. Since you are already familiar with the parts of a paragraph, this task should be very manageable.

- Next, fill in the essay outline. Each part of the essay should correspond to a similar part in the paragraph.

CONTINUED >

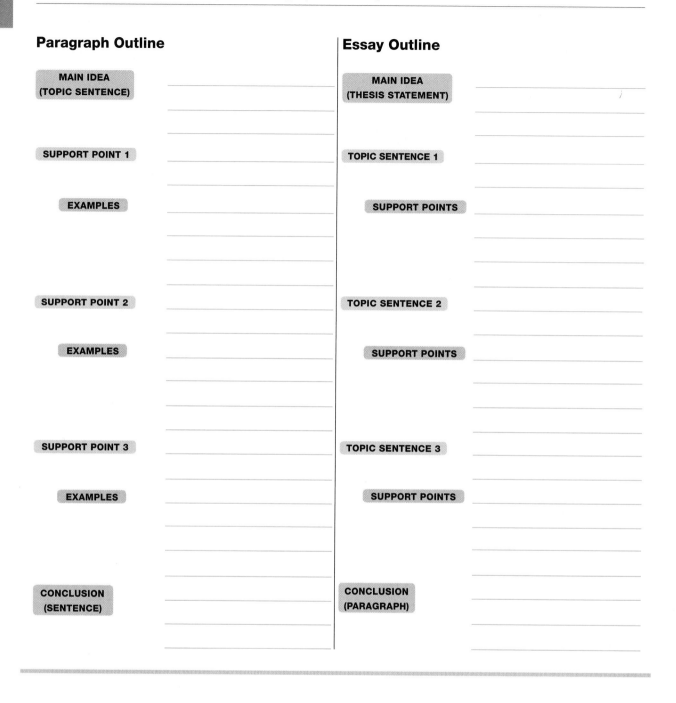

In the two outlines that you just filled in, you can see how the transition from paragraph to essay is very logical. Take a closer look:

- The main idea (topic sentence) in the paragraph outline becomes the thesis statement in the essay outline.
- Each support point in the paragraph outline becomes a topic sentence for a body paragraph in the essay outline.
- Each related example in the paragraph outline becomes a support point in the essay outline.

USING TRANSITIONAL EXPRESSIONS IN ESSAY OUTLINES

In an essay, moving from one paragraph to another requires a **transitional word or expression** such as *To begin with*, *In the second place*, and *Finally*.

As you know, transitional words or expressions help your reader follow the development of your ideas as they move from point to point. When these expressions help you move from paragraph to paragraph, they are called **major transitional expressions**. When they help you move from support point to support point within a paragraph, they are called **minor transitional expressions**.

Although you can add transitional expressions while drafting your essay, it is a much better practice to add them *directly on your outline*. For an essay outline, write a major transitional expression beside each topic sentence. This simple step will ensure that you include transitional expressions as you move from paragraph to paragraph.

You may also write a minor transitional expression beside each support point on your outline. This step will ensure smooth transitions within your body paragraph as you move from one support point to another.

Minor Transitional Expressions

For example,
For instance,
Specifically,
In particular,
In addition,
Next,
Furthermore,
Moreover,
Also,
Plus,
In fact,
To illustrate,
Another illustration…
Another example…

Major Transitional Expressions

↓

Group 1
First,
To begin with,
For starters,
In the first place,

Group 2
Second,
Next,
In the second place,
Equally important,

Group 3
Finally,
Last,
Third,
Most important,

Conclusion
In conclusion,
In brief,
In review,
In sum,
In summary,
To sum up,
To conclude,

MAIN IDEA

First, ←

TOPIC SENTENCE 1

SUPPORT POINTS   *For example,*

Furthermore,

Also,

Equally important, ←

TOPIC SENTENCE 2

SUPPORT POINTS   *For instance,*

Moreover,

Another illustration

Finally, ←

TOPIC SENTENCE 3

SUPPORT POINTS   *Specifically,*

Plus,

In fact,

To sum up, ←

CONCLUDING IDEA

Power Tip
After you have written down your three topic sentences, you may want to change their order. There are two basic approaches to ordering topic sentences: 1) begin with the most powerful idea and end with the least powerful idea; 2) begin with the least powerful idea and end with the most powerful idea. Both of these methods can work well; select the one that is more appropriate for your topic.

Power Tip
Consider using a pencil or a pen with erasable ink to keep your outline neat and legible.

Power Tip
To get a head start on mastering conclusions, see Chapter 9, pages 205–8.

FILLING IN AN ESSAY OUTLINE

The steps for filling in an essay outline are quite similar to the steps for filling in a paragraph outline. After you brainstorm your ideas, transfer them to your outline. Remember to select your most powerful ideas and make sure that they fit with the other items in your outline.

Fill in the *main idea* and *topic sentences* first so that you know where you're going. Then, when you're sure that the main idea and topic sentences are clearly connected, add the support points.

Now, here are the steps for filling in an essay outline:

Step 1: Write in the main idea (thesis statement) for your essay.

Step 2: Write in the three topic sentences, one for each body paragraph. Make sure that each topic sentence connects clearly to the main idea.

Step 3: Write in the support points for one topic sentence at a time. Make sure that each support point connects clearly to the paragraph's topic sentence.

Step 4: Add major transitional expressions beside topic sentence. Optionally, add minor transitional expressions beside each support point.

Step 5: Add a concluding idea.

ACTIVITY 2

Now, it's time to begin your writing process for a short essay. Do the following:

- Select one of the broad topics listed below and begin to narrow it for a short essay. (For more information on narrowing a broad topic, see Chapter 3, page 45.) Or, you may select one of the topics below that has already been narrowed.

- Brainstorm on the topic, using your favorite method such as clustering, listing, flowcharting, or freewriting. (For more on brainstorming methods, see Chapter 3, pages 48–57.)

- Continue brainstorming until you have filled your page with ideas or until you are confident that you have enough ideas for your composition.

- Using an outline form for a short essay (downloadable at **bedfordstmartins.com/touchstones**, Useful Forms), move your brainstorming ideas to the outline, following the recommended steps above. Remember:

  - Write the main idea first.
  - Write in the topic sentences for the three supporting paragraphs and make sure they are clearly connected to the main idea.
  - Write the support points for each topic sentence.
  - Add transitional expressions.
  - Write the concluding idea.

Broad Topics	**Narrowed Topics**
1. sports	**1.** Discuss the advantages and/ or disadvantages that you had while growing up.
2. fashion	

3. Web sites

4. mistakes

5. work

6. dreams

7. dating

8. illness/medical care

9. heroes

10. travel

2. Discuss the most important people in your life right now.

3. Discuss the tour of your town or city that you would give to a visitor.

4. Discuss how you have changed or stayed the same in the last five years.

5. Discuss the most important things you'd like to accomplish in your life.

Moving from Paragraphs to Essays: Two Methods

Most of the time, when you write an essay for college, you do so because you were assigned an essay in the first place. As you begin the writing process, you select a topic that is appropriate for a short essay (one to three pages).

However, in some cases, you may wish to expand a paragraph that you've already written into an essay. If this is your goal, you may use one of two methods to expand your paragraph. The first method involves *expanding each support point* of the paragraph; the second method involves *expanding the main idea* of the paragraph.

The following pages will introduce you to these two methods.

METHOD 1: EXPAND THE SUPPORT POINTS OF YOUR PARAGRAPH

The first method for moving from paragraph to essay is to expand each support point of the paragraph into a complete and separate "body" paragraph in the essay. In the samples below, each highlighted section of the paragraph corresponds to a separate paragraph in the essay, highlighted in the same color.

The Paragraph

Although college students sometimes miss the company of their family dog and may be tempted to get a dog of their own, they should think carefully before making this decision. In the first place, a student should consider what breed to adopt. A small dog can be easier to have around, but not all breeds are the same. A Jack Russell terrier might look like an easy, small pet, but it is a high-energy creature. A schnauzer, on the other hand, can be a good choice because of its adaptability. Second, a student should consider her schedule. If classes require her to be on campus from 8:00 A.M. till 5:00 P.M., a dog might not be a good idea. Dogs, especially young dogs, need attention. A cat might be able to handle an empty house all day, but not a dog. Some students manage this by running home between classes or over lunch. Finally, a student

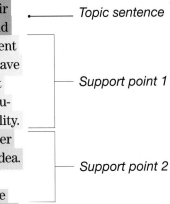

Topic sentence

Support point 1

Support point 2

Support point 3

should consider her living space. The landlord should be consulted to see if dogs are allowed. Roommates should be consulted. If your dog is going to ruin a roommate's life because she has allergies, be considerate. If you live alone, there are still neighbors to think about. Take the time to knock on doors and talk to people. You may even find someone who can take the dog out on a short walk once a day. If you consider the matter with care, a dog can be a great companion for the college student.

Concluding sentence

The Essay

Introduction

Two days after I got to college at the University of Georgia, I felt a pang of homesickness that I almost couldn't bear. I told my new friends about it and they admitted that they, too, had bouts of homesickness. One afternoon, walking by the park near the dorms, I saw a dog playing fetch with his owners. It gave me such joy to watch that happy creature playing that I knew I was going to get a dog as soon as I could. It took a year. I had to move out of the dorms and wait until my situation was right. I learned, however, that getting a dog while you are in college can

Thesis

be a good decision as long as you consider what breed of dog to get, your class schedule, and your living situation.

Support point 1

In the first place, before getting a dog, a student should consider what breed is most appropriate for the living environment. Generally, a small dog is easier to have around, but there are important differences among breeds of small dogs. For example, a Jack Russell terrier might look like an easy pet, but it is a high-energy dog. A second example is the Border collie. This smart working dog would not make a good college pet because it needs to stay mentally and physically active all day long. A schnauzer, however, might be a good choice. My neighbor has a schnauzer who is just as happy sleeping on the couch as he is on the end of a leash. Another good choice might be the placid golden retriever. Even though this is a larger breed, the golden generally has an easygoing disposition and will wait all day for its owner to return without destroying the house. A phone call to a local vet or a little research on the Internet can help you gain an understanding of the breeds and their temperaments. Finding a breed whose temperament suits your own, as well as your lifestyle, can make a more successful relationship.

Support point 2

Second, a student should consider his schedule. For instance, if your chosen field of study requires you to be on campus from 8:00 A.M. till 5:00 P.M., a dog might not be a good idea. Dogs, especially young dogs, need constant attention. Owner interaction is key to socializing any breed of dog. It's from you that the animal learns how to treat other people and other animals, how to behave in public, and how to behave at home. A cat might be able to handle an empty house all day, but a solitary, bored dog is likely to develop destructive habits. Furthermore, if it's possible, a student should consider running home between classes to spend some time with the dog. Fifteen minutes of fetch can calm your dog for several hours, depending on what breed you've chosen and its temperament. Another way to handle your absences is a dog-walking service. Doggie daycare is a new trend in pet ownership as more and more people work full-time. Some services even take pets out to hiking trails, where they can be off leash. Whatever method you choose to keep your dog sufficiently engaged, some method will be necessary if you want a healthy and well-behaved dog.

Finally, you should consider your living situation. In particular, if you live in an apartment with no yard, you need to reconsider the idea of a dog. Unless you're going to come home several times during the day to take your dog out, it's almost cruel to force an animal to live in a small space. Second, you also need to consult your lease to see if dogs are allowed. If the rule is unclear, call the landlord. If you ignore this step, you could end up being evicted. Having a dog to care for on top of needing a new place to live is a not a happy scenario. If the landlord approves a dog, your roommates should be advised next. If a dog is going to ruin a roommate's life because she has allergies or is afraid of dogs, consider your decision carefully. Dogs can destroy relationships because people tend to feel strongly about them, one way or the other. Next, if you live alone, there are neighbors to think about. If your pet is a barker and you plan to leave him in the yard for hours at a time, there will be complaints. If you take the time to knock on doors and talk to people, you can see positive results. You may end up with someone who can take the dog out on a short walk once a day. Last, you should consider that a dog means more yard care. There is cleanup to manage, which should happen at a minimum of every two days. Bored dogs can be hard on flower beds, too, digging holes or stomping on plants.

Support point 3

In summary, a dog can be a terrific addition to the college life. My dog ended my homesickness. Once I had him, I felt like I had a family. Taking him for walks and hikes and to the dog park also helped me meet a whole new set of friends. If you consider the breed carefully, as well as your class schedule and your living situation, a dog can be a great companion for any college student.

Conclusion

ACTIVITY 3

Fill in the two outlines on the next page based on the sample paragraph and essay that you've just read. Do the following:

- Fill in the paragraph outline first. Since you are already familiar with the parts of a paragraph, this task should be very manageable.
- Next, fill in the essay outline. Each part of the essay should correspond to a similar part in the paragraph.

CONTINUED >

Paragraph Outline

TOPIC SENTENCE _____
_____
_____

SUPPORT POINT 1 _____
_____

EXAMPLES _____
_____
_____

SUPPORT POINT 2 _____
_____

EXAMPLES _____
_____

SUPPORT POINT 3 _____
_____

EXAMPLES _____
_____

CONCLUSION _____

Essay Outline

THESIS STATEMENT _____
_____
_____
_____

TOPIC SENTENCE 1 _____
_____

SUPPORT POINTS _____
_____
_____
_____
_____

TOPIC SENTENCE 2 _____
_____

SUPPORT POINTS _____
_____
_____
_____

TOPIC SENTENCE 3 _____
_____

SUPPORT POINTS _____
_____
_____
_____
_____

CONCLUSION _____
_____
_____

ACTIVITY 4: Teamwork

Working with a few of your classmates, answer each of the following questions about the paragraph and essay used to illustrate method 1.

1. In the essay's first body paragraph (light green), what new information and details have been added? Identify at least three new items.

2. In the essay's second body paragraph (medium green), what new information and details have been added? Identify at least three new items.

3. In the essay's third body paragraph (dark green), what new information and details have been added? Identify at least three new items.

4. Identify the paragraph's topic sentence and the essay's thesis statement. Explain how these two sentences are similar and different. What new information has been added to the essay's first paragraph? Discuss whether you think this added information begins the essay in an interesting and effective manner.

5. What new information has been added to the essay's conclusion? Explain how the paragraph's concluding sentence and the essay's conclusion are similar and different. Discuss whether you think the added information ends the essay in an interesting and effective manner.

ACTIVITY 5

Select a paragraph that you have already written for this class and expand it into an essay using method 1. In other words, do the following:

- Select a paragraph whose ideas you can expand effectively.
- Brainstorm until you have gathered enough ideas to expand each support point into a separate body paragraph, as in the samples you just read.
- Fill in an outline for your essay (you may download an outline form from **bedfordstmartins.com/touchstones**, Useful Forms).
- Draft and revise your essay.

METHOD 2: EXPAND THE MAIN IDEA OF YOUR PARAGRAPH

The second method for moving from paragraph to essay is to expand the main idea of your paragraph and add new support points that were not part of your original composition. In this way, your original paragraph stays the same and becomes one body paragraph within the essay.

In the samples that follow, notice that the paragraph stays exactly the same and becomes the first body paragraph, in light green, in the essay. Then, the second and third body paragraphs provide new information that was not part of the original paragraph.

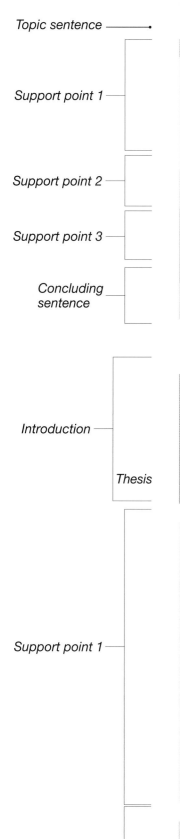

Topic sentence

Support point 1

Support point 2

Support point 3

Concluding sentence

Introduction

Thesis

Support point 1

The Paragraph

My summer job after high school really motivated me to get a college education. In the first place, I got my summer job because my friend was continually talking about his iPad, and I wanted to buy one. The Top Shop, a hat booth on Main Street, was hiring, and I got the job. But by noon on my first day, I learned that the hat booth was an oven. I was roasting. Plus, I had to be on my feet all day, from 9:00 in the morning until 4:00 in the afternoon. During the lunch hour when the street was quieter, I fought boredom. In the second place, each week I'd come home and tally what I'd saved. In Montana, minimum wage is $7.67 an hour. As a result, it took over a month to save up for my iPad. Finally, buying the iPad took half my summer wages. I ended up on campus as a freshman with very little spending money. It might have been smarter to save all my wages to bring to school, and then buy the iPad later in the year, or even the following summer. From this job experience, I learned that my future needs to include challenging work and decent money— and a college education is the best way to get there.

The Essay

I've sold a lot of things since I was 16. I started out selling hats to tourists visiting Yellowstone National Park during their summer vacation. Then I sold tools in the Ace Hardware store in my neighborhood. The next summer, I sold coffee drinks in a café. To this day, I have not had a summer job I liked. My background in retail really motivated me to get a college degree. The lack of challenge in my retail jobs, the low wages, and the effort involved in saving money reinforced my commitment to pursuing a college degree in engineering.

My summer job after high school really motivated me to get a college education. In the first place, I got my summer job because my friend was continually talking about his iPad, and I wanted to buy one. The Top Shop, a hat booth on Main Street, was hiring, and I got the job. But by noon on my first day, I learned that the hat booth was an oven. I was roasting. Plus, I had to be on my feet all day, from 9:00 in the morning until 4:00 in the afternoon. During the lunch hour when the street was quieter, I fought boredom. In the second place, each week I'd come home and tally what I'd saved. In Montana, minimum wage is $7.67 an hour. As a result, it took over a month to save up for my iPad. Finally, buying the iPad took half my summer wages. I ended up on campus as a freshman with very little spending money. It might have been smarter to save all my wages to bring to school, and then buy the iPad later in the year, or even the following summer. From this job experience, I learned that my future needs to include challenging work and decent money— and a college education is the best way to get there.

My next retail job was at Ace Hardware. To begin with, I liked learning about the tools, especially the construction power tools like table saws, jigsaws, and nail guns. I enjoyed paint mixing, too. I liked operating the mixer, and I liked following paint recipes to mix the right color. However, what I didn't like about the job were the slow hours between 1:00 and 5:00 P.M. Since most people are working during the day, the store's best customers during these hours were kids coming in for candy bars or ice cream sandwiches. This was my first experience of getting paid for doing nothing. I loved the money, but it didn't feel right to be so bored on the job. Some days, I stood in back and watched the clock for a quarter of an hour. The dullness made me feel like my life was slipping past me. The second thing that bothered me about this job was the wage. It was so low that my savings were usually gone by Christmas, and I ended up using most of my money for gas and occasional trips to McDonalds with my friends. When I complained to my dad or my uncle, they would tell me, well, that's why it's called a job. I thought a lot about that answer. I didn't want to believe that all jobs had to be dull and low paying. That experience only reinforced my commitment to get a college degree.

Support point 2

My last retail job, the summer after my junior year, was in a coffee shop. Though this job was also retail, I was selling drinks instead of hats or tools. I liked this job better because I was rarely staring at the clock. The place was busy; we were at the entrance to a national park, so we got lots of tourists in the café. My time as a barista flew by. I got very good at working the espresso maker. I had regulars who worked in neighboring shops and knew my shift because they liked the way I made their drinks. This gave me my first taste of pride in my work. By the end of the summer, however, I could make lattes in my sleep. I had mastered the hardest part of that job, which was to put out good product during a stressful, crowded rush. The challenge was over. Also, I was again working for minimum wage. My savings were gone by Christmas, and I had to go back to work to make it through spring. I longed to feel this same kind of pride, with satisfied customers, only I wanted to use my brain and make enough to really save for the future. I had a friend whose dad was an engineer for the city, and I began to talk to him about his work. He worked long hours, but he seemed truly excited by the projects he was developing, a remodeled city hall and several highway projects for the mountain pass.

Support point 3

Though I set out to write this essay just to discuss the horrible jobs I had before I got to college, I see now that each of those jobs taught me a valuable lesson. I saw firsthand that unskilled labor can lack challenge and financial rewards. Next summer, I hope to get my first engineering internship with a local engineering firm. I know the hours will be long and I may have to do a lot of things I don't like doing, but I can get through it. In summary, I think I can survive any challenges as long as I am working toward a satisfactory goal and a life beyond retail.

Conclusion

ACTIVITY 6

Fill in the two outlines below based on the sample paragraph and essay that you've just read. Do the following:

- Fill in the paragraph outline first.
- Next, fill in the essay outline. Each part of the essay should correspond to a similar part in the paragraph.

Paragraph Outline

TOPIC SENTENCE _____

_____

_____

SUPPORT POINT 1 _____

_____

EXAMPLES _____

_____

SUPPORT POINT 2 _____

_____

EXAMPLES _____

_____

SUPPORT POINT 3 _____

_____

Essay Outline

THESIS STATEMENT _____

_____

_____

_____

_____

_____

TOPIC SENTENCE 1 _____

_____

SUPPORT POINTS _____

_____

_____

_____

_____

TOPIC SENTENCE 2 _____

_____

SUPPORT POINTS _____

_____

_____

_____

_____

TOPIC SENTENCE 3 _____

_____

EXAMPLES _____   **SUPPORT POINTS** _____

_____   _____

_____   _____

_____

_____

_____

CONCLUSION _____   **CONCLUSION** _____

_____   _____

_____   _____

ACTIVITY 7: Teamwork

Working with a few of your classmates, answer the following questions about the paragraph and essay used to illustrate method 2.

1. What is the topic sentence of the paragraph? What is the thesis statement of the essay? How are these sentences similar or different? Why is the thesis statement more appropriate for a full essay?

2. What two new topic sentences have been added to the essay (in the second and third body paragraphs)? How are the ideas in these topic sentences related to the topic sentence of the first body paragraph?

3. Are any of the support points or examples in the new body paragraphs present in the original paragraph? If so, what are they?

If you use method 2 when moving from paragraph to essay, you will need to know how to expand your main idea. Here are a few examples:

Main Idea (paragraph):	Love is an emotion that has played an important role in my life.
Thesis (essay):	Several powerful emotions have ruled my life.
Main Idea (paragraph):	Eating junk food has been the cause of my poor health.
Thesis (essay):	Irresponsible eating habits have been the cause of my poor health.
Main Idea (paragraph):	Facebook offers great ways for family and friends to stay in touch.
Thesis (essay):	The Internet has provided a variety of ways for family and friends to stay in touch.

ACTIVITY 8

Select a paragraph that you have already written for this class and expand it into an essay using method 2. In other words, do the following:

- Expand your main idea into a broader thesis that will allow you to add new support points that were not part of your original paragraph.
- Brainstorm until you have gathered enough ideas for your new body paragraphs.
- Fill in an outline for your essay (outline forms are downloadable from **bedfordstmartins.com/touchstones**, Useful Forms).
- Draft and revise your essay.

Power Tip

For help writing opening and concluding paragraphs, see Chapter 9, pages 196–204 and 205–8.

Power Tip

For more in-depth coverage of problems in outlines, see Chapter 5, pages 111–16.

Solving Problems in Essay Outlines

After completing your outline—and before drafting your composition—it is a good idea to double-check the outline to make sure that it is free of three common problems:

- an item that does not fit
- an item that repeats another item
- an item that is unclear

An Item That Does Not Fit

An item does not fit when it is not clearly connected to the idea that it is supporting. In an essay outline, this happens in two cases: 1) when one of the topic sentences does not fit clearly with the main idea, and 2) when a support point in an individual paragraph does not fit clearly with the paragraph's topic sentence. Look at the following example:

MAIN IDEA	To succeed in college, I had to learn to balance my personal life and my academic life.
TOPIC SENTENCE 1	To begin with, I had to go out less in the evenings and on weekends in order to study.
TOPIC SENTENCE 2	Next, I had to find a new part-time job that fit with my school schedule.
TOPIC SENTENCE 3	Finally, I had a fight with my girlfriend and we ended our two-year relationship.

Notice that the third topic sentence does not fit clearly with the main idea because it does not connect the author's relationship with his girlfriend to his academic life. He must make this connection clear in his topic sentence, or it will not fit. A better example might be, *Finally, my girlfriend and I had to plan our time together to fit around my homework and class schedule.*

When you have finished an outline, first read each support point together with the main idea to make sure the point fits the main idea. Then, check the related examples under each support point to make sure they belong. If they do not, change them so that they fit better.

An Item That Repeats Another Item

An item repeats another item when both items express the same basic idea. Often, we do not recognize this repetition because we have changed the words. Look at the following example:

MAIN IDEA	To succeed in college, I had to learn to balance my personal life and my academic life.
TOPIC SENTENCE 1	To begin with, I had to go out less in the evenings and on weekends in order to study.
TOPIC SENTENCE 2	Next, I had to find a new part-time job that fit with my school schedule.
TOPIC SENTENCE 3	Finally, I had to resist the urge to party and play in order to stay at home and finish my homework.

Notice that topic sentences 1 and 3 express the same basic idea even though the words have been changed. The author will need to substitute one of these topic sentences with a new topic sentence that expresses a distinct idea.

An Item That Is Unclear

An item is unclear (or *vague*) when it expresses an idea that is not specific enough. An unclear item in your outline can lead to a serious breakdown of organization. Always try to correct any unclear items *before* you attempt to write your paragraph. Take a look at the following example:

MAIN IDEA	To succeed in college, I had to learn to balance my personal life and my academic life.
TOPIC SENTENCE 1	To begin with, I had to go out less in the evenings and on weekends in order to study.
TOPIC SENTENCE 2	Next, I had to do the right thing every time to maintain a balance.
TOPIC SENTENCE 3	Finally, I had to find a new part-time job that fit with my school schedule.

In the second topic sentence, notice the unclear phrase *do the right thing every time*. Reading this phrase, we have to guess at what the author means. Although the author may know what he intends to say, he should state his idea clearly so that someone who does not know him could understand, too. If not, he runs the risk of writing a vague paragraph in his essay.

Below is the complete sample outline from above that has been made error-free. Notice that all the topic sentences fit with the main idea, no item repeats another item, and no item is unclear.

MAIN IDEA	To succeed in college, I had to learn to balance my personal life and my academic life.
TOPIC SENTENCE 1	To begin with, I had to go out less in the evenings and on weekends in order to study.
TOPIC SENTENCE 2	Next, I had to train myself to attend class every day even when I felt like ditching school.
TOPIC SENTENCE 3	Finally, I had to find a new part-time job that fit with my school schedule.

The following activity will give you practice in identifying multiple problems in an outline.

ACTIVITY 9: Mastery Test or Teamwork

In each outline below, cross out and label any item that does not fit, repeats another item, or is unclear.

1. Tip: Find three errors in the following outline.

MAIN IDEA	Although my father wanted me to become an architect like him, I discovered that my academic and professional interests were different from his.
TOPIC SENTENCE 1	In the first place, I tried architecture but it wasn't for me.
SUPPORT POINTS	– I was never good at drawing or math calculations.
	– I took an Intro to Architecture class and hated it.
	– I don't have the basic skills used in architecture.
	– I worked in my dad's office one summer and was bored.
TOPIC SENTENCE 2	In the second place, I got interested in geology when I was a kid.
SUPPORT POINTS	– I loved collecting rocks and minerals.
	– I loved going to the library.
	– I loved the geology class I took in high school.
TOPIC SENTENCE 3	Third, when I switched my major to geology in college, I knew I had found my career path.
SUPPORT POINTS	– The courses I took in my junior and senior year.
	– My professors saw my passion for geology and encouraged me.
	– I attended a five-week geology course at the Grand Canyon and loved it.
	– I've already picked out two graduate schools with strong geology departments.

2. Tip: Find four errors in the following outline.

MAIN IDEA	My parents' lives are very different from my own.
TOPIC SENTENCE 1	To begin with, the way my parents grew up.

SUPPORT POINTS
- They lived in adobe huts with no electricity.
- They had to quit school and work in the fields.
- They had a poor lifestyle.
- They ate simple food with poor nutrition.

TOPIC SENTENCE 2 Second, my parents have traditional beliefs.

SUPPORT POINTS
- They have their own beliefs.
- They believe in traditional gender roles.
- They believe in keeping their Mexican heritage pure.

TOPIC SENTENCE 3 Third, my parents had limited opportunities for growth.

SUPPORT POINTS
- They never traveled outside Mexico and the United States.
- They are now in their 60s.
- They did not have a chance to become computer literate.
- They did not go to college.

3. Tip: Find three errors in the following outline.

MAIN IDEA My Internet addiction was taking over my life.

TOPIC SENTENCE 1 For starters, I was going broke and getting into debt on different Web sites.

SUPPORT POINTS
- buying too much on eBay
- eBay had a lot of great deals.
- losing too much gambling on Win Palace
- ordering video games at Players' Choice

TOPIC SENTENCE 2 Next, I was spending all my time online.

SUPPORT POINTS
- playing video games
- bidding on eBay
- checking out my friends' Facebook walls
- It was getting real bad.

TOPIC SENTENCE 3 Finally, I lost my real friendships to "virtual" friendships.

SUPPORT POINTS
- only met girls on OkCupid
- too much virtual dating
- preferred interactive gaming Web sites to hanging with friends
- tweeting to strangers instead of real conversations

BRINGING IT ALL TOGETHER:
Moving from Paragraphs to Essays

In this chapter, you have learned how to move from writing paragraphs to writing essays. Confirm your knowledge by filling in the blank spaces in the following sentences. If you need help, review the pages listed after each sentence. Finally, check off each item to confirm your understanding of the material.

✔ Academic paragraphs and essays share three features: 1) _____ _____, 2) _____ _____, and 3) _____. (page 174)

✔ A standard college essay contains three main features: 1) _____ _____, 2) _____, and 3) _____. (page 174)

✔ In an academic paragraph, the main idea is written in the _____. In a short essay, the main idea is written in the _____. (page 177)

✔ There are two methods for expanding an academic paragraph into an essay. Method 1 involves expanding _____ of the paragraph into a separate body paragraph in the essay. Method 2 involves expanding _____ of the paragraph, and adding _____ that were not a part of your original composition. (pages 181, 185)

✔ Three common problems in essay outlines are 1) _____, 2) _____, and 3) _____. (page 190)

JOURNAL WRITING: 10–15 minutes

Describe the different places where you study. Discuss what they look like, where they are located, and the advantages or disadvantages of each of these places. Are they quiet? Noisy? Spacious? Cramped? Open all hours or only part of the day? Last, discuss a few places where you would like to study but have not yet. Explain why these places attract you for studying and when you will begin studying there.

CHAPTER 9

Composing and Revising Your Essay

Test your understanding of how to compose and revise your essay by completing this quiz first. You may know more than you think.

For each question, select all the answers that apply.

WHAT DO YOU KNOW?

1. **What are some useful ways to get your reader's attention in the introduction?**
   ___ Start with a question.
   ___ Start with a big generalization.
   ___ Start with a story.
   ___ Start by repeating the assignment word for word.

2. **What should your essay's thesis statement do?**
   ___ State the main idea as clearly, directly, and powerfully as possible.
   ___ State any difficulties you're having with the assignment.
   ___ Identify the topic for the essay.
   ___ Express a controversial opinion.

3. **What is the major difference between a topic sentence (paragraph) and a thesis statement (essay)?**
   ___ A topic sentence has more words.
   ___ A topic sentence identifies support points.
   ___ The idea in a thesis statement has a broader scope.
   ___ A thesis statement is more creative.

4. **What are some strategies for writing a fresh, thoughtful conclusion?**
   ___ Restate the main idea as simply and mechanically as possible.
   ___ Give the reader some advice.
   ___ Go slightly off topic to distract the reader.
   ___ Make a prediction about your topic in the future.

5. **When you revise your essay, what should you make sure?**
   ___ that you have not accidentally changed the idea in the thesis statement
   ___ that you have not accidentally changed the ideas in the topic sentences for the paragraphs
   ___ that the topic sentences introduce new ideas not listed in your outline
   ___ that the examples and details fit the topic sentences and support points

Composing an Academic Essay

As you learned in the last chapter, creating an error-free outline gives you a big advantage in writing your essay. If you follow the parts of your outline step by step, you'll be on your way to achieving a clearly organized composition.

Here is a review of the parts of an essay outline and how those parts become the actual essay. (See Chapter 8, pages 177–80, for a more in-depth explanation of the essay outline.)

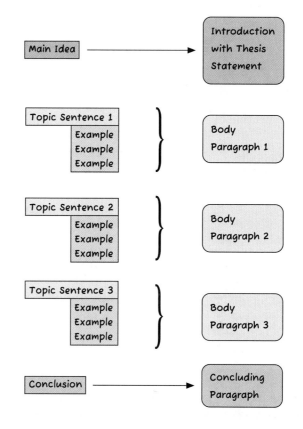

Now, let's look closely at each step in drafting the essay.

Power Tip
Remember that before you outline your essay, you will most likely brainstorm for ideas and narrow your topic. To refresh your skills in generating essay topics through brainstorming or in narrowing a topic, see Chapter 3, pages 45–57.

Writing the Introduction

To begin your essay, you will need to write an introductory paragraph with a thesis statement (more on this later in the chapter). The introduction has two basic purposes:

1. to "hook" your reader
2. to present your thesis

Let's look at these tasks one at a time.

HOOKING THE READER

When you "hook" your reader's attention, you get him or her interested in your essay by opening with a clever idea. You can usually develop this hook in a few carefully crafted sentences; you do not want the hook to get out of control and become a distraction for the reader. Remember, the *main point* of the introduction is to deliver the thesis statement for your essay.

You can hook your reader by using one of five strategies. Start the introduction with:

1. a question or series of questions
2. a story (about yourself or someone else)
3. a comparison (*x* is like *y*)
4. an imaginary scenario (*What if . . .*, *Imagine that . . .*)
5. a quotation

To understand how these strategies work, let's look at some sample opening paragraphs. As you read the following samples, consider how effective each might be in "hooking" the reader, getting him or her interested in your topic. (Note that the thesis statement is underscored in all of them.)

Starting with a Question or a Series of Questions

What is five feet three, dressed in bright yellow or green, and sure to make you smile? The answer is my best friend, Ben. <u>I have never met anyone who connects so naturally with others as Ben.</u>

Starting with a Story (about yourself or someone else)

Every other week, Birdie Laughlin takes out the pills she needs to control her diabetes and high blood pressure and cuts them in half so that they can stretch to another week. Every day, she rubs soothing clove oil onto her sore gums and rotting teeth because she cannot afford dental care. And because she cannot afford doctor's visits, she and her children take vitamin C tablets every morning and cross their fingers. "We just can't get sick," Birdie says. "Period." <u>Like the millions of other uninsured and underinsured Americans, Birdie is forced to take chances with her health every day.</u>

Starting with a Comparison (x is like y)

Some people say that Wikipedia is like a big, nasty stew that no one should eat because anyone can throw anything into the mix. Although I see their point, I think Wikipedia can be quite tasty and nutritious if it's sampled carefully. I treat it like a buffet, reading widely about a topic to get my mental juices flowing. Then, I check any information I might want to use against other sources. <u>In short, Wikipedia is a good tool for learning about the world if readers use it in a careful way.</u>

Starting with an Imaginary Scenario (What if . . . , Imagine that . . .)

Imagine that this is your daily commute: You leave your home, walk two or three blocks to a sparkling, space-age train station, and board a comfortable and clean bullet train. During your commute, you have no worries about traffic or delays. Instead, you read, call or text on your cell, or just relax. In mere minutes, you're at your destination. More and more communities want to make this scenario a reality, and it's not hard to see why: High-speed rail service is good for people, the environment, and society as a whole.

Starting with a Quotation

The writer and humorist Mark Twain once observed, "The dog is a gentleman; I hope to go to his heaven, not man's." I completely agree. Spending time with a dog can be a stress-free, peaceful experience. In fact, my gentle, wise, and kind dog, Nate, is better company than many people I know.

ACTIVITY 1: Teamwork

Reread the five introductions above and decide which one you think will "hook" the reader most effectively. Then, get together with a few of your classmates and discuss your choices. Have a debate to see if you can agree on the introduction or strategy that most effectively hooks the reader. Be ready to share your ideas with the whole class.

ACTIVITY 2

Read each of the following introductions and identify the hooking strategy that is used. Then, read the thesis statement (underscored) and decide what the main idea for the essay is. In the space provided, use your own words to explain the main idea for the essay. (You may use a few key words from the thesis statement, but do not copy the entire sentence.)

1. The Indian political leader Mahatma Gandhi once said, "Happiness is when what you think, what you say, and what you do are in harmony." As a female growing up in the 1950s, I was raised to always be polite, which sometimes meant speaking and acting in contradiction to what I believed. With time and experience, however, I have learned to live more honestly, and I have truly found the happiness that Gandhi spoke of.

Strategy used:

_____

Main idea (thesis) for this essay, in your own words:

_____

2. Imagine a future in which friendly robots clean our homes to our specifications, lovingly care for our pets and children, and even laugh at our jokes. That future is already here, to some extent. Recently, researchers have demonstrated robots that interact with humans and show emotions, essential qualities for being able to meet our personal and practical needs.

Strategy used:

_____

Main idea (thesis) for this essay, in your own words:

_____

_____

3. He was born to a single mother and lived in poverty for most of his childhood. Growing up, he struggled in school until a few teachers took him under their wing and made sure he got extra help. As a teenager, he started to work evenings and weekends to help his mother make ends meet. Eventually, he became the first person in his family to attend college, where he took a special interest in public policy. This is the story of Carlos Trevo, one of the top candidates for mayor of our economically devastated city. Because no other candidate understands the trials of struggling families better than Mr. Trevo, I believe that he is in the best position to lead our city in these trying times.

Strategy used:

_____

Main idea (thesis) for this essay, in your own words:

_____

_____

4. Who set the arson fire at Maria's Hair Salon? How did those huge piles of trash end up near the gates of the city park? Who broke into City Sounds and stole thousands of dollars' worth of audio equipment? If some city officials get their way, we may soon get the answers to questions like these. These officials are proposing the installation of surveillance cameras around town. Although this plan has obvious benefits, not everyone wants to live life under surveillance.

Strategy used:

_____

Main idea (thesis) for this essay, in your own words:

_____

_____

CONTINUED >

5. My grandmother used to compare old friendships to old shoes. Both are comfortable, if not always exciting. New friendships, in contrast, can be like wearing high heels. Since I moved to a trendy neighborhood downtown, I'm trying to balance on some very tall stilettos. All the gossip and intrigue among my new friends makes me shaky and uncertain, like I might trip and take a big fall.

Strategy used:

_____

Main idea (thesis) for this essay, in your own words:

_____

_____

ACTIVITY 3: Teamwork

Reread the five introductions above and decide which one you think will "hook" the reader most effectively. Then, get together with a few of your classmates and discuss your choices. Have a debate to see if you can agree on the introduction or strategy that most effectively hooks the reader. Be ready to share your ideas with the whole class.

ACTIVITY 4

Use one of your completed outlines from Chapter 8, and on a separate sheet of paper (or on a computer), begin to draft your essay. First, write three different introductions, using three of the hooking strategies. When you have finished, select the one introduction that you think will most effectively hook your reader. Do not write the thesis statement yet.

WRITING AN EFFECTIVE THESIS STATEMENT

Once you have hooked your reader's attention, it's time to present the main idea of your essay. You want to do this as clearly, directly, and powerfully as possible in one complete sentence. This sentence is called the **thesis statement**.

The thesis statement in an essay answers the question, "What is the main point I want to make about my topic?" You will find the answer in your brainstorming and, in some cases, in discussion with your peers and your instructor. Each essay contains just one thesis statement, presented in the introduction.

To write a thesis statement, simply transfer the main idea from your outline, making sure that it is a complete sentence with a subject and a verb. You may modify the language in the sentence to make it more original and interesting, but do not accidentally change the meaning. (More on this later.)

Once you have written the thesis statement, you should verify that it does two things: 1) It identifies the topic, and 2) it expresses your particular idea, point of view, or feeling about the topic.

Thesis Statement versus Topic Sentence

As you may have noticed, the purpose of a basic thesis statement and that of a basic topic sentence are very similar. The major difference between them is the scope of the idea presented. For example, a topic sentence should express an idea that can be fully developed in just one paragraph. In contrast, a thesis statement should express an idea that will require several paragraphs — plus an introduction and a conclusion — to fully develop.

Now, take a look. In each of the following thesis statements, the assigned topic has a single underline and the student's particular idea, point of view, or feeling has a double underline. Each idea is large enough in scope to develop over the course of a short essay.

ASSIGNED TOPIC *Discuss the influential people in your life.*

MAIN IDEA My aunt and my coach have influenced me.

THESIS STATEMENT My aunt Reese and Coach Baldwin have influenced me to make family and sports the center of my life.

ASSIGNED TOPIC *Discuss something you would like to change about your past.*

MAIN IDEA I'd like to change the time I wasted in school.

THESIS STATEMENT If I could change one thing about my past, I'd take all the wasted educational opportunities and turn them into educational accomplishments.

ASSIGNED TOPIC *Discuss money.*

MAIN IDEA I learned my financial habits from my parents.

THESIS STATEMENT My financial habits have all come from my parents' example of poor money management.

> **Power Tip**
> If you are writing an essay in response to an assigned topic, it is important that the thesis (and the entire essay) respond *directly* to the topic. For instance, you can use some key words from the topic to show that your response is direct and focused. For more information on using key words from the assignment, see Chapter 5, page 99.

ACTIVITY 5

In each of the following thesis statements, underline the assigned topic once. Then, double-underline the student's particular idea, point of view, or feeling about the topic.

CONTINUED >

EXAMPLE:

ASSIGNED TOPIC   *Discuss your romantic experiences.*

MAIN IDEA   I usually fall in love with unavailable girls.

THESIS STATEMENT   Most of my romantic experiences have been disappointing because I usually fall in love with unavailable girls.

1. **ASSIGNED TOPIC**   *Discuss your present or future life partner.*

   MAIN IDEA   My life partner must have an open mind.

   THESIS STATEMENT   My future life partner must possess an open mind about religion, gender roles, and raising children.

2. **ASSIGNED TOPIC**   *Discuss something you are passionate about.*

   MAIN IDEA   I am passionate about rescuing animals.

   THESIS STATEMENT   Since I was a child, my greatest passion in life has been rescuing hurt and abandoned animals.

3. **ASSIGNED TOPIC**   *Discuss a human hardship.*

   MAIN IDEA   I've had experience with poverty.

   THESIS STATEMENT   Coming from a developing nation, I've had lots of personal experience with the hardship of poverty.

4. **ASSIGNED TOPIC**   *Discuss changes you would make in your current housing situation.*

   MAIN IDEA   I would like my roommates to be more responsible.

   THESIS STATEMENT   My current housing situation could be much better if my three roommates were more responsible.

5. **ASSIGNED TOPIC**   *Discuss sacrifices as a part of life.*

   MAIN IDEA   I've made many sacrifices to help my family.

   THESIS STATEMENT   Everyone has to make sacrifices in life, but the sacrifices I've made for my family have been excessive and unfair.

AVOIDING COMMON PROBLEMS WITH THESIS STATEMENTS

When writing thesis statements for essays, be careful to avoid the same problems that can occur with topic sentences in paragraphs (see Chapter 6, pages 124–30). These problems are:

1. accidentally changing the meaning of your main idea (by leaving out key words, changing key words, or adding new information that's not clearly connected to the main idea)

2. asking a question (this might make your original point or opinion about the topic unclear)

3. making an announcement (this might keep you from expressing your original point or opinion about the topic)

4. writing a sentence fragment (this is ungrammatical and you might leave out your original point or opinion)

Power Tip
For more on fragments, see Chapter 16, page 361, and Chapter 18, page 423.

ACTIVITY 6

Read the following thesis statements. Identify the main problem by writing it on the line that follows. If the thesis statement is effective, then write "okay."

EXAMPLE: Main idea: There are various ways to quit smoking.

Thesis statement: In this essay, I will discuss ways to quit smoking.

Problem: _This thesis statement makes an announcement._

1. **Main idea:** Pets in nursing homes can help residents.

   Thesis statements

   a. Pets are good medicine in nursing homes.

   Problem: _____

   b. Everyone should have a pet.

   Problem: _____

   c. Do pets help nursing home residents?

   Problem: _____

   d. Nursing home residents are doing better when they keep pets.

   Problem: _____

   e. In my essay, I will talk about pets in nursing homes.

   Problem: _____

2. **Main idea:** My uncle Jarvis has been a role model for me.

   Thesis statements

   a. My uncle Jarvis has been a role model for me throughout my life.

   Problem: _____

   b. A role model who has truly shaped my life.

   Problem: _____

   c. My uncle Jarvis is our family historian.

   Problem: _____

   d. Does everyone need a role model?

   Problem: _____

   e. My brother is an excellent role model for his children.

   Problem: _____

CONTINUED >

3. **Main idea:** Today, vegetarian diets have become tasty as well as healthy.

Thesis statements

a. A healthy diet does not have to be bland, nor must it cost a lot of money.

   Problem: _____

b. What makes vegetarian diets today tasty as well as healthy?

   Problem: _____

c. Becoming not just healthy but also more tasty.

   Problem: _____

d. Vegetarian diets are healthier and tastier than ever.

   Problem: _____

e. In this essay, I will explain how a vegetarian diet can be healthy and tasty.

   Problem: _____

ACTIVITY 7

In the draft of your essay, add a thesis statement to your introduction. Underline your topic once, and then double-underline your particular idea, point of view, or feeling about the topic.

Writing the Body Paragraphs

To develop your essay fully, you will need to write two or more body paragraphs. As you know from Chapter 6, the key features of academic paragraphs are:

- a topic sentence that expresses the main idea for that paragraph
- support points that develop your topic
- related examples and additional details that develop each support point as precisely and colorfully as possible
- transitional expressions that allow you to move smoothly from one support point, example, or detail to another

Power Tip
For more on using transitional expressions in essays, see Chapter 8, page 179.

Power Tip
For more on writing complete and error-free essay outlines, see Chapter 8, pages 180–81.

When writing the body paragraphs, be careful to follow your outline. If the outline is complete and error-free, you have a good chance of writing successful body paragraphs that develop your essay's main idea. (To learn more about revising and editing your body paragraphs, see pages 210–13 of this chapter.)

ACTIVITY 8

Write the body paragraphs of your essay one at a time, following your outline. Remember to add transitional expressions between the paragraphs and within the paragraphs (see Chapter 8, page 179).

Writing the Conclusion

After you have written an introduction and two or more body paragraphs, you will need to complete your essay with a conclusion. If you do not add a conclusion, your last body paragraph will leave readers hanging, and they will not have the sense of a satisfying finish.

The conclusion for an academic essay can be short or long, depending on the specific requirements of the assignment. Many instructors are satisfied if you briefly restate your main idea; other instructors expect the conclusion to be a well-developed paragraph in which you consolidate and explore the best ideas from the essay. Because instructors have different expectations for the conclusion, be sure to ask for clarification if you are uncertain about what to include.

Here are five strategies for writing a brief conclusion:

1. giving advice to the reader
2. making a prediction
3. ending with some thought-provoking questions
4. making a personal growth statement
5. finishing the story that you used in your introduction (if you began with a story)

Following are sample conclusions for each strategy. Each conclusion corresponds to one of the sample introductions on pages 197–98 of this chapter.

Giving Advice to the Reader

Often, when we're feeling lonely, we call an old friend, browse Facebook, or even go to the neighborhood café. While human beings can be great company, dogs can be even better. My own dog, Nate, has been one of my closest and best companions. I hate to think of people depriving themselves of such a good, unconditional friendship. Everyone should consider getting a pet, and in my opinion, a dog is the best pet to have.

Making a Prediction

High-speed rail service may take several years to implement in certain communities, especially those with no current train service. Rail advocates will have to be willing to work through bureaucracies and opposition. However, I predict that high-speed rail eventually will become one of the major modes of transportation between cities and their suburbs because rail service offers the best option for reducing traffic, making commuting more pleasant, and reducing auto emissions.

Ending with Some Thought-Provoking Questions

Should you use Wikipedia? Aren't there better sources of information? You will have to answer those questions for yourself, and the answers will depend at least to some degree on what you are using the information for. But when I want to get a quick, fun overview of any topic, I will continue to enjoy grazing (carefully) from the Wikipedia buffet.

Making a Personal Growth Statement

Often, I think how grateful I am that I met Ben that day in math class. He has taught me so much: how to reach out to others, how to make life fun, and, most important, how to be a good friend. I hope that I will continue to learn from our relationship, and I hope that I will always be as good a friend to Ben as he is to me.

Finishing the Story That You Used in Your Introduction

Birdie Laughlin continues to struggle with caring for herself and her children, and with the fear and uncertainties that go along with being uninsured. Over the past month, she has developed a pain in her side, and though she knows she shouldn't ignore it, she is afraid to go to the doctor. "What if it's something bad?" she asks. Almost worse, Birdie says, is the fear that she won't be able to afford to treat it. She continues to take chances because she doesn't have any other choice, at least for now.

ACTIVITY 9: Teamwork

Reread the five conclusions above and decide which one leaves you thinking most deeply about the topic. Then, get together with a few of your classmates and discuss your choices. Have a debate to see if you can agree on the conclusion that leaves the reader thinking most deeply about the topic. Be ready to share your ideas with the whole class.

ACTIVITY 10

Read each of the following conclusions and identify the strategy used.

1. Although in some ways I am still the same polite person that I was growing up in the 1950s, I have come to understand the great costs of trying to be someone I am not. Now, many years, one divorce, and a few unhappy friendships later, I try to live according to my beliefs in every way that I can. I don't worry that others won't accept me because I don't believe in God or because I object to remarks that I find offensive. I have found happiness in being myself and in knowing that true friends love and accept me for who I am.

Strategy used:

2. I look forward to the day when I'll wake up to a fun game of chess with my robot, who will then make my favorite breakfast while remarking on news items I read to him from the paper. I truly believe that such a day is coming soon, thanks to all of the recent innovations in creating robots who can react to our emotions and have their own feelings. Perhaps I should start getting the guest room ready!

Strategy used:

3. Mr. Trevo has not forgotten his roots as a struggling child in this city. Almost every day, he visits his old neighborhood and checks in on his mother, who still lives on the same street, though in a much better apartment, thanks to her son's successes. Mr. Trevo also continues to work in the city's neighborhoods, both as a public official and as a volunteer. He is proud of the city where he found his way to a bright future, and we should be proud to call him our mayor.

Strategy used:

4. Would citywide surveillance cameras invade privacy? Maybe. Would they send a message that no one can be trusted? Quite possibly. There is no doubt that the cameras are controversial, and they are strongly opposed by those who fear being observed by "Big Brother." After carefully considering the pros and cons of the cameras, however, I have come to the conclusion that the cameras' value in deterring and helping to solve crimes outweighs their drawbacks. Yes, we would in some ways be living life under surveillance, but I believe that we would also be considerably safer.

Strategy used:

5. My new friendships still seem like high heels — fun even if sometimes uncomfortable. However, I have kept some good advice in mind, and I will share it with you: Always be open to the excitement of new friendships, but never lose touch with your old pals. Yes, it's fun to run around town in the heels, but we can never do without the comfortable slippers that are waiting for us back home.

Strategy used:

ACTIVITY 11: Teamwork

Reread the five conclusions above and decide which one leaves you thinking most deeply about the topic. Then, get together with a few of your classmates and discuss your choices. Have a debate to see if you can agree on the conclusion that leaves the reader thinking most deeply about the topic. Be ready to share your ideas with the whole class.

ACTIVITY 12

Add a concluding paragraph to the draft of your essay. First, practice writing three different conclusions, using three different strategies. When you have finished, select the one conclusion that you think is the most interesting and powerful and add it to your essay.

Revising and Editing Your Essay

When you have gained some mastery over the writing process, you will be able to produce **unified** essays that stay on track and include only information that supports the main idea. However, it's not uncommon for beginning writers to get off track while composing an essay of three to five pages, so it's especially important that you take sufficient time to revise your draft.

Revision ("re" + "vision") means looking over your compositions with a fresh eye to identify and fix any problems with unity. You will also want to check carefully for problems with grammar, mechanics (spelling, punctuation, formatting), and word choice.

The best way to make sure that you've fixed these problems is to perform your revision as carefully as you have performed the other steps in the writing process. Many students rush their revision or skip it altogether, which can seriously harm their finished product.

REVISING FOR UNITY IN AN ACADEMIC ESSAY

When you revise an essay, you need to check for unity on two levels: the "macro," or big-picture, level, and the "micro," or up-close and detailed, level. **Macro unity** means that your thesis statement and your topic sentences—the larger structures of your essay—all fit together clearly. **Micro unity** refers to the unity *within each body paragraph*: All the parts of each body paragraph (topic sentence, support points, and examples) must fit together clearly.

It's a good idea to check the macro unity of your essay first. This will ensure that the ideas in your introduction and body paragraphs flow in a smooth and logical manner. If your essay is not unified at the macro level, your reader may become confused and frustrated—and may stop reading.

If you used a complete and error-free outline to draft your essay, it's easy to check for *macro unity*. Specifically, you need to ensure that you did not accidentally change the meaning of your thesis statement or topic sentences when you drafted your essay.

An outline also helps you check for *micro unity* within each of the essay's paragraphs. Make sure that your support points are clearly connected to the paragraph's topic sentence. The related examples and details should also develop those support points clearly and effectively. The paragraphs should be free of fragments, run-ons, and points that do not fit.

Now, compare the following outline with the sample problems after it. You will see how the author of the outline ran into some problems as she drafted her essay.

MAIN IDEA	My best friend, Ben, connects naturally with others.
TOPIC SENTENCE 1	<u>First,</u> Ben attracts people easily.
SUPPORT POINTS	– He wears attention-getting clothing. – He can start a conversation with anyone. – He has an irresistible sense of humor.
TOPIC SENTENCE 2	<u>Second,</u> Ben keeps his connections strong by being a good friend in every way.
SUPPORT POINTS	– He is a good listener. – He would do anything for his friends. – He buys perfect gifts.

Problem 1: A Flawed Thesis Statement

In her draft, the student accidentally changed the meaning of her thesis statement. Take a look:

MAIN IDEA	My best friend, Ben, connects naturally with others.
THESIS STATEMENT	I have never met anyone who is as popular as Ben.

These two ideas may sound similar, but they are different enough to cause confusion for the reader. Being popular does not necessarily mean that a person connects naturally with others. With the current thesis statement, the body paragraphs would need to give examples of Ben's popularity (*All the girls want to be his girlfriend; all the guys want to be his best friend . . .*) and NOT of his special ability to connect with others.

Fix this problem by rewriting the thesis statement so that it clearly expresses the main idea for the essay:

MAIN IDEA	My best friend, Ben, connects naturally with others.
THESIS STATEMENT	I have never met anyone who connects so naturally with others as my best friend, Ben.

Problem 2: A Topic Sentence That Does Not Fit

In her draft, the student also accidentally changed the meaning of her topic sentences. Take a look:

TOPIC SENTENCE 1 (OUTLINE)	First, Ben attracts people easily.
TOPIC SENTENCE 1 (DRAFT)	First, Ben is an attractive guy.

Once again, these ideas may sound similar, but their meaning is quite different. "Ben attracts people easily" suggests a special ability that Ben has. "Ben is an attractive guy" describes his personality or physical appearance in a more general way. The support points and examples for these two topic sentences would be quite different.

Fix this problem by rewriting the topic sentence so that it clearly connects with the main idea of the essay:

| TOPIC SENTENCE 1 (OUTLINE) | *First, Ben attracts people easily.* |
| TOPIC SENTENCE 1 (DRAFT) | *First, Ben attracts people easily.* |

ACTIVITY 13

Check for *macro unity* in the draft of your essay. Make sure that the thesis statement expresses your main idea accurately. Then, confirm that the topic sentence in each paragraph connects clearly to the thesis statement.

Problem 3: Body Paragraphs That Are Not Unified

As you learned above, *micro unity* refers to the unity *within each body paragraph*: All the parts of each body paragraph (topic sentence, support points, and examples and details) must fit together clearly. There are several common ways that you can get off track when drafting a paragraph. These include:

- accidentally changing your meaning when you write a topic sentence
- accidentally changing a support point, combining it with an example, or forgetting it altogether
- forgetting a transitional expression
- including examples and details that do not fit

For a more in-depth explanation of these problems, and more activities, see Chapter 6.

Power Tip
Peer review can be a powerful way to get feedback on your essay. For more about how to conduct peer review, see Chapter 7, pages 156–58.

CHECKLIST FOR REVISING AND EDITING YOUR ESSAY

Use this checklist to revise and edit your essay.

- ❑ Does your essay have an introduction, fully developed body paragraphs, and a conclusion?
- ❑ Does your introduction include a clearly worded thesis statement that presents your essay's main idea as well as your opinion or point of view about that idea?
- ❑ Does each body paragraph have a topic sentence?
- ❑ Does each body paragraph contain support points that develop the topic effectively?
- ❑ Does your conclusion include a statement that sums up your main idea or leaves your reader thinking more deeply about your ideas?
- ❑ Have you remembered to use transitional expressions?
- ❑ Did you correct any grammar or spelling errors in your essay?

ACTIVITY 14: Mastery Test or Teamwork

Compare the outline below with the essay that follows.

- First, check the *macro unity* of the essay. Make sure that the ideas in the thesis statement and the topic sentences have not accidentally been changed.
- Next, check the *micro unity* of each body paragraph. Work slowly and carefully on one paragraph at a time, comparing each part to the outline. Make sure the support points connect clearly to each topic sentence. Watch out for items that have been changed, have been left out, or do not fit. Check the transitions.
- When you find an error, do the following:

  - Write the type of error in the margin. (For example, *detail does not fit*.)
  - For a flawed thesis statement or topic sentence, cross out the flawed sentence. Then, rewrite the sentence in the space above it.
  - For a missing transitional expression, write in the expression in the space above the sentence.
  - For a detail that does not fit, cross out the detail.

(Hint: Look for two errors at the *macro* level and six errors at the *micro* level.)

MAIN IDEA	In my freshman English class, I was proactive with my research assignment.
TOPIC SENTENCE 1	In the first place, I found all my sources by the end of week one.
SUPPORT POINTS	– For instance, I went to the library and got help. – Next, I worked in the library for six hours. – Finally, I met with my instructor to go over my sources.
TOPIC SENTENCE 2	Second, I analyzed all the sources by the end of week two.
SUPPORT POINTS	– As an illustration, I used reading strategies. – Furthermore, I got help in the Learning Center. – Finally, I discussed my results with my instructor.
TOPIC SENTENCE 3	Last, I finished writing my draft by the end of week six.
SUPPORT POINTS	– For example, I wrote the outline first. – Next, I drafted the three sections of the essay. – Last, I revised my thesis and wrote the conclusion.

CONTINUED >

On the first day of the semester, my English instructor told us that more students drop or fail the class because of the research paper than for any other reason. She said that the assignment required independent work outside of class, and that some students procrastinate and then give up at the last minute. Her warning was scary but effective. I decided right then that I would not be one of those students.

In the first place, I found all my sources by the end of the first week of class. For instance, I went to the college library to get help. Our instructor suggested that we talk to one of the research librarians to get started. Since my English class is my last class of the day, I headed straight to the library after class ended. The library was almost empty, and the research librarian seemed really happy to have a "customer." She spent time showing me all the research tools I could use (databases, books, periodicals, and so on) to find my sources. No one interrupted us the whole time. She said that would never happen later in the semester when lots of students come for help. Next, after taking a short break, I returned to the library and stayed there until closing time a few hours later. I snuck some food into the library in my backpack, and I was able to snack when the librarian wasn't looking. I was determined to find good sources for my assignment. I mostly used the online databases, which had plenty of high-quality articles for my research. When I needed additional help, I simply asked the librarian. Finally, some of my friends asked if I could help them with their research paper, but I didn't have time. The next morning, I was so excited that I showed up at 8:00 A.M. for my instructor's office hour to go over my sources. Not surprisingly, I was the only person seeking help at 8:00 A.M. on the second day of the semester. Professor Tynan was amazed by my enthusiasm, and she took almost the whole hour to review my sources and make recommendations. In the end, I only had to replace one source, and I did that the same afternoon in the library. Like the old saying "Strike while the iron is hot," my proactive approach meant that I accomplished my task quickly and got the assistance I needed.

Second, I analyzed all my sources by the end of the second week of class. As an illustration, I used a number of reading strategies that I learned in my reading class. For example, I started with the easiest sources to warm up my critical reading skills. I used different colored highlighters to mark important passages in the articles, I made notes in the margins, and I wrote a summary of each article on a separate sheet of paper. Working in this systematic and efficient way, I was able to finish each source in about one hour. I knew that I could save time if I got some help in the Learning Center. In all, I went to the center three times, and the tutors were able to give me extra time because the center (like the library) was almost empty. They helped me paraphrase difficult passages from the articles, and they checked my summaries for accuracy after I had written them. Finally, I showed up for another office hour with Professor Tynan to show her my work. Once again, I was the only student there. I brought her some fresh donuts that I'd picked up on the way to school, but she said she was on a diet. She took the time to review my analyses and summaries. Then, she discussed the articles with me and helped me prioritize them in terms of importance for my topic. As a bonus, she made suggestions about how I might organize my paper. When I left her office, I felt confident about my progress for the week.

Last, nothing could stop me. For example, I made a formal outline and checked it with the professor after class. As part of the outline, I wrote my "working thesis," knowing that I would need to modify it as I drafted the essay and became more knowledgeable about my topic. I was ready to draft the three sections of the essay. The first section

CONTINUED >

took about four hours on a Sunday afternoon. I took a break at one point to watch 15 minutes of a football game on television. The writing went so smoothly that I decided to repeat the strategy on the next two Sunday afternoons. Targeting my goals in this way motivated me, and I finished the three sections on schedule. Last, I revised the thesis with real confidence, which was satisfying. Writing the conclusion was also a pleasure because I felt like my opinions were well informed and persuasive. I rewrote the conclusion several times until the style and the vocabulary reflected my commitment and sensitivity to the issues. By the end of week five, I felt empowered and successful.

One final meeting with the professor and a few hours for revision and proofreading, and my research paper was finished. Not only did I turn it in by the sixth week of the semester, but the professor returned it within three days with enthusiastic comments and a score of 94. Then, she told the entire class about my accomplishment and encouraged others to "emulate" (her word) my proactive approach. In the future, she said, she would tell her students my story on the first day of the semester as an alternative to procrastination.

Formatting Your Essay

As important as your essay's content is, the format of your essay—how it looks on the page—is very important as well. If it is presented in a sloppy way, your instructor might take points off your grade. A sloppy paper doesn't express your seriousness about the assignment. Be sure to make a good impression.

Most instructors expect you to follow a certain format when you present an essay (check with your instructors for details). Usually, this includes listing your name, your professor's name, the class that the paper is for, and the date on the first page of your paper. Each page should have a page number, and your essay should have a title. In the end, your final edited and revised—and formatted—essay will look something like this:

1″

½″
Sweeney 1

Beth Sweeney

Double-space

Professor Juzwiak

English 110

9 Oct. 2012

Title (centered)

My Friend Ben, The Natural Connector

What is five feet three, dressed in bright yellow or green, and sure to make you smile? The answer is my best friend, Ben. I have never met anyone who connects so naturally with others as Ben.

Double-space

Indent ½ inch

First, Ben attracts people easily. For example, although he's not exactly tall or handsome, his clothing always gets attention. A case in point is his choice of T-shirts, which make ◄—1″—► people stop, think, and sometimes laugh. One of the shirts is bright yellow and says, "Make Cupcakes, Not War." Another ◄—1″—► is neon green and says, "Procrastinators of the World, Unite . . . Tomorrow." Also, people are always walking up to Ben to ask him where he gets his colorful, striped sneakers. He has several pairs in different styles, and sometimes he paints and decorates plain sneakers to create original designs. In addition to dressing for attention, Ben can start a conversation with anyone, at school or anyplace else. We met because he introduced himself to five people, including me, within the first few minutes of a freshman math class. Also, he likes to strike up conversations at restaurants and other gathering places. One time, while we were having dinner, he overheard our waitress mentioning to another table of guests her love of singing. When she came back to our table, Ben, who has an amazing voice himself, asked her about her singing . . .

Note: The bottom margin of each page should be one inch.

✎ **ACTIVITY 15**

Return to your essay. Revise and edit it carefully. Make sure that it is formatted correctly.

BRINGING IT ALL TOGETHER:
Composing and Revising Your Essay

In this chapter, you have learned how to compose and revise an academic essay. Confirm your knowledge by filling in the blank spaces in the following sentences. If you need help, review the pages listed after each sentence. Finally, check off each item to confirm your understanding of the materials.

✔ There are at least five strategies to "hook" a reader's attention in an introduction. The strategies are to start with _____

_____, _____, _____, _____,

or _____. (page 197)

✔ To be effective, a thesis statement must identify the essay's _____.
It must also express the writer's _____
about the topic. (page 201)

✔ When writing a thesis statement, avoid the following four common
errors: 1) _____, 2) _____
_____, 3) _____, and 4) _____
_____. (pages 202–3)

✔ There are at least five strategies for writing effective conclusions in an essay. These strategies help to leave the reader thinking more deeply about your topic. The strategies are 1) _____,
2) _____, 3) _____
_____, 4) _____, and 5) _____
_____. (page 205)

✔ When you revise an essay, you need to check for unity on two levels:
_____ unity and _____ unity. (page 208)

✔ Macro unity ensures that the essay's _____ and each
body paragraph's _____ clearly fit together. (page 208)

✔ Micro unity ensures that each body paragraph's _____ connect clearly to the paragraph's _____. It also ensures that you've included transitional expressions, and that the _____ and _____ in the paragraph develop the support points clearly and effectively. (page 208)

✔ Formatting your essay means listing your name, your professor's name, the class that the paper is for, and the date on the first page of your paper. Each page should also have _____, and you should give your essay _____. (page 214)

JOURNAL WRITING: 10–15 minutes

Part of being a successful college student is making mistakes and learning from those mistakes. When you learn something of value—however small—from your mistakes, they don't need to be failures. In this journal entry, discuss a mistake that you have made in college, even a small one. Describe what happened and how you could have handled the situation better. Finally, explain what lesson you learned from your mistake (if any) and how this lesson might help you in future situations.

Case Study: Writing a Successful Academic Essay

To get a clear sense of how the writing process works, take a look at the following case study that outlines Benji T.'s process of brainstorming, drafting, composing, and revising.

For his essay, Benji was assigned the following broad topic:

Write an essay about social media.

NARROWING

Power Tip
To review brainstorming techniques and how to narrow your ideas for a topic, see Chapter 3, pages 45–57.

Benji knew that his favorite method for getting his ideas down was *clustering*. In order to narrow his broad topic, he produced the following cluster:

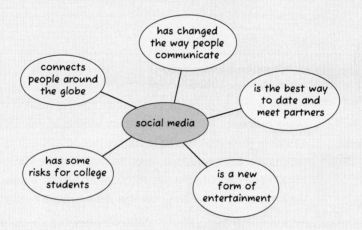

After carefully reviewing his options, Benji selected the following narrowed topic for his short essay:

Social media has risks for college students.

BRAINSTORMING

To explore his narrowed topic, Benji once again used *clustering*. Notice that his cluster has *layers* of ideas:

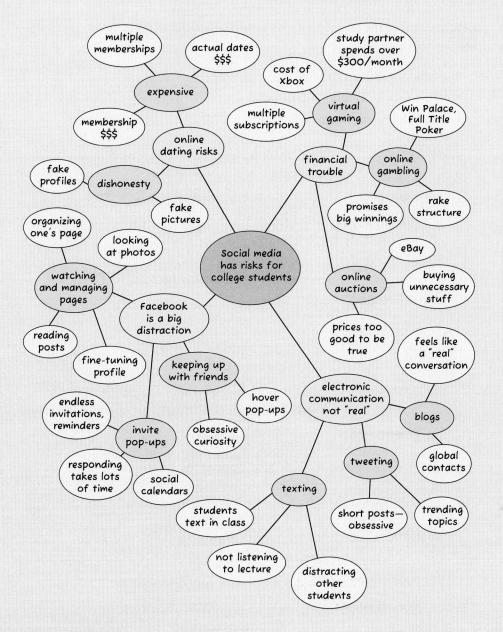

OUTLINING

After exploring his narrowed topic, Benji followed these steps to complete his outline form:

- First, he filled in the main idea.
- Then, he picked his big ideas for the topic sentences and wrote them down one at a time, as complete sentences, adding a transitional expression to each one.
- Next, he added support points for each topic sentence.

Power Tip

To review how to outline your ideas, see Chapter 5, pages 104–8.

Before drafting his essay, Benji reviewed his outline carefully for problems. He checked for:

- items that did not fit
- items that repeated other items
- items that were vague

	MAIN IDEA	Social media sites can be risky for college students.
item does not fit—not a <u>risk</u>	**TOPIC SENTENCE 1**	First, Facebook is ~~very popular~~.
	SUPPORT POINTS	– organizing pages – invite pop-ups – following friends
item repeats another item		– ~~too many invitations~~
	TOPIC SENTENCE 2	Second, life online causes financial trouble.
item does not fit—not <u>financial</u>	**SUPPORT POINTS**	– virtual gaming – ~~fun pastimes~~ – online auctions
	TOPIC SENTENCE 3	Most important, electronic communication distracts from more important forms of communication.
	SUPPORT POINTS	– texting in class – blogging vs. real conversations
item is unclear		– ~~talking is awesome~~

Then, Benji corrected the errors that he found in his outline:

MAIN IDEA	Social media sites can be risky for college students.
TOPIC SENTENCE 1	First, Facebook is very distracting.
SUPPORT POINTS	– organizing pages – invite pop-ups – following friends
TOPIC SENTENCE 2	Second, life online causes financial trouble.
SUPPORT POINTS	– virtual gaming – online gambling – online auctions
TOPIC SENTENCE 3	Most important, electronic communication distracts from more important forms of communication.
SUPPORT POINTS	– texting in class – blogging vs. real conversations – short tweets—obsessive

COMPOSING

Finally, Benji followed his outline step by step and wrote the following draft of his essay. You can see his proofreading and editing comments, which he added after composing the essay.

One phrase you rarely hear these days is "I don't know." At a party or in the park, if you want to know something or do something, you can find out more about it with just a few clicks on your smartphone, Kindle Fire, or iPad. Shopping and socializing, too, have become possible anywhere, anytime, thanks to technology. You can even keep yourself entertained by playing online games with someone on another continent by using any number of devices. However, there are risks to social media, especially for busy students. If students aren't careful, there are lots of ways that they can get in trouble.

Did I accidentally change the meaning of my thesis statement?

First, social networking sites can be very distracting. For example, Facebook is one of the most popular sites and it is dangerous because it is so addictive. Some critics call it the biggest time waster in the world. Students can spend hours looking at photographs and reading posts on pages of everyone they know. Some students become obsessed with organizing and fine-tuning their own Facebook pages as well. They want to choose the right pictures and arrange them in the right order, they want to write the funniest status updates. Most often, this time would be better spent studying. Another distraction is Facebook's invite pop-up. Facebook sends invitations and reminders of when events are happening and who is having a birthday. Reading and responding to dozens of invites and notices takes time. Students can end up spending hours planning their social calendars. Facebook offers the very tempting distraction of keeping up with friends, whether they are nearby or far away. Reading status updates can be addictive. As well, each time you hover on a friend's name, several mutual friends pop up. The site is designed to engage your curiosity. Curiosity can get the better of anyone when it comes to friends, even friends you don't know very well. Some of my friends don't use Facebook at all even though I've tried to get them interested. It's best to limit time on Facebook so that it doesn't distract you from the more important things in your life such as preparing for tests, writing essays, or doing other homework.

Is this a comma splice?

Add a transitional expression.

Does this detail really fit?

A second danger of life online is that it's easy to get into financial trouble. In particular, I used to live in Las Vegas and started gambling as soon as I was 21. Virtual gaming can cost a lot of money. Microsoft recently raised the cost of a subscription to Xbox Live from 50 dollars a month to 60. Often, students belong to several of these gaming sites, which allow them to play virtual games with people all over the globe.

Did I accidentally change the meaning of my support point?

Is this a fragment? ———

Several monthly subscriptions can quickly add up. My study partner for biology spends over 300 dollars a month in gaming subscriptions, and he never has money for food. Furthermore, online gambling can be a costly form of entertainment. Sites like Win Palace or Full Tilt Poker. They can lure students by offering lucrative winnings. The poker game Texas Hold 'Em is very popular right now. It can also be expensive. For example, if a room offers a cash pot, they require a deposit, and the poker rooms take a fee from that pot. In one night, a student can lose his spending money for the entire semester. Last, online auctions present a real financial danger to bored college students. This type of virtual shopping involves bidding for a product. Sometimes, students end up buying items they don't actually need.

I don't think this detail really fits. ———

A friend of mine buys all her clothes on eBay and saves lots of money. For example, eBay is a popular auction site that offers whatever items people want to sell. A student can find anything from an e-reader to a new pair of ski boots. Once you've made a bid, it's difficult not to obsessively check it several times an hour. Plus, students might end up spending money they need for essentials such as food and rent.

Add a transitional expression. ———

Most important, electronic services like texting, blogs, and microblogs can distract students from more important forms of communication. Students are masters at texting. Some can text under their desks in class. The professor can't tell that the student is only half listening. When a student is texting during a lecture, he isn't fully engaged in the communication between the professor and the class. Another popular, fast way to communicate is through blogs. Posting to a blog can feel like having a conversation. Readers can respond by leaving a comment. However, the drawback to all these conversations is that students end up with more virtual relationships than real-world relationships. Spending all one's energy on distant friends takes away from time that could be spent making new friends sitting right next to you. A third form of electronic communication is found in Twitter. Twitter is a microblog service, which means a user can write short posts about any topic. Also, students love the trending topics on Twitter. Students may love to text, tweet, and blog, but these services can't take the place of sharing a conversation across the table with somebody you've just met, or raising your hand in class and asking the professor an intelligent question.

Add examples of risks.

Is my conclusion interesting enough to keep my audience thinking about the topic? ———

In summary, college students should avoid excessive use of social media. These sites can be risky and cause problems.

REVISING

Finally, Benji revised his essay, correcting his errors and making the necessary changes. He submitted the following finished essay. (Note: His corrections are underlined.)

Thompson 1

Benji Thompson
Professor White
English 110
10 Nov. 2012

Social Media: The Risks for Students

One phrase you rarely hear these days is "I don't know."
At a party or in the park, if you want to know something or do
something, you can find out more about it with just a few
clicks on your smartphone, Kindle Fire, or iPad. Shopping and
socializing, too, have become possible anywhere, anytime,
thanks to technology. You can even keep yourself entertained
by playing online games with someone on another continent
by using any number of devices. However, there are risks to
social media, especially for busy students. If students aren't
careful, the Internet can rob them of precious time and
hard-earned money, and it can decrease the quality of their
relationships.

First, social networking sites can be very distracting. For
example, Facebook is one of the most popular sites, and it is
dangerous because it is so addictive. Some critics call it the
biggest time waster in the world. Students can spend hours
looking at photographs and reading posts on pages of
everyone they know. Some students become obsessed with
organizing and fine-tuning their own Facebook pages as well.
They want to choose the right pictures and arrange them in
the right order, and they want to write the funniest status
updates. Most often, this time would be better spent studying.
Another distraction is Facebook's invite pop-up. Facebook
sends invitations and reminders of when events are happening
and who is having a birthday. Reading and responding to
dozens of invites and notices takes time. Students can end up
spending hours planning their social calendars. Finally,
Facebook offers the very tempting distraction of keeping up
with friends, whether they are nearby or far away. Reading
status updates is addictive. As well, each time you hover on
a friend's name, several mutual friends pop up. The site is

Thompson 2

designed to engage your curiosity. Curiosity can get the better of anyone when it comes to friends, even friends you don't know very well. It's best to limit time on Facebook so that it doesn't distract you from the more important things in your life such as preparing for tests, writing essays, or doing other homework.

A second danger of life online is that it's easy to get into financial trouble. In particular, virtual gaming can cost a lot of money. Microsoft recently raised the cost of a subscription to Xbox Live from 50 dollars a month to 60. Often, students belong to several of these gaming sites, which allow them to play virtual games with people all over the globe. Several monthly subscriptions can quickly add up. My study partner for biology spends over 300 dollars a month in gaming subscriptions, and he never has money for food. Furthermore, online gambling can be a costly form of entertainment. Sites like Win Palace or Full Tilt Poker can lure students by offering lucrative winnings. The poker game Texas Hold 'Em is very popular right now. It can also be expensive. For example, if a room offers a cash pot, they require a deposit, and the poker rooms take a fee from the pot. In one night, a student can lose his spending money for the entire semester. Last, online auctions present a real financial danger to bored college students. This type of virtual shopping involves bidding for a product. Sometimes, students end up buying items they don't actually need. For example, eBay is a popular auction site that offers whatever items people want to sell. A student can find anything from an e-reader to a new pair of ski boots. Once you've made a bid, it's difficult not to obsessively check it several times an hour. Plus, students might end up spending money they need for essentials such as food and rent.

Most important, electronic services like texting, blogs, and microblogs can distract students from more important forms of communication. As an illustration, students are masters at texting. Some can text under their desks in class. The professor can't tell that the student is only half listening.

Thompson 3

When a student is texting during a lecture, he isn't fully engaged in the communication between the professor and the class. Another popular, fast way to communicate is through blogs. Posting to a blog can feel like having a conversation. Readers can respond by leaving a comment. However, the drawback to all these conversations is that students end up with more virtual relationships than real-world relationships. Spending all one's energy on distant friends takes away from time that could be spent making new friends sitting right next to you. A third form of electronic communication is found in Twitter. Twitter is a microblog service, which means users can write short posts about any topic. It is addictive because the conversation moves very quickly. Also, students love the trending topics on Twitter because reading them feels like joining a global conversation. The topics scroll live on the right of a student's homepage, giving him the most current news stories from across the world. However, the obsessive, addictive nature of Twitter robs students of valuable time that could be better spent communicating about personal and academic subject matter with their classmates and peers. Students may love to text, tweet, and blog, but these services can't take the place of sharing a conversation across the table with somebody you've just met, or raising your hand in class and asking the professor an intelligent question.

In summary, while life online has changed our world in many ways, some of them very positive, it also has dangers that we need to be aware of. Being distracted by Facebook, spending too much money online, and holding almost exclusively virtual conversations can consume precious time and money, and can diminish personal relationships. One simple solution is to limit Facebook time, set limits on online spending, and become more aware of the opportunities to meet new people. College is about learning, having new experiences, and meeting new people in the real world, not just "hanging out" in a virtual world.

PART TWO

Expanding Your Academic Writing

CHAPTER 10

Using Language Effectively

WHAT DO YOU KNOW?

1. **In academic writing, what are imprecise or unclear details likely to do?**

   ___ weaken your writing

   ___ strengthen your writing

   ___ give your writing more authority

   ___ give poetic meaning to your ideas

2. **What is the role of precise details in academic writing?**

   ___ to help a paragraph or an essay come to life

   ___ to answer important questions about the subject

   ___ to fill in space on the page

   ___ to help develop an idea

3. **If your writing appeals to your audience's five senses (sight, hearing, smell, taste, touch), what kind of details will it be strong in?**

   ___ quoted details

   ___ comparative details

   ___ emotive details

   ___ sensory details

4. **Words like *awesome, everything, a lot, sort of,* and *stuff* are vague. What kinds of problems can they cause in your academic writing?**

   ___ Your writing will sound sophisticated.

   ___ Your exact meaning may be unclear.

   ___ Your writing will sound more authentic.

   ___ Your writing may leave important questions unanswered.

5. **What are the following three expressions called?**

   A sucker is born every minute.

   It's not rocket science.

   Look before you leap.

   ___ metaphors

   ___ similes

   ___ clichés

   ___ emotive details

Recognizing Imprecise and Unclear Language

In everyday conversation, we use many imprecise expressions to communicate our thoughts. These expressions are so familiar to us that we do not recognize how unclear they may be. Here are some examples:

> Our team practiced <u>a lot</u> before the game. (How much, exactly?)
> The assignment was <u>really</u> hard. (How hard, specifically?)
> I <u>rarely</u> see my parents. (How often, precisely?)
> My boss hired <u>someone</u> I don't like. (Who, specifically?)
> There was some <u>stuff</u> I didn't understand. (What, exactly?)

Notice that each underlined expression is imprecise, leaving an unanswered question.

When we use such expressions, we assume that the listener will understand the meaning we intend. However, this is not always the case. Take a look at this dialogue.

> **Jake:** I watch a lot of TV.
> **Debra:** How much?
> **Jake:** About two hours every night.
> **Debra:** You call that a lot? I watch television from the time I get home at 5 until I fall asleep around midnight.

We can see that the expression *a lot* has a different meaning for each speaker. For Jake, two hours of television viewing is a lot; for Debra, it is not.

Fortunately, in a conversation, one speaker can ask the other for clarification of an idea. When you write, however, your reader may not be able to ask for clarification. Therefore, you must use precise and clear language to communicate your ideas completely and effectively.

As a college writer, you should understand that imprecise expressions can weaken your writing. The following chart contains some of the most common examples. Keep in mind that you cannot avoid these words absolutely, but you can be aware of when you use them and try to replace them with more precise words.

Imprecise Expressions

IMPRECISE QUANTITIES/ DEGREES	IMPRECISE OBJECTS	IMPRECISE LOCATIONS	IMPRECISE PERSONS
a couple	anything	anywhere	anybody
a few	everything	here / there	anyone
a little less	it	nowhere	no one
a little more	something	places	nobody
a lot of	stuff	someplace	people
a ton of	things	somewhere	somebody

(continued)	IMPRECISE FREQUENCY	IMPRECISE QUALITIES	IMPRECISE SLANG
about	always	bad	all that
almost	at times	beautiful	awesome
around	frequently	big	cool
fairly	infrequently	good	hot
generally	occasionally	happy	like that
kind of	often	nice	sweet
loads of	rarely	okay	totally
many		pretty	way
nearly		sad	
plenty of		short	
really		small	
roughly		tall	
some		ugly	
sort of			

slang: informal language often used between friends or within other social groups. *Dis* for *disrespect* is an example of slang.

Power Tip

To personalize this chart and make it more useful for you, use a highlighter to mark some of the expressions that you use most often in your speaking and writing. Also, you might add other expressions to the lists.

Adding Precise Details to Your Writing

In Chapters 6 and 9, you learned that a well-developed academic paragraph or essay should include details about the examples presented for each support point. In adding details, college writers tend to fall into one of three categories:

1. Some college writers add insufficient details; as a result, they end up with short, poorly developed paragraphs.
2. Other writers add imprecise or unclear details that can confuse the reader and leave many questions unanswered.
3. The best writers work hard to include precise and colorful details.

On the following pages, you will see examples of all three of these possibilities.

Let's begin by looking at an outline for a paragraph. It shows where details should be added when the paragraph is written.

ASSIGNED TOPIC	*Discuss a student organization or sports team you've been part of in college.*
MAIN IDEA	I am a reporter for the college newspaper.
TRANSITIONAL EXPRESSION	To begin with,
SUPPORT POINT 1	I became more informed about campus events and politics.

– learned about college sports
– learned about educational and administrative politics } **ADD DETAILS**
– learned about student government

TRANSITIONAL EXPRESSION   Second,

SUPPORT POINT 2   I improved my academic skills.
– research skills
– fieldwork skills   ADD DETAILS
– composition skills

TRANSITIONAL EXPRESSION   Last,

SUPPORT POINT 3   I made important new relationships.
– Jena, my best friend
– Professor Marks,
  supervisor and mentor   ADD DETAILS
– Q. T. Samuels, professional
  journalist

Now, let's consider three paragraphs based on this outline. The related examples for each support point from the outline are underlined in yellow. As you can see, these examples contain varying levels of details.

A Paragraph with Insufficient Details

At the start of my sophomore year, I joined my college newspaper as a reporter, and I have benefited from this work in many ways. To begin with, I became more informed about campus events and politics. For example, I learned about college sports. Also, I learned about educational and administrative politics. In addition, I learned about student government. Second, working as a reporter helped me improve several academic skills. In particular, I gained new research skills. I also gained valuable fieldwork skills. To top it off, I improved my composition skills. Last, I made important new relationships as a reporter. I met my best friend Jena. I found a mentor in the newspaper's supervisor, Professor Marks. I also met a local professional journalist, Q. T. Samuels. Although reporting for the college newspaper has taken time out of my busy study schedule, the rewards have been numerous and worthwhile.

Compare the examples in this paragraph to the examples in the outline above. You will see that the writer has not added any details. As a result, the paragraph lacks precise information and *personality*; we do not get a sense of a strong, individual voice behind this writing. We get the impression that the writer doesn't really care about the ideas in the paragraph.

A Paragraph with Imprecise and Unclear Details

At the start of my sophomore year, I joined my college newspaper as a reporter, and I have benefited from this work in many ways. To begin with, I became more informed about campus events and politics. For example, I learned a lot of things about college sports. Also, I met people involved in different types of politics. In addition, I became well-informed about everything to do with student government on our campus. Second, working as a reporter helped me improve several academic skills. In particular, I gained some awesome new research skills that I used a lot in my classes. I started doing fieldwork in some cool places, which helped me see some connections between academic work and the real world. To top it off, my composition skills got really good because I was using them a lot. Last, I made important new relationships as a reporter. I met my best friend Jena, who is totally awesome. I found a mentor in the newspaper's supervisor, Professor Marks. He knows how to relate to students and supported me in important ways. I also met a local professional journalist, Q. T. Samuels, who showed me things about being a professional reporter. Although reporting for the college newspaper has taken time out of my busy study schedule, the rewards have been numerous and worthwhile.

In this paragraph, the writer has added details, but the language is imprecise and unclear. As a result, many of the details leave an unanswered question:

a lot of things (What things, precisely?)
people (What people, exactly?)
different types of (What types, specifically?)
everything to do with (What, precisely?)
some awesome new research skills (What skills, exactly?)
used a lot in my classes (How were they used, specifically?)
some cool places (What places, precisely?)
some connections (What connections, exactly?)

got really good (How were they good, specifically?)
using them a lot (How much were they used, precisely?)
totally awesome (Awesome in what ways, exactly?)
he knows how to relate (How does he relate, specifically?)
in important ways (What ways, precisely?)
showed me things (What things, exactly?)

A Paragraph with Precise Details

At the start of my sophomore year, I joined my college newspaper as a reporter, and I have benefited from this work in many ways. To begin with, I became more informed about campus events and politics. For example, I learned that our college's football team was the division champion three years in a row. Also, I met Delores Mann, our college president, who taught me that educational politics involve regular negotiations for resources at the state and local levels. In addition, I learned that our student government representatives participate directly in these negotiations with school and state administrators. Second, working as a reporter helped me improve several academic skills. In particular, by doing background research on student rights campaigns, I became more proficient in using online databases and search engines. As a reporter, I also had to conduct frequent interviews. My social welfare class requires similar fieldwork, and my experience helped me gather field data efficiently. In addition, writing articles for the paper honed my composition skills and made it easier for me to write class essays. Last, I made important new relationships as a reporter. I met my best friend Jena, who shares my academic interest in anthropology. I found a mentor in the newspaper's supervisor, Professor Marks, who offers his students excellent academic and personal advice. He has already written one letter of recommendation for me that helped me obtain a scholarship. I also met a local professional journalist, Q. T. Samuels, who invited me to "shadow" her for a day on the job. Although reporting for the college newspaper has taken time out of my busy study schedule, the rewards have been numerous and worthwhile.

In this last paragraph, the writer has taken the time to add clear and precise details. As a result, the information is powerful, and the paragraph has personality: we get a sense of a strong, individual voice behind the writing. Notice that the new details are specific and exact. For example:

our college's football team (a specific team)
division champion (a precise accomplishment)
three years in a row (an exact number)
Delores Mann, our college president (a precise name and title)
negotiations for resources (a specific activity)
participate directly in these negotiations (a specific activity)
school and state administrators (exact groups)

research on student rights campaigns (a specific activity)
using online databases and search engines (precise resources)
conduct frequent interviews (a specific activity)
social welfare class (an exact class)
gather field data (a specific activity)
writing articles for the paper (a specific activity)
honed my composition skills (an exact accomplishment)

ACTIVITY 1

For each sentence pair below, do the following:

- Read the sentences carefully.
- Decide which sentence contains an unclear detail or details. Write "unclear" in the space after the sentence and circle the unclear word(s) or phrase(s).
- Decide which sentence contains precise details. Write "precise" in the space after the sentence and circle the precise word(s) or phrase(s).

EXAMPLE:

a. After eating raw oysters, Bill felt (kind of odd).   *unclear*
b. After eating raw oysters, Bill felt (faint and feverish).   *precise*

1. a. My aquarium had clouds of yellow algae floating in it. _____

   b. My aquarium had something weird floating in it. _____

2. a. Our coach makes a funny sound every time he shouts at the team. _____

   b. Our coach hisses through his nostrils every time he shouts at the team. _____

3. a. The long-distance track team runs
a very long way three times a week.   _____

  b. The long-distance track team runs 12 miles
three times a week.   _____

4. a. As the crowd pushed and shoved into the
stadium, someone shouted, "Help!"   _____

  b. As the crowd pushed and shoved into the
stadium, a young woman carrying a baby
shouted, "Help!"   _____

5. a. When Alex got his exam back, his expression
indicated that something was wrong.   _____

  b. When Alex got his exam back, his expression
indicated that he was displeased with his grade.   _____

ACTIVITY 2

For each pair of paragraphs below, do the following:

- Read the paragraphs carefully.
- Decide which one contains unclear details. Write "unclear" above the
  paragraph and underline all the unclear details.
- Decide which paragraph contains precise details. Write "precise"
  above the paragraph and underline all the precise details.

1. Paragraph A: _____

  During his first month of active combat there, he had a lot of
  bad experiences. Somebody always seemed to have his back when
  he went out there, but he still felt funny about doing it. In one place,
  he encountered some stuff that he couldn't believe, and when he got
  back there, he just let go.

  Paragraph B: _____

  During his first month of active combat in Afghanistan, Reginald
  had two violent encounters with local Afghan civilians. His fellow
  soldiers always watched his movement carefully when he went out on
  reconnaissance missions in the Afghan villages, but he still felt frightened about walking though the residential streets armed with a gun.
  In one village, he encountered two burned-out Army trucks with no
  sign of the soldiers who had been driving them. When he got back to
  the barracks, he broke down from exhaustion and anxiety and cried.

2. Paragraph A: _____

  Briana finally got a promotion at Bank of America after she had
  been working there for one year. She had continued to serve clients
  more efficiently and courteously to impress her supervisor, Mr. Diggs.

CONTINUED >   For more practice with
choosing precise language,
visit **bedfordstmartins.com
/touchstones**.

She even organized the supply drawers and filed receipts that she was not required to and stayed one hour late every day. Briana even wrote a self-evaluation of her job performance and gave it to Mr. Diggs to prove that she was conscious of her duties and how well she fulfilled them — and exceeded them. He appreciated her initiatives to serve the customers better and to support her co-workers, and he awarded her a promotion to head teller with a raise of two dollars per hour.

Paragraph B: _____

She finally got a promotion at the company after she had been working there for a while. She had made a lot of effort to impress him, doing things that she was not required to do and staying extra hours. She even wrote something up and gave it to him to prove that her job performance was truly awesome. He appreciated all the stuff that she had done and gave her what she asked for.

3. **Paragraph A:** _____

When he visited the place for the first time, he was overwhelmed with unusual emotions. He saw all the abandoned animals in their cages, doing stuff that seemed really sad. And there were a lot of animals there, more than he could have imagined. Suddenly, he decided to do it, and within a short time he was leaving the place with a totally awesome dog. However, when he got home, the dog showed signs of dangerous behavior. He hadn't had much experience with dogs, so he called the people back and asked them what to do. They said to bring it back so that they could figure out what to do.

Paragraph B: _____

When my cousin Ramon visited the San Diego animal shelter for the first time, he felt overwhelmed with guilt and sorrow. He saw over one hundred abandoned dogs and cats, puppies and kittens, in their cages, more than he could have imagined. After just five minutes, he decided to adopt a dog, and within less than one hour he was leaving with a speckled black-and-white pit bull terrier. However, when he got home, the dog started growling uncontrollably and snapped at Ramon three times. Ramon had never had a dog before—only a cat—so he called the staff at the animal shelter to ask for advice on handling the dog. They said to bring the dog back so that they could reevaluate its personality and behavior.

Eliminating Clichés from Your Writing

A cliché is a popular saying or expression that has been overused. In casual conversation, we often use clichés in communicating our ideas; our listeners understand what we mean and are not bothered by our use of the cliché. For example, if we say, _It's a no-brainer_, most people will understand our point. However, in academic writing, a cliché is usually considered imprecise and often unclear, as well as unoriginal. Students who rely on clichés in their writing may be perceived as lazy and ineffective writers because they have not taken the time to find precise and original language to express their ideas.

Some common clichés among students today include *a sucker is born every minute; back to the drawing board; bang for your buck; been there, done that; be there for someone; get a reality check; hard act to follow; have someone's back; hit the ground running; it's not rocket science; no such thing as a free lunch; push someone's buttons; push the envelope; reinvent the wheel; show your true colors; sounds like a plan; take it like a man; take the easy way out; talk the talk, walk the walk; talk to the hand; think outside the box; to be clueless; under the gun; wake up on the wrong side of the bed; what you see is what you get;* and *work like a dog.*

ACTIVITY 3

Underline all the clichés in the following passage. (Hint: There are 10 clichés in the passage.)

My boss at the Discount Shoe Center needs to get a reality check. For example, he hired four new employees for Black Friday and expected them to hit the ground running. However, he did not ask them about their previous experience in shoe sales, stocking, or checkout. Well, what you see is what you get, and when the doors opened on Friday morning at 6:00 A.M., those four new employees looked like deer in the headlights. My boss shouted at them to help the customers and stay busy, but they were clueless. The regular employees were running around like a bunch of chickens with their heads cut off and working like dogs. I think my boss really got a taste of his own medicine this time! Hiring experienced employees and giving them some training before Black Friday should have been a no-brainer. Next time, he will look before he leaps.

ACTIVITY 4

In the following passage, underline the ideas that have been used to replace the 10 clichés from the previous passage.

My boss at the Discount Shoe Center needs to take his job responsibilities and performance more seriously. For example, he hired four new employees for Black Friday and expected them to be highly skilled at their job. However, he did not ask them about their previous experience in shoe sales, stocking, or checkout. Well, these underprepared employees could not meet the demands of the job, and when the doors opened on Friday morning at 6:00 A.M., they froze in panic and confusion. My boss shouted at them to help the customers and stay busy, but they did not know how to help. The regular employees rushed around trying to serve the customers to the best of their ability.

CONTINUED >

I think my boss learned a valuable lesson from this experience. The need to hire experienced employees and give them adequate training before Black Friday should have been obvious to him. Next time, he will plan more carefully.

ACTIVITY 5: Teamwork

Underline the clichés in the following passage. Then, on a separate piece of paper, rewrite the passage, replacing each cliché with an idea that is more clear and precise. Use your imagination and have fun rewriting the passage.

My brother decided to drop out of college so that he could get more bang for his buck. He says that his goal is to become rich and college is throwing a monkey wrench in his plans. I warned him that there is no free lunch. He told me that he was already thinking outside of the box and had an idea for a catering service for dogs and cats. He would make fresh, organic pet food out of raw meat, brown rice, and vegetables and deliver it to wealthy pet owners on a daily or weekly basis. I said it sounded like a plan, but I cautioned him not to reinvent the wheel. I went on the Internet and showed my brother another pet catering company. At first he was disappointed, saying that the other company would be a hard act to follow. I advised him not to give up but reminded him that to be successful in business he would have to walk the walk, not just talk the talk. Well, he decided to go back to the drawing board and come up with a new idea. I am still encouraging him to return to college (maybe to get a business degree), but he knows that whatever he does, I'll have his back.

ACTIVITY 6

Take out the essay that you wrote for Chapter 9 (or a paragraph that you wrote for Chapter 6). Reread your composition carefully and eliminate any clichés that you find. Then, replace those clichés with ideas that are more clear and precise.

Cake 1: Plain

Developing Precise and Colorful Details

As a college writer, you should aim for details that are precise and colorful. It's easy enough to write ordinary or general details. But colorful and precise details will help to engage your reader and express your ideas more accurately.

For example, look at the two cakes pictured here. The basic ingredients and taste of the two cakes may be similar, but only one cake shows a professional quality of work. Although cake 1 has the main characteristics of a cake (layers and frosting), the baker has not made a special effort to create an extraordinary dessert. In contrast, cake 2 is clearly special; the baker has added precise and creative details (different-sized layers, colors, flowers, and intricate patterns) to excite the imagination and appetite of her guests.

Like a special cake, a college writing assignment should be well developed and of professional quality. In addition to the basic characteristics of a paragraph (topic sentence, support points, and related examples), an outstanding piece of writing must have something extra: It must have precise (specific) and creative details that grab readers' attention and make them hungry to read more. Although there are many strategies for developing precise and colorful details, we will focus on six in this chapter. Notice that each type of detail has a specific purpose:

1. **Concrete details:** identifying persons, places, and things
2. **Action details:** energizing your verbs
3. **Quoted details:** recording what people say
4. **Sensory details:** describing what you see, hear, smell, taste, and touch
5. **Emotive details:** exploring emotions
6. **Comparative details:** using metaphors and similes

Cake 2: Colorful and creative

USING CONCRETE DETAILS

Looking at the chart on pages 230–31, you will see that most of the words do not name specific persons, places, or things. (Notice especially the words under *Imprecise persons*, *Imprecise locations*, and *Imprecise objects*.) These words are *abstract*. When you use abstract words in your writing, you may end up with details that are imprecise and unclear. Take a look at the underlined words in this sentence:

My wife wants to go <u>somewhere special</u> for our anniversary.

In this sentence, the phrase *somewhere special* is abstract because it does not identify a specific place; for the reader, it is unclear what this special place might be. However, we can replace this abstract phrase with a more precise detail:

My wife wants to go to a <u>tropical resort</u> for our anniversary.

The phrase *tropical resort* identifies a more specific place. Any detail that names a specific person, place, or thing is called a *concrete* detail. Now, the reader has a clear idea about where the writer would like to go. However, the writer can make this detail even clearer by naming an actual tropical resort:

My wife wants to go <u>Club Med in Cancun</u> for our anniversary.

Club Med in Cancun tells the reader exactly where the wife would like to go.

Terminology Tip

Words that name people, places, or things are known as *nouns*. For more details, see Chapter 15, pages 338–39.

Terminology Tip

Club Med is known as a *proper noun* because it names a specific (brand-name) resort. Proper nouns begin with capital letters. For more on proper nouns, see Chapter 15, page 339.

Basic Guidelines for Using Concrete Details

- Avoid the abstract words in the chart on pages 230–31.
- Identify specific persons, places, and things.
- Whenever possible, use a proper noun to *name* specific people, places, and things.

ACTIVITY 7

For each sentence below, do the following:

- Underline the imprecise or abstract word(s) or phrase(s).
- Rewrite the sentence, replacing any words or phrases you underlined with precise and colorful concrete details. (You may find words other than nouns that can be made more specific.)

EXAMPLE: After buying the used car, Sue found <u>something odd</u> in the trunk.

After buying the used car, Sue found a mechanical monkey in the trunk.

1. Despite not having a college degree, my sister managed to get a pretty good job.

2. New college students have to manage many things, but it's worth it.

3. Melissa has so much stuff on her desk that she can't get things done.

4. Everyone has to bring two things to the baby shower.

5. Getting those things done to my car will cost a lot.

ACTIVITY 8: Teamwork

With two or three classmates, do the following:

- Read the paragraph below, underlining all the imprecise and unclear details.

For more practice using concrete details, visit **bedfordstmartins.com /touchstones** and go to *Exercise Central*.

- Working as a team, rewrite the paragraph, making persons, places, and things more concrete and adding other precise and colorful details.
- Have one person write the new paragraph on a separate sheet of paper.
- When all the teams in the class have finished writing, have a person from your team read the paragraph out loud to the class.

> Sometime after school, a few of us decided to get our things and go somewhere chill. When we got there, we spread out our stuff and made it real. A little while later, someone showed up and started doing something we couldn't believe. We didn't know whether to laugh or be afraid, but somebody called on her cell phone to ask for help. They showed up pretty soon and took care of everything.

ACTIVITY 9

Write a paragraph. Using as many concrete details as possible (specific persons, places, and things), discuss or describe one of the following:

- whatever you can see out the window nearest to you
- your college's cafeteria *OR* bookstore
- your favorite electronic device
- your dream car or vehicle
- a store where you love to shop

USING ACTION DETAILS

Good writing has energy. One of the best ways to energize your details is to use precise and colorful verbs. Inexperienced writers often rely on common and inexpressive verbs rather than searching for more original and powerful verbs. Take a look at the underlined verb in this example:

> Desperate to make the final out, the outfielder <u>jumped</u> to catch the fly ball.

The verb *jump* paints a basic picture of the outfielder's action, but it doesn't show his determination in a powerful way. However, we can replace this verb with a more precise and colorful action:

> Desperate to make the final out, the outfielder <u>leapt</u> to catch the fly ball.

Here, the verb *leap* creates a stronger image of the outfielder's physical action and his determination. However, if the writer of this sentence is especially creative, she might experiment with other powerful verbs. For example:

> Desperate to make the final out, the outfielder <u>rocketed</u> to catch the fly ball.

Terminology Tip
A *verb* expresses an *action* or a *state of being*. Go to Chapter 15, pages 340–41, to learn more about verbs.

Here, the verb *rocket* paints a powerful picture of the outfielder's movement. It also suggests his superhuman determination to catch the ball and win the game.

Basic Guidelines for Using Action Details

- When describing an action, close your eyes and try to imagine the specific image that you want to create in readers' minds.
- Use a portable or online thesaurus to help you find more precise and original verbs. (A thesaurus is a dictionary that, for each word, gives words with similar meanings. Check with your instructor if you are unsure about whether to use an unfamiliar word.)
- In a notebook, keep a list of new verbs that you would like to incorporate into your vocabulary.
- When possible, try to replace state-of-being verbs (*am, is, are, was, were*) with action verbs (like *stomped* or *stormed*). A good time to make these changes is when you are proofreading and editing your writing. (For more advice on proofreading, see Chapter 7.) You will learn more about verbs in Chapters 15 and 16.

ACTIVITY 10

For each sentence below, do the following:

- Underline the inexpressive verb or verbs.
- Rewrite the sentence, using one or more precise and colorful action verbs.

EXAMPLE: The dirt was so hard that I had to <u>hit</u> it several times with a shovel.

The dirt was so hard that I had to pound it several times with a shovel.

1. Chasing the suspect at a speed of 120 miles per hour, the policewoman lost control of her squad car and went into a ditch.

2. Within inches of the end zone, the receiver tried to get around the defense and score a touchdown.

3. The lead actor became so impassioned during the second act that he stepped back too far and fell off the stage into the orchestra pit.

4. As Nina was carrying the three-layer birthday cake to the table, she tripped on the rug and dropped it.

_____

_____

5. When the ancient elevator reached the second floor, its cord snapped and it fell to the basement.

_____

_____

ACTIVITY 11: Teamwork

With two or three classmates, do the following:

- Read the paragraph below, underlining all the common and inexpressive verbs.
- Working as a team, rewrite the paragraph, making verbs more vivid and powerful and adding other precise and colorful details.
- Have one person write the new paragraph on a separate sheet of paper.
- When all the teams in the class have finished writing, have a person from your team read the paragraph out loud to the class.

    Our aircraft had to make an emergency landing, touching down on the runway. After the plane came to a stop, the passengers on board got up and behaved weirdly. The guy sitting next to me stepped over me like the plane was on fire. His briefcase came open and papers came out all over the place. Some passengers were moving up and down the aisles, talking crazy. One passenger tried to open the emergency exit, but she couldn't do it. Finally, the captain spoke over the loudspeaker and told the passengers to take their seats. Dazed, the passengers returned to their seats.

ACTIVITY 12

Write a paragraph. Using as many action details as possible, discuss or describe one of the following:

- the fans at a major sports event
- a busy skateboard park
- a crowded mall where gunshots are heard
- a freeway chase with vehicles and helicopters
- firefighters engaged in fighting a high-rise fire

For more practice using action details, visit **bedfordstmartins.com /touchstones** and go to _Exercise Central._

USING QUOTED DETAILS

Power Tip
Adding quotations to your writing can be an important part of a college research paper. For more on including research in your writing, go to Chapter 14.

Many writing assignments require you to discuss people—friends, family members, co-workers, historical figures, or people in the news. If the person you are writing about said something interesting or important, you might want to record that person's words in your paragraph. The more precise you are in recording a person's words, the more powerful your writing will be. Take a look at the underlined phrase in this example:

> When I made the Dean's Honor Roll, my counselor said <u>something that made me feel good</u>.

The underlined phrase is imprecise and unclear. The reader will have to guess what the counselor actually said. However, we can replace this phrase with a more precise detail:

> When I made the Dean's Honor Roll, my counselor said <u>that I will have excellent academic opportunities if I continue to earn such high grades</u>.

With this sentence, the reader has a much clearer understanding of what the counselor said. However, the absence of quotation marks tells us that these may not be her actual words. If you remember a person's actual statement—and if this statement is especially memorable—record it precisely and put it in quotation marks:

> When I made the Dean's Honor Roll, my counselor said, <u>"With such high grades, you can get into a graduate program at a top research university like Stanford or Yale."</u>

The underlined section is called a **direct quotation** because it records the counselor's exact words. Clearly, this quotation presents powerful details that are missing in the other versions of the sentence. What the counselor actually said is much more interesting than the writer's general idea of what she said.

Basic Guidelines for Using Direct Quotations

- Put quotation marks at the beginning and end of the quotation.
- If the quotation is a complete sentence, capitalize the first word of it. For example: *Bill's father said, "Don't forget to take your lunch."*
- If the quotation is not a complete sentence, you do not need to capitalize it. For example: *All of us were told about the "mysterious green glow" that shone in Petrie Forest at night.*
- Use a comma to separate the quotation from the identification of the speaker—for example, *Tom said, "Go away."* or *"Go away," Tom said.* Notice that in both examples, the closing quotation mark is after the period or comma.

For more help with understanding how and when to use quotations, go to **bedfordstmartins .com/touchstones**.

ACTIVITY 13

For each sentence below, do the following:

- Underline the imprecise or unclear detail recording a person's words.
- Rewrite the sentence, using a precise and colorful *direct quotation*, in quotation marks.

EXAMPLE: The professor said <u>something complimentary</u> to me.

The professor said, "You have outstanding critical thinking ability."

1. I answered the phone, and an unfamiliar voice on the line yelled something crazy.

_____

_____

2. After I got my hair done at a new beauty salon, my best girlfriend took one look at my hair and gave her opinion.

_____

_____

_____

3. When I called the credit card company to ask why my credit card had been declined, the representative told me a surprising fact.

_____

_____

_____

4. After being crowned Miss Nebraska, the contestant reported an astonishing fact to the judges.

_____

_____

5. The coach told the star quarterback that his career was finished.

_____

_____

ACTIVITY 14: Teamwork

With two or three classmates, do the following:

- Read the paragraph below, underlining all the imprecise and unclear details recording a person's words.

CONTINUED >

- Working as a team, rewrite the paragraph, using the most precise and colorful quoted details you can think of. You may want to add other details too.
- Have one person write the new paragraph on a separate sheet of paper.
- When all the teams in the class have finished writing, have a person from your team read the paragraph out loud to the class.

When Jackson came late to class for the third day in a row, the professor said something that shocked us all. At first, Jackson couldn't even respond, but then he found his courage and spoke back. After considering his remark, the professor made one more observation, and then Jackson left the room. The student sitting behind me leaned forward and whispered her thoughts in my ear.

ACTIVITY 15

Write a paragraph. Using as many quoted details as possible, discuss or describe one of the following:

- a fight that you had with someone
- the conversation you would have with a famous person if you met that person face-to-face
- the conversation you would have with a deceased person if that person could come back to life
- a discussion you had with a professor
- a conversation that made you laugh or feel good

USING SENSORY DETAILS

Terminology Tip
Adjectives describe nouns (persons, places, or things). For instance, in the phrase *happy child*, *happy* is an adjective that describes the noun *child*. For more on adjectives, see Chapter 15, page 342.

We use our five senses (sight, hearing, smell, taste, touch) to connect with the world around us. When we read, we look for details that help our senses connect with the writer's world. These details are called *sensory* because they describe the way things look, sound, smell, taste, and feel. Unfortunately, many writers use imprecise sensory details. Look at the underlined adjective in this example:

By the end of the Super Bowl, the quarterback's uniform was <u>dirty</u>.

In this sentence, the adjective *dirty* gives an unclear picture of the quarterback's uniform. The person reading this sentence will have to guess what the uniform really looked like. However, we can replace the imprecise adjective with more specific and original details:

By the end of the Super Bowl, the quarterback's uniform had <u>brown and green stains</u> on it.

Now, the reader has a clearer picture of how the quarterback's uniform actually looked. However, an especially creative writer might search for even more powerful images:

> By the end of the Super Bowl, the quarterback's uniform was <u>covered in mud and grass stains</u>, <u>with splotches of blood and dark yellow mucus</u>.

In this example, we can clearly see how the addition of precise and colorful details gives the writing more power and personality. We have not only a vivid picture of the quarterback's uniform but also a snapshot of the whole game.

Basic Guidelines for Using Sensory Details

- Close your eyes and try to imagine the sights, sounds, smells, tastes, and feelings of a situation or scene. Think of descriptions that will re-create the situation or scene in readers' minds.
- Use a portable or online thesaurus to help you find more precise and original descriptions. (Remember to check with your instructor if you are unsure about whether to use an unfamiliar word.)
- When you want to describe something vividly, work through the five senses one at a time and think of details that connect to each.

ACTIVITY 16

For each sentence below, do the following:

- Underline the imprecise or unclear sensory detail.
- Rewrite the sentence, using precise and colorful sensory details.

EXAMPLE: The woman on the bus gave me <u>an unpleasant look</u>.

The woman on the bus frowned angrily at me.

1. When I tried to make a call on Jessica's cell phone, it kept making a strange sound.

2. Doug finally reopened his gym locker after one year and was surprised by a strong smell.

3. After her two-hour hike through the jungle, Naomi felt something odd on her skin.

CONTINUED >

4. We decided to order the "Margarita Surprise," but the drink tasted bad.

5. The towels in the youth hostel looked nasty.

ACTIVITY 17: Teamwork

With two or three classmates, do the following:

- Read the paragraph below, underlining all the imprecise and unclear details.
- Working as a team, rewrite the paragraph, adding the most precise and colorful sensory details you can think of. You may want to add other details too.
- Have one person write the new paragraph on a separate sheet of paper.
- When all the teams in the class have finished writing, have a person from your team read the paragraph out loud to the class.

The strange package was delivered by UPS and came from Tanzania. Alicia had no idea what could be in the package, and she was afraid to open it. First, she shook it and held it up to her ear. She heard an unusual sound coming from inside. She set the package down and cut open the plastic wrapping. At that moment, a strange odor rose up and invaded her nostrils. The smell was so intense that it left an unpleasant taste in her mouth. Finally, she cut open the top of the package and lifted the lid. Inside, she saw a disgusting sight.

ACTIVITY 18

Write a paragraph. Using as many sensory details as possible, discuss or describe one of the following:

- a great vacation experience
- a picnic or a celebration in the park
- a student event on your campus
- a party that you attended
- a favorite amusement park
- being in (or visiting someone in) the hospital

For more practice using sensory details, visit **bedfordstmartins.com /touchstones** and go to *Exercise Central.*

USING EMOTIVE DETAILS

In college, you will sometimes be asked to write on topics that bring up strong emotions for you. Good writers take the time to explore such feelings and find precise details to describe them; these details are called *emotive*. Strong emotive details capture your emotions in a powerful way that allows the reader to connect deeply with your experiences. Once again, you can begin by recognizing imprecise expressions that may weaken your writing. For example, look at the underlined words in the following sentence:

When my parents divorced and my father moved out, I felt <u>very sad</u>.

In this sentence, the phrase *very sad* gives an unclear picture of the writer's feelings. The person reading this sentence will have to guess the writer's exact emotions. However, we can replace the imprecise expression with more specific emotive details:

When my parents divorced and my father moved out, I felt <u>lonely and confused</u>.

The underlined expression here gives a clearer sense of the writer's feelings. However, the writer could still explore even deeper levels of the emotional experience:

When my parents divorced and my father moved out, I felt <u>that my happiness had been an illusion and that life would be forever uncertain and painful</u>.

The underlined phrase contains powerful emotive details that help the reader connect with the writer's deepest feelings.

Basic Guidelines for Using Emotive Details
- Avoid the abstract words from the chart on pages 230–31.
- Close your eyes and recall your deepest feelings in as much detail as possible.

ACTIVITY 19

For each sentence below, do the following:

- Underline the imprecise or unclear emotive detail.
- Rewrite the sentence, using precise and colorful emotive details.

EXAMPLE: When he won a second gold medal in the Special Olympics, Miguel <u>was upbeat</u>.

When he won a second gold medal in the Special Olympics, Miguel became overwhelmed with disbelief and joy.

CONTINUED >

1. After dropping three of his four classes, Edmond felt down.

   _____

   _____

2. Jenny was glad when she won a two-week, all-expenses-paid vacation to Paris.

   _____

   _____

3. When Derk's life sentence was reduced to ten days in jail, he was pleased.

   _____

   _____

4. Since Carlos had been in love with Brenda all his life, he felt bad when she married his best friend.

   _____

   _____

5. When the missing child was found after six months, the parents felt good.

   _____

   _____

   _____

ACTIVITY 20: Teamwork

With two or three classmates, do the following:

- Read the paragraph below, underlining all the imprecise and unclear emotive details.
- Working as a team, rewrite the paragraph, adding the most precise and colorful emotive details you can think of. You may want to add other details too.
- Have one person write the new paragraph on a separate sheet of paper.
- When all the teams in the class have finished writing, have a person from your team read the paragraph out loud to the class.

     As infants, Miriella and Gabriella had been separated during their country's civil war. Thirty years later, they were finally reunited at Kennedy Airport in New York City. Before getting off her plane, Miriella felt strange. Surprisingly, Gabriella felt something totally different as her plane landed. However, the second the sisters saw one another, they both felt the same feelings. As they hugged each other, they both cried and felt nice. Miriella looked at her sister and said, "Now, I am finally alive." This made Gabriella feel pleased.

For more practice using emotive details, visit **bedfordstmartins.com /touchstones** and go to *Exercise Central.*

ACTIVITY 21

Write a paragraph. Using as many precise and colorful emotive details as possible, discuss or describe one of the following:

- a time when you disappointed yourself
- a time when someone you loved let you down
- a reunion you had with someone you love
- the death, serious illness, or injury of a loved one
- a time when you were so angry you almost lost control

USING COMPARATIVE DETAILS: METAPHORS AND SIMILES

Metaphors are a common feature of language, and most people use them without knowing it. The best way to understand metaphors is to look at some examples.

Let's begin with a sentence that would benefit from the addition of a metaphor:

The A+ I received on my first essay was more than just a grade.

While this sentence makes a clear statement, the phrase *more than just a grade* does not give the reader a colorful image of the importance of the A+ grade. However, the writer might use a more creative description. Notice the underlined words:

The A+ I received on my first essay was a shining trophy.

In this sentence, the phrase *a shining trophy* is a metaphor that gives the reader an immediate and powerful image of the grade's importance. A metaphor is a creative comparison of two items with similar characteristics.

Sometimes, creative comparisons (comparative details) use the words *like* or *as*:

The A+ I received on my first essay was like a shining trophy.
The A+ I received on my first essay was as beautiful as a shining trophy.

Comparisons that include either *like* or *as* are known as **similes**.

Basic Guidelines for Using Creative Comparisons (Comparative Details)

- Do not overload your writing with these comparisons. One or two distinctive comparisons in a paragraph are usually sufficient.
- Try to avoid overused comparisons like those in the following list. (These are known as *clichés*, expressions that used to sound original and creative but have lost their spark because of overuse.) For more on clichés, see pages 236–38 in this chapter.

Some Overused Comparisons (Clichés)

avoid something like the plague   pretty as a picture
blind as a bat   sick as a dog
cool as a cucumber   sleep like a log
dull as dishwater   smart as a whip
like a bull in a china shop   tough as nails

ACTIVITY 22

For each of the following sentences, fill in the blank with a comparative detail.

EXAMPLE: During final exams, Nicholas often hides away in his room
for days like _____a monk_____.

1. Paul swears that he would die without his BlackBerry. He says it is like _____ to him.

2. When the hiker got lost in Death Valley, the sun felt like _____ on his head.

3. Missy's new car is as eye-catching as _____.

4. The professor's lecture was so boring it was like listening to _____.

5. That test was so hard it was like _____.

ACTIVITY 23: Teamwork

With two or three classmates, do the following:

- Rewrite the paragraph below, filling in the blank spaces with the most creative and colorful comparative details you can think of. (For this activity, we will ignore the guideline of not overloading your writing with these comparisons.)
- Have one person write the new paragraph on a separate sheet of paper.
- When all the teams in the class have finished writing, have a person from your team read the paragraph out loud to the class.

Professor Hicks is the most helpful and talented professor on campus. First, his course syllabus is as clear as _____. He lays out all the course requirements and the grading criteria with the precision of a _____. Then, on the first day of class, he takes the time to make all the students feel as comfortable as if they were _____. He comes across as very relaxed and confident, more like a _____ than a college professor. He also makes some incredibly funny jokes, which get the students cracking up like _____. However, when he starts to lecture about political science, you realize immediately that Professor Hicks is as smart as _____ and knows his subject matter like

For more practice using comparative details, visit **bedfordstmartins.com /touchstones** and go to *Exercise Central.*

a _____. To all his past and present students, Professor Hicks is a _____.

ACTIVITY 24

Write a paragraph. Using some precise and colorful comparative details, discuss or describe one of the following:

- driving on my city's freeways is like . . .
- my first day of college (*OR* on the job) was like . . .
- writing a college essay is like . . .
- falling in love is like . . .
- losing someone you love is like . . .

ACTIVITY 25

Look back at a paragraph or essay that you developed in Chapter 6 or 9. Reread the composition and underline or highlight any imprecise or unclear details. Then, using the strategies discussed in this chapter, rewrite the details to make them more precise and colorful. As a reminder, you might use one or more of the following:

- **Concrete details:** identifying persons, places, and things
- **Action details:** energizing your verbs
- **Quoted details:** recording what people say
- **Sensory details:** describing what you see, hear, smell, taste, and touch
- **Emotive details:** exploring emotions
- **Comparative details:** using metaphors and similes

BRINGING IT ALL TOGETHER:
Using Language Effectively

In this chapter, you have explored ways of making your writing effective through the use of precise and colorful details. Confirm your knowledge by filling in the blank spaces in the following sentences. If you need help, review the pages listed after each sentence.

✔ If you use _____ or _____ details in an academic paragraph or essay, you may leave many questions unanswered and confuse your audience. If you have _____ details, your writing will lack personality and your readers will think that you don't care about the ideas. (pages 231–32)

CONTINUED >

✔ _____ are popular sayings or expressions that have been over-used. In academic writing, they are usually considered _____ and _____, as well as _____. (pages 236–37)

✔ _____ details identify specific persons, places, and things. To be as specific as possible, use _____ nouns whenever possible. (pages 239–40)

✔ _____ details use energetic, expressive verbs. (page 241)

✔ _____ details record the exact words spoken by people. (page 244)

✔ _____ details describe the way things look, sound, smell, taste, and feel. (page 246)

✔ _____ details describe feelings as powerfully and precisely as possible. (page 249)

✔ _____ details include metaphors and similes. (page 251)

✔ A _____ directly compares one thing to another; for example, *My straight-A's report card was a peace flag to my parents.* (page 251)

✔ A _____ uses *like* or *as* to make comparisons; for example, *I waved my straight-A's report card like a peace flag at my parents.* (page 251)

JOURNAL WRITING: 10–15 minutes

As a student, you may sometimes feel overwhelmed by the demands of college life. One strategy for keeping a balanced perspective on your academic performance is to recognize your small successes at the end of each day. For this journal entry, write about a few small things that you did successfully in the last few days: finishing a homework assignment, performing well on a quiz, participating thoughtfully in a group discussion, making it to class on time, etc. Discuss the value of each of these small successes.

CHAPTER 11

Basic Writing Patterns

Test your understanding of basic writing patterns by completing this quiz first. You may know more than you think.

For each question, select all the answers that apply.

WHAT DO YOU KNOW?

1. When you speak or write, you often use *patterns of development* to express your ideas effectively. Which three of the following are writing patterns?

    ___ narration

    ___ impressionism

    ___ description

    ___ definition

2. If you are telling a story in your writing, what pattern are you probably using?

    ___ narration

    ___ comparison and contrast

    ___ definition

    ___ argument

3. If your writing includes powerful sensory details (sights, sounds, smells, tastes, and textures), what pattern are you probably using?

    ___ argument

    ___ comparison and contrast

    ___ description

    ___ exemplification

4. If you are providing well-developed examples to support your points, what pattern are you probably using?

    ___ exemplification

    ___ process

    ___ description

    ___ cause and effect

5. If you explain how to do something step-by-step, what pattern are you probably using?

    ___ description

    ___ narration

    ___ process

    ___ cause and effect

Introduction to the Patterns of Development

In everyday conversations, we use a number of patterns to develop our ideas and communicate them effectively. Below are the most common patterns, which may be familiar to you:

- **Description** (used to describe something)
- **Narration** (used to tell a story)
- **Exemplification** (used to give examples of something)
- **Process** (used to explain the steps in doing something)
- **Definition** (used to explain what something means)

If your business class requires you to write a product description, you will probably use *description*. If you tell the story of how your grandmother emigrated to the United States, you will probably use *narration*. If you give your friends convincing examples of the qualities that make a successful student, you will use *exemplification*. If you explain to your father how to download music to his iPod, you will probably use *process*. If you are required to define the blood–brain barrier for a biology class, you will probably use *definition*.

As you can tell from these examples, we use **patterns of development** frequently in daily life and in academic writing. These patterns can guide your work and ensure your success, just as an architect creates a blueprint to design a building. Confident writers understand the power of each pattern and use a variety of patterns fluidly.

Once you understand the most common patterns, you will be able to understand and use the more advanced ones as well. The advanced patterns are:

Terminology Tip
The patterns of development are sometimes called the *modes* or *rhetorical modes*.

- **Cause and effect** (used to explain the origin and outcome of an event or occurrence)
- **Comparison and contrast** (used to identify the similarities and/or differences between things)
- **Argument** (used to state and defend a position on an issue)

Understanding Description

We often include descriptions in what we say and write to make our ideas colorful and easy to understand. Descriptions appeal to our five senses, telling us how things look, sound, smell, taste, and feel. Without description, we would have difficulty communicating effectively. For example, if you ask a friend to locate your car in a parking lot, he might not be able to find it unless you provided a description of your car: *a dark blue Honda Civic with a dent in the driver's door.*

For college assignments, good description gives your writing personality and precision. Whether you are describing the brushstrokes in a Van Gogh painting for an art history class or cell division for a biology exam, you will need to demonstrate your *powers of observation* in what you write. These observations—impressions captured through the five senses—help your reader understand your topic and follow your points.

To write a successful description, you should keep the following strategies in mind:

1. Use **precise nouns** and **vivid adjectives** to identify the objects in your description. For example, instead of writing *a bottle of ketchup*, write *a sticky plastic bottle of Heinz ketchup with a dried crust around the lid.* For more on using powerful concrete details, see pages 239–41.

2. Use **precise verbs** and **vivid adverbs** to describe any movement or action in what you're describing. For example, instead of writing *the motorcycle went through the intersection*, write *the motorcycle raced loudly through the intersection.* For more on using powerful action details, see pages 241–43.

3. Although sight may be the most obvious sense to use, use **all five senses** to provide valuable information. Include as many sensual details as possible that describe sounds, smells, tastes, and textures. For example, instead of *the salad tasted delicious*, you could write *the crunchy lettuce, small, sweet tomatoes, and creamy ranch dressing made the salad taste delicious.* For more on using powerful sensory details, see pages 246–48.

4. Decide whether your description will be based on **memory** (something that you saw or experienced in the past), on **current observation** (something that you see or experience in the present moment), or on **imagination** (something that is not yet real but created in your mind).

5. Some descriptive writing assignments ask you to describe your feelings, thoughts, opinions, and/or beliefs in response to a situation or event. When you describe what you *feel*, this type of description is called **subjective**. In other words, you describe how you—a human subject—feel in response to an event or situation. Be sure to ask your instructor if you are allowed to include your feelings and thoughts as part of your description.

6. Try dividing the thing you are describing into two or more **major parts**. Then describe each part fully, one at a time. This strategy will help you slow down and stay focused on each part of your description.

WRITING A DESCRIPTIVE PARAGRAPH

In some cases, a description may be quite short (a few words or several sentences). In other situations, it might require a full paragraph or a short essay. When selecting something to describe, remember to consider the length of your assignment: an academic paragraph (one page or less) or a short essay (one to three pages).

Power Tip
Review Chapter 15, "The Building Blocks of Language," pages 342–43, for an explanation of adjectives and adverbs, the building blocks of language that describe things and actions.

Power Tip
In a descriptive paragraph or essay, consider using one of the following organizational strategies: 1) Start with the most important details and end with the least important details; 2) Start with the least important details and end with the most important details; 3) Start with the details that are in the background and end with the details in the foreground or focal point; 4) Start with the details in the foreground or focal point and end with the details in the background. Each of these strategies can work well; select the one that you think serves your description most effectively.

For more practice using descriptive language in your writing, visit **bedfordstmartins .com/touchstones** and go to *Exercise Central*.

Let's begin by looking at a descriptive paragraph. Notice that the writer selected a topic that could be effectively and fully described in one page or less.

My cluttered garage overflows with old junk. On the left are shelves crowded with worn automotive supplies, uselessly saved. There are half-used motor oil cans and rusty funnels once used to pour the oil into an old green Toyota that we no longer own. Under one shelf is a worn, dirty floor mat from a battered Ford pickup. On the back wall are shelves with used-up paint supplies. There are cans of encrusted blue and yellow paint from long-forgotten redecorating projects, paintbrushes with their bristles stuck together, and carelessly folded, ancient drop cloths spotted with hardened blue and yellow paint. On the bottom shelf sadly sit paint cans whose covers are so caked that they can't be opened anymore, not even with a large screwdriver. To the right are garden supplies. Cracked green and white hoses, old plastic flowerpots with dried-up soil, and corroded trowels randomly litter the area. Below are rusty rakes and pitchforks that were once used for a vegetable garden that we don't have anymore. Although everything has its place, I don't know why we are keeping all this useless rubbish.

Power Tip

For an example of a description by a professional writer, see paragraph 5 of "Dream Homes" by Joyce Zonana, page 621.

ACTIVITY 1

Choose one of the topics below and write a descriptive paragraph. Remember to follow the steps in the writing process: narrow the topic, brainstorm, outline, draft, and revise. (To review these steps, see Chapters 3–7.)

Power Tip

For more ideas on narrowing a topic and picking a topic that works for you, review Chapter 3, pages 45–48.

1. Find an image that you would like to describe. This image could be a personal or family photograph; an image from a magazine, newspaper, Web site, or college textbook; or one of the photographs on page 262 or 269 of this chapter.

2. Describe a favorite video game, Web site, or YouTube video.

3. You've just won an all-expenses-paid fantasy date with the person of your choice. Describe this date — whom you would take and everything you would do.

4. Describe the most beautiful person you've ever met. Describe in detail what makes this person especially beautiful, inside and out.

5. Describe yourself. You can discuss the way you see yourself, the different ways that other people probably see you, how you would like to be seen, and so on.

WRITING A DESCRIPTIVE ESSAY

Power Tip

For more help moving from paragraphs to essays, see Chapter 8.

Once you have mastered writing a descriptive paragraph, you should be able to transition smoothly to a short descriptive essay. To begin, you will need to select a topic that you can describe fully and effectively in one to three pages. Next, you will need to plan for an introductory paragraph with a thesis statement, two or more body paragraphs, and a concluding paragraph.

Writing a Thesis Statement for a Descriptive Essay

As you learned in Chapter 9 (page 201), a thesis statement must do two things. It must 1) identify the topic and 2) express your original point or opinion about the topic. In a description, the topic is the thing you are describing; your point or opinion is the *impression* you want to get across to your reader. (This is often known as the *dominant impression*.) Take a look at the following examples.

TOPIC (THING DESCRIBED)	THESIS STATEMENT (DOMINANT IMPRESSION UNDERLINED)
the local animal shelter	The animal shelter in my town is designed for the health and happiness of its resident animals.
my closet	My bedroom closet looks like a volcanic eruption of clothes, shoes, and old junk.
my favorite video game, "Call of Duty"	My favorite video game, "Call of Duty," depicts a highly realistic war zone.

Below is an example of a short descriptive essay that contains the required features discussed above. Read it carefully and complete the activity that follows.

My First Rally

What do you think of when you imagine a political rally? Balloons, screaming fans, and a candidate who will say anything to please his audience? Many people think all political candidates are liars or bores, or both. But when I attended my first political rally, I discovered something different. It was an exciting, multifaceted event, a great opportunity for people-watching and partying. The sights and sounds of my first rally ignited my senses and imagination.

First, I was awed by the crowds of people. Everywhere, shouting, screaming human beings filled the empty parking lot where the rally was to be held. To the right, people were dressed in costumes from 1776. They sported tri-cornered hats and knee breeches. To the left, some spectators were dressed up like Groucho Marx. They wore big, black-framed glasses and false mustaches. In front of me, a six-year-old girl was perched on her father's shoulders. She held a blue poster advertising the candidate's name. Behind me, in the rear of the crowd, a high school marching band showed off their bright white uniforms, and eight-year-old schoolchildren wore red and blue T-shirts. I was amazed and captivated by all these people.

Second, I began to notice the sounds. At the podium, a man in a white dress shirt and a megaphone urged the spectators to come closer. He yelled that the candidate would be at the rally soon, and he asked the crowd for contributions. At the left and right were loudspeakers, with music playing a conglomeration of classic rock and country. When I arrived, the music of the Beatles suggested that baby-boom voters were one of the targets of this candidate. Then, Johnny Cash almost broke my eardrums singing "Ragged Old Flag." Finally, for the eighteen-year-olds, Lady Gaga boomed. The spectators sang along, off-key in some cases, with the recordings. The sound was overwhelming.

Finally, I looked for the candidate, but he was nowhere to be found. People began muttering about leaving, and some did leave, taking their posters with them. I stayed because I wanted to see how it all would end. And, eventually, the candidate drove in on a big white bus with his picture on the side. Red, white, and blue signs with his name waved back and forth in the bright sunshine, and red and white helium-filled balloons flew overhead. Then, the candidate began speaking about everything he wanted to change in our political system. He said that if he were elected, he would lower taxes and reduce the deficit. Also, he criticized his opponents, and he promised not to forget the people who had supported him. Last, he climbed back on the bus and drove off to his next rally.

In twenty or thirty years, the political rally may become a thing of the past. More and more people will stay politically informed and involved through the Internet. So, if you have a chance, get out and attend a political rally while this great American tradition is still alive. You may not find the experience completely satisfying, but at least you will experience it for yourself and not only in the pages of a history book.

ACTIVITY 2

Fill in the following outline based on the sample essay. First, write in the thesis statement and the main idea for each body paragraph (expressed in the topic sentence). Then, try to identify the major parts of the description in each body paragraph.

THESIS STATEMENT   _____

_____

MAIN IDEA 1   _____

MAJOR PARTS   _____

_____

_____

_____

MAIN IDEA 2   _____

MAJOR PARTS   _____

_____

MAIN IDEA 3	I looked for the candidate.
MAJOR PARTS	white bus
	candidate's speech

ACTIVITY 3: Teamwork

Working with two or three of your classmates, compare what you wrote for the outline in the previous activity. If your outlines have any major differences, discuss them and see if you can come to an agreement about the appropriate content for the outline.

ACTIVITY 4

Choose one of the topics below and write a descriptive essay. Remember to follow the steps in the writing process: narrow the topic, brainstorm, outline, draft, and revise. (To review these steps, see Chapters 3–9.)

1. Describe an exciting event that you attended. (This could be a personal event, like a memorable family holiday or vacation — or a public one, like a sporting event or a school graduation.)

2. Describe your college campus.

3. Describe your ideal life partner and the life that you would lead together.

4. Go to a place that will stimulate your emotions, imagination, and intelligence: a busy emergency room, the food court in a mall, an animal shelter, a locker room after a big game, a dance club, a cemetery, a used car dealership, etc. Describe this place.

5. Describe your perfect living environment. Think about the structure, the interior, the exterior, the location, and so on.

Power Tip

When selecting a topic for your descriptive essay, keep in mind the strategies listed on page 259 of this chapter.

ACTIVITY 5

Choose one of the photographs on page 262 and write an academic essay (or paragraph) in which you describe the image. Do the following:

- First, brainstorm about what you see, writing down every single detail in the photograph. (You may not be able to use them all, but write them down so that you know your options.)

- Divide the photo into major parts and brainstorm on one part at a time. This will keep you focused and help you get better results.

- Write an outline for your essay (or paragraph). Each "major part" of the photograph can be a support point. This will help your description to flow logically from one "major part" of the photo to another.

- Compose, revise, and proofread your writing.

To review these steps, see Chapters 3–9.

Power Tip

You might also use other powerful images to write about. Ask your instructor if you can use a photo that you find yourself, either online or in a book or a magazine.

Photograph 1

Photograph 2

For more practice working
with *description*, visit
bedfordstmartins
.com/touchstones.

Photograph 3

Understanding Narration

One of the most important uses of language is storytelling, or *narration*. Since the dawn of history, storytelling has helped humans make sense of their world and has kept them entertained. In its simplest form, a story answers the question, "What happened?" However, at its most advanced, a story creates a compelling reality—with characters, settings, and actions—that can transport the reader to a different place and time.

Narration is an important element of college writing assignments. As a nursing student, you may be asked to narrate the hospital experience of a critically ill patient; as a history student, you may be asked to narrate the events leading up to the American Civil War; as an astronomy student, you may be asked to narrate the life cycle of a supernova; as a psychology student, you may be asked to narrate some of your childhood experiences. The possibilities are endless.

To write a successful narration, keep the following strategies in mind:

1. In a paragraph or short essay, you may be able to establish your **characters** only briefly; however, don't forget to provide at least one idea or observation that will bring each character powerfully to life. For example, *My cousin Natalie moves through life like a steamroller, flattening friendships and relationships as she goes.*

   Power Tip
   Sometimes, a key bit of **dialogue** can bring your characters to life. For more on using quoted details effectively, see Chapter 10, pages 244–46.

2. Something meaningful or interesting must happen to your characters. What happens to them is known as the **plot** or dramatic action. (This action can be exciting, suspenseful, humorous, tragic, inspiring, or something else.)

   When developing your plot, think in terms of a beginning, middle, and end. The **beginning** establishes the characters and setting and the initial action leading up to the main action. The **middle** relates the main dramatic action, usually with a climax or high point. The **end** relates the outcome or aftermath of the action—and especially what happens to the characters.

   Since the plot is often considered the most important element of a narrative, make sure that the parts of your plot are completely developed and logically connected. This will make it easier for your reader to follow and enjoy the story.

3. The **setting**, or location, of the story may be essential to your plot or merely a backdrop. For example, if your story is about the time you got lost in the woods, a description of the setting will be essential to your plot. On the other hand, if your story is about an argument you had with your boyfriend, the apartment where the argument took place may be little more than a backdrop to the action. Either way, be sure to describe the background for your reader, however briefly. If the setting is essential to the story, you'll need to use colorful and precise details to describe it effectively.

   Power Tip
   For more information on using precise details in your writing, see Chapter 10, pages 231–34.

4. Decide whether your narration will be based on **fiction** (an imaginary story), **nonfiction** (a true story), or a **combination** of these (a story based on true events but enhanced with made-up elements). Your instructor may specify which of these approaches is acceptable for the assignment.

WRITING A NARRATIVE PARAGRAPH

In some cases, a narration may be quite short (a few words or several sentences). In other situations, it might require a full paragraph or a short essay. When selecting a story to narrate, remember to consider the length of your assignment: an academic paragraph (one page or less) or a short essay (one to three pages).

Let's begin by looking at a narrative paragraph. Notice that the writer selected a story that could be effectively and fully narrated in one page or less.

> For a while, I was the most popular babysitter in our neighborhood, but I didn't tell anyone about the afternoon I lost track of my little brother, Jimmy. To begin with, we were throwing rocks into the creek. We had a big yard, bordered on one side by Cherry Creek. It ran from one corner all the way up the hill to our driveway. The driveway was higher than the water, so you could throw rocks over the side and listen to the splash. I asked Jimmy if he wanted something to drink. He said he didn't. When I got back with my lemonade, Jimmy was gone. Immediately, I began to worry. I called his name as I ran along the creek to the far corner of our yard. Jimmy didn't respond. My next idea was to go down into the water. I was glad I had on flip-flops, because it didn't matter if they got wet. I scrambled down the rocky path and headed upstream, towards the big culvert. We were not allowed to go in the culvert, because it ran under the road. The road was our boundary. I had looked everywhere else, however. I sloshed through the dark mouth of the pipe. I was tall, even at fourteen, but I could easily stand up inside it and the water was knee deep on me. I worried about Jimmy, who was small for his age, although he was a good swimmer. When I came out the other side, I was technically trespassing. I could hear noise around the bend. Finally, I saw him up ahead, playing ball with a big brown dog. He hadn't even bothered to take off his gym shoes! When we got home, Jimmy told me that the dog came out of the culvert with a ball in his mouth, and Jimmy followed him. I learned that you can't turn your back on a nine-year-old, not even to get a glass of lemonade.

culvert: a drain or covered channel that crosses under a road or railway

Power Tip
For an example of a narration by a professional writer, see paragraphs 10–26 of "The New Mecca" by George Saunders, page 589.

Power Tip
For more ideas on narrowing a topic and picking a topic that works for you, review Chapter 3, pages 45–48.

ACTIVITY 6

Choose one of the topics below and write a narrative paragraph. Remember to follow the steps in the writing process: narrow the topic, brainstorm, outline, draft, and revise. (To review these steps, see Chapters 3–7.)

1. Tell a story about a time when you got into big trouble for doing something you should not have done.

2. Tell a story about something that happened to you that changed you forever.

3. Tell a story about the most kind or unselfish thing you ever did.

4. Tell a story about the most embarrassing thing that ever happened to you.

5. Tell a story about an interesting encounter you had with a stranger.

WRITING A NARRATIVE ESSAY

When writing a narrative essay, you will use techniques similar to those for writing a narrative paragraph (see page 264). To begin, you will need to select a topic that you can narrate fully and effectively in one to three pages. Next, you will need to plan for an introductory paragraph with a thesis statement, two or more body paragraphs, and a concluding paragraph.

Power Tip

For more help moving from paragraphs to essays, see Chapter 8.

Writing a Thesis Statement for a Narrative Essay

As you learned in Chapter 9 (page 201), a thesis statement must do two things. It must 1) identify the topic and 2) express your original point or opinion about the topic. In a narrative, the topic is the basic story you are telling; your point or opinion is the main *purpose* for telling this particular story to your reader. Take a look at the following examples.

TOPIC (BASIC STORY)	THESIS STATEMENT (WITH PURPOSE OF STORY UNDERLINED)
winning $10,000 in the Quick Pick	Winning $10,000 in the Quick Pick <u>taught me that easy money can be more trouble than it's worth.</u>
failing my math midterm	When I failed my math midterm, <u>it was a wake-up call to the responsibilities of college life.</u>
immigrating to the U.S. at the age of six	Immigrating to the U.S. at the age of six <u>forced me to grow up fast.</u>

Below is an example of a short narrative essay that contains the required features discussed above. Read it carefully and complete the activity that follows.

Being an Effective Elementary School Teacher

What do you do with an eight-year-old who has a bloody nose? How would you handle the situation in front of a roomful of third graders? I completed my student teaching last semester in a third-grade classroom where I faced one challenge after another. The semester completed my degree in elementary education, but even more important, it taught me the skills necessary to be a success in the classroom.

On my first day in Mrs. Underhill's third-grade class, I gave directions for a reading activity. As I spoke to the class, Mrs. Underhill observed from the back of the room. The activity was simple. Working in pairs, students had ten minutes to read a short book to each other. Then, they had ten minutes to ask each other three questions printed on a hand-out. Before I got through my second sentence, hands shot in the air. I called on a little boy, who asked what happened if he didn't like the story he was assigned. I explained to the class that liking the story did not matter; students must each read what they were assigned. I completed the directions and handed out the books. Immediately, a little girl, Caralee, raised her hand to tell me that she did not like her story. She wanted to pick another one. It was frustrating, since I had just explained this situation. Yet it is also true that this sort of repetition is common at the elementary school level. Students need to be told directions and rules several times. Consequently, I didn't let any frustration into my voice as I explained again that she must use the book she had been given. From this experience, I learned that patience is the most valuable trait a schoolteacher can possess.

On another day, I was alone with the class. Suddenly, a boy named Cody tripped over his untied shoelace, hit a chair, and fell to the floor screaming. He had a bloody nose. The classroom went totally still. The sight of blood makes me nauseous and for a second I thought I might pass out. However, my instincts kicked in. I knew that in order to prevent hyperventilation, you breathed into a paper bag. I didn't have a paper bag, so I covered my mouth with my hands and breathed very slowly. Next, I hurried to Cody's side and led him to the sink at the back. I crouched down to speak eye-to-eye with him, telling him to please stop crying. To my surprise, he listened. Ignoring the jump in my stomach, I had him put his head back as I wet some paper towel to make a compress. I gently held it to his nose. Thankfully, Mrs. Underhill appeared at that moment and led him to the nurse's office. The class was staring at me. I told them in a steady voice that Cody was fine, and he would be back soon. They went back to their desks to complete their math. I still felt a little queasy, but I felt proud that I had survived. My instincts had taken over. Furthermore, I learned I could trust myself not to panic and to calm the others.

Finally, I remember another day when rain kept us inside for recess. I sensed that the kids were going crazy. Ezra, the class clown, jumped onto his chair and started doing a hula dance. He loved distracting others and I knew I was about to lose control of the class. "Third graders!" I shouted as I crossed the room to ease Ezra off his chair. Then, I turned around and told the class that the hula dance was a perfect rainy day activity. Imitating Ezra, but with my feet on the floor, I began to hula, inviting everyone to do it with us. Soon twenty third graders were jumping in place, swinging their hips in a circle like they had invisible hula hoops! Next, I directed them to do jumping jacks. This was a great way to get out some of their pent-up energy, not to mention what it did for me. A little cardio exercise was like a twenty-ounce latte! We did the hokey-pokey, and finally played a game of Duck, Duck, Goose. We filled the whole twenty-minute recess with physical activity. Afternoon science was a breeze; I got better focus from the students, and they asked great questions. Best of all was how bonded we felt to one another. We had done something spontaneous, energetic and fun, and as a result, the kids were eager to listen and to please.

In conclusion, I advise anyone interested in elementary school teaching to understand that the job is demanding and unpredictable. Thinking on your feet is critical. But even that won't work if a teacher doesn't have patience. He or she must also be able to trust

hyperventilation:
abnormal and rapid breathing that results in feeling faint or dizzy

his or her instincts, which takes courage. Lastly, the elementary school teacher ought to be a high-energy person, committed to putting energy into every day, even the rainy ones.

ACTIVITY 7

Fill in the following outline based on the sample essay. First, write in the thesis statement and the main idea for each body paragraph (expressed in the topic sentence). Then, try to identify the major parts of the narration in each body paragraph.

THESIS STATEMENT _____

_____

MAIN IDEA 1 (beginning) my first day in Mrs. Underhill's third-grade

class _____

  MAJOR PARTS _____

_____

_____

MAIN IDEA 2 (middle) _____

_____

  MAJOR PARTS _____

_____

MAIN IDEA 3 (end) another day when the rain kept us inside for

recess _____

  MAJOR PARTS _____

_____

_____

_____

> **Power Tip**
> In an essay-length narrative, you may want to devote a separate body paragraph to each part of your story: one for the beginning (characters, setting, initial action); one for the middle (main dramatic action and climax); and one for the end (outcome or aftermath).

ACTIVITY 8: Teamwork

Working with two or three of your classmates, compare what you wrote for the outline in the previous activity. If your outlines have any major differences, discuss them and see if you can come to an agreement about the appropriate content for the outline.

> For more practice working with *narration*, visit **bedfordstmartins .com/touchstones**.

ACTIVITY 9

Power Tip
When selecting a topic for your narrative essay, keep in mind the strategies listed on page 263.

Choose one of the topics below and write a narrative essay. Remember to follow the steps in the writing process: narrow the topic, brainstorm, outline, draft, and revise. (To review these steps, see Chapters 3–9.)

1. Tell the story about the first time you fell in love.

2. Tell the story about a challenging experience you had in school.

3. Tell the story about a difficult time in your relationship with your parents or parental guardians.

4. Tell the story about an important competitive event that you participated in.

5. Tell the story about a very big problem you faced at some point in your life.

ACTIVITY 10

Choose one of the photographs from the facing page and write an academic essay (or paragraph) in which you tell a story about the image. Do the following:

- First, brainstorm about the characters in the story. Who are the people in the image? Use your imagination and have fun.
- Next, brainstorm about the setting for the story. Based on the image, where is the story taking place? Give the place a name.
- Next, brainstorm about the events that make up the story (the plot).
- Remember, narration can be tragic, dramatic, suspenseful, humorous, inspirational, or something else.
- Write an outline for your essay (or paragraph).
- Compose, revise, and proofread your writing.

To review these steps, see Chapters 3–9.

Understanding Exemplification

In life, we are constantly called upon to provide examples to prove a point or illustrate an idea. If you ask for a raise at work, you'll need to provide examples of your achievements to justify that raise; if you brag that you found great sales on Black Friday, someone will probably want examples of your purchases.

In college, strong examples are the backbone of successful writing, so you should learn to recognize when examples are required and how to judge the effectiveness of your examples. For instance, if you are writing a paper against the death penalty, you'll want to provide examples of prisoners who were executed unjustly; if you are writing a paper on Renaissance paintings,

Photograph 1

Photograph 2

Photograph 3

Power Tip
In an exemplification paragraph or essay, consider using one of the following organizational strategies: 1) Start with the most powerful examples and end with the least powerful examples; 2) Start with the least powerful examples and end with the most powerful examples. Each of these strategies can work well; select the one that you think serves your composition more effectively.

you'll want to provide examples of those paintings that show the conventions and innovations of Renaissance art.

WRITING AN EXEMPLIFICATION PARAGRAPH

In some cases, the examples you provide may be quite short (a few words or several sentences). In other situations, they might require a full paragraph or a short essay. When selecting a topic for exemplification, remember to consider the length of your assignment: an academic paragraph (one page or less) or a short essay (one to three pages). Make sure that you can provide an adequate number of well-developed examples within the required length. If you don't have enough examples—or if your examples are poorly developed—your exemplification may lack credibility or persuasiveness.

Let's begin by looking at an exemplification paragraph. Notice that the writer selected a topic that could be effectively and fully exemplified in one page or less.

Power Tip
For an example of exemplification by a professional writer, see paragraphs 3–4 of "Twitterholics Anonymous" by Mona Eltahawy, page 608.

> During my childhood, I had opportunities for unsupervised play that many children today do not have. For starters, I remember that there was an empty lot on the corner near my family's apartment. Boys and girls of all ages and abilities congregated there to play softball. We were welcomed by the older children no matter what our skills were, and we played for hours. All we needed was a bat and a ball. Because we used a large softball, we didn't even need a glove. No adults were involved. Next, I remember riding on my bike to several local parks, one quite far away. At the park, I would ride down a set of shallow steps, bumpety-bump, until I arrived at the bottom. Other times, I simply rolled down the grassy hill next to the steps. My mother would have been appalled, if she had known, but she knew nothing about what I did. I simply told her that I had gone on a bike ride. I made sure I was home for dinner, so she did not suspect anything, or if she did, she didn't say anything. Finally, I spent a lot of time designing and making cut-outs of different outfits for paper dolls that I had created. I made dresses, shorts, and blouses. The paper clothes were ordinary, but no one cared. No one watched me, encouraged me, or discouraged me. I had been sent out to play, and that's what I did. Nowadays, many children go on supervised play dates. In contrast, I had uninterrupted time during my childhood in which to grow and develop independence.

ACTIVITY 11

Power Tip
For more ideas on narrowing a topic and picking a topic that works for you, review Chapter 3, pages 45–48.

Choose one of the topics below and write an exemplification paragraph. Remember to follow the steps in the writing process: narrow the topic, brainstorm, outline, draft, and revise. (To review these steps, see Chapters 3–7.)

1. Give examples of mistakes you have made in your life.

2. Give examples of what you find beautiful in life.

3. Give examples of things that make you angry.

4. Give examples of how your favorite performer or athlete delivers a great performance.

5. Give examples of things that your loved one does to make you happy *OR* things that you do to make him/her happy.

WRITING AN EXEMPLIFICATION ESSAY

Once you have mastered writing an exemplification paragraph, you should be able to transition smoothly to a short exemplification essay. To begin, you will need to select a topic that you can exemplify fully and effectively in one to three pages. Next, you will need to plan for an introductory paragraph with a thesis statement, two or more body paragraphs, and a concluding paragraph.

Power Tip
For more help moving from paragraphs to essays, see Chapter 8.

Writing a Thesis Statement for an Exemplification Essay

As you learned in Chapter 9 (page 201), a thesis statement must do two things. It must 1) identify the topic and 2) express your original point or opinion about the topic. In exemplification writing, the topic is the thing for which you will provide examples. Your point or opinion should suggest what the examples will prove or illustrate. Take a look at the following examples.

TOPIC (THING TO BE EXEMPLIFIED)	THESIS STATEMENT (THE POINT OR OPINION IS UNDERLINED)
the good study habits I've learned	The good study habits I've learned require patient and discipline, but the results are worth the effort. (Note: The examples will show that patience and discipline are required.)
signs of falling in love	There are certain signs of falling in love that can be both pleasurable and disturbing. (Note: The examples will show that the signs are both pleasurable and disturbing.)
Internet scams	In recent years, Internet scams have increased in number and complexity. (Note: The examples will show the number and complexity of the scams.)

Below is an example of a short exemplification essay that contains the required features discussed above. Read it carefully and complete the activity that follows.

My Worst Job

I remember the insurance office where I worked during the summers when I was a college student. I had come in for an interview with the man in charge—Mr. Patroski—and I had lied to him. I had told him that I wouldn't abandon the office when it came time to go back to school in the fall. In truth, it was only a summer job to me, and I did plan to leave in the fall. He must have been desperate for a worker because he said he believed me. Unfortunately, I would pay for my dishonesty. My summer job at the insurance office turned out to be the worst work experience I have ever had.

In the first place, I was very bad at what I had to do, and I didn't really get much better at it. For example, my main job was to type checks that were going out to claimants that had car insurance with the company. The claimants had had an auto accident, had gone through the process of getting estimates for repair, and now would receive their payment. The office really didn't have an official training program, but one of the women (they were all women who worked in the office) showed me how to type the checks. They had to be perfect—no misspellings, no cross-outs. If I made a typing mistake, I had to void the check and start over. At the end of the day, my voided checks had to be turned in. I was a very inaccurate typist, and I made lots of mistakes. I was ashamed to turn in my voided checks at the end of the day. No one said anything, but I knew what the other workers thought, and I was not used to feeling disapproval.

Second, the other women were distrustful of me. At my initial interview, I had been told by Mr. Patroski that I would be paid according to the current pay scale. This meant that I was being paid more than other women who had been there for many years and had started at a much lower salary. This was all right with me, but Mr. Patroski told me that I shouldn't mention what I was being paid to the other women because they would resent it. I never told them, but I think that they knew about the pay difference, and they treated me with suspicion and resentment as a result. They didn't invite me to have lunch with them, and they didn't exactly welcome me. There wasn't anything I could do about it except quit the job, but I needed the money for college.

Last, the worst thing about the job was that there wasn't enough to do. Most days, there were a few checks to type, but only a few. Sometimes, when the regular receptionist was out sick, I was assigned to sit at her desk and greet visitors. But there weren't many visitors. I had to look busy, so I couldn't bring a book to read. I couldn't retype checks that I had already typed because the checks were numbered, and someone would know. I spent a lot of time arranging the papers on my desk and going to the restroom. Eventually, I was assigned more elaborate typing jobs, but even those did not take up enough time. I was always glad when the end of the day came and I was released from the burden of trying to look as if I had been working hard.

Still, it was a job, and it paid fairly well. And, surprisingly, Mr. Patroski told me at the end of the summer, when I told him that I was quitting, that he had suspected that I wouldn't stay all year. He didn't seem upset, and he even told me that I had a job for the next summer, if I wanted one. I did work at the insurance office the next summer. Evidently, he had been worried about his employees taking vacations, and he must have wanted more employees than he really needed. The

For more practice working with *exemplification*, visit **bedfordstmartins .com/touchstones**.

same problems—bad mistakes, resentment by the other workers, and not enough to do—occurred the next summer, but I was relieved that at least I didn't have to lie this time.

ACTIVITY 12

Fill in the following outline based on the sample essay. First, write in the thesis statement and the main idea for each body paragraph (expressed in the topic sentence). Then, try to identify the major examples in each body paragraph.

THESIS STATEMENT _____

MAIN IDEA 1 I was very bad at what I had to do.

MAJOR EXAMPLES I was a poor typist.

_____

_____

_____

MAIN IDEA 2 _____

MAJOR EXAMPLES _____

_____

MAIN IDEA 3 _____

MAJOR EXAMPLES _____

_____

_____

_____

ACTIVITY 13: Teamwork

Working with two or three of your classmates, compare what you wrote for the outline in the previous activity. If your outlines have any major differences, discuss them and see if you can come to an agreement about the appropriate content for the outline.

ACTIVITY 14

Choose one of the topics below and write an exemplification essay. Remember to follow the steps in the writing process: narrow the topic, brainstorm, outline, draft, and revise. (To review these steps, see Chapters 3–9.)

Power Tip
When selecting a topic for your exemplification essay, keep in mind the strategies listed on page 270 of this chapter.

CONTINUED >

1. Give examples of the formative experiences of your childhood—those experiences that made you *the* person you are today.

2. Give examples of the small "good things" and "privileges" that you experience every day of your life but don't ordinarily think about.

3. Give examples of the things you worry most about.

4. Give examples of friends or family members who have made good *OR* bad choices in their lives.

5. Give examples of how you manage your time effectively *OR* how you manage your time poorly.

Understanding Process

In process writing, you explain or describe each step in a series of actions. There are two types of process writing: the "how to" type and the "how it happens" type.

In the "how to" approach, you give specific *instructions* to the reader, teaching him or her how to do something. The following are examples of "how to" writing topics:

> How to manage your bank account online
> How to sell items on eBay
> How to select a manageable class schedule

In "how to" writing, the reader is an imaginary *participant* in the process. To help the reader complete the process successfully, you must provide clear step-by-step instructions and precise details.

In the "how it happens" approach, you *explain* how an event occurs. The following are examples of "how it happens" writing topics:

> How the competition on *Dancing with the Stars* works
> How a solar eclipse occurs
> How the Olympic tryouts work

In "how it happens" writing, the reader is an imaginary *observer* of the process. To help the reader understand fully how the process occurs, you must provide clear step-by-step explanations and precise details.

WRITING A PROCESS PARAGRAPH

In some cases, the process you relate may be quite short (a few words or several sentences). In other situations, it may require a full paragraph or a short essay. When selecting a process for your writing, remember to consider the length of your assignment: an academic paragraph (one page or less) or a short essay (one to three pages). Make sure that you can provide clear step-by-step instructions or explanations within the required length. If you rush the instructions or explanations, the process may not be clear and engaging for your reader.

Let's begin by looking at a "how to" process paragraph. Notice that the writer selected a topic that could be effectively and fully explained in one page or less.

> Painting a room is one job that a beginning do-it-yourselfer can do. To begin, preparation is key. The first step is to cover the floor as well as furniture that you can't or don't want to move. The object is to protect these areas from paint splatters. Use a drop cloth, preferably a cloth one to prevent slipping. Next, take off all electrical covers from outlets, remove doorknobs, and use masking tape to mark all areas that you don't want to paint, such as windows and doors. Finally, you are ready to paint the room. You can use a brush to paint the edges of the woodwork. Then, use a roller to do the ceiling and then the walls. You may need more than one coat of paint, especially if you are painting a light color over a dark color. You should allow the initial coat to dry for at least two hours before applying the second coat. Last comes the cleanup. Throw away your paintbrush and roller, or rinse them under running water. Seal the paint can with a hammer, and be sure to label the can with an identification of the room that you just painted. Now you're ready to put back the switchplates, doorknobs, and furniture and to enjoy the room.

ACTIVITY 15

Choose one of the topics below and write a process paragraph. Remember to follow the steps in the writing process: narrow the topic, brainstorm, outline, draft, and revise. (To review these steps, see Chapters 3–7.)

1. From one of your college classes, explain a process: how to solve an algebraic equation, how to complete a biology lab, how to conjugate verbs in a foreign language, how to write an essay, how to draw something, etc.

2. Pick a team or group that you are a member of (a sports team, choral group, professional team, church group, etc.) and explain how the team or group members work together to achieve success.

3. Explain how to do something that you hate to do.

4. Explain how to arrange a date and make that date successful.

5. Explain how to participate effectively in a college class.

WRITING A PROCESS ESSAY

Once you have mastered writing a process paragraph, you should be able to transition smoothly to a short process essay. To begin, you will need to select a process that you can explain fully and effectively in one to three pages.

Power Tip

For an example of process by a professional writer, see paragraphs 5–7 of "The Art of Being a Neighbor" by Eve Birch, page 580.

Power Tip

For more ideas on narrowing a topic and picking a topic that works for you, review Chapter 3, pages 45–48.

Power Tip

For more help moving from paragraphs to essays, see Chapter 8.

Next, you will need to plan for an introductory paragraph with a thesis statement, two or more body paragraphs, and a concluding paragraph.

Writing a Thesis Statement for a Process Essay

As you learned in Chapter 9 (page 201), a thesis statement must do two things. It must 1) identify the topic and 2) express your original point or opinion about the topic. In process writing, the topic is the process you will explain. Your point or opinion should suggest why the process is important or what will be involved. Take a look at the following examples.

TOPIC (PROCESS TO BE EXPLAINED)	THESIS STATEMENT (THE POINT OR OPINION IS UNDERLINED)
how to do an efficient workout at the gym	In order to work out efficiently at the gym, you should devote a specific amount of time to each step in the workout.
how to interpret a poem	Although many students are afraid of writing about poetry, interpreting a poem is manageable if you follow a few important steps.
how Internet search engines work	Internet search engines seem to have miraculous powers, but understanding how they work is easy if you know their basic operational steps.

Below is an example of a short "how it happens" process essay that contains the required features discussed above. Read it carefully and complete the activity that follows.

How to Become an Auctioneer

A flood of words that can barely be understood by the eager customers—that's the auctioneer's chant. Then the word "Sold!" means that the auction is over. Propelled by the weak economy and televised reality shows, more and more people want to be auctioneers rather than customers. The steps in becoming a professional auctioneer can vary according to state regulations and personal preference, but anyone interested in this career should be familiar with the requirements and options.

The first step in learning to be an auctioneer is to find out what your state requires. For example, Ohio requires an apprentice auctioneer's license. To get this license, you have to be at least eighteen years of age, have a good reputation, and get a licensed auctioneer to sponsor you for at least one year, during which you have to call the bids in at least twelve auctions. Also, you have to take a course of study in auctioneering and pass an examination. These are typical prerequisites, but you should make sure that you know the requirements in your state.

Next, an auctioneer school, whether required by law or not, is a very good idea. There are actually many schools across the United States that offer auctioneer training. Students learn the ethics of auctioneering, how to speak in public, how to advertise an auction, and how to avoid breaking the law. At first, they may not know how to market a client's merchandise, but they can learn the techniques of determining its value and appealing to the customers who are likely to buy the products. They also learn how to work with many different types of people and answer questions from customers. An auctioneer is selling himself or herself as an expert in the field of the seller's merchandise.

Finally, no matter what type of auction is being held, the student must learn the auctioneer's chant. In the chant, the auctioneer rhythmically repeats numbers and words to show how much money the customers have bid. At the beginning of each class at an auctioneer school, the students typically have tongue-twister practice drills and counting exercises to sharpen up their skill at the auctioneer's chant. Then, the students learn to quickly run words and numbers together. "Filler words" like "Illyagive" instead of "Will you give" make the auctioneer seem incomprehensible, but good auctioneers can be readily understood. To do a good auctioneer's chant demands simplicity, clarity, rapidity, and tempo, all of which can be learned at an auctioneer school.

Becoming an auctioneer can be fun and financially rewarding. It's exciting to see shy students become confident public speakers. Also, auctioneers are typically paid by commission, taking 10–15% of the total of any auction, so they can earn quite a bit of money. Sometimes, they work part-time until they become experienced, and they can work as an apprentice with a knowledgeable auctioneer so that they can learn directly what the job entails. In most states, you don't need anything more than a high school diploma to enroll in an auctioneer school and become licensed. Anyone looking for a career should consider becoming an auctioneer.

ACTIVITY 16

Fill in the following outline based on the sample essay. First, write in the thesis statement and the main idea for each body paragraph (expressed in the topic sentence). Then, try to identify the major steps explained in each body paragraph.

THESIS STATEMENT _____

_____

_____

_____

MAIN IDEA 1 _____

_____

MAJOR STEPS _____

_____

_____

CONTINUED >

MAIN IDEA 2 _____

_____

MAJOR STEPS _____

_____

_____

_____

MAIN IDEA 3 _____

_____

MAJOR STEPS You start with tongue-twister drills.

Then you learn to run numbers and words together.

You should be understood by your customers.

ACTIVITY 17: Teamwork

Working with two or three of your classmates, compare what you wrote for the outline in the previous activity. If your outlines have any major differences, discuss them and see if you can come to an agreement about the appropriate content for the outline.

ACTIVITY 18

Power Tip

When selecting a topic for your process essay, keep in mind the strategies listed on page 274 of this chapter.

Choose one of the topics below and write a process essay. Remember to follow the steps in the writing process: narrow the topic, brainstorm, outline, draft, and revise. (To review these steps, see Chapters 3–9.)

1. Explain the process of developing a new friendship.

2. Explain the process of going on a date and making that date successful.

3. Explain the process of finding a job and getting hired.

4. Pick a competitive TV show you like to watch (like *Dancing with the Stars* or *American Idol*). Explain the competitive process—what the competitors must do, how they are judged, how they are eliminated, and so on.

5. Pick a social media Web site, such as Facebook or Twitter. Explain the process for using this Web site effectively.

For more practice working with *process*, visit **bedfordstmartins .com/touchstones**.

Understanding Definition

In writing a definition, you explain the meaning of a word or idea. Most people think of definitions as short, formal explanations of meaning such as those found in a dictionary. However, if you are writing a paragraph or an essay, a short dictionary definition will not allow you to develop your assignment adequately.

Instead, you will probably be asked to develop a more complex and creative definition. For example, a *technical* definition may require you to define the full meaning of a scientific or technological term, such as *symbiosis* or *software*. A *personal* definition might ask you to define what a particular term, such as *success* or *love*, means for you. A *contextual* definition may ask you to define a term in a specific framework, such as *depression in postpartum women* or *capitalism in modern Russia*. In each case, the key to a successful definition is exploring as many levels of meaning as possible and using precise vocabulary and examples to discuss them. Think of each level of meaning as a distinct "part" of your definition and develop it fully.

WRITING A DEFINITION PARAGRAPH

In some cases, a definition may be quite short (a few words or several sentences). In other situations, it may require a full paragraph or a short essay. When selecting a word or idea to define, remember to consider the length of your assignment: an academic paragraph (one page or less) or a short essay (one to three pages). Make sure that you can provide a fully developed definition—with multiple layers of meaning.

Let's begin by looking at a definition paragraph. Notice that the writer selected a topic that could be effectively and fully explained in one page or less.

> When people change their social class by moving to a higher class, that is considered "upward mobility." The concept of upward mobility has several important aspects. To begin with, moving to a higher social class tends to be connected with some changes. It usually involves a rise in income, and it can lead to children earning more than their parents. The family is also likely to improve their health status and education. Next, there are several ways to affect upward mobility. If people are in a low social class, they can raise their status by education, great effort, and special skills. Talent can affect upward mobility, but race, gender, and good fortune can also be important. Finally, there are special opportunities for upward mobility in certain areas. Politics is an example of one such area, with Bill Clinton, Abraham Lincoln, and Benjamin Franklin serving as good examples. Athletics and entertainment are other areas that offer special opportunities. In the United States, the population believes, in general, that effort and intelligence are important to advancement; the wealth and status of one's family are not all-important.

ACTIVITY 19

Power Tip
For more ideas on narrowing a topic and picking a topic that works for you, review Chapter 3, pages 45–48.

Choose one of the topics below and write a definition paragraph. Remember to follow the steps in the writing process: narrow the topic, brainstorm, outline, draft, and revise. (To review these steps, see Chapters 3–7.)

1. Define *self-respect*.

2. Define *sex appeal*.

3. Define *determination*.

4. Define *depression*.

5. Define *loyalty*.

WRITING A DEFINITION ESSAY

Power Tip
For more help moving from paragraphs to essays, see Chapter 8.

Once you have mastered writing a definition paragraph, you should be able to transition smoothly to a short definition essay. To begin, you will need to select a definition that you can develop fully and effectively in one to three pages. Next, you will need to plan for an introductory paragraph with a thesis statement, two or more body paragraphs, and a concluding paragraph.

Writing a Thesis Statement for a Definition Essay

As you learned in Chapter 9 (page 201), a thesis statement must do two things. It must 1) identify the topic and 2) express your original point or opinion about the topic. In definition writing, the topic is the word or idea you will define. Your point or opinion should suggest the scope or direction of your definition. Take a look at the following examples.

TOPIC (WORD OR IDEA TO BE DEFINED)	THESIS STATEMENT (THE POINT OR OPINION IS UNDERLINED)
success	My definition of success probably has nothing to do with most people's ideas about success; for me, success is defined by how many people I help in life.
love	In my experience, love can be defined as four major types or categories: self-love, romantic love, agape or brotherly love, and spiritual love.
the Renaissance	The cultural period known as the Renaissance has been defined in many different ways by scholars, but for me it is the freeing of human desire and its artistic expression in painting, literature, and architecture.

Below is an example of a short definition essay that contains the required features discussed above. Read it carefully and complete the activity that follows.

Procrastination

Mark Twain once said, "Never put off until tomorrow what you can do the day after tomorrow." He must have been a good procrastinator. About twenty percent of the population say they are habitual procrastinators. They can be found in all walks of life—in the workplace, on a college campus, even at home. They are difficult to live with. To someone who does things on time, they are very hard to understand. Basically, procrastination is the act of unnecessarily delaying essential jobs until later.

The best way to understand procrastination is to consider a range of examples. First, people who procrastinate do everything late. For instance, they fail to pay bills promptly, they invariably have to ask for an extension from the IRS to pay their income taxes, and they are consistently behind schedule for medical and dental checkups. Also, anything that has to be done by a specific date is a problem for them. For example, they miss out on chances to buy concert tickets and don't do their shopping for Christmas until Christmas Eve. Moreover, they look for chances to interrupt their work, such as inspecting their e-mail; on the surface, they show concern about answering e-mails, but really they are avoiding doing their other work, which is probably more important. Finally, many college students are procrastinators; even though their teachers use intermediate deadlines for long-term projects, they manage to miss them.

The origin of procrastination is not genetic; instead, procrastinators are reacting to certain family patterns. For example, some procrastinators are responding to the dictatorial methods of one or both of their parents. These techniques prevent their children from learning the independence that they need in order to be able to take action on their own. Some children may fight back against such behavior on the part of their parents, procrastinating as a form of rebellion. They may rely more on their friends, who may be more tolerant of their delays, apologies, and explanations. Moreover, their behaviors may extend into adulthood, long after their parents no longer exercise the same authority. Some procrastinators are perfectionists; they are afraid to act because they are afraid to fail and disappoint their parents (even when the parents are no longer present). It requires a huge amount of emotional force to change any of these habits.

Procrastination causes a range of problems beyond the delay itself. First, it exasperates others, especially friends and family, who cannot understand or forgive the procrastinators' constant lateness and breaking of deadlines. These people get annoyed or angry when they have to fix the messes caused by the procrastinator. Second, some procrastinators also develop drinking or other problems, because they have difficulties with self-control. Next, many also experience high stress and lack of sleep because of their worry about how they are going to meet deadlines. Also, they delay getting help for medical issues, just as they delay getting to other things. The effects of procrastination are disastrous for everyone, especially the procrastinators themselves.

To break the habit of procrastination is not easy. However, procrastinators will find the effort well worth it. As Christopher Parker said, "Procrastination is like a credit card: it's a lot of fun until you get the bill."

ACTIVITY 20

Fill in the following outline based on the sample essay. First, write in the thesis statement and the main idea for each body paragraph (expressed in the topic sentence). Then, try to identify the major parts of the definition in each body paragraph.

THESIS STATEMENT _____

_____

MAIN IDEA 1 _____

MAJOR PARTS _____

_____

_____

_____

MAIN IDEA 2 Procrastination is not genetic; instead, procrastinators are reacting to certain family patterns.

MAJOR PARTS _____

Procrastination is a form of rebellion.

Their behaviors may extend into adulthood.

MAIN IDEA 3 _____

MAJOR PARTS _____

_____

_____

_____

ACTIVITY 21: Teamwork

Working with two or three of your classmates, compare what you wrote for the outline in the previous activity. If your outlines have any major differences, discuss them and see if you can come to an agreement about the appropriate content for the outline.

For more practice working with *definition*, visit **bedfordstmartins .com/touchstones**.

ACTIVITY 22

Choose one of the topics below and write a definition essay. Remember to follow the steps in the writing process: narrow the topic, brainstorm, outline, draft, and revise. (To review these steps, see Chapters 3–9.)

Power Tip
When selecting a topic for your definition essay, keep in mind the strategies listed on page 279 of this chapter.

1. Define *college success.*
2. Define *family bonds.*
3. Define a *life-changing event.*
4. Define *personal style.*
5. Define *the American Dream.*

BRINGING IT ALL TOGETHER:
Basic Writing Patterns

In this chapter, you have learned about the basic patterns of development frequently used in academic and professional writing. Confirm your knowledge by filling in the blank spaces in the following sentences. If you need help, review the pages listed after each sentence.

✔ Successful writers often rely on several basic and advanced patterns of development to elaborate their ideas. Five basic patterns are 1) _____, 2) _____, 3) _____, 4) _____, and 5) _____. Three advanced patterns are 1) _____, 2) _____, and 3) _____. (page 256)

✔ When writing a _____, include as many sensory details as possible, including sounds, smells, tastes, and textures. (pages 256–57)

✔ When writing a narration, you will need to develop the dramatic action, or _____, and characters. You will also need to describe the location, or _____, for the action. (page 263)

✔ When using exemplification, make sure to provide _____ examples. Also be sure to provide enough _____ or your exemplification may lack credibility or persuasiveness. (page 270)

CONTINUED >

✔ If you provide careful step-by-step instructions in your writing, the pattern you are using is _____. (page 274)

✔ The key to a successful definition is exploring as many levels of _____ as possible and using precise _____ and _____ to discuss them. (page 279)

JOURNAL WRITING: 10–15 minutes

In college, it's important to manage your daily responsibilities and to develop a long-range academic plan. This plan may include picking your major, identifying transfer schools, researching sources of financial aid, and developing a time frame for the completion of your course work. For this journal entry, write about any ideas or plans you have for your long-range educational goals. What would you like to accomplish, when would you like to accomplish it, and how will you accomplish it? Discuss any actual plans you have made (perhaps with the help of a counselor) and/or any dreams you have for your academic future.

CHAPTER 12

Advanced Writing Patterns

Test your understanding of advanced writing patterns by completing this quiz first. You may know more than you think.

For each question, select all the answers that apply.

WHAT DO YOU KNOW?

1. **If you are explaining the origins or results of a situation, what pattern are you probably using?**
   ___ comparison and contrast
   ___ process
   ___ description
   ___ cause and effect

2. **If you are exploring the similarities and differences between two things, what pattern are you probably using?**
   ___ description
   ___ cause and effect
   ___ comparison and contrast
   ___ argument

3. **If you are defending a position on an issue, what pattern are you probably using?**
   ___ exemplification
   ___ definition
   ___ narration
   ___ argument

4. **In order to express their ideas effectively, what do most professional writers use?**
   ___ just their favorite pattern
   ___ a combination of patterns
   ___ none of the patterns
   ___ the pattern that their audience will prefer

5. **What form of evidence is most common in student writing?**
   ___ examples from personal experience
   ___ examples from assigned readings
   ___ common sense
   ___ newspaper articles

Advanced writing patterns—cause and effect, comparison and contrast, and argument—require more planning and careful thought to execute than most of the basic writing patterns. This chapter discusses the main features of these advanced patterns and also discusses mixing two or more patterns.

Understanding Cause and Effect

Why is health care so expensive in the United States? How does a person's diet affect his health, mood, and performance? What would happen if, to save costs, college libraries operated four days a week instead of five? These questions try to determine the causes and effects of an action, event, or situation.

In cause-and-effect writing, you explain the origin (cause) and the result or outcome (effect) of a particular situation, phenomenon, or event. There are three approaches to this writing pattern: **pure cause**, **pure effect**, or **combined cause and effect**.

In **pure cause**, you show only the origins of something. Look at these examples:

> There are several causes of diabetes.
> Three factors prompted the collapse of the U.S. housing market.

In **pure effect**, you show only the results or outcomes of something. Look at these examples:

> An oil spill has many devastating effects on marine life.
> I have noticed several benefits from my new study routine.

In **combined cause and effect**, you show both the origin and the outcome of something. Consider these examples:

> Several factors are responsible for the nuclear disaster in Chernobyl; furthermore, the disaster will impact human, animal, and plant life for generations to come.
> The causes of illiteracy are both political and economic, and the effects of illiteracy on the illiterate can be devastating.

As you will see, the key to successful cause-and-effect writing is to clarify the main origins and/or outcomes of a situation, phenomenon, or event—and to provide sufficient examples and details to illustrate them.

WRITING A CAUSE *OR* EFFECT PARAGRAPH

In some cases, the explanation of causes and/or effects may be quite short (just a few words or several sentences). In others, it may require a full paragraph or a short essay. When selecting a situation, phenomenon, or event whose causes and/or effects you will write about, remember to consider the length of your assignment: an academic paragraph (one page or less) or a short essay (one to three pages). Make sure that you can explain the causes and/or the effects fully and effectively—providing sufficient examples and details—within the required page length.

Pure Cause

Let's begin by looking at a pure cause paragraph. Notice that the writer selected a topic that could be explained fully and effectively in one page or less.

> Birds contribute to the health and beauty of a garden, but some gardeners have difficulty attracting birds. The three primary causes of bird inactivity are the wrong seed mix, poor feeder placement, and predators. The number one reason birds don't come to a feeder is because of what's inside of it. Bird enthusiasts should avoid using seed mixes with grains that birds don't like such as corn, oats, flax, and buckwheat. Instead, black-oil sunflower seed will attract a nice variety of songbirds such as goldfinches, chickadees, woodpeckers, and nuthatches. Secondly, a common cause of low bird activity is the placement of the bird feeder itself. Feeders should not be placed too close to large branches, which can provide jumping-off points for squirrels or predators. A feeder placed on a shrub is ideal because its branches are too fragile to hold predators but can hold small birds. As well, a feeder too close to a busy doorway will cause commotion that can scare birds away. Finally, the third cause of bird inactivity is a high population of predators, such as house pets or neighborhood cats. Cats are the worst backyard predator. Gardeners should remember that even if they don't have a cat, a neighbor might. They should try hanging feeders in trees that are out of a predator's range, as in a side yard protected by a fence. If a gardener understands and addresses the common causes of bird inactivity, she should be able to attract and keep a healthy population of birds in her garden.

Power Tip
For an example of cause and effect by a professional writer, see paragraphs 18 and 19 of "Death Knell for the Lecture" by Daphne Koller, page 593.

Pure Effect

Now take a look at a pure effect paragraph. Notice that the writer selected a topic that could be explained fully and effectively in one page or less.

> Watching too much television can have serious consequences, especially for children. The most common effects of too much television are obesity, low mood, and lack of energy. First, as surprising as it sounds, the effect of watching too much television can be obesity. Because television requires a child to be immobile, kids who watch a lot of TV are not getting the exercise they need to burn off calories. Also, children tend to eat unhealthy snacks while watching TV. The more they sit and eat high-calorie foods, the more weight they gain. The second effect of watching too much television can be a low mood. When the television is finally turned off, many kids are argumentative and slow to cooperate with parents or caregivers. Even in the classroom, after instructional videos or rainy-day movies, kids have

a hard time refocusing and being ready for the next learning activity. Part of the problem is simply the transition from the inactive mode of television viewing to the more active pace of life. The third effect of too much screen time can be a low energy level. Some kids simply get used to the sedentary life and want no part of sports or active games such as tag or hide-and-seek. Once a child who watches lots of television identifies herself as an inactive person, she will have a difficult time seeing herself as a soccer player or a runner. Active kids have more energy and better focus. The American Academy of Pediatrics (AAP) suggests that older kids watch no more than 1–2 hours of TV or video per day, and that kids under age 2 watch no television at all. Given the serious effects of TV watching on children, these are excellent recommendations.

ACTIVITY 1

Power Tip
For more ideas on narrowing a topic and picking a topic that works for you, review Chapter 3, pages 45–48.

Choose one of the topics below and write a pure cause or pure effect paragraph. Remember to follow the steps in the writing process: narrow the topic, brainstorm, outline, draft, and revise. (To review these steps, see Chapters 3–7.)

1. Discuss the causes of driving accidents.
2. Discuss the causes of family drama.
3. Discuss the causes of student debt.
4. Discuss the effects of missing class.
5. Discuss the effects of Internet addiction.
6. Discuss the effects of poor communication with your boyfriend or girlfriend.

Power Tip
Remember: *Causes* show origins; *effects* show results.

WRITING A CAUSE-AND-EFFECT ESSAY

Power Tip
For more help moving from paragraphs to essays, see Chapter 8.

Once you have mastered writing a cause or effect paragraph, you should be able to transition smoothly to a short cause-and-effect essay. To begin, you will need to select a situation, phenomenon, or event whose causes and effects you can explain fully and effectively in one to three pages. Next, you will need to plan an introductory paragraph with a thesis statement, two or more body paragraphs, and a concluding paragraph.

Writing a Thesis Statement for a Cause-and-Effect Essay

As you learned in Chapter 9 (page 201), a thesis statement must do two things. It must 1) identify the topic and 2) express your original point or opinion about the topic. In cause-and-effect writing, the topic is the situation, phenomenon, or event you will explain. Your point or opinion should suggest why understanding the causes and effects is important. Take a look at the following examples.

TOPIC (SITUATION, PHENOMENON, OR EVENT)	THESIS STATEMENT (THE POINT OR OPINION IS UNDERLINED)
global warming	The major causes of global warming are man-made; however, the effects impact all life forms on earth and the planet itself.
academic failure	Most college students are familiar with the causes of academic failure, but its lasting effects may come as a surprise to them.
poor health	It's crucial to understand the causes of poor health in order to prevent the devastating effects that may come from it.

Below is an example of a cause-and-effect essay that contains the required features discussed above. Read it carefully and complete the activity that follows.

The Causes and Effects of Freshmen's Unhealthy Habits

Many students find that by second semester they need larger clothes, they are falling asleep in class and in the library, or they are spending a lot of time in the health clinic. College freshmen are under stress as they adjust to new routines and expectations away from home. Symptoms of poor health are often dismissed as typical for first-year students. Understanding the causes of freshmen's unhealthy habits and their effects can lead to beneficial changes in these habits.

The cause of first-year college students' poor health is related to their inability to handle stress. In the first place, freshmen have to manage a complex class schedule. They suddenly have three to five classes to attend, with no parental supervision. Keeping track of when to be where can be a real challenge to those new to a big campus. Getting lost or overwhelmed is not uncommon. Secondly, students must keep track of homework. Assignment due dates and exam schedules are the key to good grades. Freshmen must plan for study time, which may include group work meetings. This takes effort and organization to be prepared on time. Thirdly, students must plan to register for upcoming required courses. By midterm, freshmen have to be looking years ahead at their planned field of study. Some classes are offered only one semester per year, so missing that class could delay graduation. Careful planning is the only way to graduate in four years, but many incoming students lack this skill.

The most common effects of a freshman's inability to handle stress are poor eating habits, lack of exercise, and lack of sleep. In the first place, student cafeterias are filled with starchy food. No one monitors what students are eating, and they tend to overload their trays with high-carb, high-fat foods such as those found at the dessert bar. The effect is the "freshman fifteen"—gaining fifteen pounds during the first year of college—that can make students sluggish and uncomfortable. Secondly, with the stress of many classes and deadlines, exercise can be difficult to fit into the schedule. Freshmen often skip this essential step in maintaining good health. Physical exercise is not a priority, and many campuses don't require much gym time. In fact, for many students, a game of cards or billiards counts as the recreation requirement, but these activities do not increase the heart rate. The third effect of poor stress management is lack of sleep. Freshmen are busy all day with school and work obligations, so nighttime becomes reserved for study. Late-night cramming is considered normal behavior, but a persistent lack of sleep creates fatigue and inability to concentrate. People who are not well rested tend to compensate for their low energy through having quick-fix snacks and beverages to get them through the day. Over time, these foods and beverages, such as a shot of caffeine and a chocolate croissant, can increase fatigue, insomnia, and weight gain, contributing to students' struggles. The tired student is also susceptible to infections, and can end up spending a lot of time in the health clinic.

The competing pressures of college life do not disappear after graduation. If anything, stress is compounded by real-world responsibilities such as paying rent, buying groceries, and maintaining relationships. Learning to balance is the key to handling stress, and it starts in college. Freshmen can learn to manage a complex schedule with a healthy diet, exercise, and sleep. A well-organized planner can be the freshman's best defense against bad habits, and practice will improve these balancing skills. After all, healthy habits can last just as long as unhealthy ones.

ACTIVITY 2

Fill in the following outline based on the sample essay. First, write in the thesis statement and the main idea for each body paragraph (expressed in the topic sentence). Then, try to identify the major causes or effects explained in each body paragraph.

THESIS STATEMENT _____

_____

_____

MAIN IDEA 1   The cause of first-year college students' poor health

is primarily an inability to handle stress.

MAJOR CAUSES   managing a complex class schedule

keeping up with homework

planning ahead for future classes

MAIN IDEA 2   _____

_____

_____

MAJOR EFFECTS   _____

_____

_____

_____

For more practice working with *cause and effect*, visit **bedfordstmartins .com/touchstones**.

ACTIVITY 3: Teamwork

Working with two or three of your classmates, compare what you wrote for the outline in the previous activity. If your outlines have any major differences, discuss them and see if you can come to an agreement about the appropriate content for the outline.

ACTIVITY 4

Choose one of the following topics and write a cause-and-effect essay. Remember to follow the steps in the writing process: narrow the topic, brainstorm, outline, draft, and revise. (To review these steps, see Chapters 3–9.)

> **Power Tip**
> Remember: *Causes* show origins; *effects* show results.

1. Discuss the causes and effects of poverty or money problems.

2. Discuss the causes and effects of divorce.

3. Discuss the causes and effects of getting married at a young age.

4. Discuss the causes and effects of difficult relationships between students and their parents.

5. Discuss the causes and effects of immigration (moving to another country).

Understanding Comparison and Contrast

When you **compare** things, you notice their *similarities*. When you **contrast** things, you notice their *differences*. Every day, you compare and contrast countless items and situations in your life. For example, when you dress each morning, you compare and contrast possible clothing choices, noticing how the colors, designs, and uses of the items are similar and/or different. Throughout the day, you constantly notice similarities and differences—in the foods you eat, the friends you spend time with, the forms of entertainment you choose, and so on.

In comparison-and-contrast writing, you identify the similarities and/or differences between things (usually two things). There are three approaches to this writing pattern: **pure comparison**, **pure contrast**, or **combined comparison and contrast**.

In **pure comparison**, you show only the similarities between items. Look at these examples:

> French and Italian are similar languages.
> The assassinations of Lincoln and Kennedy have important similarities.

In **pure contrast**, you show only the differences between items. Look at these examples:

> The Olympics and Special Olympics (for disabled athletes) have some differences.
> New York City and Los Angeles have two distinct cultures.

In **combined comparison and contrast**, you show both the similarities and the differences between items. Consider these examples:

> World War I and World War II are historically similar and different.
> Rhythm and blues and jazz have some interesting similarities and differences.

As you will see, the key to successful comparison-and-contrast writing is to clarify the main similarities and/or differences between two or more things—and to provide sufficient examples and details to illustrate these.

WRITING A COMPARISON *OR* CONTRAST PARAGRAPH

In some cases, a comparison or contrast may be quite short (a few words or several sentences). In other situations, it may require a full paragraph or a short essay. When selecting two things to compare or contrast, remember to consider the length of your assignment: an academic paragraph (one page or less) or a short essay (one to three pages). Make sure that you can demonstrate the similarities or differences fully and effectively—providing sufficient examples and details—within the required page length.

Pure Comparison

Let's begin by looking at a pure comparison paragraph. Notice that the writer selected a topic that could be effectively and fully explained in one page or less.

> College dorm life is similar to summer camp in many ways. Both involve a group of girls or boys sharing a bathroom and sleeping quarters, and both establish lifelong friendships. The first way dorm life is like summer camp is in the shared bathroom experience. This might seem like an obvious detail, but sharing a bathroom with a floor full of your peers can be a bonding experience. Brushing your teeth or washing your face next to your roommate makes both dorm life and summer camp feel like a sleepover. Strolling back to your room or cabin in slippers and pajamas also contributes to the feeling of a big slumber party. In both cases, the experience makes the new routine more comfortable. Secondly, dorm life and summer camp are similar because both involve roommates. My college assigns four girls to a dorm suite, which is similar to the six campers in a cabin at summer camp. There are often competitions between suites, just as there are competitions between cabins at camp. Living in the same dorm suite or cabin can feel like belonging to a team. This, too, can be a unifying experience. Finally, the dorm

room and summer camp establish friendships that can last a lifetime. Often, roommates and cabin mates have intimate conversations that can only occur when people live close together day after day. Often, even if roommates don't have the same classes or don't participate in the same camp activities, they will discuss their daily experiences. Students walk the same routes, and they know the same teachers or counselors, as well as the same students or campers. Because my college and my summer camp in Maine are both small, they are even more similar than they would be if I went to a big university in another state. Overall, I appreciate the way dorm life feels like summer camp, because it makes the experience less alienating.

Power Tip

For an example of comparison and contrast by a professional writer, see paragraph 7 of "Wading toward Home" by Michael Lewis, page 585.

Pure Contrast

Now take a look at a pure contrast paragraph. Notice that the writer selected a topic that could be effectively and fully explained in one page or less.

My parents approach money in contrasting ways. While my mother believes in spending money when she has it, my dad wants to save it. To begin with, my mom likes to leave big tips. She thinks waiters and waitresses work the hardest job in the world. She believes in tipping twenty percent, even for poor service. If she is really impressed, she wants to tip twenty-five percent. My dad, on the other hand, regularly tips fifteen percent. If he isn't happy with the service, he will tip much less, or skip the tip altogether. Secondly, my mother loves to buy souvenirs. On any trip we take, even if it's just to the hot springs thirty miles away, mother will buy us a key chain, a stuffed animal, or even a postcard to remember the experience. Dad thinks such purchases are a waste of money. He never buys mementos and doesn't like to enter the gift shop. He thinks the very idea is a scam. He avoids places that are meant for tourists. Finally, mom always participates in fund-raisers. Anyone who comes to our door selling popcorn, cookies, or coffee for the high school orchestra or the neighborhood elementary school play will make a sale with mom. She will spend at least twenty dollars, because she believes that if everybody on the block spent that much, the money would help a club, organization, or school a lot. Dad, however, thinks that such fund-raising efforts are manipulative. He feel that kids asking for money is a way to make him feel guilty. He is not a stingy man, but he believes that what he gives in taxes is enough to make him a good Samaritan. Overall, the differences in my parents' approach to finances is enough to prove that opposites do indeed attract.

ACTIVITY 5

Choose one of the topics below and write a pure comparison or pure contrast paragraph. Remember to follow the steps in the writing process: narrow the topic, brainstorm, outline, draft, and revise. (To review these steps, see Chapters 3–7.)

Power Tip

For more ideas on narrowing a topic and picking a topic that works for you, review Chapter 3, pages 45–48.

CONTINUED >

1. Compare or contrast the food at two fast-food restaurants.
2. Compare or contrast driving your own car and taking public transportation.
3. Compare or contrast two of your friends.
4. Compare or contrast your native language and English.
5. Compare or contrast studying on campus and studying at home.

WRITING A COMPARISON-AND-CONTRAST ESSAY

Power Tip
For more help moving from paragraphs to essays, see Chapter 8.

Once you have mastered writing a comparison or contrast paragraph, you should be able to transition smoothly to a short comparison-and-contrast essay. To begin, you will need to select two things whose similarities and differences you can demonstrate fully and effectively in one to three pages. Next, you will need to plan an introductory paragraph with a thesis statement, two or more body paragraphs, and a concluding paragraph.

Writing a Thesis Statement for a Comparison-and-Contrast Essay

As you learned in Chapter 9 (page 201), a thesis statement must do two things. It must 1) identify the topic and 2) express your original point or opinion about the topic. In comparison-and-contrast writing, the topic is the two things whose similarities and differences you will demonstrate. Your point or opinion should suggest how they are similar or different. (In other words, don't just state that the two things *are* similar and different; rather, give a clue about *how* they are similar or different.) Take a look at the following examples.

TOPIC (TWO THINGS TO COMPARE AND CONTRAST)	THESIS STATEMENT (THE POINT OR OPINION IS UNDERLINED)
health food and junk food	Health food and junk food have <u>obvious</u> differences, but <u>the fact that they can both be delicious</u> makes them similar.
men's sports and women's sports	<u>In the early twentieth century</u>, men's and women's sports were significantly different; however, <u>at the start of the twenty-first century</u> they have become quite similar.
Spanish and Italian	As Romance languages, Spanish and Italian have many features in common; however, their differences <u>make learning them unique challenges</u>.

Below is an example of a comparison-and-contrast essay that contains the required features discussed above. Read it carefully and complete the activity that follows.

Two-Year or Four-Year College—What's the Difference?

Film director Woody Allen once said, "My education was dismal. I went to a series of schools for mentally disturbed teachers." Although Allen's observation is humorous, it also brings up a serious issue: Where does a student get a good education? A first consideration for many prospective college freshmen is whether to attend a community college or a four-year college or university. While the differences between these two educational experiences are well known and fairly obvious, their similarities may be a more important factor in deciding which type of institution to attend.

A community college is different from a university in size, atmosphere, and how approachable the professors are. In the first place, a community college is smaller. Getting around can be a lot easier on a smaller campus, and students need less time to get from class to class. This helps to make the college experience more manageable and less overwhelming. It's easier to find offices and services as well. Secondly, a community college differs from a university in terms of the relaxed atmosphere. Many community college students are working people, or nontraditional students. Many are supporting families. As a result, instructors will not assign six to seven hours of homework per night. Expectations are still high; professors demand college-level work and they expect it on time. But if a student has a sick child, or has a work schedule crisis, professors tend to be more flexible about letting students make up assignments than professors at four-year schools. Thirdly, the professors at a community college are more approachable. Professors at a four-year school have many obligations outside of teaching, such as committee work and the pressure to publish original research. They keep specific office hours and may not be available at any other time. At a community college, the pressure on professors is often lower. While they are still busy, they are often much more available to give extra help or to answer questions.

Though it may seem like the two college experiences are different, they both offer opportunities to meet new people, to learn effective time management, and to get a good education. Firstly, both community college and university offer lots of opportunities to meet new people. There are sports and extracurricular activities such as theater and music at both places. Both places generally offer a central student union building or area where students can gather, buy coffee, or have a meal. And both places offer service opportunities, like tutoring or mentoring other students. Secondly, the demands of both university and community college life teach students to manage their time. Students must figure out how and when to get homework done, balancing classes with jobs and social life. The lessons students learn about time management are valuable no matter where they are learned. Finally, both campus experiences have quality education as their main goal. Whether students are pursuing a bachelor's degree or an associate's degree, they will be doing homework and participating in classes at both kinds of campuses. In effect, whether they are surrounded by three thousand students or thirty thousand, all graduating students end up with more life skills than they had going into higher education.

My first semester in college was at a state university—my parents' alma mater. Since my parents were paying the bills, there was no question about which school I would attend. However, I felt overwhelmed by the huge lecture classes and the crowded dorms. As a result, I dropped out without completing the semester. A year later, I decided to enroll in my local community college, and I found the environment less intimidating and easier to navigate. My advice to all prospective college students is to assess carefully the similarities and differences between two- and four-year schools, and to make a choice that fits your needs rather than the expectations of others.

ACTIVITY 6

Fill in the following outline based on the sample essay. First, write in the thesis statement and the main idea for each body paragraph (expressed in the topic sentence). Then, try to identify the major similarities or differences explained in each body paragraph.

THESIS STATEMENT _____

_____

_____

_____

MAIN IDEA 1 _____

_____

MAJOR DIFFERENCES Community college is smaller.

_____

_____

_____

MAIN IDEA 2 _____

_____

_____

For more practice working with *comparison and contrast*, visit **bedfordstmartins .com/touchstones**.

MAJOR SIMILARITIES   Both offer sports and extracurricular activities, a

student gathering place, and service opportunities

ACTIVITY 7: Teamwork

Working with two or three of your classmates, compare what you wrote for the outline in the previous activity. If your outlines have any major differences, discuss them and see if you can come to an agreement about the appropriate content for the outline.

ACTIVITY 8

Choose one of the topics below and write a comparison-and-contrast essay. Remember to follow the steps in the writing process: narrow the topic, brainstorm, outline, draft, and revise. (To review these steps, see Chapters 3–9.)

1. Compare and contrast two neighborhoods where you have lived.
2. Compare and contrast your college and your high school.
3. Compare and contrast two reality TV shows or talk shows.
4. Compare and contrast your parents and yourself.
5. Compare and contrast yourself five years ago and yourself now.
6. Compare and contrast two romantic relationships you have had.
7. Compare and contrast life in your native country and life in the United States.
8. Compare and contrast two sports teams or musical groups.

ACTIVITY 9

Select one of the pairs of photographs on the following two pages to compare and contrast in an academic paragraph or a short essay. Remember to follow the steps in the writing process: narrow the topic, brainstorm, outline, draft, and revise. (To review these steps, see Chapters 3–9.)

Pair 1

Pair 2

Pair 3

Understanding Argument

Arguing or defending a position is one of the most important uses of language. In everyday life, we routinely defend our positions on issues, both small and large: why we believe in freedom of speech, why we deserve a raise at work, why a certain musician or book is superior to another one, and so on. The success of our position depends on good reasoning skills, strong evidence, and a careful use of language to clarify our points.

In academic writing, argumentation may be the most important and widely used pattern of development. Forming an argument requires you to demonstrate your critical thinking ability—that is, the ability to see multiple sides of an argument, the ability to introduce appropriate and persuasive evidence, and the ability to make sound judgments based on that evidence. Since many instructors consider argumentation the "gold standard" of academic work, practicing your argumentative writing skills in this class will prepare you for your assignments in other classes.

Take a look at the following samples of argumentative writing assignments:

Argue whether the U.S. invasion of Iraq was justified.
Argue whether smoking should be banned entirely on your college
    campus.
Argue for or against the legalization of medical marijuana.

Defending your position means providing your best reasons for being for or against an issue. Look at the reasons given for this position on the legalization of medical marijuana:

The use of medical marijuana should be legalized because . . .

- it prevents dangerous weight loss in patients by stimulating appetite and reducing vomiting.
- it helps patients endure acute physical pain.
- it offers patients some relief from mental suffering.

The best approach to successful argumentation is to state your position clearly, give the major reasons for your position, and provide sufficient evidence to support your reasons. Also, keep in mind the following points:

1. When preparing your argument, make a list of the possible **counterarguments** that might be used to challenge your position. For example, some readers might have concerns that the legalization of medical marijuana may soften the laws on drug use in general. You might acknowledge these concerns in a statement like the following:

   > Although many people are concerned that the legalization of medical marijuana may lead to a softening of laws on drug use in general, current statistics show that this is not likely to happen.

   Anticipating how others might oppose your argument can help you explain your position more clearly. You may choose to include some key counterarguments in your composition, or you may simply make a list and keep them in mind to help you focus your own points.

2. In order to make a successful argument, you will need to provide strong **evidence** to support your position. The most common form of evidence for student writing is examples from your personal experience or studies. Additional forms of evidence may include facts and statistics or quotations from experts or key people involved in the issue. (You may obtain such quotations from textbooks, reliable Web sites, or interviews that you conduct.)

3. Respect the intelligence and conscience of your audience by using **valid evidence** and **careful reasoning**. Never try to "trick" your audience into accepting your position, either by presenting faulty evidence or appealing to any prejudices they might have.

WRITING AN ARGUMENT PARAGRAPH

In some cases, an argument may be quite short (a few words or several sentences). In other situations, it may require a full paragraph or a short essay. When selecting a topic for your argument, remember to consider the length of your assignment: an academic paragraph (one page or less) or a short essay (one to three pages). Make sure that you can defend your position fully and effectively—providing sufficient reasons and examples—within the required page length.

Let's begin by looking at an argument paragraph. Notice that the writer selected a topic that could be effectively and fully defended in one page or less.

> To show appreciation for enrolling and paying thousands of dollars in tuition and fees, students should be granted free parking permits at campus parking lots. In the first place, it isn't fair to charge students for permits, because they already pay a lot of money to attend school. These fees ought to include parking. Although some may say that the university needs the permit fee to maintain the parking lot, I would argue that the maintenance budget should come from another source. Secondly, students are essential to the university system. Although some funding at state schools comes from the state itself, without student tuition and fees, the professors and support staff would not have jobs or salaries. Free parking, on a first-come, first-served system, would show the school's gratitude to the student body. Thirdly, students are the majority population on campus. At the University of Tennessee, there are 28,000 students and only 10,000 faculty and staff. Clearly students are driving the majority of cars, and therefore need the most parking. At the very least, the university should make the outer lots free. They could charge a small fee for the closer lots, which are the most convenient, but leave some of the distant lots free for those willing to take the bus in to campus. Free parking for students would take a lot of restructuring, but it's the right thing to do. It would lower students' financial burden, and it would make students feel appreciated. It would increase their school spirit, while also recognizing that they are the most important population on campus. Even if all university parking can't be free, the system could be reformed to offer more flexibility and advantages to students.

Power Tip
For an example of an argument by a professional writer, see paragraphs 5–12 of "Death Knell for the Lecture" by Daphne Koller, page 593.

Power Tip
In an argument paragraph or essay, consider using one of the following organizational strategies: 1) Start with your most powerful reasons and end with the least powerful reasons; 2) Start with the least powerful reasons and end with the most powerful reasons. Each of these strategies can work well; select the one that you think serves your argument more effectively.

Power Tip
For more ideas on narrowing a topic and picking a topic that works for you, review Chapter 3, pages 45–48.

Power Tip
For more help moving from paragraphs to essays, see Chapter 8.

ACTIVITY 10

Choose one of the topics below and write an argument paragraph. Remember to follow the steps in the writing process: narrow the topic, brainstorm, outline, draft, and revise. (To review these steps, see Chapters 3–7.)

1. Argue whether all cell phones should be powered off during college classes.

2. Select a popular Web site (Facebook, eBay, Zoosk, etc.) and argue whether it is useful or a waste of time (or something in between).

3. Argue whether students who work full- or part-time jobs are at a disadvantage in college.

4. Argue whether participating in a student organization, club, or sports team is a valuable part of a college education.

WRITING AN ARGUMENT ESSAY

Once you have mastered writing an argument paragraph, you should be able to transition smoothly to a short argument essay. To begin, you will need to select a topic and a position that you can defend fully and effectively in one to three pages. Next, you will need to plan for an introductory paragraph with a thesis statement, two or more body paragraphs, and a concluding paragraph.

Writing a Thesis Statement for an Argument Essay

As you learned in Chapter 9 (page 201), a thesis statement must do two things. It must 1) identify the topic and 2) express your original point or opinion about the topic. In argument writing, the topic is the issue that you will take a position on. Your point or opinion should identify your position on the issue. Take a look at the following examples.

Power Tip
Try using *although* or *even though* to create a contrast in your thesis statement. This strategy acknowledges both sides of the argument and can engage your audience more effectively. See Chapter 9, page 200, for more information on how to create a contrast in the thesis statement.

TOPIC (THE ISSUE)	THESIS STATEMENT (THE POINT OR OPINION IS UNDERLINED)
pet medical insurance	**Although** many people think that pet medical insurance is a money-making gimmick, I believe that it makes good financial sense for some pet owners.
steroid use in professional sports	**Even though** popular consensus is against the use of steroids in professional sports, I believe that it enhances performance and improves the competition.
increased taxation for wealthy Americans	**Although** many Republicans argue that higher taxation for wealthy Americans is unfair, I am a firm believer in its fairness and benefits for the U.S. economy.

Below is an example of an argument essay that contains the required features discussed above. Read it carefully and complete the activity that follows.

Why Go Vegetarian

Many people think that vegetarians are depriving themselves of essential nutrients and pleasurable eating experiences by choosing not to eat meat. However, this idea is based largely in ignorance. Vegetarians who eat right get plenty of protein and probably more essential nutrients than their meat-eating friends. Many cultures around the world do not eat meat and are happy and healthy, enjoying delicious meals every day that are comprised of lentils, nuts, cheeses, and grains as well as fruits and vegetables. Vegetarians are not deprived, but rather are following a healthy way of life that is good for the body and the environment, and that promotes goodwill among all creatures.

To begin with, vegetarianism is good for the human body. For instance, vegetables are high in fiber, which is good for digestion. Also, they contain essential vitamins such as vitamin A, or beta carotene, found in carrots and spinach but not in meat. Plus, the omega-3 fatty acids that are so important to blood health can be found in walnuts, soybeans, and flaxseed, foods that vegetarians are likely to eat. Many people argue that the vegetarian diet lacks protein, but there are many excellent non-meat protein sources. For example, beans are very high in protein. Sauteed pinto beans or hummus from garbanzo beans can be as satisfying as a steak dinner. Another great source of protein is the soybean, and its by-product, tofu. Many vegetarians use baked tofu, fried tofu, and even tofu dip as their primary source of protein. Further-more, red meat can be unhealthy for the body, especially when con-sumed more than three times a week. It slows digestion and contributes to weight gain because of its high fat content. Consuming meat has also been linked to cancer.

Secondly, a vegetarian diet is good for the earth. By far the most significant thing vegetarianism does is make people more aware of the food they eat. In search of fresh produce, they are more likely to shop at local farmer's markets, or look for a store that will supply the most vibrant vegetables and wholesome grains. This can help support locally grown food and sustainable agriculture practices that don't damage the soil and water with harmful pesticides the way that large commercial farms do. As well, eating locally means reducing carbon waste from transportation and consumption of foods that are out of season. Non-seasonal food has traveled a long way, usu-ally from a warmer country. It has been picked by someone earning a low wage, and it has taken fossil fuels to get to the grocery store. However, the good news is that the opposite is also true. Eating food that is in season and locally grown means that someone nearby grew, tended, harvested, and transported it locally, without wasting fossil fuels or exploiting workers.

Finally, a vegetarian diet encourages a feeling of goodwill among all living creatures. Many vegetarians don't want to contribute to the poor treatment of animals so commonly found in corporate agriculture.

Chicken farming is one example. Take a look at any poultry transport truck from a commercial farm, where the terrified animals are jammed in cubicles, and you will see for yourself what kind of life they have. Many vegetarians do not want to contribute to such cruelty. It is true that meat eaters can also avoid contributing to the commercial abuse of animals by simply eating locally grown meat. But vegetarians want to go one step further. They believe that eating our fellow creatures does not promote a sense of global community. By opting out of the established food chain, they proudly create more balance and more health in general, not more suffering.

In summary, the vegetarian diet has a lot of benefits. Rather than detracting from good health, a diet that consists of no meat can actually promote health and well-being. As well, by eating and shopping locally for the freshest produce, people who adopt vegetarianism are also supporting agricultural practices that are good for the earth. And because it can involve a deep respect for animals, vegetarianism can create a feeling of fellowship among all creatures on earth. People who eat no animal-based food are not deprived. They are treating themselves to one of the healthiest lifestyles available to the human race.

ACTIVITY 11

Fill in the following outline based on the sample essay. First, write in the thesis statement and the major reason for each body paragraph (expressed in the topic sentence). Then, try to identify the support points given in each body paragraph.

THESIS STATEMENT

_____

_____

MAJOR REASON 1   _____

SUPPORT POINTS   _____

_____

_____

_____

_____

MAJOR REASON 2   A vegetarian diet is good for the earth.

SUPPORT POINTS   Vegetarianism makes people more aware of the food they eat.

It encourages eating locally grown food.

It helps cut down on carbon emissions and other wasteful practices.

MAJOR REASON 3   _____

_____

For more practice working with *argument*, visit **bedfordstmartins.com /touchstones**.

SUPPORT POINTS

_____

_____

_____

ACTIVITY 12: Teamwork

Working with two or three of your classmates, compare what you wrote for the outline in the previous activity. If your outlines have any major differences, discuss them and see if you can come to an agreement about the appropriate content for the outline.

ACTIVITY 13

Choose one of the topics below and write an argument essay. Remember to follow the steps in the writing process: narrow the topic, brainstorm, outline, draft, and revise. (To review these steps, see Chapters 3–9.)

1. Argue whether the amount of work given to college students is fair and beneficial to their education.

2. Argue whether the cost of college is fair to students and their families.

3. Argue whether spending two years on General Educational requirements is beneficial to college students.

4. Argue whether online college classes can provide as good an educational experience as traditional classes.

5. Argue whether your college provides a good educational experience for its students.

Mixing the Patterns

Professional writers often use a mixture of patterns in their writing to communicate their ideas effectively. Mixing the patterns of development is an advanced writing strategy that is essential to the success of most professional and academic writing. Take a look at the following example of how a combination of patterns might work for a topic:

ASSIGNED TOPIC _Report on this year's winner of the Heisman Trophy._

To give an accurate and helpful account of this event, the writer may need to use a combination of patterns. For example, she might:

1. define the "Heisman Trophy" (definition)

2. give examples of the winner's achievements that helped him win the award (exemplification)

Heisman Trophy: an annual award given to the most outstanding player in college football

3. tell the story of how the winner got started in football and how his career advanced (narration)

4. describe some of the winner's best moves on the field (description)

5. argue that the winner was or was not the right choice for the award this year (argument)

6. compare and/or contrast the winner to past winners (comparison and contrast)

By combining these patterns, the writer will communicate the information more effectively than if she used a single pattern only.

As a beginning college writer, you will find it useful to decide on a **primary pattern** for a writing assignment and one or more **support patterns** that will help you develop your ideas. Here is an example:

ASSIGNED TOPIC	*Compare and contrast the experiences of legal and illegal immigrants in the United States.*
PRIMARY PATTERN	Comparison and contrast (Explain the similarities and differences in the experiences of legal and illegal immigrants in the United States.)
POSSIBLE SUPPORT PATTERN	Definition (Define "legal immigrant" and "illegal immigrant.")
POSSIBLE SUPPORT PATTERN	Exemplification (Give strong examples of both experiences.)
POSSIBLE SUPPORT PATTERN	Narration (Tell the stories of some legal and/or illegal immigrants you know.)
POSSIBLE SUPPORT PATTERN	Argument (Argue whether the differences in their experiences are fair.)

ACTIVITY 14: Teamwork

With your classmates, discuss the following topics. How would you use each of the suggested patterns to communicate the information effectively? In the spaces provided, briefly describe how you would use each pattern. Then, identify the primary pattern that you would use and explain why.

1. **Topic:** Discuss the pressures that cause some students to drop out of college, and then discuss what can happen to them when they have dropped out.

   Patterns that may help you communicate your ideas effectively:

   Narration: _____

   Cause and Effect: _____

   Exemplification: _____

Primary Pattern (Which of these patterns is the most important to the success of this assignment?): _____

Explain your choice: _____

_____

2. **Topic:** Discuss how to get accepted to the four-year college or university of your dreams.

    Patterns that may help you communicate your ideas effectively:

    Description: _____

    Process: _____

    Cause and Effect: _____

    Primary Pattern (Which of these patterns is the most important to the success of this assignment?): _____

    Explain your choice: _____

    _____

3. **Topic:** Discuss the similarities and differences of younger and older college students.

    Patterns that may help you communicate your ideas effectively:

    Exemplification: _____

    Comparison and Contrast: _____

    Definition: _____

    Primary Pattern (Which of these patterns is the most important to the success of this assignment?): _____

    Explain your choice: _____

    _____

ACTIVITY 15: Teamwork

For each of the following topics, discuss with your classmates which patterns of development would help you communicate the ideas most effectively. Then, decide which pattern would be your primary pattern and write it in the space provided. Next, decide which supporting patterns would work best for the topic and write them in the spaces provided. (Note: You do not have to agree with your classmates on your final choices.)

1. **Topic:** Discuss the similarities and differences between people who speak only one language and people who speak more than one.

    Patterns of development for the writing:

    Primary Pattern: _____

    Support Pattern: _____

    Support Pattern: _____

    Support Pattern: _____

CONTINUED >

For more practice working with all of the patterns of development, visit **bedfordstmartins .com/touchstones.**

2. **Topic:** Discuss whether parents should restrict the use of certain Web sites for their teenage sons or daughters.

Patterns of development for the writing:

Primary Pattern: _____

Support Pattern: _____

Support Pattern: _____

Support Pattern: _____

3. **Topic:** Explain all the things that can happen when a person receives his or her first credit card.

Patterns of development for the writing:

Primary Pattern: _____

Support Pattern: _____

Support Pattern: _____

Support Pattern: _____

ACTIVITY 16

Select one of the topics from the preceding two activities and write an academic paragraph or a short essay in response to it. Remember to follow the steps in the writing process: narrow the topic, brainstorm, outline, draft, and revise. (To review these steps, see Chapters 3–9.)

BRINGING IT ALL TOGETHER:
Advanced Writing Patterns

In this chapter, you have learned about the advanced patterns of development frequently used in academic and professional writing. Confirm your knowledge by filling in the blank spaces in the following sentences. If you need help, review the pages listed after each sentence.

✔ In cause-and-effect writing, you explain the _____ and the result or_____ of a particular situation, phenomenon, or event. There are three approaches to this writing pattern: _____, _____, or _____.
(page 286)

✔ In a thesis statement for cause-and-effect writing, your point or opinion should suggest _____.
(page 288)

✔ Comparison-and-contrast writing identifies the _____ and/or _____ between things (usually two things). There are three approaches to this writing pattern: _____, _____, or _____. (page 291)

✔ In a thesis statement for comparison-and-contrast writing, your point or opinion should suggest _____. (page 294)

✔ In academic writing, _____ may be the most important and widely used pattern of development. Forming an argument requires students to demonstrate their _____. (page 300)

✔ When preparing an argument, make a list of the possible _____ that might be used to challenge your position. (page 300)

✔ The most common form of evidence for student writing is examples from your _____. Additional forms of evidence may include _____ or _____ from experts or key people involved in the issue. (page 301)

✔ In a thesis statement for argument writing, the topic is _____ that you will take a position on. Your point or opinion should identify _____. (page 302)

✔ Successful writers often use a _____ in their writing to communicate their ideas effectively. (page 305)

JOURNAL WRITING: 10–15 minutes

Most of your time at college is probably spent in classrooms. However, college campuses try to offer an array of activities and resources outside of the classroom: the library, computer labs, athletics facilities, theater arts, student organizations and clubs, food vendors, and so on. For this journal entry, write about what you do on your college campus when you are not in the classroom. Where do you hang out and what do you do there? Are you satisfied with this use of your time? If you are an evening student, would you like to get more involved on your campus? If so, in what ways?

CHAPTER 13

Paraphrase and Summary

Test your understanding of paraphrase and summary by taking this quiz first. You may know more than you think.

For each question, select all the answers that apply.

WHAT DO YOU KNOW?

1. What is the definition of a *paraphrase*?

___ putting an author's idea in quotation marks
___ using an author's idea without giving the author credit
___ restating the author's idea in your own words
___ restating an entire reading in a few words

2. Which of the following are strategies for paraphrasing?

___ using words that are familiar to you
___ using your own words
___ using only someone else's words
___ using big and unfamiliar words

3. What ideas are commonly paraphrased in college?

___ main ideas
___ ideas that everyone knows
___ difficult ideas
___ minor details

4. Which of the following items usually introduces a *paraphrase*?

___ a signal phrase
___ quotation marks
___ details
___ a *works cited* list

5. Which of the following describes a *summary*?

___ It presents the "big picture" of what you've read.
___ It includes everything in quotation marks.
___ It begins and ends with a story.
___ It is the same length as the original text.

Writing a Paraphrase

To **paraphrase** is to restate an author's ideas *in your own words and writing style*. When you are able to express an author's ideas in your own words, this demonstrates that you have understood the ideas.

PARAPHRASING MAIN IDEAS AND DIFFICULT IDEAS

In college, you will generally paraphrase two types of ideas: main ideas and difficult ideas. Paraphrasing an author's **main ideas** is useful for creating a summary (see page 315) and demonstrating (to your instructor) that you have understood the basic meaning of a reading. Paraphrasing an author's **difficult ideas** helps you make sense of those ideas and demonstrates (to your instructor) that you are capable of understanding them.

When restating an author's ideas in your own words and writing style, remember these tips and guidelines:

1. Divide the original passage into smaller "chunks" that you can work with individually.

2. Find new words to replace the author's words. Whenever possible, use words that you already know. If you use a thesaurus to find words, be sure to check the meaning of those words in a dictionary. You may also change the form of a word—for example, from *free* (an adjective) to *freedom* (a noun).

3. Only paraphrase the key ideas from a passage; you should not include minor details.

4. You may change the order of the ideas so that they flow smoothly in your paraphrase.

5. Never add any of your own ideas to the author's ideas.

As an example, take a look at the following passage from "Quitting Hip-Hop" by Michaela Angela Davis. (The full reading is in Chapter 33, page 623.) We will paraphrase the underlined sentence.

> I am a 40-year-old fly girl. My 13-year-old daughter, Elenni, and I often look for the same next hot thing—that perfect pair of jeans, a she's-gotta-have-it shoe, the ultimate handbag, and the freshest new sound in music, which is, more often than not, hip-hop. Though we are nearly three decades apart in age, we both feel that hip-hop is the talking drum of our time; it teaches us and represents us. <u>But, just as some of our African ancestors sold their people to European slave traders for a few used guns and porcelain plates, it seems as if the images of women of color in much of today's hip-hop music have been sold off to a greedy industry for a few buckets of "ice" and a stack of "cheese."</u>

First, let's break the long sentence into more manageable chunks and delete any unnecessary details:

> But, just as [some of our African ancestors sold their people] to [European slave traders] for a few used guns and porcelain plates, it

311

seems as if the [images of women of color] in much of [today's] [hip-hop music have been sold off] to a greedy industry ~~for a few buckets of "ice" and a stack of "cheese."~~

In the paraphrase below, follow the color coding to see how different key ideas from the original passage were restated. Notice that the order of some of the ideas has been changed to help the paraphrase flow smoothly but the author's original meaning has not been changed.

[In slave times], [some Africans sold other Africans into slavery]; likewise, [in modern times], [some hip-hop artists exploit] [images of black women] [for profit].

IDENTIFYING THE ORIGINAL AUTHOR AND SOURCE

Power Tip
Here are some other verbs commonly used in signal phrases: (*The author*) *states, says, reports, recounts, shows, tells us, explains, emphasizes, suggests, opines, points out, asserts, claims, argues* . . .

Power Tip
For more on using and identifying sources in your writing, see Chapter 14, Using Research in Your Writing.

When you paraphrase, be sure to use "bookends" to begin and end your paraphrase. Every paraphrase must begin with a **signal phrase** that identifies the author and end with a **parenthetical citation** that identifies the page number where you found the original sentence. Together, these two features identify the source of the ideas. Without these two features, your writing would seem to "steal" the author's ideas without giving her credit for them (a serious academic offense). Take a look:

SIGNAL PHRASE

Davis observes that in slave times, some Africans sold other Africans into slavery; likewise, some modern hip-hop artists exploit images of black women for profit (47).

PARENTHETICAL CITATION

ACTIVITY 1

First, read the passage below from Davis's article, "Quitting Hip-Hop." Then, follow the instructions below the passage.

> Today is my day, too. And the danger with what's currently going on in hip-hop is not as simple as a mere generation gap. Increasingly, the male-dominated industry tends to view women as moneymakers (as in the kind you shake). Few of us are in a position to be decision makers. As a result of this imbalance, many popular hip-hop CDs and videos feature a brand of violence and misogyny that is as lethal as crack and as degrading as apartheid. And though I would love to maintain my "flyest mom ever" status, my daughter's self-esteem and that of every young sister in the world is at risk. I'm willing to risk my public image to help recover theirs. If there's not a shift in how the hip-hop industry portrays women, then our 20-year relationship is officially O-V-E-R.

Each of the original sentences below has its key parts underlined and numbered. In the paraphrase that follows each sentence, underline and number each restated part of the original. For this exercise, you may assume that the passage appears on page 47 of the original reading.

1   2   3
EXAMPLE: **Original sentence:** <u>Few of us</u> <u>are in a position</u> <u>to be decision makers</u>.

1
Paraphrase: The author states that <u>not many people</u>

2   3
<u>have the power</u> to influence the <u>hip-hop industry</u> (47).

1
1. **Original sentence:** And <u>the danger with what's currently going on in</u>

2
<u>hip-hop</u> is <u>not as simple as a mere generation gap</u>.

Paraphrase: Davis reports that current dangerous trends in hip-hop

cannot be explained as mere generational differences (47).

1
2. **Original sentence:** Increasingly, <u>the male-dominated industry</u> tends to

2
<u>view women as moneymakers</u> (as in the kind you shake).

Paraphrase: Davis argues that the men who control hip-hop

see women as a moneymaking opportunity (47).

1
3. **Original sentence:** As a result of this imbalance, <u>many popular hip-hop</u>

<u>CDs and videos feature a brand of violence and misogyny</u> that is

2
<u>as lethal as crack and as degrading as apartheid</u>.

Paraphrase: Davis observes that hip-hop products often promote

violence and hatred of women, both of which are dangerous and also

humiliating (47).

1
4. **Original sentence:** And though <u>I would love to maintain my "flyest mom</u>

2
<u>ever" status</u>, <u>my daughter's self-esteem and that of every young sister</u>

<u>in the world is at risk</u>.

Paraphrase: Davis says that although she would like to keep her image

as a "cool" mom, she is more concerned about the harm hip-hop

does to the self-esteem of young women (47).

1
5. **Original sentence:** <u>If there's not a shift in how the hip-hop industry</u>

2
<u>portrays women</u>, then <u>our 20-year relationship is officially O-V-E-R</u>.

Paraphrase: According to Davis, if hip-hop doesn't change its images

of women, she will end her long support of the genre (47).

ACTIVITY 2: Teamwork

First, read the next passage from Davis's article, "Quitting Hip-Hop," shown here. Then, follow the instructions below the passage.

> Recently while watching a new video in which yet another half-dressed girl gyrated and bounced, Elenni turned to me and asked, "Why can't that girl just have on a cute pair of jeans with a halter top? Why does she always have to have on booty shorts? And why can't she just dance instead of grinding on the hood of a car? What does that have to do with the song?" I had no easy answers. Although the images of the women were both demeaning and predictable, the beats were undeniably hot. Therein lies the paradox at the heart of my beef with hip-hop: songs that make you bounce can carry a message far and wide, irrespective of what that message is. And far too often the message is that most young women of color are "bitches" or "hoes." I was backed into a corner, forced to choose between my love for hip-hop and my need to be respected and to pass the ideals of self-respect on to my daughter. No contest.

Paraphrase each of the following sentences from the passage:

- Begin by underlining the chunks of the sentence to be paraphrased.
- Next, paraphrase each underlined chunk, one at a time.
- Then, fit the parts together so that the paraphrase flows smoothly.
- Finally, add "bookends" to the beginning and end of your paraphrase — a signal phrase at the beginning and a parenthetical citation at the end (see page 312). Assume the passage appears on page 47 of the original.

EXAMPLE: **Original sentence:** <u>I had</u> <u>no easy answers.</u>

Paraphrase: Davis states that she couldn't explain clearly (47).

1. **Original sentence:** Recently while watching a new video in which yet another half-dressed girl gyrated and bounced, Elenni turned to me and asked, "Why can't that girl just have on a cute pair of jeans with a halter top? Why does she always have to have on booty shorts? And why can't she just dance instead of grinding on the hood of a car? What does that have to do with the song?"

   Paraphrase: _____

   _____

2. **Original sentence:** Although the images of the women were both demeaning and predictable, the beats were undeniably hot.

   Paraphrase: _____

   _____

3. **Original sentence:** Therein lies the paradox at the heart of my beef with hip-hop: songs that make you bounce can carry a message far and wide, irrespective of what that message is.

For more practice working with paraphrases, visit **bedfordstmartins.com /touchstones.**

Paraphrase: _____

_____

_____

4. **Original sentence:** And far too often the message is that most young women of color are "bitches" or "hoes."

    Paraphrase: _____

    _____

5. **Original sentence:** I was backed into a corner, forced to choose between my love for hip-hop and my need to be respected and to pass the ideals of self-respect on to my daughter.

    Paraphrase: _____

    _____

    _____

Writing a Summary

Writing a _summary_ is the best way to form a "big picture" of what you've learned from your reading assignment. For a basic summary, you must identify the author's main ideas, paraphrase each idea, and then join these paraphrases smoothly. Finally, you'll need to add bookends (a signal phrase or a parenthetical citation) at the beginning and the end of your summary to make it complete and correct.

To write a summary, follow these steps:

1. Find the author's main ideas. Paraphrase each idea, but do not include bookends (a signal phrase or parenthetical citation).

2. Decide how you want to order the paraphrases in your summary. You should pick the ordering system that allows the ideas to flow most smoothly and logically. Here are two options:

    - Follow the same order as the author.
    - Order the ideas from most important to least important.

3. Begin the summary with a signal phrase, the first bookend.

4. As you write the summary, add transitional expressions to join the main ideas smoothly. Some common transitional expressions are _next, furthermore, finally, secondly, consequently,_ and so on. For a longer list, go to Chapter 5, pages 103–7.

5. Finish the summary with a parenthetical citation, the second bookend.

Now, let's look at an example. The following article ("Farewell, Fair Weather," by Charles Blow) discusses problems related to extreme weather conditions in the United States. The article has 13 short paragraphs; however, once we group related paragraphs, we see that the article has five "units," each with a main idea and supporting examples.

For more practice working with summaries, visit **bedfordstmartins .com/touchstones**.

We are now firmly ensconced in the Age of Extreme Weather.

According to the Center for Research on the Epidemiology of Disasters, there have been more than <u>four times as many weather-related disasters in the last 30 years</u> than in the previous 75 years. <u>The United States has experienced more</u> of those disasters than any other country.

Just this month, a swarm of tornadoes shredded the central states. California and Florida have been scorched by wildfires, and a crippling drought in the Southeast has forced Georgia to authorize plans for new reservoirs.

<u>Who do we have to thank for all this? Probably ourselves.</u>

Last year, the Intergovernmental Panel on Climate Change issued reports concluding that "human influences" (read greenhouse-gas emissions) have "more likely than not" contributed to this increase. The United States is one of the biggest producers of greenhouse-gas emissions.

Furthermore, a White House report about the effect of global climate change on the United States issued Thursday (years late and under court order) reaffirmed that <u>the situation will probably get worse</u>: In addition to temperature extremes, "precipitation is likely to be less frequent but more intense. It is also likely that future hurricanes will become more intense, with higher peak speeds and more heavy precipitation. . . ."

<u>This increase</u> is deadly and disruptive—and <u>could become economically unbearable.</u>

According to the National Hurricane Center, 10 of the 30 costliest American hurricanes have struck since 2000, even after adjusting the figures for inflation and the cost of construction.

In 2005, the year of Hurricane Katrina, the estimated damage from storms in the United States was $121 billion. That is $39 billion more than the 2005 supplemental spending bill to fight the wars in Afghanistan and Iraq.

About $3 billion has been allocated to assist farmers who suffer losses because of droughts, floods, and tornadoes, among other things.

And a recent report in *The Denver Post* said the Forest Service plans to spend 45 percent, or $1.9 billion, of its budget this year fighting forest fires.

This surge in disasters and attendant costs is yet another reason <u>we need to declare a coordinated war on climate change</u> akin to the wars on drugs and terror. It's a matter of national security.

By the way, hurricane season begins Sunday.

THESIS

This is a period of unpredictable, dangerous weather.

MAIN IDEA 1

Paraphrase: Over the last three decades, the number of disasters caused by weather has increased greatly over previous decades, especially in the United States.

Examples of those disasters

MAIN IDEA 2

Paraphrase: Americans are largely to blame.

Examples of how humans—and especially Americans—have caused the problem

MAIN IDEA 3

Paraphrase: The problems will likely get bigger.

Examples of problems to come

MAIN IDEA 4

Paraphrase: Weather-related disasters may increasingly be causing economic hardship.

Examples of economic hardships

Examples of economic hardships

Examples of economic hardships

Examples of economic hardships

CONCLUSION

Paraphrase: We must take the battle against climate change seriously.

Now, here is a summary of the article "Farewell, Fair Weather." Notice that "bookends" (underlined) and transitional expressions (in grey) have been added.

> **SIGNAL PHRASE**
>
> In his article "Farewell, Fair Weather," <u>Charles Blow</u> claims that a period of unpredictable, dangerous weather has arrived. Over the last three decades, the number of disasters caused by weather has increased greatly over previous decades, especially in the U.S. Blow thinks that Americans are largely to blame and that the problems will likely get bigger. Furthermore, the weather-related disasters cause significant economic hardship. Consequently, we must take the battle against climate change seriously <u>(12)</u>.
>
> **PARENTHETICAL CITATION**

Power Tip

If your instructor requires you to write a summary, she will usually explain how long the summary should be and what information it should contain.

ACTIVITY 3: Teamwork

Working with a partner, choose one or more of the following readings from the list below (see Part Four of this book) and summarize them using the steps given above.

1. "The Art of Being a Neighbor," by Eve Birch, page 580
2. "Death Knell for the Lecture," by Daphne Koller, page 593
3. "Twitterholics Anonymous," by Mona Eltahawy, page 608
4. "This (Illegal) American Life," by Maria Andreu, page 618

BRINGING IT ALL TOGETHER:
Paraphrase and Summary

In this chapter, you have learned how to paraphrase and summarize. Confirm your knowledge by filling in the blank spaces in the following sentences. If you need help, review the pages listed after each sentence.

✔ To paraphrase is to _____ an author's ideas in _____ and _____. (page 311)

✔ When you are able to express an author's ideas in your own words, this demonstrates that you have _____. (page 311)

✔ When paraphrasing, divide the original passage into smaller _____ that you can work with individually. (page 311)

CONTINUED >

✔ Whenever possible, use words that you _____ in your paraphrase. (page 311)

✔ Only paraphrase the _____ ideas from a passage; you should not include _____. (page 311)

✔ When paraphrasing, never add any of _____ to the author's ideas. (page 311)

✔ Writing a summary is the best way to form a _____ of what you've learned from your reading assignment. (page 315)

✔ For a basic summary, you must identify the author's _____. (page 315)

✔ As you write the summary, order the ideas and add _____ to join the main ideas smoothly. (page 315)

✔ Always add a _____ to identify the author of the original piece of writing that you are paraphrasing or summarizing. Add a _____ at the end to indicate what page number it comes from. These "bookends" give credit to the original author and show that you are not stealing her ideas. (page 315)

JOURNAL WRITING: 10–15 minutes

You may have noticed that college instructors have a wide variety of teaching styles. Some may lecture in a formal, traditional way while others use more interactive teaching methods, such as small-group discussions. Some of your professors may write on the board while others use PowerPoint slides and Web sites. For this journal entry, write about the teaching styles of one or two of your college instructors. What do you like or dislike about their methods? Why are their methods effective or ineffective in helping you learn the subject?

CHAPTER 14

Using Research in Your Writing

Test your understanding of how to use research in your writing by completing this quiz first. You may know more than you think.

For each question, select all the answers that apply.

WHAT DO YOU KNOW?

1. **What is a list of sources that appears on the last page of your paper called?**

    ___ a *works cited* page
    ___ a parenthetical citation
    ___ a page of your notes
    ___ nothing

2. **What should you do when picking a topic for a paper?**

    ___ choose a topic that interests you
    ___ narrow your topic
    ___ formulate an opinion on the topic
    ___ keep the topic as broad as possible

3. **Which of the following are examples of plagiarism?**

    ___ copying others' words without giving them credit
    ___ using a commonly known idea or fact
    ___ failing to put other people's direct quotations in quotation marks
    ___ paraphrasing another person's words and giving them credit

4. **Working with sources is unique to writing what kind of paper?**

    ___ a journal entry
    ___ a personal essay
    ___ a research paper
    ___ a short story

5. **What should a works cited page include?**

    ___ all the sources you read
    ___ all the works you cite in your essay
    ___ all the sources your reader should look up on the topic
    ___ the most important sources you used in your essay

Using Research in Your Writing

For some writing assignments, you will need more than just your own opinion to support your point of view. You will need outside sources—the insights and opinions of experts—to lend support and authority to your position.

Begin the process of writing a research paper by finding a topic and gathering appropriate sources. Then, evaluate which sources are reliable and relevant to your topic and which are not. Next, organize your research. According to what you find, create a thesis and an outline for your essay. You will need to incorporate your sources correctly into your writing—avoiding *plagiarism*, or using other people's words and ideas without giving them credit. You will also need to cite the sources correctly at the end of your paper. Usually for this, you will use a Works Cited list. As always, you will revise, edit, and proofread your essay before you submit it.

Now, we will go through these processes in more detail.

FINDING A TOPIC

Power Tip
For more information on formulating a topic, see Chapter 3, pages 45–48.

If you are not assigned a subject for your research paper, it is helpful to find a topic that you care about. If you're interested in it, the research will be easier to do. You will care about what you discover.

If you are assigned a topic, try to pick an aspect of the topic that interests you. To do this, you may need to find out a little more about the subject first.

For example, James O'Connor, a freshman in an ecology class, was asked to write about the effects of acid rain. James knew from high school biology class that acid rain has negative effects on ecosystems, and that one cause of acid rain was emissions from automobiles. Other than this, his knowledge was vague.

James's assignment is a perfect one for research. First of all, he needs to narrow his topic. The topic of "acid rain" is too vast to fit into a three- to five-page paper. Before he can figure out how to limit the subject, James needs to know more about it. Secondly, James needs to formulate an opinion on the topic, so that he can write a thesis. Thirdly, once he knows his opinion or position, James needs to strengthen it with credible outside sources.

Power Tip
When you are not assigned a specific number of outside sources, aim to use two or three.

credible: worthy of belief or confidence; trustworthy

BEGINNING AT THE LIBRARY

Power Tip
Check your college library's Web page to see if it offers such services.

Even in the electronic age, libraries are the place to start any research project. Aside from their resources, one of their best assets is their librarians. Reference librarians are expert researchers. Many university research librarians will meet with students by appointment to help them with their projects. You can use these sessions to familiarize yourself with all that the library has to offer and you can ask specific questions about your assignment.

Secondly, libraries are hubs of information. Books are only one of the resources they offer. There are also hundreds of electronic databases, such as InfoTrac, JSTOR, or LexisNexis. Databases are catalogs of articles, usually from scholarly journals, on any subject imaginable. They often offer the most current information, and they are usually accessible from your home computer, even if you live off campus.

Narrowing a Topic

After a brief introductory meeting with the research librarian, James begins his research in the library computer lab. He starts with the search engine Google. James types in "acid rain." Immediately, he gets a list of URLs ("uniform resource locators") and links to resources on the Internet, including one to the Web site of the Environmental Protection Agency (EPA). The site explains how acidity levels in rain accumulate, plus what to do about acid rain. After clicking on the link and reading the information, James realizes that, while good, it is too general for a three- to five-page paper. He needs to narrow his search.

He adds "US parks" to his search words. This time he notices a site that mentions studies in the Great Smoky Mountains National Park (GSMNP) in Tennessee. He learns that acid rain in this park has been widely studied. In fact, of the national parks that have been studied, the GSMNP has seen the highest impact from air pollution. Already, James has narrowed his topic. Now he can focus on the effects of acid rain in the Great Smoky Mountains. (Because James found good, reliable studies and articles on Google, he does not use the bigger databases at the library this time.)

By avoiding amateur sites and Wikipedia, James is practicing the second step of research, *evaluating his sources.* Next to finding a topic, this is the most important step in using outside sources.

EVALUATING SOURCES

Generally, evaluating a source—Web or other—means considering its credibility. A *first* sign that a Web site is credible is the existence of a *by line,* or a clear statement about who wrote it. A site with an author (sometimes called a "signed" site) is more credible because the author takes responsibility for its content. A *second* sign of credibility is a relatively recent date listed on a Web site. Try to use the most current sources available and avoid material that is more than ten years old.

Third, look for objectivity—an absence of what is called *bias* or *prejudice.* Many Web sites are trying to sell a product or an idea. If you are looking into whether veterinarians should use hi-tech equipment, consulting the Web site of a veterinary equipment company might not be a good idea. Most likely, the company will present biased information because it wants to make a profit.

Objective sources to consider would be news services such the Associated Press, *New York Times,* or any other reliable paper. Newspapers try to be unbiased when presenting facts. Although many argue that there are no truly objective sources, you must judge for yourself. Document every source you use so that your readers can also make their own evaluation.

> **Power Tip**
> For more on narrowing a topic, see Chapter 3, pages 45–46.
>
> **Power Tip**
> *A note on Wikipedia:* In most college courses, Wikipedia is not considered a reliable source. It is a free online encyclopedia with many authors. In fact, any reader, regardless of expertise, can edit a page. Anyone who finds biased or incorrect information can correct it. However, the fact that information can be biased or incorrect makes it an unreliable source. Unless a professor has specifically approved Wikipedia, students should avoid it. If you are unsure, check with your instructor.

> **bias:** a particular inclination or prejudice. A bias can be negative or positive, for or against something.

ACTIVITY 1: Teamwork

For each question, read the assigned topic and the list of sources. Assume all the sources have relevant information. Which source(s) will be most credible? Put a check mark beside the best choice(s) for use in a research paper.

CONTINUED >

Remember, you want the least biased, most objective sources of information you can find. Then, discuss with your classmates, being prepared to support your answers.

1. Your topic is how large pharmaceutical companies control the price of medicine. Which of the following sources will be best for your paper?

   a. a blog about the cost of drugs, with unsigned and undated entries

   b. an article in *Newsweek* magazine, dated 2012

   c. information from the Web site of Pfizer, a large pharmaceutical company

   d. information from the Web site of the FDA (U.S. Food and Drug Administration)

2. Your topic is the use of steroids in racehorses. Which of the following sources will be best for your paper?

   a. an article in the *Los Angeles Times*, dated 2001

   b. information from the Web site for a popular racetrack

   c. a recent report by two veterinarians in *Horse Journal* magazine

   d. information from the autobiography of a famous jockey

3. Your topic is the treatment of animals used in rodeos. Which of the following sources will be best for your paper?

   a. an unsigned letter to the editor in *Rodeo News* magazine

   b. an article by Dr. James Farnesworth, professor of veterinary medicine, in *Cowboy's Digest*, dated 2013

   c. a report issued by a rodeo promotions group

   d. an editorial in the campus newspaper written by a student bronco rider, dated 2011

4. Your topic is the danger of bikes on campus. Which of the following sources will be best for your paper?

   a. a signed Web page from the National Highway Traffic Safety Administration discussing bike safety

   b. an article defending bike safety on DiscountBikes.com

   c. a recent article in a campus newspaper, citing specific bicycle-related incidents on campus

   d. an interview with two bicycle safety experts in *Bicycle* magazine, dated 2012

After browsing several books in the library stacks, as well as reading various newspaper articles, James has plenty of credible sources to choose from. The park has also been studied by ecology students like himself. He determines that his four main sources will be: two newspaper articles from the online version of the *Knoxville News Sentinel*, an unsigned Web site from the National Park Service, and the Environmental Protection Agency's page on acid rain.

ORGANIZING YOUR RESEARCH

One of the easiest ways to organize the information you have collected is with a note card system. This system is easily duplicated on various computer programs, such as Microsoft Word.

1. Using three-by-five index cards, create one or more cards for each source.
2. Put the author's last name in the top right corner.
3. In the top left corner, record the title of the article or book. If there is no author, you reference the source by the title alone.
4. Below these headers, write important information from your source. Use quotation marks around any words that are the source's.

The idea here is to collect all the information you will need both to include in your paper and to offer anyone trying to check your sources, such as your professor. Eventually, this information on sources will be put on your Works Cited page, the last page of your paper on which you list your sources.

As James makes his notes, he must decide if he will paraphrase, summarize, or quote his source material. There may be more than one note card for each source. At this stage of the process, James wants to limit the material he has to work with. That way, when he sits down to write a draft, he won't be overwhelmed with information. He can use his note cards to get straight to his point. A good goal is two note cards per page.

Power Tip
For more on forming paraphrases and summaries, see Chapter 13.

WRITING A THESIS AND AN OUTLINE

After James has made his note cards, he needs to formulate a thesis. This step is the most creative, for this is where he synthesizes the information he has compiled. It is at this point that you may find you care more than you realized about the way a problem or an issue is resolved. That's a good thing.

As James carefully reads each of his sources, he learns that acid rain is caused by high levels of sulfates in the atmosphere and that sulfates come from vehicle emissions. James begins to form an opinion: He decides that it makes sense to charge an entrance fee to the national park in order to limit the number of vehicles. Fewer vehicles means a reduction of emissions in the park.

He will organize his paper by using the patterns of cause and effect and argument. First, he will explain the causes of acid rain. Second, he will examine the effects, especially in the Great Smoky Mountains National Park. Finally, he will offer an argument for limiting the number of visitors to this park. His thesis becomes:

Power Tip
For more information on writing a thesis, see Chapter 9, pages 200–203.

Power Tip
For more on using patterns in your writing, see Chapters 11 and 12.

Imposing an entrance fee on all vehicles that pass through the Great Smoky Mountains National Park is a good way to help control the serious environmental problem of acid rain.

Next, James writes an outline:

Power Tip
For more on how to write an essay outline, see Chapter 8, pages 177–80.

MAIN POINT 1 Causes of acid rain

SUPPORT POINTS
– pollutants sulfur dioxide and nitrogen oxides
– toxic to humans
– toxic to forests and lakes

MAIN POINT 2	Effects of acid rain in the GSMNP
SUPPORT POINTS	– most impacted national park – visibility – water quality
MAIN POINT 3	How to reduce acid rain in the GSMNP
SUPPORT POINTS	– history of entrance fee – reduce number of visitors – entrance fee might help

Working with Sources

In a research paper, when you use source material, you must *document* it (give source information for it) to give credit to its authors and their ideas.

Unless your instructor has told you otherwise, use the Modern Language Association (MLA) style in your paper. The MLA style requires that you follow certain rules for documenting sources, and your instructor may ask you to use a handbook that includes these rules.

A NOTE ON PLAGIARISM

Failure to document your sources is a form of **plagiarism**, which is dishonest and a serious academic offense. Plagiarism is more than "borrowing" another person's work, whether that person is a student or a professional. It is stealing, and it can happen when you paraphrase, summarize, or use direct quotations incorrectly—even if you do so by accident.

As a general rule, you should document all words, ideas, and numbers that come from someone other than you. This also includes tables, graphs, and art such as photographs or drawings—including images that you find on the Internet. However, if the information is widely known by many people, you don't need to document it.

Some common forms of plagiarism include:

- copying other people's words, ideas, numbers, or art without giving them credit;
- cutting and pasting from the Internet without using quotation marks and citing the Web page or its author;
- failing to put other people's direct quotations in quotation marks;
- giving incorrect information about a source;
- in paraphrasing, changing other people's words but copying their original sentence structure;
- copying so many words or ideas from one source that it takes up the majority of your paper.

Power Tip
For more information, and to take tutorials on how to avoid plagiarism, go to **bedfordstmartins .com/touchstones**.

USING DIRECT QUOTATIONS

Using direct quotations is a precise way to support what you are trying to say. They often give your opinion a lot of additional authority, so they are very helpful—and common—in research papers.

By using correct form for your quotations and documenting them, you indicate that the material is a quotation, copied word for word from the original.

Long Quotations

When the direct quotation you want to use is more than four prose lines long, you will use a **block quote**. A block quote indents one inch from the left and uses no quotation marks. For example:

Ozone pollution should not be confused with the ozone layer in the earth's atmosphere. According to the National Park Service:

> Ground level ozone is a colorless gas created when nitrogen oxides mix with hydrocarbons in the presence of sunlight. Power plants, automobiles, and factories are the main producers of nitrogen oxides. Most ozone pollution originates outside the park and travels to the Smokies on prevailing winds. ("Great Smoky Mountains")

As in this example, a block quotation:

- is introduced by a signal phrase and a colon,
- is double spaced,
- uses the original text's exact words,
- has its parenthetical citation ("Great Smoky Mountains") after the quote's final punctuation (in this case a period).

Use block quotations sparingly, or else you will be relying on your secondary source too much and your essay will lack authority. For a three- to four-page paper, two block quotations is plenty.

Short Quotations

With a short quotation, you can quote as little as a brief phrase or as much as two or three sentences if they are not more than four lines long. The parenthetical citation comes before the end punctuation. Note that directly quoted material always needs a signal phrase, or an introductory remark that signals to the reader that quoted material is being presented. Look at the following example:

Ozone pollution should not be confused with the protective ozone layer in Earth's atmosphere. Rather, as the National Park Service notes, ground level ozone is a "colorless gas" produced when "nitrogen oxides mix with hydrocarbons in the presence of sunlight" ("Great Smoky Mountains").

USING IN-TEXT CITATIONS (MLA STYLE)

Power Tip
As you use different kinds of sources, different citation needs will come up. Refer to a handbook for more detailed information, or go online to **bedfordstmartins.com /touchstones** and take a tutorial.

In-text citations indicate that the ideas you've used come from another source. Sometimes they are known as **parenthetical references**. They are the words and/or numbers inside the parentheses at the end of the quoted material—for example, "Great Smoky Mountains" in the two quotations on page 325. By using in-text citations correctly, you avoid plagiarizing.

Together with the Works Cited page, in-text citations allow any reader to find—and consult—your original sources if they would like to.

Here are some common scenarios with in-text citations:

1. One of the **most common in-text citation** formats includes the author's last name and the page number: (Smith 12).

2. For **two sources by the same author**, use the author's last name followed by a comma and the abbreviated title, as well as the page number if the source has page numbers:

    > Acid rain can harm forests by "reducing nutrient levels and increasing the level of toxic substances in the soil" (Chandler, "Effects of Air Pollution").

3. If a source **lacks page numbers**, use just the author's last name:

    > The Environmental Protection Agency states that the air in some office buildings is "100 times more polluted than the air outside" (Socha).

4. Many **electronic sources**, including library databases, will lack page numbers and sometimes even authors. Use an abbreviated title for the source, in quotation marks:

    > The EPA states that human beings have put so many "different chemicals into the air that they have changed the mix of gases in the atmosphere" ("What Causes Acid Rain").

5. Sometimes you'll quote **a source from within another source**. This is called a *secondary source* and is handled with the abbreviation *qtd.*

    > Tennessee senator Lamar Alexander said that the push to limit acid rain in the park needs to intensify, noting, "People don't come to see the Smoggy Mountains. They come to see the Smoky Mountains" (qtd. in "Tourism Summit").

FORMING THE WORKS CITED PAGE

The final stage of writing the essay is to assemble the **Works Cited page**. This page should include all the works you **cite** (refer to) in your essay. Together with the in-text citations, this page helps your reader to trace your research.

-   Type "Works Cited," with no italics or underlining, at the top of a separate piece of paper, after the last page of your essay.
-   Use the same one-inch margins as for the rest of your paper.

- Double-space the entries, without skipping any lines between them.
- Indent five spaces for the second lines of citations (and the third, fourth, and so on).
- Make certain that the spellings of names and so on correspond to those in your in-text citations.

Note that when you use an online source, you must include abbreviations that indicate no page numbers ("n. pag.") when necessary. Other abbreviations include "n.d." for no date of publication listed and "n.p." for no publisher listed. You must also include the date you accessed the information, as Web sites are often updated and the material can change.

Here are some common types of entries, shown with a template plus example(s):

Book

Template:
> Last name, First name. *Title of Book.* City of Publication: Publisher, Year of Publication. Medium of Publication.

Example:
> Henley, Patricia. *The Hummingbird House.* Denver: MacMurray, 1999. Print.

Journal

A journal is a type of trade magazine, or a periodical publication for professionals in a given field. Its audience is not general but specific.

Template:
> Author(s). "Title of Article." *Title of Journal* Volume.Issue (Year): pages. Medium of publication.

A print journal. *Example:*
> Burgess, Anthony. "Politics in the Novels of Graham Greene." *Literature and Society.* Spec. issue of *Journal of Contemporary History* 2.2 (1967): 93-99. Print.

A print journal accessed online. Note that the date the article was accessed is included after the medium, "Web." *Example:*
> Wheelis, Mark. "Investigating Disease Outbreaks under a Protocol to the Biological and Toxin Weapons Convention." *Emerging Infectious Diseases* 6.6 (2000): 595-600. Web. 8 Feb. 2009.

Newspaper

Template:
> Author(s). "Title of Article." *Title of Newspaper.* Day Month Year: pages. Medium of publication.

Print article. *Example:*
> Wielaard, Robert. "Europe Warns Iran on Holocaust Denial." *Rochester Democrat and Chronicle* 16 Dec. 2005: 11A. Print.

Newspaper editorial. *Example:*

> "Earthquake in Pakistan." Editorial. *New York Times* 13 Oct. 2005, late
> ed.: A26. Print.

Newspaper article accessed online. Note that the date the article was accessed is included after the medium, "Web." *Example:*

> Barnes, Susan B. "Podcasters Reach Out in Their Own Digital Show."
> *Rochester Democrat and Chronicle* 19 June 2005. Newsbank. MCC
> Libraries, Rochester, NY. n. pag. Web. 19 Dec. 2005.

Web Sites

Power Tip
For more examples of
correct citations, consult
a grammar handbook,
or go online to
**bedfordstmartins.com
/touchstones** and take
a tutorial.

The latest edition of the MLA style manual no longer requires writers to provide URLs for Web entries. However, if your instructor asks for them, include them in angle brackets after the entry and end with a period. For long URLs, break lines only at slashes. Use the abbreviations "n.d." (no date) or "n.p." (no publisher) if there is no date or no publisher listed.

Page on a Web site. *Example:*

> "What Is Acid Rain?" *epa.gov.* United States Environmental Protection
> Agency, n.d. Web. 29 Feb. 2012 <http://www.epa.gov/acidrain/
> education/site_students/whatisacid.html>
> "How to Make Vegetarian Chili." *eHow.* Demand Media, Inc., n.d. Web.
> 24 Feb. 2009.

Article from online journal. *Example:*

> Dolby, Nadine. "Research in Youth Culture and Policy: Current Conditions and Future Directions." *Social Work and Society: The
> International Online-Only Journal* 6.2 (2008): n. pag. Web. 20
> May 2009.

Writing the Research Essay

Finally, James used his outline to draft his research paper. Then, he met with his instructor to discuss it. Based on her feedback, James revised, proofread, and edited his essay. The following is the result.

O'Connor 1

James O'Connor

Professor Appel

Ecology 101

1 Mar. 2012

Solving the Problem of Acid Rain in the Great Smoky

Mountains National Park—Before It's Too Late

Human impact on the environment is a growing problem. In the last several years, we've seen melting polar ice caps and unpredictable weather patterns due to global warming. Closer to home, levels of acid rain are rising. This rise is directly related to toxic emissions from local cities, factories, and vehicles. In particular, the Great Smoky Mountains National Park (GSMNP) in Tennessee is showing the effects of acid rain, as measured in several recent studies. Many people, including park ecologists, are concerned about the damage incurred on this national treasure and are eager to find a solution to it. Examining the causes and effects of acid rain in the Great

Smoky Mountains National Park proves that imposing an entrance fee on all vehicles that pass through the park would be a good way to help control this serious environmental problem.

According to the United States Environmental Protection Agency Web site, acid rain is weather contaminated by pollutants. The main causes of acid rain are sulfur dioxide and nitrogen oxides. High in the atmosphere, these chemicals mix and react with oxygen and water. Then, they become part of the rain, sleet, snow, and fog in the weather system. In particular, nitrogen oxide is toxic at ground level and can contribute to asthma and bronchitis in humans. Furthermore, both pollutants produce high levels of aluminum, which is toxic for forests and bodies of water. Aluminum in the soil limits the ability of trees to absorb the water that they need to grow and thrive. High aluminum levels in lakes and streams destroy populations of phytoplankton, mayflies, rainbow trout, smallmouth bass, frogs, spotted salamanders, and

O'Connor 2

crayfish, among others ("Acid Rain"). Acid rain has a direct negative impact on the environment of humans and non-humans alike.

> The source has no listed author and no page numbers, so the writer uses a shortened title.

The effects of acid rain in the GSMNP have been monitored for several decades. Studies have shown that this national park receives the highest contamination from acid rain of any monitored park. According to the National Park Service, the problems in the GSMNP are caused by local cities, especially industrial sites and power plants. These pollutants travel along weather patterns. Then, they hit the mountains that tend to "trap and concentrate human-made pollutants in and around the national park" ("Great Smoky Mountains"). The first significant effect of acid rain is to decrease visibility from a normal range from 93 miles to 25 miles. Pollutants in the air create a "uniform whitish haze," which is different from the low-lying clouds for which the "smoky" park was named ("Great Smoky Mountains"). A second effect of acid rain in the park is on the water quality. Twelve of the high-elevation streams in the park are on the Tennessee impaired waterways list, because of their high acidity. According to researchers at the University of Tennessee, the acid levels spike each time it rains (Simmons). Steve Moore, chief fisheries biologist for the GSMNP, calls these rising levels of acidity one of the most "critical issues in park resource protection" (qtd. in Simmons). Some estimates suggest that within another three decades, none of the bodies of water at high elevations will be able to support fish (Simmons).

> The paragraph contains several short, direct quotations.

Finding a way to solve the problem of acid rain in the GSMNP is the question facing national park service ecologists. For example, the National Park Service Web page claims that the main source of the problem is "inadequate pollution control equipment in power plants, factories, and automobiles" ("Great Smoky Mountains"). One simple step toward limiting acid rain would be to limit the number of visitors

> James offers his own ideas on how to solve the problem by blending source material with his own argument. When writing a research paper, do not forget to state your own opinion.

O'Connor 3

to the park by imposing an entrance fee on automobiles. In fact, we could say that with over nine million visitors a year, the park needs better restrictions in general ("Great Smoky Mountains") to keep it safe from human impact. The GSMNP is the most visited national park in the United States, and yet it is the only major park without an entrance fee. This is because the park land was once privately owned and to charge an entrance fee would require action by the Tennessee legislature ("Great Smoky Mountains"). However, trucks should not be allowed through the park. All travelers should be encouraged to enter and explore on foot. Keith Bellows, editor-in-chief of *National Geographic Traveler,* agrees. Speaking at the 2008 Great Smoky Mountains Tourism Summit, Bellows warned that high visitation to the park threatens to destroy "the very characteristics that appeal to tourists in the first place" (qtd. in "Tourism Summit").

In conclusion, acid rain is a real problem facing the Great Smoky Mountains National Park, not in the future but now. Not only does it pose human health risks, but it has had negative effects on the pristine ecosystems found in this treasured national park. Due to its location, the park feels the effects of local industry and traffic emissions. If major steps to reduce acid rain are not taken soon, the area stands to lose what originally made it great. A step in the right direction is to ban trucks and reduce vehicle visitors by imposing an entrance fee on all automobiles going through the park.

O'Connor 4

Works Cited

"Great Smoky Mountains." *nps.gov*. National Park Service.

　　U.S. Department of the Interior, n.d. Web. 29 Feb. 2012.

Simmons, Morgan. "Monitoring Water in the Smokies."

　　Knoxnews.com. Knoxville News Sentinel. 20 May 2010.

　　Scripps Interactive Newspapers Group, n.pag. Web.

　　28 Feb. 2012.

"Tourism Summit Focuses on Sustaining Area's Natural

　　Beauty." *Knoxnews.com*. Knoxville News Sentinel. 29 Apr.

　　2008. Scripps Interactive Newspapers Group, n.pag. Web.

　　1 Mar. 2012.

"What Is Acid Rain?" *epa.gov*. United States Environmental

　　Protection Agency, n.d. Web. 29 Feb. 2012.

BRINGING IT ALL TOGETHER:
Using Research in Your Writing

In this chapter, you have learned about how to use research in your writing. Confirm your knowledge by filling in the blank spaces in the following sentences. If you need help, review the pages listed after each sentence.

✔ Using outside sources in your essay lends support and _____ to your position. (page 320)

✔ After finding a topic you're interested in researching, you must find and _____ sources. (page 321)

✔ To support your thesis, you should try to find the least _____, most _____ sources that you can. (page 321)

✔ A great way of organizing your research is 1) _____ _____, 2) _____ _____, and 3) _____ _____. (page 323)

✔ Plagiarism is considered a form of _____. It can happen when you _____, _____, or _____ incorrectly—even if you do so by accident. (page 324)

✔ When you want to say something precisely, copying word for word from your original source, you will need to use a _____. When a _____ is more than four prose lines long, you will need to use a _____. (page 325)

✔ In-text citations indicate that the ideas you've used come from another source, and are also known as _____. (page 326)

✔ A Works Cited page is the last page of your essay, and it includes _____. (page 326)

JOURNAL WRITING: 10–15 minutes

Some students dress, style their hair, and even apply makeup as though college were a fashion show. Other students like to present themselves in professional attire, both for self-confidence and to make a good impression on others. On the other hand, many students believe that getting an education has nothing to do with clothing or personal style, so they dress simply for comfort and convenience. For this journal entry, write about your attitudes toward clothes and personal appearance in college. Do you think how you dress and present yourself can affect your success in college? Why or why not?

PART THREE
Grammar for Academic Writing

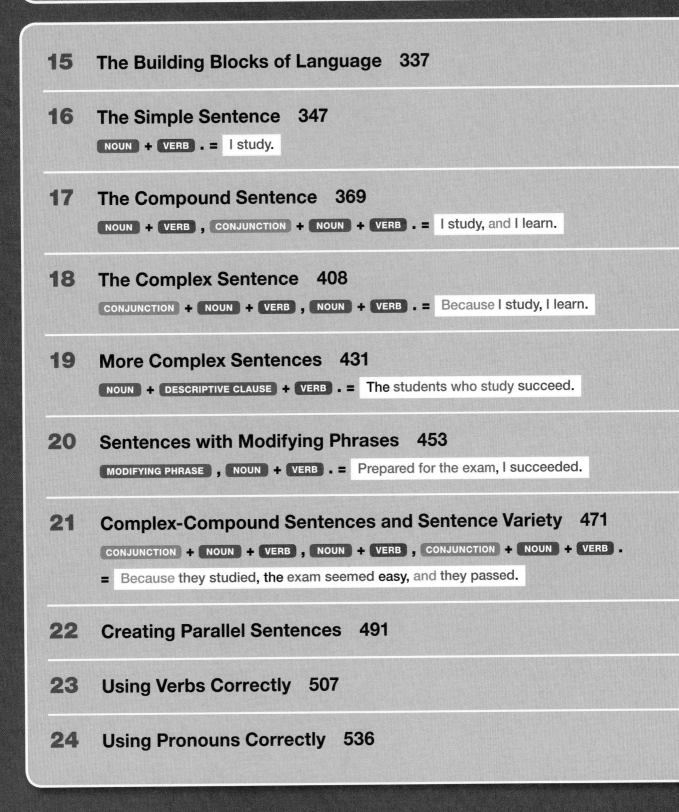

CHAPTER 15

The Building Blocks of Language

Test your understanding of sentence parts by completing this quiz first. You may know more than you think.

For each question, select all the answers that apply.

WHAT DO YOU KNOW?

1. **A noun is a word that identifies a person, place, or thing. Which of the following are types of nouns?**

    ___ concrete nouns

    ___ abstract nouns

    ___ proper nouns

    ___ simple nouns

2. **What are two types of verbs that do not express an action?**

    ___ complex verbs

    ___ helping verbs

    ___ simple verbs

    ___ linking verbs

3. **Which of the following are categories of descriptive words?**

    ___ nouns

    ___ adjectives

    ___ pronouns

    ___ adverbs

4. **Which of the following are types of connecting words?**

    ___ prepositions

    ___ verbs

    ___ pronouns

    ___ conjunctions

5. **Which of the following words are pronouns?**

    ___ *she*

    ___ *you*

    ___ *the*

    ___ *I*

In this chapter, you will learn about these important sentence parts:

Foundation Words	Descriptive Words	Connecting Words
NOUNS	ADJECTIVES	PREPOSITIONS
VERBS	ADVERBS	CONJUNCTIONS

The Building Blocks of Language

From infancy into childhood, we learn language in stages. Each stage gives us new building blocks with which to express our ideas, eventually in complete sentences.

The first stage generally takes place between the ages of one and two. In this stage, infants use single words to identify *things* (**nouns**) and *actions* (**verbs**). We call these **foundation words** because they are the foundation of all verbal communication.

With just nouns and verbs, infants begin to build simple "sentences." Take a look:

NOUN	VERB
kids	play
dog	bites

Power Tip

Although the examples of baby talk on this page contain a noun and a verb and are quite understandable, they are not complete, correct sentences.

Corrected: *The kids play. The dog bites.*

In the next stage of language building, children find words to *describe* things and actions (**adjectives** and **adverbs**). Take a look:

big **kids play**

The **adjective** *big* describes *kids.*

dog bites hard

The **adverb** *hard* describes *bites.*

We call these **descriptive words**, and we use them to *add onto* the foundation of nouns and verbs. (Notice that ***adjective*** and ***adverb*** both begin with the prefix *ad-*, showing that they are an *added* layer.)

In the third stage, children discover words that connect all the other words (**prepositions** and **conjunctions**). Take a look:

big kids play in the park

The **preposition** *in* connects *play* to *the park.*

dogs and cats bite hard

The **conjunction** *and* connects *dogs* and *cats.*

KEY TO BUILDING BLOCKS
FOUNDATION WORDS
NOUNS
VERBS
DESCRIPTIVE WORDS
ADJECTIVES
ADVERBS
CONNECTING WORDS
PREPOSITIONS
CONJUNCTIONS

At this point, a child possesses the main building blocks of language. As you will see in the next chapter, every sentence that we speak or write is a combination of these six building blocks:

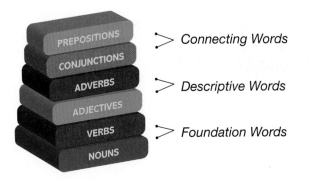

     > *Connecting Words*

     > *Descriptive Words*

     > *Foundation Words*

The chapters in this part of the book include a color-coded key that identifies foundation, descriptive, and connecting words. This color-coding will help you understand how words combine to form sentences. The key is shown on the facing page in the margin. Watch for it as you work through the chapters in Part Three.

Foundation Words: NOUNS

A **noun** is a word that identifies a person, place, or thing. There are three types of nouns (concrete, abstract, and proper) and a noun substitute (pronoun).

Concrete nouns identify physical objects that can be seen or touched, such as *desk, pencil, laptop, shirt, dress, shoe,* and so on. Simply look around you: Any object that you can see or touch has a name for it, and that name is a concrete noun.

Abstract nouns do not identify physical objects. Instead, they identify feelings or sensations (*love, fear, sadness, hunger,* and so on), ideas (*fun, trouble, intelligence, success,* and so on), or activities (*shouting, thinking, jogging, lying,* and so on). Remember: Because you can't touch any of these things, they are considered abstract.

Proper nouns are the names given to specific people, places, or things, such as *Michael Jackson, Philadelphia,* or *Toyota.* Proper nouns always begin with a capital letter.

Pronouns are convenient *substitutes* for the other types of nouns. The most common pronouns are *personal* pronouns: *I, you, he, she, it, they,* and *we.* As an example, *she* could be a convenient substitute for *the woman.*

Here is a review of the four types of nouns:

CONCRETE	ABSTRACT	PROPER	PRONOUN
things you can see or touch	feelings, ideas, activities	specific people, places, things	a noun substitute

 **ACTIVITY 1**

WARMUP

In the blank spaces provided, add additional examples to each of the following lists.

Concrete Nouns	Abstract Nouns	Proper Nouns	Pronouns
sofa	serenity	San Diego	I
pasture	energy	Brad Pitt	you
lake	fear	Walmart	they
fork	respect	Kellogg's	we
___	___	___	___
___	___	___	___
___	___	___	___
___	___	___	___

KEY TO CHALLENGE METER
WARMUP
EASY
MODERATE
ADVANCED
MASTERY

Identify the difficulty level of each activity using the key above.

 **ACTIVITY 2**

EASY

For each word, identify the noun type.

EXAMPLE: pudding _____concrete_____

1. wine _____
2. loyalty _____
3. Minnesota _____
4. we _____
5. joy _____

6. George Washington _____
7. I _____
8. glove _____
9. sea _____
10. Pablo _____

Foundation Words: VERBS

Most of the verbs in the English language are **action verbs**, and they are easy to recognize: *run, cry, drink, talk*, and so on. However, a few verbs do not express an action, so they are more difficult to recognize as verbs. These are called **linking verbs** and **helping verbs**. Take a look:

NOUN LINKING VERB (not an action)

Tonya   was . . .

NOUN **HELPING VERB** (not an action)

Parents   should . . .

As you can see from these examples, linking and helping verbs do not express an action, *nor are they complete.* They must be followed by more information to make sense. This additional information usually comes in the form of an adjective (with linking verbs) or another verb (with helping verbs).

NOUN **LINKING VERB** **ADJECTIVE**
Tonya   was   bored.

NOUN **HELPING VERB** **ANOTHER VERB**
Parents   should   listen.

Power Tip

A *linking verb* is often followed by a word that describes the subject. ("Bored" describes Tonya.) A *helping verb* is always followed by another verb, which is considered the *main verb* of the sentence. ("Listen" is the main verb, and "should" helps or supports this verb.) Together, the helping verb and the main verb make up the complete verb.

Common Linking Verbs

am, is, are, was, were (states of being)

appear, become, feel, get, grow, look, seem, smell, sound, taste

Common Helping Verbs

am, is, are, was, were

do, does, did

have, has, had

can, could, may, might

must, shall, should, will, would

ACTIVITY 3
WARMUP

In each sentence, circle the action verb.

EXAMPLE: The spider (spun) a web.

1. Our class discussed the story.
2. Thomas waited for the bus.
3. She whistles at boys.
4. The player slipped on the ice.
5. Lizbeth listens carefully in class.

ACTIVITY 4
EASY

Fill in the blank spaces with a *linking verb* to complete each sentence. Refer to the box containing linking verbs above for more help.

CONTINUED >

For more practice with nouns and verbs, go to **bedfordstmartins.com /touchstones**.

EXAMPLE: The sunset _____*is*_____ beautiful.

1. I _____ bored.

2. The apples _____ tart.

3. The contestants _____ nervous.

4. The film _____ interesting.

5. The sky suddenly _____ dark.

Now, fill in the blank spaces below with a *helping verb* to complete each sentence. Refer to the box containing helping verbs on page 341 for more help.

EXAMPLE: Curtis _____*might*_____ leave.

6. We _____ study.

7. The economy _____ improve.

8. I _____ complete my report.

9. Flight 206 _____ arrived.

10. Professor Bernard _____ taking attendance.

Descriptive Words: ADJECTIVES and ADVERBS

Adjectives describe nouns or pronouns. Take a look:

broken leg   She **is** intelligent.

torn dress   They **are** early.

laptop computer

ACTIVITY 5

EASY

In each sentence, circle the adjective. Then, in the space to the right, write the noun that the adjective is describing.

EXAMPLE: The restaurant served (cold) steaks. ___*steaks*___

1. Maddie bought a red truck. _____

2. We prefer strong coffee. _____

3. Matt Damon is a popular actor. _____

4. William Shakespeare wrote many plays. _____

5. Facebook can create dangerous situations. _____

Adverbs describe verbs (actions). Take a look:

dance the tango gracefully   quickly turned

fall hard   increasingly cost

ACTIVITY 6
EASY

In each sentence, circle the adverb. Then, in the space to the right, write the verb that the adverb is describing.

EXAMPLE: The hurricane formed (rapidly). _formed_

1. It rained steadily. _____
2. My plan worked beautifully. _____
3. Tom read the magazine article thoughtfully. _____
4. Soft meditation music relaxes me instantly. _____
5. Many people use credit cards unwisely. _____

Adverbs can also describe adjectives and other adverbs:

especially lucky   very quickly

Many adjectives can be changed to adverbs by adding *-ly*.

Adjective describing the noun *voice*
Dexter has a quiet voice.

Adverb describing the verb *speaks*
Dexter speaks quietly.

Here are some other examples:

quiet → quickly   beautiful → beautifully
smooth → smoothly   happy → happily
soft → softly   loud → loudly

ACTIVITY 7
EASY

In each sentence, circle the word that describes the underlined word. Then, in the space after the sentence, write *adjective* or *adverb* to identify the circled word. Your choice will depend on whether the underlined word is a noun or a verb.

CONTINUED >

For more practice with adjectives and adverbs, go to **bedfordstmartins.com /touchstones**.

EXAMPLE: Jeremy has (neat) handwriting. _adjective_

1. John bought a used computer. _____

2. The alarm rang suddenly. _____

3. We heard soft music. _____

4. The actress screamed hysterically. _____

5. Rain falls frequently in Seattle. _____

Connecting Words: PREPOSITIONS and CONJUNCTIONS

Prepositions (words like _at, by, for, in, on, to, with_) and **conjunctions** (words like _and, but, or, so_) are used to connect the other building blocks of language. Because these words are used for connecting, they are usually followed by other words.

> PREPOSITION
>
> Your purse is on . . .

> CONJUNCTION
>
> I took aspirin and . . .

In each example, you would need to add more information to complete the thought:

> Your purse is on the bed.

> I took aspirin and cough syrup.

PREPOSITIONS

A preposition is usually part of a **prepositional phrase**. For example:

> PREPOSITION
>
> Your purse is on the bed.
>
> PREPOSITIONAL PHRASE

A prepositional phrase always begins with a preposition, and it usually ends with a noun. As you will learn in Chapter 16, prepositional phrases can tell us _when, where_, and sometimes _how_ an action occurs.

ACTIVITY 8
WARMUP

In each sentence, circle the preposition. Then, underline the entire prepositional phrase.

EXAMPLE: (On) July 4, we always eat barbecue.

1. My notebook is under the desk.
2. With 400 dollars, I can buy a computer.
3. Derek jogs in the park.
4. Before summer, I will lose five pounds.
5. The murder is under investigation.

ACTIVITY 9
WARMUP

In each sentence, circle the preposition and then complete the prepositional phrase.

EXAMPLE: We walked (along) ___the beach___ .

1. I found my car keys under _____ .
2. Most people order their hamburgers with _____ .
3. The quarterback threw the football into _____ .
4. The diamond necklace was packaged in _____ .
5. We arrived at the hotel without _____ .

CONJUNCTIONS

Again, conjunctions, like prepositions, usually need to be followed by more information. Here are some examples:

NOUN + **NOUN**	The restaurant serves steak and lobster.
ACTION + **ACTION**	You can walk or drive to school.
ADJECTIVE + **ADJECTIVE**	Edward is smart but lazy.
CAUSE + **OUTCOME**	We studied, so we passed the exam.

ACTIVITY 10
WARMUP

In each sentence, circle the conjunction. Then, underline the two items that are connected by the conjunction.

CONTINUED >

For more practice with prepositions and conjunctions, go to **bedfordstmartins.com /touchstones**.

EXAMPLE: The students <u>passed the final exam</u>(but)<u>failed the class</u>.

1. Janice is gifted and modest.
2. For breakfast, you can have cereal or eggs.
3. We overslept, so we were late.
4. The school will be closed and locked.
5. Is the patient sick or well?

BRINGING IT ALL TOGETHER:
The Building Blocks of Language

In this chapter, you have learned about the building blocks of language. Confirm your knowledge by filling in the blank spaces in the following sentences. If you need help, review the pages listed after each sentence.

✔ _____ and _____ are known as *foundation words* because they are the foundation of all verbal communication. (page 338)

✔ A noun is a word that identifies a person, place, or thing. There are three types of nouns—_____, _____, and _____—and a noun substitute: _____. (page 339)

✔ There are three types of verbs. An _____ verb expresses an action and is easy to identify. A _____ verb must be connected to more information, usually an adjective. A _____ verb must be connected to another verb. (pages 340–41)

✔ _____ and _____ are descriptive words. _____ describe nouns or pronouns, and _____ describe verbs (or adjectives and other adverbs). (pages 342–43)

✔ _____ and _____ are used to connect the other building blocks of language. (page 344)

CHAPTER 16

The Simple Sentence

Before you read this chapter, it's a good idea to test your understanding of simple sentences. You may know more than you think.

WHAT DO YOU KNOW?

Circle "Yes" if each word group below is a complete, correct sentence. Circle "No" if it is incomplete. Then, explain your choice.

1. **She smiled at me.**

   Yes   No

   Explanation: _____

   _____

2. **A bright yellow rose growing in Aunt Jenny's flower garden.**

   Yes   No

   Explanation: _____

   _____

3. **The new stores in the mall across town.**

   Yes   No

   Explanation: _____

   _____

4. **Walking down a winding path toward the lake.**

   Yes   No

   Explanation: _____

   _____

5. **It hurts.**

   Yes   No

   Explanation: _____

   _____

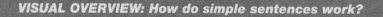

Both of these are simple sentences. You'll find out why in this chapter.

NOUN + **VERB** . = Dancers practice.

PREPOSITIONAL PHRASE , **ADJECTIVE** + **NOUN** + **VERB** + **ADVERB** .
= Before a performance, professional dancers practice rigorously.

BUILD IT: Short Simple Sentences

Now that you have mastered the building blocks of language, it's time to put everything together. In the following sections, you will build short and then longer simple sentences using nouns, verbs, adjectives, adverbs, conjunctions, and prepositions.

Did you know that a complete, correct sentence may have as few as **two words**? One of these words must be a noun, and the other must be a verb. The noun is the **subject** of the sentence. In sentences with just two words, you can think of the subject as the *actor* and the verb as the *action*. Here's an example:

SUBJECT   **VERB**

Detectives investigate.

This is a complete, correct sentence because it has a subject and a verb, and it expresses a complete thought. Yes, it could contain more information, but it does not have to.

ACTIVITY 1
EASY

Create ten simple sentences, matching subjects and verbs from the columns below. Begin by creating five sentences from the two columns on the left. Then, create five sentences from the two columns on the right. Remember to start each sentence with a capital letter and end it with a period. The first sentence is written for you.

Subject	Verb	Subject	Verb
buffalo	sailed	I	reveal
lightning	passes	artists	knocks
time	roam	opportunity	understand
Columbus	lecture	mirrors	fade
professors	struck	memories	create

_____ Buffalo roam.

_____   _____

_____   _____

_____   _____

In some sentences, the verb must be followed by another noun in order to express a complete thought and make sense. The second noun usually answers the question "What?" Take a look:

NOUN   **VERB**   **NOUN**

Pilots   use _____ [What?]

In this case, the simple sentence must have at least three words to be complete. The second noun is called the *object*, and it receives the action. Here is the complete sentence:

SUBJECT   **VERB**   **OBJECT**

Pilots   use   radar.

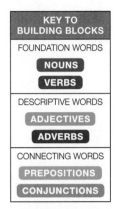

KEY TO BUILDING BLOCKS

FOUNDATION WORDS
NOUNS
VERBS

DESCRIPTIVE WORDS
ADJECTIVES
ADVERBS

CONNECTING WORDS
PREPOSITIONS
CONJUNCTIONS

ACTIVITY 2
MODERATE

Create ten simple sentences by combining subjects, verbs, and objects from the columns below. Begin by creating five sentences from the three columns on the left. Then, create five more sentences using the three columns on the right. Remember to start each sentence with a capital letter and end it with a period. The first sentence has been written for you.

Subject	Verb	Object	Subject	Verb	Object
farmers	contains	hate	water	stole	me
love	appreciate	property	bleach	understands	millions
bats	destroy	calories	she	eases	stains
cheesecake	eat	rain	aspirin	removes	thirst
tornadoes	conquers	mosquitoes	a thief	quenches	headaches

KEY TO CHALLENGE METER

WARMUP

EASY

MODERATE

ADVANCED

MASTERY

Identify the difficulty level of each activity using the key above.

_____ Farmers appreciate rain.   _____

_____   _____

_____   _____

_____   _____

ACTIVITY 3: Teamwork

MODERATE

For each of the following pairs of words, decide whether the verb must be followed by another noun in order to make sense. If the two words already express a complete thought, just add a period. If another noun is required, add the noun and a period to complete the sentence.

EXAMPLE: Maria collects _____ *stamps.* _____

1. Dogs bury _____
2. Officers arrested _____
3. Harold sneezed _____
4. Congress passes _____
5. Bananas ripen _____
6. Mechanics repair _____
7. Milk sours _____
8. We arrived _____
9. Melinda photographs _____
10. Zoologists study _____

As you learned in Chapter 15, a sentence with a linking verb or a helping verb must also have at least three words. Take a look:

NOUN	LINKING VERB	ADJECTIVE
Terrence	seems	sorry.

NOUN	HELPING VERB	MAIN VERB
We	should	leave.

ACTIVITY 4

MODERATE

Fill in the blank spaces with a *linking verb* and an *adjective* to complete each sentence.

EXAMPLE: Allison _____ *looks beautiful* _____.

1. The students _____.
2. The Rocky Mountains _____.
3. Hurricane Opal _____.
4. Martin's truck _____.
5. Miriam's daughter _____.

> **Common Linking Verbs**
>
> *am, is, are, was, were* (states of being)
>
> *appear, become, feel, get, grow, look, seem, smell, sound, taste*

Now, add a *helping verb* and *another verb*.

EXAMPLE: Uncle Theodore _____*might visit*_____ .

6. The boss _____ .

7. Jeffrey and Lynda _____ .

8. The motorcycle _____ .

9. Ross's brother _____ .

10. Some customers _____ .

> **Common Helping Verbs**
>
> *am, is, are, was, were*
>
> *do, does, did*
>
> *have, has, had*
>
> *can, could, may, might*
>
> *must, shall, should, will, would*

ACTIVITY 5
MODERATE

In each of the following sentences, underline the subject and circle the verb. Then, in the space provided, write *action*, *linking*, or *helping* to identify the verb type. (Note: If you find a helping verb, circle it, but do not circle the verb that follows it.)

EXAMPLE: The children (seem) restless. ___*linking*___

1. The sun is rising. _____

2. Chelsea bought a computer. _____

3. Shrimp contains cholesterol. _____

4. The room became quiet. _____

5. California's capital is Sacramento. _____

6. The Auburn Tigers might win. _____

7. Friendships need nurturing. _____

8. The Petersons are building a house. _____

9. The committee considered alternatives. _____

10. Familiarity breeds contempt. _____

ACTIVITY 6: Teamwork
ADVANCED

For each of the following word groups, decide if more information is needed to express a complete thought. If not, just add a period. If more information is necessary, add <u>one more word</u> and a period. Then, in the space provided, write *action*, *linking*, or *helping* to identify the verb type.

EXAMPLE: Calvin ordered ___*steak*.___   Verb type: ___*action*___

1. Vanessa should _____   Verb type: _____

2. Mike's train arrived _____   Verb type: _____

3. The passengers carried _____   Verb type: _____

CONTINUED >

Power Tip
You may use very short sentences in your college writing, but do not overuse them. Too many might suggest that your thinking and writing are simplistic. Effective writers save very short sentences for special emphasis.

4. The roses seem _____   Verb type: _____

5. Their quarterback might _____   Verb type: _____

6. The Grand Canyon is _____   Verb type: _____

7. The earthquake destroyed _____   Verb type: _____

8. Christie will _____   Verb type: _____

9. Professor Baxter became _____   Verb type: _____

10. Voters elected _____   Verb type: _____

BUILD IT: Longer Simple Sentences

You already know that a sentence may have as few as two or three words. However, we usually write longer sentences to communicate our ideas. These sentences generally include some of the other building blocks of language such as descriptive words and connecting words.

ADDING DESCRIPTIVE WORDS: ADJECTIVES AND ADVERBS

As human beings, we like to describe things, and we use a lot of descriptive words to do this. Descriptive words—**adjectives** and **adverbs**—also add length to our sentences. As an example, let's start with a very short simple sentence:

> **NOUN** **VERB**
> Teachers grade.

Now, let's add an **adjective** to describe *what type* of teachers grade:

> **ADJECTIVE** **NOUN** **VERB**
> College teachers grade.

Now, let's add an **adverb** to describe *how* college teachers grade.

> **ADJECTIVE** **NOUN** **VERB** **ADVERB**
> College teachers grade hard.

Power Tip
Remember that *ad*verbs and *ad*jectives *add* meaning to verbs and nouns.

Let's briefly review what you learned in Chapter 15. **Adjectives** describe nouns and pronouns. Take a look:

weak **coffee**   slick **road**

concerned **friend**   honest **politician**

yellow **rose**

Adverbs describe actions (verbs). Take a look:

drive slowly   arrive soon

speak quietly   apologize sincerely

hug tightly

ACTIVITY 7
EASY

In each sentence, add a descriptive word. Then, write *adjective* or *adverb* in the space after the sentence to indicate whether the word describes a noun or a verb.

EXAMPLE: The truck stopped _____*suddenly.*_____ *adverb*_____

1. Jennifer sang _____ to the baby. _____

2. Late for work, Peter drove _____ _____

3. The professor spoke _____ to the late student. _____

4. We found a _____ textbook on Amazon. _____

5. The dentist found a _____ tooth on the X-ray. _____

ACTIVITY 8
MODERATE

Use each of the following descriptive word pairs and write a short sentence. You will need to add a subject and a verb.

EXAMPLE: impatient, loudly *The impatient customer complained loudly.*

1. beautiful, shyly _____

2. young, happily _____

3. angry, rudely _____

4. irritated, sarcastically _____

5. frightened, quickly _____

ACTIVITY 9
ADVANCED

As sentences become longer, we still need to be able to recognize the subject and the verb. In the following sentences, cross out the adjectives and adverbs. Then, underline the subject and circle the verb.

EXAMPLE: ~~Active~~ people ~~generally~~ (live) ~~longer~~ lives. (Cross out three descriptive words.)

CONTINUED >

1. The inventor of the lightbulb was the famous Thomas Edison. (Cross out one descriptive word.)

2. Pioneers bravely traveled across the American wilderness. (Cross out two descriptive words.)

3. A terrible potato famine forced Irish immigration to the United States. (Cross out three descriptive words.)

4. Wilbur Wright flew only a short distance on his first flight. (Cross out three descriptive words.)

5. During Prohibition, many people made alcoholic products illegally. (Cross out three descriptive words.)

ADDING CONNECTING WORDS: CONJUNCTIONS

FOUNDATION WORDS
NOUNS
VERBS

DESCRIPTIVE WORDS
ADJECTIVES
ADVERBS

CONNECTING WORDS
PREPOSITIONS
CONJUNCTIONS

compound: made up of two or more parts

Some simple sentences have *more than one* subject or *more than one* verb. In these cases, we use **conjunctions** (*and, or, but*) to join these **compound subjects** and **compound verbs**. Take a look:

SUBJECT   **VERB**
Ryan   sneezed.

Now, let's add another subject:

COMPOUND SUBJECT   **VERB**
Ryan and Allison   sneezed.

Now, let's add another verb:

SUBJECT   **COMPOUND VERB**
Ryan   sneezed and coughed.

Note that a sentence can have *both* a compound subject and a compound verb.

COMPOUND SUBJECT   **COMPOUND VERB**
Ryan and Allison   sneezed and coughed.

The conjunctions *but* and *or* are also used to form compound subjects and verbs. Take a look:

COMPOUND SUBJECT
A credit card or a check is acceptable.

COMPOUND VERB
Anne enjoys coffee but dislikes tea.

ACTIVITY 10
EASY

In each of the following sentences, complete the compound subjects and compound verbs by filling in the blanks.

EXAMPLE (NOUN): _____Kaylee_____ and _____Damion_____ are my new neighbors.

EXAMPLE (VERB): I _____swept_____ and _____mopped_____ the kitchen floor.

Add two nouns.

1. _____ and _____ are tonight's specials.

2. _____ or _____ will drive me to the airport.

3. _____ or _____ would be a great vacation spot.

Add two verbs.

4. To get to California, Frank will _____ or _____.

5. To relieve stress, many people _____ or _____.

6. The attorney _____ the witness and _____ him.

ACTIVITY 11
MODERATE

Select any five of the following word pairs and write a simple sentence with a compound subject or a compound verb. Use the conjunctions *and*, *or*, or *but* to connect the subjects and the verbs.

EXAMPLE (NOUN): hamburgers, fries ___Hamburgers and fries are an all-___ ___American combination___.

EXAMPLE (VERB): add, taste ___Charlie added salt to the soup and tasted it___.

Nouns

1. coffee, tea _____.

2. Los Angeles, New York City _____
_____.

3. liver, beets _____.

Verbs

4. fell, hurt _____.

5. lost, found _____.

6. saved, bought _____.

For more practice with building simple sentences, visit this book's Web site at **bedfordstmartins.com /touchstones**.

ACTIVITY 12

ADVANCED

In each of the following sentences, underline the subject and circle the verb. The clue in parentheses will tell you when there are compound subjects and/ or compound verbs. It may be helpful to cross out any descriptive words first.

EXAMPLE: Neil Armstrong and Buzz Aldrin (walked) on the moon on July 20, 1969. (compound subject)

1. A light rain after a dry spell makes roads slick.

2. Yellowstone National Park has more than 500 geysers.

3. Salads often contain many hidden calories in the salad dressing.

4. Tornadoes and hurricanes are serious weather threats. (compound subject)

5. A brisk walk improves cardiovascular health and reduces stress. (compound verb)

6. Almonds and walnuts provide valuable antioxidants. (compound subject)

7. Smoking is forbidden in many public areas.

8. Many female Hindus and Muslims wear a veil. (compound subject)

9. Moisture in the air condenses and falls as rain. (compound verb)

10. The bulbs and leaves of daffodils contain toxic crystals. (compound subject)

BUILD IT: Even Longer Simple Sentences

As you have seen, sentences become longer when we add descriptive words, compound subjects, and compound verbs. The longest simple sentences usually have one or more prepositional phrases that tell us *when*, *where*, and sometimes *how* an action occurs.

ADDING CONNECTING WORDS: PREPOSITIONS

Let's start with a short simple sentence:

FOUNDATION WORDS
NOUNS
VERBS
DESCRIPTIVE WORDS
ADJECTIVES
ADVERBS
CONNECTING WORDS
PREPOSITIONS
CONJUNCTIONS

SUBJECT   **VERB**

Waves   crashed.

You already know that this is a complete, correct sentence. However, we might want to add more information about where, when, or how the waves crashed. So, let's add a preposition:

SUBJECT	VERB	PREPOSITION
Waves	crashed	onto . . .

Now that we have added the preposition *onto*, we must complete the thought. If we do not complete the thought, the sentence will not make sense.

SUBJECT	VERB	PREPOSITIONAL PHRASE
Waves	crashed	onto the shore.

The preposition *onto* connects the verb *crashed* with information about *where* the waves crashed. The preposition **plus** the words that complete the thought are called the **prepositional phrase**. A prepositional phrase always begins with a preposition (a single word) and usually ends with a noun.

PREPOSITION	NOUN

Waves crashed <u>onto</u> <u>the shore</u>.

COMMON PREPOSITIONS

about	before	except	off	throughout
above	behind	for	on	to
across	below	from	onto	toward
after	beneath	in	out	under
against	beside	inside	outside	until
along	between	into	over	up
among	beyond	like	past	upon
around	by	near	since	with
as	down	next	than	within
at	during	of	through	without

WARMUP

In each of the following sentences, add a single preposition to complete the sentence.

EXAMPLE: We waited in the pouring rain ___*for*___ twenty minutes.

1. Thousands of homes were damaged _____ the tornado outbreak.

2. The out-of-control car crashed _____ a fence.

3. We could see several huge fish _____ the surface of the water.

4. Let's keep this little secret _____ us.

5. I still like to wish _____ a star.

Terminology Tip
The noun at the end of a prepositional phrase is known as the **object of the preposition**.

Power Tip
Because the phrase *onto the shore* describes the verb *crashed,* it is functioning as an adverb. Prepositional phrases can also function as adjectives, as in this sentence: *The cat <u>on the bed</u> is friendly*. The phrase *on the bed* functions as an adjective describing the noun *cat*.

Power Tip
The preposition *to* followed by a verb does *not* create a prepositional phrase. Rather, it expresses the infinitive form of a verb, such as *to run, to think, to dream,* or *to read*.

Power Tip
Remember that many prepositional phrases have only two words: the preposition and a noun. For example, "*before* midnight," "*of* wood," "*on* Tuesday," "*in* time," "*at* work," or "*with* love."

ACTIVITY 14
EASY

In each of the following sentences, add a prepositional phrase. (Hint: To write a prepositional phrase, start with a preposition from the chart on page 357 and then complete the thought.)

EXAMPLE: A beautiful rainbow appeared ___*in the sky*___ .

1. It rained steadily _____ .
2. You may set that package _____ .
3. Jeremy found his truck keys _____ .
4. The play *Hamlet* was written _____ .
5. We celebrate Valentine's Day _____ .

ACTIVITY 15
MODERATE

To complete each of the following sentences, add a prepositional phrase at the beginning.

EXAMPLE: *for an hour* , I listened to my friend complain.

1. _____ , the ceremony will begin.
2. _____ , police officers discovered burglary tools.
3. _____ , Alex got in his truck and headed to his girlfriend's apartment.
4. _____ , the power suddenly went out.
5. _____ , Georgia always attends her yoga class.

In some sentences, two or more prepositional phrases may also be connected to make a string of prepositional phrases. Take a look:

a string of two [PREPOSITIONAL PHRASES]

[SUBJECT] [VERB]
We   built **our house** on the side of a hill.

ACTIVITY 16: Teamwork
ADVANCED

Working with other students, underline the complete string of prepositional phrases in each sentence. Then, count the number of prepositional phrases in the string and write that number in the blank space.

EXAMPLE: One of the best-selling novels of all time was *Gone with the Wind*. 2

1. Margaret Mitchell began writing *Gone with the Wind* in 1926 after a car accident. ___

2. The story takes place in Clayton County in Georgia during the Civil War. ___

3. Mitchell's manuscript was noticed in 1935 by an editor from Macmillan. ___

4. Mitchell earned a Pulitzer Prize in 1937 for this exceptional novel about the South. ___

5. Actor Clark Gable played the role of Rhett Butler in the film version of Mitchell's novel in 1939. ___

IDENTIFYING SUBJECTS WHEN THERE ARE PREPOSITIONAL PHRASES

Sometimes, a prepositional phrase may come between the subject and the verb. Take a look:

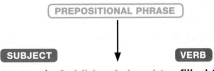

The sound of children's laughter filled the house.

In this case, the prepositional phrase describes the subject. However, a subject is never in a prepositional phrase.

FOUNDATION WORDS
- NOUNS
- VERBS

DESCRIPTIVE WORDS
- ADJECTIVES
- ADVERBS

CONNECTING WORDS
- PREPOSITIONS
- CONJUNCTIONS

ACTIVITY 17

EASY

Add a prepositional phrase between the subject and the verb. (Hint: You may use the suggested preposition in parentheses.)

EXAMPLE: A bouquet __of roses__ was delivered to Tanisha's office. (of)

1. We ordered two cups _____ at the café. (of)

2. This orange spiced tea _____ has a delicate flavor. (from)

3. The man _____ looks very suspicious. (with)

4. A novel _____ was made into a hit movie. (about)

5. A snake _____ frightened our guests half to death. (in)

ACTIVITY 18
MODERATE

Power Tip
Remember that the noun in a prepositional phrase can never be the subject of the sentence.

In each of the following sentences, cross out the prepositional phrase between the subject and the verb. Then, underline the subject and circle the verb.

EXAMPLE: The cup ~~of coffee~~ (scalded) my lip.

1. One of Lorin's daughters got into Harvard.

2. The music for *Star Wars* won an Academy Award.

3. Hikers on the Pacific Crest Trail often see bears.

4. The recipe for cranberry walnut bread calls for yeast.

5. The weather in Santa Barbara is mild.

ACTIVITY 19: Teamwork
ADVANCED

Power Tip
Remember that *or* is a conjunction, not a preposition.

In each of the following sentences, cross out all the prepositional phrases. Then, in the spaces provided, write the subject and the verb.

EXAMPLE: The story ~~of D. B. Cooper~~ is one ~~of America's favorite mysteries.~~
(Cross out two prepositional phrases.) Subject: _story_ Verb: _is_

1. On November 24, 1971, "Dan Cooper" bought a one-way ticket on Flight 305 from Portland, Oregon, to Seattle, Washington. (Cross out four prepositional phrases.) Subject: _____ Verb: _____

2. Inside his briefcase, Cooper carried eight cylinders with attached wires. (Cross out two prepositional phrases.)
Subject: _____ Verb: _____

3. During the flight to Seattle, one of the flight attendants received a note from Cooper. (Cross out four prepositional phrases.)
Subject: _____ Verb: _____

4. In the note, Cooper demanded parachutes and $200,000 in twenty-dollar bills for a ransom. (Cross out three prepositional phrases.)
Subject: _____ Verb: _____

5. Shortly before 6:00 p.m., the plane landed at the Seattle-Tacoma airport for the ransom. (Cross out three prepositional phrases.)
Subject: _____ Verb: _____

6. The operations manager for Northwest Orient Airlines delivered parachutes and a knapsack with the cash to the rear stairs of the aircraft. (Cross out four prepositional phrases.) Subject: _____
Verb: _____

7. At approximately 8:13 p.m., over the area of southwest Washington, Cooper apparently jumped from the aircraft with his knapsack of money. (Cross out six prepositional phrases.) Subject: _____
Verb: _____

8. Over the years, none of the FBI or other investigators has solved the mystery of D. B. Cooper's true identity. (Cross out three prepositional phrases.) Subject: _____ Verb: _____

For more practice with prepositions, go to **bedfordstmartins.com /touchstones**.

ACTIVITY 20: Mastery Test

MASTERY

In each sentence of the paragraph, do the following:

- Underline the subject and circle the verb (including any helping verbs). Watch for compound subjects and compound verbs.
- If you have trouble identifying a subject or a verb, remember to cross out any prepositional phrases in the sentence.
- If you are still having trouble, try crossing out any descriptive words.

(1) During the financial crisis in 2007, a new type of vacation gained popularity. (2) The "staycation" is a vacation at home. (3) The benefits of this new trend are largely financial. (4) In general, families can save a significant amount of money on travel and lodging. (5) The stress of travel through airports or on the highway is also reduced. (6) This new trend can introduce families to attractions in their own community. (7) For example, one family might take advantage of a swimming hole or a hiking trail. (8) Another might go to a nearby mall and shop for hours. (9) Perhaps a new restaurant in town needs support from local residents. (10) One of the most popular "staycation" activities is a trip to the movie theater. (11) On the other hand, some families simply rent a movie and take it home. (12) The key to a successful "staycation" is local relaxation and fun.

FIX IT: Solving Problems in Simple Sentences

You already know that a complete sentence must have a *subject* and a *verb* and express a complete thought. If a sentence is **missing a subject or a verb**, it will be a **fragment** (an incomplete sentence).

FIXING FRAGMENTS THAT ARE MISSING VERBS

Take a look at the following word groups and see if you notice a problem.

A tree.
My car.
The teacher.

FOUNDATION WORDS

NOUNS
VERBS

DESCRIPTIVE WORDS

ADJECTIVES
ADVERBS

CONNECTING WORDS

PREPOSITIONS
CONJUNCTIONS

Each of these fragments is **missing a verb**. We don't know what is happening to the tree, the car, or the teacher. It is easy to recognize and fix this problem. Just add a verb to each subject:

> A tree fell.
>
> My car stalled.
>
> The teacher talked.

Some fragments can also be quite long, making it more difficult to recognize a missing verb. The following fragments contain descriptive words and prepositional phrases but are missing a verb.

> In my yard, a tree during a storm.
>
> During rush-hour traffic, my car on the freeway.
>
> After class, the French teacher about my homework.

To fix these longer fragments, we need to add a verb:

> In my yard, a tree fell during a storm.
>
> During rush-hour traffic, my car stalled on the freeway.
>
> After class, the French teacher talked about my homework.

ACTIVITY 21
EASY

Power Tip

If necessary, cross out the descriptive words and the prepositional phrases to help you find the subject.

In each of the following fragments, underline the subject. Then, rewrite the entire fragment, adding a verb and any other information that you want in order to make a complete sentence.

EXAMPLE: The <u>driver</u> of a bright blue sports car.

The driver of a bright blue sports car revved the engine.

1. A young woman in a pencil-thin skirt and high heels.

_____

_____

2. A flooded street at the corner of Main and Elm.

_____

_____

3. Afterward, several weary employees.

_____

4. Several unsold homes in my neighborhood.

_____

_____

5. On the newest version of the menu, scrambled eggs with ham.

_____

_____

FIXING FRAGMENTS THAT HAVE INCOMPLETE VERBS

Sometimes, a sentence will contain only part of a verb. Any sentence with an **incomplete verb** is also a **fragment**. Take a look at the following examples and see if you notice a problem.

> Raul taking piano lessons.
>
> The restaurant looking for a cook.

Each of these examples is a fragment because the verb is incomplete. A verb ending with *-ing* is not a complete verb by itself. It needs one of the following helping verbs to make it complete: *am, is, are, was, were*. Take a look:

> Raul <u>was</u> taking piano lessons.
>
> The restaurant <u>is</u> looking for a cook.

Each of these sentences is now complete and correct because it contains a subject and a complete verb (a helping verb plus the main verb). Now, take a look at the following examples and see if you notice a problem.

> The packages delivered on time.
>
> Jessica stung by a bee.

Each of these sentences is also a fragment because the verb is incomplete. To fix this type of incomplete verb, add one of the same helping verbs: *am, is, are, was, were*.

> The packages <u>were</u> delivered on time.
>
> Jessica <u>was</u> stung by a bee.

ACTIVITY 22

MODERATE

In each of the following fragments, underline the subject and circle the incomplete verb. Then, turn each fragment into a sentence by completing the verb.

EXAMPLE: Several <u>customers</u> (complaining) about the store hours.

> *Several customers are complaining about the store hours.*

1. Some mothers beginning to dress like their daughters.

   _____

2. <u>Mothers</u> relating to their daughters with copycat clothing choices.

   _____

3. Sociologists expressing caution about this habit of dressing in a younger manner.

   _____

   _____

Power Tip

If necessary, cross out the descriptive words and the prepositional phrases to help you find the subject.

CONTINUED >

4. Every generation of young girls trying to establish its own unique style.

_____

_____

5. Today's mothers making it hard for their daughters to do this.

_____

_____

FIXING FRAGMENTS THAT ARE MISSING SUBJECTS

Remember that if a sentence is **missing a subject**, it will also be a **fragment**. Take a look at the following examples and see if you notice a problem.

> Driving to the Grand Canyon.
>
> To cook a perfect steak.
>
> Awarded the first-place trophy.

Each of these examples is a fragment because there is **no subject**. We don't know _who_ or _what_ drives to the Grand Canyon, cooks a perfect steak, or was awarded a trophy. To correct each fragment, add a subject and make sure the verb is complete and correct:

> Anna will drive to the Grand Canyon.
>
> Martin cooks a perfect steak.
>
> Keitha was awarded the first-place trophy.

Once again, if the fragment is long, it may be more difficult to recognize that a subject is missing. Here's an example:

> To finish her essay before the deadline at the end of the semester.

This long group of words provides a lot of information, but there is no subject. (We don't know _who_ or _what_ is finishing her essay.) Therefore, this is not a complete, correct sentence. To fix the problem, simply add a subject and adjust the verb so that it is complete and correct:

> Teresa finished her essay before the deadline at the end of the semester.

▮▮▮ ACTIVITY 23
MODERATE

Turn each fragment into a complete sentence by adding a subject. If necessary, adjust the verb.

EXAMPLE: Has discovered an interest in cooking.

Brianna has discovered an interest in cooking.

1. Watching a cooking show on television several months ago.

2. Watched with fascination the creation of a chocolate soufflé.

3. Bought the ingredients and made a chocolate soufflé at home.

4. Turned out light, rich, and delicious.

5. Impressed with her new cooking skills.

> In order to master the simple sentence, you need to remember two key rules:
>
> 1. A grammatically correct sentence must have a subject and a complete verb, and it must express a complete thought.
> 2. A complete, correct sentence may be very short or quite long; the length of a sentence has nothing to do with its completeness and correctness.

ACTIVITY 24: Teamwork

ADVANCED

Working with some of your classmates, explain why each of the following word groups is or is not a complete, correct sentence.

EXAMPLE: The Tuskegee Airmen, one of the most famous groups of African American pilots. *missing verb*

1. During World War II, racial discrimination common in the U.S. military.

2. Not allowed to serve as pilots in the American military forces.

3. Finally, in 1941, an African American combat unit created by the Army Air Corps.

4. Located at the Tuskegee Institute in Macon County, Alabama.

5. They trained at the Tuskegee Army Air Field.

CONTINUED >

6. Learned to fly P-47 Thunderbolts and P-51 Mustangs.

_____

7. The Tuskegee training program inspected by Eleanor Roosevelt.

_____

8. An African American instructor pilot took the First Lady on a half-hour

flight. _____

_____

9. Went on to fly successful missions during World War II.

_____

10. The Tuskegee Airmen later honored for their accomplishments with the

U.S. Congressional Gold Medal. _____

ACTIVITY 25: Mastery Test or Teamwork

MASTERY

Read the following paragraphs carefully, looking for fragments. Then, do the following:

- Each time you find a fragment, write **F** above the number.
- Then, rewrite each fragment, turning it into a complete sentence. (You may need to add a subject or a verb, or you may need to complete a verb. However, do not join any sentences together.)
- If a sentence is already complete and correct, write **OK** above the number.

The first sentence of each paragraph has been edited for you.

The paragraph below has nine fragments, including the one that has been edited for you.

a. (1) The Pacific Crest Trail, a 2,600-mile hiking trail in the
western United States. (2) The trail leads hikers from the border of
Mexico to the border of Canada. (3) Runs through seven national
parks in California, Oregon, and Washington. (4) The highest point
on the trail Mt. Whitney, at an elevation of more than 14,000 feet.
(5) Hikers experience blazing desert heat and chilling mountain

temperatures. (6) Captures the imagination and dreams of many long-distance hikers. (7) Takes about six months to reach the Canadian border. (8) The hike very strenuous at times. (9) Hikers must cross swift and icy streams. (10) Also must climb steep snow fields. (11) Bears often prowling in the camping areas at night. (12) Still, hundreds of hikers attempt the trail every year. (13) The beautiful views and wilderness experiences worth every hardship.

The paragraph below has 14 fragments, including the one that has been edited for you.

     F was
b. (1) Alicia 18 years old last February. (2) Her parents warned her about texting behind the wheel of her car. (3) Ignored her parents' warnings. (4) She felt confident in her multitasking abilities. (5) Was on her way to class one spring day. (6) Enjoying the beautiful spring weather. (7) Excited about her shopping trip with her friends after class. (8) She was in the middle of a text to her friend. (9) Drifted off the road and onto the right shoulder. (10) Alicia overcorrected. (11) Jerked the steering wheel hard to the left. (12) Witnesses watched in horror. (13) Alicia's car flipped end over end several times. (14) Alicia wearing her seatbelt. (15) Unfortunately, still suffered severe brain trauma. (16) For several days, her friends praying for her recovery. (17) But her injuries were too severe. (18) Alicia pronounced dead about a week after the accident. (19) Never came out of her coma. (20) Now, her friends coping with the loss of a beautiful and happy young woman. (21) And behind the wheel of their own cars, putting their cell phones away.

For more practice with fixing fragments, go to bedfordstmartins.com /touchstones.

BRINGING IT ALL TOGETHER:
The Simple Sentence

In this chapter, you have learned about the simple sentence and about fragments. Confirm your knowledge by filling in the blank spaces in the following sentences. If you need help, review the pages listed after each sentence.

✔ A complete, correct sentence must have a _____ and a _____, and it must express a _____. (page 348)

✔ Some sentences have more than one subject or more than one verb. More than one subject is called a _____. More than one verb is called a _____. (page 354)

✔ The longest simple sentences usually have one or more _____ _____. (page 356)

✔ The subject of a sentence will *never* be found in a _____ _____. (page 359)

✔ A sentence fragment may be caused by any one of the following problems: _____, _____, or _____. (pages 361–64)

✔ The _____ of a sentence has nothing to do with its completeness or correctness. (page 365)

CHAPTER 17

The Compound Sentence

Before you read this chapter, it's a good idea to test your understanding of compound sentences. You may know more than you think.

WHAT DO YOU KNOW?

Circle "Yes" if each word group below is a complete, correct sentence. Circle "No" if it is incomplete. Then, explain your choice.

1. **The weather forecast calls for rain, the wedding has been moved indoors.**

   Yes   No

   Explanation: _____

2. **We went fishing yesterday, and we caught several trout.**

   Yes   No

   Explanation: _____

3. **Homemade cookies and breads make wonderful gifts, everyone should know how to cook a few special treats.**

   Yes   No

   Explanation: _____

4. **Johnny Carson hosted *The Tonight Show* for 30 years, he won six Emmy Awards for his work.**

   Yes   No

   Explanation: _____

5. **The polar bear is the world's largest carnivore; it can weigh up to 1,500 pounds.**

   Yes   No

   Explanation: _____

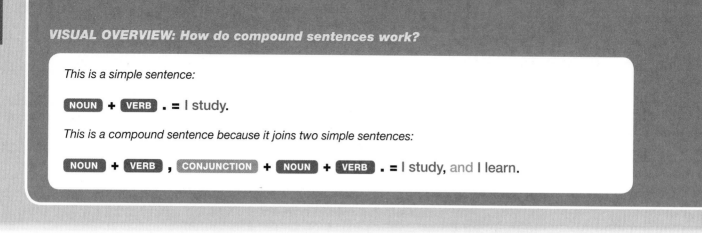

This is a simple sentence:

NOUN + **VERB** . = I study.

This is a compound sentence because it joins two simple sentences:

NOUN + **VERB** , **CONJUNCTION** + **NOUN** + **VERB** . = I study, and I learn.

BUILD IT: Short Compound Sentences

In the previous chapter, you learned that a **simple sentence** may have as few as two words: a subject (noun) and a verb. Here are two examples:

> Matt jogs. Annie runs.

In this chapter, you will learn how to write and recognize compound sentences. A **compound sentence** is two or more simple sentences joined together. Often, these sentences are joined using **a comma and a conjunction**. Take a look:

> SIMPLE SENTENCE 1   SIMPLE SENTENCE 2
> Matt jogs, and Annie runs.
> COMMA AND CONJUNCTION

In the short compound sentence above, the coordinating conjunction *and* functions like glue to hold the two simple sentences together. English has just seven **coordinating conjunctions**: *and, but, so, or, yet, nor,* and *for.* Each of these conjunctions expresses a *different type of relationship* between two simple sentences. The most common conjunctions are *and, but, so,* and *or.*

- Use **and** to <u>combine</u> two similar ideas:

> IDEA 1   IDEA 2
> **Time passes, and memories fade.**

These two ideas both express the effects of time.

- Use **but** to <u>contrast</u> two different ideas:

> IDEA 1   IDEA 2
> **Michael frowned, but Dana smiled.**

These two ideas express different types of action.

- Use **so** to <u>show a result</u>:

  IDEA 1   IDEA 2

  Our team scored, so we cheered.

  Here, the second idea is a result of the first idea.

- Use **or** to <u>show alternatives</u>:

  IDEA 1   IDEA 2

  You can leave, or you can stay.

  These two ideas express alternative options or possibilities.

  To sum up, the four types of relationships are **combination** (*and*), **contrast** (*but*), **result** (*so*), and **alternatives** (*or*). The following exercise will help you recognize the different relationships between two ideas in compound sentences.

> **Coordinating Conjunctions**
>
> *and, but, or, so, for, nor, yet*

ACTIVITY 1

EASY

First, add a conjunction (*and, but, so,* or *or*) to complete each compound sentence. Then, circle the type of relationship the conjunction suggests between the two ideas.

EXAMPLE: I am on a diet, ___so___ I will not eat that brownie.   (combination, contrast, (result), alternatives)

1. The forecast called for a severe thunderstorm, _____ we received only a light rain.   (combination, contrast, result, alternatives)

2. You should put more air in your tire, _____ you will ruin it.   (combination, contrast, result, alternatives)

3. Thomas opened his Internet business a few months ago, _____ he is already making a profit.   (combination, contrast, result, alternatives)

4. It sounds like a promising investment deal, _____ there are significant risks.   (combination, contrast, result, alternatives)

5. Bill rode his skateboard into the blackberry bushes, _____ he scraped his arms and legs. (combination, contrast, result, alternatives)

In a compound sentence, the conjunction that you use will determine the kind of idea that can go in the second sentence. For example:

COMBINATION	They sold their house, and they moved away.
CONTRAST	They sold their house, but they lost money.
RESULT	They sold their house, so they had to find another place to live.

In each sentence, the first idea is the same. However, the kind of idea that goes in the second sentence changes according to the conjunction used.

For more practice with compound sentences, go to **bedfordstmartins .com/touchstones**.

KEY TO CHALLENGE METER

WARMUP

EASY

MODERATE

ADVANCED

MASTERY

Identify the difficulty level of each activity using the key above.

Power Tip
In this chapter, we discuss *and, or, but,* and *so.* The remaining conjunctions — *yet, for,* and *nor* — are used less frequently. If you would like to learn more about these three conjunctions, go to **bedfordstmartins.com /touchstones**.

ACTIVITY 2

MODERATE

First, add a conjunction (*and, but, so,* or *or*) to complete each of the following compound sentences. Do not use a conjunction more than once in a set. Then, circle the type of relationship the conjunction suggests between the two ideas.

EXAMPLE:

    a. Kristen lost her purse, _*but*_ someone returned it to her. (combination, (contrast), result, alternatives)

    b. Kristen lost her purse, _*so*_ she called the lost and found office. (combination, contrast, (result), alternatives)

    c. Kristen lost her purse, _*and*_ she also lost her cell phone. ((combination), contrast, result, alternatives)

1. a. Logan needs a vacation, _____ he is dreaming of Las Vegas. (combination, contrast, result, alternatives)

    b. Logan needs a vacation, _____ his funds are rather limited. (combination, contrast, result, alternatives)

    c. Logan needs a vacation, _____ he will lose his mind. (combination, contrast, result, alternatives)

2. a. Annie rides a motorcycle to work, _____ she checks the weather forecast every morning. (combination, contrast, result, alternatives)

    b. Annie rides a motorcycle to work, _____ she always wears a helmet. (combination, contrast, result, alternatives)

    c. Annie rides a motorcycle to work, _____ she drives her car during bad weather. (combination, contrast, result, alternatives)

3. a. Carbonated drinks have a high sugar content, _____ many also contain caffeine. (combination, contrast, result, alternatives)

    b. Carbonated drinks have a high sugar content, _____ dieters should avoid them. (combination, contrast, result, alternatives)

    c. Carbonated drinks have a high sugar content, _____ sugar-free varieties are plentiful. (combination, contrast, result, alternatives)

4. a. Tyler has cerebral palsy, _____ he walks with a cane. (combination, contrast, result, alternatives)

    b. Tyler has cerebral palsy, _____ he does not let his condition deter him from his goals. (combination, contrast, result, alternatives)

    c. Tyler has cerebral palsy, _____ he counsels other people with CP. (combination, contrast, result, alternatives)

5. a. Jose is a police officer, _____ he is also a single parent. (combination, contrast, result, alternatives)

   b. Jose is a police officer, _____ he sometimes must work the night shift. (combination, contrast, result, alternatives)

   c. Jose is a police officer, _____ he wants to be a teacher. (combination, contrast, result, alternatives)

ACTIVITY 3: Teamwork

ADVANCED

With classmates, discuss what type of idea is necessary to complete each compound sentence. Then, write a simple sentence in the space provided to complete each sentence.

EXAMPLE:

a. Enrique has the flu, so *he stayed home from work yesterday* .

b. Enrique has the flu, but *he went to work anyway* .

c. Enrique has the flu, and *he also has a cold* .

1. a. Pepperoni pizzas are on sale, so _____.

   b. Pepperoni pizzas are on sale, but _____.

   c. Pepperoni pizzas are on sale, and _____.

2. a. I must leave for work by 6:00 a.m., or _____.

   b. I must leave for work by 6:00 a.m., but _____.

   c. I must leave for work by 6:00 a.m., so _____.

3. a. A hurricane is headed our way, and _____.

   b. A hurricane is headed our way, so _____.

   c. A hurricane is headed our way, but _____.

DISTINGUISHING COMPOUND SUBJECTS/VERBS AND COMPOUND SENTENCES

In Chapter 16, you learned about compound subjects and verbs. In this chapter, you are learning about compound sentences. It is very important that you do not confuse these two things. Compound subjects and verbs can appear in **one simple sentence**. In contrast, compound sentences must contain **two or more simple sentences**.

First, let's review compound subjects and verbs found in **one simple sentence**.

- A compound subject:

   Toby and Jessica whispered.

Two subjects are performing the *same* action. Notice that when the conjunction (*and*) joins two subjects, **no comma is used**.

KEY TO BUILDING BLOCKS
FOUNDATION WORDS
NOUNS
VERBS
DESCRIPTIVE WORDS
ADJECTIVES
ADVERBS
CONNECTING WORDS
PREPOSITIONS
CONJUNCTIONS

- A <u>compound verb</u>:

Toby <u>whispered</u> and <u>smiled</u>.

One subject is performing *two* actions. Notice that when the conjunction (*and*) joins two verbs, **no comma is used**.

- A <u>compound subject</u> and a <u>compound verb</u>:

ONE COMPOUND SUBJECT	ONE COMPOUND VERB
Toby and Jessica	whispered and smiled.

Here, *two* subjects are both performing *two* actions. Notice that when the conjunction (*and*) joins two <u>subjects</u> or two <u>verbs</u>, **no comma is used**.

Next, let's look at a **compound sentence**, which must contain two or more simple sentences.

SENTENCE 1		SENTENCE 2	
Toby	whispered, and	Jessica	smiled.
1ST SUBJECT	1ST VERB	2ND SUBJECT	2ND VERB

In a compound sentence, there will always be at least <u>two separate</u> subjects involved in at least <u>two separate</u> actions. Notice that when a conjunction joins two simple <u>sentences</u>, **a comma is required**. Here's another example, with the conjunction *but*:

Marcus voted, but his candidate lost.

Power Tip
Note that you can also create compound adjectives (*Beautiful and talented Rhonda* danced), compound adverbs (*Rhonda danced <u>smoothly and gracefully</u>*), and compound prepositional phrases (*Rhonda danced <u>at home and at the ballet studio</u>*).

ACTIVITY 4
EASY

For each simple sentence below, do the following:

- Underline the subjects and circle the verbs.
- Rewrite the sentences, turning them into compound sentences by giving each subject its own verb. Make sure to put a comma before the conjunction.

EXAMPLE:

Simple sentence: <u>Jared</u> and <u>Morgan</u> (wrote) the report and (sent) it to the regional office.

Compound sentence: *Jared wrote the report, and Morgan sent it to the regional office.*

1. **Simple sentence:** Theresa and her mother enjoy reading and watching movies.

   Compound sentence: _____

2. **Simple sentence:** The police officer and her partner caught the burglar and arrested him.

   Compound sentence: _____

3. **Simple sentence:** Kevin and his wife want a new car but are worried about the cost.

   Compound sentence: _____

4. **Simple sentence:** Professor Kendall and his students love the play *Hamlet* but do not like the film version.

   Compound sentence: _____

 **ACTIVITY 5**

MODERATE

Rewrite the following simple sentences, turning each of them into a compound sentence. You will need to invent a second subject to complete the compound sentence. Remember to add a comma when you write the compound sentence.

EXAMPLE:

Simple sentence: Toby tripped on his shoelace and laughed.

Compound sentence: *Toby tripped on his shoelace, and his friends laughed.*

1. **Simple sentence:** James ordered a large diet soda and paid for his drink.

   Compound sentence: _____

2. **Simple sentence:** I lost my credit card but found it on the floor of the grocery store.

   Compound sentence: _____

3. **Simple sentence:** Annie picked some blackberries and made a blackberry pie.

   Compound sentence: _____

4. **Simple sentence:** Bettina bought a door prize ticket and won the trip to New York City.

   Compound sentence: _____

CONTINUED >

5. **Simple sentence:** The second baseman missed an easy catch and yelled in frustration.

   Compound sentence: _____

   _____

FOUNDATION WORDS
NOUNS
VERBS
DESCRIPTIVE WORDS
ADJECTIVES
ADVERBS
CONNECTING WORDS
PREPOSITIONS
CONJUNCTIONS

In some cases, you can express the same ideas as *either* a simple sentence *or* a compound sentence. For example:

- A simple sentence:

  ONE SUBJECT **ONE COMPOUND VERB**
  The guests   left but returned.

This sentence has only <u>one</u> simple subject and <u>one</u> compound verb.

- A compound sentence:

  SENTENCE 1   **SENTENCE 2**
  The guests   left, but   they   returned.
  1ST SUBJECT **1ST VERB**   **2ND SUBJECT** **2ND VERB**

This sentence has <u>two separate</u> subjects and <u>two separate</u> verbs. The pronoun *they* refers to *guests*, but it counts as a separate subject.

   If both of these sentences express the same ideas, and if both of them are grammatically correct, which is the better choice? The simple sentence states matter-of-factly that the guests left but returned. In the compound sentence, special emphasis is given to the fact that the guests returned.

Power Tip

In the compound sentence, notice that the second sentence uses the pronoun *they* to refer to *guests*. Whenever the subjects of the two sentences of a compound sentence are the same, make sure that the subject of the second sentence is expressed by a pronoun that matches the subject in the first sentence. (For more on pronouns, see Chapter 15, page 339, and Chapter 24.)

ACTIVITY 6

ADVANCED

From the two simple sentences provided, create (1) a simple sentence with a compound verb and (2) a compound sentence with a pronoun for the second subject. Make sure to include the required comma in the compound sentence.

EXAMPLE:

Simple sentences: Willard plays tennis. Willard wants to be a professional tennis player.

Simple sentence with compound verb: Willard plays tennis and wants to be a professional tennis player.

Compound sentence: Willard plays tennis, and he wants to be a professional tennis player.

1. **Simple sentences:** The hotel suite is luxurious. It has a private balcony.

   Simple sentence with compound verb: _____

   _____

   Compound sentence: _____

   _____

2. **Simple sentences:** Tornadoes form very quickly. They are very destructive.

   Simple sentence with compound verb: _____

   _____

   Compound sentence: _____

   _____

3. **Simple sentences:** Miriam lost her wallet. She later found it in her car.

   Simple sentence with compound verb: _____

   _____

   Compound sentence: _____

   _____

4. **Simple sentences:** Enrique failed the midterm exam. He still passed the course.

   Simple sentence with compound verb: _____

   _____

   Compound sentence: _____

   _____

5. **Simple sentences:** We advertised for a Spanish-speaking assistant. We never found one.

   Simple sentence with compound verb: _____

   _____

   Compound sentence: _____

   _____

USING A SEMICOLON IN PLACE OF A CONJUNCTION

Conjunctions are the usual type of "glue" used to form compound sentences. However, there is another type of glue used to form compound sentences: the **semicolon** (;). Consider the following pair of ideas:

SENTENCE 1   SENTENCE 2

Receiving gifts is pleasant. Giving them is even better.

The period between the two sentences creates a full stop, suggesting that the two ideas are not closely related. However, since we know that the ideas *are* closely related, we can join them to make a compound sentence. There are just two ways to do this:

1. With a coordinating conjunction (preceded by a comma):

> SENTENCE 1   SENTENCE 2
> Receiving gifts is pleasant, but giving them is even better.

2. With a semicolon:

> SENTENCE 1   SENTENCE 2
> Receiving gifts is pleasant; giving them is even better.

The semicolon <u>joins</u> the two ideas, suggesting that there is a special relationship between them. This relationship is reinforced by the lack of capitalization of the first word in the second sentence.

The most important rule to remember as you start to use the semicolon to connect sentences is this: It must always *follow* a complete sentence, and it must *be followed* by another complete sentence. Take a look:

> SENTENCE 1   SENTENCE 2
> The bill came. We paid.

> SENTENCE 1   SENTENCE 2
> The bill came; we paid.

Many students try to use the semicolon to replace commas. **Avoid this mistake!** As a "soft" period, the semicolon is nearly as powerful as a "hard" period (a full stop), and you must respect its authority.

Power Tip
Although the semicolon has other uses as described in Appendix C, its main use is to connect two sentences. We recommend that you master this use of the semicolon before attempting others.

ACTIVITY 7
MODERATE

Form compound sentences from each pair of simple sentences by (1) using a comma and a conjunction and (2) using a semicolon.

EXAMPLE:

Simple sentences: The meals at this café are delicious. I dine here often.

Compound sentence with a conjunction: The meals at this café are delicious, and I dine here often.

Compound sentence with a semicolon: The meals at this café are delicious; I dine here often.

1. **Simple sentences:** My favorite dish is the salmon salad. It's healthy and reasonably priced.

   Compound sentence with a conjunction: _____

Compound sentence with a semicolon: _____

_____

2. **Simple sentences:** The salmon is grilled. The seasoning is perfect.

Compound sentence with a conjunction: _____

_____

Compound sentence with a semicolon: _____

_____

3. **Simple sentences:** I have brought my friends to this café. Everyone loves it.

Compound sentence with a conjunction: _____

_____

Compound sentence with a semicolon: _____

_____

Power Tip
When joining two simple sentences, use a semicolon *only if* the relationship between the two sentences is absolutely clear. If it's not, use a comma and a joining word to clarify the relationship.

Many students have difficulty deciding when a semicolon is a better choice than a conjunction. Take a look at these two sentences:

Writing is easy, but revising is difficult.

Writing is easy; revising is difficult.

Some writers would say that the contrast between writing and revising is absolutely clear, so the conjunction *but* is not necessary. Other writers would say that the conjunction emphasizes the contrast. Both versions are appropriate. If you were faced with this choice, you would have to decide which version you like better.

Power Tip
Most writers avoid using a semicolon to replace *so* (a result), *or* (alternatives), and *but* (when it expresses a strong contrast). In general, you will not use semicolons very often. In fact, most writers use many more conjunctions than semicolons.

ACTIVITY 8: Teamwork

ADVANCED

For each item below, do the following:

- Work individually to form two compound sentences from each pair of simple sentences. Do this in two ways: (1) with a conjunction, and (2) with a semicolon. Make sure the conjunction is preceded by a comma.
- Working with classmates, decide which compound sentence is more effective.

EXAMPLE:

Simple sentences: Crater Lake National Park lies in Oregon. It is one of Oregon's most popular tourist destinations.

Compound sentence with a conjunction: Crater Lake National Park lies in Oregon, and it is one of Oregon's most popular tourist destinations.

Compound sentence with a semicolon: Crater Lake National Park lies in Oregon; it is one of Oregon's most popular tourist destinations.

CONTINUED >

For more practice with conjunctions and semicolons, go to **bedfordstmartins.com /touchstones**.

1. **Simple sentences:** In approximately 5700 BC, Mt. Mazama erupted. It formed a deep crater.

   Compound sentence with a conjunction: _____

   _____

   Compound sentence with a semicolon: _____

   _____

2. **Simple sentences:** Over many centuries, the crater filled with water. Crater Lake was formed.

   Compound sentence with a conjunction: _____

   _____

   Compound sentence with a semicolon: _____

   _____

3. **Simple sentences:** Crater Lake is nearly 2,000 feet deep. It is America's deepest lake.

   Compound sentence with a conjunction: _____

   _____

   Compound sentence with a semicolon: _____

   _____

4. **Simple sentences:** Crater Lake is naturally a deep blue color. Visitors are awed by its beauty.

   Compound sentence with a conjunction: _____

   _____

   Compound sentence with a semicolon: _____

   _____

5. **Simple sentences:** For tourists, Crater Lake is an awe-inspiring sight. For Native Americans, the lake is a sacred place.

   Compound sentence with a conjunction: _____

   _____

   Compound sentence with a semicolon: _____

   _____

BUILD IT: Longer Compound Sentences

So far, the sentences that you've written in this chapter have been rather short. In your academic writing, the compound sentences will sometimes be much longer. As with shorter sentences, it is important that you select the appropriate conjunction and use correct punctuation when writing longer compound sentences.

A compound sentence can become longer for three reasons:

1. The two simple sentences in it include descriptive words and prepositional phrases.

2. The two simple sentences contain a compound subject and/or a compound verb.

3. Three simple sentences are connected instead of two.

ADDING DESCRIPTIVE WORDS AND PREPOSITIONAL PHRASES

First, let's review how simple sentences become longer. In Chapter 16, you learned that a simple sentence can have as few as two words (a subject and a verb). When a writer adds descriptive words (adjectives and adverbs) and prepositional phrases, the simple sentence becomes longer. (Remember, a prepositional phrase begins with a preposition and typically ends with a noun. For more information, see Chapter 16, pages 356–58.)

The longest simple sentences can have three or more prepositional phrases along with descriptive words. Look at the following example:

SUBJECT AND A VERB INCLUDED	My cat sleeps.
DESCRIPTIVE WORDS ADDED	My old cat sleeps soundly.
PREPOSITIONAL PHRASES ADDED	My old cat sleeps soundly at the foot of my bed.
ANOTHER PREPOSITIONAL PHRASE ADDED	During the night, my old cat sleeps soundly at the foot of my bed.

FOUNDATION WORDS
NOUNS
VERBS

DESCRIPTIVE WORDS
ADJECTIVES
ADVERBS

CONNECTING WORDS
PREPOSITIONS
CONJUNCTIONS

Power Tip
For a list of common prepositions, see Chapter 16, page 357.

Similarly, compound sentences can contain descriptive words and prepositional phrases. Take a look:

SENTENCE 1

During the night, my old cat sleeps soundly at the foot of my bed, and in the morning, he eagerly wakes me for his favorite breakfast of kitty tuna delight.   **SENTENCE 2**

ACTIVITY 9
MODERATE

For each pair of simple sentences below, do the following:

- Add a prepositional phrase to the end of each simple sentence.
- Use a conjunction to join the two sentences that you have created, making sure to precede it with a comma.

EXAMPLE:

Simple sentences: Lorin needed a break. She went on a road trip.

Add a prepositional phrase to sentence 1: Lorin needed a break from her job.

CONTINUED >

Add a prepositional phrase to sentence 2: She went on a road trip to the Grand Canyon.

Combine the previous two sentences to make a compound sentence:
Lorin needed a break from her job, so she went on a road trip to the Grand Canyon.

1. **Simple sentences:** Ingrid looked for a new apartment. She found an acceptable studio.

   Add a prepositional phrase to sentence 1: _____

   Add a prepositional phrase to sentence 2: _____

   Combine the previous two sentences to make a compound sentence:
   _____

2. **Simple sentences:** I ordered a new laptop computer. It arrived.

   Add a prepositional phrase to sentence 1: _____

   Add a prepositional phrase to sentence 2: _____

   Combine the previous two sentences to make a compound sentence:
   _____

3. **Simple sentences:** Garrett crashed his bicycle. He received only minor injuries.

   Add a prepositional phrase to sentence 1: _____

   Add a prepositional phrase to sentence 2: _____

   Combine the previous two sentences to make a compound sentence:
   _____

INCLUDING COMPOUND SUBJECTS AND VERBS

Earlier in this chapter, you studied the difference between two sentence types:

1. a simple sentence that contains a **compound subject** and/or a **compound verb**

2. a **compound sentence** that contains two simple sentences

Now, if we put these two types together, we get a third possibility:

3. a compound sentence made up of two simple sentences, each of which contains a compound subject and/or a compound verb

Let's take a closer look.

Here is a simple sentence with a compound subject and a compound verb:

`A COMPOUND SUBJECT`   `A COMPOUND VERB`

The <u>mayor</u> and his <u>aide</u> <u>stepped</u> to the podium and <u>waved</u>.

<u>Both</u> subjects are involved in <u>two</u> connected actions. Notice that <u>no comma</u> is used to join a compound subject or a compound verb.

Here is a compound sentence:

`SENTENCE 1`   `SENTENCE 2`

The mayor stepped to the podium, and his aide waved.

`1ST SUBJECT` `1ST VERB` `CONJUNCTION` `2ND SUBJECT` `2ND VERB`

These are <u>two separate</u> subjects involved in <u>two separate</u> actions. As you know, a comma is required when joining two simple sentences with a conjunction.

Here is a compound sentence in which each simple sentence has a compound subject and a compound verb:

`1ST COMPOUND SUBJECT`   `1ST COMPOUND VERB`

The disgraced <u>mayor</u> and his loyal <u>aide</u> <u>stepped</u> to the podium and <u>waved</u>, but the angry <u>citizens</u> and <u>reporters</u> <u>stood</u> and <u>waited</u> for an explanation.

`CONJUNCTION` `2ND COMPOUND SUBJECT` `2ND COMPOUND VERB`

When we join simple sentences that have compound subjects and compound verbs, the resulting compound sentence can be quite long. Notice, however, that there is still only <u>one</u> comma in the previous sentence; we do not need a comma to join a compound subject or a compound verb.

ACTIVITY 10: Teamwork

ADVANCED

With classmates, do the following for each set of simple sentences:

- Discuss how to combine each pair of simple sentences to make one simple sentence with a compound subject and/or a compound verb. Write the two simple sentences in the spaces provided.

- Select a conjunction (or use a semicolon) to form a compound sentence from the two simple sentences. Write the compound sentence in the space provided, making sure to place the comma correctly.

EXAMPLE:

Simple sentences:

a. Multnomah Falls is located on the Columbia River. Horsetail Falls is located on the Columbia River.

CONTINUED >

    b. Both waterfalls can be viewed up close. Both waterfalls are popular tourist attractions.

Combined to form compound subjects/verbs:

a. Multnomah Falls and Horsetail Falls are located on the Columbia River.

b. Both waterfalls can be viewed up close and are popular tourist attractions.

Compound sentence: Multnomah Falls and Horsetail Falls are located on the Columbia River; both waterfalls can be viewed up close and are popular tourist attractions.

1. **Simple sentences:**

    a. Destin, Florida, is famous for its sugar-white beaches. Ft. Walton Beach, Florida, is famous for its sugar-white beaches.

    b. The Gulf waters can be dangerous. They have cost many swimmers their lives.

    Combined to form compound subjects/verbs:

    a. _____

    b. _____

    Compound sentence: _____

2. **Simple sentences:**

    a. Ben wanted to skip school. He wanted to go fishing instead.

    b. He went to school anyway. He attended his history class.

    Combined to form compound subjects/verbs:

    a. _____

    b. _____

    Compound sentence: _____

3. **Simple sentences:**

    a. Blueberries are loaded with antioxidants. Raspberries are loaded with antioxidants.

    b. They taste delicious on ice cream. They make refreshing smoothies.

    Combined to form compound subjects/verbs:

    a. _____

    b. _____

For more practice with compound sentences, go to **bedfordstmartins.com /touchstones**.

Compound sentence: _____

_____

_____

4. **Simple sentences:**
   a. Rock climbing requires great endurance. Long-distance hiking requires great endurance.
   b. Both activities build confidence. Both activities are rewarding.

   Combined to form compound subjects/verbs:

   a. _____

   b. _____

   Compound sentence: _____

   _____

   _____

5. **Simple sentences:**
   a. Deep breathing calms the mind. Sustained stretching calms the mind.
   b. Both help people relieve stress. Both help people stay focused.

   Combined to form compound subjects/verbs:

   a. _____

   b. _____

   Compound sentence: _____

   _____

   _____

JOINING THREE SIMPLE SENTENCES INSTEAD OF TWO

Most compound sentences join two simple sentences. Sometimes, however, a compound sentence will join three simple sentences. In this case, the sentence will have <u>three separate subjects</u> and <u>three separate verbs</u>. Also, two conjunctions will be needed to join the three sentences. In some instances, you may use a semicolon to replace one of the conjunctions.

Consider this example:

SIMPLE SENTENCE 1	We planned to take a bus to the airport.
SIMPLE SENTENCE 2	We were running late.
SIMPLE SENTENCE 3	We took a taxi instead.
COMPOUND SENTENCE	We planned to take a bus to the airport, but we were running late, so we took a taxi instead.
WITH SEMICOLON	We planned to take a bus to the airport, but we were running late; we took a taxi instead.

FOUNDATION WORDS
NOUNS
VERBS
DESCRIPTIVE WORDS
ADJECTIVES
ADVERBS
CONNECTING WORDS
PREPOSITIONS
CONJUNCTIONS

ılıl **ACTIVITY 11**

MODERATE

Select appropriate conjunctions (or use a semicolon) to connect the following simple sentences. Start by joining the first two sentences, and then the third sentence should be easier to add. Write the complete compound sentence in the space provided.

Note: Each compound sentence will have at least two commas, unless you use a semicolon in place of one of the conjunctions. If the compound sentence begins with a prepositional phrase, the sentence will have an additional comma.

EXAMPLE: Shontika is good at math. Kaylee is good at writing. They study together.

Compound sentence: Shontika is good at math, and Kaylee is good at writing, so they study together.

1. Joyce is allergic to seafood. Daniel is a vegetarian. They rarely go out to dinner together.

   Compound sentence: _____

   _____

2. Residents should evacuate the area now. They could become trapped by the approaching hurricane. Rescuers would be risking their lives.

   Compound sentence: _____

   _____

3. Katy is very interested in hiking. Her husband prefers indoor activities. Katy hikes with her friends.

   Compound sentence: _____

   _____

4. Two years ago, Roger was diagnosed with high blood pressure. He immediately improved his diet and started an exercise program. His blood pressure is now excellent.

   Compound sentence: _____

   _____

5. At the end of each semester, Professor Hudson needs a vacation. He travels to the mountains and goes fishing. He always returns to college refreshed and energized.

   Compound sentence: _____

   _____

ACTIVITY 12: Teamwork

ADVANCED

With classmates, unscramble each set of three simple sentences, following these steps:

- Discuss the sentences and put them in the correct order.
- Decide which conjunctions will join the sentences smoothly. You might use a semicolon in place of a conjunction.
- Working individually, write the compound sentence in the space provided. Make sure your commas are correctly placed.

EXAMPLE: I put the brownies in the oven. After almost an hour, I smelled the odor of burned brownies. I called my sister and became involved in a long conversation.

Compound sentence: *I put the brownies in the oven, and I called my sister and became involved in a long conversation; after almost an hour, I smelled the odor of burned brownies.*

1. After the repair, the truck was still running rough. My mechanic replaced the carburetor in my truck. He replaced the carburetor again and did not bill me for the additional parts or labor.

   Compound sentence: _____

   _____

   _____

   _____

2. The backup quarterback is doing quite well. The Badgers no longer have a star quarterback. During a brutal sack, the star quarterback suffered a broken collarbone.

   Compound sentence: _____

   _____

   _____

   _____

3. The bolt traveled through the driveway and flattened all four of his truck's tires. Lightning struck the pine tree next to Jeff's house. The lightning had traveled directly to the steel-belted radial tires.

   Compound sentence: _____

   _____

   _____

   _____

CONTINUED >

4. We were very annoyed and complained to the manager. She refused to take any action. During dinner at an expensive restaurant, several patrons talked loudly on their cell phones.

   Compound sentence: _____

   _____

   _____

5. The payments became very difficult in the worsening economy. They made a painful decision and sold their condo. Ten years ago, Todd and his wife purchased a vacation condo in Vail, Colorado.

   Compound sentence: _____

   _____

   _____

   _____

RECOGNIZING CORRECT PUNCTUATION IN SIMPLE AND COMPOUND SENTENCES

So far, you have learned four rules for punctuating simple and compound sentences. The following is a review, with examples.

- If a sentence begins with a prepositional phrase, a comma usually follows this phrase:

  PREPOSITIONAL PHRASE

  On Saturday morning, **we left for our vacation.**

  COMMA

- No comma is used when forming a compound subject or a compound verb:

  | COMPOUND SUBJECT, NO COMMA | COMPOUND VERB, NO COMMA |

  <u>Elton</u> and <u>Hannah</u> <u>renovate</u> old homes and <u>resell</u> them.

- When a conjunction is used to join two simple sentences, a comma should precede the conjunction:

  SENTENCE 1   SENTENCE 2

  You may sleep **in our guest bedroom,** or you can stay **at a motel.**

  COMMA & CONJUNCTION

- The semicolon follows a complete sentence, so it should not be used to replace a comma:

INCORRECT	Bob moved to Colorado; and he learned to ski.
CORRECT	Bob moved to Colorado, and he learned to ski.
	Bob moved to Colorado. He learned to ski.
	Bob moved to Colorado; he learned to ski.

SEMICOLON REPLACES
A PERIOD

ACTIVITY 13: Teamwork

ADVANCED

Carefully examine and discuss each of the following groups of sentences. Only one sentence has the correct punctuation. Put a check mark beside it.

EXAMPLE:

a. Online dating sites are popular these days but many user profiles contain lies.

b. Online dating sites are popular these days; but many user profiles contain lies.

c. Online dating sites are popular these days, but many user profiles contain lies. ✓

1. a. Many people exaggerate their height they often add two inches to their real height.

   b. Many people exaggerate their height; they often add two inches to their real height. ✓

   c. Many people exaggerate their height, they often add two inches to their real height.

2. a. On the average, "recent" photos are old, and some are one or two years old. ✓

   b. On the average, "recent" photos are old and, some are one or two years old.

   c. On the average, "recent" photos are old; and some are one or two years old.

3. a. In many online profiles, users exaggerate their annual income. ✓

   b. In many online profiles users exaggerate their annual income.

   c. In many online profiles; users exaggerate their annual income.

4. a. Another touchy area is weight, lies are common in this area.

   b. Another touchy area is weight lies are common in this area.

   c. Another touchy area is weight; lies are common in this area. ✓

5. a. Some people even lie about their marital status but, these lies are less common.

   b. Some people even lie about their marital status, but these lies are less common. ✓

   c. Some people even lie about their marital status; but these lies are less common.

CONTINUED >

For more practice with punctuation in compound sentences, go to **bedfordstmartins.com /touchstones**.

6. a. Not everyone is completely honest, so online dating sites must be used with caution. √

   b. Not everyone is completely honest so, online dating sites must be used with caution.

   c. Not everyone is completely honest; so online dating sites must be used with caution.

ACTIVITY 14: Mastery Test or Teamwork

In the following paragraph, form seven compound sentences, using *and*, *or*, *but*, or *so*. First, identify each pair of sentences that can be joined, and then decide which conjunction will join the sentences most effectively. The first one has been done for you.

Olympic National Park is located in the northwestern corner

of the state of Washington. Relatively few people know about Olympic

National Park/It **, but it** offers many outdoor activities for visitors. The

park encompasses nearly a million acres. It includes the rugged

and rocky beaches of the Pacific Ocean. It offers snow-capped

mountains and stunningly beautiful rain forests. Hiking trails are

abundant. Hikers may find some of the trails challenging. At times, the

trail is covered by high tide. Some coastline trails require the use of

fixed ropes. Coastline trails can be dangerous. Other trails are more

user-friendly. The nine-mile Ozette Loop has a three-mile boardwalk.

In the winter, skiers will enjoy the small alpine ski area at Hurricane

Ridge. The ski area is run by a nonprofit organization. The lift passes

are not expensive. History buffs will find the area's past quite fascinating.

Native Americans once lived in the park area. They used the peninsula

for fishing and hunting. Valuable artifacts have been found in the

park. Despite its location in the northwestern tip of Washington,

Olympic National Park is well worth the journey.

FIX IT: Solving Problems in Compound Sentences

So far in this chapter, you have learned that there are just two types of "glue" to form compound sentences: a **conjunction** (preceded by a comma) and a **semicolon**. Remember that there are only seven coordinating conjunctions (*and, or, but, so, yet, nor, for*), and that <u>no other words can be glue</u>. Let's review:

A conjunction with a comma as glue:

SENTENCE 1   SENTENCE 2

Class started**,** so we opened **our** books.

A semicolon as glue:

SENTENCE 1   SENTENCE 2

Class started**;** we opened **our** books.

and
or
but
so
■
,

UNDERSTANDING HOW RUN-ONS AND COMMA SPLICES OCCUR

If you forget to use glue when joining two simple sentences, or if you try to use other words or punctuation marks as glue, you will create a **run-on** or a **comma splice**. Both are errors. Take a look:

1. Trying to join two sentences with no glue:

   Class started we opened **our** books.
                   ↑

Although these sentences are very short, they are two separate sentences with two separate subjects and two separate verbs. If we <u>run them together</u> without glue, we have a **run-on**.

2. Trying to use a comma by itself as glue:

   Class started, we opened **our** books.
                   ↑

When sentences are so short, some writers believe that they can be joined with a comma. However, remember that <u>a comma by itself is never glue</u>. If we "splice" (join) these two sentences with a comma only, we have a **comma splice**.

3. Trying to use other words as glue:

   Class started **then** we opened **our** books.
                     ↑

   Class started, <u>then</u> we opened **our** books.
                     ↑

In English, there are many words that seem like glue but are not. In this example, *then* has been used in place of a coordinating conjunction. As a result, the first example is a **run-on**, and the second example is a **comma splice**. In both cases, the sentences do not have the glue they need to be joined correctly.

Power Tip
A run-on and a comma splice are really the same grammatical error. In both cases, two separate sentences are joined without glue. In the case of a comma splice, the writer has added a comma as glue, but you now know that a comma by itself is never glue.

ACTIVITY 15
MODERATE

Carefully examine each of the following items. Then, decide whether each is

- a correct compound sentence,
- a run-on, or
- a comma splice.

Write the appropriate label in the space provided. Then, fix incorrect sentences by adding glue (a comma and conjunction or a semicolon) or by forming two separate sentences.

EXAMPLE:

Many job-seekers make serious mistakes during their searches; these mistakes often cost them the position. comma splice

1. Some people apply for only one job at a time, this mistake limits opportunities. _____CS_____

2. References are important they should be chosen carefully. __run__

3. Interviewees should have a neat briefcase, sloppiness creates an unfavorable impression. __CS__

4. Temporary positions should not be overlooked; they can lead to full-time positions. __CCS__

5. During interviews at restaurants, employers watch how the interviewee treats the food service staff, rudeness reflects an inconsiderate attitude. __CS__

6. Insulting a previous employer or company rival is another serious mistake it reflects a lack of loyalty and tact. _____

7. Potential employers now routinely check social networks, and compromising photographs or posts will paint a negative impression of job-seekers. __CCS__

8. A follow-up call or e-mail about the status of the position is acceptable, numerous calls or e-mails make the job-seeker appear rude or desperate. __CS__

9. A polite thank-you note following the interview is appropriate it will remind the employer of the interview and reflect consideration and good manners. _____

10. Good positions generate significant competition, treating the employer with tact and polish will earn job-seekers an extra advantage.

_____

UNDERSTANDING WORDS THAT CAN CAUSE RUN-ONS AND COMMA SPLICES

Many run-ons and comma splices are caused when we try to use <u>words that are not conjunctions</u> as glue. As you already know, there are only seven words that can truly be used as glue: *and, but, or, so, for, nor,* and *yet*. However, what often confuses students is that there are lots of other words that *seem* like glue.

Below are some words that are commonly *misused* as glue. They are divided into four groups to help you remember them.

PERSONAL PRONOUNS	DEMONSTRATIVE PRONOUNS	ADDITIVE EXPRESSIONS	TRANSITIONAL EXPRESSIONS
I	this	also	as a result
you	that	for example	consequently
he	these	for instance	furthermore
she	those	next	however
it		plus	in addition
we		then	instead
they			moreover
			nevertheless
			otherwise
			therefore

Power Tip
The additive expressions listed here can also be used as transitional expressions. However, we distinguish them here because they cause run-ons and comma splices in a particular way.

Let's look at each of these groups individually to understand why the words often *seem* like glue.

Personal Pronouns

The personal pronouns in the list above cause more run-ons and comma splices than any other group of words. Therefore, it is very important that you understand why. Take a look at the following run-on:

FOUNDATION WORDS
NOUNS
VERBS
DESCRIPTIVE WORDS
ADJECTIVES
ADVERBS
CONNECTING WORDS
PREPOSITIONS
CONJUNCTIONS

Serena needed **transportation** she bought **a motorbike.**

1ST SUBJECT 1ST VERB   2ND SUBJECT 2ND VERB

Notice that there are two separate sentences here with two separate subjects and two separate verbs. Therefore, we need some glue to join them.

Many of the sentences we write are about people. If the sentence is compound, often the first subject will name a person or persons and the second subject will be a <u>personal pronoun</u> that <u>refers back</u> to the first subject. Take a look:

Serena needed **transportation** she bought **a motorbike.**

Because *she* refers to *Serena*, many writers believe that it is glue that can join the two simple sentences. However, *she* is the subject of the second simple sentence, even though it refers back to *Serena*. Therefore, we still need some glue to join these two sentences, or we need to break them into separate sentences:

COMMA AND COORDINATING CONJUNCTION ADDED	Serena needed **transportation,** so she bought **a motorbike.**

or

SEMICOLON ADDED	Serena needed **transportation;** she bought **a motorbike.**

or

PERIOD ADDED	Serena needed **transportation.** She bought **a motorbike.**

The last option (using a period) does correct the run-on; however, it does not <u>join</u> the two simple sentences to form a compound sentence.

Sometimes, the personal pronoun that causes the problem refers back to a noun in the first sentence that is not the subject:

We saw Serena **yesterday** she invited **us to come with her.**

This sentence can be fixed in the same ways as the sentence above.

ACTIVITY 16

MODERATE

For each of the run-ons or comma splices below, do the following:

- Circle the personal pronoun.
- Draw an arrow connecting the pronoun to the subject or other noun to which it refers.
- Rewrite the run-on or comma splice in the space provided, adding a conjunction or a semicolon to make it a correct compound sentence. If you use a conjunction, don't forget to add the required comma.

EXAMPLE:

Dan held a high-stress job in the financial industry he was experiencing heart palpitations and headaches.

Dan held a high-stress job in the financial industry, and he was experiencing heart palpitations and headaches.

1. Dan approached his boss about a short vacation, she denied his request.

2. Dan's boss, Ms. Burrows, is a workaholic she never takes vacations herself.

3. Ms. Burrows works 12-hour days, she expects her employees to do the same.

4. One morning, Dan awoke with a pounding heart, he told his wife about his health worries.

5. Amanda told Dan, "I have a plan you and I are playing hooky today."

6. Amanda called Dan's office with a story about the flu, it was a convincing story.

7. Dan and Amanda took a drive in the mountains they took a picnic lunch with them.

8. Beside a stream, they dangled their feet in the water, its coolness felt soothing.

CONTINUED >

9. Amanda and Dan lay on the grass and watched the clouds drift by they talked all afternoon.

10. Dan had made an important realization, he wrote a letter of resignation.

Demonstrative Pronouns

FOUNDATION WORDS
NOUNS
VERBS

DESCRIPTIVE WORDS
ADJECTIVES
ADVERBS

CONNECTING WORDS
PREPOSITIONS
CONJUNCTIONS

Demonstrative pronouns (*this, that, these, those*) usually refer to <u>things, places, or ideas</u>. Demonstrative pronouns do not cause as many run-ons and comma splices as personal pronouns do, but they are often more difficult to spot. Take a look at the following comma splice:

SENTENCE 1	SENTENCE 2

My teacher didn't read my essay, that upset me.

| 1ST SUBJECT | 1ST VERB | | 2ND SUBJECT | 2ND VERB |

This example also contains two separate sentences with two separate subjects and two separate verbs. However, it may be difficult to recognize the pronoun *that* as a separate subject.

When a demonstrative pronoun is used as a subject in a compound sentence, it often <u>refers back</u> to a thing, a place, or an idea in the first part of the sentence. This thing, place, or idea may consist of more than one word. Take a look:

My teacher didn't read my essay, that upset me.

That is a pronoun, and just like all pronouns, it refers to something else (a person, place, thing, or idea). To understand what *that* refers to, ask yourself, "What upset me?" What upset you was the fact that your teacher did not read your essay. Because the pronoun *that* refers back to the idea in the first part of the sentence, many writers believe that it is glue, but it is not. We still need some glue to join these sentences, or we need to break them into separate sentences:

COORDINATING CONJUNCTION ADDED	My teacher didn't read my essay, and that upset me.
or	
SEMICOLON USED	My teacher didn't read my essay; that upset me.
or	
PERIOD USED	My teacher didn't read my essay. That upset me.

Power Tip
If there is any chance that a reader might not understand what you are referring to with a demonstrative pronoun, replace it with more specific words. For example, take a look at this replacement for *that*: *My teacher didn't read my essay, and <u>her lack of interest in my work</u> upset me.*

The last option (using a period instead of a coordinating conjunction or semicolon) does correct the comma splice; however, it does not <u>join</u> the two simple sentences to form a compound sentence.

ACTIVITY 17

MODERATE

For each of the run-ons or comma splices below, do the following:

- Circle the demonstrative pronoun.
- Underline the thing, place, or idea to which the demonstrative pronoun refers.
- Rewrite the run-on or comma splice in the space provided, adding a conjunction or a semicolon to make it a correct compound sentence. If you use a conjunction, don't forget the required comma.

EXAMPLE:

Aunt Anna collects porcelain <u>animals</u> (these) are her most cherished possessions.

Aunt Anna collects porcelain animals, and these are her most cherished

possessions.

1. My supervisor wrote me a letter of appreciation that made my day.

_____

_____

2. After the accident, James had bruises and scratches those were his only injuries.

_____

_____

3. During the midterm exam, Dana had a terrible headache; this distracted her greatly.

_____

_____

4. I am usually not a fan of grilled hot dogs these were absolutely delicious.

_____

_____

5. For question number 11 on the quiz, I chose B that was the wrong answer.

_____

_____

FOUNDATION WORDS
NOUNS
VERBS

DESCRIPTIVE WORDS
ADJECTIVES
ADVERBS

CONNECTING WORDS
PREPOSITIONS
CONJUNCTIONS

Additive Expressions

Sometimes, we write a sentence and then decide to add more information to it. We often use additive expressions (*also*, *for example*, *next*, *plus*, *then*, and so on) to join this information to our sentence. However, if this additional information is expressed with a separate subject and a separate verb, it cannot be joined to the first simple sentence with an additive expression. <u>Additive expressions are never glue.</u> Look at the following comma splice:

SENTENCE 1   SENTENCE 2
Daniel repairs **old bicycles**, then he donates **them to needy children.**
1ST SUBJECT 1ST VERB   2ND SUBJECT 2ND VERB

Additive expressions are tricky because they seem so much like glue! However, you know that the <u>only glue</u> for joining sentences is (1) a conjunction (*and*, *but*, *or*, *so*, *for*, *nor*, or *yet*) preceded by a comma or (2) a semicolon. To fix the previous comma splice, you could use a conjunction in place of the additive expression or use a semicolon followed by the additive expression. If a conjunction is used, a comma must precede it. If an additive expression is used, a comma usually follows it. Take a look:

CONJUNCTION USED   Daniel repairs **old bicycles,** and he
                             donates **them to needy children.**

or

SEMICOLON AND ADDITIVE   Daniel repairs **old bicycles;** then,
EXPRESSION USED   he donates **them to needy children.**

In some cases—most commonly with *then*—you can use both a conjunction and an additive expression. Take a look:

Daniel repairs **old bicycles,** and then he donates **them to needy children.**

ACTIVITY 18

MODERATE

For each of the run-ons or comma splices below, do the following:

- Circle the additive expression (*also*, *for example*, *next*, *plus*, *then*, and so on).

- Rewrite the run-on or comma splice in the space provided, using one of the correction methods described. (If you add a conjunction, make sure to put a comma before it. If you use a semicolon followed by an additive expression, make sure that a comma follows this expression.)

EXAMPLE:

Shontelle had just been laid off at work, (also), she had very little money set aside for the upcoming holiday season.

Shontelle had just been laid off at work; also, she had very little

money set aside for the upcoming holiday season.

1. Shontelle enjoys giving special gifts to everyone for example, she even buys gifts for the postal carrier and for her hairstylist.

   _____

   _____

2. She decided to trim her gift list this year, also, she would give handmade gifts.

   _____

   _____

3. Shontelle is quite a good cook for example, she is famous among her friends for her delicious pastries.

   _____

   _____

4. Her cookbooks contain recipes for many tasty breads, cakes, and cookies also, she knows a wonderful recipe for scones.

   _____

   _____

5. At the supermarket, Shontelle bought the ingredients for scones, then, she set aside a day for baking.

   _____

   _____

6. Shontelle baked a large batch of scones next, she wrapped them in airtight plastic wrap.

   _____

   _____

7. She wrapped the gifts creatively, for example, she used holiday wrapping paper to cover shoe boxes.

   _____

   _____

8. Her friends loved her delicious scones plus they appreciated her thoughtfulness.

   _____

   _____

Transitional Expressions

You already know that we use a conjunction to join two related simple sentences. Transitional expressions (*as a result, consequently, furthermore, however, in addition,* and so on) do exactly the same thing; in fact, transitional expressions are really just "grown-up" conjunctions. The only difference is

FOUNDATION WORDS
NOUNS
VERBS
DESCRIPTIVE WORDS
ADJECTIVES
ADVERBS
CONNECTING WORDS
PREPOSITIONS
CONJUNCTIONS

that <u>transitional expressions are never glue</u>. A transitional expression by itself can never join two separate sentences. Take a look at this run-on:

SENTENCE 1

The judge sentenced the vandals to three days in jail furthermore
1ST SUBJECT **1ST VERB**

SENTENCE 2

the vandals had to pay restitution.
2ND SUBJECT **2ND VERB**

First, notice that this example consists of two separate sentences with two separate subjects and two separate verbs. The writer has tried to use *furthermore* as glue to join the two simple sentences, but we know that a transitional word can never be glue. Often, a writer will add a comma with the transitional word:

> The judge sentenced the vandals to three days in jail<u>, furthermore</u> the vandals had to pay restitution.

However, you already know that a comma can never be glue. Even though the writer has used a comma and a transitional word together here, there is still <u>no glue</u> to hold the two simple sentences together. <u>If you want to use a transitional expression in a compound sentence, the best way to do so is with a semicolon.</u> Take a look:

> The judge sentenced the vandals to three days in jail<u>;</u> furthermore, the vandals had to pay restitution.

This sentence is now a correct compound sentence; the semicolon provides the glue that joins the two simple sentences. Also, notice the added comma after *furthermore*.

New comma rule: When a transitional expression begins a sentence (including a sentence that is part of a compound sentence), this expression should be followed by a comma. (Remember that prepositional phrases that begin sentences also are followed by a comma.)

Power Tip
Transitions are an important tool for helping readers to follow your ideas. For more advice on using them, see Chapter 5, pages 103–4, and Chapter 6, pages 136 and 141–42.

ACTIVITY 19
MODERATE

For each of the following run-ons or comma splices, do the following:

- Circle the transitional expression (*as a result, consequently, furthermore, however, in addition,* and so on).
- Rewrite the run-on or comma splice in the space provided, turning it into a correct compound sentence. Use a semicolon as glue, and remember to put a comma after the transitional expression.

EXAMPLE:

> Tami's spending was out of control,(furthermore) she was deeply in debt.
> *Tami's spending was out of control; furthermore, she was deeply in debt.*

1. Tami was careless with her credit cards; therefore, she had over
   $20,000 in credit card debt.

2. At times, she was unable to make minimum payments; as a result, the
   interest charges increased dramatically.

3. Tami despaired; however, her best friend suggested credit counseling.

4. Tami followed her counselor's financial advice; furthermore, she
   destroyed all her credit cards.

5. After four years, Tami was debt-free; in addition, she has started
   a retirement account to save money.

The following chart shows that conjunctions and transitional expressions are
used to show the same *four types of relationships* between ideas.

Relationships Shown by Conjunctions and Transitional Expressions

	COMBINATION	CONTRAST	RESULT	ALTERNATIVES
Coordinating conjunctions	and (nor)	but (yet)	so (for)	or
Transitional expressions	furthermore in addition moreover	however nevertheless	as a result consequently therefore	instead on the other hand otherwise

Let's take a closer look:

Combination

Ellen was promoted to manager, and she received a raise in salary.

Ellen was promoted to manager; furthermore, she received a raise in salary.

In the first sentence, the conjunction is the glue. In the next sentence, the
semicolon is the glue, not the transitional expression.

Both compound sentences mean the same thing. Just like the conjunction *and*, the transitional expressions *furthermore, in addition,* and *moreover*
combine two **similar** ideas.

For more practice with fixing
run-ons and comma splices,
go to **bedfordstmartins.com
/touchstones**.

Power Tip
If you were the writer of any of these pairs of sentences, you would have to choose the version you like best; it is a matter of personal style and taste.

Contrast

Ellen was promoted to manager, but the new position required longer working hours.

Ellen was promoted to manager; however, the new position required longer working hours.

In the first sentence, the conjunction is the glue. In the next sentence, the semicolon is the glue, not the transitional expression.

Both compound sentences mean the same thing. Just like the conjunction *but*, the transitional expressions *however, instead,* and *nevertheless* **contrast** two **different** ideas.

Result

Ellen was promoted to manager, so she had more responsibilities.

Ellen was promoted to manager; as a result, she had more responsibilities.

In the first sentence, the conjunction is the glue. In the next sentence, the semicolon is the glue, not the transitional expression.

Both compound sentences mean the same thing. Just like the conjunction *so*, the transitional expressions *as a result, consequently,* and *therefore* show a **result** of one idea from another.

Alternatives

Ellen might accept the promotion to manager, or she might decline the offer.

Ellen might accept the promotion to manager; on the other hand, she might decline the offer.

In the first sentence, the conjunction is the glue. In the next sentence, the semicolon is the glue, not the transitional expression.

Both compound sentences mean the same thing. Just like the conjunction *or*, the transitional expressions *instead, on the other hand,* and *otherwise* show **alternative** options or possibilities.

As a beginning writer, you should not feel pressured to use either transitional expressions or semicolons. If you are more comfortable using conjunctions, focus your practice on writing compound sentences with conjunctions. Some excellent writers do not use many transitional expressions or semicolons.

ACTIVITY 20: Teamwork

ADVANCED

Correct each of the following run-ons or comma splices in two ways:

- For the first correction, add a conjunction. Make sure that a comma precedes the conjunction.

- For the second correction, add a semicolon and a transitional expression. Make sure that a comma follows the transitional expression.

EXAMPLE:

"Silent Night" is a Christmas carol familiar to almost everyone, few people know its origin.

"Silent Night" is a Christmas carol familiar to almost everyone, but few people know its origin.

"Silent Night" is a Christmas carol familiar to almost everyone; however, few people know its origin.

1. In 1816, in a small village in Austria, a young priest named Joseph Mohr wrote "Silent Night" as a poem he did not write the melody.

2. Two years later, Mohr was an assistant pastor in Oberndorf and needed a song for the Christmas Eve service he asked his musician friend Franz Gruber to write the melody for "Silent Night."

3. Mohr and Gruber delivered the first performance of "Silent Night" together that Christmas Eve at the St. Nicholas Church, the song soon spread around the world.

4. "Silent Night" made its way to America in 1839 it has been translated into 300 different languages.

CONTINUED >

5. This lovely Austrian song, "Stille Nacht! Heilige Nacht!," is now performed every Christmas Eve in Oberndorf, on that night, the tiny village is crowded with visitors from all over the world.

_____

_____

_____

_____

_____

_____

ACTIVITY 21: Mastery Test or Teamwork

MASTERY

Read each of the following paragraphs carefully, looking for run-ons and comma splices. Then, rewrite each error to fix the problem, using one of the following methods: (1) adding a conjunction (with a comma, if one is missing), (2) adding a semicolon alone, (3) adding a semicolon followed by an additive or transitional expression and a comma, or (4) using a period. The first sentence of each paragraph has been edited for you.

This paragraph has six comma splices (including the one that has been edited for you) and four run-ons.

a. (1) In June 2008 in Gosforth, Newcastle Upon Tyne, in the

United Kingdom, six tiny mallard ducklings were swept away from

; however,

their mother in an underground drain, this story has a happy ending.

(2) The mother duck followed her babies for about a mile she

could hear their frantic cries from storm drains. (3) This heroic mother

walked across busy roads, school fields, and even a metro rail

line, she survived the dangerous journey. (4) Finally, the babies

stopped in a neighborhood in Gosforth. (5) One of the residents,

Peter Elliott, noticed the mother duck, she was standing over a

manhole and would not leave that spot. (6) Mr. Elliott could not

understand the duck's strange behavior then, his daughter went to see the duck and heard the cries of the ducklings. (7) Mr. Elliott finally understood the situation, he enlisted the help of a neighbor. (8) They took off the manhole cover, with a small net, they lifted each duckling from the drain and reunited each with its mother. (9) The neighborhood was quite dangerous for the ducks, Mr. Elliott relocated the mother mallard and her babies to a nearby lake. (10) Mr. Elliott calls the mother duck the real hero in this story this brave mother followed her babies' cheeping from manhole covers and drains she would not leave them.

This paragraph has seven comma splices and five run-ons (including the one that has been edited for you).

  b. (1) The story of Scotland's Susan Boyle is a real-life fairy tale; she went from obscurity to fame overnight. (2) In April 2009, Susan Boyle auditioned for Britain's reality TV show *Britain's Got Talent.* (3) She took the stage as a rather frumpy woman, she was 47 years old. (4) Based on the judgmental expressions on the faces of the audience and judge Simon Cowell, everyone expected Susan Boyle to flop. (5) She did not look at all like a polished performer, this woman amazed everyone in the audience. (6) She sang the first few notes of "I Dreamed a Dream" from the musical *Les Miserables* in a strong, rich voice Simon Cowell's expression changed instantly from boredom to amazement. (7) In the audience, mouths fell open Susan's beautiful voice brought the audience to their feet they cheered and clapped for her unexpected and thrilling performance. (8) This now-famous audition video became an instant viral hit, it has been viewed several hundred million

CONTINUED >

times. (9) Susan Boyle sang well in the remaining appearances
on *Britain's Got Talent*, she did not win first place, she still landed
a recording contract. (10) Her first CD debuted in November
2009, within six weeks, it was the biggest-selling CD in the world.

(11) Susan Boyle continues to sing professionally she has truly
dreamed a dream it has come true.

BRINGING IT ALL TOGETHER:
The Compound Sentence

In this chapter, you have learned how to build compound sentences and
punctuate them correctly. You have also learned how to avoid two common
problems in these sentences: run-ons and comma splices. Confirm your
knowledge by filling in the blank spaces in the following sentences. If you need
help, review the pages listed after each sentence.

✔ A compound sentence is two or more related simple sentences joined
together. Just two types of "glue" are used to form compound sentences. These two types of glue are _____ and
_____. (pages 370, 377)

✔ There are seven coordinating conjunctions in the English language.
They are _____, _____, _____, _____,
_____, _____, and _____. (page 370)

✔ Each coordinating conjunction expresses a specific type of relationship between the two simple sentences. _____ combines
two similar ideas. _____ contrasts two different ideas.
_____ shows a result. _____ shows alternatives.
(pages 370–71)

✔ In a compound sentence, there must always be two separate
_____ and two separate _____. When punctuating
a compound sentence, a _____ must always come before the
conjunction. (page 374)

✔ A semicolon can be used to join two simple sentences that have a special connection, but it must always follow a _____. (page 378)

✔ If you try to join two simple sentences with no glue (without a conjunction or a semicolon), the result will be a _____, a major grammatical error. (page 391)

✔ If you try to join two simple sentences with only a comma, the result will be a _____, a major grammatical error. (page 391)

✔ Four groups of words are often used *incorrectly* as glue when joining simple sentences. These groups of words are: _____, _____, _____, and _____. (page 393)

CHAPTER 18

The Complex Sentence

Before you read this chapter, it's a good idea to test your understanding of complex sentences. You may know more than you think.

WHAT DO YOU KNOW?

Circle "Yes" if each word group below is a complete, correct sentence. Circle "No" if it is incomplete. Then, explain your choice.

1. **When fog blanketed the airport; all flights were postponed.**

   Yes   No

   Explanation: _____

2. **Unless you make reservations by March.**

   Yes   No

   Explanation: _____
   _____

3. **If you need assistance, I will help.**

   Yes   No

   Explanation: _____

4. **After Fred removed the turkey from the oven he let it cool.**

   Yes   No

   Explanation: _____
   _____

5. **Because Ann could afford the sports car, she bought it.**

   Yes   No

   Explanation: _____
   _____

Both of these are complex sentences. They have the same basic meaning, but they are also different. You'll learn why in this chapter.

`CONJUNCTION` + `NOUN` + `VERB` , `NOUN` + `VERB` . = Because I study, I learn.

`NOUN` + `VERB` + `CONJUNCTION` + `NOUN` + `VERB` . = I learn because I study.

BUILD IT: Complex Sentences

In the previous chapter, you learned that <u>coordinating conjunctions</u> (*and, but, or,* and *so,* and less commonly *for, nor,* and *yet*) work like glue to join simple sentences into **compound sentences**. Take a look:

SIMPLE SENTENCES	`SENTENCE 1` The music played.	`SENTENCE 2` We danced.
COMPOUND SENTENCE	`SENTENCE 1` `SENTENCE 2` The music played, and we danced.	

↑
`COORDINATING CONJUNCTION PRECEDED BY COMMA`

In this chapter, you will study **subordinating conjunctions**, another group of words that work like glue to join simple sentences into what are known as **complex sentences**. Take a look:

SIMPLE SENTENCES	`SENTENCE 1` `SENTENCE 2` The music played. We danced.	
COMPLEX SENTENCE	`SENTENCE 1` `SENTENCE 2` When the music played, we danced.	

↑
`SUBORDINATING CONJUNCTION`

From these examples, you can already see that coordinating and subordinating conjunctions work in a very similar way. However, you should keep some differences in mind:

- There are **more** subordinating conjunctions than coordinating conjunctions.
- Subordinating conjunctions have different rules for **punctuation**.
- If you do not correctly punctuate sentences with subordinating conjunctions, you can create a **sentence fragment**.

Subordinating conjunctions are like a **glue gun**. Whenever you use a glue gun instead of using glue from a bottle, you need to be especially

> **Common Subordinating Conjunctions**
>
> *after, although, as, because, before, even though, even if, if, since, unless, until, when, while*

careful because you have more power and more risk of making a mistake. Likewise, when you use subordinating conjunctions instead of coordinating conjunctions, you also have more power and more risk of making a mistake.

UNDERSTANDING COORDINATING VERSUS SUBORDINATING CONJUNCTIONS

In Chapter 17, you learned that we use coordinating conjunctions to

- combine similar ideas
- contrast different ideas
- show a result
- show alternatives

This chart reviews the relationships shown by coordinating conjunctions and those shown by subordinating conjunctions. Examples of these relationships follow.

Relationships Shown by Conjunctions

	COMBINATION	CONTRAST	RESULT	ALTERNATIVES/ POSSIBILITIES
Coordinating conjunctions	and (nor)	but (yet)	so (for)	or
Subordinating conjunctions	after as before when while	although even though	because since	if (even if) unless (until)

In each of the following sentence pairs, both sentences express the same idea. However, the first sentence uses a **coordinating conjunction**, and the second uses a **subordinating conjunction**. In the second (complex) sentence, the subordinating conjunction comes at the <u>beginning</u> of the sentence. The comma is in the <u>middle</u> of both sentences.

<u>Combining</u> two similar ideas

The team practiced, and the coach took notes.

While the team practiced, the coach took notes.

<u>Contrasting</u> two different ideas

Sue has a 4.0 GPA, but she did not get accepted to Yale.

Although Sue has a 4.0 GPA, she did not get accepted to Yale.

Showing a <u>result</u>

Movie tickets cost $12, so we rent videos.

Because movie tickets cost $12, we rent videos.

Power Tip
Avoid using both *although/even though* and *but* in the same sentence. You need just one of these expressions per sentence.

Incorrect: *Although I left the house early, but I was still late for work.*

Correct: *Although I left the house early, I was still late for work.*

Showing <u>alternatives</u> or <u>possibilities</u>

You must attend class, or you will be dropped.

Unless you attend class, you will be dropped.

Note that the parts of a sentence joined by a coordinating conjunction have equal weight:

You must take a cab, or you must walk.

However, when you begin one sentence part with a subordinating conjunction, it often has less weight (emphasis) than the other part. In other words, it becomes *subordinate* (less important).

Unless you take a cab,

you must walk.

Terminology Tip

The part of the sentence that begins with the subordinating conjunction (*Unless you take a cab*) is known as a **dependent clause**, or **subordinate clause**, because it cannot stand alone as its own sentence. An **independent clause**, or **main clause** (*you must walk*), can stand alone as a sentence. If a dependent/subordinate clause is not attached to a sentence, it is a sentence fragment. For more on fragments, see pages 423–24.

ACTIVITY 1
EASY

Combine each pair of simple sentences in two ways:

- as a compound sentence, using a coordinating conjunction, and
- as a complex sentence, using a subordinating conjunction.

For a list of conjunctions, see the chart on the facing page.

EXAMPLE: Leah longed for a weekend of shopping and relaxing with her friends. She was behind on her homework.

Compound sentence: Leah longed for a weekend of shopping and relaxing with her friends, but she was behind on her homework.

Complex sentence: Although Leah longed for a weekend of shopping and relaxing with her friends, she was behind on her homework.

1. She could take the weekend off. She would fall even further behind.

Compound sentence: _____

Complex sentence: _____

KEY TO CHALLENGE METER	
WARMUP	
EASY	
MODERATE	
ADVANCED	
MASTERY	

Identify the difficulty level of each activity using the key above.

CONTINUED >

2. Leah wants to succeed in college. She decided to keep working.

   Compound sentence: _____

   _____

   Complex sentence: _____

   _____

3. Her friends spent Saturday at the mall. Leah stayed home and studied.

   Compound sentence: _____

   _____

   Complex sentence: _____

   _____

4. Leah wrote essays for her English and psychology classes. She had time for laundry and housecleaning.

   Compound sentence: _____

   _____

   Complex sentence: _____

   _____

5. Monday morning arrived. Leah was prepared and in a great mood.

   Compound sentence: _____

   _____

   Complex sentence: _____

   _____

ACTIVITY 2
EASY

First, complete each compound sentence. Then, rewrite each compound sentences as a complex sentence, using a subordinating conjunction at the beginning. For a list of subordinating conjunctions, see page 410.

EXAMPLE:

Compound sentence: This is last year's camera model, so it  is on sale.

Complex sentence: Because this is last year's camera model, it is on sale.

1. **Compound sentence:** Madison decided to buy a new cell phone, but she

   _____

   Complex sentence: _____

   _____

2. **Compound sentence:** Workers accidentally cut a power line, so we

   _____

   Complex sentence: _____

   _____

For more practice with complex sentences, go to **bedfordstmartins.com /touchstones**.

3. **Compound sentence:** My best friend had two tickets to the concert,

   but he _____

   Complex sentence: _____

   _____

4. **Compound sentence:** Miguel entered his sunset photograph in the

   photo contest, and he _____

   Complex sentence: _____

   _____

5. **Compound sentence:** We forgot to go to the post office on Monday,

   so Jared's _____

   Complex sentence: _____

   _____

UNDERSTANDING RELATIONSHIPS SHOWN BY SUBORDINATING CONJUNCTIONS

Different subordinating conjunctions signal different meanings and relationships in complex sentences. The following sections describe some of the most important relationships.

Expected and Unexpected Results

In the examples below, we will start with the simple sentence, *We canceled our hike.*

KEY TO BUILDING BLOCKS

FOUNDATION WORDS

NOUNS

VERBS

DESCRIPTIVE WORDS

ADJECTIVES

ADVERBS

CONNECTING WORDS

PREPOSITIONS

CONJUNCTIONS

To show an <u>expected result (a reason)</u>

Since it was raining, we canceled our hike.

When we use *since* or *because* to form a complex sentence, we want to show an **expected result**. For example, when it rains, you usually do not take hikes.

Note that in sentences like this one, *since* and *because* mean the same thing. It does not matter which one you use.

Because it was raining, we canceled our hike.

To show an <u>unexpected result (a contrast)</u>

Although it was raining, we went on our hike.

When we use *although* or *even though* to form a complex sentence, we want to show an **unexpected** result (a contrast). For example, when it rains, you usually do not take hikes.

Note that *although* and *even though* mean the same thing. It does not matter which one you use.

Even though **it was raining, we went on our hike.**

ACTIVITY 3

MODERATE

Examine each of the following pairs of complex sentences and decide whether each sentence shows an <u>expected</u> result (a reason) or an <u>unexpected</u> result (a contrast). Then, use **since/because** or **although/even though** to complete the sentence.

EXAMPLE:

    a. _____*Since*_____ green tea contains healthful antioxidants, Tracy drinks it daily.

    b. _____*Although*_____ green tea contains healthful antioxidants, Tracy dislikes it.

1. a. _____*S*_____ local residents were ordered to evacuate, the neighborhood was empty.

    b. _____*A*_____ local residents were ordered to evacuate, many refused to leave their homes.

2. a. _____*A*_____ Taylor Swift was nominated for a Grammy, she did not win the award.

    b. _____*S*_____ Taylor Swift was nominated for a Grammy, she attended the ceremony.

3. a. _____*B*_____ the airbags were defective, several thousand vehicles were recalled.

    b. _____*A*_____ the airbags were defective, the manufacturer did not issue a recall.

ACTIVITY 4

MODERATE

For each of the following items, complete the first sentence with an expected result. Complete the second sentence with an unexpected result (a contrast).

EXAMPLE:

    a. Because Trina was on a strict diet, *she did not order the pasta on the menu.*

    b. Although Trina was on a strict diet, *she ordered the pasta on the menu.*

1. a. Since Cameron had lost his receipt, _____

_____

    b. Although Cameron had lost his receipt, _____

_____

2. a. Because the tornado missed the college campus, _____

_____

b. Even though the tornado missed the college campus, _____

_____

3. a. Since the vehicle has more than 300,000 miles on it, _____

_____

b. Although the vehicle has more than 300,000 miles on it, _____

_____

4. a. Since the head football coach was warned by the referee, _____

_____

b. Even though the head football coach was warned by the referee,

_____

5. a. Because last month's sales figures were down, _____

_____

b. Although last month's sales figures were down, _____

_____

Conditions and Possibilities

We use the subordinating conjunctions *if* and *unless* to set up a condition or a possibility:

> If you do this, then . . .
>
> Unless you do this, then . . .

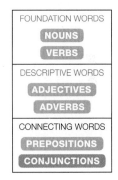

A **condition** can be a requirement or a hypothesis. It indicates a situation or task that must occur in order for a particular result or outcome to take place. While this may sound complicated, most of us use *if* and *unless* frequently in our conversations to state conditions. Take a look:

> If Raul works your shift, you can take the day off.
>
> Unless Raul works your shift, you cannot take the day off.

Most writers have no difficulty using the conjunctions *if* and *unless*. Just be sure that the outcome makes sense given the condition.

ACTIVITY 5

MODERATE

Examine each of the following pairs of complex sentences and decide which sentence should begin with **if** and which should begin with **unless**. Write your answers in the spaces provided.

CONTINUED >

EXAMPLE:

    a. _____*If*_____ Logan pays me back today, I can put gas in my car.

    b. ____*Unless*____ Logan pays me back today, I will not be able to put gas in my car.

1. a. _____ the credit card payment is made by the fifteenth of the month, interest will be charged.

    b. _____ the credit card payment is made by the fifteenth of the month, no interest will be charged.

2. a. _____ Stefan begins an exercise program, he may be at risk for a heart attack.

    b. _____ Stefan begins an exercise program, he will improve his cardiac health.

3. a. _____ there is still construction on the freeway, it's better to take the back roads to work.

    b. _____ there is still construction on the freeway, it's better to take the freeway to work.

4. a. _____ the economy improves soon, we can expect layoffs at all levels.

    b. _____ the economy improves soon, we will receive our usual yearly raise.

5. a. _____ it rains soon, the drought will destroy this year's corn crop.

    b. _____ it rains soon, this year's corn crop will be saved.

ACTIVITY 6

MODERATE

Complete each of the following sentences. In order to determine a logical outcome for each sentence, pay close attention to the subordinate conjunction that begins the sentence.

EXAMPLE:

    a. If I am promoted to manager, *I will have to take a leadership course.*

    b. Unless I am promoted to manager, *I will not have to take the leadership course.*

1. a. If the fog lifts within the next hour, *The plane will take off.*

    b. Unless the fog lifts within the next hour, *I'm going to be late for a meeting.*

2. a. Unless you will buy my dinner, _____

    b. If you will buy my dinner, _____

For more practice with subordinating conjunctions, go to **bedfordstmartins .com/touchstones**.

3. a. If the suspect confesses to the robbery, _____

_____

b. Unless the suspect confesses to the robbery, _____

_____

4. a. Unless you take a taxicab from the airport, _____

_____

b. If you take a taxicab from the airport, _____

_____

5. a. If the library book is returned by tomorrow, _____

_____

b. Unless the library book is returned by tomorrow, _____

_____

RECOGNIZING CORRECT PUNCTUATION IN COMPLEX SENTENCES

So far in this chapter, you have seen one way to form a complex sentence: by <u>beginning</u> the sentence with a subordinating conjunction. Here is an example:

> Because **we are expecting company, we must clean the house.**

However, you could also put a subordinating conjunction <u>in the middle</u> of a sentence:

> **We must clean the house** because **we are expecting company.**

Most students would write the second version of this sentence because it sounds more conversational or **informal**. The first version sounds more **formal**. However, both sentences emphasize the fact that the house must be cleaned. (For more on emphasis in sentences with subordinating conjunctions, see page 411.)

Now, notice the important difference in punctuation:

FORMAL Because **we are expecting company, we must clean the house.**

INFORMAL **We must clean the house** because **we are expecting company.**

When you <u>begin</u> a complex sentence with a subordinating conjunction, you must put a comma in the middle of the sentence. When the subordinating conjunction comes in the middle of the sentence, usually a comma will not come before it.

FOUNDATION WORDS
NOUNS
VERBS

DESCRIPTIVE WORDS
ADJECTIVES
ADVERBS

CONNECTING WORDS
PREPOSITIONS
CONJUNCTIONS

Note that a comma never follows a subordinating conjunction regardless of this conjunction's position in a sentence:

INCORRECT

Because, we are expecting company, we must clean the house.

INCORRECT

We must clean the house because, we are expecting company.

ACTIVITY 7

MODERATE

Examine each of the following sentences and determine whether the punctuation is correct. Write **C** next to the sentence if the punctuation is correct. Otherwise, rewrite the sentence, correcting the punctuation.

EXAMPLE: If, I were you, I would not play with that porcupine.

If I were you, I would not play with that porcupine.

1. We had to bring our plants inside the house, because the weather turned very cold.

_____

2. No refund is available for this airline ticket; unless you bought traveler's insurance.

_____

3. After he called in sick again, my cousin lost his job. *Correct*

_____

4. While Sam was eating, a fly flew into his soup.

_____

5. The Tuskegee Airmen faced discrimination although, they were excellent pilots.

_____

BUILDING SENTENCE VARIETY

In Chapter 17, you learned about two ways to form **compound sentences**: (a) with a coordinating conjunction and a comma, or (b) with a semicolon (alone or with a transitional expression followed by a comma). Take a look:

> COMMA AND COORDINATING CONJUNCTION

(a) Professor Jones was in a hurry, but she made time to talk to me.

> SEMICOLON WITH TRANSITIONAL EXPRESSION AND COMMA

(b) Professor Jones was in a hurry; however, she made time to talk to me.

In this chapter, you have learned to form **complex sentences** in two ways: (c) more formally, by placing a subordinating conjunction at the beginning of a sentence, and (d) more informally, by placing a conjunction in the middle of a sentence.

> SUBORDINATING CONJUNCTION AT BEGINNING

(c) Although Professor Jones was in a hurry, she made time to talk to me.

> SUBORDINATING CONJUNCTION IN MIDDLE

(d) Professor Jones made time to talk to me although she was in a hurry.

In a basic sense, all four of these sentences express the same ideas. So which one is best for your writing? While there is no simple answer to this question, you should consider two things:

1. **Style:** If you like a more <u>casual</u> style of writing, you will probably prefer sentences **a** and **d**. Both of these sentences reflect the way we speak; they are more conversational in tone. If you like a more <u>formal</u> style of writing, you might prefer sentences **b** and **c**.

2. **Meaning:** Very thoughtful writers might notice a small difference in meaning among these sentences. Sentences **c** and **d** give a special emphasis to the fact that Professor Jones made the time. Perhaps the writer wants to express surprise about this fact.

However, the best recommendation is to <u>use a variety</u> of these sentence types in your writing. Varied sentence patterns will keep your readers interested in the same way that music with varied rhythms keeps listeners interested. The more you practice and use these four sentence types, the more dynamic your writing will become.

Let's review conjunctions and transitional expressions that can be used to create sentence variety.

Words Used for Sentence Variety

	COMBINATION	CONTRAST	RESULT	ALTERNATIVES/ POSSIBILITIES
Coordinating conjunctions	and (nor)	but (yet)	so (for)	or
Subordinating conjunctions	after as before when while	although even though	because since	if (even if) unless (until)
Transitional expressions (see Chapter 17)	furthermore in addition moreover	however nevertheless	as a result consequently therefore	instead on the other hand otherwise

ACTIVITY 8: Teamwork

ADVANCED

Combine each pair of sentences in the four ways shown in the example. Remember: Correct punctuation is necessary for the success of your sentences. To help you get started, the type of relationship for each pair of sentences has been provided in parentheses.

EXAMPLE: A military jet roared over our house. Our windows rattled. (combination)

    a. **Compound — with coordinating conjunction and comma:**
      A military jet roared over our house, and our windows rattled.

    b. **Compound — with semicolon and transitional expression:**
      A military jet roared over our house; moreover, our windows rattled.

    c. **Complex — with subordinating conjunction at beginning of sentence:** When a military jet roared over our house, our windows rattled.

    d. **Complex — with subordinating conjunction in the middle of sentence:** Our windows rattled when a military jet roared over our house.

1. Many people have severe peanut allergies. Most airlines no longer serve peanuts to passengers. (result)

    a. **Compound:** _____

    b. **Compound:** _____

    c. **Complex:** _____

    d. **Complex:** _____

2. Spain's Running of the Bulls is a dangerous event. Many people participate in it. (contrast)

    a. Compound: _____

    _____

    b. Compound: _____

    _____

    c. Complex: _____

    _____

    d. Complex: _____

    _____

3. Kevin graduated from law school with honors. He accepted a position with a prestigious firm in New York City. (combination)

    a. Compound: _____

    _____

    b. Compound: _____

    _____

    c. Complex: _____

    _____

    d. Complex: _____

    _____

4. Sharks were sighted near the beach. It was temporarily closed. (result)

    a. Compound: _____

    _____

    b. Compound: _____

    _____

    c. Complex: _____

    _____

    d. Complex: _____

    _____

5. Tourists in national parks should not feed the wildlife. They may be injured by animals. (alternatives/possibilities)

    a. Compound: _____

    _____

    b. Compound: _____

    _____

    c. Complex: _____

    _____

    d. Complex: _____

    _____

ACTIVITY 9: Mastery Test or Teamwork

In the following paragraph, form up to seven complex sentences, using the **subordinating conjunctions** from the chart in the margin. First, identify each pair of sentences that can be joined, and then decide which conjunction will join the sentences most effectively. Remember that the conjunction may be placed at the beginning of the complex sentence or in the middle between the two simple sentences. The first one has been done for you.

On March 20, 1980, a magnitude 4.2 earthquake shook Washington's Mt. St. Helens. Geologists became concerned. ~~Numerous~~ *when numerous* smaller earthquakes were recorded in the following week. Then, on March 27, Mt. St. Helens erupted. This event was minor compared to the impending disaster. Earthquakes continued to shake the mountain. Geologists became even more concerned. The nature of the movements began to change to those associated with gas or magma. A dangerous bulge on the side of Mt. St. Helens appeared. Authorities expected a major eruption. Local residents were ordered to evacuate the area. Not everyone obeyed the order. Harry R. Truman was 83 years old and had lived at Spirit Lake near Mt. St. Helens for 54 years. He steadfastly refused to leave his home. He did not believe the geologists' predictions. On May 18, at 8:32 A.M., Mt. St. Helens experienced a catastrophic eruption. The blast destroyed nearly everything in a 230-square-mile fan-shaped area. The north side of the mountain collapsed. An enormous debris avalanche was created. This avalanche raced down the mountain at speeds of over 150 miles per hour. Harry R. Truman's body was never found. Volcanologist David A. Johnston was manning an observation station six miles from Mt. St. Helens that morning. He thought he was in a safe location. However, he was also killed. In all, 57 people lost their lives in North America's most deadly and costly volcanic eruption.

For more practice with compound and complex sentences, go to **bedfordstmartins.com /touchstones**.

FIX IT: Solving Problems in Complex Sentences

In Chapter 16, you learned about an error that writers occasionally make when writing simple sentences: fragments. A fragment is a word group that is missing a subject or verb, or that doesn't express a complete thought. Fragments can also occur in complex sentences. The following sections explain common causes of fragments in complex sentences and how you can fix these errors.

FIXING FRAGMENTS CAUSED BY A MISPLACED PERIOD

By now, you know that the following simple sentence is complete and correct:

FOUNDATION WORDS
NOUNS
VERBS

DESCRIPTIVE WORDS
ADJECTIVES
ADVERBS

CONNECTING WORDS
PREPOSITIONS
CONJUNCTIONS

SUBJECT **VERB**
Shane reads **books.**

However, take a look at the following example:

Shane reads **books** because.

Few people would write this fragment. It is obvious that this group of words is not a complete thought. Most writers would automatically complete the thought by adding more information:

Shane reads **books** because they stimulate **his mind.**

However, many writers get confused when they <u>begin</u> a sentence with a subordinating conjunction. They might create the following fragment:

Because they stimulate **his mind.**

When we <u>begin</u> a simple sentence with a subordinating conjunction, we must add a comma and complete the thought:

Because they stimulate **his mind,** Shane reads **books.**

Writers sometimes create fragments accidentally when they add <u>an unnecessary period</u>. Take a look:

SIMPLE SENTENCE   **FRAGMENT**
Shane reads **books.** Because they stimulate **his mind.**
                ↑

        FRAGMENT   **SIMPLE SENTENCE**
Because they stimulate **his mind.** Shane reads **books.**
                    ↑

Fortunately, this type of fragment is very simple to correct. Just remove the period or replace it with a comma:

MORE INFORMAL: Remove the period.

Shane reads books because they stimulate his mind.
↑

MORE FORMAL: Replace the period with a comma.

Because they stimulate his mind, Shane reads books.
↑

ACTIVITY 10
EASY

In each of the following items, mark an **F** above or beside the fragment. Then, correct the fragment by connecting it to a simple sentence. Remember to (1) remove the period between the fragment and the simple sentence to which you want to connect the fragment or (2) replace this period with a comma. Do not change the other simple sentence.

EXAMPLE:

F
After Sara read an online journal about California's John Muir Trail. She dreamed of hiking this 211-mile trail herself. She was very excited.

After Sara read an online journal about California's John Muir Trail,

she dreamed of hiking this 211-mile trail herself. She was very

excited.

1. Since the trail is rugged and mountainous. Sara had to get in shape. On weekends, she trained in the hills near her home in Tennessee.

2. Sara needed to dehydrate food. Because she would have to hike several days at a time between post offices. She had to carry several days' worth of food with her at a time.

3. When the day finally came for her adventure. Sara began her hike from Yosemite National Park. The mountains and the valley were spectacularly beautiful.

4. The trails were rocky and steep at times. Even though her muscles ached. She loved the incredible views at nearly every turn in the trail.

_____

_____

5. Sara hiked onward for nearly three weeks. When she reached the end of the trail. She felt a mixture of overwhelming pride and serenity.

_____

_____

ACTIVITY 11: Teamwork

MODERATE

In each of the following items, mark an **F** above or beside the fragment. Then, correct the fragment by connecting it to a simple sentence. Remember to (1) remove the period between the fragment and the simple sentence to which you want to connect the fragment or (2) replace this period with a comma. Do not change the other simple sentence(s).

EXAMPLE:

My niece's wedding was held in Breckenridge, Colorado. Several family members decided to rent a luxurious home in the mountains for the event. Even though the home cost us a little more than a hotel. ꜰ We loved the comfortable home with the view of the Rocky Mountains.

My niece's wedding was held in Breckenridge, Colorado. Several family members decided to rent a luxurious home in the mountains for the event. Even though the home cost us a little more than a hotel, we loved the comfortable home with the view of the Rocky Mountains.

1. Restaurants can be dangerous places for the calorie-conscious consumer. If you order fettuccini Alfredo. You will be consuming about 1,200 calories. A double cheeseburger, medium fries, and a small milkshake contain about 1,600 calories.

_____

_____

_____

2. Although special sales at supermarkets may seem to offer great deals. Shoppers should find out the regular price for any sale item. Some super-markets double the price of certain products. Then they offer the product for an enticing 50 percent off sale.

CONTINUED >

3. Two years ago, Juanita took a class in jewelry making at a local craft store. Because she wanted to wear unique jewelry and also save money. Now she designs and sells her own jewelry. She plans to open a boutique soon.

4. Tailgating is a dangerous driving habit. Since the tailgaters do not allow sufficient space between their vehicle and the one ahead. The chances of a rear-end accident are increased. Drivers should always allow enough space between vehicles for safe stopping in emergency situations.

5. After David added support to the foundation of his grandparents' old farmhouse. He renovated the inside of the house. His hard work paid off. Now his wife and children have a beautiful and solid home.

FIXING FRAGMENTS CAUSED BY A MISPLACED SEMICOLON

Complex sentences can be more informal or more formal:

MORE INFORMAL	We will paint the house unless it rains.
MORE FORMAL	Unless it rains, we will paint the house.

As noted earlier, less experienced writers sometimes add unnecessary periods to both types of sentences.

FOUNDATION WORDS
NOUNS
VERBS

DESCRIPTIVE WORDS
ADJECTIVES
ADVERBS

CONNECTING WORDS
PREPOSITIONS
CONJUNCTIONS

	[FRAGMENT]
INCORRECT	We will paint the house. Unless it rains.

	[FRAGMENT]
INCORRECT	Unless it rains. We will paint the house.

Another common error when writing such sentences is to add a semicolon:

	[FRAGMENT]
INCORRECT	We will paint the house; unless it rains.

	[FRAGMENT]
INCORRECT	Unless it rains; we will paint the house.

Just like a misplaced period, a misplaced semicolon in a complex sentence causes a fragment. The rule is very simple: <u>Never use a semicolon in a complex sentence.</u> You can correct the previous fragments in the following ways:

MORE INFORMAL: Remove the semicolon.

We will paint the house unless it rains.

MORE FORMAL: Replace the semicolon with a comma.

Unless it rains, we will paint the house.

ACTIVITY 12

MODERATE

In each of the following items, mark an **F** above or beside the fragment. Then, correct the fragment by connecting it to a simple sentence. Remember to (1) remove the semicolon between the fragment and the simple sentence to which you want to connect the fragment or (2) replace this semicolon with a comma. Do not change the other simple sentence.

EXAMPLE:

                                F
After she works out at the gym; Lynda has a smoothie at the fruit bar. She loves this delicious and healthful treat.

After she works out at the gym, Lynda has a smoothie at the fruit bar.

She loves this delicious and healthful treat.

1. It's not unusual for people to tackle physically challenging sports; after they reach their seventies and eighties. Age is more a matter of physical and mental fitness than years.

CONTINUED >

For more practice with fixing fragments, go to **bedfordstmartins .com/touchstones**.

2. Because a defensive football player grabbed the opponent's face mask during a tackle; the referee blew his whistle. The home team was penalized 15 yards.

_____

_____

_____

3. If you are stung by a jellyfish in the ocean; you can treat it with meat tenderizer. This will neutralize the venom.

_____

_____

4. Many Native American ceremonies are considered sacred. Non-Native Americans are usually not allowed to attend these ceremonies; unless they are invited by members of the tribe.

_____

_____

_____

5. Although parents generally encourage their children to have sportsmanlike behavior; parents themselves sometimes demonstrate poor sportsmanship. These parents end up becoming very poor role models for their children.

_____

_____

_____

_____

ACTIVITY 13: Mastery Test or Teamwork

MASTERY

In each of the following paragraphs, mark an **F** above any fragments that you find. Then, correct each fragment by connecting it to another sentence. Remember to remove incorrect periods or semicolons and replace them with commas when necessary.

The following paragraph has six fragments, including the one that has been marked for you.

a. (1) In April 2003, while hiking alone in Utah's Canyonlands

National Park Aron Lee Ralston had a serious accident. (2) He became

trapped. (3) When a falling boulder landed on his right forearm and pinned him against the canyon wall. (4) Because Ralston had not told anyone about his hiking plans or destination. (5) Nobody was looking for him. (6) For five days, Ralston tried to free himself. (7) Although his situation seemed hopeless. (8) Ralston's will to live was strong. (9) If he were to survive; he would have to amputate his right arm. (10) After he used his knife to cut off his arm. (11) He hiked out for help. (12) His courageous and inspirational feat is now the subject of a film called *127 Hours*.

The following paragraph has eight fragments, including the one that has been marked for you.

b. (1) Although Nashville's Grand Ole Opry began its run as a radio show in 1925, it quickly became a popular country music stage show. (2) After the show moved from place to place a number of times. (3) It found a home at the Ryman Auditorium in 1943. (4) The show remained at the Ryman Auditorium; until it moved to a much larger theater in 1974. (5) Its new home is the Grand Ole Opry House east of downtown Nashville. (6) Because the move from the Ryman to the Opry House broke tradition. (7) A six-foot circular piece of the Ryman stage was incorporated into the new stage at the Opry House. (8) When contemporary singers like Carrie Underwood and Brad Paisley perform on stage; they will be standing on the same stage as legends Patsy Cline, Hank Williams, and Roy Acuff. (9) In May 2010, the Grand Ole Opry House was flooded. (10) After the Cumberland River rose over its banks. (11) Although the Opry House was closed during the flood; the show was moved to another location and went on as scheduled. (12) After cleanup and restoration were completed; the Grand Ole Opry returned to its home and continues to entertain music fans from all over the world.

BRINGING IT ALL TOGETHER:
The Complex Sentence

In this chapter, you have learned what subordinating conjunctions do, how they are used, and how they can cause problems in academic writing. Confirm your knowledge by filling in the blank spaces in the following sentences. If you need help, review the pages listed after each sentence.

✔ To form complex sentences, we use a powerful glue called a _____ conjunction. (page 409)

✔ Like coordinating conjunctions, subordinating conjunctions can show four kinds of relationships between ideas. These are _____, _____, _____, and _____. (page 410)

✔ The conjunctions *since* and *because* show an _____ result. The conjunctions *although* and *even though* show an _____ result. (pages 413–14)

✔ In a complex sentence, the subordinating conjunction will be placed either at _____ of the sentence or in _____ of the sentence. (page 417)

✔ Punctuation rule: If a complex sentence <u>begins</u> with a subordinating conjunction, a _____ is required in the middle of the sentence. (page 417)

✔ Punctuation rule: If a complex sentence has the subordinating conjunction <u>in the middle</u> of the sentence, no _____ is usually required. (page 417)

✔ Punctuation rule: A misplaced _____ or a misplaced _____ can cause a subordinating clause fragment. Never use a _____ in a complex sentence. (pages 423–27)

CHAPTER 19

More Complex Sentences

Before you read this chapter, it's a good idea to test your understanding of complex sentences with descriptive clauses. You may know more than you think.

WHAT DO YOU KNOW?

Circle "Yes" if each word group below is a complete, correct sentence. Circle "No" if it is incomplete. Then, explain your choice.

1. **The book that you ordered has arrived.**

   Yes   No

   Explanation: _____

   _____

2. **The pitcher who led the team to a national championship.**

   Yes   No

   Explanation: _____

   _____

3. **The camera that I want, is now on sale.**

   Yes   No

   Explanation: _____

   _____

4. **My next-door neighbor, who owns a beautiful fishing boat.**

   Yes   No

   Explanation: _____

   _____

5. **Our annual family vacation which takes place during the Fourth of July holiday has been postponed.**

   Yes   No

   Explanation: _____

   _____

Descriptive clauses add more information to sentences. Also, they are another way to "glue" sentences together. You'll learn how to use them in this chapter.

NOUN + DESCRIPTIVE CLAUSE + VERB . = The students who study succeed.

NOUN , DESCRIPTIVE CLAUSE , VERB .

= The evening students, who are at school until 10 P.M., get home late.

BUILD IT: Complex Sentences with Descriptive Clauses

In the previous two chapters, you learned that **coordinating conjunctions** (*and, but, or, so,* and so on) and **subordinating conjunctions** (*although, because, since, unless,* and so on) work like glue to join simple sentences. Here are some examples with the word *that*:

SENTENCE 1 SENTENCE 2
The mirror fell. It cracked.

Joined with a Coordinating Conjunction
The mirror fell, and it cracked.

Joined with a Subordinating Conjunction
When the mirror fell, it cracked.

In this chapter, you will study other words that work like glue to join simple sentences. Here's an example with the glue word *that*:

SENTENCE 1 SENTENCE 2
The mirror fell. It cracked.

Joined with a Pronoun
The mirror that fell cracked.

You can think of this as putting one sentence within another. The main idea (expressed in the **main clause**) is that the mirror cracked. The **descriptive clause** tells us *which* mirror cracked.

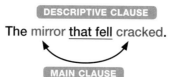

DESCRIPTIVE CLAUSE
The mirror that fell cracked.
MAIN CLAUSE

Terminology Tip
Because the clause *that fell* describes the noun *mirror*, it is functioning as an adjective. For more on adjectives, see Chapter 16, page 352.

In addition to *that*, the glue words used to form complex sentences with descriptive clauses are *which, who, when,* and *where.*

Note that the descriptive clause always comes right after the word it describes (in this case, *mirror*). Like a jigsaw puzzle, a complex sentence formed with a descriptive clause must have all of its pieces connected in the right order to make sense.

Terminology Tip
The descriptive clauses discussed in this chapter are **dependent clauses**, or **subordinate clauses**: They cannot stand alone as a sentence. Rather, they are *subordinate* to the main clause, which *can* stand alone as a sentence.

ACTIVITY 1
EASY

Join the following sentence pairs by making one a descriptive clause beginning with **that** and the other a main clause. Follow these steps:

- First, underline the repeated item in each simple sentence. Use this to begin your complex sentence.
- Form a descriptive clause using **that**, and put this clause <u>in the middle</u> of your new sentence.
- Underline the descriptive clause in your new sentence and double-underline the main clause.

EXAMPLE: <u>The dog</u> kept me awake. <u>The dog</u> barked all night.

<u>The dog</u> <u>that barked all night</u> <u>kept me awake</u>.

1. The book is on sale at the bookstore. The book was banned.

2. The painting is a fake. The painting sold for $50,000.

3. The meteorite frightened local residents. The meteorite landed in the lake.

4. The photograph won first place. The photograph captured a tornado.

5. A family stays together. A family plays together.

KEY TO CHALLENGE METER	
WARMUP	
EASY	
MODERATE	
ADVANCED	
MASTERY	

Identify the difficulty level of each activity using the key above.

The word *which* is another glue word used to create descriptive clauses. When you use *which*, the descriptive clause must be set off by commas. Take a look:

SENTENCE 1   SENTENCE 2

The museum was built in 1952. The museum is now closed.

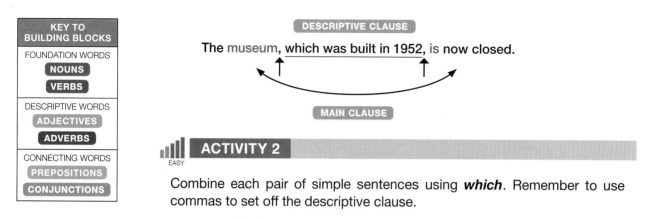

DESCRIPTIVE CLAUSE

The museum, which was built in 1952, is now closed.

MAIN CLAUSE

ACTIVITY 2

EASY

Combine each pair of simple sentences using **which**. Remember to use commas to set off the descriptive clause.

EXAMPLE: My first car is now an antique. My first car was a 1963 Ford.

My first car, which was a 1963 Ford, is now an antique.

1. This motor home gets excellent gas mileage. This motor home has a diesel engine.

   _____

   _____

2. The movie *Dirty Dancing* has become a cult classic. The movie starred Patrick Swayze.

   _____

   _____

3. Mt. Hood offers alpine skiing all year long. Mt. Hood is located in Oregon.

   _____

   _____

4. The Gulf Coast is a frequent target of hurricanes. The Gulf Coast was struck by Hurricane Katrina in 2005.

   _____

   _____

5. The longest-running television game show is *The Price Is Right*. The longest-running game show aired its first show in 1956.

   _____

   _____

Terminology Tip
If the information in a descriptive clause is essential for the main meaning of the sentence, the clause is called **restrictive**. If the information is optional, the clause is called **nonrestrictive**.

THAT AND *WHICH* CLAUSES

Many students have difficulty deciding when to use *that* or *which* to form a descriptive clause. However, the rule is actually quite simple:

1. Use *that* for information that is essential (absolutely necessary) for the main meaning of your sentence.

2. Use *which* for information that is optional (not absolutely necessary) for the main meaning of your sentence.

Now, look at the following two sentences, each with a descriptive clause (underlined):

> The book <u>that I am reading</u> is a mystery.

> The book, <u>which is fascinating,</u> is a mystery.

The first sentence, by using *that*, shows that the information in the descriptive clause is essential to the main meaning in the sentence: Not just *any* book is a mystery, but *specifically* the book that I am reading.

The second sentence, by using *which*, shows that the information in the descriptive clause is optional. The fact that the book is fascinating is bonus information. It's helpful but not absolutely necessary for the main meaning of the sentence. The commas that set off this clause also suggest that the information is optional. (Always use commas to set off a clause that begins with *which*.)

ACTIVITY 3
MODERATE

Combine each pair of simple sentences to make a complex sentence.

- First, underline the repeated item in each simple sentence. Use this noun to begin your complex sentence.
- Form a descriptive clause using ***that*** or ***which***, and put this descriptive clause <u>in the middle</u> of the sentence.
- If you use ***which***, set off the descriptive clause with commas.
- Circle the descriptive clause in your complex sentence.

EXAMPLE: <u>The forest fire</u> is now under control. <u>The forest fire</u> destroyed more than 500 acres of pine trees.

The forest fire⟨that destroyed more than 500 acres of pine trees⟩ is now under control.

1. The truck caused a two-hour traffic jam. The truck spilled its load of watermelons.

_____

_____

2. The Appalachian Trail is popular with long-distance hikers. The Appalachian Trail is more than 2,000 miles long.

_____

_____

3. The homes were damaged in the flood. The homes lay in the valley.

_____

4. The Apollo 13 mission was a failed attempt to land on the moon. The Apollo 13 mission is the subject of a popular 1995 movie.

_____

CONTINUED >

For more practice with *that* and *which*, go to **bedfordstmartins.com /touchstones**.

5. The automobiles were recalled by the manufacturer. The automobiles had defective exhaust systems.

_____

_____

WHO CLAUSES

Terminology Tip
The glue words *that*, *which*, and *who* are known as **relative pronouns**, and descriptive clauses formed with them are known as **relative clauses**.

The word *who* is used to form descriptive clauses about people. Take a look:

SENTENCE 1   SENTENCE 2

The firefighter saved the child. The firefighter was called a hero.

DESCRIPTIVE CLAUSE

The firefighter who saved the child was called a hero.

ACTIVITY 4
EASY

Combine each of the following pairs of simple sentences using **who**. No commas are needed.

EXAMPLE: The man witnessed the accident. The man was waiting for a bus.

The man who was waiting for a bus witnessed the accident.

1. The customers received a 50 percent discount. The customers had special gold coupons.

_____

_____

2. The police officer solved the crime. The police officer investigated the vandalism.

_____

3. The marathon runner crossed the finish line last. The marathon runner got lost.

_____

4. People should not throw stones. People live in glass houses.

_____

5. The driver received a ticket. The driver did not pull over for the ambulance.

_____

The glue word *who* can introduce essential or optional information in a sentence. Take a look:

DESCRIPTIVE CLAUSE

The singer who won the contest is only 12 years old.

DESCRIPTIVE CLAUSE

The singer, who is only 12 years old, won the contest.

Even though both of these descriptive clauses begin with *who*, the second one is set off by commas. This shows that the information in the clause is optional; it is not absolutely necessary for the main meaning of the sentence.

However, in the first sentence, the information in the clause is essential for the main meaning: Not just *any* singer is only 12 years old but *specifically* the singer who won the contest. Therefore, the clause is not set off by commas.

ACTIVITY 5

MODERATE

Combine each pair of simple sentences to make a complex sentence.

- First, underline the repeated item in each simple sentence. Use this noun to begin your complex sentence.
- Form a descriptive clause using **who**, and put this clause in the middle of the sentence.
- If the information in the descriptive clause is essential, do not use commas. If the information in the descriptive clause is optional, set off the descriptive clause with commas.
- Circle the descriptive clause in your complex sentence.

EXAMPLE: Jon's mother just entered college. Jon's mother is 89 years old.

Jon's mother, who is 89 years old, just entered college.

1. The passerby was never identified. The passerby pulled the struggling swimmer from the lake.

2. Professor Martinez allows pets in the classroom. Professor Martinez loves animals.

3. Protestors will be arrested. Protestors trespass on private property.

4. Elsie won the lottery. Elsie has bought only one lottery ticket in her life.

5. Anyone is eligible to win the Caribbean cruise. Anyone buys a raffle ticket.

Power Tip
A semicolon should not appear in a complex sentence. Take a look:

Incorrect: *We elected Justine Campbell; who has a good record of public service.*

Correct: *We elected Justine Campbell, who has a good record of public service.*

For more on semicolon usage, see Chapter 17, pages 377–79.

FOUNDATION WORDS
NOUNS
VERBS

DESCRIPTIVE WORDS
ADJECTIVES
ADVERBS

CONNECTING WORDS
PREPOSITIONS
CONJUNCTIONS

PLACING DESCRIPTIVE CLAUSES IN SENTENCES

Descriptive clauses can appear in the middle or at the end of a sentence. The important thing is that they appear <u>directly after</u> the word they describe. Otherwise, a <u>misplaced modifier</u> may result.

Take a look at the following examples. The descriptive clause appears first in the middle and then at the end of the sentence. The descriptive clause is underlined. An arrow indicates the word being described.

DESCRIPTIVE CLAUSE IN THE MIDDLE	The report <u>that was submitted</u> is inaccurate.
DESCRIPTIVE CLAUSE AT THE END	We must correct the report <u>that was submitted</u>.
DESCRIPTIVE CLAUSE IN THE MIDDLE	Breakfast, <u>which was free</u>, included weak coffee.
DESCRIPTIVE CLAUSE AT THE END	Weak coffee came with breakfast, <u>which was free</u>.
DESCRIPTIVE CLAUSE IN THE MIDDLE	The girl <u>who won the spelling bee</u> is my cousin.
DESCRIPTIVE CLAUSE AT THE END	My cousin is the girl <u>who won the spelling bee</u>.

Power Tip

Notice that when a *nonrestrictive* clause is in the middle of a sentence, commas are used both <u>before</u> and <u>after</u> it. However, when a *nonrestrictive* clause is at the end of a sentence, we need <u>only one</u> comma: the one <u>before</u> the clause.

📶 **ACTIVITY 6**
MODERATE

Combine each pair of simple sentences to make a complex sentence.

- Turn the second sentence into a descriptive clause beginning with **that**, **which**, or **who**, and put it <u>at the end</u> of your complex sentence.
- If the information in the descriptive clause is essential, do not use a comma. If the information in the descriptive clause is optional, set off the descriptive clause with a comma.
- Circle the descriptive clause.

Power Tip

When *who* is followed by a noun or another pronoun, it usually becomes *whom*. Take a look: *Hillary Clinton, whom my mother admires, was First Lady from 1993 to 2001.* For more practice with *who* and *whom*, go to **bedfordstmartins.com /touchstones**.

EXAMPLE: My new neighbor is Blake. Blake is a former NBA player.

My new neighbor is Blake, who is a former NBA player.

1. We bought the car. The car has 200,000 miles on the engine.

2. The firm needs to hire more salespeople. The salespeople speak Spanish.

3. My wife made reservations at the new restaurant. The new restaurant opens next month.

4. We must turn the project over to someone. Someone has experience in international sales.

_____

_____

5. The professor ordered a textbook. The textbook was too advanced for the class.

_____

WHEN AND *WHERE* CLAUSES

The word *when* is used to form descriptive clauses about time (hours, days, and so on). The word *where* is used to form descriptive clauses about places. In the following examples, the noun that appears in both simple sentences has been underlined. When the sentences are combined, this noun is followed immediately by the descriptive clause, which begins with *when* or *where*.

> I will never forget that day. My son was born on that day.
>
> DESCRIPTIVE CLAUSE
>
> I will never forget that day when my son was born.

> The farmland belonged to Chad's family. The new mall was built on the farmland.
>
> DESCRIPTIVE CLAUSE
>
> The farmland where the new mall was built belonged to Chad's family.

ACTIVITY 7
MODERATE

Combine each pair of sentences using **when** or **where**. No commas are needed. (*Hint:* First, underline the noun that appears in both simple sentences. Then, begin your complex sentence with this noun followed by **when** or **where**.)

EXAMPLE: The restaurant is one block from my office. The fire occurred at the restaurant.

> *The restaurant where the fire occurred is one block from my office.*

1. The day was Valentine's Day. Jeff proposed on that day.

_____

2. The company provides day care for employees' children. Celeste works for the company.

_____

CONTINUED >

3. The stream is becoming too crowded with gold seekers. Allen pans for gold in the stream.

_____

_____

4. The mountain cabin had a view of the Rockies. Pierre and Kate stayed in the mountain cabin.

_____

_____

5. The specific time was not recorded. The volcano erupted at the specific time.

_____

_____

_____

Descriptive clauses formed with *where* and *when* can also contain essential or optional information. Again, punctuation helps us understand which ideas are necessary to the main meaning of the sentence and which ideas are optional. Take a look:

> DESCRIPTIVE CLAUSE

Police began **the search at the site** where the painting disappeared.

> DESCRIPTIVE CLAUSE

I will **always** remember **the day** when I started college.

In these sentences, there are **no commas**, so we know that the information contained in the descriptive clauses is essential to understand the main meaning of the sentence. In the first sentence, the police did not begin the search at just *any* site; they began the search *specifically* at the site where the painting disappeared. In the second sentence, it's not just *any* day that the writer will remember but *specifically* the day when the writer started college.

Now, look at these sentences:

> DESCRIPTIVE CLAUSE

This **valley,** where Frank has lived all his life, **is** now polluted.

> DESCRIPTIVE CLAUSE

On weekday mornings, when my family sleeps, I do yoga.

In these sentences, the writer has set off the descriptive clauses **with commas**, telling us that the information in these clauses is optional. In the first sentence, the fact that Frank has lived in the valley all his life is interesting but not essential to the writer's main point: that the valley is now polluted. In the second sentence, the fact that the writer's family is sleeping is interesting but not essential to the writer's main point: that the writer does yoga on weekday mornings.

📶 **ACTIVITY 8**

MODERATE

Combine each pair of simple sentences to make a complex sentence.

- Turn the second sentence into a descriptive clause beginning with **where** or **when**, and put it in the middle or at the end of your complex sentence.
- If the information in the descriptive clause is essential, do not use commas. If the information in the descriptive clause is optional, set off the descriptive clause with commas.
- Circle the descriptive clause.

EXAMPLE: The coffee shop has a view of the lake. I do my homework at the coffee shop.

The coffee shop (where I do my homework) has a view of the lake.

1. The battleground of Gettysburg is right near my uncle's house. Many soldiers were killed at Gettysburg.

   _____

   _____

2. The day will live on forever for me. I met my wife on that day.

   _____

3. Jared wants to retire in Georgia. He can fish every day in Georgia.

   _____

4. It is important to choose a hotel. Internet access is available.

   _____

5. Please make your dental appointment at a time. There is no conflict with your college classes at the time.

   _____

   _____

BUILD IT: Longer Sentences with Descriptive Clauses

We started this chapter by looking at complex sentences with only a few words. Let's go back to an earlier example:

TWO SENTENCES	The mirror fell. It cracked.
JOINED WITH A DESCRIPTIVE CLAUSE	The mirror that fell cracked.

We can make complex sentences more informative by adding descriptive words (adjectives and adverbs) and prepositional phrases to the different parts of the sentence.

| FOUNDATION WORDS |
| NOUNS |
| VERBS |
| DESCRIPTIVE WORDS |
| ADJECTIVES |
| ADVERBS |
| CONNECTING WORDS |
| PREPOSITIONS |
| CONJUNCTIONS |

The mirror   that fell   cracked.

WHICH MIRROR?   **HOW DID IT FALL?**   **HOW WAS IT CRACKED?**

The antique mirror that fell during an earthquake cracked extensively.

Now, let's put the pieces of the puzzle together:

The antique mirror that fell during an earthquake cracked extensively.

For a review of adjectives and adverbs, see Chapter 16, pages 352–53. For more on prepositions and prepositional phrases, see Chapter 16, pages 356–58.

ACTIVITY 9: Teamwork

ADVANCED

Working in a group of three students, expand each of the sentences below, following these steps:

- Each student should take one part of the sentence.
- Working individually, each student should think of descriptive words and/or a prepositional phrase to add to that part of the sentence.
- Starting at the beginning of the sentence, each student should read his or her part aloud, including the added words.
- When everyone has finished, each student should write down the complete sentence, being sure to include any necessary commas.

EXAMPLE: The employee + who parked + received a reprimand.

The unlucky employee who carelessly parked in the boss's

parking space received a stern reprimand.

1. The meadow + where the horses graze + is blooming.

   _____

   _____

2. The day + when I fell + amuses my friends.

   _____

   _____

3. The driver + who crashed his car + received a ticket.

   _____

   _____

4. Our friend + made pizza + which he burned.

   _____

   _____

5. My professor + who rides a unicycle + crashed.

   _____

   _____

For more practice with *that, which, who, when,* and *where,* go to **bedfordstmartins.com /touchstones**.

**ACTIVITY 10: Mastery Test or Teamwork**

In the following paragraph, form seven complex sentences, using ***that***, ***which***, ***who***, ***when***, or ***where***. First, identify each pair of sentences that can be joined, and then decide which word will join the sentences most effectively. The first one has already been done for you.

> Did you know that there is a walking route across America? ̶I̶t̶ ^that^
> begins in Delaware and ends in California. This little-known trail is the
> American Discovery Trail. It was established in the early 1990s through
> the efforts of the American Hiking Society and *Backpacker* magazine.
> The goal of the American Discovery Trail is to provide hikers with an
> opportunity to enjoy uniquely American experiences. These experiences
> include historical sites, scenic views, wilderness, and cities. The trail
> includes 6,800 miles of trails. The trails are divided into a northern
> route and a southern route. The northern route takes hikers through
> Chicago. The southern route goes through St. Louis. Both routes lead
> to Denver. There, the two trails rejoin. The trail winds through many state
> parks. There, hikers can set up their tents. The first people to hike the entire
> length of the trail were Ken and Marcia Powers. Ken and Marcia Powers
> walked the trail in just 231 days. Most hikers take six months to a year
> to complete the trail. Those who have taken this long walk have said
> that it has changed their lives.

FIX IT: Solving Problems in Complex Sentences with Descriptive Clauses

In this section, you will learn how to find and fix fragments in complex sentences that contain descriptive clauses. Remember from earlier chapters that fragments are word groups that are missing a subject or verb or that do not express a complete thought.

FIXING FRAGMENTS

By now, you know that the following sentence is complete and correct:

> `SUBJECT` `VERB`
>
> A rainbow appeared.

FOUNDATION WORDS
NOUNS
VERBS
DESCRIPTIVE WORDS
ADJECTIVES
ADVERBS
CONNECTING WORDS
PREPOSITIONS
CONJUNCTIONS

Power Tip
You might be wondering why this sentence needs another verb in addition to *appeared*. The reason is that *appeared* is no longer the main verb in the sentence. The words *that appeared* function as an adjective describing the rainbow: *What rainbow? The rainbow that appeared.*

Now, decide whether the following example is a complete, correct sentence:

> The rainbow that appeared.

The answer is *no*. By adding *that*, we have created a **descriptive clause**: It is part of a sentence, but it can't stand alone as a sentence. In other words, it is a **fragment**.

To fix this fragment, we must complete the thought by adding a verb to the main clause:

MISSING VERB

> The rainbow [that appeared] _____.

In other words, we must answer the question, What happened with the rainbow that appeared? Take a look:

> The rainbow [that appeared] astonished us.

To check whether we have successfully completed the complex sentence, cover the descriptive clause and read the main clause:

> The rainbow [   ] astonished us.

This makes sense. The main clause has been completed successfully.

Notice that you cannot correct a descriptive clause fragment by adding descriptive words:

> The rainbow [that appeared] so suddenly.

To see why, remove the descriptive clause and read the main clause:

> The rainbow [   ] so suddenly.

This does not make sense. The words *so suddenly* describe how the rainbow *appeared*, so it belongs in the descriptive clause:

> The rainbow [that appeared so suddenly] _____.

To complete this sentence, add a verb to the main clause:

> The rainbow [that appeared so suddenly] astonished us.

Also, we cannot complete a descriptive clause fragment with a prepositional phrase:

> The rainbow [that appeared] after the storm.

To see why, remove the descriptive clause and read the main clause:

> The rainbow [   ] after the storm.

This does not make sense. The prepositional phrase *after the storm* describes when the rainbow *appeared*, so it belongs in the descriptive clause:

> The rainbow [that appeared after the storm] _____.

To complete this sentence, add a verb to the main clause:

The rainbow [that appeared after the storm] astonished us.

Remember that the *length* of a word group does not determine whether it is a complete and correct sentence. When descriptive clause fragments are long, they can be tricky to recognize. Take a look:

Oregon's Timberline Lodge, [where the U.S. Olympic Ski Team often goes to train].

If we remove the descriptive clause, we can see that the remaining word group is not a complete sentence:

Oregon's Timberline Lodge, [   ].

Now, let's form a complete sentence by adding a verb and other words to complete the thought:

Oregon's Timberline Lodge, [where the U.S. Olympic Ski team often goes to train], is open for skiing all year long.

ACTIVITY 11
MODERATE

For each item below, do the following:

- First, put brackets around the descriptive clause.
- Then, decide whether the word group is a complete sentence or a fragment.
- If the word group is a complete sentence, write **correct** on the line provided.
- If the word group is a fragment, rewrite it with more information as a complete, correct sentence on the line provided.

EXAMPLE: George Washington, [who was America's first president.]

George Washington, who was America's first president, is

pictured on the one-dollar bill.

1. Professor Bates, who was born in Paris, France.

_____

_____

2. Niagara Falls, which is in New York State near the Canadian border.

_____

_____

3. Martin Luther King Jr., who delivered his famous "I Have a Dream" speech in Washington, D.C., in 1963.

_____

_____

CONTINUED >

4. Grand Canyon National Park, where tourists can walk above the canyon on a glass skywalk.

5. Seattle, Washington, which has an annual rainfall of more than 36 inches.

6. Everyone who lives within 100 yards of the river was evacuated.

7. Scott's best friend, Byron, who habitually texts while driving.

8. Soy milk, which has significantly more calcium than regular milk.

Often, writers create descriptive clause fragments accidentally, by putting a period where it does not belong. Take a look:

> **INCORRECT**   My sister and I went shopping at the new mall. <u>Where we found some great shoes on sale.</u>
>
> DESCRIPTIVE CLAUSE FRAGMENT

When you find a descriptive clause fragment in your writing, usually the easiest way to fix it is to join it to another sentence—either the sentence that comes before it or the sentence that comes after it.

> **CORRECT**   My sister and I went shopping at the new mall, where we found some great shoes on sale.

Sometimes, when you connect the fragment to another sentence, you may have to remove an extra word. For example:

> DESCRIPTIVE CLAUSE FRAGMENT
>
> **INCORRECT**   <u>The apartment complex where we used to live.</u> It has been torn down.

When joining this fragment to the sentence that follows, we must remove the extra subject *it*. Take a look:

> **CORRECT**   The apartment complex where we used to live has been torn down.

ACTIVITY 12

For each item below, do the following:

- First, mark an **F** above the fragment.
- Then, correct the fragment by connecting it to a simple sentence. Remember to remove the period or replace the period with a comma. Also, you may need to remove an extra word.
- Do not change the other simple sentence.

EXAMPLE: Everyone ran for cover at that moment. When it suddenly began
F
to rain. The picnic was ruined.

Everyone ran for cover at that moment when it suddenly began

to rain. The picnic was ruined.

1. We came across a rustic old cabin in the woods. Where an old man lived with his pet wolf. The man was quite an interesting character.

2. The new tile that we ordered for the kitchen. It was the wrong color. We had to send it back.

3. Mandy enjoys collecting antique teacups. Which she finds at yard sales and flea markets. She has more than 500 teacups.

4. The customers who bought the faulty cell phones. They are quite angry. They are demanding a refund.

5. Last weekend, Susan and her mother went to a crafts fair. Where they bought crocheted scarves, homemade jelly, and handmade jewelry. They enjoy finding unique gifts for friends and family.

For more practice correcting fragments in complex sentences, go to **bedfordstmartins.com /touchstones**.

Power Tip
In descriptive clauses,
the glue words are *that*,
which, *where*, *when*,
and *who*.

Sometimes, you will not be able to fix a descriptive clause fragment by joining it to another sentence. Take a look:

DESCRIPTIVE CLAUSE
FRAGMENT

Sara wanted to have pizza for dinner. <u>Larry, who prefers more healthful meals.</u> They ordered a vegetarian pizza.

If we try to connect this descriptive clause fragment to one of the other sentences, the results will not make sense. In this case, there are two other methods for correcting the fragment. First, we could simply delete the glue word *who*:

CORRECT SIMPLE
SENTENCE

Sara wanted to have pizza for dinner. <u>Larry prefers more healthful meals.</u> They ordered a vegetarian pizza.

The second method is to add more information to the fragment to make it a complete, correct sentence:

Sara wanted to have pizza for dinner. Larry, who prefers more healthful meals, <u>decided to compromise</u>. They ordered a vegetarian pizza.

ADDED INFORMATION

ACTIVITY 13: Teamwork

ADVANCED

In each item below, do the following:

- First, mark an **F** above or beside the fragment.
- Then, correct the fragment by (1) joining it to another sentence, (2) deleting the glue word, or (3) adding more information to make the fragment a complete sentence.
- Copy the other sentence(s) without any changes.

EXAMPLE: Our company began offering free meditation classes. Which are ^*F*^
held in the courtyard. Management hopes that reducing stress
will help employees remain healthy.

Our company began offering free meditation classes, which are

held in the courtyard. Management hopes that reducing stress will

help employees remain healthy.

1. Drivers who take a shortcut through our apartment complex parking lot. They are creating a very dangerous situation. Children often ride bicycles or play kickball in this area.

2. Professor Rogers came up with a way to use textbooks. Textbooks that are outdated or no longer being used. He collects them and sends them to needy schools or orphanages.

_____

_____

_____

3. To renovate the courthouse, the city must hire a contractor. Someone who has experience in renovating buildings more than 100 years old. City leaders want to maintain the building's charm.

_____

_____

_____

4. On a dark and rainy night, we drove past a dog. A dog that was standing forlornly on the side of the road, miles from any house. We could not leave this lost creature, so we stopped and let him into our car and into our family.

_____

_____

_____

_____

5. The new community center will be constructed beside the river. A place where people can swim or just enjoy the view. It will also be a lovely place for weddings and family reunions.

_____

_____

_____

ACTIVITY 14: Mastery Test or Teamwork

MASTERY

Read each of the following paragraphs carefully, looking for fragments. Then, rewrite each error you find to fix the problem, using one of the following methods:

- Connect the fragment to another sentence.
- Delete the glue word.
- Add more information to make the fragment a complete sentence.

If the revised sentences require commas, be sure to include them. The first item in each paragraph has been edited for you.

CONTINUED >

The following paragraph has six fragments (including the one that has been edited for you).

a. (1) Amtrak's USA Rail Pass is a good way to see America/ (2) A̶t̶ *at* a cost that is quite reasonable. (3) This pass provides a good opportunity for travelers. (4) These travelers who would like to stop for a day or more at various locations along their route. (5) The passes, which are available in trip lengths from 15 days to 45 days. (6) The passes must be used within 180 days. (7) Although the number of stops is limited for each pass, travelers have an opportunity to create their own custom tours. (8) Travelers could, for example, stop in West Glacier, Montana. (9) Where they can visit Glacier National Park. (10) Another fun option is to take the Sunset Limited. (11) Which begins or ends in New Orleans, Louisiana. (12) This rail pass is perfect for adventurers. (13) These adventurers who have a little extra vacation time and a desire to see the United States.

The following paragraph has eight fragments (including the one that has been edited for you).

b. (1) Researchers are studying people/ (2) P̶e̶o̶p̶l̶e̶ who live to be over 100 years old. (3) In general, there are three key characteristics. (4) The characteristics that centenarians share. (5) First, to live a long life, they have to have a passion for something. (6) Which can be a hobby or a profession. (7) Researchers interviewed many centenarians. (8) Who were active in reading, creating artwork, playing musical instruments, or pursuing other hobbies. (9) Another secret to a long life is to have a goal or event. (10) The kind of goal or event that they can look forward to, such as a wedding, a family reunion, or a holiday. (11) Many people can think of an isolated elderly friend or family member. (12) The person who passed away right after spending a major event or a holiday alone. (13) Thus, our state of mind can influence our longevity. (14) Finally, people who live to be 100 tend to live in an area. (15) In this area, where they are surrounded by loving family and friends. (16) Loneliness and depression can cause stress. (17) The kind of stress that can shorten lives. (18) To live to be 100, then, we should strive to maintain a passionate hobby, to have goals, and to maintain close relationships with family and friends.

BRINGING IT ALL TOGETHER:
More Complex Sentences

In this chapter, you have learned what descriptive clauses are, how they are used, and how they can cause problems in academic writing. Confirm your knowledge by filling in the blank spaces in the following sentences. If you need help, review the pages listed after each sentence.

✔ To form complex sentences with descriptive clauses, we can use five glue words. They are _____, _____, _____, _____, and _____. (page 432)

✔ A descriptive clause by itself does not express a complete thought, so it cannot be a _____. (page 433)

✔ When a descriptive clause begins with the word _____, it must always be set off by commas. (page 435)

✔ A descriptive clause that is *not* set off by commas contains information that is _____ to the main meaning of the sentence. (page 435)

✔ A descriptive clause that *is* set off by commas contains information that is _____ for the main meaning of the sentence. (page 435)

✔ Descriptive clauses can be placed either in _____ of a sentence or at _____ of a sentence. (page 438)

✔ A descriptive clause that is used as a complete sentence is a _____, a major grammatical error. (page 444)

CONTINUED >

✔ To correct a descriptive clause fragment, you must add a
_____ to complete the main clause. (page 444)

✔ Descriptive clause fragments are sometimes caused by putting a
_____ at the end of a descriptive clause. (page 446)

✔ There are three ways to correct a descriptive clause fragment.
These ways are: 1) _____,
2) _____, and 3) _____. (pages 446–48)

CHAPTER 20

Sentences with Modifying Phrases

Before you read this chapter, it's a good idea to test your understanding of sentences with modifying phrases. You may know more than you think.

WHAT DO YOU KNOW?

Circle "Yes" if each word group below is a complete, correct sentence. Circle "No" if it is incomplete. Then, explain your choice.

1. **Smiling, Bill waved.**

   Yes   No

   Explanation: _____

2. **Stepping on the brake, my car stopped.**

   Yes   No

   Explanation: _____

3. **To stay healthy, they exercised.**

   Yes   No

   Explanation: _____

4. **Looking up in the sky, the sun blinded me.**

   Yes   No

   Explanation: _____

5. **Lost in the jungle, the rescue crew arrived to save them.**

   Yes   No

   Explanation: _____

Modifying phrases offer other ways to add information to different sentence parts. You'll learn how to use them in this chapter.

MODIFYING PHRASE , NOUN + VERB . = Prepared for the exam, I succeeded.

NOUN , MODIFYING PHRASE , VERB .

= **The** students, studying together for long hours, succeeded.

BUILD IT: Sentences with Modifying Phrases

In Chapters 17 through 19, you learned how to combine simple sentences into compound or complex sentences. In this chapter, you will learn a new and useful method of combining simple sentences. Let's begin with a brief review.

SIMPLE SENTENCE 1   SIMPLE SENTENCE 2
Amy rushed through her homework. She made several errors.

You already know that these two simple sentences can be combined to form a **compound** sentence. Take a look:

Amy rushed through her homework, so she made several errors.

Amy rushed through her homework; as a result, she made several errors.

Or, you can combine the two simple sentences to make a **complex** sentence:

When Amy rushed through her homework, she made several errors.

Amy, who rushed through her homework, made several errors.

As you have learned, both compound and complex sentences always have two separate subjects and two separate verbs. However, if you do not want to repeat a subject, you can combine the two simple sentences by turning one of them into a **modifying phrase**.

MODIFYING PHRASE   SIMPLE SENTENCE
Rushing through her homework, Amy made several errors.

SUBJECT BEING DESCRIBED

Terminology Tip
A **phrase** is a word group that does not have both a subject and a verb. *Rushing through her homework* is a phrase because it is missing a subject — we don't know who or what is rushing through her homework.

When you begin a sentence with a phrase, the phrase works like a coat hanger: You will "hang" the rest of your sentence on it.

Usually, modifying phrases appear at the beginning of sentences—though they sometimes come later in the sentence instead (for example, *Amy, rushing through her homework, made several errors*). Beginning a sentence with a modifying phrase is a good way to add variety to your writing, especially if a lot of your sentences start with subjects followed by verbs.

Read these two examples aloud. Can you hear a difference between them?

`SUBJECT` `VERB`   `SUBJECT` `VERB`

Jack left the room angrily. He slammed the door.

`MODIFYING PHRASE`   `SUBJECT` `VERB`

Leaving the room angrily, Jack slammed the door.

The first example sounds almost robot-like. The second example sounds more musical. The following sections of this chapter will help you make your writing more "musical" by showing you how to begin sentences with different modifying phrases.

In this chapter, you will learn to begin sentences with three types of modifying phrases:

- an *-ing* phrase (*present participle* phrase)
- a *to* phrase (*infinitive* phrase)
- an *-ed* phrase (*past participle* phrase)

These phrases all work in the same basic way, but their meanings vary somewhat, as you will see.

BEGINNING A SENTENCE WITH AN *-ING* PHRASE

Verbs ending in *-ing* (*dancing, sleeping, driving,* and so on) are typically used for one action that is **ongoing** at the time another action occurs. In the following sentence, the *-ing* verb (*weeding*) leads into or sets up the second action, so the *-ing* verb comes first, followed by the second action (*found*), which occurs while the *-ing* verb action is taking place.

`ONGOING ACTION`   `SECOND ACTION`

Weeding the garden, Iris found an arrowhead.

If you wish to combine two simple sentences by turning one of the sentences into an *-ing* phrase, begin by identifying the verb in each of the simple sentences:

Iris weeded the garden. She found an arrowhead.

Next, use the base form of the first verb (*weed* in this case) and add *-ing* to it. Begin your sentence with the *-ing* phrase:

Weeding the garden . . .

Terminology Tip
Weeding is what is known as a **present participle**.

Power Tip
Some writers prefer to add the word *while* to the beginning of an *-ing* phrase. For example: *While weeding the garden, Iris found an arrowhead.*

Now, add a comma and "hang" the rest of your sentence on the phrase:

Weeding the garden, Iris found an arrowhead.

The second part of the sentence begins with the subject *Iris* instead of *she* because *Iris* doesn't appear in the first part of the sentence, and it is a more specific name for the subject.

KEY TO CHALLENGE METER	
WARMUP	
EASY	
MODERATE	
ADVANCED	
MASTERY	

Identify the difficulty level of each activity using the key above.

ACTIVITY 1
WARMUP

Complete each sentence below by following these steps:

- Add a verb to the subject.
- Add any additional information to complete the thought.

EXAMPLE: Listening to the music on the radio, Jessica *sang along* .

1. Struggling to stay awake during class, Roberto _____.
2. Pouring hot coffee into my cup, the waitress _____.
3. Writing his research paper late at night, Stefan _____.
4. Suffering from a bad headache, Dwight _____.
5. Tasting the soup on the stove, Katherine _____.

ACTIVITY 2
EASY

Combine each pair of simple sentences by turning the first sentence into an *-ing* phrase. Follow these steps:

- Underline the verb in each simple sentence.
- Put the first verb in the *-ing* form and use it to write an *-ing* phrase that will begin your new sentence.
- Add a comma after the phrase.
- Hang the rest of your sentence on the phrase. (You may need to change the subject of the second part of the sentence.)

EXAMPLE: Ben <u>saw</u> dark clouds on the horizon. He <u>sensed</u> danger.

Seeing dark clouds on the horizon, Ben sensed danger.

1. Ben turned on the radio. He heard a tornado warning.

_____

2. He scanned the horizon. He saw a funnel cloud forming.

_____

3. Ben gathered his family. He led them into the basement.

_____

4. Ben heard a terrible roaring sound. He feared a direct hit.

_____

5. The tornado spared Ben's home. The tornado damaged only a few trees.

_____

ACTIVITY 3: Teamwork

MODERATE

For each of the following items, use the two verbs and the subject provided to write a sentence that begins with an -*ing* phrase. Follow these steps:

- Put the first verb in the -*ing* form and use it to begin your sentence with a phrase.
- Add a comma after the phrase.
- Use the subject and the second verb to complete the thought. (You may put the second verb in the past, present, or future tense.)

> **Power Tip**
> For advice on forming various verb tenses, see Chapter 23.

EXAMPLE:

First verb: watch   **Subject:** Cassandra   **Second verb:** laugh

Watching her favorite sitcom, Cassandra laughed out loud.

1. First verb: talk   **Subject:** Evan   **Second verb:** disturb

_____

2. First verb: ride   **Subject:** Annie   **Second verb:** fall

_____

3. First verb: interview   **Subject:** reporter   **Second verb:** ask

_____

4. First verb: paint   **Subject:** artist   **Second verb:** use

_____

5. First verb: sing   **Subject:** rock star   **Second verb:** forget

_____

BEGINNING A SENTENCE WITH A *TO* PHRASE

When a verb is written in the *to* form (*to dance, to sleep, to drive,* and so on), it often shows a **desired action** or goal. In such cases, you will find a desired action or goal (the *to* phrase) in the first part of the sentence and a necessary action in the second part of the sentence:

> **Terminology Tip**
> A verb that is written in the *to* form is called an **infinitive**. The *to* in an infinitive should not be confused with the preposition *to,* which typically shows direction: *I went to the store.*

~~DESIRED ACTION~~   ~~ACTION THAT MUST BE TAKEN~~

To save money on gasoline, Brian rides his bicycle to work.

When you begin sentences like these with a *to* phrase, it is the same as beginning the sentence with *In order to* . . . Take a look:

> To save money on gasoline, Brian rides his bicycle to work.
>
> <u>In order to</u> save money on gasoline, Brian rides his bicycle to work.

Both of these sentences are correct, and they have the same meaning. You may use either form you prefer.

If you wish to combine two simple sentences by turning one of the sentences into a *to* phrase, begin by identifying the *to* + verb combination in the first simple sentence:

> The boss wants <u>to improve</u> productivity. She hired a consultant.

Use this combination to form the phrase that will begin your new sentence:

> To improve productivity . . .

Now, add a comma and "hang" the rest of your sentence on the phrase:

> To improve productivity, the boss hired a consultant.

The second part of the sentence begins with *the boss* instead of *she* because *the boss* doesn't appear in the first part of the sentence, and it is a more specific name for the subject.

ACTIVITY 4
WARMUP

Complete each sentence below by following these steps:

- Add a verb to the subject.
- Add any additional information to complete the thought.

EXAMPLE: To reheat his soup, Charlie *used the microwave* _____ .

1. To lose a few pounds, Ted _____ .
2. To get a deal on a new car, Amanda _____ .
3. To fully understand the story, students _____ .
4. To learn Spanish, Edward _____ .
5. To save money, Nicole _____ .

ACTIVITY 5
EASY

Combine each pair of simple sentences by turning the first sentence into a *to* phrase. Follow these steps:

- Underline the *to* + verb combination in the first simple sentence.
- Use this combination to form the phrase that will begin your new sentence.

- Add a comma after the phrase.
- Hang the rest of your sentence on the phrase. (You may need to change the subject of the second part of the sentence.)

EXAMPLE: Many people want <u>to save</u> money on holiday gifts. They shop online for the best prices.

To save money on holiday gifts, many people shop online for the

best prices.

1. Kyle wanted to find time to exercise. He got up an hour earlier in the morning.

_____

_____

2. The students wanted to pass the final exam. They formed an evening study group.

_____

_____

3. Lana decided to earn extra spending money. She sold some of her antiques on eBay.

_____

_____

4. Shane needed to overcome his fear of public speaking. He joined a debating club.

_____

_____

5. Susan likes to keep fresh herbs on hand. She has a small herb garden on her patio.

_____

_____

ACTIVITY 6: Teamwork

MODERATE

For the following items, use the two verbs and the subject provided to write a sentence that begins with a *to* phrase. Follow these steps:

- Put the first verb in the *to* form and use it to begin your sentence with a phrase.
- Add a comma after the phrase.
- Use the subject and the second verb to complete the thought. (You may put the second verb in the past, present, or future tense.)

CONTINUED >

EXAMPLE:

First verb: flavor   **Subject:** the chef   **Second verb:** add

To flavor the fish, the chef added garlic and fresh dill.

1. **First verb:** solve   **Subject:** the investigator   **Second verb:** search

2. **First verb:** rescue   **Subject:** the firefighter   **Second verb:** climb

3. **First verb:** determine   **Subject:** the doctor   **Second verb:** order

4. **First verb:** catch   **Subject:** fisherman   **Second verb:** use

5. **First verb:** finish   **Subject:** the novelist   **Second verb:** write

BEGINNING A SENTENCE WITH AN *-ED* PHRASE

KEY TO
BUILDING BLOCKS

FOUNDATION WORDS
NOUNS
VERBS

DESCRIPTIVE WORDS
ADJECTIVES
ADVERBS

CONNECTING WORDS
PREPOSITIONS
CONJUNCTIONS

When a verb in a modifying phrase is written in the *-ed* form (*embarrassed, married, angered,* and so on), it indicates the **condition** of someone or something. In a sentence that begins with an *-ed* phrase, you will find the description of the condition in the first part of the sentence and the person or thing being described, and what the person/thing did, in the last part of the sentence:

CONDITION   PERSON DESCRIBED   PERSON'S ACTION
Frustrated with his slow computer, Chan ordered a new one.

Frustrated is what is known as a *past participle.* Keep in mind that an *-ed* phrase can have an irregular past participle that doesn't end in *-ed.* (You will learn more about the irregular forms of verbs in Chapter 23.) Take a look:

PAST PARTICIPLE OF *STING*
Stung by a bee, Darrin let out a yelp.

PAST PARTICIPLE OF *LOSE*
Lost in the unfamiliar city, we consulted a map.

To combine two simple sentences by turning one of the sentences into an *-ed* phrase, begin by identifying the complete verb in the first simple sentence:

Lucas was confused about the assignment. He asked his instructor for clarification.

Drop the helping verb *was* and use the part participle to form the phrase that will begin your new sentence:

Confused about the assignment . . .

Power Tip
For more on identifying complete verbs (including helping verbs and the verbs that follow them), see Chapter 15, pages 340–41, and Chapter 23.

Now, add a comma and "hang" the rest of your sentence on the phrase:

Confused about the assignment, Lucas asked his instructor for clarification.

The second part of the sentence begins with the subject *Lucas* instead of *he* because *Lucas* doesn't appear in the first part of the sentence, and *Lucas* is a more specific name for the subject.

ACTIVITY 7
WARMUP

Complete each sentence by following these steps:

- Add a verb to the subject.
- Add any additional information to complete the thought.

EXAMPLE: Concerned about her algebra grades, Nikki <u>found a tutor</u>   .

1. Interested in getting a pilot's license, Carly _____.
2. Startled by the loud noise, Frank _____.
3. Annoyed by the loud children, the old woman _____.
4. Distracted by the television show, Ellen _____.
5. Excited about his winning lottery ticket, Dave _____.

ACTIVITY 8
EASY

Combine each pair of simple sentences by turning the first sentence into an *-ed* phrase. Follow these steps:

- Underline the complete verb in the first simple sentence.
- Drop the helping verb (if there is one) and use the past participle to form the phrase that will begin your new sentence.
- Add a comma after the phrase.
- Hang the rest of your sentence on the phrase. (You may need to change the subject of the second part of the sentence.)

EXAMPLE: Hanna <u>was asked</u> to support breast cancer research. She signed up for a three-day Walk for the Cure.

<u>Asked to support breast cancer research, Hanna signed up for</u>

<u>a three-day Walk for the Cure.</u>

1. Hanna was challenged by the many hills on the first day. She was surprised at how much her legs ached.

_____

_____

CONTINUED >

2. The pain reminded Hanna of the suffering of cancer victims. Hanna kept on walking.

_____

_____

3. Hanna was determined to finish the walk. She tried not to think about her aching legs.

_____

_____

4. Hanna was encouraged by the other walkers. She found a hidden strength.

_____

_____

5. Hanna was moved to tears when she finished the walk. She signed up for next year's walk.

_____

_____

ACTIVITY 9: Teamwork

MODERATE

For each of the following items, use the two verbs and the subject provided to write a sentence that begins with an -ed phrase.

- Put the first verb in the -ed form and use it to begin your sentence with a phrase.
- Add a comma after the phrase.
- Use the subject and the second verb to complete the thought. (You may put the second verb in the past, present, or future tense.)

EXAMPLE:

First verb: injure   **Subject:** the baseball player   **Second verb:** limp

Injured during the double play, the baseball player limped to the dugout.

1. **First verb:** annoy   **Subject:** our cat   **Second verb:** scratch

2. **First verb:** distract   **Subject:** my English professor   **Second verb:** forgot

3. **First verb:** discourage   **Subject:** the sales manager   **Second verb:** reduce

4. **First verb:** frighten   **Subject:** Alvin   **Second verb:** jump

5. **First verb:** convince   **Subject:** the police officer   **Second verb:** arrest

ACTIVITY 10: Mastery Test or Teamwork

In each of the following paragraphs, combine pairs of simple sentences by turning one of the simple sentences into a modifying phrase. First, identify a pair of sentences that can be combined, and then decide which one will become a modifying phrase.

(*Hint:* Combine five pairs)

a. Serena felt disorganized and too busy. She was taking college classes and working full-time. She did not have enough time to spend with her husband and children. Serena was frustrated. She bought a book on how to get organized. The book taught her how to get control of her life. She had to consolidate her errands. She set aside one day each week for chores such as doing car maintenance, filling prescriptions, and going to the bank. In addition, she assigned some of these errands to her husband and children. She wanted to avoid wasting time at the grocery store every day. She wrote out a weekly menu plan and shopped for groceries only once a week. She turned off the television and banned cell phones at the dinner table. She forced her family to turn their attention to each other. These changes in her life helped give Serena more time for her work, her education, and, most important, her family.

(*Hint:* Combine six pairs)

b. On August 7, 1993, a mother and her children traveled from Mississippi to Destin, Florida. They looked forward to a relaxing vacation. They checked into a room on the seventh floor of a condo. Early the next morning, two-year-old Hays woke up. He was wearing only a T-shirt and a diaper. He found his way outside the room and onto the balcony while his mother lay sleeping. Hays wanted to see over the balcony. He climbed up on top of a cart that had been left outside. Little Hays fell seven stories to the parking lot below. Bystanders were horrified at the sight of the unconscious child. They called 911. Hays was rushed to a local hospital. Hays was examined thoroughly. Amazingly,

CONTINUED >

For more practice with using modifiers, go to **bedfordstmartins.com /touchstones**.

he had no injuries. Officials believe that his diaper helped save him.
The diaper inflated during the fall. The diaper cushioned the impact. His
grateful family calls his survival a miracle.

FIX IT: Fixing Problems in Sentences with Modifying Phrases

In this section, you will learn how to recognize and fix a common problem in sentences with modifying phrases: dangling modifiers.

RECOGNIZING DANGLING MODIFIERS

FOUNDATION WORDS
NOUNS
VERBS
DESCRIPTIVE WORDS
ADJECTIVES
ADVERBS
CONNECTING WORDS
PREPOSITIONS
CONJUNCTIONS

Take a look at the following sentence and see if you can spot a problem with its meaning:

> Exhausted after a long day of shopping, the coffee shop looked good.

There is something odd about this sentence, but you may have to look very closely to figure out the problem. Let's begin by examining a simple sentence:

> The coffee shop looked good.

The meaning of this sentence is clear and simple. However, if we add a modifying phrase to the beginning of the sentence, we have to be sure that the two parts of the sentence fit together. Sometimes, especially when we are writing quickly, we may write a sentence where the two parts do not fit together. As a result, the sentence will not make perfect sense:

> Exhausted after a long day of shopping, the coffee shop looked good.

According to this sentence, who or what was exhausted after a long day of shopping? While your imagination may tell you that a *person* was exhausted, the sentence actually says that the *coffee shop* was exhausted. This is an odd idea.

To be absolutely clear, we must add a subject that makes sense:

> Exhausted after a long day of shopping, Allison thought the coffee shop looked good.

When you begin a sentence with a modifier, remember two rules:

- The subject of the sentence must come immediately after the comma.
- The subject of the sentence must connect with the condition of action in the modifier.

Take a look:

A. Knitting a scarf, my cat played with the yarn.

B. Knitting a scarf, I let my cat play with the yarn.

According to sentence A, the *cat* was knitting a scarf, but this idea doesn't make sense. When we write or read such a sentence, we usually allow our imagination to fill in the *real* subject of the action. Instead, we should recognize that the sentence does not make sense and needs to have an appropriate subject added. Sentence B is correct because it tells us that *I* was knitting a scarf. In this case, the subject of the action is 100 percent clear.

When an appropriate subject is missing or unclear, we cannot be 100 percent sure who or what is connected to the action or condition in the modifier. So, the modifier is left **dangling** or *unattached* to a subject that makes sense.

ACTIVITY 11

Do the following for each group of sentences below:

- Read all three sentences.
- In the space provided, write a question that will help you identify the correct subject. (See the example below.)
- Circle the subject or subjects that fit with the action or condition in the modifier.

EXAMPLE:

Topped with nuts and a cherry, David served dessert.

Topped with nuts and a cherry, David's (dessert) looked delicious.

Topped with nuts and a cherry, the guests enjoyed dessert.

Question: *Who or what was topped with nuts and a cherry?*

1. Dunking the basketball with a flourish, the crowd cheered the point guard.

   Dunking the basketball with a flourish, the coach yelled at the point guard.

   Dunking the basketball with a flourish, the point guard grinned.

   Question: _____

2. Confused about how to use commas, the English professor helped Dawn.

   Confused about how to use commas, Dawn made an appointment with her English professor.

   Confused about how to use commas, a visit to Dawn's English professor helped.

   Question: _____

CONTINUED >

3. Drinking milk from a saucer, my mother spoke to the stray kitten.

   Drinking milk from a saucer, the stray kitten seemed grateful to my mother.

   Drinking milk from a saucer, I watched my mother speak softly to the stray kitten.

   Question: _____

4. To lose a few pounds, Sam's breakfast now consists of grapefruit and cereal.

   To lose a few pounds, Sam's usual pancakes were replaced by grapefruit and cereal.

   To lose a few pounds, Sam now eats grapefruit and cereal for breakfast.

   Question: _____

5. Sentenced to ten days in jail, the mischievous college student hung his head.

   Sentenced to ten days in jail, the defense attorney comforted her client.

   Sentenced to ten days in jail, the judge punished the mischievous college student.

   Question: _____

FIXING DANGLING MODIFIERS

If you find that you have written a dangling modifier, you will need to do *one* of the following things:

1. Change the <u>second part</u> of the sentence by adding a new subject.
2. Change the <u>first part</u> of the sentence (the modifier) by adding a subject and a complete verb.

Let's consider these options one at a time.

Changing the Second Part of the Sentence

Take a look at a new example:

> Hiking in Yellowstone National Park, the views were beautiful.

Clearly, it does not make sense to say that *the views* were hiking. As you read sentences like this, *do not let your imagination do the work that the sentence should be doing*. The first way to fix this error is to leave the modifier the same but <u>change the second half of the sentence</u>. In doing this, we must <u>add a subject</u> that fits with the action *hiking*. For example:

MODIFIER STAYS THE SAME   **NEW SUBJECT**

<u>Hiking in Yellowstone National Park</u>, we enjoyed the beautiful views.

Now it is clear that *we* were hiking. This makes perfect sense. Notice, too, that the new subject, *we*, requires a new verb, *enjoyed*. We did what? We enjoyed the views.

ACTIVITY 12

MODERATE

Correct each dangling modifier below by following these steps:

- Copy the modifying phrase that opens the sentence, leaving it the same.
- Put a comma after this phrase.
- Add a subject that fits with the action in the modifier.
- Add a verb and complete the thought.

Note: You may need to change other words in the second part of the sentence.

EXAMPLE: Reading a mystery novel, John's cat jumped onto his lap.

Reading a mystery novel, John was startled when his cat jumped onto his lap.

1. Walking along a trail by a creek, a bald eagle circled above the hikers.

2. To win the prize money, more than 500 boxes of cookies had to be sold by our scout troop.

3. Parked near the baseball field, a foul ball landed on an expensive sports car.

4. Checking her cell phone, the text message from her mother had not arrived.

5. Stuck in a traffic jam for more than three hours, my stomach began to grumble.

Changing the Modifier

The second method for correcting a dangling modifier is to <u>change the modifier</u> but leave the second half of the sentence the same. In doing this, we must

<u>add a subject</u> that fits with the action in the modifier. We must also make sure that there is a <u>complete verb</u>. Let's return to a familiar example:

Hiking in Yellowstone National Park, the views were beautiful.

Now, we will <u>add a subject</u> to the first part of this sentence. We will also add the helping verb *were* before *hiking* to make the verb complete. (For more on helping verbs, see Chapter 15, pages 340–41.) Notice that the second half of the sentence remains unchanged:

While we were hiking in Yellowstone National Park, the views were beautiful.

Notice also that the <u>subordinating conjunction</u> *while* has been added to the opening phrase. By adding this information to the modifier, we have created a complex sentence with two separate subjects and two separate verbs.

| **1ST SUBJECT** | **1ST VERB** | | **2ND SUBJECT** | **2ND VERB** |

While we were hiking in Yellowstone National Park, the views were beautiful.

Now it is clear that *we* were hiking.

ACTIVITY 13
ADVANCED

Correct each dangling modifier below by following these steps:

- Rewrite the modifier, adding an appropriate subordinating conjunction (see the Subordinating Conjunctions box at left) and a new subject. Change the verb as necessary.
- Add a comma.
- Leave the second half of the sentence the same.

EXAMPLE: Adding too much salt, the soup became inedible.

Because I added too much salt, the soup became inedible.

1. Running to catch a Frisbee, a branch tripped Steve.

_____

2. Blowing up the balloon too fully, it popped.

_____

3. Accelerating rapidly at the green light, my coffee spilled.

_____

_____

4. Searching all morning, my cell phone turned up in my jacket pocket.

_____

_____

> **Common Subordinating Conjunctions**
>
> *after, although, as, because, before, even though, even if, if, since, unless, until, when, while*

5. Typing in a hurry, the report had several typographical errors.

_____

_____

ACTIVITY 14: Mastery Test or Teamwork

Read each of the following paragraphs carefully, looking for dangling modifiers. Then, rewrite each error to fix the problem, using one of the following methods:

- Leave the opening modifier the same, but change the second half of the sentence.
- Add more information to the opening modifier, but leave the second half of the sentence the same.

Be sure to put any commas in the correct places. The first error in each paragraph has been edited for you.

The following paragraph has four dangling modifiers (including the one that has been edited for you).

> _Caleb does crossword puzzles._

a. (1) To improve his vocabulary, ~~crossword puzzles are Caleb's~~

~~favorite strategy.~~ (2) These puzzles introduce him to words that he

otherwise might not come across. (3) Learning the meaning of new

words, his reading comprehension improved. (4) Further, he has

become a better speaker. (5) Knowing the precise meaning of words,

his conversations with others are clearer. (6) Caleb has found that his

spelling has also improved. (7) Known as a poor speller in high school,

Caleb's spelling is now very accurate. (8) Caleb has his father

to thank for this beneficial hobby. (9) To help keep his mind sharp,

Caleb's father did a crossword puzzle every morning at breakfast.

The following paragraph has six dangling modifiers (including the one that has been edited for you).

b. (1) Hiking in the wilderness provides great exercise as well as a

unique connection to nature. (2) The wilderness is not without its dangers,

> _humans can startle bears._

however. (3) Hiking along a scenic trail, ~~bears can be startled by humans.~~

(4) Preferring to avoid human contact, humans are generally not attacked

by bears. (5) If a bear feels threatened, however, it may act to protect

itself or its cubs. (6) Blowing a whistle, singing, or talking loudly,

CONTINUED >

For more practice with correcting dangling modifiers, go to **bedfordstmartins.com/touchstones.**

bears are warned of the presence of humans. (7) Warned of approaching humans, a bear's usual response is to run away. (8) If hikers come across a bear near the trail, they should remain calm and should never run. (9) Able to run at speeds over 30 miles per hour, humans have no chance of outrunning a bear. (10) Hikers should stand their ground, wave their arms, and make noise. (11) Bears sometimes charge humans but often bluff and veer off at the last second. (12) Attacked by bears, playing dead is often a successful strategy. (13) The best strategy to avoid encounters with bears is to make noise and to travel in groups.

BRINGING IT ALL TOGETHER:
Sentences with Modifying Phrases

In this chapter, you have learned about sentences formed with modifying phrases. You have also learned how to avoid common problems caused by modifying phrases. Confirm your knowledge by filling in the blank spaces in the following sentences. If you need help, review the pages listed after each sentence.

✔ One way to combine two simple sentences is to turn one of them into a modifying phrase. Three common modifying phrases are _____ phrases, _____ phrases, and _____ phrases. (page 455)

✔ Modifying phrases are usually at _____ of a sentence, although they may also come elsewhere in a sentence. (page 455)

✔ One common problem in sentences with modifying phrases is the _____ modifier. When this problem occurs, the _____ of the sentence is not clear. (pages 464–65)

✔ There are two basic ways to correct a dangling modifier. You can:
1) _____, or
2) _____
_____. (page 466)

CHAPTER 21

Complex-Compound Sentences and Sentence Variety

Before you read this chapter, it's a good idea to test your understanding of complex-compound sentences. You may know more than you think.

WHAT DO YOU KNOW?

Circle "Yes" if each complex-compound sentence below is punctuated correctly. Circle "No" if the punctuation is incorrect. If you circle "No," explain the problem.

1. **After it stops raining. The sun will come out, and we might see a rainbow.**

   Yes   No

   Explanation: _____

2. **Because animals in national parks are wild, visitors should keep their distance, and they should certainly never attempt to feed or pet these animals.**

   Yes   No

   Explanation: _____

3. **Beth graciously accepted her niece's homemade brownie; even though she was on a diet, for she did not want to disappoint the little girl.**

   Yes   No

   Explanation: _____

4. **If I were in your shoes, I would not buy that expensive and complicated camera, but I would buy that excellent point-and-shoot camera.**

   Yes   No

   Explanation: _____

5. **Because he has a generous heart, Al lent his truck to his cousin; but he asked his cousin to return the truck with a full tank of gas.**

   Yes   No

   Explanation: _____

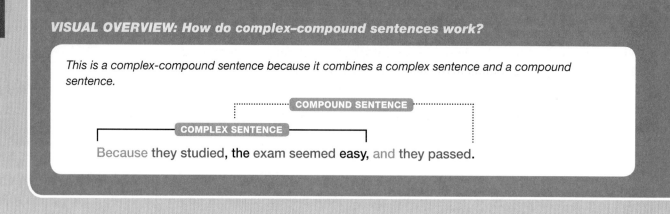

This is a complex-compound sentence because it combines a complex sentence and a compound sentence.

COMPOUND SENTENCE

COMPLEX SENTENCE

Because they studied, the exam seemed easy, and they passed.

BUILD IT: Complex-Compound Sentences

So far in this book, you have learned about several types of "glue" that allow you to join simple sentences. For example, in Chapter 17, you learned two ways to form a compound sentence:

1. With a comma and a coordinating conjunction as glue:

COMMA AND COORDINATING CONJUNCTION

Mirella asked for a raise, but her boss refused.

2. With a semicolon alone or a semicolon and a transitional expression (followed by a comma) as glue:

SEMICOLON WITH TRANSITIONAL EXPRESSION AND COMMA

Mirella asked for a raise; however, her boss refused.

In Chapter 18, you learned two ways to form a complex sentence, using a subordinating conjunction as glue:

1. With the subordinating conjunction at the beginning of the sentence (and a comma in the middle):

SUBORDINATING CONJUNCTION

Because her evaluation was strong, Mirella asked for a raise.

2. With the conjunction in the middle of the sentence (and no comma):

SUBORDINATING CONJUNCTION

Mirella asked for a raise because her evaluation was strong.

In this chapter, you will learn to form a complex-compound sentence by joining three simple sentences using two different types of glue. Take a look:

Her evaluation was strong.
Mirella asked for a raise.   } three simple sentences
Her boss refused.

KEY TO BUILDING BLOCKS
FOUNDATION WORDS
NOUNS
VERBS
DESCRIPTIVE WORDS
ADJECTIVES
ADVERBS
CONNECTING WORDS
PREPOSITIONS
CONJUNCTIONS

First, join the first two simple sentences with a subordinating conjunction at the beginning (and a comma in the middle) to create a complex sentence:

> SUBORDINATING CONJUNCTION
>
> Because **her** evaluation was **strong,** Mirella asked **for a raise.**

Then, use a comma and a coordinating conjunction to add the third simple sentence:

> SUBORDINATING CONJUNCTION   COMMA AND COORDINATING CONJUNCTION
>
> Because **her** evaluation was **strong,** Mirella asked **for a raise, but her boss refused.**

In the following illustration, you can see why this combination is called a complex-compound sentence.

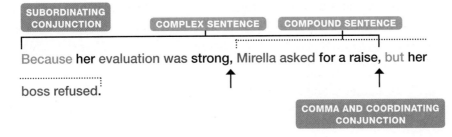

> SUBORDINATING CONJUNCTION   COMPLEX SENTENCE   COMPOUND SENTENCE
>
> Because **her** evaluation was **strong,** Mirella asked **for a raise, but her boss refused.**
>
> COMMA AND COORDINATING CONJUNCTION

Notice that for the compound sentence, you may also use a semicolon and a transitional expression (followed by a comma) as glue:

> SUBORDINATING CONJUNCTION   SEMICOLON WITH TRANSITIONAL EXPRESSION AND COMMA
>
> Because **her** evaluation was **strong,** Mirella asked **for a raise; however, her boss refused.**

Complex-compound sentences are particularly useful when you want to link three closely related ideas. Although you could separate these ideas into two or more shorter sentences, this approach would not emphasize the relationship among the ideas as powerfully.

Furthermore, including complex-compound sentences in your writing demonstrates a high level of critical thinking and grammar mastery.

ACTIVITY 1
MODERATE

Combine each set of three simple sentences to form a complex-compound sentence.

- Begin the complex-compound sentence with a subordinating conjunction and use a coordinating conjunction to add the last simple sentence. (Remember to use commas correctly.)
- Then, rewrite the complex-compound sentence, replacing the coordinating conjunction with a semicolon and a transitional expression. (Remember to use commas correctly.)

CONTINUED >

Coordinating Conjunctions

and, but, or, so, for, nor, yet

Common Transitional Expressions

as a result, consequently, furthermore, however, in addition, instead, moreover, nevertheless, on the other hand, otherwise, therefore

Common Subordinating Conjunctions

after, although, as, because, before, even if, even though, since, unless, until, when, while

KEY TO CHALLENGE METER	
WARMUP	
EASY	
MODERATE	
ADVANCED	
MASTERY	

Identify the difficulty level of each activity using the key above.

EXAMPLE: Eating out is expensive. I cook my own food. The recipes are simple.

Since eating out is expensive, I cook my own food, but the recipes are simple.

Since eating out is expensive, I cook my own food; however, the recipes are simple.

1. The work is difficult, I love my job. It pays well.

_____

_____

_____

_____

2. Joe finished the book. He returned it to the library. He had to pay a late fee.

_____

_____

_____

_____

3. My steak was undercooked. I sent it back. It came back overcooked.

_____

_____

_____

_____

4. Math anxiety is common. There are strategies to overcome it. Many students have used them successfully.

_____

_____

_____

_____

5. The laptop computer was clearly defective. The store manager replaced it with a newer model. The customer was pleased with this solution.

_____

_____

_____

_____

_____

ACTIVITY 2: Teamwork

Combine each set of three simple sentences to form a complex-compound sentence.

- Begin the complex-compound sentence with a subordinating conjunction and use a coordinating conjunction to add the last simple sentence. (Remember to use commas correctly.)
- Then, rewrite the complex-compound sentence, replacing the coordinating conjunction with a semicolon and a transitional expression. (Remember to use commas correctly.)

EXAMPLE:

A grade point average is an important indicator of college success.

Many employers do not consider an applicant's GPA.

They do look closely at the college courses an applicant took.

Although a grade point average is an important indicator of college success, many employers do not consider an applicant's GPA, but they do look closely at the college courses an applicant took.

Although a grade point average is an important indicator of college success, many employers do not consider an applicant's GPA; however, they do look closely at the college courses an applicant took.

1. Smartphones are very beneficial for college students.

   These devices have become a significant classroom distraction.

   Smartphone use can cause students to miss important lecture points.

   _____

   _____

   _____

   _____

   _____

   _____

   _____

2. Martin was becoming increasingly concerned about the cost of his daughter's wedding.

   He offered the bride and groom $10,000 to elope.

   The couple preferred to have an extravagant wedding.

elope: to run away, often to get married in secret

CONTINUED >

3. The hotel's Web site promised a fantastic price on a premium room with a view.

Several hidden costs, such as expensive meals and Internet surcharges, made our final bill unusually high.

We will now be suspicious of so-called great deals from this hotel.

FORMING COMPLEX-COMPOUND SENTENCES WHEN THE CONJUNCTION APPEARS IN THE MIDDLE

As you saw on page 472 of this chapter, the subordinating conjunction may be in the middle of a complex sentence (with no comma). Take a look again at this example:

SUBORDINATING CONJUNCTION

Mirella asked **for a raise** because **her evaluation was strong.**

You may expand this sentence into a complex-compound sentence by adding a sentence through either of the methods you have practiced. Take a look:

SUBORDINATING CONJUNCTION   **COMMA AND COORDINATING CONJUNCTION**

Mirella asked **for a raise** because **her evaluation was strong,** but her boss refused.

SUBORDINATING CONJUNCTION	SEMICOLON WITH TRANSITIONAL EXPRESSION AND COMMA

Mirella asked **for a raise** because **her** evaluation was **strong;** <u>however,</u> **her** boss refused.
                                     ↑   ↑

ACTIVITY 3
MODERATE

Combine each set of three simple sentences to form a complex-compound sentence.

- When joining the first two simple sentences, put a subordinating conjunction in the middle. Use a coordinating conjunction to add the last simple sentence. (Remember to use commas correctly.)

- Then, rewrite the complex-compound sentence, replacing the coordinating conjunction with a semicolon and a transitional expression. (Remember to use commas correctly.)

EXAMPLE:

Jaime decided to join the army.

He wanted to serve his country.

His parents worried about his decision.

Jaime decided to join the army because he wanted to serve his country, but his parents worried about his decision.

Jaime decided to join the army because he wanted to serve his country; however, his parents worried about his decision.

1. We got in line at the electronics store at 6:00 A.M.. *even though*

   The store did not open until 10:00 A.M., *so*

   We were able to purchase one of the few "doorbuster" laptop specials.

   _____

   _____

   _____

   _____

   _____

2. The dentist took X-rays.

   He suspected a cavity.

   He did not find one.

   _____

   _____

   _____

   _____

CONTINUED >

3. Traffic on the freeway was moving slowly.

There were no accidents.

The trip home took a long time.

_____

_____

_____

4. I decided to challenge the parking ticket in court.

My car had been parked legally.

The grumpy judge made me pay the fine.

_____

_____

_____

_____

5. Rebecca applied to ten universities.

Her grade point average and SAT scores were low.

She now has three schools to choose from.

_____

_____

_____

_____

BUILD IT: Sentence Variety

In Chapters 16 through 21, you have learned several important sentence forms. All these sentence forms (except the simple sentence) use one or more types of "glue" to combine simple sentences. Here is a quick review of these sentence forms, with the glue highlighted in orange:

- Simple sentence (Chapter 16):

  The professor canceled class. She gave extra homework.

- Compound sentence (Chapter 17):

  The professor canceled class, but she gave extra homework.
  The professor canceled class; however, she gave extra homework.

- Complex sentence, with subordinate clause (Chapter 18):

  Even though the professor canceled class, she gave extra homework.
  The professor gave extra homework *even though* she canceled class.

- Complex sentence, with descriptive clause (Chapter 19):

  The professor *who* canceled class gave extra homework.

- Sentence with a modifying phrase (Chapter 20):

  Canceling class, the professor gave extra homework.

- Complex-compound sentence (Chapter 21):

  Although the professor canceled class, she gave extra homework, *so*
  I started studying right away.

Power Tip
Although sentence variety can enhance your writing, you do not need to use all the forms described here. It is more important to master a few of these forms than to use all of them carelessly or incorrectly.

The chart below summarizes the types of words and phrases that serve as glue in moving beyond simple sentences.

		COMBINATION	CONTRAST	RESULT	ALTERNATIVES
Coordinating conjunctions	1	and (nor)	but (yet)	so (for)	or
Subordinating conjunctions	2	after as before when	although even though while	because since	if unless
Transitional expressions	3	furthermore in addition moreover	however nevertheless	as a result consequently therefore	instead on the other hand otherwise
		THINGS	PEOPLE	PLACES	TIMES
Relative pronouns	4	that which	who	where	when
		ONGOING ACTION	DESIRED GOAL	CONDITION	
Modifying phrases	5	*-ing* phrase	*to* phrase	*-ed* phrase	

Once you are able to write complete, correct sentences with confidence (whatever forms these sentences may be), it's time to move on to the next phase of becoming a successful college writer: building sentence variety in your writing. This means using different sentence forms to create a kind of music or rhythm in your writing. This "music" will entertain your readers and help keep them engaged in your writing and your ideas. Also, the term *building* suggests that you do not simply wait for sentence variety to happen magically in your writing, but that you look for opportunities to create sentence variety in your work.

The following exercises will give you practice in forming different kinds of sentences in different ways.

ACTIVITY 4

EASY

Power Tip
In some cases, you may wish to divide sentences instead of combining them. Dividing sentences can be useful when you discover excessively long, confusing sentences in your work.

Combine each pair of simple sentences below to create two different sentence forms. Then, decide which sentence form you like better—which form expresses the ideas more effectively—and put a check mark beside it. You may use the "glue" chart on page 479 to help you make your choices.

EXAMPLE:

Belonging to student organizations can be beneficial.

Many students are too busy to join them.

Although belonging to student organizations can be beneficial, many

students are too busy to join them. ✓

Belonging to student organizations can be beneficial; however, many

students are too busy to join them.

1. Many people fear flying in airplanes.

   Air travel is statistically safer than automobile travel.

   _____

   _____

   _____

   _____

2. Male cats can be prone to urinary tract problems related to their diets.

   They should not be fed too much dry food or seafood.

   _____

   _____

   _____

   _____

3. In our fast-paced lives, it is difficult to find time to work out.

   Exercise is vital to ensure energy and good health.

   _____

   _____

   _____

   _____

ACTIVITY 5

MODERATE

Combine each group of simple sentences below in two different ways. Follow these guidelines:

- Your first solution must be a complex-compound sentence.
- Your second solution should combine two of the simple sentences and leave the third one separate.

Finally, decide which sentence form you like better—which form expresses the ideas more effectively—and put a check mark beside it.

EXAMPLE:

My bank now charges five dollars a month for ATM use.

I can't stop using ATMs.

This charge seems excessive to me.

Although my bank now charges five dollars a month for ATM use, I can't stop

using ATMs; however, this charge seems excessive to me.

My bank now charges five dollars a month for ATM use. I can't stop using

ATMs, but this charge seems excessive to me. ✓

1. I love homemade spaghetti.

   I have tried many times to make a delicious sauce. *but*

   My recipe is never as good as my mother's.

   _____

   _____

   _____

   _____

   _____

   _____

2. Our flight was delayed for two hours.

   Heavy fog had settled over the airport.

   We entertained ourselves by shopping at the airport boutiques.

   _____

   _____

   _____

   _____

   _____

   _____

CONTINUED >

3. The buffet restaurant began offering "all you can eat" meals.

   Many customers left food on their plates.

   The manager started charging a higher price.

   _____

   _____

   _____

   _____

   _____

   _____

ACTIVITY 6: Teamwork

ADVANCED

Combine each group of simple sentences below in two different ways. Follow these guidelines:

- Combine three of the sentences into a complex-compound sentence. Leave the fourth sentence as it is.

- Try dividing the four sentences into two pairs. Then, combine each of these pairs. You will end up with two sentences.

Finally, decide which sentence form you like better—which form expresses the ideas more effectively—and put a check mark beside it.

EXAMPLE:

Ernesto tried out for the college basketball team.

He didn't make it.

The coach said that he could be a substitute at practice.

Ernesto thinks that might improve his skills for next year's tryouts.

When Ernesto tried out for the college basketball team, he didn't make it;

however, the coach said that he could be a substitute at practice. Ernesto

thinks that might improve his skills for next year's tryouts.

Ernesto tried out for the college basketball team; however, he didn't make

it. The coach said that he could be a substitute at practice, and Ernesto

thinks that might improve his skills for next year's tryouts. ✓

1. Stefan's cat Lucy had a fever.

   He took her to the vet's office.

   The veterinarian did not know the cause of the fever.

   He prescribed an antibiotic for Lucy.

_____

_____

_____

_____

_____

_____

2. We needed to repair the front porch of our old house.

The porch was worn and sagging.

Our neighbor recommended a good carpenter.

The carpenter did an excellent job and charged us a reasonable price.

_____

_____

_____

_____

_____

3. Calvin promised his parents that he would never text while driving.

He eventually broke his promise.

One day he nearly hit a young child.

Calvin now leaves his cell phone in the glove compartment when he drives.

_____

_____

_____

_____

_____

_____

_____

ACTIVITY 7: Mastery Test or Teamwork

MASTERY

For each of the paragraphs below, try to achieve the recommended number of combinations. You may use any sentence forms you wish to make the combinations, but try to use a variety of forms. The first combination includes an example.

CONTINUED >

Make four combinations in the paragraph below, including the example.

a. ~~Attending~~ _{Although attending} college while working full-time is difficult. ~~Many~~ _{, many} adults who have full-time day jobs enroll in evening classes. They desire to learn and improve their lives. They make the extra effort to attend classes and do homework. They may be very tired after a long day of work. They find the resolve to drive to campus and stay awake for a two- or three-hour class. However, the results of their efforts are not guaranteed. Many returning adult students never stay in college long enough to earn a degree. For those who do, the sense of pride and accomplishment is unbeatable.

Make nine combinations in the paragraph below.

b. Automobiles were invented more than a century ago. They were used as a practical form of transportation. The automobile has evolved into a statement more of style than of function. Many people view the family minivan as a sign of domestic responsibility. They don't want to be caught driving a minivan. Trucks have long been considered tough and useful. Some truck owners feel capable, powerful, and even manly. It is not unusual to see custom paint jobs and brilliant chrome on trucks. Their owners would never dream of using them as work vehicles. They might get scratched. Some people want to project an image of freedom and youth. They purchase sleek sports cars and convertibles. Then there are the cars that reflect success, wealth, and a certain "coolness." These come with a high price tag. These brands are easily recognizable and often envied by others. These others cannot afford them. For style-conscious drivers, cars have become a kind of personal bumper sticker.

FIX IT: Punctuation Errors in Complex-Compound and Other Sentences

When you speak, most of your listeners are willing to "go with the flow" of your ideas. You use pauses and inflections to signal the end of a thought. It is unlikely that one of your listeners will interrupt you to ask, "Is there a period or a comma after that idea?"

However, when you write, your reader does not have the advantage of your vocal cues to know where one idea ends and another begins. As you know, without **accurate punctuation**, your written ideas may merge together in an unclear and confusing manner.

As you achieve greater sentence variety in your writing, you will also be working to master accurate punctuation in your sentences. You have already seen in this chapter that achieving accurate punctuation is really not the impossible task that many writers assume it is. The following activities will help you review these important punctuation rules and ensure that you use them consistently and correctly.

ACTIVITY 8
MODERATE

For each of the following sentences, add any necessary commas. If a sentence does not require any additional commas, write *correct* on the line provided.

EXAMPLE: Our final exam is scheduled on Wednesday, June 5; however I already bought a ticket to leave for Paris on Monday, June 3.

Our final exam is scheduled on Wednesday, June 5; however,

I already bought a ticket to leave for Paris on Monday, June 3.

1. Although Ms. Ramsey usually conducts the sales meetings, she turned that task over to her assistant.

2. We found the class lectures quite boring, but the textbook was interesting.

3. The suspect has refused to meet with detectives unless her attorney is present.   *Correct*

CONTINUED >

4. Jack wanted to graduate by December; however, he had to drop one of his classes.

_____

_____

5. Even though the motorcycle has 30,000 miles on the odometer, the engine is in remarkably good shape.

_____

_____

ACTIVITY 9

ADVANCED

For each of the following sentences, add any necessary commas.

EXAMPLE: Studying for her math exam until four in the morning Beatrice overslept and missed the exam.

Studying for her math exam until four in the morning, Beatrice

overslept and missed the exam.

1. Grabbing the microphone away from the mayor, an angry citizen faced the crowd and called for the mayor to step down.

_____

_____

2. Winters are very long in Norway, so some Norwegians pass the time by skate-sailing, which is a sport involving ice skates and a large sail.

_____

_____

3. Driving too quickly on the icy road, Matthew felt his truck go into a skid so he turned the steering wheel to correct the skid, and slowly eased up on the accelerator.

_____

_____

_____

4. Our company has made excellent profits this year although it is a new and relatively small company; therefore, we are all proud of our success.

_____

_____

_____

5. Since there are mountains to the north and south of the Columbia River a wind tunnel effect is created, making parts of this river an excellent location for windsurfing.

6. Hoping to deter thieves from breaking into the warehouse, the owners posted signs from a security company even though they had no such service.

7. Driving through Oregon on our road trip last summer, we visited Powell's Books, which is a huge new and used bookstore that covers an entire city block.

8. Although winter snowmobiling is a popular sport, the loud noise frightens wildlife and shatters the natural quiet of the wilderness; therefore, snowmobiles are now banned in many areas.

ACTIVITY 10: Mastery Test or Teamwork

For each of the paragraphs below, add any necessary commas or semicolons.

Find nine missing commas and three missing semicolons.

a. (1) Located in southeastern California the Mojave Desert contains extremes in elevation and climate consequently this region is sometimes referred to as the Devil's Playground. (2) Consisting of about 25,000 square miles the Mojave Desert includes Mount Whitney which is the highest mountain in the contiguous United States. (3) People

CONTINUED >

who climb this mountain often struggle to breathe the thin air near its summit. (4) Contrasting with Mount Whitney's impressive 14,505-foot summit Death Valley has an elevation of 282 feet below sea level therefore it is the lowest elevation in North America. (5) Since this beautiful desert has freezing temperatures as well as very hot temperatures it is common to see both pine trees and cacti here. (6) Because this area has such extreme contrasts it attracts many tourists and photographers in fact U.S. Highway 395 through Owens Valley is one of the most scenic drives in America.

Find 14 missing commas and three missing semicolons.

b. (1) A common theme in popular films is a character's transformation from a corrupt or uncaring person to one with integrity and sensitivity. (2) To see a good example of this transformation theme study the 1992 film titled *Thunderheart*. (3) When the film opens we see FBI agent Ray Levoi who is played by actor Val Kilmer driving into Washington, D.C. (4) Wearing expensive sunglasses and driving a sleek convertible Levoi appears far removed from his mixed roots as a Sioux in fact he denies this heritage because he is ashamed of his alcoholic Sioux father. (5) When Levoi is assigned to help investigate a murder on a Sioux reservation in the Badlands we see Levoi's character slowly change. (6) Levoi initially insists that he is not a member of the Sioux people however a tribe elder recognizes him as the reincarnated Thunderheart who died during the battle of Wounded Knee. (7) As Levoi becomes more involved in the tribe he rejects the corruption of the local FBI office and he sides with the tribe. (8) Levoi's unity with the Sioux people becomes complete when he stands with them against armed FBI agents and other government officials. (9) After the corrupt

agents have been arrested and taken to jail Levoi is free to return

to the Washington, D.C., bureau however he hesitates at the

crossroads leaving the viewer with the impression that he might remain

on the reservation with "his people."

BRINGING IT ALL TOGETHER:
Complex-Compound Sentences and Sentence Variety

In this chapter, you have learned how to build complex-compound sentences and create sentence variety. You have also learned how to avoid punctuation errors that commonly occur with complex-compound and other sentences. Confirm your knowledge by filling in the blank spaces in the following sentences. If you need help, review the pages listed after each sentence.

✔ One way to form a compound sentence is with a _____ and a _____ as glue. (page 472)

✔ Another way to form a compound sentence is with a _____ and a _____ as glue. (page 472)

✔ You can use a subordinating conjunction to form a complex sentence. The subordinating conjunction may be at the _____ of the sentence or in the _____. (page 472)

✔ To form a complex-compound sentence, you can join _____ simple sentences using _____ different types of _____. (page 472)

✔ You can achieve greater sentence variety in your writing by combining simple sentences with five different types of glue. The types of words and phrases that can serve as glue are 1) _____, 2) _____, 3) _____, 4) _____, and 5) _____. (page 479)

CONTINUED >

✔ A crucial difference between successful oral and successful written communication is _____. (page 485)

✔ When you write, you must use accurate _____ to make sure that your readers can follow the flow of your ideas. (page 485)

CHAPTER 22

Creating Parallel Sentences

Before you read this chapter, it's a good idea to test your understanding of parallelism. You may know more than you think.

WHAT DO YOU KNOW?

Circle "Yes" if each sentence below is parallel. Circle "No" if it is not. Then, rewrite the sentence, making it parallel.

1. **To reach the Caribbean, we drove to Boston, flew to Miami, and a boat to Aruba.**

   Yes   No

   Rewrite: _____

2. **The dentist recommended filling a cavity, fitting a crown, and scheduling a root canal.**

   Yes   No

   Rewrite: _____

3. **The new restaurant in town serves seafood, steaks, and you can get sushi too.**

   Yes   No

   Rewrite: _____

4. **Jim is taller than his brother's height.**

   Yes   No

   Rewrite: _____

5. **We will neither sell our vacation home nor buy a new one.**

   Yes   No

   Rewrite: _____

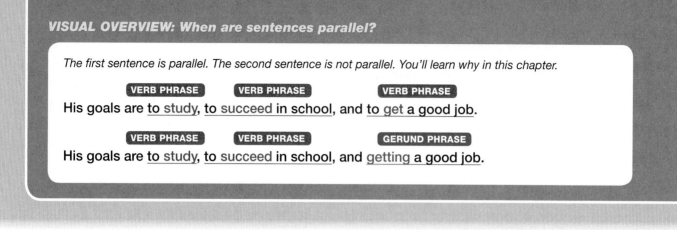

The first sentence is parallel. The second sentence is not parallel. You'll learn why in this chapter.

| VERB PHRASE | VERB PHRASE | VERB PHRASE |

His goals are to study, to succeed in school, and to get a good job.

| VERB PHRASE | VERB PHRASE | GERUND PHRASE |

His goals are to study, to succeed in school, and getting a good job.

BUILD IT: Creating Parallel Sentences

Have you ever set up a row of dominos so that it will fall smoothly and quickly when the first domino is tipped over? If you have, you know that all the dominos must be lined up evenly (parallel) if the trick is going to work. If one domino is *not* lined up evenly (*un*parallel), the dominos will not fall smoothly. They will stop before reaching the end of the row.

Similarly, when you write a sentence that contains a series of items, each of those items must be "lined up" evenly with the others. This means that all of the items must have the *same grammatical structure*. For example, if a series of items in a sentence includes two verbs and one noun, the sentence's structure is not even. Instead, to be even, the sentence must have three verbs. Then it shows correct **parallel** structure.

CREATING PARALLELISM WITH SINGLE-WORD ITEMS

When the items in a sentence are parallel, you can read quickly and smoothly from the beginning of the sentence to the end.

Each of the following sentences contains a series of three single-word items (for example, in the first sentence: *talks, whistles, sings*). As well, in each sentence the items in the series have the same grammatical structure.

| KEY TO BUILDING BLOCKS |
| FOUNDATION WORDS |
| NOUNS |
| VERBS |
| DESCRIPTIVE WORDS |
| ADJECTIVES |
| ADVERBS |
| CONNECTING WORDS |
| PREPOSITIONS |
| CONJUNCTIONS |

| VERB | VERB | VERB |

The parrot talks, whistles, and sings.

| NOUN | NOUN | NOUN |

My old car needs brakes, tires, and a battery.

| ADJECTIVE | ADJECTIVE | ADJECTIVE |

A college professor should be prepared, punctual, and lively.

 **ACTIVITY 1**

EASY

Create a simple sentence using each group of three items. Be sure that your sentence is parallel.

EXAMPLE: juice, coffee, cereal

My favorite breakfast includes juice, coffee, and cereal.

1. tall, blond, handsome

2. pens, pencils, highlighters

3. danced, drank, partied

4. responsible, respectful, hardworking

5. underwear, socks, handkerchiefs

Identify the difficulty level of each activity using the key above.

CREATING PARALLELISM WITH PHRASES

If a sentence contains a list of single-word items (like _vegetables_, _beans_, and _pasta_), the parallelism between them is easy to recognize. However, if a sentence contains a list of phrases (groups of two or more words), the parallelism may be harder to manage. Some common types of phrases to watch out for are prepositional phrases, verb phrases, noun phrases, adjective phrases, and gerund phrases.

In the following examples, each preposition, verb, noun, adjective, or gerund is highlighted while each whole phrase is underlined. These examples are parallel.

Power Tip
For more on nouns, verbs, adjectives, and prepositions, see Chapters 15 and 16.

Parallel Prepositional Phrases

PREPOSITIONAL PHRASE   PREPOSITIONAL PHRASE   PREPOSITIONAL PHRASE

Explorers have traveled <u>around the world</u>, <u>under the sea</u>, and <u>to the moon</u>.

Parallel Verb Phrases

VERB PHRASE

The assignment required students to <u>conduct interviews</u>, <u>collect specimens</u>, and <u>write a lab report</u>.

VERB PHRASE   VERB PHRASE

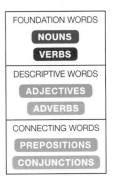

FOUNDATION WORDS
NOUNS
VERBS

DESCRIPTIVE WORDS
ADJECTIVES
ADVERBS

CONNECTING WORDS
PREPOSITIONS
CONJUNCTIONS

Parallel Noun Phrases

NOUN PHRASE   NOUN PHRASE   NOUN PHRASE

Joe's favorite attire is <u>cowboy boots</u>, <u>ripped jeans</u>, and <u>a muscle shirt</u>.

Parallel Adjective Phrases

Boy Scouts must be respectful **ADJECTIVE PHRASE** to others and their leader, mindful **ADJECTIVE PHRASE** of their surroundings, and neat **ADJECTIVE PHRASE** in their appearance and uniform.

Parallel Gerund Phrases

This summer, we plan on painting **GERUND PHRASE** the house, planting **GERUND PHRASE** a garden, and building **GERUND PHRASE** a deck.

ACTIVITY 2

MODERATE

Create a sentence using each group of three items. Follow these steps:

- Write out the sentence.
- Underline the first word of each phrase to ensure that your sentence is parallel. (Note: If the phrases in a sentence are noun phrases, underline the main noun in each phrase instead.)
- Then, write one of the following terms to identify the type of phrases used in the sentence: *prepositional phrases, verb phrases, noun phrases, adjective phrases, gerund phrases.*

EXAMPLE: traveled to Paris, climbed the Eiffel Tower, fell in love

Last summer, my cousin traveled to Paris, climbed the Eiffel Tower, and fell in love.

Type of phrases: verb phrases

1. in my backpack, under my desk, on the floor

_____

_____

Type of phrases: _____

2. unpleasant in the morning, approachable during the day, delightful in the evening

_____

_____

Type of phrases: _____

3. ordered wine, toasted our anniversary, kissed each other

_____

_____

Type of phrases: _____

4. applying for a home loan, buying a house, moving in

_____

_____

Type of phrases: _____

5. an old laptop, a broken iPod, a cheap cell phone

_____

_____

Type of phrases: _____

CREATING PARALLELISM IN COMPARISONS

In some sentences, we compare two items such as _my final exam in Algebra_ and _a bad dream_ by including words commonly used to make comparisons such as _like, as (as . . . as), than, similar to, in the same way that,_ and so on. For example, _Her eyes were as blue as cornflowers._ (Note that the word _than_ is often paired with an adjective: _more than, less than, better than,_ etc.)

Items being compared may be single-word items or phrases, but they should always be parallel since they have equal value in the sentence. In other words, the comparisons should have the same grammatical structure. Take a look:

Parallel Comparisons with Noun Phrases

NOUN PHRASE   NOUN PHRASE

My final exam in Algebra was (similar to) a bad dream.

Parallel Comparisons with Adjective Phrases

ADJECTIVE PHRASE

Police officers need to be (as) sensitive to community issues (as) they are

serious about crimes.

ADJECTIVE PHRASE

Parallel Comparisons with Gerund Phrases

GERUND PHRASE   GERUND PHRASE

Owning your own home is (like) having your own castle.

ACTIVITY 3
ADVANCED

Create a sentence using each pair of items. Follow these steps:

- Write out the sentence, using one of the following comparative expressions: _like, as (as . . . . as), similar to, than (more than, less than, better than,_ etc.).

CONTINUED >

- Underline the first word of each phrase to ensure that your sentence is parallel. (Note: If the phrases in a sentence are noun phrases, underline the main noun in each phrase instead.)
- Circle the word or words that show the paired expression.
- Then, write one of the following terms to identify the type of phrases used in the sentence: *prepositional phrases, verb phrases, noun phrases, adjective phrases, gerund phrases*.

EXAMPLE: a well-carved pumpkin, a work of art

A well-carved <u>pumpkin</u> is (like) a <u>work</u> of art.

Type of phrases: noun phrases

1. eating dark chocolate, experiencing ecstasy

Type of phrases: _____

2. powerful song, medicine for the soul

Type of phrases: _____

3. falling in love, winning the lottery

Type of phrases: _____

4. a selfish adult, a spoiled child

Type of phrases: _____

5. graduating from college, fulfilling a dream

Type of phrases: _____

CREATING PARALLELISM WITH PAIRED EXPRESSIONS

In English, there are some paired expressions that require parallelism. These expressions link to equal elements in the sentence and show the relationship between them. Five of these paired expressions are:

either . . . or
neither . . . nor
both . . . and
not only . . . but also
rather . . . than

When you use the first part of a paired expression, be sure you always use the second part, too. Otherwise, your sentence might not make sense. The following paired expressions are parallel.

Parallel Prepositional Phrases

PREPOSITIONAL PHRASE   PREPOSITIONAL PHRASE

My parents will buy their new home (either) in the desert (or) on the coast.

Parallel Verb Phrases

VERB PHRASE

For our geology project, we would (rather) collect minerals (than) photograph rock strata.

VERB PHRASE

Parallel Noun Phrases

NOUN PHRASE   NOUN PHRASE

(Neither) the professor's weekly lectures (nor) her midterm and final exams are especially difficult.

Parallel Adjective Phrases

ADJECTIVE PHRASE   ADJECTIVE PHRASE

My new boyfriend is (both) easy on the eyes (and) gentle on the spirit.

Parallel Gerund Phrases

GERUND PHRASE

For relaxation, Janine enjoys (not only) going to the beach (but also) watching a movie.

GERUND PHRASE

ACTIVITY 4
ADVANCED

Create a sentence using each pair of items. Follow these steps:

- Write out the sentence, using one of the paired expressions: *either . . . or*, *neither . . . nor*, *both . . . and*, *not only . . . but also*, *rather . . . than*.
- Underline the first word of each phrase to ensure that your sentence is parallel. (Note: If the phrases in a sentence are noun phrases, underline the main noun in each phrase instead.)
- Circle the words that show the paired expression.
- Then, write one of the following terms to identify the type of phrases used in the sentence: *prepositional phrases*, *verb phrases*, *noun phrases*, *adjective phrases*, *gerund phrases*.

CONTINUED >

EXAMPLE: preparing several days in advance, reviewing at the last minute

For tests, Albert likes (not only) <u>preparing</u> several days in advance (but also) <u>reviewing</u> at the last minute.

Type of phrases: gerund phrases

1. tried out for the basketball team, applied for an athletic scholarship

   _____

   Type of phrases: _____

2. going to the beach, going to class

   _____

   Type of phrases: _____

3. in the morning, in the afternoon

   _____

   Type of phrases: _____

4. true to his friends, true to himself

   _____

   Type of phrases: _____

5. lucky in love, lucky in business

   _____

   Type of phrases: _____

FIX IT: Correcting Faulty Parallelism

When the items in a sentence are not parallel, you cannot read quickly and smoothly from the beginning of the sentence to the end, and your understanding may be interrupted. You may wonder what the writer is trying to say, or the sentence might sound awkward.

FIXING FAULTY PARALLELISM WITH PHRASES

As you know, some common types of phrases are prepositional phrases, verb phrases, noun phrases, adjective phrases, and gerund phrases. When these are not parallel, they can be harder to recognize because they involve more words. One easy way to identify them is to ask if the same part of speech (preposition, noun, verb, etc.) starts each phrase. If the answer is no, then you probably have a faulty sentence.

Prepositional Phrases Not Parallel

| PREPOSITIONAL PHRASE | PREPOSITIONAL PHRASE | NOUN PHRASE |

Global warming affects life on the land, in the air, and the sea.

Parallel

| PREPOSITIONAL PHRASE | PREPOSITIONAL PHRASE | PREPOSITIONAL PHRASE |

Global warming affects life on the land, in the air, and in the sea.

Verb Phrases Not Parallel

VERB PHRASE   VERB PHRASE

Marco has a law degree, runs his own business, and

studying political science at night.

GERUND PHRASE

Parallel

VERB PHRASE   VERB PHRASE

Marco has a law degree, runs his own business, and

is studying political science at night.

VERB PHRASE

Noun Phrases Not Parallel

NOUN PHRASE   NOUN PHRASE

The Marine wore a combat helmet, a tactical vest, and

had ballistic goggles.

VERB PHRASE

Parallel

NOUN PHRASE   NOUN PHRASE   NOUN PHRASE

The Marine wore a combat helmet, a tactical vest, and ballistic goggles.

Adjective Phrases Not Parallel

ADJECTIVE PHRASE   ADJECTIVE PHRASE

Successful students are regular in their class attendance, respectful to

their teachers, and cooperate with their classmates.

VERB PHRASE

Parallel

ADJECTIVE PHRASE

Successful students are regular in their class attendance,

respectful to their teachers, and cooperative with their classmates.

ADJECTIVE PHRASE   ADJECTIVE PHRASE

Gerund Phrases Not Parallel

GERUND PHRASE

Three strategies that improved my grades were <u>studying</u> with classmates, <u>meeting</u> with the professor, and active before exams.

GERUND PHRASE   ADJECTIVE PHRASE

Parallel

GERUND PHRASE

Three strategies that improved my grades were <u>studying</u> with classmates, <u>meeting</u> with the professor, and <u>exercising</u> before exams.

GERUND PHRASE   GERUND PHRASE

ACTIVITY 5

MODERATE

In each of the following sentences, underline the item that is not parallel. Then, rewrite the sentence, changing the nonparallel item so that it is parallel with the other two items. Finally, write the type of phrases that are used in the sentence with parallelism.

EXAMPLE: My class moved from the Administration Building to the Library Building and <u>finally the Science Building</u>.

My class moved from the Administration Building to the Library

Building and finally to the Science Building.

Type of phrases: prepositional phrases

1. The Tour de France bicycle race goes through towns, over mountains, and the coast.

    _____

    _____

    Type of phrases: _____

2. On weekends, my wife and I like eating at our favorite restaurant, shopping at the mall, and a picnic in the park.

    _____

    _____

    Type of phrases: _____

3. Our babysitter plays with the kids, bakes cookies with them, and bedtime stories are a must.

    _____

    _____

    Type of phrases: _____

4. Paris is our favorite European city because it has great museums, the cafés are romantic, and beautiful sights.

_____

_____

Type of phrases: _____

5. Newlyweds should be sensitive to their partner's needs, responsible about money, and help with housecleaning.

_____

_____

Type of phrases: _____

FIXING FAULTY PARALLELISM IN COMPARISONS

When you compare two or more things, be sure to have the same grammatical structure on both sides of the comparison. Otherwise, the sentence will not make sense.

Gerund Phrases Not Parallel

> `GERUND PHRASE`
> Owning your own home is (like) your own castle.

Parallel

> `GERUND PHRASE`   `GERUND PHRASE`
> Owning your own home is (like) having your own castle.

Remember that the items being compared may be single-word items or phrases (prepositional phrases, verb phrases, noun phrases, adjective phrases, or gerund phrases).

ADVANCED   **ACTIVITY 6**

Revise each of the sentences below for correct parallelism. Do the following for each item:

- First, circle the word or words that are used to make the comparison: *like, as . . . as, similar to*.

- Second, underline the two items that are being compared. If these items are phrases, be sure to underline all the words that make up each phrase.

CONTINUED >

- Third, decide whether you want to change the first item or the second item.
- Fourth, rewrite the sentence to make the two items parallel.
- Last, write the type of phrase that is used in the sentence with parallelism.

EXAMPLE: Paying five dollars a gallon for gas is (like) robbery.

Paying five dollars a gallon for gas is like getting robbed.

Type of phrases: *gerund phrases*

1. Winning the lottery is like a lightning strike: The odds of either happening to you are slim.

Type of phrases: _____

2. Resort vacations are as fabulously luxurious as they are an outrageous expense.

Type of phrases: _____

3. Modern skyscrapers in New York are similar to seeing ancient pyramids in Egypt.

Type of phrases: _____

4. Einstein was as hardworking and determined as he had a lot of intelligence and creativity.

Type of phrases: _____

5. Learning French is similar to Spanish because they are both Romance languages.

Type of phrases: _____

FIXING FAULTY PARALLELISM IN PAIRED EXPRESSIONS

In paired expressions, you are looking to create parallel structure in all parts of speech. In addition, if you leave off the first or the second part of the expression (*either . . . or, neither . . . nor,* etc.), you may end up with an unbalanced sentence.

Gerund Phrases Not Parallel

> **GERUND PHRASE**
>
> For relaxation, Janine enjoys (not only) the beach (but also) watching a movie.

Parallel

> **GERUND PHRASE**
>
> For relaxation, Janine enjoys (not only) going to the beach (but also) watching a movie.
>
> **GERUND PHRASE**

ACTIVITY 7

ADVANCED

Revise each of the sentences below for correct parallelism. Do the following for each item:

- First, circle the paired expression used in the sentence.
- Second, underline the two items being paired. If these items are phrases, be sure to underline all the words that make up each phrase.
- Third, decide whether you want to change the first item or the second item.
- Fourth, rewrite the sentence to make the two items parallel.
- Last, write the type of phrases that are used in the sentence with parallelism.

EXAMPLE: For our daily vegetables, we can (both) drink vegetable juice (and) leafy greens.

For our daily vegetables, we can both drink vegetable juice and eat leafy greens.

Type of phrases: verb phrases

CONTINUED >

1. The sporting goods store has neither camping equipment nor stocks bug repellent.

_____

Type of phrases: _____

2. Denise would rather work part-time than a big college debt.

_____

Type of phrases: _____

3. The cruise ship not only has a water slide but also bowling is free.

_____

Type of phrases: _____

4. The college gym has both free weights and you can do cardio training.

_____

Type of phrases: _____

5. We would rather plant a cactus garden than watering roses all the time.

_____

Type of phrases: _____

ACTIVITY 8: Mastery Test or Teamwork

MASTERY

In the following paragraphs, underline each sentence that contains items that are not parallel. Then, rewrite each sentence below, making it parallel. Remember to decide which item you will change before attempting to rewrite the sentence.

Find two sentences that are not parallel.

a. (1) Libraries are valuable assets to their communities. (2) They exist to provide their communities with access to books, CDs, movies, and there are also computers. (3) Patrons can read books, browse the Internet, or search online for jobs. (4) Those who cannot afford to take college classes have access to reference books, can check out textbooks, and free online courses. (5) There are books and software programs to help people learn how to knit, cook, or fix a bicycle.

_____

_____

_____

Find three sentences that are not parallel.

    b. (6) Libraries provide not only education and entertainment but also offering social opportunities. (7) Many libraries have special programs for teens and senior citizens. (8) Both teens and seniors benefit from interacting with their peers, learning about new books, and they develop computer skills. (9) Some libraries have very colorful and active children's sections. (10) These allow children to have fun either playing with friends or quiet reading.

_____

_____

_____

_____

_____

_____

BRINGING IT ALL TOGETHER:
Creating Parallel Sentences

In this chapter, you have learned how to write clear and correct parallel sentences. Confirm your knowledge by filling in the blank spaces in the following sentences. If you need help, review the pages listed after each sentence.

✔ When you write a sentence that contains a series of items, all those items must be _____. (page 492)

✔ In a sentence with correct parallelism, all items in a series must have the same _____. For example, if the series includes two verbs and one noun, this sentence is not parallel; the series must have three verbs for the sentence to be "even," or parallel. (page 492)

✔ When writing parallel sentences, some common types of phrases to watch out for are _____ phrases, _____ phrases, _____ phrases, _____ phrases, and _____ phrases. (page 493)

CONTINUED >

✔ In English, there are certain paired expressions that require parallelism. Five of these paired expressions are 1) _____,
2) _____, 3) _____, 4) _____,
and 5) _____. (page 496)

✔ If an item in a list is not parallel (does not have the same grammatical structure as the others), this error is called _____
parallelism. (page 498)

CHAPTER 23

Using Verbs Correctly

Before you read this chapter, it's a good idea to test your understanding of verbs. You may know more than you think.

WHAT DO YOU KNOW?

Circle "Yes" if each word group below is a complete, correct sentence. Circle "No" if it is incorrect. If "No," explain the problem.

1. **Recently, my sister and I go on a cruise to Mexico.**

   Yes   No

   Explanation: _____

2. **If I were you, I would of taken the job in Dallas.**

   Yes   No

   Explanation: _____
   _____

3. **The condition of the roads are poor.**

   Yes   No

   Explanation: _____
   _____

4. **Benjamin always does a good job when he landscapes yards.**

   Yes   No

   Explanation: _____
   _____

5. **We waited nearly an hour for our food, and the waiter does not even apologize.**

   Yes   No

   Explanation: _____
   _____

Verbs tell us when something happens or happened. You'll learn more details in this chapter.

PRESENT TENSE

The students study.

PAST TENSE

The students studied.

BUILD IT: Sentences with Correct Verbs

As you learned in Chapter 16, **verbs** often express actions, although some verbs have other functions. In this chapter, you will learn about how verbs change form to express different times, and you will also learn about some problems that can occur with verbs.

RECOGNIZING STANDARD AND NONSTANDARD VERBS

When we speak, we sometimes use *nonstandard English*, which does not follow the rules of written academic English. Take a look at this example:

NONSTANDARD ENGLISH	Trisha be a vegetarian. She don't eat meat.
STANDARD ENGLISH	Trisha is a vegetarian. She doesn't eat meat.

You may hear nonstandard English in conversation, television shows, movies, and music. Rap and hip-hop artists, for example, often mix standard and nonstandard English in their songs. Look at the lyrics of "Hard Times," by hip-hop group Run-D.M.C. (Nonstandard verbs—and their standard versions—appear in red.)

(standard English: are spreading)

Hard times spreading just like the flu

Watch out, homeboy, don't let it catch you

P-p-prices go up, don't let your pocket go down

(standard English: have)

When you got short money you're stuck on the ground

Turn around, get ready, keep your eye on the prize

And be on point for the future shock

Hard times are coming to your town

So stay alert, don't let them get you down

They tell you times are tough, you hear that times are hard

But when you work for that ace you know you pulled the right card

Hard times got our pockets all in chains   (standard English: have)

I'll tell you what, homeboy, it don't have my brain   (standard English: doesn't)

All day I have to work at my peak

Because I need that dollar every day of the week

Hard times can take you on a natural trip

So keep your balance, and don't you slip

Hard times is nothing new on me   (standard English: are)

I'm gonna use my strong mentality   (standard English: going to)

Like the cream of the crop, like the crop of the cream

B-b-beating hard times, that is my theme

Hard times in life, hard times in death

I'm gonna keep on fighting to my very last breath   (standard English: going to)

This song communicates a powerful message, and Run-D.M.C. shows that breaking the rules of grammar can sometimes be empowering in our personal and artistic lives. However, if you know *only* nonstandard English, you may be limiting your opportunities for both personal and professional success.

Standard English (which follows the rules of written academic English) helps you to express your ideas with great precision and clarity, and it is the form of English expected in most school and work settings. Therefore, as a college writer, you should commit to learning and using standard English. Doing so will help you achieve academic success and allow you to communicate more effectively in your personal and professional lives.

If you are more comfortable with nonstandard English than with standard English, you can improve your academic writing simply by focusing on verbs, as you'll do in this chapter.

KEY TO BUILDING BLOCKS

FOUNDATION WORDS

NOUNS
VERBS

DESCRIPTIVE WORDS

ADJECTIVES
ADVERBS

CONNECTING WORDS

PREPOSITIONS
CONJUNCTIONS

BUILD IT: Basic Verb Usage, Present and Past Tenses

As you have learned, every sentence must have a subject and a verb. The verb must be in the correct form to match

- the tense (time) of the action in a sentence *and*
- the subject. (More on this later.)

The simple present tense is used for

- regular actions (*I **take** the train every day*),
- facts (*Jonas **likes** rich desserts*), and
- feelings experienced right now and certain actions happening right now (*We **feel** exhausted. I **hear** the doorbell*).

The simple past tense is used for actions completed in the past (*I **walked** four miles every day*).

The correct form of a verb is determined by the spelling. About 90 percent of all verb problems are caused by two simple errors: the absence or unnecessary addition of an *-s* or an *-ed* ending. You will learn more about these problems and other common mistakes later in this chapter.

USING THE PRESENT TENSE

Again, the simple present tense is used for regular actions, for facts, and for feelings and some actions at the present moment. Present tense verbs follow a very simple spelling rule. Take a look:

Grabbing onto the Slippery -s

Notice that the only difference in the two forms of the verb *play* is that an *-s* comes at the end when the subject is *he, she,* or *it* (or some equivalent). We call this "the slippery *-s*" because, like a snake or a lizard, it can slip out of sight easily when we are not paying attention. Most students know how to spell verbs in the present tense, but they sometimes forget to write the *-s*. (And sometimes they add it when it's not needed.) Because the slippery *-s* is a major cause of verb errors, you should grab ahold of it in your mind and not let go.

The Slippery -s

░███ ACTIVITY 1
EASY

For each sentence below, do the following:

- In the space provided, write the correct present tense form of the verb in parentheses.
- If the verb ends in -s, circle the *s* or mark it with a highlighter.

EXAMPLE: Miranda _____read(s)_____ (read) the newspaper every morning.

1. Ramon _____ (eat) grapefruit for breakfast every morning.

2. Our neighbor _____ (own) a beautiful sailboat.

3. The students _____ (enjoy) sentence-combining exercises.

4. Carly _____ (walk) to work every day.

5. The Joneses _____ (live) in a four-story house.

KEY TO CHALLENGE METER
WARMUP
EASY
MODERATE
ADVANCED
MASTERY

Identify the difficulty level of each activity using the key above.

Recognizing Irregular Present Tense Verbs: Be, Have, *and* Do

You should be aware of three "irregular" verbs that we use frequently. These verbs are irregular because they follow spelling rules that are different from the rules for regular verbs (like *play*, *walk*, and *bake*). Fortunately, most students use and spell them correctly.

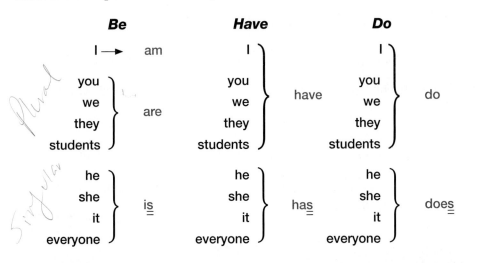

Notice that the slippery **-s** is found in the same place for these irregular verbs.

Power Tip
Often, the *-s* ending moves from the verb to the subject when the subject becomes plural.

Singular Subject: The girl plays.

Plural Subject: The girls play.

You will have to add an *-es* instead of an *-s* to the end of some verbs, such as those that end in *-ch* or *-sh*: *teach →
teaches*; *catch →
catches*; *fish → fishes*;
wish → wishes.

ACTIVITY 2
MODERATE

For the passage below, do the following:

• In the spaces provided, write the correct present tense forms of the verbs in parentheses.

• If a verb ends in *-s*, circle the *s* or mark it with a highlighter.

The first space in the passage has been filled in for you.

(1) Why _____are_____ (be) parents and teachers so afraid

of allowing children to fail? (2) Failure ___has___ (have) its

CONTINUED >

Power Tip
In everyday speech, we sometimes leave out *be* verbs (*am/is/are/was/were*). Avoid this error in your writing.

Incorrect: *I sick.*
          He happy.

Revised: *I am sick.*
          He is happy.

For more practice with irregular present tense verbs, go to **bedfordstmartins.com /touchstones.**

benefits. (3) Occasionally, children _____*do*_____ (do) not put forth

sufficient effort on a task or an assignment. (4) In this case, failure

_____*is*_____ (be) a natural consequence that teaches children

responsibility and accountability. (5) In other cases, when children

_____*do*_____ (do) their best work and still fail, they learn three

things. (6) First, they learn that not everything ___*is*___ (be)

easy for them. (7) Second, they learn that they ___*have*___

(have) weaknesses. (8) Awareness ___*is*___ (be) the first step

in improving that weakness. (9) Third, if they still fail after trying again

and again, they learn that, like everyone else, they ___*have*___

(have) limitations. (10) Limitations ___*are*___ (be) opportunities

to learn alternative methods of success. (11) A parent or teacher who

shields children from failure ___*does*___ (do) not allow them to

develop valuable educational, coping, and compensation skills.

(12) Failure _____*is*_____ (be) not a bad thing. (13) Failure

___*has*___ (have) a way of teaching us important lessons.

Power Tip
If English is not your first language, see Appendix A for special advice on verb usage and other grammar topics.

USING THE PAST TENSE

Again, the simple past tense is used for actions completed in the past (*I **walked** four miles every day*). All regular past tense verbs follow a simple rule. Take a look:

Power Tip
Remember these spelling points:

If a verb ends in *e*, you usually add just a *d* to form the past tense.

If a verb ends in a consonant (*b, c, d, f, g,* and so on), both the *e* and the *d* must be added.

A final *y* usually must change to *i* before *ed* is added, unless a vowel precedes the *y* — for example, *convey* → *conveyed.*

Base Form		Past Tense
look		look__ed__
laugh	+ ed	laugh__ed__
spell		spell__ed__
love		lov__ed__
type	+ d	typ__ed__
refuse		refus__ed__
cry		cr__ied__
try	– y + ied	tr__ied__
marry		marr__ied__

For more practice with regular past tense verbs, go to **bedfordstmartins.com /touchstones**.

Keeping an Eye on the Elusive -ed

Notice that all of these verbs—regardless of their present tense spelling—end in *-ed* in the past tense. Most students know this, but they may forget to add the *-ed*. (Often, they *hear* the *-ed* in their head, but they don't *see* that it's missing on the page.) For this reason, we call this the "elusive *-ed*." Like the "slippery *-s*," it is a major cause of verb errors, so remember to keep a close eye on it in your writing.

elusive: difficult to see, find, or grasp

ACTIVITY 3
EASY

For each sentence below, write the correct past tense form of the verb in parentheses.

EXAMPLE: On July 20, 1969, two American astronauts ___landed___ (land) the *Apollo 11* spacecraft on the surface of the moon.

1. The *Apollo 11* mission was ___lanched___ (launch) from the Kennedy Space Center in Florida on July 16, 1969.

2. The crew ___included___ (include) Neil Armstrong, Edwin "Buzz" Aldrin Jr., and Michael Collins.

3. Michael Collins, the command module pilot, ___remained___ (remain) in orbit while Armstrong and Aldrin landed the lunar module on the moon's surface.

4. The lunar module was ___called___ (call) *Eagle*.

5. When Neil Armstrong ___stepped___ (step) onto the moon's surface, he said the famous words, "That's one small step for (a) man, one giant leap for mankind."

6. Armstrong and Aldrin ___explored___ (explore) the moon's surface for more than 21 hours.

7. In addition, the astronauts ___collected___ (collect) nearly 50 pounds of lunar rocks.

8. The astronauts ___returned___ (return) to Earth on July 24, 1969.

9. With the aid of parachutes, their capsule ___slashed___ (splash) down in the Pacific Ocean.

10. The three astronauts were ___honored___ (honor) as American heroes.

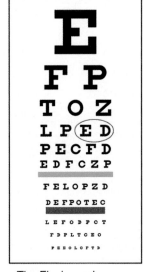

The Elusive -ed

IRREGULAR PAST TENSE VERBS

Now it is time to prepare for some memorization work. Many past tense verbs have an "irregular" form that is not spelled with an *-ed* ending. Some of these irregular spellings you already know by heart. The following chart shows many of the most common irregular past tense verbs.

Irregular Past Tense Verbs

BASE FORM	PAST TENSE FORM	BASE FORM	PAST TENSE FORM	BASE FORM	PAST TENSE FORM
be	was/were	have	had	send	sent
become	became	hear	heard	set	set
begin	began	hide	hid	shake	shook
bite	bit	hold	held	show	showed
blow	blew	hurt	hurt	shrink	shrank
break	broke	keep	kept	shut	shut
bring	brought	know	knew	sing	sang
build	built	lay (*to put down*)	laid	sink	sank
buy	bought			sit	sat
catch	caught	lead	led	sleep	slept
choose	chose	leave	left	speak	spoke
come	came	let	let	spend	spent
cost	cost	lie (*to recline*)	lay	spring	sprang
dive	dived, dove	light	lit	stand	stood
do	did	lose	lost	steal	stole
draw	drew	make	made	stick	stuck
drink	drank	mean	meant	sting	stung
drive	drove	meet	met	strike	struck
eat	ate	pay	paid	swim	swam
fall	fell	put	put	take	took
feed	fed	quit	quit	teach	taught
feel	felt	read	read	tear	tore
fight	fought	ride	rode	tell	told
find	found	ring	rang	think	thought
fly	flew	rise	rose	throw	threw
freeze	froze	run	ran	understand	understood
get	got	say	said	wake	woke, waked
give	gave	see	saw	wear	wore
go	went	seek	sought	win	won
grow	grew	sell	sold	write	wrote

ACTIVITY 4
MODERATE

First, read the passage below. Then, in the spaces provided, write the correct past tense forms of the verbs in parentheses. If necessary, you may refer to the chart above; however, try to complete the activity first using your own knowledge.

The first space in the passage has been filled in for you.

For more practice with irregular past tense verbs, go to **bedfordstmartins.com /touchstones**.

(1) In 1983, Sally Ride _____became_____ (become) the first American woman in space on the shuttle *Challenger*. (2) In a way, fortune ___chose___ (choose) Ride's career as an astronaut for her. (3) In 1976, Ride ___heard___ (hear) about NASA's open call for new astronauts. (4) Along with 8,000 other hopefuls, Ride ___put___ (put) in an application. (5) Happily, she ___got___ (get) selected, one of just six women who ___won___ (win) the prestigious opportunity to become an astronaut. (6) In 1977, Ride ___began___ (begin) her official training with NASA. (7) She ___spent___ (spend) an intensive year in training, learning many exciting new skills. (8) For example, she ___flew___ (fly) an aircraft for the first time and loved it so much that flying ___became___ (become) a favorite hobby. (9) She ___drove___ (dive) from 13,000 feet in a parachute. (10) She ___went___ (go) through gravity and weightlessness training. (11) She ___swam___ (swim) long distances in bulky gear to learn water survival techniques. (12) Before actually going into space, Ride also ___held___ (hold) the position of communications officer for the shuttle *Columbia*'s second and third flights. (13) She ___sent___ (send) messages from mission control to the shuttle crews in space. (14) In addition, Dr. Ride was part of a team that ___built___ (build) a remote mechanical arm for handling satellites in space. (15) Finally, in 1983, she ___rode___ (ride) into space for the first time on the shuttle *Challenger*. (16) One year later, she ___made___ (make) her second flight, again on the *Challenger*. (17) Unfortunately, her third mission was put on hold after the *Challenger* disaster in 1986, which ___shook___ (shake)

CONTINUED >

Power Tip
To help you memorize irregular past tense verb forms, you can use a number of proven strategies, such as priority lists, visual aids, auditory aids, and tactile aids. For more information on these strategies, visit **bedfordstmartins .com/touchstones**.

the world. (18) As a result of the disaster, NASA _____ put

(put) the shuttle program on hold, and Ride _____ took _____ (take)

an administrative position with NASA's long-range planning team in

Washington, D.C. (19) One year later, Ride _____ quit _____ (quit)

her job at NASA to become a Science Fellow at Stanford University.

(20) In total, Ride _____ had _____ (have) 343 cumulative hours of

space flight and will always be remembered as America's first female

astronaut.

FIX IT: Common Verb Problems

The following sections discuss some errors that often occur with use of the present and past tenses.

SUBJECT-VERB AGREEMENT ERRORS

A verb is said to "agree" with its subject when it is in the correct form for that subject according to the rules of English grammar. As you have already learned, when the subject is *he, she,* or *it* (or some equivalent of *he, she,* or *it,* such as *Jonas* or *the iPod*), the verb must end in **-s** in the present tense (*play***s***).

Making sure that verbs agree with their subjects can be tricky in certain instances, such as with the verbs *be, have,* and *do* (see page 511). Here, we'll look at some other situations where agreement problems may occur. As you'll see, these errors are often made in the present tense.

Verbs Separated from the Subject

As you learned in earlier chapters, words or word groups often separate the subject of a sentence from its verb. Let's look at some examples.

> **PREPOSITIONAL PHRASE**
> The roses <u>in the crystal vase</u> look wilted.

For more on prepositional phrases, see Chapter 16.

> **DESCRIPTIVE CLAUSE**
> The technician <u>who fills my prescriptions</u> has found a less expensive medication.

For more on descriptive clauses, see Chapter 19.

MODIFYING PHRASE

The students, <u>growing restless</u>, steal glances at the clock.

For more on modifying phrases, see Chapter 20.

When words come between the subject and the verb, you need to make the verb agree with the subject, not with the word that comes right before the verb. Crossing out prepositional phrases, descriptive clauses, modifying phrases, and other such word groups can help you identify the subject and its verb. Take a look:

Power Tip
On pages 516–21, only subjects (not other nouns) are highlighted in blue.

INCORRECT   The report on last year's sales are now available.

          [*IT* EQUIVALENT]   [*-S* ENDING ON VERB]

REVISED   The report ~~on last year's sales~~ is now available.

The subject of the sentence is *report*, not *sales*, as we can see by crossing out the prepositional phrase. The verb *is* agrees with *report*.

ACTIVITY 5

MODERATE

For each sentence below, do the following:

- Cross out any prepositional phrases, descriptive clauses, or modifying phrases.
- Underline the subject, and circle the verb.
- If the verb agrees with the subject, write "OK" in the space provided.
- If the verb does not agree with the subject, rewrite the sentence in the space provided, using the correct form of the verb.

EXAMPLE: The <u>cost</u> ~~of these shoes~~ (are) unusually high.

      The cost of these shoes is unusually high.

1. One of the employees have problems getting to work on time.

2. The story that you read to the students were hilarious.

3. That set of crystal looks very expensive.

4. The student who's always dropping his books disturb the whole class.

5. The mayor, getting annoyed at the personal questions about his finances, snap at the reporters.

Verbs before the Subject

In some sentences, the verb comes before the subject. For example, such reversals happen in questions and in statements that begin with *There is* or *There are.*

Take a look at the following questions:

Where is my cell **phone?**

Who are your college **professors?**

The subjects are the words in blue, not *Who* or *Where.* If you are confused about how to identify subjects in questions, turn the questions around:

> ┌──────────────┐ ┌──────────────┐
> │ *IT*   │ │ **-S ENDING**│
> │ **EQUIVALENT**│ │ **ON VERB** │
> └──────────────┘ └──────────────┘

My cell phone is . . .

> ┌──────────────┐ ┌──────────────┐
> │ *THEY*   │ │ **NO -S ENDING**│
> │ **EQUIVALENT**│ │ **ON VERB** │
> └──────────────┘ └──────────────┘

Your college professors are . . .

As we can see, the subjects and verbs in these examples agree. Now, take a look at the following statements:

There is a large **tear** on that shirt.

There are several good **restaurants** in town.

Again, the subjects here are blue. If you are confused about how to identify subjects in statements that begin with *There is* or *There are,* turn the statements around:

> ┌──────────────┐ ┌──────────────┐
> │ *IT*   │ │ **-S ENDING**│
> │ **EQUIVALENT**│ │ **ON VERB** │
> └──────────────┘ └──────────────┘

A large tear is on that shirt.

> ┌──────────────┐ ┌──────────────┐
> │ *THEY*   │ │ **NO -S ENDING**│
> │ **EQUIVALENT**│ │ **ON VERB** │
> └──────────────┘ └──────────────┘

Several good restaurants are in town.

As we can see, the subjects and verbs in these examples agree.

ACTIVITY 6

MODERATE

For each sentence below, do the following:

- Underline the subject, and circle the verb. If you have trouble identifying the subject, you may want to turn the question or statement around.

- If the verb agrees with the subject, write "OK" in the space provided.

- If the verb does not agree with the subject, rewrite the sentence in the space provided, using the correct form of the verb.

For more practice on subject-verb agreement, go to **bedfordstmartins.com /touchstones**.

EXAMPLE: There (is) several reasons for my current financial situation.
<u>There are several reasons for my current financial situation.</u>

1. What is your favorite movies?

   _____

2. Here is the French fries that you ordered.

   _____

3. Where are your grandparents from?

   _____

4. There is many ways to approach this project.

   _____

5. Who is the top candidates in the presidential race?

   _____

Verbs with Compound Subjects

As you learned in Chapter 17, **compound subjects** consist of more than one subject. Often, compound subjects are joined with the conjunction *and*. Take a look:

[COMPOUND SUBJECT]
Maria **and** Edward exercise **regularly.**

However, if *or* is used as the conjunction, the verb needs to agree with the subject that is closest to the verb. Consider these examples:

[*THEY* EQUIVALENT] [NO -*S* ENDING ON VERB]
My father **or my** <u>brothers</u> open **the store in the morning.**

[*HE/SHE* EQUIVALENT] [-*S* ENDING ON VERB]
My brothers **or my** <u>father</u> opens **the store in the morning.**

[*HE/SHE* EQUIVALENT] [-*S* ENDING ON VERB]
My sister, brothers, **or** father opens **the store in the morning.**

ACTIVITY 7
EASY

For each sentence below, do the following:

- In the space provided, write the correct present tense form of the verb in parentheses.
- If the verb ends in -*s,* circle the *s* or mark it with a highlighter.

CONTINUED >

EXAMPLE: Matt or Dante _____*is*_____ (be) responsible for the budget report.

1. Paul and Paula ____*are*____ (be) the only set of fraternal twins in the family.

2. The tomatoes and the corn ____*needs*____ (need) to be picked.

3. A baked potato or rice ____*goes*____ (go) well with roasted chicken.

4. Brad, Denise, and Raul ____*belong*____ (belong) to a travel club.

5. The chef or the restaurant owner _____ (recommend) a good wine with the entrée.

Indefinite Pronoun Subjects

Indefinite pronouns refer to general people or things. Most indefinite pronouns, like those in the following list, take the *he/she/it* form of the verb; in other words, there is an *-s* at the end of the verb.

anybody	**everyone**	**one**
anyone	**everything**	**somebody**
anything	**neither**	**someone**
each	**no one**	**something**
either	**nobody**	
everybody	**nothing**	

Everybody loves my aunt Zelda.

Nothing ever happens in this dull town.

However, some indefinite pronouns (such as *many, several,* and *few*) take the *they* form of the verb; in other words, there is no *-s* at the end of the verb.

Few approve of the new policy.

It's a good idea to minimize your use of indefinite pronouns, not only because they can cause agreement problems but also because they can lead to overgeneralizations. (For more information, see Chapter 24, pages 548–49.)

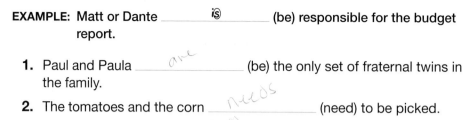

ACTIVITY 8

EASY

For each sentence, do the following:

*   In the space provided, write the correct present tense form of the verb in parentheses.

*   If the verb ends in *-s,* circle the *s* or mark it with a highlighter.

EXAMPLE: Each of the waiters ____*carries*____ (carry) two trays.

1. Everyone ___*enjoys*___ (enjoy) a day off.

2. Something ___*looks*___ (look) out of place.

3. Nobody ___*understood*___ (understand) the instruction manual.

4. Someone _____ (complain) about the speed bumps nearly every day.

5. No one _____ (seem) sorry that class was canceled.

ERRORS BASED ON PRONUNCIATION

When we speak, we sometimes run words together in our pronunciation. Then, when we write these words, we try to spell them the way we pronounce them. This is how we end up with nonstandard verbs like *gonna, wanna, gotta, should of, would of,* and *could of.* Study the following examples:

NONSTANDARD ENGLISH	STANDARD ENGLISH
Our team is gonna win the game.	Our team is going to win the game.
I wanna lose some weight.	I want to lose some weight.
They gotta find a new apartment.	They have got to find a new apartment.
Julio should of studied.	Julio should have studied.
We would of forgotten the date.	We would have forgotten the date.
Sheila could of found a better job.	Sheila could have found a better job.

FOUNDATION WORDS
NOUNS
VERBS
DESCRIPTIVE WORDS
ADJECTIVES
ADVERBS
CONNECTING WORDS
PREPOSITIONS
CONJUNCTIONS

It is common to see these nonstandard verb forms in personal e-mails. However, you should eliminate them from your academic and professional writing.

ACTIVITY 9
MODERATE

Rewrite each of the following sentences to eliminate nonstandard verbs. There may be more than one nonstandard verb in each sentence.

EXAMPLE: I could of finished my homework, but I didn't wanna miss the ball game.

I could have finished my homework, but I didn't want to miss

the ball game.

1. If we're gonna get to the airport on time, we gotta leave right now.

_____

2. Do you wanna see my history notes?

_____

CONTINUED >

For more practice with fixing nonstandard verbs, go to **bedfordstmartins.com /touchstones.**

3. I could of helped you paint the house; you should of asked me.

4. If you're gonna tell that scary story, I just gotta leave the room.

5. Dale would of bought your old car; he doesn't wanna buy a new one.

SHIFT ERRORS

Some errors result from accidental shifts (inconsistencies) in verb tense or in other verb usages. The following sections will examine these shifts and how they happen.

Shifts in Verb Tense

As you have learned, we use verb tenses to show when an action took (or takes) place. Take a look at these examples:

AN ACTION IN THE PAST	A clerk lost my registration forms.
A REGULAR ACTION (PRESENT TENSE)	Nora travels to France every summer.

If we are describing several actions that took (or take) place *together*, we need to be sure that the verb tenses match. Take a look:

TWO RELATED ACTIONS IN THE PAST	A clerk lost my registration forms and apologized for the mistake.
TWO RELATED, REGULAR ACTIONS (PRESENT TENSE)	Nora travels to France every summer and studies French.

In both sentences, the verbs are consistent (the same) in tense. However, if we change one of the verbs to a different tense without a good reason for doing so, the sentence will not make sense:

Incorrect Shift in Verb Tense

(PAST)   (PRESENT)

A clerk lost my registration form and apologizes for the mistake.

(PAST)   (PRESENT)

Nora traveled to France every summer and studies French.

This unnecessary change in verb tense usually happens when we are not paying close attention to the spelling of our verbs.

Sometimes, a sentence may contain two actions that happen at different times. In this case, a change in verb tense may make sense:

> | AN ACTION IN THE PAST | | A CURRENT STATE (PRESENT TENSE) |
>
> Randall **moved** to California last spring, but he **misses** his home in Texas.

Randall moved to California in the past, but he misses Texas now, in the present. This change in verb tense makes perfect sense.

ACTIVITY 10

For each sentence below, do the following:

- Decide whether or not the verb tense is consistent.
- If the tense is consistent, write a **C** in the margin.
- If the tense is inconsistent, cross out one of the verbs and write the correct verb tense above it.

installed
EXAMPLE: I was very proud after I ~~install~~ a pet door for my dog, Pepper.

1. One night last week, I woke up in the middle of the night when I hear a loud crash from the kitchen. *(heard)*

2. Pepper, my dog, was in the bedroom with me. He starts to growl.

3. Terrified, I grab Pepper and my cell phone, and we escaped out the bedroom window.

4. I called 911 to report an intruder. The police find a raccoon in my kitchen, rummaging through the trash can. *(found)*

5. The police officers laughed. They told me to shut the pet door at night.

Shifts When Telling a Story

Incorrect shifts in verb tense can occur when telling stories. Writers usually use the past tense when telling a story. Writers can also tell stories in the present tense to heighten the dramatic energy. However, sometimes we may begin a story in the *past* tense but then get so involved in the action or details that we shift to the *present* tense without realizing it, creating an incorrect shift.

> My happiest memory <u>was</u> leading my high school basketball team to victory in the regional championship. Imagine this scene: Just 30 seconds <u>remained</u> on the clock. The gymnasium <u>was</u> packed with fans. My team, Lincoln Heights, and the rival team, Bonaventure, <u>struggle</u> for control of the ball as Bonaventure <u>fights</u> to hold on to its one-point lead. Sweat <u>drips</u> in my eyes and nearly <u>blinds</u>

Power Tip
For more information on narration, see Chapter 11.

For more practice with using consistent verb tense, go to **bedfordstmartins.com /touchstones**.

me. Suddenly, the ball <u>flies</u> in front of me, and I <u>intercept</u> it. I <u>see</u> three seconds on the clock and <u>make</u> a wild, half-blind toss toward the net — SCORE!

At other times, writers get so swept up in the drama of a story that they jump back and forth between tenses. Read this version of the basketball story and notice how the verb tenses start shifting back and forth.

My happiest memory <u>was</u> leading my high school basketball team to victory in the regional championship. Imagine this scene: Just 30 seconds <u>remained</u> on the clock. The gymnasium <u>was</u> packed with fans. My team, Lincoln Heights, and the rival team, Bonaventure, <u>struggle</u> for control of the ball as Bonaventure <u>fights</u> to hold on to its one-point lead. Sweat <u>dripped</u> in my eyes and nearly blinded me. Suddenly, the ball <u>flies</u> in front of me, and I <u>intercepted</u> it. I <u>see</u> three seconds on the clock and <u>made</u> a wild, half-blind toss toward the net — SCORE!

This sort of "out of control" shift in verb tense is a common problem for inexperienced writers. If you are ever unsure about your use of verb tense when writing a story, ask your instructor for guidance.

ACTIVITY 11

ADVANCED

For the passage below, do the following:

- Read the first sentence and decide whether the story is in the past or present tense.
- Read the rest of the passage, crossing out any verbs that are not in the correct tense.
- In each place where you have crossed out a verb, write the correct verb form above it.

You should find five verb tense errors.

(1) Selena Quintanilla Perez was a talented Latino singer from Texas.

(2) Although she sang beautifully in Spanish, Selena's first language was English. (3) When she was a child, Selena's father, Abraham Perez, played in a band. (4) He recognizes Selena's singing talent and helps her launch her career. (5) Her first album is released when she was only 12 years old. (6) In 1987, she won Female Vocalist of the Year at the Tejano Music Awards. (7) Sadly, Selena's life is cut short at the age of 23 when she was murdered by one of her employees.

(8) Singer and actress Jennifer Lopez stars in a 1997 film about Selena's life called *Selena*.

Interrupting a Story with Current Information or Facts. Again, most stories are told in the past tense. Sometimes, however, we may want to interrupt the action of a story with current information or facts. This information may make more sense in the present tense. As you read the following story, notice that the action is in the past tense (the verbs underlined in yellow) and that current information and facts are in the present tense (underlined in purple):

> When the patrol car flashed its lights behind my brother and me, I sensed that something wasn't right. My brother, who was driving, has a spotless record and drives conservatively. He also keeps his registration tags and his vehicle maintenance up to date, so I knew that the cops hadn't chosen us because of a traffic violation, old tags, or an extinguished taillight. My brother pulled carefully onto the shoulder of the road and turned off the engine. As the cops approached from both sides, they aimed their flashlights in the backseat like they were searching for something. Suddenly, I remembered what my cousin always said about the police in our town: They are often guilty of racial profiling, stopping innocent drivers just because of their race. My brother and I happen to be Latino, so I prepared myself for the worst . . .

The brother's driving record and responsible behavior, the profiling by police, and the race of the writer and his brother are *current* and *factual* details, so it makes sense to keep them in the present tense.

ACTIVITY 12

ADVANCED

For the passage below, do the following:

- Read the passage to confirm that it's generally in the past tense.
- Look for any sentences that contain current information or facts.
- In these sentences, cross out any verbs that should be in the present but are in the past tense. Above them, write the correct present tense verbs.
- Correct any incorrect shifts to the present tense by crossing out the verb and writing the past tense form above it.

You should find four errors.

(1) Glenn Cunningham passed away in 1988 at age 78, but he was still considered, even now, one of the greatest runners in American history. (2) When he was eight years old, his legs were badly injured in a schoolhouse fire that burned most of the flesh off his legs and all of his toes on his left foot. (3) Despite the doctors' recommendation, Glenn and his parents refuse to allow the

CONTINUED >

amputation of his legs. (4) Glenn was determined to walk again. (5) At first, he crawled, dragging his almost useless legs behind him. (6) Gradually, he forced himself to stand, and then to walk, and finally to run. (7) He ran so well that in 1932 he competed in the Olympics, taking fourth place in the 1,500-meter run. (8) Two years later, he set a world record by running one mile in 4:06.8. (9) In 1936, he won the silver medal in the Olympic 1,500-meter run. (10) Not everyone reached their goals in their lifetime, and it was the same for Glenn, who never broke the four-minute mile. (11) Nevertheless, his life and story were an inspiration to us today.

Terminology Tip
Helping verbs "help" other (main) verbs. For more information, see Chapter 15, pages 340–41.

Using *Can/Could* and *Will/Would*.   *Can* shows an <u>ability</u> to do something, and *will* shows an <u>intention</u> (plan) to do something. Take a look:

| **AN <u>ABILITY</u> TO FLY** | Antonio can fly a helicopter. |
| **AN <u>INTENTION</u> TO APPLY** | Antonio will apply for the position in Chicago. |

Could and *would* are often used to express an ability or an intention in the past tense:

| **AN <u>ABILITY</u> TO FLY** | When Antonio was in the army, he could fly a helicopter. |
| **AN <u>INTENTION</u> TO APPLY** | Antonio told his family that he would apply for the position in Chicago. |

Power Tip
Notice that when you use *can, could, will,* and *would,* the verb that appears after these helping verbs does not change form; instead, it is always in the base form (for example, *fly,* not *flew*).

extracurricular: occurring outside of class

In the following passage, you can see how the writer keeps the verb tense consistent, using *can* and *will*. Notice that the underlined verbs in the first sentence establish this story in the present tense:

I am still a student, so I have to follow my parents' house rules. For example, I can go out only two nights a week, Friday and Saturday. On the other nights, I can invite friends to the house to study. My parents will allow me to have a part-time job, but I can work up to only 20 hours per week. If my grades start to slip, I will have to cut back on hours at work or quit. My parents will also let me participate in one extracurricular activity, like a sports team or student government. However, if I neglect my studies because of this activity, I will have to give it up. These rules may seem strict, but I know they can help me succeed, so I will obey them. When I live on my own, I can make my own house rules, but as long as I live at home, I will respect my parents' wishes.

For more practice with using consistent verb tenses, go to **bedfordstmartins.com /touchstones**.

Now, watch what happens when this story changes to the past tense. The helping verbs change to *could* and *would*, and they stay consistent. Once again, notice how the underlined verbs in the first sentence establish this story in the past tense:

> When I was a high school student, I had to follow my parents' house rules. For example, I could go out only two nights a week, Friday and Saturday. On the other nights, I could invite friends to the house to study. My parents would allow me to have a part-time job, but I could work up to only 20 hours per week. If my grades started to slip, I would have to cut back on hours at work or quit. My parents would also let me participate in one extracurricular activity, like a sports team or student government. However, if I neglected my studies because of this activity, I would have to give it up. These rules may have seemed strict, but I knew they could help me succeed, so I would obey them. I knew that when I lived on my own, I could make my own house rules, but as long as I lived at home, I would respect my parents' wishes.

Some writers have difficulty staying consistent when using these helping verbs. In conversation, we often jump back and forth between *can/could* and *will/would*, and most people don't notice. In our writing also, we sometimes jump back and forth between these forms for no reason. Such illogical shifts in tense can be confusing and frustrating for our readers.

ACTIVITY 13

ADVANCED

For the passage below, do the following:

- Read the first sentence and decide whether the writing is in the past or present tense.
- Read the rest of the passage, crossing out any ***can/could/will/would*** helping verbs that are not in the correct tense.
- In each place where you have crossed out a helping verb, write the correct verb form above it.

You should find four errors.

(1) Many people are finding creative ways to earn extra income at home. (2) One of the most popular methods is to use an online auction site such as eBay or Webstore. (3) People could sell unwanted clothes, books, electronic equipment, jewelry, or antiques. (4) There is generally someone who will be interested in these items. (5) Also, those with artistic talents could sell their own artwork or crafts. (6) Another effective

CONTINUED >

way to earn money is to set up a Web site and turn a hobby into a business. (7) Someone who is skilled at cooking can set up a local catering business. (8) Someone who is good at repairing cars could do basic automobile repair and maintenance in the local area. (9) Of course, these kinds of businesses require a business license.

(10) Finally, one doesn't have to be a professional photographer to earn money with photographs. (11) Anyone could submit photographs to agencies such as Shutterstock or iStockphoto and earn royalties when others download photos. (12) With the use of the Internet, anyone can turn unwanted items or a special skill into extra cash.

Could and *would* are also used when we express wishes or hypotheticals:

A WISH   I wish I could fly a helicopter.

A HYPOTHETICAL   If I were you, I would apply for the position in Chicago.

hypothetical: related to an idea or situation that has not actually happened, or to an imagined possibility

In college, some writing topics ask you to express your wishes or imagine hypotheticals. You can recognize these topics by the presence of *could* and *would*:

If you **could** travel anywhere, which country **would** you like to visit?
If you **could** spend a day with one famous person, who **would** it be?
If you **could** change one thing about the world, what **would** it be?
If you **could** have the career of your dreams, what **would** it be?

When you express a wish or hypothetical, you should use *could* and *would* consistently; do not jump back and forth unnecessarily between *can/could* and *will/would*. In the following paragraph, the writer has made this mistake:

If I could spend a day with one famous person, it would be Bill Gates, chairman and former CEO of Microsoft. For starters, I would like him to give me an "insider's" tour of the Microsoft headquarters. I would like to start my tour in Bill's executive office. I can sit in his chair and pretend that I am in command of the world's greatest software empire. I can also pick up the phone and surprise my girlfriend with a call from Bill's office. Then, I would like Bill to escort me to the "inner sanctum," where top-secret software design takes place. I will meet with Microsoft's elite designers — some of the highest-paid engineers in the world — and tell them what I don't like about Windows 8, the newest version of Windows. I could give them some tips on how to improve it. I would like to finish my tour by viewing exhibits on Microsoft's products and history at the company's visitor center. Bill can guide me through the exhibits, sharing the details of his company's many inventions.

When we read this passage quickly, it may *sound* correct because we are used to shifting verb tenses in our casual conversation. However, if you turn in a paper with tense shifts like those above, it will likely be marked down. Here is the same passage revised for consistent verb tense:

> If I could spend a day with one famous person, it would be Bill Gates, chairman and former CEO of Microsoft. For starters, I would like him to give me an "insider's" tour of the Microsoft headquarters. I would like to start my tour in Bill's executive office. I could sit in his chair and pretend that I am in command of the world's greatest software empire. I could also pick up the phone and surprise my girlfriend with a call from Bill's office. Then, I would like Bill to escort me to the "inner sanctum," where top-secret software design takes place. I would meet with Microsoft's elite designers—some of the highest-paid engineers in the world—and tell them what I don't like about Windows 8, the newest version of Windows. I could give them some tips on how to improve it. I would like to finish my tour by viewing exhibits on Microsoft's products and history at the company's visitor center. Bill could guide me through the exhibits, sharing the details of his company's many inventions.

ACTIVITY 14

ADVANCED

For the passage below, do the following:

- Read the passage and determine the general tense of the writing.
- Cross out any **can/could/will/would** helping verbs that are not in the correct tense.
- In each place where you have crossed out a helping verb, write the correct verb form above it.

You should find four errors.

(1) If I could play hooky for one day, I would get in my car and just drive. (2) I will not have a particular destination in mind. (3) I would just follow my whims. (4) I would leave early in the morning and stop for breakfast at some mom-and-pop café along a country road. (5) If I wanted to, I can order pancakes or waffles, and nobody would shake a finger at me and remind me of my diet. (6) I would bring some CDs and sing my favorite songs at the top of my voice. (7) I will take a book along with me. (8) Perhaps I would stop at a coffee shop and order a large latte with cinnamon and whipped cream. (9) I would read for an hour or two and get lost in another world. (10) I might end the day at a

CONTINUED >

mall. (11) If I had a little extra money in my pocket, I can buy a new pair of shoes or a new CD. (12) Playing hooky would certainly be fun, but unfortunately, if I got caught, I could certainly get into a lot of trouble.

Shifts in Voice

In most sentences that we write, the subject takes some kind of action. Take a look:

SUBJECT

A foul <u>ball</u> struck a baseball fan.

In this sentence, the ball took action: It struck a fan. Such sentences are said to be in the **active voice**.

In some cases, however, the subject is <u>acted upon</u>:

SUBJECT

A baseball <u>fan</u> was struck by a foul ball.

These sentences are said to be in the **passive voice**. Notice that when we form the passive voice, a *be* helping verb precedes the main verb (*struck* in this example).

Generally, it's a good idea to avoid the passive voice because it is less direct than the active voice. However, writers may choose the passive voice in some circumstances—for example, when they do not know who or what took action:

The senator was heckled by someone in the audience.

Also, avoid shifting between the active and passive voices. Take a look at these examples:

SHIFT IN VOICE	My parents often took me to baseball games, and I was sometimes taken by my grandparents to the beach.
REVISED	My parents often took me to baseball games, and my grandparents sometimes took me to the beach.

ACTIVITY 15

ADVANCED

Edit the following passage to eliminate five shifts to the passive voice. (In other words, the entire passage should be in the active voice.)

(1) Every winter, our entire family makes camp stew, which is similar to Brunswick stew, in a large cast-iron pot outside. (2) Everyone has

For more practice with avoiding shifts in voice, go to **bedfordstmartins.com /touchstones**.

a job. (3) My father cuts hickory wood into kindling and builds a fire

in the yard. (4) The meat is prepared by my mother. (5) She pre-cooks

several pounds each of beef, pork, and chicken. (6) My sisters and I peel

the potatoes, but cutting the potatoes into cubes is a task shared by

everyone. (7) My brother always volunteers for the eye-stinging task

of chopping the onions. (8) First, we cook the meat, potatoes, and

onions, and then the tomatoes and spices are added. (9) When it is

time to cook the stew, everyone takes turns stirring. (10) An old boat

paddle is used to stir the pot. (11) About this time, other relatives and

friends arrive, and they also take their traditional turn stirring the pot.

(12) Finally, my father declares that the stew is ready and that it's the

best batch we have ever made. (13) The first bowls of hot stew are

enjoyed by everyone.

ACTIVITY 16: Mastery Test or Teamwork

MASTERY

Read each of the following paragraphs carefully, looking for verb errors. Then, rewrite each error to fix the problem. The errors will include:

- missing -*s* endings and other subject-verb agreement problems. (See pages 510 and 516–21.)
- missing -*ed* endings on regular past tense verbs. (See page 513.)
- incorrect forms of irregular verbs, both present and past tense. (See pages 513–16.)
- verb errors based on pronunciation. (See page 521.)
- inconsistent tense and/or voice. (See pages 522–31.)

The first error in each paragraph has been edited for you.

The following paragraph has 13 verb errors (including the one that has been edited for you).

a. (1) Despite the high cost of gasoline, the use of recreational

        continues

vehicles (RVs) ~~continue~~ to be popular for a number of reasons. (2) First,

RVs be economical. (3) They are an inexpensive alternative to high-priced

airline tickets, especially for large families. (4) In addition, the use of

CONTINUED >

RVs eliminate the need for expensive hotel rooms. (5) Campsites are considerably less expensive than hotel rooms, and in some locations campgrounds is even free. (6) RV users can also save money on food. (7) Anyone who has eaten at restaurants three times a day knows how expensive dining out can be. (8) Simple and economical meals can be prepare in the RV since most is equipped with a gas stove, oven, microwave, refrigerator, and sink. (9) Second, families can travel in a familiar and homey place. (10) They could sleep in their own clean and comfortable beds rather than enduring hard or lumpy hotel mattresses. (11) Because RVs have toilets and even showers, families can also avoid inconvenient restroom stops at gas stations, which are often unclean. (12) Third, since children are gonna get bored or restless on long trips, they can bring along more toys, books, or games to keep them occupied. (13) They could play board or video games, watch movies, listen to satellite radio, or even access the Internet on their computers. (14) A fourth advantage to RV travel is that pets can easily accompany their families on vacations, something that would eliminate costly boarding fees as well as the anxiety pets might feel when left behind. (15) Finally, RVs provide families the opportunity to be closer to nature. (16) Most camping areas and RV parks are locate near outdoor recreational areas, which were usually quite scenic. (17) In addition, they offer hiking, boating, fishing, horseback riding, and other outdoor activities. (18) When all of these advantages are considered, the cost of driving an RV seem like a bargain.

The following paragraph has 15 verb errors (including the one that has been edited for you).

b. (1) In 1888, John Robert Gregg developed Gregg shorthand, which is a writing method that ~~use~~ *uses* short symbols for sounds instead of letters. (2) The Gregg shorthand system include "brief forms," which are simple symbols that stand for an entire word or phrase. (3) Gregg design his shorthand as a method for copying spoken words quickly and accurately. (4) For many years, before the invention of tape recorders and dictation machines, administrative assistants use shorthand to record letters dictated by their employers and to take notes during meetings. (5) Also, courtroom proceedings were recorded in shorthand by court reporters. (6) Today, with so much electronic recording technology, some people consider shorthand obsolete; however, it can still be a very useful skill, professionally and personally. (7) Journalists could use shorthand to make quick, accurate notes during interviews or press conferences, saving them the time it take to transcribe audio recordings. (8) Police officers and investigators can use shorthand during their interviews of victims or suspects. (9) Those who gotta copy information during a phone call would find shorthand useful. (10) How many times have people missed important details when talking to someone from a phone company, a utility company, city hall, a real estate company, or an attorney's office? (11) Sometimes, people write so hurriedly that they had trouble reading their own handwriting. (12) Shorthand is especially useful for students, who have all experienced the struggle to capture key ideas when a professor has spoken too fast. (13) It is true that using a tape recorder is the most accurate way of recording class lectures, but it took

CONTINUED >

a long time to transcribe notes from a recording. (14) Busy students would certainly benefit from using shorthand in the classroom. (15) Fortunately, shorthand is easy to learn because it involved natural writing movements. (16) Further, complete mastery of shorthand is not necessary because common words and brief forms can be combine with complete words to increase note-taking speed. (17) Shorthand is a skill that everyone should take the time to learn because it have daily applications in the business world and in the classroom.

BRINGING IT ALL TOGETHER:
Using Verbs Correctly

In this chapter, you have learned about using verbs correctly and avoiding common problems caused by incorrect verb usage. Confirm your knowledge by filling in the blank spaces in the following sentences. If you need help, review the pages listed after each sentence.

✔ Nonstandard English tends to be used in _____ _____. Standard English should be used in _____. (pages 508–9)

✔ The _____ tense is used for regular actions, facts, and feelings and some actions at the present moment. Often, verb errors in this tense happen because of the absence or unnecessary addition of an _____ ending. (page 510)

✔ The _____ tense is used for action completed in the past. Often, verb errors in this tense happen because of the absence or unnec-essary addition of an _____ ending. (pages 512–13)

✔ Irregular past tense verbs are not spelled with an _____ ending. (page 513)

✔ When the ending on a present or past tense verb does not match the subject, this is called an error in _____. (page 516)

✔ Spelling verbs the way you (incorrectly) pronounce them—such as *wanna*, *gonna*, *should of*, *could of*—is an error based on _____. (page 521)

✔ Jumping back and forth unnecessarily between present and past tense verbs creates incorrect _____ in verb tense. (page 522)

✔ A story told in the past tense may shift into the present tense to include _____. (page 525)

✔ The past tense of *can* is _____. The past tense of *will* is _____. If you are using *will/can* or *would/could* in your writing, you should not _____ illogically. (pages 526–29)

CHAPTER 24

Using Pronouns Correctly

Before you read this chapter, it's a good idea to test your understanding of pronouns. You may know more than you think.

Circle "Yes" if each word group below is a complete, correct sentence. Circle "No" if it is incorrect. If "No," explain the problem.

1. **Clark wants a hybrid vehicle because you can get better gas mileage.**

    Yes   No

    Explanation: _____

2. **Everyone in our department has finished their work early.**

    Yes   No

    Explanation: _____

3. **Danny and me are planning to go to Las Vegas this weekend.**

    Yes   No

    Explanation: _____

4. **Somebody has a flat tire on their car.**

    Yes   No

    Explanation: _____

5. **Nobody in our office has received his or her evaluation yet.**

    Yes   No

    Explanation: _____

Pronouns (noun substitutes) take different forms. You'll learn these forms — as well as how to avoid errors when using them — in this chapter.

SUBJECT   OBJECT

I study with him.

POSSESSIVE

His grades are improving.

BUILD IT: Pronoun Usage

A **pronoun** is a word that *takes the place* of a noun (a person, place, or thing):

NOUN   NOUN

Raul   tried   golf.

He   tried   it.
PRONOUN   PRONOUN

Often, a pronoun *refers back to* (renames) a specific noun that has already been mentioned:

Raul tried golf. It was very difficult.

Pronouns can also replace and refer to *noun phrases* (a noun plus descriptive words or a prepositional phrase). Take a look:

NOUN PHRASE   NOUN PHRASE

The entire team   wanted   an opportunity to play the Broncos again.

Everyone   wanted   that.
PRONOUN   PRONOUN

WHY WE USE PRONOUNS

We use pronouns for convenience, so that we do not have to repeat a noun or a noun phrase over and over. Take a look at the following passage, in which two noun phrases are repeated in every sentence:

My cousin Angel from Puerto Rico bought a classic 1968 Ford Mustang.
My cousin Angel from Puerto Rico won the classic 1968 Ford Mustang on eBay.
When the classic 1968 Ford Mustang arrived by ship, my cousin Angel from

Terminology Tip
As you learned in Chapter 16, a pronoun is a type of noun that functions as a noun substitute. In English grammar, the noun that a pronoun refers back to is known as an *antecedent*.

Puerto Rico inspected the classic 1968 Ford Mustang. My cousin Angel from Puerto Rico discovered that the classic 1968 Ford Mustang was not the classic 1968 Ford Mustang shown on eBay. My cousin Angel from Puerto Rico called the seller about the classic 1968 Ford Mustang and learned that the wrong classic 1968 Ford Mustang had been shipped. My cousin Angel from Puerto Rico returned the classic 1968 Ford Mustang and waited for the right classic 1968 Ford Mustang to be shipped.

Of course, most people would substitute single-word nouns (*Angel, Mustang*) and shorter noun phrases (*my cousin, the car*) for the longer noun phrases:

My cousin Angel from Puerto Rico bought a classic 1968 Ford Mustang. My cousin won the car on eBay. When the Mustang arrived by ship, Angel inspected the car. Angel discovered that the car was not the Mustang shown on eBay. Angel called the seller about the Mustang and learned that the wrong car had been shipped. My cousin returned the car and waited for the right Mustang to be shipped.

This version is more efficient, but it still sounds wordy and repetitive. The most efficient way to communicate this information is to replace some of the nouns and noun phrases with pronouns (*he, it,* and so on):

My cousin Angel from Puerto Rico bought a classic 1968 Ford Mustang. He won it on eBay. When the car arrived by ship, Angel inspected it. He discovered that it was not the Mustang shown on eBay. He called the seller about this and learned that the wrong car had been shipped. Angel returned the Mustang and waited for the right one to be shipped.

In this version, the writer has achieved a nice balance of nouns and pronouns to make the information smoother and easier to digest.

In conversation, we use pronouns as a shortcut to communicate quickly and efficiently. Pronouns are common in academic writing, too; however, in the writing that we do for college, we must use pronouns with extra care, making sure to balance the need for efficiency with the need for *clarity* at all times.

TYPES OF PRONOUNS

The goal of this chapter is to help you avoid common pronoun errors. To achieve this goal, we will focus on three major groups of pronouns:

1. *specific* and *general* pronouns
2. *subject* and *object* pronouns
3. *possessive* pronouns

Specific versus General Pronouns

Pronouns can be used to identify both *specific* people and things and *general* people and things. Look at the examples in the following chart:

SPECIFIC		GENERAL	
People	**Things**	**People**	**Things**
I you he she we they	it this that they these those	anybody anyone everybody everyone no one nobody one somebody someone	anything everything nothing one something

ACTIVITY 1

WARMUP

In each of the following sentences, underline the pronoun(s). Then, label the pronouns as follows:

- Write **SP** above the pronouns that refer to specific people.
- Write **ST** above the pronouns that refer to specific things.
- Write **GP** above the pronouns that refer to general people.
- Write **GT** above the pronouns that refer to general things.

SP
EXAMPLE: Floyd decided that <u>he</u> wanted an herb garden.

1. Floyd did not know anything about how to create one.

2. Floyd turned to friends for advice, and they suggested that he go to a local greenhouse.

3. Someone at the greenhouse recommended basil, dill, and parsley; these are useful spices for everyday cooking.

4. Floyd planted the herbs in small pots on the patio. Everything he planted grew well.

5. He now uses fresh herbs in nearly everything he cooks.

KEY TO CHALLENGE METER

WARMUP	📊
EASY	📊
MODERATE	📊
ADVANCED	📊
MASTERY	📊

Identify the difficulty level of each activity using the key above.

Subject and Object Pronouns

Many specific pronouns can take subject or object forms, depending on their role in the sentence. Subject pronouns act as the subject of the sentence: who or what the sentence is about. Look at these examples:

SUBJECT	Charlotte dislikes dogs.
SUBJECT PRONOUN (REPLACES *CHARLOTTE*)	She dislikes dogs.

Power Tip
In the sentences in this chapter, the blue highlighting is used for pronouns *and* for the words that pronouns replace.

For more practice with pronouns, go to **bedfordstmartins.com /touchstones**.

Power Tip
Note that the pronouns *she/her* and *he/him* identify someone as male or female; *she* and *her* can refer only to females, and *he* and *him* can refer only to males.

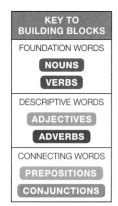

KEY TO BUILDING BLOCKS
FOUNDATION WORDS
NOUNS
VERBS
DESCRIPTIVE WORDS
ADJECTIVES
ADVERBS
CONNECTING WORDS
PREPOSITIONS
CONJUNCTIONS

Objects receive the action of a verb:

OBJECT	A dog bit Charlotte.
OBJECT PRONOUN (REPLACES *CHARLOTTE*)	A dog bit her.

In these examples, *Charlotte* and *her* receive the action of *bit*. Notice that the object pronoun has a different form from the subject pronoun: *her* instead of *she*.

Objects can also complete prepositional phrases:

OBJECT PRONOUN

Joseph handed the report <u>to me</u>.

PREPOSITIONAL PHRASE (UNDERLINED)

For more on prepositions and prepositional phrases, see Chapter 16, pages 356–61.

Subject and Object Pronouns

Subject		Object
I	→	me
we	→	us
you	→	you
he/she	→	him/her
it	→	it
they	→	them

ACTIVITY 2
EASY

In each of the following sentences, label the underlined pronouns as **S** for subject pronoun or **O** for object pronoun.

                                                 o

EXAMPLE: For my friend Lorin and <u>me</u>, exchanging gifts was getting out of control.

1. <u>We</u> used to exchange gifts for birthdays and for every major holiday, such as Christmas, Valentine's Day, and even St. Patrick's Day since <u>we</u> are both Irish.

2. Although the gifts were not very expensive, <u>they</u> did cost <u>us</u> more and more each year.

3. When Lorin moved out of state, <u>we</u> spent even more time and money on gifts because <u>they</u> had to be wrapped and mailed.

4. Finally, Lorin said, "I would like for <u>us</u> to give each other the gift of no gift."

5. Now, <u>we</u> just send each other cards instead of gifts, and <u>we</u> don't

miss <u>them</u> at all.

ACTIVITY 3
MODERATE

In each sentence below, circle the correct subject or object form of the pronouns in parentheses.

EXAMPLE: Last summer, my friend Jared and (Ⓘ / me) went on a weekend fishing trip to a nearby lake.

1. For Jared and (I / me), fishing is a favorite form of relaxation, but (he / him) and I did not relax at all on this trip.

2. Jared and (I / me) rented a canoe, which neither of (we / us) knew how to use.

3. When Jared stood up in the canoe, (he / him) caused (I / me) to fall overboard.

4. When (I / me) fell out of the canoe, Jared lost his balance, and into the water (he / him) went as well.

5. (We / Us) were rescued by nearby fishermen, but (they / them) laughed hard at (we / us).

Possessive Pronouns

Specific pronouns that have subject and object forms also have possessive forms. Possessive pronouns (*my, mine, ours, yours,* and so on) show ownership. Take a look at the following examples:

That is my boat. That boat is mine.

Our apartment is small and cramped, but yours is spacious.

The oak tree has lost its leaves.

Possessive Pronouns

SUBJECT PRONOUNS	POSSESSIVE PRONOUNS
I	my, mine
we	our, ours
you	your, yours
he	his
she	her, hers
it	its
they	their, theirs

Power Tip
You do not need to add an apostrophe (') to show possession when you use a possessive pronoun.

Incorrect: *This cabin is <u>your's</u>; <u>our's</u> is across the lake.*

Revised: *This cabin is <u>yours</u>; <u>ours</u> is across the lake.*

ıllıll
EASY
ACTIVITY 4

In each of the following sentences, underline the possessive pronoun(s).

EXAMPLE: Several of <u>my</u> co-workers and I came up with an economical way to enjoy <u>our</u> lunch hour.

1. We formed a lunch club, and on Mondays, Calvin brings his delicious chili and cornbread for our group.

2. On Tuesdays, I bring my grilled chicken salad because of its popularity with my co-workers.

3. Every Wednesday, Lisa brings her tasty lasagna or another casserole to our lunch table.

4. On Thursday, Nathan shares one of his soups; his homemade chicken noodle soup is a favorite of mine.

5. Kaylee brings her homemade bread, deli meats, and cheese on Fridays and tells us, "Make the sandwich of your choice."

FIX IT: Common Pronoun Problems

The final passage on page 538 shows how an experienced writer uses pronouns to identify *specific* people and things (Angel, the Mustang, etc.). When used with care, these pronouns can make your academic writing clear and efficient.

Be aware, however, that even specific pronouns, which are friends of the academic writer, can cause problems if used carelessly. The following sections discuss common problems with pronouns.

UNCLEAR REFERENCE

You have learned that a pronoun refers to a noun—a specific person, place, or thing. However, if we use pronouns carelessly, the reference (what the pronoun refers to) may not be 100 percent clear to the reader. In a conversation, we can always ask for or provide clarification if a pronoun does not make sense. Take a look:

Vince: I had a blind date with a girl named Kirsten on Saturday night. I took her to dinner at a new restaurant. It was a disaster.

Earl: Yeah, I went on a blind date once, and it was a disaster, too.

Vince: No, I mean the restaurant was a disaster. The service was slow. It took almost 40 minutes to get our food, and it was cold.

Here, the pronoun *it* has an unclear reference: It might refer to *the date* or to *the restaurant*. When Earl gets confused, Vince is able to clarify that the

For more practice with pronouns, go to **bedfordstmartins.com /touchstones**.

pronoun refers to *the restaurant*. In our conversations, this sort of clarification happens all the time.

However, when we use unclear pronouns in our writing, the reader may not have the opportunity to ask for clarification. Read the following passage and see how difficult it is to follow the writer's ideas:

> The hardest thing I ever had to do was put my dog Chester to sleep. To begin with, making the decision to end Chester's life was tough. For a long time, I was in denial about it. They told me to learn more about this. I read a book on it and even saw a documentary on that. It helped me understand our responsibility to them. She explained that allowing it to suffer should not be an option. We decided to make an appointment with him to discuss this. This was the first step in coming to terms with it.

This passage is confusing because most of the pronouns have an unclear reference: we don't know *exactly* what they mean. Take a look:

> . . . in denial about it (In denial about what, exactly?)
>
> . . . They told me (Who told, exactly?)
>
> . . . to learn more about this (About what, exactly?)
>
> . . . I read a book on it (A book on what, exactly?)
>
> . . . saw a documentary on that (A documentary on what, exactly?)
>
> . . . It helped me understand (What helped, exactly?)
>
> . . . our responsibility to them (Our responsibility to whom, specifically?)
>
> . . . She explained (Who explained, exactly?)
>
> . . . allowing it to suffer (Allowing what to suffer, exactly?)
>
> . . . We decided (Who decided, exactly?)
>
> . . . an appointment with him (An appointment with whom, specifically?)
>
> . . . to discuss this (To discuss what, exactly?)
>
> . . . This was the first step (What was the first step, exactly?)
>
> . . . in coming to terms with it (Coming to terms with what, exactly?)

The reader should not have to pause to guess about what a pronoun means. If you suspect that a pronoun in your writing is unclear, replace it with a noun or noun phrase that clarifies your meaning. Compare the following version of the passage to its original:

> The hardest thing I ever had to do was put my dog Chester to sleep. To begin with, making the decision to end Chester's life was tough. For a long time, I was in denial about Chester's terminal condition. My family told me to learn more about cancer in animals. I read a book on cancer in dogs and even saw a documentary on pet euthanasia. The film helped me understand our responsibility to our terminally ill pets. The author of the book explained that allowing a pet to suffer should not be an option. My family and I decided to make an appointment with the vet to discuss Chester's situation. Making this appointment was the first step in coming to terms with my responsibility to Chester.

euthanasia: the act of humanely ending the life of a very ill creature

ooll **ACTIVITY 5**
MODERATE

For the paragraph below, do the following:

- Underline any pronouns that have an unclear reference.
- Using your imagination, rewrite the paragraph, adding more specific words in place of the unclear pronouns.

(1) When my wife and I arrived, <u>it</u> was crowded. (2) We had hoped to celebrate our anniversary in a quiet place, but they were noisy and rowdy. (3) We asked <u>him</u> if we could be moved to a quieter table, but he said <u>it</u> was not available. (4) She shrugged and ordered <u>something</u>, so I ordered <u>something</u>. (5) They were not delivered to our table for a very <u>long time</u>. (6) This did not bother my wife, who began to talk about <u>something</u>. (7) We laughed when we remembered it, and gradually <u>they</u> faded into the background. (8) We ended up truly enjoying it. (9) I will always be grateful to her for this.

OVERUSE OF *YOU*

In conversation, we often use the pronoun *you* to mean "people in general." In academic writing, however, be careful when using *you*. In the following passage, notice that the writer begins by narrating a personal experience, using the pronouns *I*, *me*, and *my* (see the words highlighted in yellow). Then, unexpectedly, she shifts to the pronouns *you* and *your* to refer to people in general (see the words highlighted in blue).

Terminology Tip
The pronoun error described here is called a **shift in person** because the pronoun shifts unexpectedly from a specific person to the generalized *you*. For more on shifts, see Chapter 23, pages 522–31.

Doing research for my history assignment was easier than I had expected. First, I found all the materials that I needed online. For instance, the librarian showed me how to use a database called LexisNexis, which contains thousands of articles and documents. All you have to do is type in keywords related to your topic, and you get hundreds of professional articles on that topic. Also, my local library now has whole books in digital format. I was able to read a digital version of <u>Women and Slavery</u> by Gwyn Campbell. You can also Google your topic, but you have to be careful about the quality of the Web sites you find with this search engine.

Power Tip
For more on standard and nonstandard English, see Chapter 23, pages 508–9.

Such shifts in pronoun usage are so common in conversational English that many students make them in their academic writing without realizing the error. However, if the subject of a sentence or a paragraph is a specific person, place, or thing, the pronouns referring to that subject should be *consistent* with it. Take a look at this revision of the previous paragraph:

Doing research for my history assignment was easier than I had expected. First, I found all the materials that I needed online. For instance, the librarian showed me how to use a database called LexisNexis, which contains thousands of articles and documents. All I had to do was type in keywords related to my topic, and I got hundreds of professional articles on that topic. Also, my local library now has whole books in digital format. I was able to read a digital version of <u>Women and Slavery</u> by Gwyn Campbell. I also Googled my topic, but I had to be careful about the quality of the Web sites I found with this search engine.

There are really only two situations in which the pronoun *you* is useful in academic writing:

1. In a direct quotation:

   Tamika said to me, "You will be getting a raise next month."

   Here, *you* refers to a specific person, not to people in general.

2. In a paragraph or essay in which you are addressing the reader directly to explain a process:

   To get the best price on an airline ticket, you should be flexible with flying dates.

   Here, *you* refers to a specific person, the reader.

Power Tip
Some instructors may prefer that students do not use *you* even when explaining a process. If you are in doubt about your instructor's preference, it's always a good idea to ask.

ACTIVITY 6

For each sentence below, do the following:

- Cross out each *you* pronoun that refers to people in general.
- Above this crossed-out word, write in the pronoun that is consistent with the specific subject of the sentence. (See Chapter 16 for more on identifying subjects.)
- You might also have to change the verb to maintain verb agreement.

EXAMPLE: I appreciate my Aunt Gracie because she is always there for ~~you.~~ *me.*

1. Jennifer prefers stairs over elevators because ~~you~~ get more exercise on the stairs.

2. When LaDonna and I arrived at work, ~~you~~ could tell that it was going to be a busy day.

3. The employees dislike the work schedule, which never gives ~~you~~ the same days off each week.

4. As David and I entered the coffee shop, ~~you~~ could smell the rich aroma of freshly brewed coffee.

5. Ty is studying medicine because as a physician ~~you~~ can make a big difference in people's lives.

ACTIVITY 7

MODERATE

For the paragraph below, do the following:

- Cross out each *you/your* pronoun that refers to people in general.
- Above each crossed-out word, write in the pronoun that is consistent with the specific subject of the paragraph.
- You might also have to change the verb to maintain verb agreement.

(1) When Shane, who is in the army, was transferred to Alaska, he was very disappointed because ~~you were~~ so far away from ~~your~~ family and friends. (2) He had heard that the temperature in the winter would drop so low that ~~you~~ would have to plug your parked car into a heating post to keep the engine operational. (3) Also, in the winter, the days are very short, so you would have only a few hours of daylight. (4) After Shane arrived in Alaska, however, he was amazed at the beauty ~~you~~ saw there. (5) As he drove to work in the mornings, moose would trot across the highway in front of you. (6) At night, he was transfixed by the brilliant displays of the northern lights. (7) When summer arrived, Shane learned to fish for salmon. (8) You could stand in the river and catch your limit within minutes. (9) It wasn't long before Shane changed his attitude about Alaska. (10) He learned to take advantage of wherever the army sends ~~you~~.

OVERUSE OF *IT*

The pronoun *it* is sometimes called the "king of the pronouns" because it is used so frequently. However, the careless use or overuse of this pronoun in academic writing can confuse readers. Take a look:

Dropping out of high school can lead to a number of problems. To begin with, a teenager can experience a sense of isolation and loneliness without the social opportunities that high school provides. For example, it really made my brother crazy when he quit school in the eleventh grade. He watched television all day to try to forget about it. Even though he still saw his old buddies on the weekends, it was painful. Worst of all, the girls stopped calling, and it

For more practice with pronouns, go to **bedfordstmartins.com /touchstones**.

became unbearable for him. It proves that dropping out of high school can be a risky choice.

In this passage, each use of the pronoun *it* leads to a lack of clarity:

> . . . it really made my brother crazy (What made him crazy, exactly?)
>
> . . . to forget about it (To forget about what, exactly?)
>
> . . . it was painful (What was painful, exactly?)
>
> . . . it became unbearable for him (What became unbearable, exactly?)
>
> . . . It proves (What proves, exactly?)

The answers to these questions might be clear *in the writer's mind*, but the reader will have to guess, which can result in confusion. A more experienced writer avoids the careless use of *it*, replacing this pronoun with more specific nouns and noun phrases. Let's see how the previous paragraph could be revised:

> Dropping out of high school can lead to a number of problems. To begin with, a teenager can experience a sense of isolation and loneliness without the social opportunities that high school provides. For example, the sudden isolation really made my brother crazy when he quit school in the eleventh grade. He watched television all day to try to forget about his growing sense of loneliness. Even though he still saw his old buddies on the weekends, losing daily contact with them was painful. Worst of all, the girls stopped calling, and the loss of dates became unbearable for him. My brother's example proves that dropping out of high school can be a risky choice.

ACTIVITY 8

ADVANCED

For the paragraph below, do the following:

- Underline unclear uses of *it*.
- Using your imagination, replace the unclear pronouns with more specific words. You may need to replace other words, too.

(1) Even a short hike in the wilderness can quickly turn unpleasant or dangerous, so hikers should be well prepared for it. (2) There are basic survival items to pack in it and bring along. (3) Hikers should be prepared to survive it for two or three days. (4) A fleece jacket and a waterproof rain suit will offer warmth and dryness if it turns cold or rainy. (5) A few energy bars and an extra bottle of water will help make it a less miserable experience. (6) It can be a less frightening event if hikers also carry

CONTINUED >

matches, a cell phone, a flashlight, and a compass. (7) In addition, hikers should carry a loud whistle; it can help rescuers locate them in the wilderness. (8) Nobody expects it on a leisurely day hike, but being prepared may be the key to it.

OVERUSE OF INDEFINITE PRONOUNS

As you saw earlier in the chapter, some pronouns are used to identify *general* people or things. These pronouns are called *indefinite pronouns*. Here they are again:

Indefinite Pronouns

GENERAL	
People	**Things**
anybody anyone everybody everyone no one nobody one somebody someone	anything everything nothing one something

Using indefinite pronouns to identify general people and things can harm your academic writing for two reasons:

1. They can lead to *overgeneralizations*.
2. They can lead to *awkward agreement*.

Next, we'll discuss both reasons in more detail.

Indefinite Pronouns and Overgeneralizing

Pronouns that identify people or things in general are called *indefinite* because they do not identify a *definite* (specific) person or thing. Take a look:

Everybody **enjoys learning new skills.**

If we make this statement, what we mean is that *most people* or *people in general* like to learn new skills. However, this statement is weak because we have incorrectly phrased it as a universal truth: Certainly, there are individuals who do not care about new skills.

Such *overgeneralizations* are common in spoken language; however, in academic writing, we need to be more specific. Therefore, whenever possible, it's a good idea to replace indefinite pronouns with nouns or noun phrases that are more specific:

WEAK	Everybody enjoys learning new skills.
MORE SPECIFIC	Most people enjoy learning new skills.
	The average person enjoys learning new skills.
	Most students enjoy learning new skills.
	Tamara and Jacob enjoy learning new skills.

Here is another example of an indefinite pronoun that leads to a clear overgeneralization:

Everything went wrong today.

If I make this a statement, I mean that *every single thing went wrong*. However, it's hard to imagine that this statement is absolutely true: Certainly, some things went right.

In your own academic writing, be careful to find specific nouns or noun phrases to express your thoughts:

WEAK	Everything went wrong today.
MORE SPECIFIC	Many things went wrong today.
	Some of my decisions went wrong today.
	Most of my computer-related tasks went wrong today.
	All my attempts to pay my bills online went wrong today.

As you can see from these examples, indefinite pronouns can lead to weak statements that are overgeneralizations. In your academic writing, whenever possible, replace an indefinite pronoun with a more specific noun or noun phrase.

ACTIVITY 9

MODERATE

For each sentence below, do the following:

- Underline the indefinite pronoun.
- Using your imagination, rewrite the sentence to replace the pronoun with more specific words. You may need to rewrite other parts of the sentence, too.

EXAMPLE: Everyone was surprised when Manuel suddenly quit his job.

Manuel's friends and family were surprised when he suddenly quit his job.

CONTINUED >

1. Mandy claims that she simply doesn't have anything to wear to the wedding.

2. Nobody understood the professor's rambling explanation.

3. During the meeting, someone brought up the subject of merit pay.

4. I want a smartphone because everybody has one.

5. Don't allow anyone to use my truck while I'm away.

Indefinite Pronouns and Awkward Agreement

If you decide to use an indefinite pronoun as the subject of a sentence, you may encounter another common problem. Take a look:

Nobody **likes to waste** their **money.**

SUBJECT   PRONOUN REFERRING BACK TO SUBJECT

Terminology Tip
When singular pronouns refer back to singular nouns/pronouns and plural pronouns refer back to plural nouns/pronouns, these words are said to agree in **number**.

Although the sentence above *sounds* correct, it contains a common pronoun error: The possessive pronoun *their* (plural) does not match with the subject *nobody* (singular). In other words, the pronoun *their* does not *agree* with the subject.

Remember that <u>most indefinite pronouns are singular</u> even though many of them have plural meanings (*everybody, everyone, everything*). There are just three ways to fix agreement errors with indefinite pronouns:

Singular subject + Singular pronoun

1. Nobody likes to waste his or her money.
2. Nobody likes to waste her money.
3. Nobody likes to waste his money.

Each of these sentences is now grammatically correct. However, each one sounds awkward:

1. *His or her* is wordy, and if you use it over and over, your writing can become cluttered.
2. *Her* by itself sounds odd because not all people are women.
3. *His* by itself also sounds odd because not all people are men.

The best way to correct the problem may be to change *nobody* to a more specific subject. Take a look:

Plural subject + Plural pronoun

Few people like to waste their money.

This sentence is a better choice for academic writing because it has a more specific subject, it has a plural pronoun to match a plural subject, and it is not awkwardly worded.

ACTIVITY 10

ADVANCED

Each sentence below has a pronoun agreement error. For each one, underline the subject pronoun and the possessive pronoun that refers back to the subject pronoun. Then, rewrite the sentence in two ways:

- First, replace the possessive pronoun, but leave the subject pronoun alone.
- Second, replace the subject pronoun, but leave the possessive pronoun alone.

You may need to change other words as well. For example, if you make the subject plural, you may need to change the verb to agree with the subject. (For more information, see Chapter 23.)

EXAMPLE: <u>Someone</u> drove <u>their</u> car through our yard.

Someone drove his or her car through our yard.

The Browns drove their car through our yard.

1. No one expects to have their vehicle broken into.

2. Everyone wants to do well on their final exams.

3. Anyone may enter their best photograph in the contest.

4. Somebody left their luggage on the shuttle bus.

5. Everybody wants their pets to stay healthy.

Power Tip
Don't think that you can *never* use indefinite pronouns, but be aware of the problems they can cause. Whenever you are tempted to use such a pronoun, ask yourself if you can find a more specific noun or noun phrase. If you still want to use an indefinite pronoun, make sure it agrees with (matches) the noun it refers back to.

For more practice with agreement of indefinite pronouns, go to **bedfordstmartins.com /touchstones**.

OTHER PRONOUN PROBLEMS

Finally, we'll look at some other problems that can occur with pronouns. We'll begin with errors in the use of subject versus object pronouns. To remind yourself of the differences between these types of pronouns, see pages 539–40.

Problems with Subject versus Object Forms

In most sentences with a single subject or object, we have no trouble understanding what type of pronoun to use. Take a look:

SINGLE SUBJECT PRONOUN	I make a daily plan every morning.
SINGLE OBJECT PRONOUN	Mom made a quilt for <u>me</u>.

When there is more than one subject or object, however, it's sometimes harder to "hear" what pronouns are correct. Take a look at the following sentences, in which the pronoun usage is incorrect:

COMPOUND SUBJECT	<u>Tara and me</u> sing in the church choir.
COMPOUND OBJECT	Dennis is going to Denver with <u>Kevin and I</u>.

Remember, if a pronoun is acting as a subject, the subject form must be used, and if a pronoun is acting as an object, the object form must be used. Let's look at corrected versions of the previous sentences:

> **SUBJECT PRONOUN**

<u>Tara and I</u> sing in the church choir.

> **OBJECT PRONOUN**

Dennis is going to Denver with <u>Kevin and me</u>.

 **ACTIVITY 11**

MODERATE

In the following paragraph, circle the correct pronouns from the choices given in parentheses.

(1) Sometimes, a song can bring back vivid, powerful memories.
(2) Recently, my sister was driving (we / us) to our parents' house for dinner. (3) (She / Her) and (I / me) were listening to the car radio when Elton John's classic "Philadelphia Freedom" began to play. (4) Suddenly, I was transported back to 1975. (5) My best friend, Laura, and (I / me) had just graduated from college, and we were driving to New York City just because we had never been there before. (6) "Philadelphia Freedom"

was a hit song at the time, and the radio played it every hour. (7) When (she/her) and (I/me) drove through Philadelphia, we rolled down the car windows, turned up the volume on the radio, and sang along with Elton John at the top of our voices. (8) This was a very exciting time for (we/us) because we felt very free. (9) (She/Her) and (I/me) were not yet tied down to jobs. (10) The future felt so bright for Laura and (I/me).

(11) When my sister pulled into my parents' driveway, she looked at me and said, "You and (I/me) need to talk. You look as if you're a million miles away."

When we make comparisons, we may also have trouble deciding between a subject or an object pronoun. What pronoun would you choose to complete the following sentence?

> Ryan speaks Spanish better than (I / me).

The object pronoun *me* might sound right, but it is incorrect. How can we tell? Let's expand the second part of the comparison:

> Ryan speaks Spanish better than (I / me) speak Spanish.

or

> Ryan speaks Spanish better than (I / me) do.

It may be clearer now that the subject pronoun *I* is the correct choice. It is correct because *I* is the <u>subject</u> that goes with the added-on verbs (*speak, do*).

Whenever you are in doubt about whether to use a subject or an object pronoun in a comparison, expand the comparison.

ACTIVITY 12
MODERATE

In each of the following sentences, circle the correct pronoun from the choices in parentheses.

EXAMPLE: Mickey is a better singer than (I / me).

1. As a speaker, you are just as entertaining as (he / him).
2. No one has worked harder on this project than (she / her).
3. Clearly, you are more worried about Jack's health than (I / me).
4. Hunter has grown so much that he is nearly as tall as (I / me).
5. I believe that you have better management skills than (he / him).

Problems with Collective Nouns

Collective nouns refer to groups of people or things. Following are some examples:

audience	crowd
class	family
committee	jury
company	team

In everyday conversation, we often use the plural possessive *their* to refer to collective nouns, but this practice usually is incorrect in academic writing. Take a look:

The committee will release their report on Tuesday.

In most cases like this one, the members of a group described by a collective noun act as one. Therefore, collective nouns usually are treated as singular. This means that pronouns referring to them usually are singular too.

Let's look at the corrected version of the previous sentence.

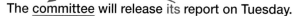

The <u>committee</u> will release its report on Tuesday.

COLLECTIVE NOUN		SINGULAR POSSESSIVE PRONOUN

And here's another correct example:

The <u>jury</u> reached its decision in two days.

COLLECTIVE NOUN	SINGULAR POSSESSIVE PRONOUN

However, collective nouns may be referred to by a plural pronoun if the members of a group are acting as individuals. In the following example, different team members took off their own helmets; they acted individually, not as one. Thus, the collective noun has a plural meaning and takes a plural possessive pronoun.

The team took off their helmets and trudged to the locker room.

◢◢◢◢ ACTIVITY 13
MODERATE

For each sentence below, do the following:

- Underline the collective noun. If the members of the collective noun are acting as one, write **O** next to the sentence.
- If they are acting as individuals, write **I** next to the sentence.
- Circle the possessive pronoun (singular or plural) that goes with the collective noun.

EXAMPLE: The <u>band</u> packed (its /(their)) instruments onto the bus. I

1. The jury reached (its / their) decision after only two hours of deliberation.

2. The audience stamped (its / their) feet in enthusiasm.

3. The committee will deliver (its / their) recommendations at the end of the week.

4. Our football team took off (its / their) helmets in celebration.

5. The entire class finished (its / their) tests in under 30 minutes.

ACTIVITY 14: Mastery Test or Teamwork

Read the following paragraph carefully, looking for pronoun errors. Then, rewrite each error to fix the problem. The errors will include the following:

- unclear pronoun references (see pages 542–44)
- shifts from specific subjects to *you* (see pages 544–46)
- overuse of *it* (see pages 546–48)
- incorrect pronoun agreement (see pages 550–51)
- incorrect use of subject versus object pronouns (see pages 552–53)

The first error has been edited for you.

The following paragraph has 11 pronoun errors (including the one that has been edited for you).

(1) Every summer, my family and ~~me~~ I spend a week in Mexico.

(2) It is not a vacation for us. (3) My family and me are members of our church's mission group, which travels to Mexico every summer to build a new house for a needy family. (4) The work is challenging because you have to work in the hot sun all day. (5) It often reaches 100 degrees or more. (6) Despite the challenges, everybody does their part to build a basic cement house with a tin roof. (7) My brother and me often compete with each other, but he always works faster and harder than me. (8) As we work, we see the terrible poverty among the people that we serve. (9) Although our family is not rich, we are aware that we have so much more than them. (10) At the end of the week, the new house is complete, and the grateful family always shows deep gratitude to me and the rest of the group. (11) For my family and I, this annual mission is very satisfying. (12) We feel very good when you give a deserving family a new house.

BRINGING IT ALL TOGETHER:
Using Pronouns Correctly

In this chapter, you have learned about using pronouns correctly. Confirm your knowledge by filling in the blank spaces in the following sentences. If you need help, review the pages listed after each sentence.

✔ A _____ is a word that takes the place of a noun. Often, a pronoun refers back to a specific _____ that has already been mentioned. (page 537)

✔ We use pronouns for _____, so that we do not have to _____. (page 537)

✔ Three major groups of pronouns are _____, _____, and _____. (page 538)

✔ When the pronoun does not refer clearly to a specific noun or noun phrase, this problem is called an _____. (page 542)

✔ One pronoun that means "people in general" and is often overused in student writing is _____. (page 544)

✔ Another pronoun is sometimes called the "king of the pronouns" because it is so often used and overused. This pronoun is _____. (page 546)

✔ _____ pronouns are used to identify general people or things. These pronouns can lead to two problems: 1) _____ and 2) _____. (page 548)

✔ In academic writing, collective nouns—such as *audience*, *crowd*, *class*, and *family*—are usually treated as singular. Consequently, the possessive pronoun used to refer to a collective noun is _____ instead of *their*. (page 554)

PART FOUR
Reading for Academic Writing

Introduction to Academic Reading

Recreational and Critical Reading

Most of the reading that we do in life falls into two general categories: *recreational reading* and *critical* (or *academic*) *reading*. The primary goal of recreational reading is pleasure; the primary goal of critical reading is knowledge.

When we read recreationally, we want to be entertained or told a good story. We might want to know more about something we care about, such as cooking, fashion, celebrity gossip, car mechanics, or sports scores. This kind of reading should never feel like work.

Academic or critical reading is more active reading: We are actively searching for information and knowledge that can help us expand our horizons. The materials that we read to gain knowledge usually require more work than our recreational reading, and we need reliable tools and procedures to be successful in this operation. Like a doctor performing surgery on a patient, we must learn how to open up a text and get inside it precisely and effectively.

Power Tip
Of course, recreational reading and critical reading are not complete opposites. For example, you can often learn important information from your recreational reading, and you can have fun with critical reading; in fact, many students experience a rush of excitement—an "intellectual high"—when they become good critical readers.

The Three Stages of Academic Reading

When you are given a reading assignment for a class, how do you get started? Do you simply open the book, read the passage, and then move on to another assignment, never thinking about the reading again? If this is your approach, you are not alone. Many students mistakenly believe that academic reading should be as effortless as recreational reading.

Now, imagine a surgeon who walks into an operating room and begins operating on an unknown patient. She makes an incision, starts poking around, adjusts a few arteries and organs, and then sutures the patient up. She leaves and never meets the patient again, unsure whether or not the operation was a success.

Obviously, this scenario is absurd. The success of an operation depends on the doctor's knowledge of the patient before surgery, her problem-solving ability during surgery, and her follow-up with the patient after surgery. In a similar manner, successful critical reading depends on your knowledge of the text *before reading,* your problem-solving ability *while reading,* and your follow-up with the text *after reading.* Take a look:

Pre-surgery	**Surgery**	**Post-surgery**

Pre-reading	**Reading**	**Post-reading**
↓	↓	↓
What is the text about?	*What do I not understand?*	*What have I learned?*
What do I already know?	*What are the main ideas?*	*What questions do I have?*
What do I want to know?	*What evidence can I use?*	*Did I read effectively?*

TOOLS OF THE TRADE

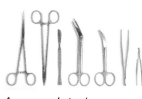

A surgeon's tools

Just like surgery, academic or critical reading is a continuous process of problem solving. A surgeon may encounter old scar tissue, unexpected tumors, and other complications; a critical reader may encounter unexpected vocabulary, complicated information, excessive details, and other obstacles. To solve these problems as they arise, both the surgeon and the critical reader need to have the correct tools on hand. Without them, the operation might be a failure. Good readers should have:

- highlighters
- sharpened pencils (with working erasers)
- sticky notes
- college-level dictionaries
- a notebook for a reading log and a vocabulary log

A critical reader's tools

PRE-READING STRATEGIES

Before you dive into your assigned reading, take a minute to survey what's ahead of you. Pausing to look over the text will give you time to absorb some important information, as well as a moment to calm down if you're feeling anxious. It will also help you to retain more information during and after reading. Begin with two strategies: breaking the reading into manageable parts, and asking three key questions.

Break the Reading into Parts

It's helpful to "preview" the text by breaking it into manageable parts and taking a quick look at them. This will help you think about how the meaning of the reading is being built. This way, you can uncover a lot of information before you even begin reading.

- **The title.** What does the title tell you? Can you guess the reading's main idea?
- **The author's biography** (if available). What does it tell you about the author's expertise or experience? How old is the text?
- **The first paragraph.** Does the first paragraph contain the reading's main idea? Read slowly to get used to the author's writing style and vocabulary.
- **The first sentence of each following paragraph.** How do you think the reading's main idea will develop?
- **The last paragraph.** Does the author summarize the main idea and supporting points?
- **The pattern of development.** Does the reading contain an argument? What other patterns does it use—comparison and contrast or cause and effect, for example?

Power Tip
For more on the patterns of development, see Chapters 11 and 12.

Ask Three Questions

Once you've broken the reading into manageable parts, it's time to ask three important questions about the reading. These will help you discover *what you already think* about the reading and its subject, and they will make the reading process much more satisfying.

To prepare for the three questions, set up a **reading log**—one of your main tools for critical reading. This log can be in a special section of your class notebook or in a separate notebook. Remember, the log should be a permanent record of your reading responses, so do not write on scratch paper, which might get lost.

At the top of the first page, write the heading "Pre-Reading" followed by the title of the reading assignment, the date, and the time that you begin working.

Next, write your answers to the three important pre-reading questions below. Answer these questions briefly each time you pre-read an assigned text:

1. **What is this text about?** Based on the parts of the text that you have just read, what subject or subjects do you think the text will discuss? You can begin by writing:

   I think this text will talk about . . .

2. **What do I already know or feel about this subject?** Do a little brainstorming on what you already know or feel about the subject or subjects of the reading. You can begin by writing:

   I already know (or feel) that . . .

Title of Reading 4/15/12
Start time: 2:35
Pre-Reading:

I think this text will talk about . . .

I already know that . . .

I would like to know more about . . .

3. **What would I like to know about this subject?** Here, you need to be creative: Think of two or three things that you would like to learn about the subject or subjects of this text. You can begin by writing:

I would like to know more about . . .

STOP! Here is a whole idea that I do not understand.

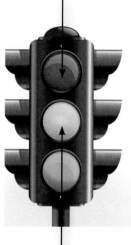

SLOW DOWN! Here is a word **that I do not understand.**

READING STRATEGIES

Now, it's time to read the whole assignment from beginning to end. You may have already read the first paragraph as part of your pre-reading. It is a good strategy to read the paragraph again slowly at least one more time.

Next, it is very important to mark any words or ideas that you do not understand. An effective way to do this is with two simple tools: a yellow highlighter and a pink highlighter.

- As you read, use the yellow highlighter to mark individual words that you do not understand. Many readers skip over unfamiliar words. If this is your habit, you may need to slow down in order to spot these words and highlight them.
- With the pink highlighter, mark any **whole ideas** that you do not understand. A whole idea may be expressed in a few words, a whole sentence, or a group of sentences. Many students skip over difficult ideas, but the meaning of these ideas is often key to understanding the assigned reading.

You can think of these colors like two of the signals on a traffic light. (You'll find out about the green light later.)

ACTIVITY 1

Working with a reading selection that is familiar to you, read the text all the way through, using yellow and pink highlighters to mark the words and ideas that you do not understand. Read slowly and carefully.

Look Up Unfamiliar Words

Each time you look up an unfamiliar word in the dictionary, you are taking an important step toward building an academic vocabulary, which is essential for college-level reading. Furthermore, as you add new words to your vocabulary, you will gain confidence in your ability to discuss and write about a variety of issues and ideas.

Many students skip over unfamiliar words when they read. They do not develop a strategy for vocabulary building, and sooner or later their lack of word knowledge gets in the way of their success as readers and writers. Don't let this happen to you.

One easy and effective strategy is to keep track of new words on yellow sticky notes. Each time you highlight an unfamiliar word, look up its definition and write it on a note. Next, stick the note in the margin of the text. Later, you can move it to a special page in your notebook where you can keep it in alphabetical order along with other words.

Here are some additional tips for building your vocabulary:

- You do not have to look up every unfamiliar word you find. However, look up an unfamiliar word if:

  - the word is necessary for understanding the meaning of a sentence
  - the word is in a sentence that you need to paraphrase
  - you think you have seen or heard the word before
  - you like the sound or the appearance of the word

- Sometimes, it is easier to remember a word if you have heard it pronounced correctly. Many online dictionaries allow you to hear the pronunciation of a word by clicking on an icon (such as the red speaker icon at Merriam-Webster.com).

- Some dictionaries have long and complex definitions. While these may be useful at some point in your education, for now you can rely on a compact student dictionary, a portable electronic dictionary, or a vocabulary-building Web site like Vocabulary.com. These sources provide clear and commonly accepted definitions.

- Have fun building your vocabulary. Some Web sites have word games, thematic word lists, "word of the day," visual definitions, and other features that can motivate you to learn new words (such as on Freerice.com).

Paraphrase Difficult Ideas

Some students skip over difficult ideas when they read. Are you one of these students? If you do this too often during a reading assignment, you may end up having no clue about what you've just read. Being "clueless" when you get to class can be frustrating and embarrassing; you may have difficulty following the instructor's lesson, participating in group discussions, and taking quizzes based on the reading.

It is important to have a concrete strategy for dealing with difficult ideas each time you encounter them. In Chapter 13 of this book, you learned that paraphrasing difficult sentences can help you make sense of them. This strategy takes a little extra time, but the improvement in your reading comprehension can be dramatic.

Start by dividing a difficult sentence into smaller "chunks," or units of information. Do this in your reading log or on a separate sheet of paper. Then, rephrase the chunks in your own words. When you are done, write the paraphrase on a pink or red sticky note and stick it in the margin of the text next to the original sentence. This will allow you to refer quickly to your paraphrase when discussing the reading in class. Later, you'll be able to move all the sticky notes to your reading log.

Power Tip
You can look up each word immediately or after you have finished reading the whole assignment.

Power Tip
You may use differently sized sticky notes depending on how much you need to write.

emulate (verb): to strive to match someone, especially by imitating that person

Power Tip
Remember, to paraphrase means to *restate* an author's ideas *in your own words and writing style*. For more on paraphrasing, see Chapter 13, pages 311–15.

Davis points out that she had to make a choice between hip-hop and the need for women to be respected (p. 47).

GO! I have identified the main idea and am ready for post-reading strategies.

Find Main Ideas

Often, college students are asked to read materials for class *with no specific instructions about what information to look for.* A professor might say, "Read Chapter 6 for our next class meeting," or "For homework, read this story. We will discuss it on Monday."

If you receive an assignment like this—with no specific instructions about what to look for in the reading—you can assume that your professor wants you to read for a basic understanding of the material. A basic understanding means that you should be able to locate and summarize the author's main ideas.

The best way to identify an author's main ideas is to read the assigned reading a second time—after you have defined unfamiliar words and paraphrased difficult ideas. The idea of reading an assignment twice may seem unreasonable, but *rereading* is a standard expectation for college-level work. If you try to deal with vocabulary, difficult ideas, and main ideas the first time you read an assignment, you might become overwhelmed and discouraged.

Here is an effective way to keep track of main ideas:

- Use a green highlighter to mark the main idea for each paragraph (or group of small paragraphs) in the assigned reading. You may want to work with a pencil at first while considering all the possibilities. However, at some point, you should commit to a choice and highlight it. Of course, you can always change your mind later (after a class discussion, for example), but independent decision making is an important part of the learning process.

- After you have identified a main idea, paraphrase it in your own words. (Follow the guidelines and strategies for paraphrasing in Chapter 13, pages 311–15.)

- Then, write the finished paraphrase on a green sticky note.

In his article "Farewell, Fair Weather," Charles Blow claims that a period of unpredictable, dangerous weather has arrived in the U.S. and should be taken seriously (p. 12).

You'll probably want to review your ideas during class discussion, so put each green sticky note in the margin alongside the appropriate paragraph in the reading. Later, if you want to write a summary of the reading assignment, you'll be able to move the sticky notes to your reading log and arrange them in a convenient order. (For more on writing a summary, see Chapter 13, pages 315–17.)

When you have identified and paraphrased the author's main ideas, you are ready to move on to the last stage of academic or critical reading. You now have a green light to move on.

POST-READING STRATEGIES

The final stage of the reading process allows you to bring together all the smaller pieces of information that you have gathered so far. In other words, post-reading activities give you the "big picture" of what you have read. As with your pre-reading and reading work, you should write down all your post-reading ideas in your log so that you can use them later. You may want them to help you prepare for class discussions, exams, or writing assignments.

As a college student, you should be able to go beyond answering basic questions about assigned readings. You should also be able to develop your own questions that demonstrate your critical thinking ability. Here, you will be introduced to four important types of questions.

Read the following paragraph and the material after it to understand more about four types of questions: <u>identification</u>, <u>synthesis</u>, <u>inference</u>, and <u>abstraction</u> questions.

The following paragraph discusses an African American culture found on several small islands off the southeastern coast of the United States. "Gullah" culture has survived for more than 200 years on these islands but is currently in decline.

But we cannot let our culture just dwindle like our population. **1**
We have to tell our young people the old stories, show them our
dances and teach them our crafts so that they will be able to pass
the culture onto their children. That is why, since 1995, we have
held an annual festival called Cultural Day on the third Saturday of **5**
September, in the hope that the people of Sapelo, living here and on
the mainland, will bring their traditional baskets, their handmade
nets and their family recipes and stories, and share Gullah culture
with a new generation. That is also why we welcome visitors to the
island. They can rent mobile homes or stay in a Hog's Hummock **10**
guesthouse not far from the dock. Although there is no visitor's center here, state tourist centers on nearby St. Simons Island or in the
towns of Meridian and Savannah can offer information on what to
do in Sapelo. For starters, you might try an old-fashioned mule tour
run by my own son, Maurice Bailey. Of course, plants and trees and **15**
wildlife abound, and those of us left on Sapelo enjoy demonstrating
our local crafts and cooking.

"On-the-Page" Questions

"On-the-page" questions identify something or synthesize information that is given clearly in the reading. **Identification** and **synthesis** questions are considered "easy" because their answers are stated directly by the author. The answers to "on-the-page" questions are not mysterious: You can find them right in the text.

1. **Identification questions ask you for a piece of information from the text.** The answer will be <u>one item</u> stated on the page.

   Example
   Question: What is something that the Gullah people have done since 1995 to preserve their culture?
   Answer: They hold the Cultural Day festival once a year. *(This answer is directly stated in the fifth line of the paragraph.)*

2. **Synthesis questions ask you to pull together different pieces of information in the text.** The answer will be <u>two or more items</u> stated on the page.

Power Tip
To synthesize means to combine or bring together several parts to make a whole.

Example

Question: What is the traditional lifestyle like in Gullah culture?

Answer: The people make their own baskets and nets, entertain themselves by telling stories, use mules, and live close to nature. *(This answer is directly stated in the seventh, eighth, fourteenth, and fifteenth lines of the paragraph.)*

ACTIVITY 2: Teamwork

Team up with some of your classmates. Next, using a reading that you are all already familiar with, separate into pairs and have each pair develop one identification question and one synthesis question. Then, trade questions and supply the answers.

"Between-the-Lines" Questions

Inference and **abstraction** questions are more challenging because you cannot point to the answers on the page. We call these "between-the-lines" questions because you have to dig below the surface to figure out the answers. For inference questions, you can use cues that the author has provided. For abstraction questions, you might need to do some additional research. In both cases, these questions reveal deeper levels of meaning in the assigned reading.

Power Tip

To infer means to figure out an answer based on clues, or to make a calculated guess.

3. **Inference questions ask you to figure something out based on what you read.** The answer is <u>suggested</u> by the author but is not stated directly.

Example

Question: Does Sapelo Island have a well-developed tourist industry?

Answer: Probably not. There is no state tourist center like on the neighboring islands, and tourist accommodations are modest (mobile homes instead of hotels). A main attraction is a mule tour run by one person. This doesn't suggest a "well-developed tourist industry."

Power Tip

To abstract means to move away from simple, concrete facts (on the page) to ask a more generalized or abstract ("big picture") question about the topic.

4. **Abstraction questions ask you to think about the reading's theme and to tie the reading to things beyond the reading.** The answer is related to a theme in the reading but is not found in the reading. Often, the answer will require additional research.

Example

Question: Are other traditional, ethnic cultures in America also struggling to survive?

This answer will require additional research.

ACTIVITY 3: Teamwork

Team up with some of your classmates. Next, using a reading that you are all already familiar with, separate into pairs and have each pair develop one inference question and one abstraction question. Then, trade questions and supply the answers. Remember that with inference questions the answer is suggested by the author but not stated directly, whereas with abstraction questions the answer requires information not provided in the text.

Developing the four types of post-reading questions every time you read an assignment is an important last step in becoming a successful college reader. Although you can have as many questions as you like, try to develop at least one question of each type (identification, synthesis, inference, and abstraction). This practice will strengthen your critical reading—and thinking—ability.

Self-Assessment Questions

Last, it is very important to chart your progress as a critical reader. Every time you complete a reading assignment, ask yourself the following questions:

- How do I feel about this reading experience?
- Did I notice any changes in my approach to critical reading?
- What was my attitude when I got stuck or confused in my reading? What is my "problem-solving attitude"?
- Did I have any "ah-ha!" moments when I figured something out or realized something?
- Do I feel like I am gaining focus and control in my critical reading skills? Why or why not?
- How often was I bored or distracted? What did I do to get back on track?
- Did the time go by slowly or quickly while I was reading? Why?
- Are my critical reading skills helping me in some other areas of my life?
- What are my goals for my critical reading at this point?

ACTIVITY 4

In your journal or reading log, write for five or ten minutes about your reading experience. Write anything that comes to mind. If you are stuck, try responding to **one or two** of the self-assessment questions listed above.

ACTIVITY 5: Teamwork

Pair with a classmate and exchange your self-assessment writing. After reading each other's ideas, discuss out loud what you have written and how you feel about your critical reading ability at this point.

BRINGING IT ALL TOGETHER:
Introduction to Academic Reading

In this chapter, you have been introduced to reading for academic writing. Confirm your knowledge by filling in the blank spaces in the following sentences. If you need help, review the pages listed after each sentence.

✔ Recreational reading should never feel like work. Critical reading is more _____ than recreational reading, and it requires reliable _____ such as highlighters, pencils, sticky notes, dictionaries, and a notebook. (pages 559–60)

✔ Two pre-reading strategies are _____ and _____. (pages 560–62)

✔ While reading, it's useful to use three colored highlighters and the same colored sticky notes. These will help you identify _____ that are unfamiliar to you, _____ that you don't understand, and _____ in the paragraphs. Once you have identified and understood these, you will most likely have a good grasp of the text. (pages 562, 564)

✔ The four types of post-reading questions fall into two categories: "on-the-page" questions and "between-the-lines" questions. They are: 1) _____, 2) _____, 3) _____, and 4) _____ questions. These questions help you to go beyond basic understanding and form your own ideas. (pages 564–67)

On Family Heritage

What is your family heritage, and how does it affect you? Do you have any customs or traditions that relate to your heritage? Do you feel that your personality has been determined by your family heritage, or do you think the general environment in which you were raised matters more? What does it mean to live in America, a country with people of so many different backgrounds living in one place?

Sherman Alexie

Blankets

Sherman Alexie is a poet, fiction writer, and filmmaker known for his portrayals of contemporary Native American life. He grew up on the Spokane Indian Reservation in Wellpinit, Washington, and now lives in Seattle.

After the surgeon cut off my father's right foot—no, half of my father's right foot—and three toes from the left, I sat with him in the recovery room. It was more like a recovery hallway. There was no privacy, not even a thin curtain. I guessed it made it easier for the nurses to monitor the postsurgical patients, but still, my father was exposed—his decades of poor health and worse decisions were illuminated—on white sheets, in a white hallway under white lights. 1

"Are you okay?" I asked. It was a stupid question. Who could be okay after such a thing? Yesterday, my father had walked into the hospital. Okay, he'd shuffled while balanced on two canes, but that was still called walking. A few hours ago, my father still had both of his feet. Yes, his feet and toes had been black with rot and disease but they'd still been, technically speaking, feet and toes. And, most important, those feet and toes had belonged to my father. But now they were gone, sliced off. Where were they? What did they do with the right foot and the toes from the left foot? Did they throw them in the incinerator? Were their ashes floating over the city? 2

"Doctor, I'm cold," my father said. 3

"Dad, it's me," I said. 4

"I know who are you. You're my son." But considering the blankness in my father's eyes, I assumed he was just guessing at my identity. 5

"Dad, you're in the hospital. You just had surgery." 6

"I know where I am. I'm cold." 7

"Do you want another blanket?" Another stupid question. Of course 8
he wanted another blanket. He probably wanted me to build a fucking
campfire or drag in one of those giant propane heaters that NFL football
teams used on the sidelines.

I walked down the hallway—the recovery hallway—to the nurses' sta- 9
tion. There were three women nurses, two white and one black. Being Native
American–Spokane and Coeur d'Alene Indian, I hoped my darker pigment
would give me an edge with the black nurse, so I addressed her directly.

pigment: skin color

"My father is cold," I said. "Can I get another blanket?" 10

The black nurse glanced up from her paperwork and regarded me. 11
Her expression was neither compassionate nor callous.

callous: unfeeling

"How can I help you, sir?" she asked. 12

"I'd like another blanket for my father. He's cold." 13

"I'll be with you in a moment, sir." 14

She looked back down at her paperwork. She made a few notes. Not 15
knowing what else to do, I stood there and waited.

"Sir," the black nurse said. "I'll be with you in a moment." 16

She was irritated. I understood. After all, how many thousands of 17
times had she been asked for an extra blanket? She was a nurse, an educated woman, not a damn housekeeper. And it was never really about an
extra blanket, was it? No, when people asked for an extra blanket, they
were asking for a time machine. And, yes, she knew she was a health care
provider, and she knew she was supposed to be compassionate, but my
father, an alcoholic, diabetic Indian with terminally damaged kidneys, had
just endured an incredibly expensive surgery for what? So he could ride
his motorized wheelchair to the bar and win bets by showing off his dis-
figured foot? I know she didn't want to be cruel, but she believed there
was a point when doctors should stop rescuing people from their own
self-destructive impulses. And I couldn't disagree with her but I could ask
for the most basic of comforts, couldn't I?

"My father," I said. "An extra blanket, please." 18

"Fine," she said, then stood and walked back to a linen closet, 19
grabbed a white blanket, and handed it to me. "If you need anything
else—"

I didn't wait around for the end of her sentence. With the blanket 20
in hand, I walked back to my father. It was a thin blanket, laundered and
sterilized a hundred times. In fact, it was too thin. It wasn't really a blanket.
It was more like a large beach towel. Hell, it wasn't even good enough for
that. It was more like the world's largest coffee filter. Jesus, had health
care finally come to this? Everybody was uninsured and unblanketed.

"Dad, I'm back." 21

He looked so small and pale lying in that hospital bed. How had that 22
change happened? For the first sixty-seven years of his life, my father had
been a large and dark man. And now, he was just another pale and sick
drone in a hallway of pale and sick drones. A hive, I thought, this place
looks like a beehive with colony collapse disorder.

**colony collapse
disorder:** the phe-
nomenon of bees
abandoning their hive

"Dad, it's me." 23

"I'm cold." 24

"I have a blanket." 25

As I draped it over my father and tucked it around his body, I felt 26
the first sting of grief. I'd read the hospital literature about this moment.
There would come a time when roles would reverse and the adult child
would become the caretaker of the ill parent. The circle of life. Such
poetic bullshit.

"I can't get warm," my father said. "I'm freezing." 27

"I brought you a blanket, Dad, I put it on you." 28

"Get me another one. Please. I'm so cold. I need another blanket." 29

I knew that ten more of these cheap blankets wouldn't be enough. 30
My father needed a real blanket, a good blanket.

I walked out of the recovery hallway and made my way through vari- 31
ous doorways and other hallways, peering into the rooms, looking at the
patients and their families, looking for a particular kind of patient and
family.

I walked through the ER, cancer, heart and vascular, neuroscience, 32
orthopedic, women's health, pediatrics, and surgical services. Nobody
stopped me. My expression and posture were that of a man with a sick
father and so I belonged.

And then I saw him, another Native man, leaning against a wall near 33
the gift shop. Well, maybe he was Asian; lots of those in Seattle. He was
a small man, pale brown, with muscular arms and a soft belly. Maybe he
was Mexican, which is really a kind of Indian, too, but not the kind that
I needed. It was hard to tell sometimes what people were. Even brown
people guessed at the identity of other brown people.

"Hey," I said. 34

"Hey," the other man said. 35

"You Indian?" I asked. 36

"Yeah." 37

"What tribe?" 38

"Lummi." 39

"I'm Spokane." 40

"My first wife was Spokane. I hated her." 41

"My first wife was Lummi. She hated me." 42

We laughed at the new jokes that instantly sounded old. 43

"Why are you in here?" I asked. 44

"My sister is having a baby," he said. "But don't worry, it's not mine." 45

"Ayyyyyy," I said—another Indian idiom—and laughed. 46

"I don't even want to be here," the other Indian said. "But my dad 47
started, like, this new Indian tradition. He says it's a thousand years old.
But that's bullshit. He just made it up to impress himself. And the whole
family just goes along, even when we know it's bullshit. He's in the deliv-
ery room waving eagle feathers around. Jesus."

"What's the tradition?" 48

"Oh, he does a naming ceremony right in the hospital. Like, it's sup- 49
posed to protect the baby from all the technology and shit. Like hospitals
are the big problem. You know how many babies died before we had good
hospitals?"

"I don't know." 50

"Most of them. Well, shit, a lot of them, at least." 51

trance: a half-conscious, dazed state of mind

charlatan: a fake

orate: to speak formally

sovereignty: self-governance

indigenous: native to a particular place

ironic: contrary to expectation, and as a result, funny or surprising

This guy was talking out of his ass. I liked him immediately.   52

"I mean," the guy said, "you should see my dad right now. He's pre-   53
tending to go into this, like, fucking trance and is dancing around my sister's
bed, and he says he's trying to, you know, see into her womb, to see who
the baby is, to see its true nature, so he can give it a name—a protective
name—before it's born."

The guy laughed and threw his head back and banged it on the wall.   54

"I mean, come on, I'm a loser," he said and rubbed his sore skull. "My   55
whole family is filled with losers."

The Indian world is filled with charlatans, men and women who   56
pretended—hell, who might have come to believe—that they were holy.
Last year, I had gone to a lecture at the University of Washington. An elderly
Indian woman, a Sioux writer and scholar and charlatan, had come to orate
on Indian sovereignty and literature. She kept arguing for some kind of
separate indigenous literary identity, which was ironic considering that she
was speaking English to a room full of white professors. But I wasn't angry
with the woman, or even bored. No, I felt sorry for her. I realized that she
was dying of nostalgia. She had taken nostalgia as her false idol—her thin
blanket—and it was murdering her.

"Nostalgia," I said to the other Indian man in the hospital.   57

"What?"   58

"Your dad, he sounds like he's got a bad case of nostalgia."   59

"Yeah, I hear you catch that from fucking old high school girl friends,"   60
the man said. "What the hell you doing here anyway?"

"My dad just got his feet cut off," I said.   61

"Diabetes?"   62

"And vodka."   63

"Vodka straight up or with a nostalgia chaser?"   64

"Both."   65

"Natural causes for an Indian."   66

"Yep."   67

There wasn't much to say after that.   68

"Well, I better get back," the man said. "Otherwise, my dad might   69
wave an eagle feather and change my name."

"Hey, wait," I said.   70

"Yeah?"   71

"Can I ask you a favor?"   72

"What?"   73

"My dad, he's in the recovery room," I said. "Well, it's more like a   74
hallway, and he's freezing, and they've only got these shitty little blankets,
and I came looking for Indians in the hospital because I figured—well, I
guessed if I found any Indians, they might have some good blankets."

"So you want to borrow a blanket from us?" the man asked.   75

"Yeah."   76

"Because you thought some Indians would just happen to have some   77
extra blankets lying around?"

"Yeah."   78

"That's fucking ridiculous."   79

"I know."   80

"And it's racist."   81

"I know."   82

"You're stereotyping your own damn people."   83

"I know."   84

"But damn if we don't have a room full of Pendleton blankets. New   85
ones. Jesus, you'd think my sister was having, like, a dozen babies."

Five minutes later, carrying a Pendleton Star Blanket, the Indian man   86
walked out of his sister's hospital room, accompanied by his father, who
wore Levi's, a black T-shirt, and eagle feathers in his gray braids.

"We want to give your father this blanket," the old man said. "It was   87
meant for my grandson, but I think it will be good for your father, too."

"Thank you."   88

"Let me bless it. I will sing a healing song for the blanket. And for   89
your father."

I flinched. This guy wanted to sing a song? That was dangerous. This   90
song could take two minutes or two hours. It was impossible to know. Hell,
considering how desperate this old man was to be seen as holy, he might
sing for a week. I couldn't let this guy begin his song without issuing a caveat.   **caveat:** an exception
or warning

"My dad," I said. "I really need to get back to him. He's really sick."   91

"Don't worry," the old man said and winked. "I'll sing one of my short   92
ones."

Jesus, who'd ever heard of a self-aware fundamentalist? The son,   93   **fundamentalist:** a
perhaps not the unbeliever he'd pretended to be, sang backup as his father   conservative believer
launched into his radio-friendly honor song, just three-and-a-half minutes,
like the length of any Top Forty rock song of the last fifty years. But here's
the funny thing: the old man couldn't sing very well. If you were going to
have the balls to sing healing songs in hospital hallways, then you should
logically have a great voice, right? But no, this guy couldn't keep the tune.
And his voice cracked and wavered. Does a holy song lose its power if its   **waver:** to sway or
singer is untalented?   flutter

"That is your father's song," the old man said when he was finished.   94
"I give it to him. I will never sing it again. It belongs to your father now."

Behind his back, the old man's son rolled his eyes and walked back   95
into his sister's room.

"Okay, thank you," I said. I felt like an ass, accepting the blanket and   96
the old man's good wishes, but silently mocking them at the same time.
But maybe the old man did have some power, some real medicine, because he peeked into my brain.

"It doesn't matter if you believe in the healing song," the old man   97
said. "It only matters that the blanket heard."

"Where have you been?" my father asked when I returned. "I'm cold."   98

"I know, I know," I said. "I found you a blanket. A good one. It will   99
keep you warm."

I draped the Star Blanket over my father. He pulled the thick wool **100**
up to his chin. And then he began to sing. It was a healing song, not the
same song that I had just heard, but a healing song nonetheless. My father could sing beautifully. I wondered if it was proper for a man to sing
a healing song for himself. I wondered if my father needed help with the
song. I hadn't sung for many years, not like that, but I joined him. I knew
this song would not bring back my father's feet. This song would not repair my father's bladder, kidneys, lungs, and heart. This song would not
prevent my father from drinking a bottle of vodka as soon as he could sit
up in bed. This song would not defeat death. No, I thought, this song is

temporary, but right now, temporary is good enough. And it was a good song. Our voices filled the recovery hallway. The sick and healthy stopped to listen. The nurses, even the remote black one, unconsciously took a few steps toward us. The black nurse sighed and smiled. I smiled back. I knew what she was thinking. Sometimes, even after all of these years, she could still be surprised by her work. She still marveled at the infinite and ridiculous faith of other people.

DISCUSS WITH YOUR PEERS

1. Reread paragraph 26. The author says he "felt the first sting of grief," but by the end of the paragraph he calls the role reversal between parent and child "poetic bullshit." How would you describe the narrator's emotional response to his father's condition? Beyond this paragraph, can you find other clues that reveal the narrator's emotions? If so, where?

2. Reread paragraphs 33 and 74–85. From these passages, it is clear that the narrator thinks about issues of race. However, to what extent is he himself also racist, if at all? You might begin by answering the question, what does it mean to be "racist"? Use details from the passages to support your opinion.

3. Reread paragraphs 47–56 and 89–97. What is the attitude of the narrator and the man he meets in the hospital about Indian traditions? Do you think their attitude is realistic and fair? Next, discuss the attitude of the father toward Indian tradition. Do you think he is a "loser" like the son claims, or is he contributing something meaningful?

4. Reread paragraph 100. Does the narrator's attitude toward tradition change in this paragraph? If so, how does it change, and why? Try to identify two or three key quotations that explain the narrator's attitude in this paragraph.

IDENTIFY THE PATTERNS

1. The primary pattern of this story is **narration**. Identify the beginning, middle, and end of the story. Where does each part start and stop? What important things happen in each part?

2. The author uses **cause and effect** at least twice in the story. First, describe the father's illness (effects) and then identify the causes of his illness. Next, describe the behavior of the nurse (effects) and then identify the likely causes of her behavior.

3. The author uses **process** in paragraph 53. Reread the paragraph, and then explain in your own words each step in the process that the father uses to name the unborn child.

4. The author uses **exemplification** in paragraph 56. Explain what the author is exemplifying and whether you think his example is a good one.

WRITE ABOUT THE READING

1. In this story, does "tradition" serve the Native Americans in a valuable way, or is it more of an obstacle in dealing with the realities of life? Use examples and details from the story to support your position.

2. Is the narrator in this story someone you would enjoy having as a friend or family member? Use examples and details from the story to support your position.

WRITE ABOUT YOUR LIFE

1. Discuss traditions that are part of your family or culture. You can describe these traditions and discuss whether they have changed and whether they still have an important role for your family or culture.

2. Discuss a family member who suffered from a severe illness and perhaps spent time in a hospital. Describe the person's condition and how you and other family members responded to the situation.

Gary Soto

Like Mexicans

In addition to many award-winning poetry collections, Gary Soto has written children's and young-adult books, novels, and the memoir *Living up the Street* (1985). He also helps promote the work of California Rural Legal Assistance and the United Farm Workers of America, organizations that assist farm workers and the rural poor. Like much of Soto's writing, the following essay draws on his experiences growing up in a working-class Mexican American family.

My grandmother gave me bad advice and good advice when I was in my early teens. For the bad advice, she said that I should become a barber because they made good money and listened to the radio all day. "Honey, they don't work *como burros*," she would say every time I visited her. She made the sound of donkeys braying. "Like that, honey!" For the good advice, she said that I should marry a Mexican girl. "No Okies, *hijo*"—she would say—"Look my son. He marry one and they fight every day about I don't know what and I don't know what." For her, everyone who wasn't Mexican, black, or Asian were Okies. The French were Okies, the Italians in suits were Okies. When I asked about Jews, whom I had read about, she asked for a picture. I rode home on my bicycle and returned with a calendar depicting the important races of the world. *"Pues sí, son Okies también!"* she said, nodding her head. She waved the calendar away and we went to the living room, where she lectured me on the virtues of the Mexican girl: first, she could cook and, second, she acted like a woman, not a man, in her husband's home. She said she would tell me about a third when I got a little older.

1

como burros
[Spanish]: like donkeys

hijo [Spanish]: son

"Pues sí, son Okies también!" [Spanish]: "Then they are also Okies!"

I asked my mother about it—becoming a barber and marrying **2** Mexican. She was in the kitchen. Steam curled from a pot of boiling beans, the radio was on, looking as squat as a loaf of bread. "Well, if you want to be a barber—they say they make good money." She slapped a round steak with a knife, her glasses slipping down with each strike. She stopped and looked up. "If you find a good Mexican girl, marry her of course." She returned to slapping the meat and I went to the backyard where my brother and David King were sitting on the lawn feeling the inside of their cheeks.

"This is what girls feel like," my brother said, rubbing the inside of **3** his cheek. David put three fingers inside his mouth and scratched. I ignored them and climbed the back fence to see my best friend, Scott, a second-generation Okie. I called him and his mother pointed to the side of the house where his bedroom was a small aluminum trailer, the kind you gawk at when they're flipped over on the freeway, wheels spinning in the air. I went around to find Scott pitching horseshoes.

meager: small or weak

I picked up a set of rusty ones and joined him. While we played, we **4** talked about school and friends and record albums. The horseshoes scuffed up dirt, sometimes ringing the iron that threw out a meager shadow like a sundial. After three argued-over games, we pulled two oranges apiece from his tree and started down the alley still talking school and friends and record albums. We pulled more oranges from the alley and talked about who we would marry. "No offense, Scott," I said with an orange slice in my mouth, "but I would never marry an Okie." We walked in step, almost touching, with a sled of shadows dragging behind us. "No offense, Gary," Scott said, "but I would *never* marry a Mexican." I looked at him: a fang of orange slice showed from his munching mouth. I didn't think anything of it. He had his girl and I had mine. But our seventh-grade vision was the same: to marry, get jobs, buy cars and maybe a house if we had money left over.

We talked about our future lives until, to our surprise, we were on the **5** downtown mall, two miles from home. We bought a bag of popcorn at Penneys and sat on a bench near the fountain watching Mexican and Okie girls pass. "That one's mine," I pointed with my chin when a girl with eyebrows arched into black rainbows ambled by. "She's cute," Scott said about a girl with yellow hair and a mouthful of gum. We dreamed aloud, our chins busy pointing out girls. We agreed that we couldn't wait to become men and lift them onto our laps.

But the woman I married was not Mexican but Japanese. It was a **6** surprise to me. For years, I went about wide-eyed in my search for the brown girl in a white dress at a dance. I searched the playground at the baseball diamond. When the girls raced for grounders, their hair bounced like something that couldn't be caught. When they sat together in the lunchroom, heads pressed together, I knew they were talking about us Mexican guys. I saw them and dreamed them. I threw my face into my pillow, making up sentences that were good as in the movies.

But when I was twenty, I fell in love with this other girl who wor- **7** ried my mother, who had my grandmother asking once again to see the calendar of the Important Races of the World. I told her I had thrown it away years before. I took a much-glanced-at snapshot from my wallet. We looked at it together, in silence. Then grandma reclined in her chair, lit a cigarette, and said, "Es pretty." She blew and asked with all her worry pushed up to her forehead: "Chinese?"

I was in love and there was no looking back. She was the one. I told   **8**
my mother who was slapping hamburger into patties. "Well, sure if you
want to marry her," she said. But the more I talked, the more concerned
she became. Later I began to worry. Was it all a mistake? "Marry a Mexican girl," I heard my mother say in my mind. I heard it at breakfast. I
heard it over math problems, between Western Civilization and cultural
geography. But then one afternoon while I was hitchhiking home from
school, it struck me like a baseball in the back: my mother wanted me
to marry someone of my own social class—a poor girl. I considered my
fiancee, Carolyn, and she didn't look poor, though I knew she came from a
family of farm workers and pull-yourself-up-by-your-bootstraps ranchers.
I asked my brother, who was marrying Mexican poor that fall, if I should
marry a poor girl. He screamed "Yeah" above his terrible guitar playing in
his bedroom. I considered my sister who had married Mexican. Cousins
were dating Mexican. Uncles were remarrying poor women. I asked Scott,
who was still my best friend, and he said, "She's too good for you, so you
better not."

I worried about it until Carolyn took me home to meet her parents.   **9**
We drove in her Plymouth until the houses gave way to farms and ranches
and finally her house fifty feet from the highway. When we pulled into the
drive, I panicked and begged Carolyn to make a U-turn and go back so we
could talk about it over a soda. She pinched my cheek, calling me a "silly
boy." I felt better, though, when I got out of the car and saw the house:
the chipped paint, a cracked window, boards for a walk to the back door.
There were rusting cars near the barn. A tractor with a net of spiderwebs
under a mulberry. A field. A bale of barbed wire like children's scribbling
leaning against an empty chicken coop. Carolyn took my hand and pulled
me to my future mother-in-law who was coming out to greet us.

We had lunch: sandwiches, potato chips, and iced tea. Carolyn and   **10**
her mother talked mostly about neighbors and the congregation at the
Japanese Methodist Church in West Fresno. Her father, who was in khaki
work clothes, excused himself with a wave that was almost a salute and
went outside. I heard a truck start, a dog bark, and then the truck rattle away.

Carolyn's mother offered another sandwich, but I declined with a   **11**
shake of my head and a smile. I looked around when I could, when I was
not saying over and over that I was a college student, hinting that I could
take care of her daughter. I shifted my chair. I saw newspapers piled in
corners, dusty cereal boxes and vinegar bottles in corners. The wallpaper
was bubbled from rain that had come in from a bad roof. Dust. Dust lay
on lamp shades and window sills. These people are just like Mexicans, I
thought. Poor people.

Carolyn's mother asked me through Carolyn if I would like a *sushi*.   **12**
A plate of black and white things was held in front of me. I took one, wide-
eyed, and turned it over like a foreign coin. I was biting into one when I saw
a kitten crawl up the window screen over the sink. I chewed and the kitten
opened its mouth of terror as she crawled higher, wanting in to paw the
leftovers from our plates. I looked at Carolyn who said that the cat was just
showing off. I looked up in time to see it fall. It crawled up, then fell again.

We talked for an hour and had apple pie and coffee, slowly. Finally,   **13**
we got up with Carolyn taking my hand. Slightly embarrassed, I tried to pull
away but her grip held me. I let her have her way as she led me down the

hallway with her mother right behind me. When I opened the door, I was startled by a kitten clinging to the screen door, its mouth screaming "cat food, dog biscuits, *sushi*...." I opened the door and the kitten, still holding on, whined in the language of hungry animals. When I got into Carolyn's car, I looked back: the cat was still clinging. I asked Carolyn if it were possibly hungry, but she said the cat was being silly. She started the car, waved to her mother, and bounced us over the rain-poked drive, patting my thigh for being her lover baby. Carolyn waved again. I looked back, waving, then gawking at a window screen where there were now three kittens clawing and screaming to get in. Like Mexicans, I thought. I remembered the Molinas and how the cats clung to their screens—cats they shot down with squirt guns. On the highway, I felt happy, pleased by it all. I patted Carolyn's thigh. Her people were like Mexicans, only different.

gawking: staring in a stupid-looking way

DISCUSS WITH YOUR PEERS

1. Reread paragraph 1, and discuss whether the grandmother's attitude about other races is racist. Then, discuss whether her advice about marriage is racist or simply traditional. Finally, are her claims about Mexican girls sexist and potentially harmful? If you are a woman, would you like to be described in this way? Explain your opinions.

2. Notice from paragraph 8 that the author's family members tend to date and marry within their own ethnic group (Mexican) and socio-economic class (poor). Moreover, they encourage him to do the same thing. Discuss what some advantages and disadvantages of this practice might be.

3. Look closely at the description of the kitten in paragraphs 12–13. The author seems fixated on the kitten as he struggles to feel comfortable in the unfamiliar environment. Discuss how the kitten is an illustration of Soto himself and what he is going through at that moment. What terrifies Soto? In what way is Soto trying to "crawl higher" and then falling and crawling up again? What is he clinging to? What is he starved for?

IDENTIFY THE PATTERNS

1. The author uses **narration** as the main pattern of development. What is the story he tells? What are the main events of the story? Does the author effectively re-create the settings and the characters? Provide specific examples.

2. Soto also uses **description** to develop his writing. Almost every sentence contains strong action verbs, colorful adjectives, and concrete nouns. Reread paragraphs 4 and 9 in particular, and underline or highlight some of the powerful details that bring the scenes and the characters to life.

3. In paragraphs 10–13, the author uses **comparison and contrast**. First, identify what two things are being compared and/or contrasted. Then, identify some of the ways in which these two things are simi-

lar and/or different. Does the author use more comparison, more contrast, or an equal amount of both? Does he provide enough information and details to make this an effective comparison and contrast?

WRITE ABOUT THE READING

Discuss whether you believe that the author, Gary, and his girlfriend, Carolyn, are likely to have a successful marriage. Use information from the story to support your point of view.

WRITE ABOUT YOUR LIFE

1. Discuss whether people should try to marry someone of their own race, ethnicity, or socioeconomic class. Support your position with specific reasons and examples.

2. Describe the relationship of an interracial couple or a couple from different socioeconomic backgrounds (you and your partner or a couple you have known). What sorts of challenges does the couple face, how do they handle the challenges, and what are some of the outcomes of those situations?

WRITE ABOUT THE THEME

1. Compare and/or contrast the narrators of the two stories and how they reject or embrace their family heritage.

2. Compare and/or contrast the family heritages—Native American and Mexican—in the two stories. What are their traditions, and how are they similar and/or different?

When was the last time you did something nice for another person? Do you make it a conscious habit to look out for the well-being of other people? As you read the following two stories, consider how looking out for others is beneficial to both the persons receiving that kindness *and* the giver. Think about how the world might be a better place if we all took more time to recognize the needs of others.

Eve Birch

The Art of Being a Neighbor

Eve Birch is a librarian in West Virginia. She also runs a remodeling business that provides work to people in need, many of whom are her neighbors.

I used to believe in the American dream that meant a job, a mortgage, cable, credit, warrantees, success. I wanted it and worked toward it like everyone else, all of us separately chasing the same thing. 1

One year, through a series of unhappy events, it all fell apart. I found myself homeless and alone. I had my truck and $56. 2

scour: to search carefully

I scoured the countryside for someplace I could rent for the cheapest possible amount. I came upon a shack in an isolated hollow four miles up a winding mountain road over the Potomac River in West Virginia. 3

It was abandoned, full of broken glass and rubbish. When I pried off the plywood over a window and climbed in, I found something I could put my hands to. I hadn't been alone for twenty-five years. I was scared, but hoped the hard work would distract and heal me. 4

I found the owner and rented the place for $50 a month. I took a bedroll, broom, rope, a gun, and cooking gear, and cleared a corner to camp in while I worked. 5

The locals knew nothing about me. But slowly, they started teaching me the art of being a neighbor. They dropped off blankets, candles, tools, and canned deer meat, and they began sticking around to chat. They asked if I wanted to meet cousin Albie or go fishing, maybe get 6 drunk some night. They started to teach me a belief in a different American dream — not the one of individual achievement but of neighborliness.

Men would stop by with wild berries, ice cream, truck parts, and bullets to see if I was up for courting. I wasn't, but they were civil anyway. The women on that mountain worked harder than any I'd ever met. They taught me the value of a whetstone to sharpen my knives, how to store food in the creek and keep it cold and safe. I learned to keep enough for an extra plate for company.   7

whetstone: a stone for sharpening tools

What I had believed in, all those things I thought were the necessary accoutrements for a civilized life, were nonexistent in this place. Up on the mountain, my most valuable possessions were my relationships with my neighbors.   8

accoutrement: an accessory

After four years in that hollow, I moved back into town. I saw that a lot of people were having a really hard time, losing their jobs and homes. With the help of a real estate broker I chatted up at the grocery store, I managed to rent a big enough house to take in a handful of people.   9

It's four of us now, but over time I've had nine come in and move on to other places from here. We'd all be in shelters if we hadn't banded together.   10

The American dream I believe in now is a shared one. It's not so much about what I can get for myself; it's about how we can all get by together.   11

DISCUSS WITH YOUR PEERS

1. Reread paragraphs 1 and 11. Discuss the two versions of the American dream. Which version of this dream is truer for you and your life? Does this story make you want to modify your idea of the American dream? Why or why not?

2. Reread paragraphs 3–5. Why is the little shack so motivational for the author? Do you think you would have a similar reaction if you were in her shoes? Why or why not?

3. Reread paragraphs 6 and 7. Does the neighbors' behavior surprise you? Why or why not? Does their behavior resemble the behavior of any neighbors you've had?

IDENTIFY THE PATTERNS

1. The author uses **definition** to explore various meanings of "the American dream." Reread paragraphs 1, 6, 8, and 11, and discuss her old definition of this dream and her new definition. How and why has her definition changed over time?

2. The author uses **process** to show how her neighbors "slowly . . . started teaching [her] the art of being a neighbor" (para. 6). Discuss the steps in the process through which her neighbors taught her this art.

CONTINUED >

3. The author uses **cause and effect** to show how her experiences with homelessness and poverty changed her. What things cause her to change (see paras. 6–8), and what are the outcomes (effects) of this change (see paras. 9–11)?

WRITE ABOUT THE READING

Explain the process by which the narrator goes from depending on others' kindness to being able to help other people in need. Describe each step in this transformation as precisely as you can, using examples and details from the story to illustrate the steps.

WRITE ABOUT YOUR LIFE

1. Discuss a time in your life when people came to your and/or your family's rescue. Describe the situation, what those people did, and what you learned from the experience.

2. Discuss how hardship can change a person or people. You may discuss a situation of hardship that happened to you or to someone you know.

Howard White

The Power of Hello

Howard White is a former University of Maryland point guard and current vice president of Jordan Brand at Nike. He founded the national Nike youth movement, "Believe to Achieve," and authored a book by the same title.

gazillion: an extremely large, incalculable number

I work at a company where there are about a gazillion employees. I can't   1
say that I know them all by name, but I know my fair share of them. I think that almost all of them know me. I'd say that's the reason I've been able to go wherever it is I've made it to in this world. It's all based on one simple principle: I believe that every single person deserves to be acknowledged, however small or simple the greeting.

When I was about ten years old, I was walking down the street   2
with my mother. She stopped to speak to Mr. Lee. I was busy trying to bull's-eye the O on the stop sign with a rock. I knew I could see Mr. Lee any old time around the neighborhood, so I didn't pay any attention to him. After we passed Mr. Lee, my mother stopped me and said something that has stuck with me from that day until now. She said, "You let that be the last time you ever walk by somebody and not open up your mouth to speak, because even a dog can wag its tail when it passes you on the street." That phrase sounds simple, but it's been a guidepost for me and the foundation of who I am.

When you write an essay like this, you look in the mirror and see **3** who you are and what makes up your character. I realized mine was cemented that day when I was ten years old. Even then, I started to see that when I spoke to someone, they spoke back. And that felt good.

It's not just something I believe in; it's become a way of life. I believe **4** that every person deserves to feel someone acknowledge their presence, no matter how humble they may be or even how important.

At work, I always used to say hello to the founder of the company **5** and ask him how our business was doing. But I also spoke to the people in the café and the people who cleaned the buildings and asked how their children were doing. After a few years of passing by the founder, I had the courage to ask him for a meeting. We had a great talk. At a certain point I asked him how far he thought I could go in his company. He said, "If you want to, you can get all the way to this seat."

I've become vice president, but that hasn't changed the way I ap- **6** proach people. I still follow my mother's advice. I speak to everyone I see, no matter where I am. I've learned that speaking to people creates a pathway into their world, and it lets them come into mine, too.

The day you speak to someone who has their head down but lifts it **7** up and smiles, you realize how powerful it is just to open your mouth and say, "Hello."

DISCUSS WITH YOUR PEERS

1. In paragraphs 1 and 4, the author repeats his core belief that "every single person" should be acknowledged. His goal is to interact—however briefly—with every individual he encounters. Do you think his ambition is realistic or exaggerated? Is this a principle that most humans should strive to achieve? Explain your opinion.

2. In paragraphs 1 and 5, the author suggests that his practice of acknowledging others has contributed to his professional success. Discuss whether you believe that acknowledging others—both supervisors and subordinates—in the workplace can increase one's chances of professional success.

3. In paragraph 6, the author says that "speaking to people creates a pathway into their world, and it lets them come into mine, too." Discuss whether or not you share the author's optimism. In other words, discuss situations in which speaking to everyone you meet might create risks or discomfort that would be better avoided.

IDENTIFY THE PATTERNS

1. The author uses **narration** to show the origin of his beliefs. Reread paragraph 2, and identify the main parts and purpose of the story that White tells about his childhood.

CONTINUED >

2. The author uses **exemplification** to illustrate how he puts his belief into practice. Reread paragraphs 5 and 6, and find examples of how the author acknowledges others.

3. The author uses **effect** to explain the outcomes or benefits of acknowledging others. Reread paragraphs 1, 3, and 7, and identify these benefits.

WRITE ABOUT THE READING

The author works hard to convince you that the practice of acknowledging others can be beneficial to both you and those you acknowledge. Discuss whether the author has successfully convinced you to try—and perhaps adopt—this behavior. Give examples from the reading to support your point of view.

WRITE ABOUT YOUR LIFE

Discuss your attitude about interacting with others, especially people you don't know. Are you as comfortable as the author in relating to everyone you meet, or are you more cautious and reserved? You may discuss actual experiences you've had interacting with others and, if appropriate, where your attitude comes from—family, environment, personality, and so on.

WRITE ABOUT THE THEME

Compare and/or contrast the types of help that are given in the two essays in Chapter 27. Discuss the relative value of these different types of help.

On Rich and Poor

As you read the following selections, think about the stark contrast between rich and poor and the very close proximity in which they exist. How does poverty affect a person's life, and how does wealth affect it? What are your own experiences with poverty and privilege? How does this compare to the poverty or the privilege of other people around the world?

Michael Lewis

Wading toward Home

Michael Lewis is a best-selling nonfiction author and an investigative journalist. His work examines success, innovation, and the financial world. The following is an excerpt from a longer feature he wrote about Hurricane Katrina in New Orleans for the *New York Times*.

Pretty quickly, it became clear that there were more than a few people left in the city and that they fell into two broad categories: extremely well-armed white men prepared to do battle and a ragtag collection of irregulars, black and white, who had no idea that there was anyone to do battle with. A great many of the irregulars were old people, like Ms. Perrier, who had no family outside New Orleans and so could not imagine where else they would go. But there were also plenty of people who, like the portly, topless, middle-aged gay couple in short shorts walking their dogs down St. Charles Avenue every day, seemed not to sense the slightest danger.

The city on high ground organized itself around the few houses turned into forts. By Saturday morning, Fort Huger was again alive with half a dozen young men who spent their day checking on houses and rescuing the two groups of living creatures most in need of help: old people and pets. Two doors down from my sister's house on Audubon Park was Fort Ryan, under the command of Bill Ryan, who lost an eye to a mortar in Vietnam, was hit by a hand grenade, and was shot through the arm and then returned home with a well-earned chestful of ribbons and medals. Him you could understand. He had passed the nights sitting on his porch with his son at his side and a rifle on his lap. "The funny thing is," he told

1

2

portly: overweight

Power Tip
In August 2005, Hurricane Katrina flooded 80 percent of the city of New Orleans, leaving almost two thousand people dead, and hundreds of thousands homeless plus jobless, many of them poor. It was the sixth-strongest Atlantic hurricane ever recorded.

me, "is that before now my son never asked me what happened in Vietnam. Now he wants to know."

The biggest fort of all was Fort Ramelli, a mansion on St. Charles Avenue. At Fort Ryan, they joked, lovingly, about Fort Ramelli. "We used to say that if a nuclear bomb went off in New Orleans, the only thing left would be the cockroaches and Bobby Ramelli," said Nick Ryan, Bill's son. "Now we're not so sure about the cockroaches." Bobby Ramelli and his son spent the first five days of the flood in his flatboat, pulling, they guessed, about three hundred people from the water.

3

The police had said that gangs of young black men were looting and killing their way across the city, and the news had reached the men inside the forts. These men also had another informational disadvantage: working TV sets. Over and over again, they replayed the same few horrifying scenes from the Superdome, the convention center, and a shop in downtown New Orleans. If the images were to be reduced to a sentence in the minds of Uptown New Orleans, that sentence would be: *Crazy black people with automatic weapons are out hunting white people, and there's no bag limit!* "The perspective you are getting from me," one of Fort Huger's foot soldiers said as he walked around the living room with an M-16, "is the perspective of the guy who is getting disinformation and reacting accordingly." He spoke, for those few days, for much of the city, including the mayor and the police chief.

4

No emotion is as absurd as fear when it is proved to be unjustified. I was aware of this; I was also aware that it is better to be absurdly alive than absurdly dead. I broke into the family duck-hunting closet, loaded a shotgun with birdshot, and headed out into the city. Running around with a 12-gauge filled with birdshot was, in the eyes of the local militia, little better than running around with a slingshot or one of those guns that, when you shoot them, spit out a tiny flag. Over the next few days, I checked hundreds of houses and found that none had been broken into. The story about the children's hospital turned out to be just that, a story. The glass door to the Rite Aid on St. Charles near Broadway—where my paternal grandfather collapsed and died in 1979—was shattered, but the only section disturbed was the shelf Stocking the Wild Turkey. The Ace Hardware store on Oak Street was supposed to have had its front wall pulled off by a forklift, but it appeared to be, like most stores and all houses, perfectly intact. Of all the stores in town, none looked so well preserved as the bookshops. No one loots literature.

5

Oddly, the only rumor that contained even a grain of truth was the looting of Perlis. The window of the Uptown clothing store was shattered. But the alligator belts hung from their carousel, and the shirts with miniature crawfish emblazoned on their breasts lay stacked as neatly as they had been before Katrina churned up the Gulf. On the floor was a ripped brown paper sack with two pairs of jeans inside: the thief lacked both ambition and conviction.

6

The old houses were also safe. There wasn't a house in the Garden District, or Uptown, that could not have been easily entered; there wasn't a house in either area that didn't have food and water to keep a family of five alive for a week; and there was hardly a house in either place that had been violated in any way. And the grocery stores! I spent some time

7

bag limit: the legal number of prey that a hunter may kill

militia: a group of citizens formed for military service

paternal: relating to the father's side of the family

inside a Whole Foods choosing from the selection of Power Bars. The door was open, the shelves groaned with untouched bottles of water and food. Downtown, twenty-five thousand people spent the previous four days without food and water when a few miles away — and it's a lovely stroll — entire grocery stores, doors ajar, were untouched. From the moment the crisis downtown began, there had been a clear path, requiring maybe an hour's walk, to food, water, and shelter. And no one, not a single person, it seemed, took it.

Here, in the most familial city in America, the people turned out to know even less of one another than they did of the ground on which they stood. Downtown, into which the people too poor to get themselves out of town had been shamefully herded by local authorities, I found the mirror image of the hysteria uptown. Inside the Superdome and the convention center, rumors started that the police chief, the mayor, and the national media passed along: of two hundred people murdered, of countless rapes, of hundreds of armed black gang members on the loose. (Weeks later, the *Times-Picayune* wrote that just two people were found killed and there had been no reports of rape. The murder rate in the city the week after Katrina hit was unchanged.) There, two poor people told me that the flood wasn't caused by nature but by man: the government was trying to kill poor people. (Another reason it may never have occurred to the poor to make their way into the homes and grocery stores of the rich is that they assumed the whole point of this event was for the rich to get a clean shot at the poor.) In their view, the whole thing, beginning with the levee break and ending with the cramming of thousands of innocent people into what they were sure were death chambers with murderers and rapists, was a setup.

8

My great-grandfather J. Blanc Monroe is dead and gone, but he didn't take with him the climate of suspicion between rich and poor that he apparently helped foster. On St. Claude Avenue, just below the French Quarter, there was a scene of indigents, old people, and gay men employed in the arts fleeing what they took to be bombs being dropped on them by army helicopters. What were being dropped were, in fact, ready-to-eat meals and water in plastic jugs. But falling from the sky, these missiles looked unfriendly, and when the jugs hit concrete, they exploded and threw up shrapnel. The people in the area had heard from the police that George W. Bush intended to visit the city that day, and they could not imagine he meant them any good — but this attack, as they took it, came as a shock. "Run! Run!" screamed a man among the hordes trying to outrun the chopper. "It's the president!"

9

foster: to create

indigent: a poor person

DISCUSS WITH YOUR PEERS

1. The author describes post-Katrina New Orleans like a war zone. Reread paragraphs 1 and 4, and identify the "enemies" in this "war." Who are they, and why are they afraid of one another? Does it make sense to you that a city would turn into a "war zone" after a natural disaster? Explain your opinion.

CONTINUED >

2. Reread paragraphs 5–7. What does the narrator expect to find when he takes his gun and goes out into the streets? What does he discover instead? Do you think his expectations were realistic? Were you surprised by what he found? Explain your opinion.

3. Reread paragraphs 8 and 9. What are some of the false stories that were spread following Katrina? Why do the poor people believe these stories? Do you think their fear is realistic or hysterical?

IDENTIFY THE PATTERNS

1. The author uses **description** to paint strong images of the aftermath of Hurricane Katrina. Reread paragraphs 5–7, and describe the scenes depicted there. Which descriptive details paint the strongest images for you?

2. The author uses **cause and effect** to show how unreasonable behavior comes from fear. Find and discuss examples of the causes (what do the people fear?) and the effects (how do they behave because of this fear?).

3. The author uses **comparison and contrast** to show the similarities and differences between the (rich) white people and the (poor) black people in New Orleans following Hurricane Katrina. Find and discuss examples of how the two groups are similar (in their ignorance and suspicion, for example) and how they are different.

WRITE ABOUT THE READING

Discuss the effects of fear and ignorance on the citizens of New Orleans after Katrina. Describe these effects and explain what they suggest about life in New Orleans.

WRITE ABOUT YOUR LIFE

1. Discuss the attitudes of wealthy people toward poor people and vice versa. Use examples from your own life and experience to support your ideas.

2. Discuss a natural disaster or crisis situation that you were a part of. How did people behave during or after the crisis? How did they treat one another? What can you learn from the behavior that you witnessed?

George Saunders

The New Mecca

George Saunders is a writer of short fiction as well as essays, novellas, and children's books. Saunders's work is characterized by satire and an adamant sense of compassion and empathy. He teaches at Syracuse University in New York State.

1   If you are like I was three weeks ago, before I went to Dubai, you may not know exactly where Dubai is. Near Venezuela? No, sorry, that is incorrect. Somewhere north of Pakistan, an idyllic mountain kingdom ruled by gentle goatherds? Well, no.

idyllic: peaceful, beautiful

2   Dubai, actually, is in the United Arab Emirates, on the Arabian Peninsula, 100 miles across the Gulf from Iran, about 600 miles from Basra, 1,100 from Kabul.

3   You might also not know, as I did not know, what Dubai is all about or why someone would want to send you there. You might wonder: Is it dangerous? Will I be beheaded? Will I need a translator? Will my translator be beheaded? Just before we're beheaded, will my translator try to get out of it by blaming everything on me?

4   No, no, not to worry. Dubai, turns out, is quite possibly the safest great city in the world. It is also the newest great city in the world. In the 1950s, before oil was discovered there, Dubai was just a cluster of mud huts and Bedouin tents along Dubai Creek: the entire city has basically been built in the last fifty years. And actually, the cool parts—the parts that have won Dubai its reputation as "the Vegas of the Middle East" or "the Venice of the Middle East" or "the Disney World of the Middle East, if Disney World were the size of San Francisco and out in a desert"—have been built in the last ten years. And the supercool parts—the parts that, when someone tells you about them, your attention drifts because these morons have to be lying (no one dreams this big or has that much available capital)—those parts are all going to be built in the next five years.

Bedouin: a nomadic Arab tribe

5   By 2010, if all goes according to plan, Dubai will have: the world's tallest skyscraper (2,300 feet); largest mall; biggest theme park; longest indoor ski run; most luxurious underwater hotel (accessible by submarine train); a huge (2,000-acre, 60,000-resident) development called International City, divided into nation-neighborhoods (England, China, France, Greece, etc.) within which all homes will be required to reflect the national architectural style; not to mention four artificially constructed island mega-archipelagoes (three shaped like giant palm trees, the fourth like a map of the world) built using a specially designed boat that dredges up tons of ocean-bottom sand each day and sprays it into place.

archipelago: a group of islands

dredge: to dig

bluster: exaggerated talk

6   Before I saw Dubai for myself, I assumed this was bluster: brag about ten upcoming projects, finally build one—smaller than you'd bragged—hope everyone forgets about the other nine.

7   But no.

8   I've been to Dubai, and I believe.

[…]

My Arrival in Heaven

The Burj Al Arab is the only seven-star hotel in the world, even though **9** the ratings system only goes up to five. The most expensive Burj suite goes for $12,000 a night. The atrium is 590 feet from floor to ceiling, the largest in the world. As you enter, the staff rushes over with cold towels, rosewater for the hands, dates, incense. The smell, the scale, the level of loving, fascinated attention you are receiving, makes you realize you have never really been in the lap of true luxury before. All the luxury you have previously had—in New York, L.A.—was stale, Burj-imitative crap! Your entire concept of *being inside a building* is being altered in real time. The lobby of the Burj is neither inside nor out. The roof is so far away as to seem like sky. The underbellies of the floors above you grade through countless shades of color from deep blue to, finally, up so high you can barely see it: pale green. Your Guest Services liaison, a humble, pretty Ukrainian, tells you that every gold-colored surface you see during your stay is actual twenty-four-karat gold. Even those four-story columns? Even so, she says. Even the thick fourth-story arcs the size of buses that span the columns? All gold, sir, is correct.

[…]

Look, Dream, but Stay Out There

[…]

Returning to the hotel at dusk, I find dozens of the low-level South Indian **10** workers, on their weekly half-day off, making their way toward the Towers, like peasants to the gates of the castle, dressed in their finest clothes (cowboy-type shirts buttoned to the throat), holding clunky circa-1980s cameras.

What are they doing here? I ask. What's going on? **11**

We are on holiday, one says. **12**

What are their jobs? When can they go home? What will they do to- **13** night? Go out and meet girls? Do they have girlfriends back home, wives?

Maybe someday, one guy says, smiling a smile of anticipatory domes- **14** tic ecstasy, and what he means is: Sir, if you please, how can I marry when I have nothing? This is why I'm here: so someday I can have a family.

Are you going in there? I ask, meaning the hotel. **15**

An awkward silence follows. In there? Them? **16**

No, sir, one says. We are just wishing to take photos of ourselves in **17** this beautiful place.

They go off. I watch them merrily photographing themselves in front **18** of the futuristic fountain, in the groves of lush trees, photos they'll send home to Hyderabad, Bangalore. Entering the hotel is out of the question. They know the rules.

I decide to go in but can't locate the pedestrian entrance. The idea, I **19** come to understand, after fifteen minutes of high-attentiveness searching, is to discourage foot traffic. Anybody who belongs in there will drive in and valet park.

Finally I locate the entrance: an unmarked, concealed, marble stair- **20** case with wide, stately steps fifty feet across. Going up, I pass a lone Indian guy hand-squeegeeing the thirty-three (I count them) steps.

atrium: a central, open room such as a lobby, often with many stories and a skylight

liaison: a representative

anticipatory: looking forward to

domestic: relating to home life

How long will this take you? I ask. All afternoon? **21**

I think so, he says sweetly. **22**

Part of me wants to offer to help. But that would be, of course, ri- **23**
diculous, melodramatic. He washes these stairs every day. It's not my job
to hand-wash stairs. It's his job to hand-wash stairs. My job is to observe
him hand-washing the stairs, then go inside the air-conditioned lobby and
order a cold beer and take notes about his stair-washing so I can go home
and write about it, making more for writing about it than he'll make in
many, many years of doing it.

And of course, somewhere in India is a guy who'd kill to do some **24**
stair-washing in Dubai. He hasn't worked in three years, any chance of
marriage is rapidly fading. Does this stair washer have any inclination to
return to India, surrender his job to this other guy, give up his hard-won
lifestyle to help this fellow human being? Who knows? If he's like me, he
probably does. But in the end, his answer, like mine, is: that would be
ridiculous, melodramatic. It's not my job to give up my job, which I worked
so hard these many years to get.

Am I not me? Is he not him? **25**

He keeps washing. I jog up the stairs to the hotel. Two smiling Nepalese **26**
throw open the huge doors, greeting me warmly, and I go inside.

DISCUSS WITH YOUR PEERS

1. Reread paragraph 9. Imagine yourself arriving as a guest at this hotel
   with your expenses already paid. How would you feel about the
   environment and the treatment you receive? Explain your answer.

2. Reread paragraphs 10–17. If you were a poor migrant laborer, would
   you want to visit places like this hotel that do not allow you to come
   inside? What do you think the Indian immigrant workers feel?

3. Reread paragraphs 22 and 23. The author suggests that the reason
   people do not step out of their privileged lifestyle to help others is
   because it would appear "ridiculous, melodramatic." Do you believe
   his claim? What are some other reasons why people do not step out
   of their privileged lifestyle to help those needier than themselves?

IDENTIFY THE PATTERNS

1. The author uses **description** to re-create the fabulous, excessive
   wealth of the hotel. How successful is his description? What are some
   of the descriptive details that make you feel like you are actually in the
   hotel lobby?

2. The author uses **cause and effect** to suggest why the Indian
   workers have come to Dubai and what happens to them when
   they arrive. What causes the Indian workers to leave their homeland
   for Dubai?

CONTINUED >

3. The author uses **argument** to explain why he doesn't reach out to help the Indian man hand-washing the stairs. Reread paragraphs 23–25, and identify the reasons that the author gives for his behavior. Do you agree with the author's decision?

WRITE ABOUT THE READING

Discuss the culture of Dubai as it is presented in this article. What attracts you and what disturbs you in this description? Based on this reading, would you like to visit Dubai? Give examples and details from the reading to support your ideas.

WRITE ABOUT YOUR LIFE

Discuss some examples of wealth and privilege that you have seen in person or in the media. Explain your feelings about this sort of wealth and privilege. Would you like to be so rich? How might it be more complicated than it seems at first?

WRITE ABOUT THE THEME

Compare and contrast the realities of the rich and poor in the two readings in Chapter 28. How do they live in each situation? How are they treated? How do they feel? What do they believe?

On Education

As you read the following selections, think about the importance of education, both in society and in your own life. What have your educational experiences been like in elementary school, high school, and college? Have you experienced any experimental or nontraditional forms of education? If so, were they effective? What are the strengths and weaknesses of traditional education, and how might traditional education be changed for the better?

Daphne Koller

Death Knell for the Lecture: Technology as a Passport to Personalized Education

Daphne Koller is a professor at Stanford University. She researches artificial intelligence and its applications in biomedical sciences. She won a MacArthur grant in 2004, and she is starting a free online course on advanced mathematics.

Our education system is in a state of crisis. Among developed countries, the United States is fifty-fifth in quality rankings of elementary math and science education, twentieth in high school completion rate, and twenty-seventh in the fraction of college students receiving undergraduate degrees in science or engineering. **1**

As a society, we can and should invest more money in education. But that is only part of the solution. The high costs of high-quality education put it off limits to large parts of the population, both in the United States and abroad, and threaten the school's place in society as a whole. We need to significantly reduce those costs while at the same time improving quality. **2**

If these goals seem contradictory, let's consider an example from history. In the nineteenth century, 60 percent of the American work force was in agriculture, and there were frequent food shortages. Today, agriculture accounts for less than 2 percent of the work force, and there are food surpluses. **3**

contradictory: at odds, incompatible

The key to this transition was the use of technology—from crop rotation strategies to GPS-guided farm machinery—which greatly increased productivity. By contrast, our approach to education has remained largely **4**

surplus: a leftover amount, an excess

unchanged since the Renaissance: From middle school through college, most teaching is done by an instructor lecturing to a room full of students, only some of them paying attention.

How can we improve performance in education, while cutting costs at the same time? In 1984, Benjamin Bloom showed that individual tutoring had a huge advantage over standard lecture environments: The average tutored student performed better than 98 percent of the students in the standard class.   **5**

Until now, it has been hard to see how to make individualized education affordable. But I argue that technology may provide a path to this goal.   **6**

augment: to increase

Consider the success of the Khan Academy, which began when Salman Khan tried to teach math remotely to his young cousins. He recorded short videos with explanations and placed them on the Web, augmenting them with automatically graded exercises. This simple approach was so compelling that by now, more than 700 million videos have been watched by millions of viewers.   **7**

At Stanford, we recently placed three computer science courses online, using a similar format. Remarkably, in the first four weeks, 300,000 students registered for these courses, with millions of video views and hundreds of thousands of submitted assignments.   **8**

What can we learn from these successes? First, we see that video content is engaging to students—many of whom grew up on YouTube—and easy for instructors to produce.   **9**

monolithic: huge; characterized by a singular, gigantic form

Second, presenting content in short, bite-size chunks, rather than monolithic hourlong lectures, is better suited to students' attention spans, and provides the flexibility to tailor instruction to individual students. Those with less preparation can dwell longer on background material without feeling uncomfortable about how they might be perceived by classmates or the instructor.   **10**

aptitude: a natural ability or talent

Conversely, students with an aptitude for the topic can move ahead rapidly, avoiding boredom and disengagement. In short, everyone has access to a personalized experience that resembles individual tutoring.   **11**

Watching passively is not enough. Engagement through exercises and assessments is a critical component of learning. These exercises are designed not just to evaluate the student's learning, but also, more important, to enhance understanding by prompting recall and placing ideas in context.   **12**

Moreover, testing allows students to move ahead when they master a concept, rather than when they have spent a stipulated amount of time staring at the teacher who is explaining it.   **13**

For many types of questions, we now have methods to automatically assess students' work, allowing them to practice while receiving instant feedback about their performance. With some effort in technology development, our ability to check answers for many types of questions will get closer and closer to that of human graders.   **14**

Of course, these student-computer interactions can leave many gaps. Students need to be able to ask questions and discuss the material. How do we scale the human interaction to tens of thousands of students?   **15**

Our Stanford courses provide a forum in which students can vote **16** on questions and answers, allowing the most important questions to be answered quickly—often by another student. In the future, we can adapt Web technology to support even more interactive formats, like real-time group discussions, affordably and at large scale.

More broadly, the online format gives us the ability to identify what **17** works. Until now, many education studies have been based on populations of a few dozen students. Online technology can capture every click: what students watched more than once, where they paused, what mistakes they made. This mass of data is an invaluable resource for understanding the learning process and figuring out which strategies really serve students best.

Some argue that online education can't teach creative problem-solving **18** and critical-thinking skills. But to practice problem-solving, a student must first master certain concepts. By providing a cost-effective solution for this first step, we can focus precious classroom time on more interactive problem-solving activities that achieve deeper understanding—and foster creativity.

foster: to encourage, promote

In this format, which we call the flipped classroom, teachers have **19** time to interact with students, motivate them, and challenge them. Though attendance in my Stanford class is optional, it is considerably higher than in many standard lecture-based classes. And after the Los Altos school district in Northern California adopted this blended approach, using the Khan Academy, seventh graders in a remedial math class sharply improved their performance, with 41 percent reaching advanced or proficient levels, up from 23 percent.

remedial: intended to fix problems

proficient: competent, skilled

A 2010 analysis from the Department of Education, based on forty-five **20** studies, showed that online learning is as effective as face-to-face learning, and that blended learning is considerably more effective than either.

Online education, then, can serve two goals. For students lucky **21** enough to have access to great teachers, blended learning can mean even better outcomes at the same or lower cost. And for the millions here and abroad who lack access to good, in-person education, online learning can open doors that would otherwise remain closed.

Nelson Mandela said, "Education is the most powerful weapon **22** which you can use to change the world."

By using technology in the service of education, we can change the **23** world in our lifetime.

DISCUSS WITH YOUR PEERS

1. Reread paragraph 1. Do the statistics about America's failing educational system surprise you? Or do they seem consistent with the educational experiences you've had and/or heard about? Explain your answer and give examples from your experience.

2. Reread paragraphs 7 and 8. Do the huge numbers of people who responded to online education surprise you? Why do you suppose that so many people responded so enthusiastically? Would you do the same?

CONTINUED >

3. Reread paragraphs 20 and 21. Why do you think that the "blended" approach to education is the most effective approach? What does it offer to students that the other two approaches don't offer?

IDENTIFY THE PATTERNS

1. The author uses **exemplification** frequently, providing specific examples to back up her claims. Identify the examples that she provides in paragraphs 1, 3, 7, and 8. Are these examples precise and powerful enough to prove her point?

2. The author uses **argument** as her primary pattern of development. Reread paragraphs 5 and 6, and identify the author's main argument. Then, reread paragraphs 9–14, and identify the major reasons the author gives for the success of technology-based instruction.

3. The author uses **definition** to clarify new terms like the *flipped classroom* and the *blended approach*. Reread paragraphs 18–21, and explain what those terms mean. Are the author's definitions clear enough, or could they be more effective? Explain your opinion.

WRITE ABOUT THE READING

Discuss what you've learned about the benefits of technology-based education from this article. Then, explain whether or not you agree with the author's optimism about this new approach to education.

WRITE ABOUT YOUR LIFE

1. Discuss both your traditional educational experiences (in a classroom with books and chalkboard) and any technology-based educational experiences (on a computer) that you've had. You might wish to compare and contrast these two experiences.

2. Discuss the success or failure of the education you've received in the United States. Does your experience prove that the American educational system is failing, or does your experience suggest otherwise?

Robert Lake

An Indian Father's Plea

Robert Lake, also known as "Bobby Lake-Thom," is a traditional native healer, spiritual teacher, and author. He is of Karuk-Seneca-Cherokee tribal descent (and part European American). He was employed at the Gonzaga University Indian Education Center III at the time this article was originally written and published. He has been educated in both Western and Native American traditions and lives in Yreka, California.

Dear teacher, I would like to introduce you to my son, Wind-Wolf. He is probably what you would consider a typical Indian kid. He was born and raised on a reservation. He has black hair, dark brown eyes, olive complexion. And like so many Indian children his age, he is shy and quiet in the classroom. He is five years old, in kindergarten, and I can't understand why you have already labeled him a "slow learner." **1**

At the age of five, he has already been through quite an education compared with his peers in Western society. At his first introduction into this world, he was bonded to his mother and to the Mother Earth in a traditional native childbirth ceremony. And he has been continuously cared for by his mother, father, sisters, cousins, uncles, grandparents, and extended tribal family since this ceremony. **2**

Wind-Wolf's educational setting has been not only a "secure" environment, but also very colorful, complicated, sensitive, and diverse. He has been with his mother at the ocean at daybreak when she made her prayers and gathered fresh seaweed from the rocks, he has sat with his uncles in a rowboat on the river while they fished with gill nets, and he has watched and listened to elders as they told creation stories and animal legends and sang songs around the campfires. He has watched the women make beaded jewelry and traditional native regalia. He has had many opportunities to watch his father, uncles, and ceremonial leaders using different kinds of songs while preparing for the sacred dances and rituals. **3**

regalia: especially fine clothing, costumes

It takes a long time to absorb and reflect on these kinds of experiences, so maybe that is why you think my Indian child is a slow learner. His aunts and grandmothers taught him to count and know his numbers while they sorted out the complex materials used to make the abstract designs in the native baskets. He listened to his mother count each and every bead and sort out numerically according to color while she painstakingly made complex beaded belts and necklaces. He learned his basic numbers by helping his father count and sort the rocks to be used in the sweat-lodge—seven rocks for a medicine sweat, say, or thirteen for the summer solstice ceremony. (The rocks are later heated and doused with water to create purifying steam.) And he was taught to learn mathematics by counting the sticks we use in our traditional native hand game. So I realize he may be slow in grasping the methods and tools that you are now using in your classroom, ones quite familiar to his white peers, but I hope you will be patient with him. It takes time to adjust to a new cultural system and learn new things. **4**

solstice: a time of year when the sun is at the greatest distance from the equator

He is not culturally "disadvantaged," but he is culturally "different." If you ask him how many months there are in a year, he will probably tell you thirteen. He will respond this way not because he doesn't know how to count properly, but because he has been taught by our traditional people that there are thirteen full moons in a year according to the native tribal calendar and that there are really thirteen planets in our solar system and thirteen tail feathers on a perfectly balanced eagle, the most powerful kind of bird to use in ceremonial healing. **5**

But he also knows that some eagles may only have twelve tail feathers or seven, that they do not all have the same number. He can probably **6** count more than forty different kinds of birds, tell you and his peers what kind of bird each is and where it lives, the seasons in which it appears, and how it is used in a sacred ceremony. He may also have trouble writing his name on a piece of paper, but he knows how to say it and many other things in several different Indian languages. He is not fluent yet because he is only five years old and required by law to attend your educational system, learn your language, your values, your ways of thinking, and your methods of teaching and learning.

So you see, all of these influences together make him somewhat shy and quiet—and perhaps "slow" according to your standards. But if Wind-Wolf was not prepared for his first tentative foray into your world, neither were you appreciative of his culture. On the first day of class, you had difficulty with his name. You wanted to call him Wind, insisting that Wolf must somehow be his middle name. The students in the class laughed at him, causing further embarrassment.

7

While you were trying to teach him your new methods, helping him learn new tools for self-discovery and adapt to his new learning environment, he may have been looking out the window as if daydreaming. Why? Because he has been taught to watch and study the changes in nature. It is hard for him to make the appropriate psychic switch from the right to the left hemisphere of the brain when he sees the leaves turning bright colors, the geese heading south, and the squirrels scurrying around for nuts to get ready for a harsh winter. In his heart, in his young mind, and almost by instinct, he knows that this is the time of the year he is supposed to be with people gathering and preparing fish, deer meat, and native plants and herbs, and learning his assigned tasks in this role. He is caught between two worlds, torn by two distinct cultural systems.

8

Yesterday, for the third time in two weeks, he came home crying and said he wanted to have his hair cut. He said he doesn't have any friends at school because they make fun of his long hair. I tried to explain to him that in our culture, long hair is a sign of masculinity and balance and is a source of power. But he remained adamant in his position.

9

To make matters worse, he recently encountered his first harsh case of racism. Wind-Wolf had managed to adopt at least one good school friend. On the way home from school one day, he asked his new pal if he wanted to come home to play with him until supper. That was OK with Wind-Wolf's mother, who was walking with them. When they all got to the little friend's house, the two boys ran inside to ask permission while Wind-Wolf's mother waited. But the other boy's mother lashed out: "It is OK if you have to play with him at school, but we don't allow those kind of people in our house!" When my wife asked why not, the other boy's mother answered, "Because you are Indians, and we are white, and I don't want my kids growing up with your kind of people."

10

So now my young Indian child does not want to go to school anymore (even though we cut his hair). He feels that he does not belong. He is the only Indian child in your class, and he is well aware of this fact. Instead of being proud of his race, heritage, and culture, he feels ashamed. When he watches television, he asks why the white people hate us so much and always kill our people in the movies and why they take everything away from us. He asks why the other kids in school are not taught about the

11

tentative: exploratory

foray: a brief journey into new territory

psychic: mental

adamant: fixed, firm, unyielding

power, beauty, and essence of nature or provided with an opportunity to experience the world around them firsthand. He says he hates living in the city and that he misses his Indian cousins and friends. He asks why one young white girl at school who is his friend always tells him, "I like you, Wind-Wolf, because you are a good Indian."

Now he refuses to sing his native songs, play with his Indian arti- 12 facts, learn his language, or participate in his sacred ceremonies. When I ask him to go to an urban powwow or help me with a sacred sweat-lodge ritual, he says no because "that's weird" and he doesn't want his friends at school to think he doesn't believe in God.

So, dear teacher, I want to introduce you to my son, Wind-Wolf, who 13 is not really a "typical" little Indian kid after all. He stems from a long line of hereditary chiefs, medicine men and women, and ceremonial leaders whose accomplishments and unique forms of knowledge are still being studied and recorded in contemporary books. He has seven different tribal systems flowing through his blood; he is even part white. I want my child to succeed in school and in life. I don't want him to be a dropout or juvenile delinquent or to end up on drugs and alcohol because he is made to feel inferior or because of discrimination. I want him to be proud of his rich heritage and culture, and I would like him to develop the necessary capabilities to adapt to, and succeed in, both cultures. But I need your help.

What you say and what you do in the classroom, what you teach 14 and how you teach it, and what you don't say and don't teach will have a significant effect on the potential success or failure of my child. Please remember that this is the primary year of his education and development. All I ask is that you work with me, not against me, to help educate my child in the best way. If you don't have the knowledge, preparation, experience, or training to effectively deal with culturally different children, I am willing to help you with the few resources I have available or direct you to such resources.

My Indian child has a constitutional right to learn, retain, and main- 15 tain his heritage and culture. By the same token, I strongly believe that non-Indian children also have a constitutional right to learn about our Native American heritage and culture, because Indians play a significant part in the history of Western society. Until this reality is equally understood and applied in education as a whole, there will be a lot more schoolchildren in grades K–2 identified as "slow learners."

My son, Wind-Wolf, is not an empty glass coming into your class to 16 be filled. He is a full basket coming into a different environment and society with something special to share. Please let him share his knowledge, heritage, and culture with you and his peers.

DISCUSS WITH YOUR PEERS

1. Reread paragraphs 5 and 6. Do you believe that what traditional "Indian" education teaches is as valuable as what traditional Western-society education teaches, such as reading, writing, math, and so on? Explain your opinion.

CONTINUED >

2. Reread paragraphs 7–11, and identify the ways in which Wind-Wolf is discriminated against. Do you believe that these forms of discrimination are still common in American culture and the U.S. school system? Use examples from your own experience to support your opinion.

3. Reread paragraph 13. What are the father's main wishes for his son? Is it fair to ask the teacher and the school to adapt their system to the special needs of one student? Explain your response.

IDENTIFY THE PATTERNS

1. The author uses **exemplification** to illustrate the son's education among his family and tribe. Reread paragraphs 2–4, and identify examples of the son's education. How effective are these examples?

2. The author uses **contrast** to show the differences between "two distinct cultural systems." Reread paragraph 8, and discuss how these two systems are different.

3. The author makes an **argument** about the constitutional rights of K–12 schoolchildren. Reread paragraph 15, and explain his argument. Do you think that he has provided strong enough evidence throughout the article to persuade the teacher and you?

WRITE ABOUT THE READING

Discuss the ways, if any, in which the traditional "Indian" education that Wind-Wolf receives could be valuable for all people today. Use examples and details from the reading to support your ideas.

WRITE ABOUT YOUR LIFE

Discuss the "education" you've received (outside of school) from your family or your native culture. What did you learn, who taught you, and how have these things benefited you? If you wish, you can compare and/or contrast this education and your school education.

WRITE ABOUT THE THEME

In each of the readings in Chapter 29, the author argues in favor of a new approach to education. Compare and/or contrast these two approaches, and make an argument for which one you think would be most beneficial for students today.

CHAPTER 30

On Responding to Violence

As you read the following selections, think about how violence—or images of violence—has affected your life or the lives of the people that you know. This may include the effects of war on returning soldiers, the influence of gang or street violence on neighborhoods, or the impact of violence in movies, television, or games on young children. What motivates people to behave violently? How do the people you know respond to violence?

Michael Hall

Running for His Life

Michael Hall is a writer for *Texas Monthly* and has been published in *The Best American Magazine Writing*, *The Best American Sports Writing*, and the *New York Times*. Gilbert Tuhabonye, whom Hall profiles in this piece, was born in the east-central African country of Burundi to a family of Tutsi tribe farmers.

He was on fire. It was three in the morning, and most of his classmates from the Kibimba school in Burundi were dead—beaten and burned alive by friends of theirs, kids and grownups they had known most of their lives. Smoldering bodies lay in mounds all over the small room. He had used some of the corpses for cover, to keep from being hit by the fiery branches tossed in by the Hutu mob outside. For hours he had heard them laughing, singing, clapping, taunting. Waving their machetes, they had herded more than a hundred Tutsi teenagers and teachers from his high school into the room before sunset. A couple dozen were still alive, moaning in pain, dreaming of death.

smolder: to burn without flame

"There weren't that many of us left," he says. "A guy said, 'I'm going out—I don't want to die like a dog.' He jumped from a window. They cut him to pieces. Then they started a fire on the roof. After a while it started falling on me, and I held up my right arm as it came down, trying to pull bodies over me. My back and arm were on fire—it hurt so bad. I decided I had had enough. I decided to kill myself by diving from a pile of bodies onto my head. I tried twice, but it didn't work. Then I heard a voice. It said, 'You don't want to die. Don't do that.' Outside, we could hear Hutus giving up and leaving. I heard one say, 'Before we go, let's make sure everyone is dead.' So three came inside. One put a spear through a guy's heart; another

1

2

601

guy tried to escape, and they caught him and killed him. I heard the voice say, 'Get out.' There was a body next to me, burned down to the bones. It was hot. I grabbed a bone—it was hot in my hands—and used it to break the bar on the window. The fires had been going for nine hours, so it was easy to break. My thinking was, I wanted to kill myself. I wanted to be identifiable. I wanted my parents to know me. I didn't want to be all burned up, like everyone else. I was jumping to let them kill me."

genocide: the systematic murder of a certain group of people

There was a fire underneath the window, set as an obstacle to escape.   3
He jumped. And somehow, in the darkness, amid the uproar of genocide, at least for a few seconds, no one saw him. His back was on fire, his legs were smoking, and his feet were raw with pain. He ran.

If you could call it running.   4

"Gilbert!" Almost a decade later, on March 30, 2003, he crossed the finish   5
line at the Capitol 10,000 in Austin to the sound of hundreds of people clapping, many calling his name. "Gilbert! Woo!" He finished ahead of some 14,000 runners, but it wasn't good enough, and the look on his face said that he knew it. Others knew it too. A woman off to the side yelled, "Coach, you're awesome! I love you! You're number one, Gilbert!" In fact, Gilbert Tuhabonye was number three, a minute and fifteen seconds behind the winner in a race he had won the previous year and was favored to win again. Gilbert turned and jogged back against the flow of the other finishers, shaking hands and high-fiving spectators, who all seemed to know the thin African. Then he ran the last fifty yards again with Richard Mendez, one of many runners he had trained. "Come on! Come on!" Gilbert said to Mendez. "High knee!" When Mendez finished, Gilbert went back and ran with Ryan Steglich, another of his charges. And then with Shae Rainer and Lisa Spenner. "Come on! Come on!" he yelled. "Butt kick!"

bask: to enjoy a pleasant atmosphere

Afterward, Gilbert, who stands five feet ten and weighs 127 pounds,   6
hung around talking to the other runners, many of whom wore T-shirts that read GILBERT'S GAZELLES TRAINING GROUP. A circle of eight stood basking in his approval, trading anecdotes about their pains and agonies, as runners do. He laughed and joked with them, accepting halfhearted high-fives and thin encouragement, which made him look down self-consciously. Eight thousand miles from home, he's a celebrity in Austin, a twenty-eight-year-old with protruding teeth and a boyish laugh, the most popular running coach in a town of rabid runners, a former national champion, both as a teenager in Africa and as a college student in West Texas. Governor Rick Perry, himself an avid runner, seeks out Gilbert to chat. Kids ask for his autograph. Rich white ladies pay him to order them to run laps. Everybody wants him to make them go faster. They've heard his mantra: It's all about form. "If you have good form," says Gilbert, "running becomes a joy. You can go farther and faster. You can run forever."

rabid: extreme

mantra: a repeated phrase, slogan

You can run forever. This, to a runner, is heaven. Gilbert's students   7
see him as a savior, upbeat after all that he's been through, relentless and optimistic when he has every right to be withdrawn and angry. A man on a mission: to win an Olympic medal, to tell his story, to show the world what one tribe did and what one man—set on fire and left to die—can do. A man with a last name (pronounced "Too-ha-bon-yay") almost too good to be true. "In Burundi," Gilbert says, "your last name has to have meaning. When

I was born, it was a very difficult time. It was right after the war. There had been a big drought, crickets attacked the crops—and then my mother broke her ankle. When I was born, she said I was special. She said, 'This is not my son. This is a son of God.' 'Tuhabonye' means 'a son of God.'"

As the runners dispersed, Jeff Kloster, who works with Gilbert at 8
RunTex, an Austin running store, brought him his warm-ups, and Gilbert took off his shirt to change. Though Jeff had seen them before, he could not take his eyes off the scars that cover Gilbert's back. The burns continue along his right arm, where they bubble the skin like large patches of candle wax, and then to his right leg, which gets darker along the sides of his calf, where the flames ate down to the bone. The scars are proof of the unthinkable: Ten years ago, on a mountaintop in Burundi, high school kids and their teachers were stuck in a room and set on fire. For nine hours Gilbert watched his friends die, breathed their burning flesh, hid under their corpses. Then he ran for his life. People speak of crucibles and the forging of character. They have no idea.

> **crucible:** a container for heating substances; also, a severe test

[. . .]

We're accustomed to African-American athletes being superior, and we're 9
accustomed to Africans, especially East Africans, being the best long-distance runners. Generally, they are. But they're human. They make mistakes. They get hypothermia, as Gilbert did in February at the Motorola Marathon in Austin, when he finished with a disappointing time of 2:26. They train wrong, as Gilbert did for the Capitol 10,000. They get tired. On a typical day, Gilbert is up at five, coaching at six, doing a morning run by seven-thirty, selling shoes all day, coaching after work, and then doing an evening run by seven; he runs an average of twenty miles a day. He tries to give time to Triph and Emma. He almost always falls short.

> **hypothermia:** subnormal body temperature

And, as unbelievable as it may seem to his students, sometimes he 10
doubts himself. "I've never seen a guy so easily psyched out," says John Conley, Gilbert's agent. "Before a race, I tell him he's done the work; he knows the strategy; he's got the speed; he's got the strength. He just has to not let the negative talk in his head get to him. It's his Achilles' heel. He thinks, 'These guys are better than me,' and he puts himself in last place. If he could be like Ali and think, 'I'm the greatest,' he'd be unbeatable."

> **Triph and Emma:** Gilbert's family members

In truth, runners don't race to beat other runners. They race against 11
themselves: to conquer their wills, to transcend their weaknesses, to beat back their nightmares. Of course, a runner will never actually beat himself; he'll never be good enough to do that. But he can get better. And so Gilbert has spent the spring and summer of this year trying to do just that, racing men who are faster than he is, knowing that this makes him better. In May he went to Indianapolis to run a half-marathon against a fast field and finished tenth, with a respectable time of 1:07:50. In June he ran the prestigious Grandma's Marathon in Duluth, Minnesota, at 2:23, but he'll need to get under 2:20 to make the Burundi Olympic team. Carrozza wants to push him even further and have him train with even faster runners. One problem, according to Carrozza, is that Gilbert has been running at slower paces with his students, essentially dumbing his body down. "He's got to refocus on himself," says Carrozza, "to balance the coaching with his training. But he doesn't have to give up coaching."

> **transcend:** to rise above

spud: a potato

That will be a relief to the Gazelles and the spud-shaped obsessives **12** on the running trails. Of course, they see Gilbert as more than just a good coach. He's a flesh-and-blood symbol, a real-life survivor, a true son of God, a man on a mission that's both infinitely greater than and remarkably similar to their own: the daily struggle to show what you're made of.

DISCUSS WITH YOUR PEERS

1. Reread paragraphs 2 and 3. Discuss the reasons that Gilbert wanted to kill himself in the Kibimba school.

2. Why do Gilbert's runners consider him a "savior"? Reread paragraphs 5, 6, and 12, and discuss how Gilbert helps and inspires his runners.

3. At times, Gilbert seems like an extraordinary human being. And yet, he is imperfect like all human beings. Reread paragraphs 9–11, and discuss Gilbert's weaknesses and personal challenges.

IDENTIFY THE PATTERNS

1. The author uses **narration** to tell what happened to Gilbert at the Kibimba school in Burundi. Reread paragraphs 1–4, and identify the key events in the story. (Try to separate key events from descriptive details.)

2. The author uses **description** to describe a typical race with the extraordinary Gilbert. Reread paragraphs 5–8, and identify the details that create his portrait.

3. The author uses **cause and effect** to suggest how Gilbert's experience of genocide in Burundi (the cause) "[forged] his character" (the effects). Reread paragraphs 8 and 11, and discuss the person that Gilbert has become since the genocide. How is his running a result of his experience in the Kibimba school?

WRITE ABOUT THE READING

What is Gilbert's mission in life, and how is he accomplishing that mission? Give examples from the reading to support your ideas.

WRITE ABOUT YOUR LIFE

1. Discuss a tragic event that happened in your life, and explain how that event shaped you as a person.

2. Discuss someone you know (personally or through the media) who is a highly motivated, success-oriented person. Describe the person's "mission" in life, what he or she is doing to accomplish that mission, and what motivates him or her.

Courtney Moreno

GSW

Emergency medical technician Courtney Moreno wrote this essay as part of a larger piece titled "Help Is on the Way: Tales of an Ambulance Driver." Originally published in *LA Weekly*, it was a finalist in the 2010 Southern California Journalism Awards.

The only time I've ever dreamed about a patient, I held the potent images in for as long as I could and was scared to share them. Some things are precious. The patient was a GSW: gunshot wound. The patient was found lying facedown in the street, with a river of blood coming out of his head. The patient was about twenty-five years old; the patient was a heavily tattooed John Doe; the patient was presumably a gang member.

John Doe: an unknown man

Police were on scene long before we were, and they didn't bother to call it in because they assumed he was dead. They staged out the area, put up the caution tape, and started hunting for clues, witnesses, the killer, and the weapon. At some point someone noticed that blood bubbles were popping out of his mouth, that he was still breathing.

For those of you who want to know, it looks exactly like the movies. I had trouble watching graphic movies before I drove an ambulance, and I can't watch them now. Funny, I guess, that most people can't do this kind of work, but can watch those movies without a problem.

We descended on him eagerly—a true case of trauma is a rare and coveted event—and the police officers watched with bemused interest. One even got a notebook ready in case the guy regained enough consciousness to reveal his or his assailant's name. It was my first GSW and I was very much a rookie at the time, but even I could've told the cop to put his notebook away.

coveted: greatly desired

bemused: displaying a sense of humor

assailant: an attacker

The bullet had gone through the patient's occipital lobe, and the larger exit wound showed that it had shot out of his left temporal lobe. The part of his brain that controlled his breathing remained, amazingly, intact. Once we had treated, packaged, and begun our transport to a trauma center, there was nothing to do but sit and watch him breathe. I matched his respirations with the bag-valve mask to help push extra O_2 in. His vitals were fine, but we all knew we were looking at a dying man, or a comatose one. His body had yet to admit the obvious.

occipital lobe: the back part of the brain

temporal lobe: the side part of the brain

When we went over a bump in the road, the trauma dressing slipped from his forehead, and a large geyser of blood and brain gushed from the exit wound. I yanked my left hand out of the way and slid my foot away from the new pool of blood. My right hand continued to bag him with oxygen as I reached for a new multitrauma dressing. *I saw brain*, I kept thinking.

geyser: a strong upward spray

I had the strangest feeling while watching him. His body was still warm and strong. His clothes had been cut off and he lay there oozing with life, impossibly alive. *Somebody loved him*, I thought. His mother, his girlfriend, his brother, his friend. Somebody thought he was invincible. He had thought he was invincible, clearly. The muscle memory in his body reeked of it.

invincible: unbeatable

Later, when it was over, when I had changed into a fresh uniform and finished my report, I took a nap in the ambulance, my arms crossed over

ER: emergency room

my chest, my sunglasses on. I looked tougher than I felt. I was shaken to my boots. He died amid the tools, machinery, and impersonal language of the ER. All that yelling across his body, but nothing anybody did seemed related to him. And where was he in the midst of it all? Forgotten. A John Doe, dead. A policeman's empty notebook page.

My partner didn't think he was worth saving. His opinion was that all gang members were a cancer on society, and they should be rounded up and allowed to kill each other, so the rest of us could be free of them. He had two years' experience on me and ordered me around constantly. That day I was too numb and exhausted to tell him what I was convinced of: that it wasn't our job to decide who lived or died. That I didn't ever want it to be my job to decide. If a person lay dying in front of me, I would try to help.   **9**

I didn't think I'd be able to fall asleep sitting in the rig, but in the end I did. I slept and I dreamed. In my dream there was a clean white room: white walls, tile floor. John Doe was lying on the floor, still naked but cleaned up: no sign of blood or brain or even the wound for that matter, and his skin and tattoos were gleaming. His eyes were closed, he wasn't yet dead but not alive either, and whatever life existed in him was in the form of a kind of coiled-up and angry tension: some part of him refused to let go.   **10**

meticulous: very detailed

serpentine: snakelike

ajar: slightly open

I got underneath him very carefully. Curled up in a ball, my head lowered, my breathing labored, I inched his torso into a sitting position by leaning my body weight into his back and pushing the ground away. It was slow, meticulous work and he was unnaturally heavy. His arms were relaxed at his side and his head was tilted back resting on my serpentine spine. His mouth was ajar and through the open channel of his throat came a kind of smoke or light. Every time I nudged him, his body relaxed a little more, and that strange substance slid out, curling up into the air around him.   **11**

That smoke, that light was grateful to be going. It was grateful to be going, and the more it left him, the lighter and more relaxed his body became. No tension, no ugliness, no holding on. Just a body on a tile floor, with smoke and light in the air around it, and me crouched underneath.   **12**

I want to be that grateful when I go.   **13**

DISCUSS WITH YOUR PEERS

1. Reread paragraphs 6 and 7. How does the author respond to the gruesome condition of the patient? Do you think her emotional response is appropriate for a rookie?

2. Reread paragraph 9. Discuss whose point of view (the narrator's or her partner's) you agree with most. Explain your position.

3. Reread paragraphs 10–12. Why do you think the author has this dream? What does her dream mean, and why does she get so "up close and personal" with the patient?

IDENTIFY THE PATTERNS

1. The author uses **description** to help the reader visualize the events. As an example, reread paragraphs 10–12, and identify the descriptive details that bring the narrator's dream to life.

2. The author uses **process** to show how police respond at a crime scene (para. 2) and how emergency medics treat a patient (paras. 4–6). Reread these paragraphs, and identify the steps in each process.

WRITE ABOUT THE READING

How does the author respond to the patient? Consider the different ways in which she responds, and discuss whether you believe these responses are appropriate. Give examples from the reading to support your ideas.

WRITE ABOUT YOUR LIFE

Discuss a form of violence that you have witnessed in your life (war or gang violence, domestic violence, images of violence in the media, etc.). Describe the causes and consequences of the violence and how you responded to it.

WRITE ABOUT THE THEME

1. Compare and contrast the types of violence portrayed in the two essays in Chapter 30. Discuss the violent event in each story, the causes of the event, and the attitudes of the people involved.

2. Compare and contrast how Gilbert in "Running for His Life" and the narrator in "GSW" cope with horrific violence. What do they each do to redeem the victims and themselves?

CHAPTER 31

On Technology

Technology affects many aspects of our lives — how we learn, how we entertain ourselves, even how we relate to one another. It can be both useful and distracting. As you read the following selections, think about how you use technology and how your life might be different without it. For instance, without social networking sites, how would your friendships and self-image be different? How does technology affect your education or your overall happiness?

Mona Eltahawy

Twitterholics Anonymous

Mona Eltahawy is an award-winning journalist and activist born in Egypt and now living in New York. She lectures and writes about human rights and the importance of technology in the Arab world. In 2011, she was arrested, assaulted, and beaten — police broke both of her arms — while reporting on the Cairo protests from the front line. After her arrest, she tweeted, "The whole time I was thinking about the article I would write."

bane: a curse

Twitter is my lifeline to the world. Twitter is the bane of my existence. Twitter connects me to everything I care about and Twitter is ruining my life. 1

Yes, yes, I'm Mona; I'm a Twitterholic, etc. etc. 2

tweet: to send a message on Twitter

Here are the places I tweet: In bed (when I wake up in the middle of the night, I'll reach out for my iPhone and check in on the Twitterverse). In the bathroom (don't ask). On the street. At bookshops. Standing in line to pay at the grocery store. You get the idea. 3

Sometimes I'll even tweet while I'm on the phone with my sister (we follow each other on Twitter) and she'll tweet back, "I can't believe you're tweeting while we're on the phone!!!" 4

Yes. It's bad. 5

Power Tip
Twitter is a micro-blog platform on which people can send 140-character messages to their followers on any subject. Many celebrities, journalists, CEOs, corporations, and politicians use Twitter to broadcast their ideas.

But in all seriousness, before we start to talk about A for Addiction, let me tell you how — for this columnist and news junkie — Twitter has become part of the backbone for my work along with my laptop and Internet connection. It has broken more stories for me than any other news "source" recently. 6

I spent almost six years as a Reuters correspondent in Cairo and   **7**
Jerusalem, honing my thirst for speed, which along with accuracy is wire
reporting's forte. Twitter gives you the first and can leave you free-falling
when it comes to the second, but if you don't know how to navigate, then
you don't belong on the Twitterhighway.

hone: to sharpen
forte: strength

I first learned of the bomb attack, which took place a few minutes   **8**
into the New Year against a Coptic Christian church in Alexandria, Egypt,
via Twitter. Granted it was a very slow news day regardless of time zone,
but on Twitter there's always someone awake somewhere.

Coptic: an Afroasiatic
language of Egypt

Twitter wasn't just the first place I heard about the uprising in Tunisia   **9**
but it was, for many days, the only place. The U.S. media mostly ignored
the worst unrest to hit the North African country in a decade. It started on
December 17, when a young man poured gasoline on himself in Sidibouzid
to protest police confiscating the fruits and vegetables he sold without a
permit, in lieu of a job he couldn't find despite having a university degree.

confiscate: to seize for
public use

This is where who you follow along that Twitterhighway matters.   **10**
Thanks to a group of activists, journalists and bloggers (sometimes they
are all in one), I got not just the latest information from Tunisia—blog
entries, video straight from demonstrations, news about arrested bloggers
and campaigns for their release—but also live updates from solidarity
protests in neighboring countries too, such as the one in Cairo.

solidarity: unity for a
cause

And then where else could I follow in real time as Boston-based   **11**
Mauritanian-American activist Nasser Weddady—who has for years run
advocacy campaigns to release activists and journalists imprisoned in the
Middle East—demanded that Alec Ross, Secretary of State Hillary Clinton's Senior Advisor for Innovation, explain why the U.S. Administration
was silent as Tunisia arrested protesters and bloggers and used live am-
munition against demonstrators.

Ross is a champion of social media and his boss often extols the   **12**
virtues of net freedom, so it was captivating to follow their discussion because here was Tunisia conducting a vicious war against Facebook users,
bloggers and other online activists to shut them down and yet it got little
of the condemnation Washington meted out to Iran when the latter went
after online activists after the 2009 elections.

extol: to praise

mete out: to distribute
in small amounts

So, of course, I'm on Twitter. I don't care about Lady GaGa or Justin   **13**
Bieber, who between them have about half of the world following them.
Twitter helps me mine the world for small gems of optimism to hold
onto—those tireless and increasingly frantic tweets from Cairo protesters corralled by police for more than seven hours, or tweets from Egyptian
Muslims who attended Christmas Eve services to show solidarity with
their Coptic compatriots and pictures showing them standing outside
churches holding candles: I demand to be moved to the edge of tears, rage
and optimism and Twitter delivers.

corralled: gathered up
and encircled

And that's exactly why it's destroying my life, my ability to write and   **14**
my ability to look away from the computer screen. I see a number up there
on the Twitter tab and I must refresh, immediately—must.know.now.

I'm glued to Twitter for hours on end. It's exhausting not just because   **15**
of the amount of time I spend on it—I don't just read, I tweet too—but
because it keeps you in a constant state of alertness. To write, you need
to move beyond that alertness, to stop refreshing that Twitter feed, and

tentacles: multiple, long-reaching arms

to wander away. Twitter never lets me wonder. Its tentacles hold me too tightly.

Just disconnect, you ask? I would lose a vital pipeline of information. But also social interaction. **16**

Writing is a lonely endeavor—the payback for the constant dripdrip-drip of distraction is an army of people across the globe. First up are the Australians, Malaysians and Indonesians. I'll catch a few hours of them before I head to bed just as the Middle East is waking up. By the time I'm awake—or if I sneak a peek in the middle of sleep—I'll get Europe and then during my day, it's the Middle East's night owls along with North American tweeps. **17**

When I'm up all night to write, I'm never alone. But when I need distance for focus and analysis, again I'm never alone. **18**

Addiction. Connection. Distraction. Twitter I love/hate you. **19**

DISCUSS WITH YOUR PEERS

1. Reread paragraphs 6 and 13. Discuss why Twitter is so important for the author. How does it help Eltahawy both professionally and personally?

2. What types of news events are especially important to the author? Consider the examples given in paragraphs 8, 9, and 11.

3. Look at the three key words in paragraph 19: "Addiction. Connection. Distraction." Explain how each of these terms is true for the author, giving examples from the reading.

IDENTIFY THE PATTERNS

1. The author uses **exemplification** to show how Twitter keeps her informed about world events. Reread paragraphs 7–13, and identify examples of these world events.

2. The author uses **cause and effect** to show how Twitter (the cause) is "destroying [her] life" (the effects). Reread paragraphs 14–18, and identify the negative effects of Twitter on the author's life.

3. The author uses **process** to show the steps involved in keeping up with people "across the globe." Reread paragraph 17, and identify these steps.

WRITE ABOUT THE READING

Discuss the author's range of attitudes and feelings about Twitter. What advice would you give her about how to manage or change her habitual Twitter usage?

1. Discuss how Twitter and/or other forms of electronic communication have changed your life.

2. Discuss how Twitter and/or other forms of electronic communication have changed societies, politics, international relations, or other public realities.

Nancy Nevins

The Cell Fish Blues

Nancy Nevins was one of the six preeminent female rock vocalists of the 1960s. Her band, Sweetwater, was the first band to play on the stage at Woodstock. Today, Nancy is a performer, songwriter, and English instructor in Los Angeles, California.

A long time ago cigarettes made everybody cool. At twelve, I lit up for **1**
the first time behind the garage with my buddies. What a trip.

Smoking was a big step into life, where I lived on the edge of un- **2**
comfortable. Cigarettes evened out rough patches—heightened the good
times, too. Smokers found other smokers. Like magnets, we hung together. Nothing matters like shared mischief. Behind the garage, we dried
and smoked banana peels, experimented with pot, and smoked tons of
cigarettes. We even ripped open tea bags and rolled the acrid leaves. Best   **acrid:** sharp-smelling
of all, I could stroll through the mall or walk anywhere dragging, exhaling,
and waving my Marlboro safety nets. No feeling maimed a changing teen-   **maim:** to injure
ager if she smoked—smoking helped everything.

If you didn't smoke cigarettes you were probably not cool. **3**

Smokers felt connected. You bummed a smoke from anyone. You **4**
smoked with music and on street corners. You smoked before and after
eating, and when driving or riding in the car, cab, train, limo, bus, or plane.
You smoked at weddings, funerals, parties, and your own graduation. You
smoked at the beach, in waiting rooms, in class, in bars and coffee shops, in
theater lobbies, and in court. You smoked before and after job interviews,
when you were hired and when you were fired. You smoked when you studied and when you watched TV. You smoked waiting for phone calls and
for escrow to close—waiting for *any* answer. At the hospital, you smoked   **escrow:** money or
before the baby was born, while the baby was born, and after the baby was   property held by a third
born. You smoked when you read books or newspapers—when you fished,   party until certain condi-
walked, bowled, golfed, or played tennis. (I knew someone who smoked in   tions are met
the shower, but he was a hard case.) You flicked your Bic at concerts where
orange tips winked across the smoking crowd. You smoked when you were   **Bic:** a plastic cigarette
worried, bored, or happy. You smoked during a troubled relationship. You   lighter
smoked when you were flirting, courting, fighting, making up, and after sex.
Sometimes, you couldn't hold my hand because there was a cigarette in it.

Times changed. Smokers morphed from cool to addicted. The broad- **5**
cast age of cancer took over; smoking's barely tolerated now. We feel

strata: socioeconomic levels

sorry for these addicts. They come from all strata. Totally un-cool now, almost every smoker I know wants to quit.

If we can't smoke anymore, what can we do?   **6**

Get a cell phone.   **7**

You feel connected. Use it in all situations. Text, talk, game, send   **8** pics, look things up. Check Facebook; tweet; make videos; watch videos. Leave your cell on your desk so you can distract yourself "whenever." You can talk or text in the car, cab, bus, train, limo, or plane. Even some bicyclists chat on their phones. Keep your cell between you and who or whatever's happening wherever you are: at a show, in court, in class, in the store, at the gym, in the doctor's office, in line, in bars and in meetings, in coffee shops, on escalators and elevators, before and after job interviews, onstage and backstage, and waiting for your therapist. Take your phone to parties, weddings, funerals (not yours, of course—unless someone conjures an "eternity" app before you go), and your graduation. Wave your phone's digital flame in solidarity at rock concerts. You belong. Let everyone know where you are. Take it shopping. Take it on your date—when it rings, moans, or buzzes, he constantly remembers you are busy. Show him the friends on your phone. Send texts across the table. *Sometimes, you can't hold my hand because there is a cell phone in it.*

There's even a possible cancer threat and addiction linked to cell   **9** phone use. And, it's easier to connect with someone who's not there than to befriend a silent stranger next to you. Strangers are dangerous; silence is, too. Moreover, cell phones give off extra waves of glamour—and armor.

Cell phones top smokers' cravings because cells are practical, too.   **10** After all, who doesn't want to share good news right away or unburden angst with unlimited minutes? Who doesn't want a calendar, constant updates, tweeting, mobile email and banking, a thousand Facebook friends, quick answers, maps, games, and instant directions? Who doesn't feel grateful for messaging in tricky affairs where you need to regroup? Who doesn't want to click a picture right away, video something on-the-spot, or sound an alarm? Who doesn't want the siren song of a well-managed life?

contrive: to invent

disassociate: to separate, pull apart

Confounding human nature, cell phones have altered social develop-   **11** ments. Past and present are contrived, blended into one. Time and distance dissolved—barely a factor. A rich cell phone life is somewhat like believing in your own ghost. Phoning in your life-story is a disassociative strategy. You keep up with everyone else's ghost, too. Make calls. Return calls. Leave and listen to messages. With one message, your presence is history and your past is present. You never have to be "here." You are always "there." Your friends are just like active mobile you.

narcissistic: extremely self-focused

A complex addiction, cell phones feel like they make busy life bet-   **12** ter, but they make true life harder. We deprive ourselves of quiet time and use messages to feed dependence and eliminate aloneness (not to be confused with loneliness). "I'm walking to class. I'm opening the door. I'm here, Mom-Dad-Tiffany-Brad." *I exist.* In narcissistic times, reporting and feeling in-control are the survivor's payoffs, not to mention fashionable and current. Nothing's going to get past you. Still, humans don't absorb life that quickly. Instant messaging is new to human history. Cell phones can't meet all needs, can't nurture all our parts. Sometimes aloneness, like presence or processing, is necessary.

Nearly extinct, Mother Nature wrestles Technology to hang onto authen-   **13** tic living and presence—technology can't undo the need for contemplation, either. Beyond nicotine's kick, cell phones seduce our self-centeredness, starve our characters, and fake our presence. They manipulate aloneness. Alone with your phone, you're never alone. You can always be found. Once, absence made the heart grow fonder—still does; yet, in new millennium life, it's "game-on" in the demand for your company. Once, other than Morse code, Pre-Cell Phone Man couldn't tap out instant messages. Humans who sought real connection traveled hard to find another person—they had to. Born face-2-face, humans knew genuine presence—body language with loud or soft words that rush or falter: the fullness of smell, sight, sound, taste, and touch—your cave or mine? A short time ago, the human being stood app-less, phone-less, and alone—gazing at stars. Without technology, we're still made like this. We're not born yet with tiny, fleshy bluetooths embedded over the ear canal.

Gazing at stars still matters. Real-time, no-task-but-you presence **14** *does, too.*

Cell phone packages deceive us. They play on images: needs and **15** wants, responsibilities and pride. Verizon, Sprint, T-Mobile, AT&T, all stroke emotions and cleverly compete for us; stimulate curiosity and the zest for newness; play on our contradictory fear of strangers and our need to belong. Like weird jailers, cell phone companies turn us into prey—fish marked in a cell-fish age. They bait appetites with hip substitutes for body language, like callers' faces on small screens in the palm of your hand; they put communication on a cool linear plane; they stunt unprogrammable, genuine interactions. Beware nicotine-less cell phones. They absorb independence, aloneness, processing skills, and presence—your money and your life (talk about the blues). For many, *smoking took life, too.* Someday a Surgeon General may warn: (Cell) Phone at Your Own Risk.

> **stunt:** to stop the growth of something

Believe it or not, I love my cell phone; yet, I wonder how those **16** who don't know anything else—kindergarteners playing with their phones—will grow. Raised in the shade of a distant intimacy—without the inspiration aloneness yields, or enough contact with the effusion of presence—they give too much to their phones. They accept norms of disembodied voices, games, and deconstructed time. Because cells (jail) offer life at a safer distance, young cell fish develop once removed from each other—a new kind of cell-ular change.

> **effusion:** a pouring forth
>
> **disembodied:** lacking a body
>
> **deconstruct:** to dismantle, take apart

Expressionless faces connect with wireless voices like it's a better **17** way to walk around—easier, simpler. Truth is, when we pass, our eyes still want to meet. In person, "hi-hey-what's-up" still crackles neutrons between us. *We exist.*

Many of us spend hours with our phones—we point out the good **18** technology does and say we can stop anytime.

We just don't want to. **19**

At times, I feel like interrupting someone walking by on her phone. **20**

Her eyes flick over me, but I know she doesn't see me. I want to ask if **21** someone's really on the other end or if she is just pretending to be talking. It'd be funny if she was pretending—then again, maybe it wouldn't be. Researchers continue brain studies of damage from cell phone use and traffic laws are tougher on driving while texting and talking. Will the socialization of cell phone dependency—its cultural consequences—come under scrutiny next? I hope so.

> **scrutiny:** close inspection

Who knows? If cell phones end up banned, smoking might make a **22** huge comeback. LOL.

DISCUSS WITH YOUR PEERS

1. Reread the last sentences in paragraphs 4 and 8, and the sentence in paragraph 14. Why are these sentences in italics? What special messages do these sentences express that are so important to the author?

2. Reread paragraph 11. The author compares excessive cell phone use to "believing in your own ghost" and "[keeping] up with everyone else's ghost, too." What does the author mean by this comparison? Do you agree or disagree with this idea? Explain your opinion.

3. Reread paragraph 15. Do you agree that cell phone companies successfully deceive and manipulate consumers? Or do they merely provide accurate information about their products? Explain your opinions.

IDENTIFY THE PATTERNS

1. The author uses **comparison and contrast** to show how smoking and cell phones are similar and different. Reread paragraphs 4 and 8, identifying the similarities. Reread paragraph 10, identifying the differences.

2. The author uses **cause and effect** to show how cell phones (the cause) have changed human experience and behavior (the effects). Reread paragraphs 12 and 13, identifying some of the ways in which cell phones have changed human experience and behavior.

3. The author uses **exemplification** throughout the reading. Look at paragraph 4. Identify the examples provided, and explain what idea these examples illustrate.

WRITE ABOUT THE READING

Discuss the ways in which cell phones have changed human experience and behavior. Give examples from the reading to support your ideas.

WRITE ABOUT YOUR LIFE

Discuss your relationship with your cell phone. How closely does the author's description represent your own experience?

WRITE ABOUT THE THEME

Discuss the advantages and disadvantages of your favorite form of electronic or online communication. Provide examples from both readings in Chapter 31, as well as from your personal experience, to support your ideas.

CHAPTER 32

On Being from Elsewhere

Where are you from? Where is home to you? Is that something you get to decide for yourself, or is it a feeling you can't help? As you read the following selections, think about what it means to be an "outsider" and what it means to be at home. Finally, think about your future: Where are you going?

Edwidge Danticat

Uncle Moïse

Edwidge Danticat was born in Haiti and immigrated to the United States with her family when she was two years old. Since childhood, she has been a prolific writer, often focusing on issues affecting Haitians both in the United States and abroad. She has won many awards, including a MacArthur Genius grant.

My uncle Moïse died last week after a six-year battle, first with prostate, then bone cancer. Of all my mother's brothers, Uncle Moïse was my favorite because he often peppered his conversations, whether in English or in Haitian Creole, with the word "Fuck!" Uncle Moïse used different variations of the word freely, even with children (*Speak up, silence is fucked up*), priests (*They can be fucks*), or my very devout and demure parents (*They're your parents, but fuck!*), who could never be swayed by his argument that the most interesting aspect of any language was its cusswords. To substantiate this, he would quote translations of the Marquis de Sade or find interesting uses of the word "fuck" in English-language poetry, his favorite being a verse from a 1971 Philip Larkin poem:

1

demure: shy

substantiate: to back up, give substance to

> They fuck you up, your mum and dad.
> They may not mean to, but they do.

Though I was not fully conscious of the influence of Uncle Moïse's speech pattern on mine, it would surface from time to time in desperate situations. Once, during a heated argument with a boyfriend, I found myself tongue-tied, yet shouting, "You fucking fuck!" then smiling, thinking this was something Uncle Moïse might have said.

2

euphemism: a polite way of saying something

calamity: a disaster

paraphrase: to restate in different words

tribulations: hardships

eulogizer: a person who speaks at a funeral

unfettered: unrestricted, free

inconsolable: not able to be comforted or calmed

en masse: as a large group

A few years into his cancer treatment, Uncle Moïse, who had been   3
both a seminary student and an army officer in Haiti, became an evangelical Christian and began to use a biblical euphemism for the word "fuck." A bad situation became a calamity. When he thought me too quiet, for example, he would now say, "Speak up, silence is a calamity." The switch became a clear sign that Uncle Moïse was taking evangelical Christianity seriously for those of us who had doubted he could. He stopped quoting de Sade and Larkin and turned to Bible verses instead, often paraphrasing Deuteronomy 32:35, "Their foot shall slide in time, for the day of calamity is at hand," or Proverbs 6:15, "Therefore shall his calamity come suddenly, suddenly shall he be broken without remedy."

As he grew sicker, Uncle Moïse timed his remaining days in Good   4
Fridays, as if to link his own personal tribulations to the passion of Christ. "I may not have another Good Friday left," he would say, even though he had already seen seventy-one. Good Friday seemed more and more like a perfect day to die in order to be guaranteed a heavenly rebirth. "All Fridays are ultimately good," he would eventually concede, "as long as you're around to see them." (In some parts of Spain, he once explained to me, you ask, "How many Aprils do you have?" to find out someone's age.)

At his wake, speaker after speaker described Uncle Moïse at differ-   5
ent periods of his life. People who knew him when he was a Haitian army officer and had to flee the national palace on a motorcycle when his boss, the dictator François "Papa Doc" Duvalier, threatened to have him killed for failing to deliver a letter on time. Others who knew him in connection with his different families (he had been married twice and it was only at his wake that many of his children from his first marriage and his son from the second met one another). While meeting many of his children for the first time myself, I thought of how Uncle Moïse loved to compartmentalize, devoting himself entirely to whatever he was involved with at the time and rarely looking back. Of his long exile from Haiti, which he rarely wanted to discuss, he would only say, "There are enough present calamities so we don't have to keep looking back on past ones." But most of Uncle Moïse's eulogizers had known him as an evangelical Christian at the church where his wake was held and spoke only of his long suffering and, just as he might have wanted, his soul's rebirth in Heaven. During the wake, I kept wishing I could get up and say that what I enjoyed most when in his company was his unfettered use of a four-letter word, but it did not seem appropriate, especially since he had abandoned the word at the end of his life.

The last time I saw Uncle Moïse, against the advice of his doctors, he   6
had driven himself from his home on Long Island to the church in Brooklyn where he was an usher. "It's a calamity sitting around and waiting to die," he had said. Nostalgic, I had thought of his risky cross-county drive as a continuation of his motorcycle flight from certain death and as further evidence of his defiant nature, which neither illness nor the Gospel had completely extinguished. A week later, he was gone.

I cried quite a bit at Uncle Moïse's funeral, mostly because my   7
mother, his younger sister, was the most inconsolable of his mourners. Exile had scattered her family, she said, and it was only death that brought us together en masse these days. My most sorrowful moment

came, however, on a Friday, three days after the funeral, when I tried to write Uncle Moïse's name in my computer and couldn't find on my American keyboard the accent key that would place the tréma over the i in his name. Then exile and loss became palpable to me. It is the calamity of living and dying in a place where it takes uncommon effort to spell a fucking name that you have known your entire life.

tréma: an accent mark

palpable: real, present

DISCUSS WITH YOUR PEERS

1. Reread paragraphs 1 and 2, and the last sentences of paragraphs 5 and 7. Why does the word *fuck* become so important for the author? What does the word represent for her? In your opinion, does her use of the word honor her uncle or disrespect him? Explain your opinion.

2. Reread paragraphs 5 and 6. How would you characterize Uncle Moïse? What are his strongest personality traits?

3. Reread paragraph 7. Explain the cause of the author's sorrow. Does it make sense that her difficulty in typing her uncle's name could bring about such a powerful emotional response? Why or why not?

IDENTIFY THE PATTERNS

1. The author uses **narration** to tell the story of Uncle Moïse's life and last years. Reread the story, and identify some of the key events in Moïse's life.

2. The author uses **exemplification** to show how her uncle uses the words *fuck* and *calamity*. Reread paragraphs 1, 3, 5, and 6, and identify the examples provided by the author.

3. The author uses **cause and effect** to show how cancer (the cause) brings about changes in Uncle Moïse's life and behavior (the effects). Reread paragraphs 3, 4, and 6, and identify the effects that cancer has on Moïse's behavior.

WRITE ABOUT THE READING

Would you like to have Uncle Moïse as your own uncle? Provide examples from the reading to support your ideas.

WRITE ABOUT YOUR LIFE

Discuss a family member or relative who has had a powerful influence on your life. If appropriate, focus on behaviors, gestures, or expressions this person used that made him or her distinctive to you.

Maria Andreu
This (Illegal) American Life

Maria Andreu is a writer, mother, and marketing consultant. She is also the co-chair of a nonprofit that works with migrant workers and their families to help provide access to social services, employment opportunities, and career training. She was born in Argentina and now lives in New Jersey.

pundit: a scholar, expert

assiduous: rigorous, intense

When the pundits began to tear into undocumented immigrants last summer, using terms like "parasites" and "criminals," my first reaction was to bury my head and turn off the TV. I had worked too hard since my own illegal Mexican border crossing thirty years ago, at the age of eight, to blow my cover now. I had assiduously cultivated myself as an American, reading the right books, sporting "the Rachel" haircut in the '90s, gossiping about reality TV with gusto on the sidelines of my children's soccer games. I was aided by pasty white skin that placed my ancestry vaguely somewhere in the northern Mediterranean countries or Eastern Europe in most people's imaginations, not among the stereotype of an illegal immigrant. 1

My parents came to New York City to make their fortune when I was a baby. Irresponsible and in their early twenties, they didn't think things through when their visa expired; they decided to stay just a bit longer to build up a nest egg. 2

But our stay got progressively longer, until, when I was six, my grandfather died in South America. My father decided my mother and I should go to the funeral and, with assurances that he would handle everything, sat me down and told me I'd have a nice visit in his boyhood home in Argentina, then be back in America in a month. 3

I didn't see him for two years. 4

rickety: falling apart, broken down

insular: enclosed, isolated

Being stranded in Argentina on the dusty Mendozan foothills where my parents had met and married, and for which they'd pined during my childhood in our little New Jersey basement apartment, was a revelation for me. While growing up different and apart in the U.S.—not being able to enter kindergarten with my friends, speaking rickety English I picked up from "Sesame Street"—my parents had assured me that one day we'd be in our real home of Argentina. But I soon realized I was even more of an oddity in the insular world of this tiny Argentine town. I missed my Barbie dolls and games of tag that went on until dusk. I missed the New York skyline and hearing the national anthem before the TV networks stopped broadcasting for the evening. I missed home. 5

We couldn't get a visa to return. My father sent us money from New Jersey, as the months of our absence stretched into years. Finally, he met someone who knew "coyotes"—people who smuggled others into the U.S. via Mexico. He paid them what they asked for, and we flew to Mexico City. 6

pungent: very strong-smelling

The coyotes hid my mother and me for weeks in a shack in Tijuana with an outhouse so pungent I held my need to use it until I was bursting. At eight years old, I only vaguely understood the danger of being in a no man's land, completely dependent on the smugglers, with nothing but my mother's mostly empty purse and the clothes we were wearing. 7

Being light-skinned like gringas would work in our favor, the coyotes told us. They drove us to the Mexican side of the border, and left us at a beach. Another from their operation picked us up there and drove us across as his family. We passed Disneyland on our way to the airport, where we boarded the plane to finally rejoin my father. 8

As a child, I had thought coming back home would be the magical end to our troubles, but in many ways it was the beginning. I chafed at the strictures of undocumented life: no social security number meant no public school (instead I attended a Catholic school my parents could scarcely afford), no driver's license, no after-school job. My parents had made their choices, and I had to live with those, seeing off my classmates as they left on a class trip to Canada, or packing to go off to college, where I could not go. 9

The year before I graduated from high school, Congress passed the amnesty law of 1987. A few months after my eighteenth birthday, I became legal and what had always seemed a blank future of no hope suddenly turned dazzling with possibility. 10

When I went for my interview at the Immigration and Naturalization Service, the caseworker looked at me quizzically when he heard me talk in unaccented English and joke about current events. Surely this American teenager did not fit in with the crowd of illegals looking to make things right. 11

At the time, I was flattered. His confusion meant I could pass as an American. But in the twenty years since, I have come to realize that I fit in with that crowd of illegal immigrants as well as with "real" Americans. I've finally come to understand there are many paths to living the American Dream, and I took one of them—mine. 12

DISCUSS WITH YOUR PEERS

1. In the first paragraph, the author says that she doesn't want to "blow [her] cover." What is this "cover," and why is it so important to her?

2. Reread paragraph 5. Discuss the author's struggle to belong in either Mendoza or New Jersey. Which place is more her home, and why? Can you empathize with her struggle? Explain your response.

3. Reread the last paragraph. The author says that she followed her own path to achieving the "American Dream." Would you say that her path was more that of an illegal immigrant or a typical, American-born citizen? Explain your answer.

IDENTIFY THE PATTERNS

1. The author uses **narration** to tell the story of her life. Reread the story, identifying the key events in the author's life.

2. The author uses **exemplification** in paragraphs 1, 5, and 9. Identify the specific examples that she provides in each paragraph, and explain what these are examples of.

WRITE ABOUT THE READING

Discuss the author's struggles and her success in dealing with those struggles. Provide examples from the reading to support your ideas.

WRITE ABOUT YOUR LIFE

1. If you immigrated to the United States from another country, discuss your feelings about both places. Which place do you consider home?

2. Interview someone you know who immigrated to the United States from another country, and discuss his or her feelings about the two places. Which place does he or she consider home?

WRITE ABOUT THE THEME

Compare and contrast the experiences of Uncle Moïse and Maria Andreu. What are the challenges they faced while living in exile, and how did they handle these challenges? Provide examples from the readings to support your ideas.

On Music

To most people, music is more than just entertainment: It is an expression of personality and culture, and it's a way that people relate to each other. As you read the following selections, consider the role that music has played in your own life. What music or musicians do you like? What do you relate to (or like) in their music? Do you think this music has shaped who you are? How has your family's or your culture's taste in music influenced your own?

Joyce Zonana

Dream Homes

Joyce Zonana is an English professor and a writer. This essay is excerpted from Zonana's book, *Dream Homes*, a memoir of her family's complicated Egyptian American heritage. She lives in Brooklyn, New York.

Before my discovery of belly dance at twenty-five, I perceived Arabic music only with my mother's ears, hearing nothing but a cacophony of empty sound. **1**

cacophony: a loud, disturbing noise

"I hate it," my mother would say. "It's ugly and sad." **2**

If my mother could have had her way, our Brooklyn apartment would have been filled only with the studiously upbeat sound of 1950s popular music, supplemented by Italian opera, *Live from the Met* on Saturday afternoons. But my mother's authority was limited; she was subject, even in the home she managed so well, to the will of her mother-in-law, my father's widowed mother, *Nonna*—the woman who, with the exception of the five years between my parents' emigration from Cairo and hers, lived with my parents from the day of their wedding in 1945 until the day they placed her in a nursing home, in 1975. **3**

supplemented: complemented by

I will never know which came first: my mother's distaste for Middle Eastern music or her conflict with her mother-in-law. I only know that in the unspoken battleground that was our home, my grandmother's music came to represent all that my mother abhorred. Given the choices—my vibrant mother or my embittered grandmother—I aligned myself with my mother, barricading myself against the sounds of my birthplace, refusing to hear my grandmother's call. **4**

abhor: to hate, detest

align: to side with, join a side

plaintive:
resembling crying

incomprehensible:
impossible to understand

discordant: not in harmony, clashing

paroxysm: an attack

keen: to make a high-pitched, crying sound

lament: to regret, feel sorrow

fathomless: bottomless, without end

encompass: to cover completely

litany: a prayer

une fille bien élevée
[French]: a well-mannered girl

avert: to turn away

elicit: to call forth

visceral: from the guts, not intellectual

For *Nonna* cherished Arabic music, listening to it daily despite my   5
mother's obvious distaste. She would sit alone in the center of the worn sofa bed that stretched along one wall of our living room, an embroidered and perfumed handkerchief in her hand, her records beside her. She had only four—scratched recordings of popular favorites by Fairuz, the Lebanese diva, and Farid Al-Atrash, an Egyptian heartthrob—yet she played them, one after another, day after day, year after year, on the old Victrola in the corner. Hearing the plaintive, mournful sounds, I could not distinguish the seemingly endless repetition of the songs themselves from the repetition caused by the needle skipping across the battered old disks. The Arabic words were incomprehensible to me, the music discordant and strange; yet for *Nonna*, locked in her memories, these were the sounds of home.

As she listened, repeating the Arabic words and humming the tunes,   6
she would begin to rock, sighing, crying, working herself into a paroxysm of pain. "Aiii," she keened as Fairuz's voice rose in an anthem of love for her lost Lebanon, "aiii." Instead of mourning Lebanon, *Nonna* lamented her sons Ezra and Isaac, my father's two brothers, who lived abroad; she mourned for a daughter who died in infancy, for a husband dead after only ten years of marriage. "Aiiiii," *Nonna* cried, the sound now rising from her chest, simultaneously deep and shrill. All that had been left behind—her country, her family, her youth, her joy—contributed to this fathomless, endless, encompassing grief. And that grief wound itself so fully into the music that those songs, whatever their lyrics or rhythm—whether folk ballad or love song or playful melody—came to represent for me an echoing litany of loss.

Terrified and threatened by the immensity of her grief, the fixity of   7
her pain, I wanted my aging *Nonna* gone, away from our home, out of our lives, so that I might give myself to the unthinking pleasures of my own young body. If I could have, I would have stopped my ears against the sound, run into my room, locked the door, and never emerged. But the only room I had was the one I shared with *Nonna*, and, trained as I was to be a good girl—*une fille bien élevée*—all I could do was avert my eyes from the sight of her huddled on the sofa. For many years, the sound of Arabic music elicited in me an immediate, visceral response: My stomach clenched and I grew rigid with distress. *Nonna* came back to me, in all her suffering. So when I stepped into that dance studio in San Francisco, I was already moving with a new freedom: I was beginning to reoccupy the body *Nonna* had so savagely possessed.

DISCUSS WITH YOUR PEERS

1. Reread paragraphs 4 and 5, and discuss why the author dislikes Arabic music.

2. The author says, "I will never know which came first: my mother's distaste for Middle Eastern music or her conflict with her mother-in-law" (para. 4). Discuss what the author means by this. Based on the details in the story, which would you guess came first?

3. Reread paragraph 7. Do you think the author's desire to have her grandmother gone is reasonable or selfish? Then, what does she mean by the "new freedom" she experiences many years after her grandmother's death? In what way can she "reoccupy" her own body?

IDENTIFY THE PATTERNS

1. The author uses **contrast** to show how Arabic music sounds different to the different characters in the story. First, find some key details that describe how the music sounds to the author and her mother. Then, locate contrasting details that describe how the music sounds to the grandmother.

2. The author uses **cause and effect** to show the grandmother's reaction to the Arabic music. Reread paragraph 6, and identify the important effects of the music on the grandmother.

WRITE ABOUT THE READING

Discuss whether Arabic music is a blessing or a curse—or both—for the grandmother. Use examples from the story to support your point of view.

WRITE ABOUT YOUR LIFE

1. Discuss a type of music that brings back powerful memories for you. Describe the music and its effects on you when you listen to it now.

2. Discuss a type of music that is important to someone you know but that does not appeal to you. How do your feelings about this music affect your opinion of this person, if at all? Why can you not relate to it?

Michaela Angela Davis

Quitting Hip-Hop

Michaela Angela Davis is a writer who focuses on issues of style, race, gender, and hip-hop culture. Davis has worked for several publications, including *Essence* and *Honey*, and was one of the founding editors of *Vibe* magazine.

I am a forty-year-old fly girl. My thirteen-year-old daughter, Elenni, and I often look for the same next hot thing—that perfect pair of jeans, a she's-gotta-have-it shoe, the ultimate handbag, and the freshest new sound in music, which is, more often than not, hip-hop. Though we are nearly three decades apart in age, we both feel that hip-hop is the talking drum of our time; it teaches us and represents us. But, just as some of our African ancestors sold their people to European slave traders for a few used guns and porcelain plates, it seems as if the images of women of color in much

1   **fly girl:** an attractive, hip woman (slang)

ice: diamonds (slang)

cheese: money (slang)

gyrate: to turn in spirals

demeaning: degrading

paradox: a contradiction, mystery

of today's hip-hop music have been sold off to a greedy industry for a few buckets of "ice" and a stack of "cheese."

Recently while watching a new video in which yet another half-dressed girl gyrated and bounced, Elenni turned to me and asked, "Why can't that girl just have on a cute pair of jeans with a halter top? Why does she always have to have on booty shorts? And why can't she just dance instead of grinding on the hood of a car? What does that have to do with the song?" I had no easy answers. Although the images of the women were both demeaning and predictable, the beats were undeniably hot. Therein lies the paradox at the heart of my beef with hip-hop: songs that make you bounce can carry a message far and wide, irrespective of what that message is. And far too often the message is that most young women of color are "bitches" or "hoes." I was backed into a corner, forced to choose between my love for hip-hop and my need to be respected and to pass the ideals of self-respect on to my daughter. No contest.

lucrative: profitable

espouse: to adopt or embrace

Look, I'm no finger-wagging conservative outsider. I was one of the founding editors of *Vibe*, the first national magazine dedicated to hip-hop music, style, and culture, so it's really hard for me to hate. I also worked as a fashion stylist, helping to create looks for everyone from LL Cool J to Mary J. Later I landed at *Honey*, a magazine for young urban women, and eventually became its editor-in-chief. I wouldn't have had my career if it weren't for hip-hop culture. And that goes for lots of black folks. In addition to its music, hip-hop has journalism, film, fashion, and other lucrative by-products that have employed and empowered hundreds, if not thousands, of us. So clearly I'm not one of those out-of-touch mothers who won't listen to current music or who espouse corny clichés like "In my day, we knew what real music was."

misogyny: the hatred of women

apartheid: government-sponsored racism, especially as promoted by the former government of South Africa

Today is my day, too. And the danger with what's currently going on in hip-hop is not as simple as a mere generation gap. Increasingly, the male-dominated industry tends to view women as moneymakers (as in the kind you shake). Few of us are in a position to be decision makers. As a result of this imbalance, many popular hip-hop CDs and videos feature a brand of violence and misogyny that is as lethal as crack and as degrading as apartheid. And though I would love to maintain my "flyest mom ever" status, my daughter's self-esteem and that of every young sister in the world is at risk. I'm willing to risk my public image to help recover theirs. If there's not a shift in how the hip-hop industry portrays women, then our twenty-year relationship is officially O-V-E-R.

I've since found creative ways to deal with my daughter's dilemma and my heartbreaking breakup: I ask Elenni why she likes a song, then I suggest alternative artists who might have a similar vibe. We look for videos that feature more progressive acts like Floetry, Jean Grae, and Talib Kweli. We listen to classics such as Public Enemy and MC Lyte, so she knows that hip-hop does have a positive history. We also participate in other urban-culture activities that affirm and satisfy us, like art exhibits, poetry slams, and yes, shoe shopping.

It's not going to be easy, leaving hip-hop behind. But I can no longer merely take what it dishes out and blame it on the boogie. The cost is just too great.

1. Reread paragraphs 1 and 4. The author compares the hip-hop industry to the European slave trade and apartheid (government-sponsored racism). In your opinion, are these fair comparisons? Is the industry's greed really as dangerous as those other forms of oppression?

2. Reread paragraphs 2 and 4. What is the mother giving up in order to support her daughter and other women? Do you think she makes a good decision for herself and other women?

3. Are you familiar with any of the artists discussed in this article? If so, do you agree or disagree with the author's argument? Give examples to support your point of view.

IDENTIFY THE PATTERNS

1. The author uses **exemplification** to support and illustrate her ideas. Reread paragraphs 3 and 5, and identify the examples that she provides. Then, explain what the examples illustrate.

2. The author uses **definition** to portray herself as a person and a mother. Reread paragraphs 1 and 3, and find three sentences in which the mother clearly defines herself. Based on these sentences, what kind of person is the author?

3. The author uses **argument** to persuade the reader that hip-hop culture needs to change. Reread paragraphs 2 and 4, and identify the author's argument against hip-hop. Does she provide enough evidence in the article to persuade you that hip-hop needs to change?

WRITE ABOUT THE READING

Would you like to have the author of this article as your own mother? Why or why not? Use examples from the reading to support your ideas.

WRITE ABOUT YOUR LIFE

If you are a fan of hip-hop music, discuss the positive or negative features of the genre and your feelings about these features. If you are not a fan of hip-hop, discuss your favorite type of music. Explain why you like this music, and discuss whether it sends positive or negative messages to its listeners.

WRITE ABOUT THE THEME

Use the two readings in Chapter 33 to compare and contrast the positive and the negative effects of music on people's lives.

APPENDIX A

Guidelines for ESL Writers

If English is not your first language, or if you grew up in a home where standard English was not spoken, every chapter in Part Three of this book will improve your grammar skills. Additionally, you may benefit from reviewing this appendix and completing the activities in it, as well as getting further practice online at this book's companion Web site, **bedfordstmartins.com /touchstones**.

Remember, too, that the more you hear and read standard English, the faster your language skills will improve. Try to listen to news broadcasts or podcasts while driving, exercising, or preparing meals. Also, read magazine or newspaper articles as often as you can.

Note: This appendix color-codes all of the building blocks of language according to the system used in Part Three. See the box at right for a reminder.

KEY TO
BUILDING BLOCKS

FOUNDATION WORDS
NOUNS
VERBS

DESCRIPTIVE WORDS
ADJECTIVES
ADVERBS

CONNECTING WORDS
PREPOSITIONS
CONJUNCTIONS

Count and Noncount Nouns

As you learned in Chapter 15, a **noun** is a word that identifies a person, place, or thing (for instance, *girl, Beatrice, city, Chicago, ball*).

Count nouns refer to people, places, or things that can be counted (for example, three *girls*, two *boys*, two *towns*, six *shoes*, seven *apples*). **Noncount nouns** refer to things—often, qualities or concepts—that can't be counted (for example, *flour, granite, honesty*). Here are some more examples:

COUNT NOUNS	NONCOUNT NOUNS
desk/desks	employment
dish/dishes	furniture
example/examples	happiness
girl/girls	homelessness
hurricane/hurricanes	information
metal/metals	mail
skirt/skirts	science
stamp/stamps	silver
stove/stoves	smoke

Note that noncount nouns usually do not have plural forms; in other words, do not add *-s* or *-es* to the end of them.

INCORRECT   furnitures, informations, advices, knowledges

CORRECT   furniture, information, advice, knowledge

ACTIVITY 1: Mastery Test

MASTERY

Identify each of the following nouns as *count* or *noncount* by writing **C** or **N** in the space provided.

EXAMPLE: automobile _____ C _____

1. sandwich _____   6. judge _____

2. desk _____   7. class _____

3. homework_____   8. horse _____

4. luggage _____   9. equipment _____

5. dress _____   10. teacher _____

FOUNDATION WORDS
NOUNS
VERBS
DESCRIPTIVE WORDS
ADJECTIVES
ADVERBS
CONNECTING WORDS
PREPOSITIONS
CONJUNCTIONS

Articles

The **articles** *a*, *an*, and *the* are small but important words that signal that a noun is coming up. Look at the following examples, in which the articles are underlined.

The cook entered the kitchen.

A cat came into the yard.

An actor won the award.

Use *a* or *an* to signal nonspecific nouns, and *the* to signal specific nouns:

A neighbor took in the mail during my trip. (the neighbor's identity is not specified)

An apple is good for your health. (any apple)

The neighbor who lives upstairs took in the mail during my trip. (the neighbor is the one who lives upstairs)

The dress I just bought was shorter than I realized. (the dress is the one that I just bought)

Terminology Tip
A and *an* are known as *indefinite articles* because they signal indefinite, nonspecific nouns. *The* is known as a *definite article* because it signals definite, specific nouns.

As you use articles, keep the following rules in mind:

1. Do not use *a* or *an* with noncount nouns.   In standard English, the following sentence would be incorrect:

INCORRECT   A luggage was lost on the airplane flight.

You do not need the article *a* before the noncount noun *luggage*. However, if you specify a quantity of a noncount noun, you may use the article:

> **CORRECT**   <u>A</u> piece of luggage was lost on the airplane flight.

2. Do not use *the* before noncount or plural nouns that mean "in general."   Take a look at the following sentences:

> **INCORRECT**   Bill thinks he knows everything and likes to give <u>the</u> advice.

> **INCORRECT**   <u>The</u> apples are good for your health.

In the first example, the intended meaning is that Bill likes to give advice in general. Therefore, the article should be dropped.

> **CORRECT**   Bill thinks he knows everything and likes to give advice.

In the second example, the intended meaning is that apples in general are good for your health. Therefore, the article should be dropped.

> **CORRECT**   Apples are good for your health.

3. In article + adjective + noun combinations, use the article (*a* or *an*) that fits the sound of the adjective, not the sound of the noun.

> **INCORRECT**   <u>An</u> flowered apron protected Danny's clothes from the barbeque.

> **CORRECT**   <u>A</u> flowered apron protected Danny's clothes from the barbeque.

4. Use *a* before consonant sounds, and *an* before vowel sounds.

- Consonant sounds include: *b, c, d, f, g, j, k, l, m, n, p, q, r, s, t, v, w, x, z,* usually *h* (as in words like *house* and *hose*), sometimes *u* (as in words like *uranium* and *useful*), and usually *y*.
- Vowel sounds include: *a, e, i, o,* sometimes *h* (as in words like *honest* and *honor*), and sometimes *u* (as in words like *umbrella* and *unusual*).

ACTIVITY 2: Mastery Test

For each blank in the following paragraph, fill in the correct article. If no article is needed, write **N.A.** in the blank.

(1) Juan decided to drive to _____ local library to see if it had any good books on his native country of Mexico. (2) On _____ way, he noticed that his car needed _____ gas, so he stopped at _____ gas station to fill his tank. (3) Then,

CONTINUED >

For more practice with nouns and articles, go to **bedfordstmartins.com /touchstones**.

he found _____ open parking space in _____ library parking lot and went in. (4) In _____ travel section, he found _____ book on _____ Mexico, which he checked out at _____ front desk. (5) He also found _____ book about _____ Los Angeles Dodgers, his favorite baseball team. (6) All in all, it was _____ good trip.

Verbs

As you learned in Chapter 23, mastering English verbs doesn't have to be difficult; you just need patience and practice. Also, as noted earlier, it's a good idea to read and listen to as much standard English as possible so that standard verb usage begins to sound more natural to you.

If you haven't already worked through Chapter 23, it's a good idea to do so now. Try to do as many of the activities in the chapter as you can. Also, you may want to review the coverage of helping verbs in Chapter 15 (pages 340–42).

This section expands on the advice contained in earlier chapters, covering issues that are most challenging for English-as-a-second-language (ESL) students.

VERBS WITH GERUNDS AND INFINITIVES

FOUNDATION WORDS
NOUNS
VERBS
DESCRIPTIVE WORDS
ADJECTIVES
ADVERBS
CONNECTING WORDS
PREPOSITIONS
CONJUNCTIONS

Gerunds are verbs that have *-ing* endings and that function as nouns. Look at these examples:

| GERUND | GERUND |
I like jogging.   Lili likes cooking.

Infinitives combine *to* and a base verb (for example, *to jog, to cook*). Look at these examples:

| INFINITIVE | INFINITIVE |
I want to jog today.   Lili likes to cook in her new kitchen.

In standard English, some verbs may be followed by a gerund or an infinitive:

| GERUND | INFINITIVE |
I like jogging.   I like to jog.

Other verbs may be followed by a gerund but not by an infinitive:

| | GERUND |
CORRECT   I enjoy looking at photographs of weddings.

| | INFINITIVE |
INCORRECT   I enjoy to look at photographs of weddings.

Yet other verbs may be followed by an infinitive but not by a gerund:

INFINITIVE

CORRECT   I promise <u>to look</u> for your uncle when I go home.

GERUND

INCORRECT   I promise <u>looking</u> for your uncle when I go home.

VERBS THAT CAN BE FOLLOWED BY A GERUND OR AN INFINITIVE			
begin	hate	remember	try
continue	like	start	
forget	love	stop	
VERBS THAT CAN BE FOLLOWED BY A GERUND BUT NOT BY AN INFINITIVE			
admit	enjoy	practice	suggest
avoid	finish	quit	
deny	imagine	recall	
discuss	miss	risk	
VERBS THAT CAN BE FOLLOWED BY AN INFINITIVE BUT NOT BY A GERUND			
agree	decide	need	promise
ask	expect	offer	refuse
beg	hope	plan	wait
claim	manage	pretend	want

ACTIVITY 3: Mastery Test

MASTERY

For each blank in the following paragraph, fill in the gerund or infinitive form of the verb in parentheses.

(1) One of the hardest things for Chung to bear in the United States is the winter. (2) In his original home, Vietnam, it was always summer, and he recalls _____ (go) to the grocery store in his flip-flops and shorts all year long. (3) He admits _____ (see) large insects, and it was often very humid, but there was never any snow or ice. (4) In New York, where he lives now, the weather is so different, and although he continues _____ (enjoy) summer, it lasts only for several months. (5) When the fall comes, he actually enjoys _____ (feel) the air become dry and crisp, but soon it turns cold. (6) He hates _____ (wear) a hat every time he goes outside. (7) And then, by December, it gets very cold, and he begins _____ (wear) boots and a heavy jacket. (8) Because Chung has no garage, he keeps his car parked in front of his house, and every morning he needs _____ (scrape)

CONTINUED >

For more practice with using verbs correctly, go to **bedfordstmartins.com /touchstones**.

the ice off his windshield. (9) His arms ache from all this scraping, and sometimes he almost doesn't manage _____ (finish). (10) If it has snowed, he must risk _____ (drive) to work because his boss expects him _____ (come). (11) When he is driving, he has to be careful to leave extra space between his car and others, because it takes longer to stop the car. (12) He has to admit that the snow is pretty, but, in general, he misses _____ (walk) outside without putting on outerwear. (13) Chung enjoys _____ (think) about the weather in his home country. (14) Maybe he should move to Florida!

NEGATIVE STATEMENTS AND QUESTIONS

The rules for forming negative statements and questions vary, depending on whether the original (positive) statement has a helping verb:

Maryam loves to sew.

Maryam has purchased a sewing machine.

As you can see, the second example has a helping verb, while the first example does not. Let's look at how to form negative statements first.

Negative Statements

To turn a sentence with a helping verb into a negative statement, put the word *not* right after the helping verb:

Maryam has not purchased a sewing machine.

Now, let's look back at the example without the helping verb:

Maryam loves to sew.

To turn this type of sentence into a negative statement, put the helping verb *do + not* before the base form of the main verb. (The base form of *loves* is *love*.) The helping verb *do* must change to *does* to agree with *Maryam*. (For more on subject-verb agreement, see Chapter 23, pages 516–21.)

Maryam does not love to sew.

If the verb in the original positive statement is a form of *be* (*am, is, are, was,* or *were*), you do not need to add the helping verb *do* before *not* when forming a negative statement.

Positive	→	**Negative**
Marco is hopeful.		Marco is not hopeful.

ACTIVITY 4: Mastery Test

MASTERY

Rewrite the following positive statements as negative statements.

EXAMPLE: You have thanked your mother for the gift.

You have not thanked your mother for the gift.

1. The early frost damaged the strawberries.

_____

2. The new album is as good as the previous one.

_____

3. Tom walked to the corner store to get the newspaper.

_____

4. His sons are working with him this summer.

_____

5. The price of gasoline has risen lately.

_____

Questions

Let's look back at the positive statements presented earlier:

Maryam loves to sew.

> **HELPING VERB**
> **(FOLLOWED BY MAIN VERB)**

Maryam has purchased a sewing machine.

To turn a sentence with a helping verb into a question, put the helping verb before the subject (_Maryam_) and change the period at the end of the sentence to a question mark:

Has Maryam purchased a sewing machine?

Now, let's look back at the example without the helping verb:

Maryam loves to sew.

To change this type of sentence into a question, put the helping verb _do_ before the subject. (Note that _do_ must change to _does_ in order to agree with _Maryam_.) Then, after the subject, provide the base form of the original verb (_loves_ → _love_). Finally, change the period at the end of the sentence to a question mark:

Does Maryam love to sew?

For more practice with forming questions and negative statements, go to **bedfordstmartins.com /touchstones**.

If the verb in the original positive statement is a form of *be* (*am, is, are, was,* or *were*), you do not need to add the helping verb *do* when forming a question. Simply move the verb to precede the subject.

Positive	→	**Question**
Marco is hopeful.		Is Marco hopeful?

ACTIVITY 5: Mastery Test

Rewrite the following positive statements as questions.

EXAMPLE: You have thanked your mother for the gift.
Have you thanked your mother for the gift?

1. The early frost damaged the strawberries.

_____

2. The new album is as good as the previous one.

_____

3. Tom walked to the corner store to get the newspaper.

_____

4. His sons are working with him this summer.

_____

5. The price of gasoline has risen lately.

_____

Prepositions

FOUNDATION WORDS
NOUNS
VERBS
DESCRIPTIVE WORDS
ADJECTIVES
ADVERBS
CONNECTING WORDS
PREPOSITIONS
CONJUNCTIONS

As you learned in Chapter 15, a **preposition** connects a word to more information about the word. Take a look:

The dog hid in the bathroom.

The preposition *in* connects the verb *hid* to more information: Where did the dog hide? In the bathroom. (*In the bathroom* is known as a prepositional phrase.)

MEANINGS OF COMMON PREPOSITIONS

Some of the most common English prepositions are *at, in,* and *on*. These prepositions may show either time or location, and you have to memorize the proper uses.

Whenever you are confused about how to use one of these prepositions, refer to the following chart.

PREPOSITION	USAGE TO SHOW TIME	USAGE TO SHOW LOCATION
at	Indicates a specific time: *The party will begin at 8:30 P.M.*	Indicates a specific place: *My parents are at their house.* *Turn left at the white building.* *Anna sat at her computer.*
in	Indicates a point in the future from now: *In a month, we will get married.* Indicates a period of time: *In 1997, I left my native country.* *In July, we often go to the beach.*	Indicates that someone or something is inside something or is in a geographic location: *Jim stayed in the kitchen.* *The car was in the garage.* *I live in Pittsburgh.*
on	Indicates a specific day or date: *Come back on Monday.*	Indicates that something rests on or hangs from a surface: *The glass rested on the table.* *Please hang the photograph on the wall.*

For a full list of common prepositions, see Chapter 16, page 357.

ACTIVITY 6: Mastery Test

For each of the following sentences, fill in the blank with the correct preposition: *at*, *in*, or *on*.

EXAMPLE: Carol lives _____*in*_____ a small apartment.

1. Pierre worked _____ the restaurant every night.

2. _____ July 15, 2008, we moved into our new house.

3. _____ 8:15 A.M., we will start the sale.

4. The cat waited patiently _____ the door until Jack let her out.

5. The debates will begin _____ three hours.

PREPOSITIONS AFTER ADJECTIVES

As you learned in Chapter 15, **adjectives** are words that describe nouns. Some English adjectives are often followed by specific prepositions. Again, you have to memorize the correct combinations, some of which are shown in the following chart.

ADJECTIVE + PREPOSITION COMBINATION	EXAMPLE
addicted to	Maya is <u>addicted to</u> TV soap operas.
afraid of	I am <u>afraid of</u> dogs.
angry about	Carlotta is <u>angry about</u> the telephone call.
angry with/at	Henry is <u>angry with/angry at</u> his wife.
confused by	The political candidates were <u>confused by</u> the polls.
excited about	The bride and groom were <u>excited about</u> their honeymoon plans.
grateful for	The mayor was <u>grateful for</u> the contribution.
happy about	I am <u>happy about</u> the good news.
interested in	He was <u>interested in</u> computer games.
pleased with	Jacqueline was <u>pleased with</u> the work of the contractor.
proud of	I am <u>proud of</u> your hard work.
responsible for	Parents are <u>responsible for</u> the health of their children.
sorry about	Angelo was <u>sorry about</u> the error.
tired of	Josie was <u>tired of</u> her children's bad behavior.

ACTIVITY 7: Mastery Test

For each of the following sentences, fill in the blank with the correct preposition.

EXAMPLE: She was pleased _____with_____ her accomplishments.

1. Harriet is confused _____ all the sales offers.

2. Kenneth is angry _____ the mistake in his bank statement.

3. I was grateful _____ the gift and proud _____ my parents for thinking of me.

4. Tom was interested _____ the book, but he was tired _____ reading.

5. The guests at the party were excited _____ the star performer.

PREPOSITIONS AFTER VERBS

Some English verbs are followed by specific prepositions. Here's just one example:

> The teacher handed in her grades.

With some verb + preposition combinations, words can come between the verb and the preposition. Take a look:

> The teacher handed her grades in.

When the verb + preposition combination is used with a pronoun (*me, you, her,* and so on), the pronoun must come between the verb and the preposition.

CORRECT	The teacher handed them in.
INCORRECT	The teacher handed in them.

With other combinations, however, the verb and the preposition cannot be separated.

CORRECT	The governor fought for the new tax law.
INCORRECT	The governor fought the new tax law for.

Again, you have to memorize the correct combinations and which ones can and cannot be separated. The following chart shows just some of the possible combinations.

VERB + PREPOSITION COMBINATIONS THAT CAN BE SEPARATED	
Combination	**Example**
bring up (raise an issue)	I wanted to bring up the subject of money. / I wanted to bring it up.
call off (cancel)	We called off the party. / We called it off.
drop off (leave at a location)	She dropped off the children at school. / She dropped them off.
fill in (add a substance until something is full/complete)	Workers filled in the gaps in the bushes with new plantings. / Workers filled them in.
fill out (complete)	Antony filled out all the blanks on the college application. / Antony filled them all out.
hand in (submit)	The students handed in their essays. / The students handed them in.
look up (find or check)	Look up the subject on the Internet. / Look it up.
pick up (collect)	You can pick up the dry cleaning after 4 P.M. / You can pick it up after 4 P.M.
put away (place something somewhere / remove from sight)	Put away the clean dishes in the cabinet. / Put them away.

CONTINUED >

Combination	Example
put off (delay)	Don't <u>put off</u> your appointment to take the car in for servicing. / Don't <u>put</u> it <u>off</u>.
take off (remove)	<u>Take off</u> your coat and stay awhile / <u>Take</u> it <u>off</u>.
throw away / throw out (discard)	Marta <u>threw away</u> her old clothes. / Marta <u>threw</u> them <u>away</u>.
turn down (lower the volume of)	Please <u>turn down</u> the television. / Please <u>turn</u> it <u>down</u>.
turn off (shut off)	I never remember to <u>turn off</u> the sprinkler. / I never remember to <u>turn</u> it <u>off</u>.
wake up (interrupt the sleep of / rise from sleep)	The party next door <u>woke up</u> her husband. / The party <u>woke</u> him <u>up</u>.

VERB + PREPOSITION COMBINATIONS THAT CANNOT BE SEPARATED	
Combination	**Example**
drop in (pay a visit)	<u>Drop in</u> anytime.
fight against (combat)	The North <u>fought against</u> the South in the U.S. Civil War.
fight for (work on behalf of / defend)	I will <u>fight for</u> my candidate in the election.
go over (review)	The teacher will <u>go over</u> today's homework.
grow up (mature)	She <u>grew up</u> in Chicago.
pay off (have good results)	All his hard work this semester <u>paid off</u>.
show up (make an appearance)	My parents <u>showed up</u> early at the wedding.

ACTIVITY 8: Mastery Test

Read each sentence pair below and do the following:

- Determine which sentence has the correct word order and circle it.
- If *both* sentences are in the correct order, write **C** next to them.

EXAMPLE: a. He threw away the trash.

   b. He threw the trash away. c

1. **a.** Clara decided to fight for her job.
   b. Clara decided to fight her job for.

2. **a.** Put away the laundry.
   b. Put the laundry away.

3. **a.** Taquita picked up her children at the mall.
   b. Taquita picked her children up at the mall.

4. a. Our new neighbors dropped in to say hello.

   b. Our new neighbors dropped to say hello in.

5. a. The group called off their concert.

   b. The group called their concert off.

Order of Adjectives

Again, **adjectives** are words that describe nouns. In the following example, the adjective *little* describes the noun *cat*:

the little cat

If you use more than one adjective to describe a noun, the adjectives must come in a certain order, or the sentence will sound funny in standard English. To a native speaker, the first example below would sound odd, while the second one would sound "right":

AWKWARD	the little black cute cat
STANDARD	the cute little black cat

Again, as you listen to and read more standard English, you too will develop a sense of what sounds right. Until then, be aware that when nouns are described by more than one adjective, the words generally come in this order:

1. Article or other word indicating number or ownership: *a, an, the, six, some, Jackie's*
2. Judgment or opinion: *pretty, smart, fragile, fashionable, ugly*
3. Size: *tiny, little, huge, big*
4. Shape or length: *circular, square, short, long, ___-shaped* (as in *egg-shaped*)
5. Age: *youthful, mature, new*
6. Color: *white, black, yellow, red*
7. Nationality/region: *Chinese, American, Italian, northern*
8. Material: *glass, aluminum, plastic*
9. Noun used as adjective: *race* in *race car; computer* in *computer desk*
10. Noun being described: *girl, dress, carrot, automobile*

FOUNDATION WORDS
NOUNS
VERBS
DESCRIPTIVE WORDS
ADJECTIVES
ADVERBS
CONNECTING WORDS
PREPOSITIONS
CONJUNCTIONS

ACTIVITY 9: Mastery Test

MASTERY

In each of the following sentences, the adjectives are scrambled. Rewrite each sentence in the space provided, putting the words in the correct order.

For more practice with using prepositions and adjectives, go to **bedfordstmartins.com /touchstones**.

EXAMPLE: Jane's daughter likes to wear pink long nightgowns.
Jane's daughter likes to wear long pink nightgowns.

1. The black race rare car was very expensive.

2. Richard liked the Italian young excellent singer.

3. A black huge spider frightened Maria, but she pretended that it was just a round small bug.

4. The little Chinese blue valuable bowl fell off the table and broke.

5. The French old popular chef created a new recipe.

Other Guidelines

This section briefly reviews some other points to be aware of if you are an ESL student or if you generally want to build your skills in standard English. Because most of these issues have been covered in more depth in earlier chapters, we provide references to those chapters.

Power Tip
A prepositional phrase cannot be the subject of a sentence.

Incorrect: _In the trees_ have many leaves.

Revised: _The trees_ have many leaves.

- Remember to include subjects in all sentences:

INCORRECT	Loves to cook.
REVISED	Jeff loves to cook.

  For more details on including subjects in sentences, see Chapter 16.

- Many English sentences begin with _There is/There are_ or _It is_. Do not leave out _There_ or _It_ in these sentences:

INCORRECT	Are many advantages to learning early. Is snowing today.
REVISED	There are many advantages to learning early. It is snowing today.

- Remember to use verbs in all sentences:

INCORRECT	I happy to introduce you to my boss.
REVISED	I am happy to introduce you to my boss.

For more details on including verbs in sentences, see Chapter 16.

- Do not use pronouns to repeat subjects within a simple sentence.

As you learned in Chapter 15, **pronouns** are noun substitutes. In the following compound sentence (joining two simple sentences), the pronoun *he* substitutes for *Ivan* so that you don't have to repeat Ivan's name.

SENTENCE 1   SENTENCE 2

Ivan likes to hunt, and he hunts every year.

NOUN   PRONOUN

Within a simple sentence, however, do not use pronouns to repeat subjects:

INCORRECT   Ivan, he hunts every year.

REVISED   Ivan hunts every year.

For more on simple sentences, see Chapter 16. For more on compound sentences, see Chapter 17.

ACTIVITY 10: Mastery Test

Correct the grammatical error in each of the following sentences. The first sentence has been corrected for you.

(1) ~~Opened~~ *Emily opened* a savings account at her local bank. (2) Wants to save some money each month from her paycheck. (3) Emily responsible with her finances. (4) Thinks a savings account would improve her financial security. (5) Are three benefits to having a savings account.

(6) The account, it would contain money for emergencies. (7) Also, would be a back-up resource if her checking account was overdrawn.

(8) Lastly, the account, it would earn interest for Emily.

More on Adjectives and Adverbs

As you saw in Chapter 15, adjectives and adverbs are descriptive words. They help you make your sentences more concrete, vivid, and interesting. In addition to their basic—or base—form, adjectives and adverbs have comparative and superlative forms that help them do their job of description even more effectively.

KEY TO BUILDING BLOCKS

FOUNDATION WORDS
NOUNS
VERBS

DESCRIPTIVE WORDS
ADJECTIVES
ADVERBS

CONNECTING WORDS
PREPOSITIONS
CONJUNCTIONS

Using Comparative and Superlative Adjectives

As you know, an **adjective** describes a person, place, or thing (a noun). It names a quality of the person, place, or thing. For example:

Jim is tall.

A **comparative adjective** lets us describe people, places, or things in comparison to one or more other people, places, or things. We can say that people, places, or things have *more* of the quality than others:

Jim is taller than the team captain.

A **superlative adjective** lets us describe people, places, or things in comparison to two or more other people, places, or things. We can say that people, places, or things have the *most* of a quality of any member of the group we are talking about; they rank first in this quality:

Jim is the tallest player on his team.

Here is a chart that shows the three forms for two different adjectives. Notice that there are two ways to do the comparative form and two ways to do the superlative form.

Power Tip
Comparatives often occur in sentences with *than* (*Jim is taller **than** the team captain*). Superlatives often occur in sentences with a phrase that mentions a group (*Jim is the tallest player on **his team***).

BASE FORM	COMPARATIVE FORM	SUPERLATIVE FORM
tall	taller	tallest
interesting	more interesting	most interesting

ACTIVITY 1: Mastery Test

MASTERY

In each of the following sentences, circle the adjective. Then, identify the adjective form (**base**, **comparative**, or **superlative**) in the space provided.

EXAMPLE: My grandmother is (wiser) than my aunt.

Adjective form: _comparative_

1. I would like to buy a used car.

Adjective form: _____

2. Luke is the youngest teacher at his school.

Adjective form: _____

3. Your boss is nicer than my boss.

Adjective form: _____

4. The smartest students in the classroom are not always the teacher's favorites.

Adjective form: _____

5. Your shoes look more comfortable than mine.

Adjective form: _____

To figure out the correct way to make a particular comparative adjective (with *-er* or with *more*) or superlative adjective (with *-est* or with *most*), first count the number of syllables in the base form of the adjective. For example:

One-syllable adjectives: *nice, tall, smart*

Two-syllable adjectives: *healthy, clever, famous*

Adjectives with three or more syllables: *generous, energetic, intelligent*

Then, follow these rules:

1. For most one-syllable adjectives, add *-er* to the base form for comparatives or *-est* for superlatives. For example:

BASE FORM	COMPARATIVE FORM	SUPERLATIVE FORM
big	big**ger**	big**gest**
blue	blu**er**	blu**est**
dark	dark**er**	dark**est**
smart	smart**er**	smart**est**

Power Tip

If the base form of the adjective ends in *-e*, add only *-r* for the comparative form and only *-st* for the superlative form (for example, *nice* → *nicer, nicest*). If the base form ends with a vowel followed by a consonant, double the consonant before adding *-er* (for example, *hot* → *hotter, hottest*).

Power Tip
For some two-syllable adjectives, you can make comparatives and superlatives both ways (for example, *friendly* → *more friendly* or *friendlier, most friendly* or *friendliest*; *gentle* → *more gentle* or *gentler, most gentle* or *gentlest*; *handsome* → *more handsome* or *hand-somer, most handsome* or *handsomest*). When you are unsure about a two-syllable adjective that does not end in *-y*, use *more* and *most* before the base form of the adjective since that will always be correct.

2. For two-syllable adjectives that end in -*y*, after changing the *y* to an *i*, add -*er* or -*est* to the base form.   For example:

BASE FORM	COMPARATIVE FORM	SUPERLATIVE FORM
healthy	health<u>ier</u>	health<u>iest</u>
tasty	tast<u>ier</u>	tast<u>iest</u>

3. For most other two-syllable adjectives, use *more* before the base form for comparatives or use *most* before the base form for superlatives.   For example:

BASE FORM	COMPARATIVE FORM	SUPERLATIVE FORM
bitter	<u>more</u> bitter	<u>most</u> bitter
famous	<u>more</u> famous	<u>most</u> famous
open	<u>more</u> open	<u>most</u> open

4. For adjectives of three syllables or more, use *more* before the base form for comparatives or use *most* before the base form for superlatives.   Here are some examples:

BASE FORM	COMPARATIVE FORM	SUPERLATIVE FORM
arrogant	<u>more</u> arrogant	<u>most</u> arrogant
energetic	<u>more</u> energetic	<u>most</u> energetic
generous	<u>more</u> generous	<u>most</u> generous
intelligent	<u>more</u> intelligent	<u>most</u> intelligent

ACTIVITY 2: Mastery Test

Write the correctly formed adjective in each space. Then, identify the form (*comparative* or *superlative*) in the space provided.

EXAMPLE: This activity is _____tougher_____ (tough) than the last one.
   Adjective form: _____comparative_____

1. The home team was _____ (strong) than the guest team.
   Adjective form: _____

2. My chemistry homework is the _____ (hard) of all.
   Adjective form: _____

3. My coach gets _____ (angry) than the other coaches.
   Adjective form: _____

4. Of all the students, Pedro was the _____ (upset) about that last test and his grade on it.

   Adjective form: _____

5. The new players are _____ (enthusiastic) than the veteran players.

   Adjective form: _____

6. Japanese cuisine is among the _____ (healthy) in the world.

   Adjective form: _____

7. Skydiving is _____ (dangerous) than surfing.

   Adjective form: _____

8. At family dinners, my brother always has the _____ (big) portions.

   Adjective form: _____

9. The Kia may be the _____ (underrated) car on the market.

   Adjective form: _____

10. Alicia is a _____ (graceful) dancer than her sister.

    Adjective form: _____

Some adjectives have irregular comparative and superlative forms, so you'll need to memorize them. Take a look:

BASE FORM	COMPARATIVE FORM	SUPERLATIVE FORM
bad	worse	worst
far	farther/further	farthest/furthest
good	better	best
little	less	least
many	more	most
much	more	most

ACTIVITY 3: Mastery Test

MASTERY

Write the correctly formed adjective in each space. Then, identify the form (*comparative* or *superlative*) in the space provided.

EXAMPLE: Rubies cost _____less_____ (little) money than diamonds.

   Adjective form: _____comparative_____

1. Yogurt is _____ (good) for my digestion than ice cream.

   Adjective form: _____

CONTINUED >

2. That soap opera actor was the _____ (bad) dancer on *Dancing with the Stars*.

   Adjective form: _____

3. Uncle Jamison takes the _____ (many) vacations of anyone I know.

   Adjective form: _____

4. That's really the _____ (good) gym in the neighborhood.

   Adjective form: _____

5. We didn't have any _____ (much) luck than you had in getting through to him.

   Adjective form: _____

Using Comparative and Superlative Adverbs

FOUNDATION WORDS
NOUNS
VERBS
DESCRIPTIVE WORDS
ADJECTIVES
ADVERBS
CONNECTING WORDS
PREPOSITIONS
CONJUNCTIONS

Power Tip
Most adjectives that end in -*ic* (such as *artistic* and *fantastic*) require a special ending of -*ally* (*artistically, fantastically*) to form an adverb.

As you know, an **adverb** describes an action (a verb). It can tell us the way an action is performed. For example:

Lucy speaks French fluently.

For many adverbs, the base form comes from adding -*ly* to an adjective. Look at these sentences:

 NOUN   ADJECTIVE
Lucy's French is fluent.

VERB   ADVERB
Lucy speaks **French** fluently.

In the first sentence, *fluent* is an adjective that describes the noun *French*. In the second sentence, *fluently* is an adverb that describes the verb *speaks*.

A **comparative adverb** lets us describe actions in comparison to one or more other actions. We can say that actions are performed in a certain *way* to a greater *degree* than other actions are. For example:

Lucy speaks French more fluently than Michelle speaks French.

A **superlative adverb** lets us describe actions in comparison to two or more other actions. We can say that an action is performed in a certain *way* to a greater *degree* than the other actions. The action ranks first in this way.

Michelle speaks French pretty fluently, and Gil does too, but Lucy speaks French the most fluently of all.

Here is a chart that shows the three forms for two different adverbs. As with adjectives, there are two ways to do the comparative and superlative forms.

BASE FORM	COMPARATIVE FORM	SUPERLATIVE FORM
fast	fast<u>er</u>	fast<u>est</u>
quickly	<u>more</u> quickly	<u>most</u> quickly

The rules for comparative and superlative forms of adverbs are similar to those for comparative and superlative adjectives:

1. For most one-syllable adverbs, add *-er* to the base form for comparatives and *-est* for superlatives:

BASE FORM	COMPARATIVE FORM	SUPERLATIVE FORM
hard	hard<u>er</u>	hard<u>est</u>
high	high<u>er</u>	high<u>est</u>
late	lat<u>er</u>	lat<u>est</u>

2. For *-ly* adverbs, which have two or more syllables, use *more* before the base form for comparatives or *most* for superlatives:

BASE FORM	COMPARATIVE FORM	SUPERLATIVE FORM
professionally	<u>more</u> professionally	<u>most</u> professionally
quickly	<u>more</u> quickly	<u>most</u> quickly
slowly	<u>more</u> slowly	<u>most</u> slowly
suddenly	<u>more</u> suddenly	<u>most</u> suddenly

ACTIVITY 4: Mastery Test

MASTERY

Write the correctly formed adverb in each space. Then, identify the form (*base*, *comparative*, or *superlative*) in the space provided.

EXAMPLE: Emma sews <u>*more professionally*</u> (professional) than Esmeralda.

       Adverb form: <u>*comparative*</u>

1. Alex studies _____ (constantly) between his classes.

    Adverb form: _____

2. My history instructor lectures _____ (passionately) than my psychology instructor.

    Adverb form: _____

3. My parents came _____ (soon) than expected.

    Adverb form: _____

CONTINUED >

4. The student in the front row responds the _____ (intelligently) of all the students in the class.

   Adverb form: _____

5. Of all the finalists in the tournament, Serena played the _____ (aggressively).

   Adverb form: _____

6. At the restaurant where I work, the chef eats the _____ (late) of anyone.

   Adverb form: _____

7. I can understand his Spanish because he speaks _____ (slowly) than you do.

   Adverb form: _____

8. On the girls' track team, Denise jumps the _____ (high) of all the pole-vaulters.

   Adverb form: _____

9. The halfback runs _____ (fast) than the quarterback.

   Adverb form: _____

10. Ted lives _____ (near) to me than I realized.

    Adverb form: _____

Some adverbs have irregular comparative and superlative forms, so you'll need to memorize them. Take a look:

BASE FORM	COMPARATIVE FORM	SUPERLATIVE FORM
badly	worse	worst
far	farther/further	farthest/furthest
little	less	least
much	more	most
well	better	best

ACTIVITY 5: Mastery Test

Write the correctly formed adverb in each space. Then, identify the form (*comparative* or *superlative*) in the space provided.

EXAMPLE: My mom jogs _____farther_____ (far) than my father.

   Adverb form: _____comparative_____

1. Derek looks _____ (well) in black than in yellow.

   Adverb form: _____

2. The old fish in my refrigerator smells the _____ (badly) of all the leftovers.

   Adverb form: _____

3. My college-age daughter reads _____ (little) than my nine-year-old.

   Adverb form: _____

4. We all worried about how he was doing, but I probably worried the _____ (much) of anyone.

   Adverb form: _____

5. The teenager in a red wheelchair went the _____ (far) of all the disabled athletes.

   Adverb form: _____

APPENDIX C

Punctuation and Capitalization

Using Correct
Punctuation 650
Using Correct
Capitalization 660

Using Correct Punctuation

Punctuation marks are like little traffic signals for your readers, telling them to pause, stop, notice where your own words stop and another's start, and so on. The following sections briefly review some punctuation uses covered in earlier chapters and introduce a few new ones.

COMMAS (,)

Let's begin by reviewing some of the comma uses that may be most familiar to you.

Commas after Introductory Words

Usually, commas come after beginning words that set up, describe, or otherwise introduce the main ideas in a sentence. Here are five types of expressions that are typically followed by commas.

1. Transitional expressions.   Look at these examples:

> <u>First of all</u>, parents need to support their children.
> <u>More important</u>, an athlete has to be in excellent physical condition.
> <u>Finally</u>, owning a pet requires being able to give love and attention.
> <u>However</u>, she carried an umbrella just in case it rained.

Sometimes, a transitional expression will appear after a semicolon (;). It should be followed by a comma in this case, too:

> My parents tried to give my sister and me toys and games; <u>nevertheless</u>, they were limited by their small income.

For more information on transitional expressions, see Chapter 7, page 153, and Chapter 17, pages 399–406.

650

2. Simple adverbs.   Look at these examples:

> <u>Happily</u>, we found everything we needed at a single store.
> <u>Nightly</u>, I dreamed that I was taking a trip.
> <u>Proudly</u>, the winners paraded around the room.

For more information on adverbs, see Chapter 15, pages 342–44.

3. Prepositional phrases.   Look at these examples:

> <u>After the prom</u>, there was a party hosted by the parents.
> <u>Behind the house</u>, the children played hide-and-seek.
> <u>In three years</u>, I expect to be out of debt.

For more information on prepositional phrases, see Chapter 15, pages 344–45.

4. Word groups beginning with subordinating conjunctions.   Look at these examples:

> <u>Since she missed the deadline</u>, she could not apply for the job.
> <u>If the car needs new tires</u>, you should buy them.
> <u>When George entered the room</u>, everyone cheered.

For more information on subordination, see Chapter 18.

5. Modifying phrases.   Look at these examples:

> <u>Fishing in the canal</u>, Harriet caught a large turtle.
> <u>Covered with the blanket</u>, I was warm and cozy.
> <u>To get our attention</u>, she screamed and waved.

For more information on modifying phrases, see Chapter 20.

Commas in Compound Sentences

As you learned in Chapter 17, a **compound sentence** is two or more related simple sentences joined together. When simple sentences are joined with a coordinating conjunction (such as *and, but, or,* or *so*), a comma must precede this conjunction. Take a look:

> SIMPLE SENTENCE 1   SIMPLE SENTENCE 2
> We lived in an apartment   , and   they lived in a house.
>   COMMA AND CONJUNCTION

However, remember that no comma is used when forming a compound subject or a compound verb:

> COMPOUND SUBJECT,   COMPOUND VERB,
> NO COMMA   NO COMMA
> Harold and Margaret washed their car and waxed it.

For more information, see Chapter 17.

KEY TO
BUILDING BLOCKS

FOUNDATION WORDS
NOUNS
VERBS

DESCRIPTIVE WORDS
ADJECTIVES
ADVERBS

CONNECTING WORDS
PREPOSITIONS
CONJUNCTIONS

Commas Setting Off Descriptive/Modifying Word Groups

You already know that when a modifying phrase begins a sentence, it must be followed by a comma. Let's review some other rules for descriptive word groups.

Remember from Chapter 19 that if you add a descriptive clause that is *not essential* to the meaning of a sentence, you usually must set it off with commas. If the clause is in the middle of a sentence, commas come before and after the clause:

World of Warcraft, which I play on my computer, is a really fun game.

If the clause is at the end of a sentence, use one comma, immediately before the clause:

I enjoy World of Warcraft, which I play on my computer.

Do not use commas to set off *essential* information:

ESSENTIAL INFORMATION

The World of Warcraft game that I play on my computer has been around for years.

Also, note these rules for modifying phrases that begin with *-ing*, *to*, or *-ed*:

- When the phrase is in the middle of a sentence, commas are used before and after it.
- When the modifying phrase comes at the end, commas generally are not used.

A modifying phrase in the middle:

Joanne, walking in the park, went slowly.

The police officer, puzzled by the driver's erratic behavior, decided to stop the car.

A modifying phrase at the end:

Joanne went slowly walking in the park.

He went to the convenience store on Sunday to buy some tissues.

For additional information on punctuating modifying phrases, see Chapter 20.

Other Uses of Commas

Here, we will introduce four additional uses of commas.

1. To separate items in a series.   When you list three or more items, separate them with commas. Take a look:

A cook can choose rye, wheat, or whole-grain flour.

Bertha purchased eggs, milk, bread, and cheese at the supermarket.

Note that for clarity, most instructors and other writing experts recommend putting a comma before the conjunctions *and* and *or* in these series.

2. To set off information that renames another item.   Sometimes, we follow a noun with a word group that renames that noun. Take a look at the underlined word group in this sentence:

> Dontelle Jackson, <u>my best employee</u>, had to go to court.

My best employee renames *Dontelle Jackson.* Here's another example:

> That's Judge Enright, <u>the one who gave me three months of probation</u>.

The underlined word group renames *Judge Enright.*

Terminology Tip
Words that rename a noun are known as *appositives*.

3. To separate parts of an address.   Look at this example:

> Fred lives at 53 Brant Court, Latham, CT 03146.

Notice that no comma appears before the zip code.

When the name of a city and state appear in the middle of a sentence, a comma should follow the state name:

> Michael went to live in Miami, Florida, to escape the hard winter.

4. To separate parts of dates.   When a date includes the month, day, and year, a comma must come between the day and the year:

> The Declaration of Independence was signed on July 4, 1776.

If a date with the month, day, and year appears in the middle of a sentence, a comma should also follow the year:

> The Declaration of Independence was signed on July 4, 1776, in Philadelphia.

When only a month and year are specified, no comma is needed between them:

> World War II ended in August 1945.

ACTIVITY 1: Mastery Test

Edit each of the following paragraphs, adding necessary commas and deleting unnecessary ones. There are 33 missing commas and 4 unnecessary commas.

(1) After 40 years of living in the same house in Pennsylvania Alice and Richard decided to move south. (2) They had a daughter Joy in Georgia

CONTINUED >

and wanted to be near her. (3) Also they wanted to move to a place where it was warmer in the winter and they wanted to be closer to their grandchildren. (4) Long before they were ready to move they started cleaning out their old house. (5) It was amazing to see how much junk they had collected, after living for so long in the same place. (6) Every day, Alice and Richard brought old tools old clothes and old pots and pans to a local charity, where they were sorted and discarded given away or sold to other people.

(7) Then it was time to put the house up for sale. (8) Alice and Richard interviewed several real estate agents and picked someone who lived up the street thinking that he knew the neighborhood. (9) He helped them decide on the asking price of the house, and held an open house for other real estate agents. (10) Alice and Richard really wanted to sell the house soon; therefore they priced it low enough to attract potential buyers. (11) Selling the house turned out, to be easier than they had expected. (12) They had three offers and one was for slightly more than the asking price.

(13) At this point Alice and Richard had to pick a moving company. (14) Their daughter who had moved several times told them about how much it would cost and they interviewed three movers. (15) They picked one settled on a date and got ready to move. (16) One thing that worried them was their beloved dog Lucky a tiny Yorkie. (17) They decided to bring him to Georgia on one plane trip leave him with their daughter and fly home. (18) Then they would drive their car down separately. (19) It all worked out better than they expected. (20) Because Lucky was so small they were able to hide him in Alice's big purse while they were on the plane and he was very good, while he stayed at Joy's house. (21) The car trip was not so bad either but Alice and Richard were very glad to arrive safely in Georgia. (22) The movers

For more practice with commas, go to **bedfordstmartins.com /touchstones**.

arrived on August 4 2012 when they said they would and unloaded everything, as they had been instructed in Joy's garage. (23) All Alice and Richard needed to do now was to find a place to live in Georgia.

COLONS (:)

Sometimes, we follow a complete sentence with examples or explanations related to the complete sentence. In such cases, a colon may be used before the examples or explanations. Take a look:

`COMPLETE SENTENCE` `COLON` `EXAMPLES`

Ruth likes three kinds of books: mysteries, political novels, and biographies.

`COMPLETE SENTENCE` `COLON`

There was one problem with Dwayne's plan to get a watchdog: He was afraid of dogs.
`EXPLANATION`

Notice that in the second example, the word group after the colon begins with a capital *H* because it is a complete sentence.

Colons are also used in the following situations:

- Between the main titles and subtitles of books, reports, and other publications. Look at these examples:

  I read a very good book on child-rearing called *Brain Rules for Baby: How to Raise a Smart and Happy Child from Zero to Age Five.*

- After greetings or *to/from* directives in letters or memos. Take a look:

  Dear Mr. Stock:
  To: The Admissions staff
  From: Eileen Roberts

📶 **ACTIVITY 2: Mastery Test**
MASTERY

Write five sentences that include colons.

SEMICOLONS (;)

As you learned in Chapter 17, a semicolon can be used instead of a conjunction to connect two closely related simple sentences. Here are two simple sentences joined with a comma and a coordinating conjunction:

| SENTENCE 1 | COMMA AND COORDINATING CONJUNCTION | SENTENCE 2 |

The current was strong , so he could not swim to shore.

Here are the same sentences joined with a semicolon:

| SENTENCE 1 | SENTENCE 2 |

The current was strong; he could not swim to shore.

In this use, a semicolon must *follow* a complete sentence and must *be followed* by another complete sentence.

For more on joining sentences with a semicolon, see Chapter 17.

Now, we'll introduce a new use of the semicolon: *to separate items in a series that already contains commas.*

As you learned on pages 652–53, in lists of three or more items, the items are separated with commas. Now, look at these examples:

> Last year, I traveled to Chicago, Illinois; Philadelphia, Pennsylvania; and Atlanta, Georgia.

> When Don went for his interview, he met with William Barnett, the director of the Humanities Division; Barbara Migar, the provost; and Sandra Chu, the vice president of admissions.

Without the semicolons, the groupings of items might not be immediately clear to readers. The semicolons clarify the groupings.

ACTIVITY 3: Mastery Test

MASTERY

Add missing semicolons to each of the following sentences, replacing commas if necessary. (You should use semicolons instead of periods to separate sentences.)

EXAMPLE: My brother was born in Ohio; my sister was born in Indiana.

1. I have all the questions you have all the answers.

2. He is from Wilmington, Delaware, his wife is from Chengdu, China, and their children were born in Baltimore, Maryland.

3. Driving from Nevada to Connecticut took four days the return took only three.

For more practice with colons and semicolons, go to **bedfordstmartins.com /touchstones**.

4. On Wednesday, there was a hailstorm in Montgomery, Alabama, a

   snowstorm in Richmond, Virginia, a tornado in Springfield, Illinois, and

   a hurricane in central Florida.

5. There was a great deal of media attention on the candidate reporters

   followed her wherever she went.

APOSTROPHES (')

Here, we will introduce three common uses of apostrophes.

1. To show ownership.   When you want to show that a singular noun (*boy*, *professor*, *Cass*) owns something, add -*'s*:

> The boy's car needed a new muffler.
> The professor's lecture was exciting.
> Cass's cat sleeps all day and eats only at night.

When you want to show that a plural noun ending in -*s* (*boys*, *professors*) owns something, add only an apostrophe:

> The boys' cars were parked at the school.
> The professors' lectures took place in the auditorium.

If a plural noun does not end in -*s* (*men*, *women*, *children*), you need to add -*'s* to form the possessive:

> The men's exercise class was closed to visitors.
> The children's pediatrician did not have office hours on Sunday.

When time expressions show ownership, apostrophes should also be used:

> This year's annual dinner was better than last year's.
> Martin gave four weeks' notice to his landlord that he was moving out.

2. To shorten words.   Sometimes, especially in speech, we shorten words by omitting letters. When writing these shortened forms, known as *contractions*, we use an apostrophe to show where letters have been left out:

LONG FORM	CONTRACTION
are not	aren't
cannot	can't
did not	didn't
do not	don't

Power Tip
You do not need to add an apostrophe to show possession when you use a possessive pronoun.

Incorrect: *This cabin is your's; our's is across the lake.*

Revised: *This cabin is yours; ours is across the lake.*

For more on possessive pronouns, see Chapter 24, pages 541–42.

I am	I'm
I will	I'll
is not	isn't
it is, it has	it's
was not	wasn't

Be careful not to misplace apostrophes when you are writing contractions:

> **INCORRECT** are'nt; is'nt   **REVISED** aren't; isn't

Some instructors prefer that students avoid contractions in papers. If you are unsure of your instructors' preferences, be sure to ask.

3. To make numbers and letters plural.   Occasionally, you will write plural forms of numbers and letters. Use apostrophes in these cases:

> Bill writes his 2's like 7's.   I got three A's and two B's last semester.

ACTIVITY 4: Mastery Test

Edit the following paragraph, adding apostrophes where necessary and fixing any incorrectly placed apostrophes. There are seven missing apostrophes and three incorrectly placed apostrophes.

(1) Raina, the manager of the fast-food restaurant, was surprised and disappointed that it got Ds on its inspections. (2) She instituted several changes. (3) First, she made sure that employees followed the rules for the different foods temperatures. (4) To encourage this, Raina provided a food thermometer so that workers could measure a hamburgers temperature before serving it. (5) Rainas signs in the mens' and womens' bathrooms that warned them about washing their hands were made larger. (6) Then, Raina called exterminators to spray the restaurant for roaches and other insects. (7) Customers had'nt complained about the tastiness of the food, so she knew her main problem was food safety. (8) On the restaurants next inspection, Raina was glad to see that it got As and Bs.

QUOTATION MARKS (" ")

When we use someone's exact words in writing, these *direct quotations* need to be enclosed in quotation marks. Take a look:

> **The comedian Steven Wright once asked, "If a word in the dictionary were misspelled, how would we know?"**
>
> **As the suspect fled, the officer yelled, "Halt! Police!"**

If we report what someone said without using his or her exact words, quotation marks are not necessary. Such reported speech is known as an *indirect quotation.*

> **The officer told the fleeing suspect to stop.**

Following are some basic guidelines for using direct quotations:

- Put the quotation marks at the beginning and end of the quotation.
- If the quotation is a complete sentence, capitalize the first word of it. For example: *Peter's father said, "Make sure you take a jacket to school."*
- If the quotation is not a complete sentence, you do not need to capitalize it. For example: *According to the MSNBC commentator, the political process "often results in gridlock."*
- Use a comma to separate the quotation from the identification of the speaker. For example: *Sarah said, "Come in." OR "Come in," Sarah said.* Notice that in both examples the closing quotation mark is *after the period or comma.*
- If a question mark is part of a quoted speaker's words, put it inside the quotation marks. For example: *Martin asked, "Why should we care about the price of gas?"*
- If a question is being posed by you, the writer, not by the quoted speaker, put the question mark outside of the quotation marks. For example: *What did Caroline mean when she referred to the "technological imperative"?*

Power Tip
When quoted material appears within other quoted material, put single quotation marks (' ') around the innermost quotation—for example: *Our supervisor's e-mail warned, "Do not, under any circumstances, open e-mail attachments from people you do not know, especially if the file name ends in 'exe.' "*

ACTIVITY 5: Mastery Test

Edit the following paragraph, adding quotation marks where necessary and fixing any incorrectly used quotation marks. You may need to fix other punctuation and some capitalization as well.

You should add eight pairs of missing quotation marks, remove two pairs of unnecessary quotation marks (for indirect quotations), fix six other punctuation errors, and correct one capitalization error.

(1) Stop! You almost hit that mailbox Stan warned. (2) Ronnie was

learning to drive, and Stan, his father, was teaching him, though Stan

For more practice with apostrophes and quotation marks, go to **bedfordstmartins.com /touchstones**.

was starting to think that "it was not such a good idea." (3) When should I put on my turn signal? Ronnie asked? (4) "Now. Stan replied.

(5) Didn't you say something about a blind spot Ronnie asked. (6) I'll show you, Stan said. (7) He told Ronnie "to pull into that empty parking lot and stop the car." (8) Like this asked Ronnie. (9) Yes, Stan said.

(10) Stan got out of the car, and he walked on the driver's side until his image disappeared from the side mirror. (11) See Stan asked.

(12) Ronnie said, now, I understand.

Using Correct Capitalization

Capital letters are large letters, like the *C* at the beginning of this sentence. Aside from capitalizing the first word of every sentence, you should also capitalize

- proper nouns
- major words in titles

As you learned in Chapter 15, proper nouns name *specific* people, places, and things. Let's take a closer look at different types of proper nouns.

Power Tip
Father, *mother*, and other family titles are capitalized when they are used in place of the person's specific name: *Yes, Father is retired.* Otherwise, such titles should not be capitalized: *My father is retired.*

- **People.** Capitalize the names of specific people, including titles preceding those names.

Uncle Charles	Ms. Burke
Mother	Professor Mancuso
Pablo Montoya	President Lincoln

  Do not capitalize titles like *president*, *vice president*, or *aunt* if they are used without a name.

- **Places/geographic features.** Capitalize the names of specific locations, monuments, and geographic features.

the White House	the Vietnam Veterans Memorial
Chattanooga, Tennessee	the Mississippi River
Main Street	Mount Rushmore
Paris	the East / the South
Yosemite National Park	the Atlantic Ocean

Do not capitalize locations like *street*, *park*, or *river* if you are not naming a specific street, park, river, or other location:

Our street is next to a park.
↑   ↑

Capitalize *north*, *south*, *east*, and *west* when they name specific regions, but do not capitalize them in directions:

The South had an agricultural economy at the time of the Civil War.
   ↑

Drive west for three miles, and then go south on I-71.
  ↑   ↑

- **Racial and ethnic groups, nationalities, and languages**

Native American	Italian
Nigerian	Brazilian
Japanese	Polish
Hispanic	Chinese

- **Organizations, teams, and other specific groups or establishments.** Capitalize the names of specific groups.

Salvation Army	Latham University
Girl Scouts	Ironworkers Union
Phillies	General Motors

Do not capitalize groups or establishments if you are not naming them specifically:

Ken dropped out of his rock band and went to college.
                    ↑   ↑

- **Religions**

Presbyterian	Buddhist	Greek Catholic
Muslim	Jewish	Baptist

- **Months, days, and holidays**

July	Tuesday	Christmas
December	Sunday	Halloween

Note that *winter*, *spring*, *summer*, and *fall* are not capitalized.

- **Brand names.** Capitalize the names of specific brands.

Procter & Gamble	Apple
Dockers	Harley-Davidson

Do not capitalize products when you are not naming a specific brand:

Juan put on his jacket and sneakers and left for town.
              ↑   ↑

- **Academic courses.** Capitalize the names of specific academic courses.

English 101
French 1
Math for Non-Majors 103
Physics 204

Unless you are naming a specific course, do not capitalize a course name unless it is a specific language, nationality, or other term that you would normally capitalize:

Last semester, I took three difficult courses: economics, geology, and English.

Power Tip
Notice that the titles of books, newspapers, movies, and television shows are italicized (or underlined). Titles of articles, essays, and short stories appear in quotation marks.

<u>In addition to capitalizing proper nouns, you should capitalize major words in the titles of publications, films, television shows, songs, and other media.</u> You should not capitalize articles (*a*, *an*, and *the*), prepositions (like *at*, *in*, *on*, *to*, and *with*), or conjunctions (*and*, *but*, *or*, and so on) unless they begin or end the title.

Ernest Hemingway's book *The Old Man and the Sea* was available at the library.

In 2006, Rachel Weisz won an Academy Award for her role in the film *The Constant Gardener.*

I watched a rerun of *Little House on the Prairie* on my new television.

The *Parkland News* wrote an editorial entitled "The Doomsday Virus."

▥ ACTIVITY 6: Mastery Test

MASTERY

Correct the capitalization errors in each of the following sentences.

EXAMPLE: In ĵune, I will graduate from ȼoral ȟigh ŝchool.

1. Jack and Molly camped at the new hampshire travel park near mount jefferson.

2. In december, the fall semester will end at hamlin college.

3. On halloween, Frank managed to read the first chapter of *a farewell to arms* even though children in costume kept knocking on our door.

For more practice with capitalization, go to **bedfordstmartins.com /touchstones**.

4. Every Spring, my favorite Aunt comes to visit us, staying near the hudson river and visiting the new york aquarium on the way.

5. If you go North on main street for five miles and then turn right at the big yellow house and keep going straight for two hundred yards, you will come to the carter county library.

Acknowledgments

Sherman Alexie. "Blankets." From *War Dances*, pp. 31–40. Copyright © 2010 by Grove Press. Reprinted by permission of Grove/Atlantic, Inc.

Maria Andreu. "This (Illegal) American Life." *Newsweek*, October 13, 2008. Copyright © 2008. Used by permission. All rights reserved.

Karen Armstrong. Excerpt from *Buddha*. Copyright © 2001 by Karen Armstrong. Used by permission of Viking Penguin, a division of Penguin Group (USA) Inc.

Eve Birch. "The Art of Being a Neighbor." From *This I Believe: Life Lessons*, by Dan Gediman et al. Copyright © 2011 by John Wiley & Sons. Reprinted by permission of the publisher.

Charles M. Blow. "Farewell, Fair Weather." *New York Times*, May 31, 2008. Copyright © The New York Times, Inc. All rights reserved. Used by permission and protected by the Copyright Laws of the United States. The printing, copying, redistribution, or retransmission of this Content without express written permission is prohibited. www.nytimes.com.

Edwidge Danticat. "Uncle Moïse." From *The Best Creative Nonfiction*, Volume 3, edited by Lee Gutkind. Copyright © 2009 by Edwidge Danticat. First published in PMS *poemmemoirstory* and reprinted by permission of Edwidge Danticat and Aragi Inc.

Michaela Angela Davis. "Quitting Hip-Hop." First published in *Essence* magazine, October 2004. Copyright © Michaela Angela Davis. Used by permission of the author.

Mona Eltahawy. "Twitterholics Anonymous." From monaeltahawy.com/blog, January 12, 2011. Copyright © 2011 by Mona Eltahawy. Reprinted by permission of Mona Eltahawy.

Mark A. Gluck, Eduardo Mercado, and Catherine E. Myers. "Emotion and Retrieval of Memories." Excerpt, p. 390, from *Learning and Memory: From Brain to Behavior*. Copyright © 2008 Worth Publishers. Used by permission of the publisher.

Michael Hall. "Running for His Life." *Texas Monthly*, August 2003. Copyright © 2003 by Texas Monthly. Reprinted by permission of Emmis Publishing LLP.

Will Kane. "Cyclist Hurt in San Francisco Crash with Mail Truck." *San Francisco Chronicle*, February 2, 2012. Reprinted by permission.

Daphne Koller. "Death Knell for the Lecture: Technology as a Passport to Personalized Education." *New York Times*, December 5, 2011. Reprinted by permission. All rights reserved.

Robert Lake. "An Indian Father's Plea." From *Teacher Magazine*, 2.1 (1990), pp. 48–53. Copyright © 1990 by Robert Lake. Reprinted by permission of Robert Lake.

Michael Lewis. Excerpt from "Wading toward Home." *New York Times*, October 9, 2005. Reprinted by permission. All rights reserved.

Courtney Moreno. "GSW." Excerpt from "Fed to the Streets." First published in *LA Weekly* as "Help Is on the Way," April 1, 2009. Copyright © 2009 by Courtney Moreno. Reprinted with permission of the Author and Foundry Literary + Media.

Nancy Nevins. "The Cell Fish Blues." Copyright © 2011 by Nancy Nevins. Reprinted by permission of Nancy Nevins.

Erica Petri. "College Students Are Still Hesitant to Whip Out the Plastic." *USA Today*, December 1, 2011. Used by permission of USA TODAY.

George Saunders. Excerpt from "The New Mecca." Copyright © 2005 by Condé Nast. Originally published in *GQ*, November 2005. Reprinted by permission.

Gary Soto. "Like Mexicans." From *The Effects of Knut Hamsun on a Fresno Boy: Recollections and Short Essays*, pp. 29–33. Copyright © 1983, 2001 by Gary Soto. Reprinted by permission of Persea Books, Inc., New York. All rights reserved.

Howard White. "The Power of Hello." From *This I Believe: Life Lessons*, by Dan Gediman et al. Copyright © 2011 by John Wiley & Sons. Reprinted by permission of the publisher.

Joyce Zonana. "Dream Homes." From *Dream Homes: From Cairo to Katrina, an Exile's Journey*. Copyright © 2008 by Joyce Zonana. Reprinted with the permission of the Permissions Company, Inc., on behalf of the Feminist Press, feministpress.org.

Photograph and Illustration Credits

Page 8 (top): © Iain Masterson/Alamy
Page 8 (bottom): © incamerastock/Alamy
Page 11: © Commercial Eye/Getty Images
Page 20: © Guardian News & Media Ltd, 2004
Page 23: © Thinkstock/Getty Images
Page 29 (left): © "Brand Cloud" Web site analysis by Idea Grove, a Dallas marketing firm
Page 29 (right): © Graphic created by Marc Archambault/papershine.com
Page 33: © Visuals Unlimited, Inc./Carol & Mike Werner/Getty Images
Page 111: © Gail Mooney/Masterfile
Page 154: © Nordic Photos/Getty Images
Page 156: © James Marshall/The Image Works
Page 158: © GlowImages/Alamy
Page 165: © JUPITERIMAGES/Polka Dot/Alamy
Page 175 (left and right): © dieKleinert/Superstock
Page 238: © FOOD AND DRINK PHOTOS/Superstock
Page 239: © Maryam at Icing Dreams/Getty Images
Page 262 (top): © AP/Wide World Photos
Page 262 (middle): © AP/Wide World Photos
Page 262 (bottom): © Lisa Clarke
Page 269 (top): © National News/Zuma Press
Page 269 (middle): © Richlam/Getty Images
Page 269 (bottom): © Phil Noble/Reuters/Landov
Page 298 (top): © Reuters/Landov
Page 298 (middle): © Gabriel Bouys/AFP/Getty Images
Page 298 (bottom): © Reuters/Hazir Reka/Landov
Page 299 (top): © Janek Skarzynski/AFP/Getty Images
Page 299 (middle): © Raul Kitagaki Jr./MCT/Landov
Page 299 (bottom): © Daniel Roland/AFP/Getty Images
Page 560 (left): © Blend Images/SuperStock
Page 560 (middle): © Bob Riha Jr./Children's Hospital Los Angeles via Getty Images
Page 560 (right): © Mark Thomas/Photo Researchers, Inc.
Page 560 (top, margin): © Shutterstock
Page 560 (middle, margin): © Alamy Creativity/Alamy
Page 560 (middle, margin): © Digifoto Alpha/Alamy
Page 560 (bottom, margin): © Corbis RF/Alamy
Page 562: © iStockphoto
Page 563 (top): © Alamy Creativity/Alamy
Page 563 (bottom): © Wavebreak Media Ltd/Alamy
Page 564 (top): © iStockphoto
Page 564 (bottom): © Stargatechris/Alamy

Journal Writing Boxes

Pages 27, 167, 318: © Edyta Pawlowska/Shutterstock
Pages 41, 194, 333: © lenetstan/Shutterstock
Pages 62, 217: © Wavebreak Media Ltd/Shutterstock
Pages 95, 254: © dotweb/Shutterstock
Pages 119, 284: © Roger Jegg: Fotodesign-Jegg.de/Shutterstock
Pages 148, 309: © EDHAR/Shutterstock

Index

Reference Material

The material in this section gives you a quick review of common issues in the writing classroom. Refer to it when you need help remembering major grammatical errors, or when you need to look up a correction symbol that your instructor has marked on your assignment. This section also lists where to find helpful lists, charts, and visuals of important subjects in the book. Finally, the last page provides a handy reference to the major parts of speech.

Comma Usage

Follow Four Comma Rules:

Remember that most simple sentences begin with a subject and a verb:

SUBJECT   VERB

The professor gave a test.

Comma Rule 1:
Use a comma after any introductory expressions that begin a sentence.
(pages 650–51)

On Friday, the professor gave a test.

Furthermore, the professor gave a test.

Normally, the professor gave a test.

Hoping for good results, the professor gave a test.

Comma Rule 2:
Use a comma in a compound sentence. (pages 370–71)

The professor gave a test, and the students performed well.

Comma Rule 3:
Use a comma in a complex sentence. (pages 409–18)

When the class finished the chapter, the professor gave a test.

Comma Rule 4:
Use a comma after all but the last item in a list of three or more items. (pages 652–53)

The professor gave a lecture, a quiz, and a test.

For more on comma usage, see Chapter 17, pages 370–71; Chapter 18, pages 409–18; and Appendix C, pages 650–55.

Fragments

There Are Three Types of Fragments:

Missing subject, missing verb, incomplete verb (pages 361–64)

- **Applied** for a student loan.
- A major **marathon**.
- The kids **ignored** by their teammates.

Incomplete thought, subordinate clause (pages 423–27)

- **Since** the lights went out.
- **Although** we bought a ticket.
- **Before** my chemistry class.

Incomplete thought, subject with relative clause (pages 443–48)

- The glass **that** shattered.
- An actor **who** volunteers.
- The market **where** we shop.

Fix It!

Add the missing information OR connect the fragment to another sentence:

Fragment →	**Fix It**
Applied for a student loan.	**Nancy** applied for a student loan.
Since the lights went out. We lit candles.	Since the lights went out, we lit candles.
The glass **that** shattered. It cut me.	The glass that shattered **cut** me.

For more on fragments, see Chapter 16, pages 361–67; Chapter 18, pages 423–29; and Chapter 19, pages 443–51.

Run-Ons and Comma Splices

Four Groups of Words Cause Run-Ons (RO) and Comma Splices (CS):

I, you, she/he, it, they, we (pages 393–94)

> The concert ended we clapped. (RO)
>
> The concert ended, we clapped. (CS)

this, that, these, those (pages 396–97)

> I passed the quiz that shocked me. (RO)
>
> I passed the quiz, that shocked me. (CS)

then, next, also, plus, for example, for instance (page 398)

> The team played hard then they rested. (RO)
>
> The team played hard, then they rested. (CS)

therefore, as a result, consequently, however, furthermore, in addition, instead, nevertheless (pages 399–400)

> Abe shouted however, no one heard him. (RO)
>
> Abe shouted, however, no one heard him. (CS)

Fix It!

Add a period OR a semicolon OR a comma with a joining word (*and, or, but, so, nor, for, yet*).

Run-On or Comma Splice →

The concert ended we clapped.

The concert ended, we clapped.

Fix It

The concert ended. We clapped.

The concert ended; we clapped.

The concert ended, and we clapped.

For more on run-ons and comma splices, see Chapter 17, pages 391–406.

Sentence Combining

Use Glue to Join Two Simple Sentences:

SIMPLE SENTENCE 1	GLUE	SIMPLE SENTENCE 2
The light turned red.	*A joining word and/or punctuation (, ;)*	The car stopped.

Form Correct Compound Sentences:

The light turned red, so **the car stopped.**

Add a comma and a coordinating conjunction:
, and   , or   (, nor)   (, yet)
, but   , so   (, for)

The light turned red; the car stopped.

Add a semicolon:
;

The light turned red; therefore, **the car stopped.**

Add a semicolon and a transitional expression:
; as a result,   ; in addition,
; consequently,   ; instead,
; furthermore,   ; nevertheless,
; however,   ; therefore,

Form Correct Complex Sentences:

When **the light turned red, the car stopped.**

Add a comma and a subordinating conjunction:

After	Because	Even though	Unless	While
Although	Before	If	Until	
As	Even if	Since	When	

The light turned red when **the car stopped.**

Add just a subordinating conjunction:

after	before	since	while
although	even if	unless	
as	even though	until	
because	if	when	

For more on sentence combining, see Chapter 17, pages 369–407, and Chapter 18, pages 408–30.

Correct Verb Usage

Make sure the subject and verb AGREE:

INCORRECT

Jenny play in the school band.

CORRECT

Jenny plays in the school band.

If you add an unnecessary *-s* or forget to add an *-s*, your subject and verb may not agree. So, watch out for the "slippery **-s**" (see page 510).

Make sure your verbs have consistent TENSE:

INCORRECT

Joe tripped on the rug and falls.

CORRECT

Joe tripped on the rug and fell.

If you add an unnecessary *-ed* ending, or forget to add an *-ed* ending, your verbs may not have consistent tense.

For more on how to form correct tense in verbs, see Chapter 23, pages 507–35.

Avoid errors based on PRONUNCIATION in informal speech:

INCORRECT	CORRECT	INCORRECT	CORRECT
You is	You are	We gonna study.	We are going to study.
We is	We are	I wanna eat.	I want to eat.
They is	They are	They gotta go.	They have to go.
You does	You do	Jan would of called.	Jan would have called.
We does	We do	Our team should of won.	Our team should have won.
They does	They do	Ben could of helped.	Ben could have helped.
People is	People are		
People does	People do		
People has	People have		

For more on correct verb usage, see Chapter 23, pages 507–35.

Correction Symbols

Your instructor may use certain symbols to mark writing and grammar problems in your papers. Following are some common symbols and their meanings. (If your instructor uses different symbols than those shown here, write those in the spaces provided.) On the right, we've shown (in bold) chapters or sections of *Touchstones* that you can refer to for more help.

YOUR INSTRUCTOR'S SYMBOL	STANDARD SYMBOL	MEANING	CHAPTER OR SECTION IN THIS BOOK
	adj	Problem with adjective use	15, 16, Appendix A, Appendix B
	adv	Problem with adverb use	15, 16, Appendix B
	agr	Agreement problem between subject and verb	23
		Agreement problem between pronoun and what it refers back to (antecedent)	24
	awk	Awkward wording	7, 10
		Awkward sentence structure	16–22
	cap	Capitalization error	Appendix C
	case	Pronoun case error	24
	cliché	Clichéd language	10
	coh	Lack of coherence/unity in writing	7, 9
	combine	Combine sentences	17–22
	coord	Coordinate sentences/coordination problem	17
	cs	Comma splice	17
	dev	Strengthen development of writing	3, 6, 8, 9
	dm	Dangling modifier	20
	frag	Fragment	16, 18, 19
	prep	Problem with prepositions/prepositional phrases	16, Appendix A
	ref	Unclear pronoun reference	24
	ro	Run-on	17
	shift	Shift in tense or voice	23
	sp	Spelling error	7
	sub	Subordinate sentences/subordination problem	18
	tense	Verb tense problem	23
	trans	Transition needed	5, 6, 8, 9
	unity	Lack of unity/coherence in writing	7, 9
	vb/verb	Verb problem	23, Appendix A
	wc	Problem with word choice	7, 9
	¶	Start a new paragraph	8
	⌢ , ; ' "" — ( ) !	Problem with punctuation	Appendix C
	⌃	Insert	
	ℯ	Delete	
	⌣	Close space	
	⌐⌐	Reverse order of letters/words	

Helpful Lists, Charts, and Visuals